Globalization and Security

Globalization and Security

An Encyclopedia

Volume 1: Economic and Political Aspects

G. Honor Fagan and Ronaldo Munck, Editors

PRAEGER SECURITY INTERNATIONAL
An Imprint of ABC-CLIO, LLC

A B C ❖ C L I O

Santa Barbara, California • Denver, Colorado • Oxford, England

Copyright 2009 by G. Honor Fagan and Ronaldo Munck

All rights reserved. No part of this publication may be reproduced, stored in a retrieval system, or transmitted, in any form or by any means, electronic, mechanical, photocopying, recording, or otherwise, except for the inclusion of brief quotations in a review, without prior permission in writing from the publisher.

Library of Congress Cataloging-in-Publication Data

Globalization and security : an encyclopedia / G. Honor Fagan and Ronaldo Munck, editors.
    p.cm.
  Includes bibliographical references and index.
  ISBN 978-0-275-99692-5 (set : hard copy : alk. paper) – ISBN 978-0-275-99693-2 (set : ebook) – ISBN 978-0-275-99694-9 (v. 1 : hard copy : alk. paper) – ISBN 978-0-275-99695-6 (v. 1 : ebook) – ISBN 978-0-275-99696-3 (v. 2 : hard copy : alk. paper) – ISBN 978-0-275-99697-0 (v. 2 : ebook) 1. Security, International—Encyclopedias. 2. Globalization–Encyclopedias. I. Fagan, G. Honor. II. Munck, Ronaldo.
  D763.M47.G56 2009
  355'.0330003–dc22   2009029695

ISBN: 978-0-275-99696-3
EISBN: 978-0-275-99697-0

13 12 11 10 09   1 2 3 4 5

This book is also available on the World Wide Web as an eBook. Visit www.abc-clio.com for details.

Praeger Security International
An Imprint of ABC-CLIO, LLC

ABC-CLIO, LLC
130 Cremona Drive, P.O. Box 1911
Santa Barbara, California 93116-1911

This book is printed on acid-free paper ∞

Manufactured in the United States of America

Contents

Abbreviations   vii

Introduction to Volume 1
   G. Honor Fagan and Ronaldo Munck   1

1   Citizenship
   Peter Kivisto   28

2   Democracy
   Harry F. Dahms   42

3   Development
   Mark T. Berger   61

4   Environmental Insecurity
   Erika Cudworth and Stephen Hobden   79

5   Finance
   Eleni Tsingou   101

6   Food Security/Fisheries
   Liza Griffin   120

7   Geopolitics
   Klaus Dodds   137

8   Global Ethics and Human Security
   Des Gasper   155

9   Human Rights
   Chiara Certomà   172

10   Imperialism
   Radhika Desai   190

11	Information Wars *John Arquilla*	206
12	Nation-State *Cory Blad*	221
13	Natural Resources: Diamonds and Human Security *Ian Smillie*	239
14	New Economy *Neil Lee*	257
15	New Wars *Helen Dexter*	275
16	Nongovernmental Organizations *Shamima Ahmed*	293
17	Regionalism in the Americas *Rosalba Icaza*	312
18	Regionalism in Eurasia *Mikhail A. Molchanov*	328
19	Regulation *Celine Tan*	349
20	Terrorism *Richard Jackson, Marie Breen Smyth, and Jeroen Gunning*	370
21	Trade *Jens L. Mortensen*	390
22	Transnational Corporations *Grazia Ietto-Gillies*	410

Glossary 429

Index 435

About the Editors and Contributors 455

Abbreviations

Doc.	Document
ICCPR	International Covenant on Civil and Political Rights
ICESCR	International Covenant on Civil and Political Rights
Res.	Resolution
UDHR	Universal Declaration of Human Rights
UN	United Nations
UNESCO	United Nations Educational, Scientific and Cultural Organization

Introduction to Volume 1

G. Honor Fagan and Ronaldo Munck

Whatever our perspective on the world around us, we cannot help wondering whether globalization and the end of the Cold War has actually brought us greater insecurity, rather than the increased security promised. The processes of internationalization unleashed by globalization have undermined the once dominant national security model. But the globalization paradigm has not itself been too concerned to map out the new global (in)security dilemmas. We have only rather generalized theories of "global risk" (Beck 1999) and wishful aspirations for a "global civil society" (Kaldor 2003). This general introduction thus seeks to develop a fruitful encounter between the globalization paradigm and the new (and old) forms of security and insecurity now becoming manifest across the world with greater intensity.

The security dilemmas we all face in the post–Cold War era can be dealt with in various ways. We could just be fatalistic and accept security concerns as an inevitable part of the human condition read in Hobbesian terms. We could also seek to mitigate security and risk challenges through amelioration and conflict containment. Or, finally, as Ken Booth and Nicholas Wheeler argue, we can pursue a "transcender logic [which] argues that human society on a global scale can construct a radically new world order, and in so doing escape the dangers of the past" (2008, 18). Whether this view is overly optimistic is a matter of opinion, but it at least offers a framework to pursue postconflict security strategies. Nor does this view deny that world politics in the twenty-first century will be characterized by deep uncertainties, growing and unpredictable risks, as well as generalized turmoil. Indeed, Booth and Wheeler point to how "the global agenda will be uniquely dominated by an era of converging global challenges, with potentially catastrophic global and local impacts" (268). There will be new challenges overlaid on old ones, combining in new and unsettling modalities. The point is, can we deal with the era of uncertainty and risk by denying it or hiding from it or simply coping with it or should we seek to address its root causes? This encyclopaedia seeks to address the complex cluster of security challenges in the era of globalization. Our focus is particularly on what is new, and our lens is a critical one that avoids facile orthodoxies. The challenges are very serious, and so our thinking must be equally serious and focused on a critical understanding of current reality and, wherever possible, on seeking mechanisms for transcending the security dilemma.

We start this introductory chapter by examining the diverse ways in which globalization has redefined the nature of security. Security threats are now increasingly global—from global warming to global hunger, to global terrorism—and thus, the national or statist security paradigm is inadequate. We expand on this theme in the next section dealing with the simultaneous "widening" of security (to take on nonmilitary threats) and its "deepening" (to go further than the nation-state into society). This leads us to a sustained review of the new human security paradigm seen by its supporters as the replacement for the national security paradigm and by its detractors as vague and unable to be operationalized. Turning to more recent dramatic events in world affairs since 2001, we consider the notion that we are entering a new era of permanent war or permanent security. Finally, we turn to the broader picture of globalization with its winners and losers and ask whether a global civil society can be constructed to take us beyond the current state of seemingly limitless insecurity as the dominant human condition.

GLOBAL SECURITY

Globalization creates greater economic, political, social, and cultural interactions across the globe and is thus a source of great dynamism. However, security analysts argue that "many different aspects of globalisation now combine to increase the dangers of a variety of transnational threats from weapons proliferation, cyber attacks, ethnic violence, global crime, drug trafficking, environmental degradation and the spread of infectious disease" (Davis 2003, 1–2). From this rather wide range of perceived threats, it is clear that two in particular are at the top of the list. The first is the environment and the cluster of issues under the label of global warming that clearly pose transnational risks (see **Environmental Insecurity** entry). The second is the issue of global terrorism (see **Terrorism** entry) with the likes of Al Qaeda being "able effectively to exploit new communications technologies, global financial networks, and the ease of movements of people" (Davis 2003, 1). Between them these twin perils are creating great turbulence by posing security threats in a conventional sense and undermining human security in a broader sense.

Globalization's security implications have led to a number of attempts at "redefining security" (Mathews 1989). Since the end of the Cold War, a narrow military conception of national security has seemed not only redundant but also inadequate. Jessica Mathews was already arguing in 1989 that "global developments now suggest the need for [a] broadening definition of **national security** to include resource, environmental and demographic issues" (162). National sovereignty had already been undermined by the increased freedom of financial flows in the 1980s and by the information and communications technology revolution (see **Internet and Human [In] Security** entry in volume 2). Environmental strains now clearly transcended national borders. From a global development perspective, there was a simultaneous move to broaden the definition of security to include economic vulnerability and dependency in the **global South** (Thomas 1987). External military threats were seen as less important in the South than economic vulnerability and state weakness. The issue of external dependence, becoming more accentuated rather than less in the era of globalization, is seen as the main context-setting element for the majority of the world's population.

Taking a broad overview of the globalization and security field, we note a fairly general recognition that there are now new security challenges that cannot be dealt with on the basis of national security or by purely military means. Even the proponents of traditional military conceptions of security accept a tendency toward the internationalization of security. Notions of collective security now come to the fore, whether dealing with **global warming** or global terrorism. The old binary opposition between the external (international) and the internal (national) can no longer be credibly sustained. Crime, drugs, people trafficking, and terrorism are as much inside as outside the national borders (see **Crime** entry in volume 2). State security is no longer effective even in its own terms, never mind from the perspective of the many millions across the world for whom their own state is the main source of insecurity. While state security is clearly an urgent issue in relation to the real or perceived terrorist threat as an overall paradigm, it is, we argue, of declining effectiveness.

Whether globalization has increased or diminished global security is not entirely or easily decidable. Jan Aart Scholte systematically goes through all the main issues at stake and finds arguments for and against on all counts (2005, chap. 9). While global connectivity may disincentive war in the **global North**, the increasingly global reach of armed forces has facilitated military intervention in the global South. While global consciousness has promoted ecological awareness, many global activities are heavily polluting. Globalization's impact on security is clearly contradictory across and at all levels. Likewise, while globalization has brought to the fore global threats and the need for transnational responses, the national security paradigm is far from defunct in practice. As David Held and others put it, "The doctrine of national security remains one of the essential defining principles of modern statehood . . . For if a state does not have the capacity to secure its territory and protect its people, then its very *raison d'être* can be called into question" (1999, 145). This verdict is clearly reflected in the U.S. response to the attack on the symbols of national political, economic, and military power in September 2001.

Critical security theorists now argue for the need "to develop a new [security] paradigm around the policies likely to enhance peace and limit conflict" (Rogers 2000, 119). This is a broad agenda indeed insofar as true global security would entail a reversal of current socioeconomic polarization, unsustainable growth patterns, and unbridled global military aggression. While this transformative view of security in the era of globalization is unlikely to be mainstreamed, there is still a considerable widening of traditional notions of security. The U.S. National Security Strategy statement of 1994 thus declared unambiguously that "not all security risks are military in nature. Transnational phenomena such as terrorism, narcotics trafficking, environmental degradation, rapid population growth and refugee flows also have security implications" (cited in Hough 2004, 14). The broadening of security from this state perspective relates to the understanding that **soft power** can often complement **hard power**. It is indeed the rise of soft power that could be seen as the defining characteristic of the era despite the more traditional hard power response to 9/11.

DEEPER SECURITY

The widening security agenda can be seen as simply increasing the state's **securitization** of such issues as migration, health, and food in a way that does not essentially challenge the traditional security paradigm in its essentials (see entries for **Migration** and **Health** in volume 2, and **Food Security/Fisheries** entry in this volume). But we might ask, what would be the implications of a deeper conception of security? In 1993 the UN Development Programme (UNDP) declared paradigmatically that "the concept of security must change—from an exclusive stress on national society to a much greater stress on people's security, from security through armaments to security through human development, from territorial to food, employment and environmental security" (cited in Hough 2004, 13). This move by the UN was congruent with its concern to promote the "human face" of globalization in contrast with the dominant powers' then-prevalent adherence to free and unrestricted market mechanisms and the multilateral economic organizations such as the World Bank and the International Monetary Fund (IMF). The step was part of the broader move toward a post–**Washington Consensus** on economic matters.

It was not only the soft power approach of the UN, though, that sought to deepen the traditional concept of security. From the mid-1990s onward, such nation-states as Canada and Ireland, as well as the Scandinavian countries, also began, at least rhetorically, to advance the notion of human security (see next section). Canada's foreign minister from 1996 to 2000, Lloyd Axworthy, consistently argued for human security in the UN and forcefully advocated the creation of the International Criminal Court. Critics could easily argue that this move was simply a middle-ranking power's bid to gain exposure in the international arena through a distinctive foreign policy. Furthermore, the policy was couched in the language of soft power in the sense of the pursuit of state interests by other means, rather than a pursuit of global interest however that might be defined. Nevertheless, despite these reservations, it has been noted, "the Canadians . . . have been in the forefront of campaigns to ban the use of land mines, and reform the UN Security Council so that it is less constrained by power politics" (Hough 2004, 14).

In the academic domain, there occurred around that same time a parallel process of deepening of security as a theoretical paradigm. In the early 1980s, the influential work of Barry Buzan had already begun the process of widening security, with his *People, States and Fear* (1983) adding the categories of economic, societal, and ecological security to that of military security. It was the state and not the individual, however, that remained the reference point for security insofar as the state was seen as the primary agent for the reduction of insecurity. By the early 1990s, this view proved unsustainable, particularly in Europe. With Ole Weaver, Buzan developed the concept of **societal security**, a notion that effectively deepened the traditional idea of state security (Buzan, Weaver, and de Wilde 1998). In post–Cold War Europe, sovereignty was less important than issues of identity (including culture, religion, and language) in societies changing rapidly, not least through the increase of mass migration. Societies were seen as complex organizations, and the challenges they faced were conceived of as much more diffuse and less easy to categorize than were, for example, the traditional security challenges made by other powers.

The deepening of security through the development of a concept of societal security was designed, however, not to replace state security but to complement it. The reconceptualization of security is thus incomplete here. There is here a reified understanding of identity as an objective given and little understanding of security as a social construction. Also at play here is an implicit **Eurocentrism** insofar as it quite uncritically privileges a Western conception of security and securitization (of, say, Islam). Above all, the deepening of the security paradigm by what has become known as the Copenhagen School seems to ignore the gendered nature of security as concept and practice. A gender perspective (see entry for **Gender** in volume 2) entails not just adding new issues (widening) but also genuinely reconceptualizing (deepening) security. To understand globalization, conflict, and security today, we require a gendered approach that can deconstruct the patriarchal state, unpack the gendered nature of **identity,** and explore the links between militarism and patriarchy (see Tickner 2001). Social relations and processes on a global scale are all inherently gendered, and, thus, security challenges affect men and women differently.

From a critical security perspective, the widening and deepening operations carried out within the mainstream paradigm since the end of the Cold War and the onset of globalization have clear limits. It has been argued that the events of 2001–2003 (9/11, Afghanistan, and Iraq) have in fact taken us back to the days when state security reigned supreme—when state security trumped the security of the individual, and state-led military power rendered soft power irrelevant. Still, Steve Smith makes a strong contrary argument that "the events of September 11 support those who wish to widen and deepen the concept of security" (2006). After all, it was not a state that declared war on the United States but, rather, a transnational network reflecting a very different conception of identity, of community, and, indeed, of security itself. What this tells us, of course, is that security is a conceptual battlefield with no agreed-on definition or parameters. That security as a concept is itself a contested discourse is hardly surprising given what is at stake in terms of how we define the problems and the responses to global security risks.

HUMAN SECURITY

We could argue that the simultaneous widening and deepening of security comes to a logical conclusion with the concept of human security now seen as a full-blown alternative to state security. The concept of human security is inseparable from the optimistic Western view following the end of the Cold War, namely, that globalization would lead to democratization and that conflict over fundamentals would become a thing of the past (see **Geopolitics** entry). In 1995, the Commission on Global Governance published its influential report *Our Common Neighbourhood,* arguing that "the concept of global security must be broadened from the traditional focus on the security of states, to include the security of people and the security of the planet" (Commission on Global Governance 1995, 338). At the same time, the concept of human security was coming to the fore in the work of the UNDP, which launched the **human development index** (HDI) focused on the welfare of individuals rather than the economy.

Economic development and military security now became intertwined in the dominant conceptual discourses (see **Development** entry). The basic underlying principle seems straightforward enough: "Since the idea of human security is to improve the lives of people rather than improve the security of national borders and key issues cross these borders, coordinated action by the international community seems essential" (King and Murray 2001–2002). Human security is a move in the realm of security that parallels the discursive shift in development theory toward sustainable development, and in international law to human rights as an overarching principle. It is a people-centered approach to security that seeks to create a situation where all will enjoy "freedom from fear and freedom from want." It is assumed to be the raison d'être of the United Nations, and many national governments have adopted it as a progressive foreign policy slogan.

Recently, considerable effort has been put into developing and operationalizing the concept of human security (Alkire 2003). Nevertheless, the effort remains quite vulnerable to the charge that "human security is like 'sustainable development'—everyone is for it, but few people have a clear idea of what it means" (Paris 2004, 250). From the perspective of the national security advisor, human security looks very much like a laundry list of desirable but utopian goals; a laudable ideal rather than a relevant policy category. It is also open to many, often conflicting interpretations. We might, for example, agree that to bring peace to a region we need to address the root causes of conflict, but then the remedies suggested might vary hugely. From a traditional **state security** perspective, the **human security** approach can only dilute the analytical power of security and presents such a vast array of different threats and complex ambitious solutions, that nothing gets done.

Beyond its vagueness, the concept of human security can also be interrogated in terms of its assumed unproblematic notion of human security itself. In 2003, the Commission on Human Security issued the landmark report *Human Security Now*. The report argued that when a state is neither willing nor able to ensure the human security of its citizens, "the principle of [international] non-interference yields to the international responsibility to protect" (Commission on Human Security 2003, ix). States or the state systems are still expected to ensure human security by intervening where "fragile, collapsed, fragmenting or generally chaotic state entities" (p. 8) do not protect human security. This approach enlists the concept of human security in a radical way to support the global governance agenda. As Mark Duffield and Nicholas Waddell put it, "*Human Security Now* argues for a bio-politics of human population based upon global forms of coordination and centralisation . . . collectively having the ability and legitimacy to support the efforts of weak and ineffective states" (2006, 15). In other words, human security can be yet another form of human control.

From this perspective, the resilience of global populations can be improved through regulatory networks, including aid programs, to ensure biopolitical regulation. This critique of the concept of human security as a form of biopolitical regulation draws on the work of Michel Foucault. Biopolitics and biopower can be seen as the appropriate regulatory mechanism for the era of global governance. As Foucault put it, "Regulatory mechanisms must be established to establish an equilibrium, maintain an average, establish a sort of homeostasis . . . security mechanisms have to be installed around the random element inherent in a population of living beings, so as to optimise a state of life" (2003, 246). Human security is ultimately about the security of the modern state. It is a hugely ambitious project to establish through **biopower** a disciplinary power over the human-as-species. In this sense, it is complementary to, rather than a radical alternative to, traditional conceptions of state security.

PERMANENT SECURITY

The benign version of human security did ultimately come to pass, however, as the optimistic global security mood of the 1990s gave way to the post-2001 moves toward what we might call an enhanced permanent security state. The modern "state of emergency" emerges when a state declares that military methods are necessary to deal with disorder that cannot be dealt with by normal political means. The panoply of counterterrorism measures declared by the president of the United States of America after the attacks on the World Trade Center and the Pentagon have been wide-ranging and designed to last. As Michael Dillon argues, "On September 11th 2001, the United States found itself subject to the recoil of the violence of globalisation. Declaring war on the terror to which New York had been subjected, the Bush administration invoked a global state of emergency to wage indefinite war on an indefinite enemy. The outcome has been a radical suspension of the law to save the law" (2002, 77). The logic of modern power is articulated most clearly by Giorgio Agamben (2005), who argues that the "state of exception," which was once a provisional measure in the West, has now become a working paradigm for government.

Globalization and security set the parameters of events prior to and since 2001. One asymmetric attack by a relatively small organization is clearly not the cause of this transformation in world affairs. Nor can it explain how or why an emergency extrapolitical regime has now become the new normality. The traditional divide between war and peace has now disappeared as the world embarks on a long war (see **Information Wars** and **New Wars** entries). President George W. Bush declared, "Our war on terror begins with Al Qaeda, but it does not end there. It will not end until every terrorist group of global reach has been found, stopped and defeated" (cited in Gross 2006, 75). The global War on Terror declared in 2001 has since transmuted in White House and Pentagon discourse into the "Long War." The change in terminology reflects a growing recognition that one cannot declare war on a form of war. But there is still no recognition that this Long War cannot be won by military means. As John Arquilla puts it, "In terms of the Long War thus far, and in what is likely to come, ideas and beliefs have, in important ways, begun to trump traditional war-fighting" (2007, 384).

The Long War, like the Cold War before it, seeks a clearly identifiable enemy that fits conventional geopolitical and military thinking (see Münkler 2005 for an overview). It does not respond to the complex array of factors creating global insecurity but, in fact, adds to them. It is not even sustainable security in conventional terms: "The current U.S. security paradigm is essentially one of "control"—a matter of responding to current and potential threats primarily by the use of military force" (Rogers 2007, 136). This exposes the severe limitations in the **Revolution in Military Affairs** (RMA) that was meant to transform U.S. military strategy after the Cold War ended. The use of weapons, high technology, and information and communications technology would put an end to war as we know it (Hirst 2001). The American way of life was now joined by an American way of war. But the RMA was disrupted by the asymmetric attacks of 2001 and their global dissemination by global information and communications technology.

The RMA and the Long War are of dubious efficacy as security drivers even in their own terms because they rest on an outdated modernization theory perspective on development—on the notion of regime change, for example—and on a technological determinism that ignores the social, political, and cultural determinants of conflict. More specifically, by demonizing the likes of Al Qaeda, the dominant security discourses cannot comprehend its nature. A quite different approach would be to examine this type of organization in terms of social movement theory and as part of global civil society. Victor Asal and his colleagues make a coherent argument that such organizations as Al Qaeda can be viewed as "transnational advocacy networks," a theoretical approach mainly applied to human rights movements (2007). After all, Al Qaeda has embraced a localized and networked form of organization, and like humanitarian networks it is alert to the importance of symbolic political action. It also works on public opinion through an adept use of the new communications technology.

The notion of a Long War against Islam as a consequence of an underlying clash of civilizations is based on no clear historical understanding of the relationship between globalization and war (on which see Barkani 2006). That globalization meant peace and that war was now a thing of the past was an illusion of the 1990s and reflected the era's "the end of history" mood (Fukuyama 1992). It is not so much that globalization itself causes war but that we need an understanding of how "war is itself a form of *interconnection*, and a historically pervasive and significant one at that. War in this sense is a **globalizing force,** and it has been for a long time" (Barkani 2006, xii). We can then go on to explore how the West and Islam are interconnected and have a mutual constitution. The modernity and hybridity of a movement such as Al Qaeda precludes any simplistic model based on Islamic fundamentalism and shows how the Long War on Terror is a recipe only for the deepening and broadening of insecurity.

BEYOND SECURITY?

We argue that to understand and deal with the issue of (in)security in the era of globalization, we need to move beyond the security paradigms explored in this introduction. The various theoretical approaches to security—from realism through **poststructuralism**—are also constantly constructing the political meaning of (in)security. We have examined in particular the broadening and deepening of the security problematic and the highly ambiguous concept of human security seen by some as liberal wishful thinking and by others as a Foucaultian control mechanism. What Booth advocates, from the perspective of the new critical security studies, is not just to turn all political problems into security issues ("securitising politics") but to "turn every security issue into a question of political theory (what might be called *politicising* security)" (2005, 14). Security is too important to all of us to be left to the so-called **securocrats** or, for that matter, to the academic specialists in security studies.

Clearly, from a globalization perspective, security cannot be divorced from the global political economy. Security and insecurity issues do not arise in sterile apolitical environments or as part of some military strategist's abstract scenario planning. To a large extent, the political economy of globalization dictates life chances, affecting whether we lead comfortable lives or suffer social exclusion (Munck 2005). As Roger Tooze argues, "It is the apparently increasingly arbitrary, random, sudden and unpredictable nature of the workings of the global economy that have heightened the sense that these matters concern our security" (2005, 143). We could go further to argue that the currently dominant neoliberal market-friendly globalization not only generates but even depends on insecurity. Competitiveness—which applies as much between people, communities, cities, nation-states, and regions as between enterprises—is explicitly creating insecurity and rejecting any notion of social protection or solidarity.

Neither can we approach security in a global context without clearly understanding the complexity and tensions in the real world. Certainly, globalization did not do away with what are mistakenly seen as premodern forms of conflict derived from racial, ethnic, tribal, or national identities. Paul James (2006) directs our attention to the complexities and contradictions that structure people's lives and social relationships in the era of globalization. There is not an abstract contest between globalization (good) and tribalism (bad), as many proponents of globalization have argued. James develops instead a counterposition "that allows us to make decisions about political-ethical directions, on the basis of an understanding about the complexities of different forms of community and polity, rather than on the basis of ideologically-driven prejudice about the essential virtues of savage globalisation" (2006, 9).

One seemingly attractive response to global insecurity would be to foster the development of a global civil society (see **Global Civil Society** entry in volume 2), which would counter the state and other forms of violence and insecurity. Such a society is defined as "the sphere of ideas, values, institutions, organisations, networks and individuals located *between* the family, the state, and the market and operating *beyond* the confines of national societies, politics and economies" (Anheier, Glasius, and Kaldor 2001, 17). This broad definition would embrace many forms of globalization-contesting movements throughout the world, including Al Qaeda. But the proponents of global civil society clearly do not wish to see **global terrorism,** or global crime, for that matter, included in their cosmopolitan sphere of civilized dialogue. Indeed, they have gone so far as supporting wars they deemed humanitarian, such wars, for example, as the bombing of Serbia by NATO forces in 1999.

Whether there can be such a thing as a **humanitarian war** goes to the heart of the relationship between globalization and security. For Mary Kaldor and others, the nature of the new wars, where criminalism and tribalism prevail, necessitates a cosmopolitan response that will likely include military force (2003). Likewise sympathetic to the view that outside agencies should intervene when a state cannot save its own citizens from violence, Iris Marion Young also argues that she finds it "disturbing that some international actors appear to assume that such commitments to human rights themselves legitimate some states making war on others" (2007, 100). The contradictions between the notion of humanitarian wars and the specter of human rights imperialism point us to the main limitation of global civil society theory, namely, that it fails to address and understand the nature of contemporary postmodern violence (Delanty 2001).

To effectively go beyond even critical security studies (see Fierke 2007 for an overview), we need to start with the so-called **theory-practice nexus**. We must accept that theory is *"for some one and for* some purpose," as Robert Cox famously put it. An **emancipatory theory** would need to explore the sources of human insecurity over and above the challenges to state security. There is today a global anxiety, or what Zygmunt Bauman calls "liquid fear" (2006), that permeates all areas of our life, creating insecurity around many of the facets of globalization and not just the new global terror that the security literature concentrates on. There are regressive structures and processes in today's global society that clearly create ever greater insecurity. These range from inequitable trade arrangements and unjust wars to polluting, sexist, and racist daily social practices. There are also progressive structures and processes striving to knit together the local communities and global networks in pursuit of a better life for all. Certainly a gap exists here, as Richard Wyn Jones argues, because "international relations specialists on the whole have been remarkably ineffective on the relationship between their work—their theories—and political practice . . . There have been no systematic considerations of how critical international theory can help generate, support or sustain emancipatory politics beyond the seminar room or conference hotel" (1999, xx). To once again marry a critical understanding of the world around us with the enduring human capacity to imagine and construct a better life would indeed be a task worth developing to ensure that the era of globalization does not become the era of insecurity it threatens to be.

GLOBALIZATION

Globalization—variously defined or not at all—is the obligatory point of reference for any discussion of contemporary economic, political, social, and cultural transformation including the critical issue of security and insecurity. Globalization is, in short, the new matrix for our era, the framework for what is and for what might be (see Castells 1996a). The next section of this introductory chapter examines the contested and often contradictory meanings that globalization takes on as dominant paradigm for our time. This is followed by a summary of the main economic transformations globalization has generated in the world around us. How this new world order might be governed politically is the subject of the final section that sets the parameters for many of the contributions to this volume.

Globalization is currently the dominant paradigm or way of seeing the world around us, both for supporters of this phenomenon and for its detractors. It is a **grand narrative** as powerful, all embracing, and visionary as any that may have preceded it, including those of classical capitalism, colonialism, or socialism. It is seen as an epoch-making moment in human history, a transition to a brave new world whether that is viewed positively or negatively. Recently, substantive and seriously researched books have been published arguing for "the truth about globalization" (Legrain 2004) or "in defence of globalization" (Bhagwati 2004) and on "why globalization works" (Wolf 2004). These works are as passionate and as important as those seeking to defend an earlier model of capitalism from the ideological challenge posed by the rise of the Soviet planned economy in the 1920s. So, what is the neoliberal case for a global market economy?

For the liberal **globalizers**, the essence of the phenomenon in question is the free movement of goods, services, capital, and labor "so that, economically speaking, there are no foreigners" (Wolf 2004, 14). They believe, quite literally, in the "magic of the market," a market they see as not only the source of material wealth but "also the basis of freedom and democracy" (Wolf 2004, 57). Liberal globalization is seen as something that encourages moral virtues. While it indeed "makes people richer," it also, according to Martin Wolf, makes people "more concerned about environmental damage, pain and injustice" (2004, 57). Be that as it may, clearly the liberal globalizer worldview goes beyond simple economics and offers an alternative to all collectivist or social views of the world. Corporations are seen as virtuous as well as dynamic agents of progressive change. Globalization will, according to this view, lead to a decline of inequality and poverty worldwide as the market works its magic. While it might have some downsides—it is accepted that no market is perfect—overall there is simply no alternative. Freedom itself—variously defined or not at all—depends on the continued expansion of the global free market.

The case against globalization is equally passionate and categorical. Globalization, from this perspective, is seen as an economic process leading to the **commodification** of life itself. There is nothing that is not for sale, from health to education, from knowledge to our genes. Behind the rhetoric of free trade supposedly lies a sinister move toward introducing barriers around privatized technology, resources, and knowledge to keep them safe for capitalist exploitation. The result, as Naomi Klein puts it, is that "globalization is now on trial because on the other side of all these virtual fences are real people, shut out of schools, workplaces, their own farms, homes and communities" (2002, xxi). The "silent takeover" (Hertz 2001) by the transnational corporations (see entry on **Transnational Corporations**) is seen by others to be an imminent threat to the very possibility of Western democracy as we have known it (see entry on **Democracy**). Corporations are taking over social functions previously carried out by the state, pressuring governments to follow their neoliberal global agenda, and leaving the political system devoid of any real choices.

It is probably impossible to adjudicate between the pro- and antiglobalization cases, especially when stated in such a polemical and absolutist manner. It might, anyway, be more productive to avoid such binary opposition and instead start from an assumption around the sheer complexity of the globalization processes. As John Urry puts it, "Global ordering is so immensely complicated that it cannot be "known" through a simple concept or set of processes" (2003, 15). The global era cannot be reduced to a simple logic of the market, or of so-called network society or of empire. The **complexity approach** allows us to move beyond such counterpositions as those between structural determinism and pure chance or, put another way, between frozen stability and ever-changingness as dominant trends. Complexity refuses all static and **reductionist** readings of globalization that should, in preference, be seen as "neither unified nor . . . act[ing] as a subject nor should it be conceived of in linear fashion" (Urry 2003, 40). It is understandable that first-generation globalization studies should have conceived of this complex process as more powerful and unified than it actually was, but from now on an approach that foregrounds the complexity approach will be more productive whatever political choices we ultimately make.

Another common opposition in the vast literature on globalization now available is between those who stress the novelty of the situation and those who stress continuity with earlier periods of capitalism's internationalization. Among the popularizers of the first position must be counted management consultant Kenichi Ohmae, who in a series of books with such titles as *The Borderless World* (1990) and *The End of the Nation State* (1995) articulated a vision of modernity's nation-state era coming to an end as the liberating forces of the global market became dominant in the 1990s. The traditional order of national economies, industrial production, welfare states, and so on, would be swept away by the new wind of free market dynamism. Ohmae stresses the revolutionary break with the past and the short time span, say, 25 years, in which these world revolutionary events took place.

Academic promoters of the globalist case are more nuanced; nevertheless, emphasis is laid very much on the novelty of the phenomenon described. Thus Anthony Giddens finds himself essentially agreeing with those for whom "the new communications technologies, the role of knowledge as a factor of production, and the new discoveries in the life sciences, signal a profound transition in human history" (2001, 4). The whole mood or tone of this discourse is revolutionary in that it conceptualizes globalization as a fundamental shift in the human trajectory that is now in full flow. There are, of course, optimistic and pessimistic renderings of the globalizing scenario, but the unifying strand is that the shifts involved in all areas of human life are irreversible and of global significance, whether we view them as benign or not.

Against the globalizers, who believe in globalization, and the antiglobalizers who believe it is real, too, even if they do not like its effects, we can posit the **sceptics,** for whom the death of the traditional order is at best overstated. None are clearer or more evidence based than the arguments of Paul Hirst and Grahame Thompson in their aptly titled *Globalization in Question* (1999), which challenges what they call the "necessary myth" that globalization represents a qualitatively new stage of capitalist development. For these authors, the globalization of production has been exaggerated, as have the forecasts of the death of the nation-state. While accepting that there is a growing international economy, they reject as fanciful the idea that multi- or transnational corporations are footloose and fancy-free. They even turn the tables on the decline-of-the-nation-state arguments by showing how in many ways the nation-state has gained in importance by managing or governing the processes of internationalization. While arguably marked by a tinge of nostalgia for a preglobalization era when so-called normal national politics prevailed, this approach is a healthy sceptical antidote to out-and-out globalizers.

Globalization today certainly shows many new traits, but one can also discern continuities with previous expansionary phases of capitalism. One way of putting it, albeit allegorically, is that "one-third of the globalization narrative is over-sold; one-third we do not understand; and one-third is radically new" (Drache 1999, 7). From a complexity theory standpoint, we might challenge this separation between being and becoming, but the drift of the argument is well taken. There is a big difference between globalization as mutually reinforcing and causally related transformations following a preestablished path, and a conception based on the notion of "**contingently related** tendencies" (Dicken, Peck, and Tickell 1997, 161). There are also extremely diverse economic, political, social, and cultural tendencies that vary widely across regions and time. There is simply no unified coherent and unilinear globalization strategy waiting to be applied comparable to the 1950s **modernization theory,** which for that era served as a widely accepted overarching paradigm for social change (see **Development** entry). Now occurring around us all the time is a complex restructuring and recomposition of the world order, an order the concept of globalization might point toward in different ways and even partially explain, but the concept cannot serve as a master framework to understand and explain it totally.

Having briefly analyzed what globalization is not, what can we say about what it is over and beyond the obvious complexity and uneven development of the phenomenon? Clearly, it is no one thing and has various interlinked economic, political, ideological, social, and cultural facets. But if there is one overarching theme, it is that of **connectivity** or interconnectedness. Following Ash Amin, we could argue that "the most distinctive aspect of contemporary globalization" is the "interconnectedness, multiplexity and **hybridization** of social life at every level" (1997, 129). This means we can no longer draw clear and firm boundaries between local and global spheres or between national and international spheres of social life. We cannot separate the "in here" of the city, community, or locality in which we live from the "out there" of global flows of money, capital, people, power, and dominance. Thus globalization should be seen not as an entity but, rather, as a set of complex interacting relationships.

Our daily activities are all influenced by these complex and interrelated facets that are stretching our social relationships to an unprecedented degree.

Another useful image to understand globalization is that of **time-space compression**. Spatial barriers—for example, in trade or communications—have fallen away to a considerable degree. Space does not even matter any more, according to some pundits. Time has also changed from being a reflection of natural processes to become instantaneous. The world has been shrinking for a long time, but this process has taken a qualitative leap forward in the last quarter of the twentieth century. We may not yet have achieved the distanceless world that Martin Heidegger once foretold, but as David Harvey puts it, we are now living through "processes that so revolutionize the objective qualities of space and time that we are forced to alter, sometimes in quite radical ways, how we represent the world to ourselves" (1989, 240). The elimination of spatial barriers and the compression of time will not, however, necessarily lead to a homogeneous spatial development. The changing spatiality of global capitalism is, if anything, more heterogeneous, differentiated, and fragmented (see two entries under **Regionalism**).

Above all else, we must stress that globalization signifies a much greater interconnectedness of social fates. As David Held and Anthony McGrew put it, "Globalization weaves together, in highly complex and abstract systems, the fates of households, communities and peoples in distant regions of the globe" (2003, 129). Our own daily lives are becoming increasingly globalized in terms of their references points, our consumption patterns, and our mental maps. We imagine the world in a different way than our ancestors did at the last turn of the century. Today for many individual and collective subjects, be they governments, companies, intellectuals, artists, or citizens, globalization is the "imagined horizon" (García Canclini 1999, 32). The repercussions, both positive and negative, of the 2004 New Year's Eve East Asian tsunami demonstrated most clearly how real the weaving together of fates across the world now is. Whichever view is taken, clearly globalization has transformed the world around us, as well as the way in which we understand it and seek to change it.

So in terms of competing paradigms, it might be premature to choose one particular rendition of globalization theory to guide us. Held and his colleagues usefully distinguish between the globalizers, the sceptics (who doubt there is much new in it), and the **transformationalists**. The latter stress the changes taking place and how an open-ended explanation of this arena may help us in getting to know the one-third of globalization that is as yet unknown. As against fixed ideal-type paradigms of a new global market, global democracy, or global civilization, Held and his colleagues prefer the "transformationalist accounts [that] emphasize globalization as a long-term historical process which is inscribed with contradictions and which is significantly shaped by **conjunctural factors**" (1999, 7). A good example of the latter are the events of September 11, 2001, in the United States and their sequel of unfolding conflicts across the world that effectively put an end to prevailing optimistic views of globalization as a new peaceful era of harmonious global development.

A transformationalist approach to globalization starts from the premise that the world is changing rapidly and in fundamental ways, even if the direction of change is not yet fully discernible. An underlying question is whether a new sense of globality means we should abandon methodological nationalism, that is, the nation-state as an obvious and self-sufficient frame of reference for understanding the changing worlds we live in. A closely associated issue is the viability of **methodological nationalism**, that is, the forms of social enquiry that precede the rise of **supraterritoriality** (e.g., the Internet and global financial markets). While accepting that a new global optic is necessary to comprehend the changing worlds around us, we cannot accept that the nation-state does not matter or that territorial forms of consciousness might not have a continuing or even increasing relevance. The point is, simply, that we now live in the era of globalization, immersed in a rapidly changing world that clearly has an impact on all the facets and levels of our lives.

GLOBALIZATION AND THE ECONOMY

It is not a belief in **economic determinism** that leads us to start with the economic world but, rather, an understanding that how people produce is crucial to social development. Early debates revolved around whether economic internationalization was indeed new at all and whether it was, in fact, even global in the true sense of the word. Certainly, there were earlier periods of capitalist development when trade and finances were truly international. Nor is there any doubt that globalization is primarily a phenomenon affecting the richer and more powerful nation-states of the West, or global North, even though its effects are as significant as any tsunami on what was once known as the developing world. The underlying political question is whether economic internationalization and the operation of freer markets is spreading development or concentrating it in ever fewer hands (see **Inequality** and **Social Exclusion** entries in volume 2). The supporters of globalization and the antiglobalization movement are predictably at opposite ends of this debate. While economic growth in China and India has accelerated along with increased integration with the global economy, overall the global South, as the developing world is now called, has suffered from **neoliberal policies** favoring the free market.

The traditional, modern world of production is now joined by the virtual or new economy (see **New Economy** entry) characteristic of the **Information Age**, with greatly enhanced communications and transportation systems. As Jan Aart Scholte puts it, "Globalization has played an important role in redistributing the relative weights of accumulation away from 'merchandise' (commercial on industrial capital) towards 'intangibles' (finance, information and communications capital)" (2000, 123). This new economy is not really a postcapitalist era in any real sense of the word; it is simply the latest manifestation of a dynamic and plastic economic system. This new economy is less bound to territory, however, and is a harbinger of a more transnational order. Multinational corporations become truly transnational corporations. The "death of space" is not just a clever business logo. This major transformation in how capitalism works has led to huge changes in the world of work and has also generated considerable opposition from social movements concerned with comodification, consumerism, effects on the environment, and the social situation of workers and agriculturalists.

Whereas the promoters of globalization in the 1990s sought to present this phenomenon of economic internationalization as something novel and breathtaking, the sceptics were quick to point out that that it was really not that unprecedented. Hirst and Thompson, for example, argued that "in some respects, the current international economy is less open and integrated than the regime that prevailed from 1870 to 1914" (1999, 2). Indeed, in that classical **gold standard** era, there was a huge expansion of trade and a veritable revolution in transportation and communications. Global markets emerged for many products, and the gold standard ensured a stable financial and payments order (see entry for **Finance**). This was largely a European world order, however, and the rest of the world was simply not included within its parameters. Furthermore, the disruption to trade caused by World War I and the **Great Crash of 1929** and the depression of the 1930s put paid to the illusion that a dynamic and stable world capitalist order could be achieved easily.

While it is indeed important to place the current phase of economic internationalization in historical context, we do need to recognize the massive socioeconomic transformations that occurred in the second half of the twentieth century. The golden age of capitalism stretching from 1950 to around 1973 saw a remarkable flourishing of productivity and a gradual move toward a genuinely global free trade order. The **Bretton Woods** international financial order, agreed to by the main powers after the World War II, was premised on fixed exchange rates and closed capital accounts. This provided the legal underpinning for the multilateral trade order, and a long era of stability and legitimacy ensued. While this trading regime was clearly stratified and incorporation into it was uneven, it did set the basis for expanded production and consumption across the globe. In a somewhat stylized manner we will now explore the various facets of economic internationalization in terms of trade, production, and finance.

From 1945 to 1985, global free trade predominated among the rich oil-exporting countries (see **Trade** entry). Following the debt crisis of the 1980s, most of the developing countries in the South followed suit and dismantled protectionist barriers. Then, in the early 1990s, they were joined by the once communist countries in the East that had to varying degrees been isolated from the capitalist market. A global market on this scale was simply unprecedented and signaled a massive expansion of capitalist relations and capitalist production and consumption patterns. Based on data for 68 countries, it was found that in 1950 the intensity of trade links was 64 percent (out of a possible 100 percent, meaning all countries traded with all), which rose to 95 percent in 1990 (Held et al. 1999, 167), marking a major increase in the intensity of trade. We can see that trade has been not only much more extensive than in the past but also much more intensive. Foreign trade is now a much more important element in most countries in terms of its overall economic significance.

With increased national enmeshment within a global trading order came a need to regulate and institutionalize that regime. The **GATT** (General Agreement on Tarrifs and Trade) was a central element in creating a stable international trading regime following World War II, in spite of its weaknesses. With trade tariffs already reduced to a minimum by the l990s, interest shifted to the domestic regulations governing competition. This led to the creation in 1995 of the **WTO** (World Trade Organization), charged with harmonizing competition and business rules across nations to promote global free trade in ever more sectors (to include, for example, services). The WTO is considerably more powerful than GATT was, and it has various sanctions it can apply. Although the WTO failed to reach agreement on an agenda for future trade talks in Seattle in 1999, it has since moved forward, albeit conflictually at times, to ensure a rules-based intensification of trade liberalization for its 132 member countries. The setback to the WTO's plans at the 2003 Cancun meeting and the 2008 trade round highlights how difficult this process will be and how little genuine consensus exists across the globe for this vital plank in the globalization project.

Along with the extension of trade went an enormous leap in production-level integration at a global level based on foreign direct investment (FDI) in particular. Perhaps the major characteristic of the postwar period was the rise of the multinational corporations (MNCs) that now account for the vast majority of the world's exports. Already in the 1970s, a **new international division of labor** had emerged, with many developing countries achieving significant levels of industrialization. However, by the 1990s, a much more marked global production and distribution system was emerging based on the estimated 650 MNCs and their nearly 850,000 affiliates across the globe. With foreign investment regulations a thing of the past, the main issue now was how to attract and retain FDI, usually through national governments offering increasing concessions. The MNCs have shifted from their 1970s concern with natural resources (see **Natural Resources** for a case study on diamonds) and labor costs to an emphasis on efficiency and strategic asset seeking. As John Dunning explains, "The strategic response of MNCs to the emerging global economy has been increasingly to integrate their sourcing, value-added and marketing activities, and to harness their resources and capabilities from throughout the world" (2000, 48).

Globalization of production can be assessed in terms of increasing FDI flows and the growing importance of the MNCs in global production. It goes further, though, insofar as the global production networks are the key technological drivers of capitalist development. The impact of these worldwide networks of innovation, production, and distribution reaches deep into domestic economies right down to the local level. It is estimated that the MNCs today account for nearly one-third of world output and are approaching three-quarters of total world trade (UNCTAD 1995). Without minimize their importance or weight in the global economy, we need to recognize that the MNCs are not footloose, as many of their critics allege. In fact, the MNCs tend to be strongly embedded both nationally and socially, and, in many ways, they seek stability rather than risk the uncertainties prevailing in unfettered financial markets, for example.

Apart from trade and production, it is the development of a global financial market that, of course, best symbolizes the advent of globalization. In the 1980s, financial deregulation (see entry on **Regulation**) was accompanied by the growth of private international banks (see entry for **Finance**). The classical gold standard era (1870–1914) had already seen the emergence of an international financial order, but this was largely confined to Europe. The post-1945 Bretton

Woods era then saw a veritable reinvention of a global financial order. Consistent with national **Keynesian economic policies**, this financial order was designed not to interfere with such domestic economic objectives as full employment. This system collapsed, however, when in 1971 the United States decided no longer to allow the U.S. dollar to be freely convertible into gold, thus undermining the system of **fixed exchange rates**. As Held and his coauthors put it, "This ushered in an era of floating exchange rates in which (in theory) the value of currencies is set by global market forces, that is, worldwide demand and supply of a particular currency" (1999, 202). Henceforth, foreign exchange markets would blossom and become a linchpin of the globalization strategy. With internationalization came deregulation of financial activities as the restrictions on capital accounts and exchange rates of the Bretton Woods order were cast aside in 1973 after a vain attempt to patch up the old system.

Global financial flows increased dramatically in the 1990s in their extension across the world and in their intensity. In the mid-1990s, some $200 million per day flowed across the globe; by the late l990s, the figure had risen to a staggering $1.5 trillion. **Deregulation** of national financial markets and the removal of capital controls in the monetarist 1980s facilitated this move toward greater financial fluidity. Unlike the situation that prevailed during the early Bretton Woods era, now the international financial order would take precedence over domestic economic policies. For many commentators, as Geoffrey Garrett puts it, "the potential for massive capital flight acts as the ultimate discipline on governments that may want to pursue autonomous economic policies" (2000, 111). Finance capital is fluid and mobile, increasingly removed from any form of control despite the volatility and potential for disorder inherent in today's global financial order, dubbed "casino capitalism" by Susan Strange (1986). In itself this element will induce insecurity into the global order.

The question we now need to ask is whether the combined impact of trade, production, and financial internationalization adds up to a qualitatively new era of capitalism we can call globalization. The globalizers who referred to a new "borderless world" (Ohmae 1995) and the "death of the nation state" (Ohmae 1995) were undoubtedly confusing tendencies, or even wishes, with reality. We are now in the midst of massive economic transformations the outcome of which is by no means certain. In spite of these provisos, however, we need to consider carefully Held and his coauthors' conclusion, based on meticulous empirical research, that "in nearly all domains contemporary patterns of globalization have not only quantitatively surpassed those of earlier epochs, but have also displayed unparalleled qualitative differences—that is in terms of how globalization is organised and reproduced" (1999, 425). Economic internationalization, in particular, has achieved a depth and extension that is simply unprecedented. Does this mean globalization is inevitable in some sense?

Certainly, nothing about economic internationalization is inevitable, and we need to avoid **teleological** interpretations that see it moving toward a predefined end, whether benign or the opposite. We have been describing not an act of God or a natural event but, rather, a process driven by particular social groups that are clearly defined. Globalization does not just happen. It is a strategy for capitalist expansion on a global scale that began under the Thatcher

(UK) and Reagan (U.S.) regimes in the 1980s. Global economic integration is today driven by powerful governments and corporations that think, design, and manage the new global order. These managers of globalization are now quite aware that free market economics has definite social and political limits and that it exacerbates risk, even for those who benefit from its unprecedented productivity. A degree of social regulation is thus increasingly seen as necessary if the free or unregulated market approach is not to end up in a state of social anarchy.

GLOBALIZATION AND POLITICS

In the political domain, the early globalization debates focused around the so-called decline—even death—of the nation-state (see entry on **Nation-State**). The national-global relationship was interpreted as a zero-sum game, where the gain of one was seen as loss for the other. By the mid-1990s, however, it was widely acknowledged that "states have significantly more room to manoeuvre in the global political economy than globalisation theory allows" (Weiss 2003, 26). This was the case not least because globalization's critics, as much as its supporters, were beginning to understand globalization as a process that could be enabling or empowering to some. Clearly, globalization was not some form of nebula hanging over the world as benign or malignant presence depending on one's point of view. The phenomenon called globalization in the 1990s could be traced back to specific economic policies developed by the rich and powerful nation-states of the West going back most immediately to the **neoliberal** (anti-statist, pro-privatization) policies dominant in the 1980s (see entry on **Imperialism**).

Thus a powerful image developed around the decline-of-the nation-state thesis. It seemed logical that increased economic internationalization would lead to a decrease of political sovereignty. The new global market form of capitalist development certainly weakened **statist** or nationalist development models. The levers of economic power were no longer, straightforwardly, in the hands of national governments. Nor do governments control the national territory in quite the same way as they did in the era of the nation-state. Even on the purely economic policy side, however, states may still steer the economy through such supply-side measures as technological innovations and training or education. Nor does the development of such pooled sovereignty as that of the EU or NATO or the WTO prove any less powerful a means to pursue the objectives of the rich nation-states. Finally, we must reject economistic visions of nation-state decline insofar as different states may clearly use their power in different ways and the different varieties of capitalism have markedly different political effects.

The changing worlds described herein need to be governed, of course. Until quite recently, the regimes of **national sovereignty** set the main parameters of **governance**. Today, global governance is required, and it sets the terms of regional, national, and even city-level governance. Nation-states had national governments ruling over the sovereign national territory through executive, legislature, and judicial branches. Political parties expressed or represented the views of the citizens (see entry on **Citizenship**). In the era of globalization, government, in the traditional sense, is being superseded by what we call governance—that is, by the way in which a state steers, rather than commands, society and where the market is allowed to play a full role in allocating resources. Less hierarchical or bureaucratic than traditional governments, contemporary governance is achieved through coordination, consultation, and community involvement, with its favored form of organization being the network. This paradigm shift from government to governance had been completed in most countries by the end of the twentieth century.

The traditional state and government were challenged as effective modalities for the new capitalism (see **New Economy** entry) primarily because as territorial-based bodies they were ill-equipped to deal with such **supraterritorial** phenomena as the Internet or offshore banking. The proliferation of supraterritorial issues has led to connections being formed above the national government level (e.g., the WTO), but also below the national government level as transnational connections flourish between cities and regions in pursuit of diverse interests that may or may not coincide with those of national governments. As Scholte explains, "As a result of this multiplication of **substate** and **suprastate** arrangements alongside regulation through states, contemporary governance has become considerably more decentralized and fragmented" (2000, 143). As with other issues or facets of globalization explored in this introduction, hybridity of organizational forms is growing in keeping with the complexity of challenges faced by contemporary capitalist development.

"The world is now more than ever enmeshed in a process of complex globalization," as Phil Cerny puts it, and "the most urgent research agenda . . . is to identify the myriad dimensions of this complex process and evaluate the structure of the intersections and interactions among them" (1999, 209). There is no neat hierarchy of spatial levels from the local to the global, through the national to the regional. Rather, all issues are multilayered, as are the strategies and structures to deal with them. In social policy, for instance, we have the term "**wicked issues**" to describe such social problems as youth crime that cannot be assigned to any one government department because the issue is multidimensional. Likewise, global warming can be seen as a wicked issue that requires a multilayered response. Since at least the end of the Cold War economic, political, and social issues and ideologies have grown more complex and less easily amenable to simple solutions. It is this move to a world beyond slogans that explains the recent paradigm shift away from the once dominant Washington Consensus.

During the first wave of neoliberal-led globalization in the 1980s and 1990s, a quite fundamentalist economic doctrine and political philosophy prevailed. This was codified around 1990 in the so-called Washington Consensus, centered upon the key tenets of trade liberalization, deregulation, privatization, and financial liberalization. The doctrine was applied with particular rigor and fervor in Latin America, where it became known widely as neoliberalism, a form of free market economics pledged to the removal of the state from any areas where it might interfere with the free workings of the market. Against all forms of national protectionism—which had been essential for industrialization in the developing world—the Washington Consensus called for removal of all tariff and other barriers so that international trade could be free. Removal of such trade barriers was intended to overcome the 1980s **debt crisis** in Latin America, and the Washington Consensus policies were imposed on debtor nations as forms of macroeconomic conditionality for further loans.

The free market silent revolution, as its supporters called it, was to meet internal contradictions and external limits. The Asian financial crisis of the late 1990s began in Thailand in 1997 but rapidly spread to the Philippines and Indonesia and later Russia and Brazil, among others. Financial deregulation created the volatile hot money markets where a collapse of confidence could spread like wildfire. Henceforth, even such fervent supporters of free market economics as Jagdish Bhagwati (2004) would also call for renewed financial controls and regulation. Then in Latin America came another financial crisis in Mexico in 1997–1998, and, most dramatically of all, the economy of Argentina virtually collapsed at the end of 2001—and Argentina had been the country where the Washington Consensus was so faithfully implemented that the peso was even tied to the U.S. dollar. Finally, around the same time a number of corporate scandals in the United States—the mostly notably newsworthy being Enron—showed that free market neoliberalism had to be saved from itself.

Toward the turn of the century the contradictions of the Washington Consensus as the political economy paradigm of the era became apparent. According to Robin Broad, "While some tenets of the old Consensus have been transformed more than others, we are unquestionably in the midst of a paradigm shift and a period of continued debate" (2004, 148). The rejection of full capital market liberalization opened the door for further questioning of key tenets of the Washington Consensus. Far from rejecting the role of the state in economic affairs, the new economic wisdom sought to restructure the state and created the "new public management" approach. The **global governance** agenda as a whole can be seen as a response to the failings of free market liberalism as well as a response to the counterglobalization movements of the late 1990s and beyond. Beyond the economic debates there seemed to be a recognition that the moral acceptance of capitalism mattered. The new consensus was a pragmatic adaptation to new conditions, but it had a distinct moral undertone.

We could say, following Richard Higgott, that "the global market place of the 1980s and the first 6–7 years of the 1990s was an 'ethics free zone'" (2000, 138). Poverty was seen as an unfortunate side effect of globalization, an adjustment pain that did not cause any moral dilemmas. But by the late 1990s, there was "in some quarters a genuine recognition of the importance of tackling ethical questions of justice, fairness and inequality" (Higgott 2000, 139). A small but probably not insignificant sign of this mood swing was the conversion of George Soros from financial speculator par excellence to caring, far-sighted articulator of **third-way** politics to save global capitalism from itself (see Soros 1999). More broadly, this was an era when the corporate social responsibility agenda took off. Perhaps the trend came about only because Nike shares plummeted when conditions in the company's overseas plants were exposed, or perhaps it was because in 1999 protestors in Seattle targeted Starbucks; even so, the swing toward a more socially responsible capitalism had begun (see **Human Rights** entry).

The shift to social responsibility does not imply that global governance is simply benign compared with the Washington Consensus. Indeed, following Ian Douglas, perhaps we should be "rethinking globalization as governance" (1999, 151). The contemporary transformations in the modalities of political rule beyond traditional government models can simply be seen as more effective ways to control global society. While the state may well have been hollowed out as an effect of economic internationalization and the traditional models of political sovereignty have been rendered void, the replacement is by no means progressive. Rather than simply accept at face value the concerned humanitarian message of the Commission on Global Governance (1995), Douglas asks us to first confront the interesting question, "To what problem is global governance the solution?" (1999, 154). The move toward networks of governance that are largely self-reliant and the emergence of the self-organizing individual may be positive in a general sense, but they may also reflect a Foucauldian drive for order and may well create new inequalities and hierarchies.

Global governance as reform and repression at the same time simply poses a more general dilemma thst goes back to early 1900s debates on reform versus revolution and the 1960s notion of **repressive tolerance**. For Foucault, for example, governance can be seen as a more effective, because more totalizing, form of control in terms of biopower. However, while it is easy to see how a nongovernmental organization (NGO) or social movement might be co-opted through engagement with the global economic agencies, their interaction is nonetheless real. Foucault might respond that this engagement and even protest against globalization is beneficial to the established order because it creates reform (the better to govern), but inaction is a totally more progressive option. Many critical thinkers now accept that globalization might open some doors for progressive social transformation as well as close others. Global governance may well be a reform of "repressive tolerance" or just a simple modernization or rationalization of control mechanisms, but it is still different from government as previously understood.

A fundamental point about the global governance paradigm or problematic from the point of view of this text is that it allows the social movements back in. The NGOs (see entry on **Nongovernmental Organizations**), the global social movements, and assorted advocacy or protest networks all play a role in the governance of the global economy. These nonstate or nontraditional sectors have, at least since the 1999 Seattle WTO debacle, been at the forefront of debate on how global governance can be ensured. At its most official level, this shift can be seen in the attempt by the United Nations to develop a **global compact** bringing together the corporate sector and issues such as human rights as well as labor and environmental standards. For Higgott, "While it sits firmly within a neo-liberal discourse for developing an interaction between the international institutions and the corporate world, it is an important recognition of the need to globalize some important common values" (2000, 140). Effectively, this initiative seeks to globalize the socially embedded liberalism of the postwar era that served to create capitalist growth and social cohesion at the same time.

As the protests against globalization grew in the late 1990s, so did the role of the NGOs or what others call **civil society organizations** (CSOs). Yet they faced the dilemma of either joining protestors in the streets or taking their critique into the conference halls and boardrooms of global governance and the corporate sector. Of course, in practice they could do both, but many more mainstream NGOs chose to seek to influence policy from within, as it were. There are signs that they were often welcomed into the capitalist tent even if their influence was not always significant. There was also a strong move toward organizing parallel or unofficial summits alongside those of the WTO and other such organizations. Although evidence is scanty because it is difficult to assess influence, one well-researched study concludes that in the early 1990s only 20 percent of unofficial summits had an impact on the official event, but by the year 2000 this proportion had risen to 40 percent (Pianta 2001, 186–87). Civil society was at least having some impact on the leading bodies of global capitalism (see **Global Civil Society** entry in volume 2).

The move toward global governance also allowed for more space to be created where social movements could intervene (Castells 1996b). To differing degrees the likes of the World Bank and other economic institutions became more porous to the demands of some social movements. The international women's movement and the environmental movement had significant successes, but the labor movement, in a less public way, was also at least able to place its perspective on the negotiating table of the global corporate sector. One of the more systematic studies that has been carried out concludes that "there is a transformation in the nature of global economic governance as a result of the MEI (**multilateral economic institutions**) – GSM (global social movements) encounter" (O'Brien et al. 2000, 3). Whatever the particular verdict on each case of engagement (and there is always a sceptical view to match any optimism), there is undoubtedly a transformation in terms of the range of economic and political institutions engaged with social movements and their demands.

CONCLUSION

The economic, political, social, and cultural transformations of the world around us have one common feature we could arguably name **reflexivity**. When referring to "reflexive modernization," Ulrich Beck sets it in terms of a "subversive, unintended and unforeseen self-questioning of the bases of political life" (2000, 101), which is created by the perception of risk that now prevails after the age of innocence. Rather than living through the "end of history," as Francis Fukuyama optimistically predicted at the end of the Cold War, we are moving into a new era of global civilization where we all have a common destiny, albeit threatened by old and new forms of global risk, whether from famine to AIDS or from global terrorism to the perils of genetic engineering. The point is that the era of globalization is characterized by intense reflexivity as individuals and institutions reflect on transformation, risks, and how to construct a better future. This does not spell an era of consensus necessarily, but all bets are off, and the rationality of modernity (see entry for **Modernity** in volume 2) does not imprison our minds and lives as it once did.

Globalization cannot explain everything or even anything on its own. The emergent global risk society, to use Beck's terminology, is neither unified, nor all-powerful, nor uncontested (even at the level of meanings). Urry quite correctly takes to task simplified and static conceptions neglected in statements that "''globalization'' is χ or alternatively that ''globalization'' does χ'' (2003, 40). In reality, nothing is linear about the development of globalization, as if it were some rerun of the teleological 1950s modernization theories based on an unproblematic expansion of a conception of modernity based on a stylized rendering of the U.S. experience. While globalization cannot, therefore, be treated as the subject of history, it can be conceived as a new matrix for global development. Thus globalization can be taken as a shorthand label for the complex economic, sociopolitical, and cultural parameters that set the terms of reference and establish a matrix for the developmentof human societies.

REFERENCES

Agamben, Giorgio. 2005. *State of Exception.* Chicago: University of Chicago Press.

Albrow, Martin. 1997. *The global age: State and society beyond modernity.* Cambridge: Polity Press.

Alkire, Sabina. 2003. A conceptual framework for human security. Working Paper 2. Oxford: University of Oxford, Centre for Research of Inequality, Human Security and Ethnicity.

Amin, Ash. 1997. Placing globalisation. *Theory, Culture & Society* 14: 123–37.

Arquilla, J. 2007. The end of war as we knew it? Insurgency, counter-insurgency and lessons for the forgotten history of early terror networks. *Third World Quarterly* 28: 369–86.

Asal, V., B. Nussbaum, and D. William Harrington. 2007. Terrorism as transnational advocacy: An organisational and tactical examination. *Studies in Conflict and Terrorism* 30: 15–40.

Barkawi, Tarak. 2006. *Globalization and war.* Lanham, MD: Rowman and Littlefield.

Bauman, Zygmunt. 2006. *Liquid fear.* Cambridge: Polity Press.

Beck, Ulrich. 1999. *World risk society.* Cambridge: Polity Press.

———. 2001. *What is globalization?* Cambridge: Polity Press.

Bhagwati, Jagdish. 2004. *In defense of globalization.* New York: Oxford University Press.

Booth, Ken. 2005. "Beyond critical security studies." In *Critical security studies and world politics,* ed. K. Booth, 272–6. Boulder, CO: Lynne Rienner.

Booth, Ken, and Nicholas Wheeler, eds. 2008. *The security dilemma: Fear, cooperation and trust in world politics.* London: Palgrave.

Broad, Robin. 2004. The Washington Consensus meets the global backlash. *Globalizations* 1: 129–84.

Buzan, Barry. 1983. *People, state and fears.* Boulder, CO: Lynne Rienner.

Buzan, Barry, O. Weaver, and J. de Wilde. 1998. *Security: A new framework.* Boulder, CO: Lynne Rienner.

Castells, Manuel. 1996a. *The rise of the network society.* Vol. 1 of *The information age.* Oxford: Blackwell.
———. 1996b. *The power of identity.* Vol. 2 of *The information age.* Oxford: Blackwell.
Castles, Stephen, and Mark J. Miller, eds. 1993. *The age of migration: International population movements in the modern world.* London: Macmillan.
Cerny, Phil. 1999. Globalization, governance and complexity. In *Globalization and governance*, ed. Aseem Prakash and Jeffrey Hart. London: Routledge.
Commission on Human Security. 2003. *Human security now.* New York: Commission on Human Security.
Davis, L. 2003. Globalisation's security implications. RAND Issue Paper.
Delanty, G. 2001. Cosmopolitanism and violence—the limits of global civil society. *European Journal of Social Theory* 4: 41–52.
Dicken, Paul, Jamie Peck, and Adam Tickell. 1997. Unpacking the global. In *Geographics of Economies,* ed. R. Lee and J. Wills. London: Arnold.
Dillon, M. 2002. Network society, network centric warfare and the state of emergency. *Theory, Culture and Society* 19: 71–79.
Douglas, Ian. 1999. Globalization as governance: Toward an archaeology of contemporary political reason. In *Globalization and governance,* ed. Aseem Prakash and Jeffrey Hart, 134–60. London: Routledge.
Drache, Daniel. 1999. Globalization: Is there anything to fear? CSGR Working Paper 23. Coventry, UK: University of Warwick.
Duffield, M., and N. Waddell. 2006. Securing humans in a dangerous world. *International Politics* 43: 1–23.
Dunning, John. 2000. The new geography of foreign direct investment. In *The political economy of globalization,* ed. Ngaire Woods, 20–53. London: Palgrave.
Eade, John, ed. 1996. *Living the global city.* London: Routledge.
Featherstone, Michael. 1995. *Undoing culture.* London: Sage.
Fierke, Karin. 2007. *Critical approaches to international security.* Cambridge: Polity Press.
Foucault, Michel. 2003. *Society must be defended.* London: Penguin Books.
Fukuyama, Francis. 1992. *The end of history and the last man.* London: Hamish Hamilton.
García Canclini, Néstor. 1999. *La globalización imaginada [Imagined globalization].* Buenos Aires: Paidós.
Garrett, Geoffrey. 2000. Globalization and national autonomy. In *The political economy of globalization,* ed. Ngaire Woods, 107–46. London: Palgrave.
Giddens, Anthony. 2001. Anthony Giddens and Will Hutton in conversation. In *On the edge: Living with global capitalism,* ed. W. Hutton and A. Giddens, 1–51. London: Vintage.
Gross, O. 2006. What emergency regime? *Constellations* 13: 74–88.
Harvey, David. 1989. *The condition of postmodernity.* Oxford: Blackwell.
Held, David, and Anthony McGrew. 2003. *Globalization and anti-globalization.* Cambridge: Polity Press.
Held, David, Anthony McGrew, David Goldblatt, and Jonathan Perraton. 1999. *Global transformations—politics, economics and culture.* Cambridge: Polity Press.

Hertz Noreena. 2001. *The silent takeover: Global capitalism and the death of democracy.* London: Arrow.
Higgott, Richard. 2000. Contested globalization: The changing context and normative challenges. *Review of International Studies* 26: 131–53.
Hirst, Paul. 2001. *War and power in the 21st century—the state, military conflict and the international system.* Cambridge: Polity Press.
Hirst, Paul, and Grahame Thompson. 1999. *Globalization in question.* Cambridge: Polity Press.
Hough, Paul. 2004. *Understanding global security.* London: Routledge.
Huntington, Samuel. 2002. *The clash of civilizations and the remaking of world order.* New York: Free Press.
James, Paul. 2006. *Globalism, nationalism, tribalism: Bringing theory back in.* London: Sage.
Kaldor, Mary. 2003. *Global civil society: An answer to war.* Cambridge: Polity Press.
Kayatekin, S. A., and D. E. Ruccio. 1998. Global fragments: Subjectivity and class politics in discourses of globalization. *Economy and Society* 27: 74–96.
King, G., and C. Murray. 2001–2002. Rethinking human security. *Political Science* 116: 4585–4610.
Klein, Naomi. 2002. *Logo fences and windows: Dispatches from the front lines of the globalization debate.* New York: Picador.
Legrain, Philippe. 2004. *Open world: The truth about globalization.* New York: Ivan Dee.
Maddison, Angus. 2001. *The world economy: A millennial perspective.* Paris: OECD.
Mathews, Jessica. 1989. Redefining security. *Foreign Affairs* 68: 12–177.
Munck, R. 2006. Global civil society: Royal road or slippery path? *VOLUNTAS* 17: 324–31.
Münkler, Herfried. 2005. *The new wars.* Cambridge: Polity Press.
O'Brien, Robert, Anne Marie Goetz, Jan Aart Scholte, and Marc Williams. 2000. *Contesting global governance: Multilateral economic institutions and global social movements.* Cambridge and New York: Cambridge University Press.
Ohmae, Kenichi. 1995. *The borderless world.* London: Collins. (Orig. pub. 1990.)
Paris, Roland. 2004. Human security: Paradigm shift or hot air? In *New global dangers: Changing dimensions of international security,* ed. M. Brown, O. Cote, S. Lynn-Jones, and S. Miller, 249–64. Cambridge, MA: MIT Press.
Pianta, Mario. 2001. Parallel summits of global civil society. In *Global civil society, 2001,* ed. Helmut Anheier, Marlics Glasius, and Mary Kaldor, 169–194. Oxford: Oxford University Press.
Ritzer, George. 1993. *The McDonaldization of society.* Newbury Park, CA: Pine Forge Press.
Robertson, Roland. 1992. *Globalization: Social theory and global culture.* London: Sage.
———. 1995. Globalization. In *Global modernities,* ed. M. Featherstone. London: Sage.
Rogers, Paul. 2000. *Losing control: Global security in the twenty-first century.* London: Pluto Press.
———. 2007. *Into the Long War.* London: Pluto Press.
Schirato, Tony, and Jenn Webb. 2003. *Understanding globalization.* London: Sage.

Scholte, Jan Aart. 2000. *Globalization: A critical introduction*. London: Palgrave.
Smith, Steve. 2005. The contested concept of security. In *Critical security studies and world politics,* ed. K. Booth. Boulder, CO: Lynne Rienner.
———. 2006. The concept of security in a globalising world. In *Globalisation and conflict: National security in a "new" strategic era*, ed. R Patman, 33–55. London: Routledge.
Therborn, Göran. 2000. Dimensions of globalisation and the dynamics of (in)equalities. In *The ends of globalization*, ed. Don Kalb, Marco van der Lan, Richard Stanning, Bout van Steenbergen, and Nic Wilterdink, 33–48. Lanham, MD: Rowman & Littlefield.
Thomas, Caroline. 1987. *In search of security: The Third World in international relations*. Brighton, UK: Harvester Wheatsheaf.
Tickner, Ann. 2001. *Gendering world politics: Issues and approaches in the post–Cold War era.* New York: Columbia University Press.
Tooze, Roger. 2005. The missing link: Security, critical international political economy and community. In *Critical Security Studies and World Politics,* ed. K. Booth, 133–58. Boulder, CO: Lynne Rienner.
UN Development Programme (UNDP). 2002. *Human development report: Deepening democracy in a fragmented world.* New York: Oxford University Press.
Urry, John. 2003. *Global complexity.* Cambridge: Polity Press.
Waters, Malcolm. 2001. *Globalization.* New York: Routledge.
Weiss, Linda. 2003. Is the state being "transformed" by globalization? In *States in the Flobal Economy: Bringing Domestic Institutions Back In*, ed. Linda Weiss. Cambridge: Cambridge University Press.
Wolf, Martin. 2004. *Why globalization works*. New Haven, CT: Yale University Press.
World Bank. 2002. *Globalization, growth, and poverty: Building an inclusive world economy.* New York: Oxford University Press.
World Commission on the Social Dimension of Globalization. 2003. *Creating opportunities for all.* Available at http://www.ito.org/public/English/wcsdg/dcs/report.pdf.
Wyn Jones, R. 1999. *Security, strategy and critical theory*. Boulder, CO: Lynne Reinner.
Young, Iris M. 2007. *Global challenges: War, self-determination, and responsibility for justice*. Cambridge: Polity Press.

1
Citizenship

Peter Kivisto

Citizenship can be succinctly defined in terms of two component features. First, it constitutes membership in a polity, and as such it inevitably involves a tension between inclusion and exclusion, between those deemed eligible for citizenship and those who are denied the right to become members. In its earliest form in ancient Greece, the polity in question was the city-state. In the modern world, it was transformed during the era of democratic revolutions into the nation-state. Second, membership brings with it a reciprocal set of duties and rights, both of which vary by place and time, though some are universal. This leads to a final point: citizenship exists only in democratic regimes, for in nondemocratic ones people are subjects rather than citizens.

Citizenship implies the dichotomizing of the "we," members of the political community, and "they," those who remain outsiders. Thus, one can aptly speak about national citizenship as entailing social closure around the political community. To borrow from Charles Tilly (1985), the role of the state is akin to that of a protection racket. While the ways that state protection addresses the insecurities of citizens is multifaceted, the two approaches bearing directly on citizenship are those that entail determining who can and who cannot enter a nation's boundaries and under what terms, and second, who can and who cannot be admitted to full societal membership by qualifying for citizenship (Béland 2005). The creation of the passport, the passage of immigration laws, and legislation determining the terms of deciding who is eligible for citizenship have been the main approaches to effecting this type of state protection.

Complicating this situation are relatively recent developments that suggest the world is entering a new era in which the nation-state's monopoly on defining citizenship is being challenged. In large part, this is attributable to the rapid expansion of people with dual or multiple citizenships and the growing willingness of governments to legalize, or at least tolerate, this situation. This increase is largely attributable to transnational migration, which though not entirely new is more significant today as a result of new communications technologies and improved transportation networks. Second, as exponents of postnationalist thought such as Yasemin Soysal (1994) contend, suprastate entities such as the United Nations and the European Union (EU) are increasingly coming to assume some of the roles traditionally located solely within the nation-state. This is particularly the case with the issue of human rights, where there is evidence of the embryonic form of a global human rights regime. This is also relevant for environmental concerns, as the Kyoto Protocol makes clear, for these are matters that transcend existing political borders. Although the EU is unique, the fact that citizens of its member states can treat their social rights as applying outside their national boundaries signals yet another development of interest.

Contrary to those postnational scholars who argue that these developments signal the decline of the nation-state, the events that have occurred during what has become known as the age of terrorism, the post-9/11 world, call this into question as the state apparatuses of the world's liberal democracies have reasserted themselves. With this in mind, the matter of how they have responded to the proliferation of dual citizenship raises interesting questions, both about each respective state's understanding of its own security needs and about whether dual citizenship poses a threat. Given the fact that social scientists and policy makers have only recently begun to focus on this topic, much of what we know at present is based on a rather limited empirical foundation. What follows, therefore, should be seen as a review of the state of the field nearing the end of the first decade of the twenty-first century.

In the past, including the recent past, dual citizenship was considered to be a problem. Today it is increasingly viewed instead as a possibility that needs to be negotiated from standpoints ranging from a simple pragmatic tolerance to active encouragement. Such a bald statement needs immediately to be qualified lest the contemporary significance of dual citizenship be misconstrued as yet another of those claims about a radical rupture between past and present—reflected, for instance, in many accounts of postmodernism, postnationalism, and various other "posts." In addition, it needs to be stressed that those actors treating the phenomenon as either a problem or a possibility include in various ways agents of states—including, of course, political elites, government bureaucrats, and cultural elites concerned with offering ideological defenses of particular national identities.

Since the birth of modern nation-states and the emergence of the idea of citizenship within the boundaries of such political entities, the issue of dual citizenship has been addressed by those elites (Kivisto and Faist 2007). Modern nation-states claim a monopoly not only on violence but on determinations of membership. Indeed, it is the state that arbitrates the distinctions between citizen and alien, between insider and outsider, between member and nonmember. States have been averse to ceding the power to decide who is and who is not qualified to become a citizen, and this has led to certain inherent dilemmas for both individuals and states. If each state establishes its own citizenship laws, individuals may well find themselves in situations where they can legally become citizens of two or more states. On the other hand, other individuals may find that they can potentially become stateless.

HISTORICAL EXCURSUS

Dual citizenship became a matter of concern in the nineteenth century chiefly because of the impact of emigration from Europe to the United States. It came to a head when immigrants seeking to become naturalized citizens of their new homeland were confronted with the challenge posed by the refusal of their states of origin to allow them to renounce their original citizenship. The refusal was at some level perplexing given the fact that both political and cultural elites at the time also tended to denounce the emigrants as traitors to the homeland. Traitors they may be, but the very same states were not prepared to release them from the obligations of citizenship. Although this may seem ironic, in fact, it was a product of rational calculation, particularly because of a desire to maintain their émigré population as a potential source for military conscription.

These sending states, quite simply, sought to reinforce their claim to determine all matters involving citizenship, ranging from the matter of inclusion to the matter of exit. For its part, concerned about what was seen as the problem of dual loyalties, American immigration law called for naturalizing citizens to renounce their previous allegiances. But as Peter Spiro (2002, 22) has pointed out, the issue not only concerned the relationship between the state and the citizen. It also involved interstate relations. Specifically, the monopoly of control over its citizenry was not questioned by other states provided that the citizen did not hold dual citizenship. If an individual did, questions were raised about the ability of the nation to do whatever it wished to its citizens because there were limits as to what could be done to citizens of other countries.

The tide of immigration was not going to be stemmed by this intrastate conflict over competing citizenship regimes. Thus, in the end a negotiated settlement had to be worked out, commencing with the treaties between the United States and various Western European nations that collectively became known as the Bancroft Treaties. The guiding principle behind these treaties was that dual citizenship should be avoided as much as possible. The states did not seek to eradicate dual citizenship entirely; rather, they attempted to contain it. In particular, from the perspective of a settler society such as the United States, it was understood that nation building could not proceed unless the huge infusion of newcomers arriving at the nation's shores could repudiate their earlier national identities and, in effect, start over.

The significance of treating national identity in civic rather than ethnic terms was that by making the choice to become an American volitional, the message was that earlier claims to primordial allegiances were to be viewed as suspect. Meanwhile, the sending states learned that it was best to cut their losses. Several factors led them to this conclusion, including the growing power of the United States, both politically and economically. Second, some states discovered that when their émigré populations maintain an interest in homeland politics, the results could be a mixed bag. While they might work to support existing regimes, they equally might work to overthrow them. Although the factors at play differed depending on the particular state in question, it was clear by the early decades of the twentieth century that a growing consensus between sending and receiving nations was emerging. This consensus was codified in 1930 in the

Hague Convention concerning Certain Questions Relating to the Conflict of Nationality, in which the signatories established the principle that all people should be citizens of one and only one state. Two things were to be avoided: promoting dual citizenship and constructing policies that resulted in statelessness.

This has been the guiding thread of state policies in the world's liberal democracies until very recently, when fissures in this consensus have developed; that being said, it was never the case that states attempted to eliminate dual citizenship altogether. In the case of a settler state like the United States, the goal was to insure that naturalized citizens did not maintain citizenship in their nation of origin. However, in other instances dual citizenship was permitted, a consequence of the competing claims of four criteria that can factor into the citizenship laws of particular states: the *jus soli* principle, the *jus sanguinis* principle, marital status, and residential location (Hansen and Weil 2002, 2). For example, children born in the United States of noncitizen parents will be both citizens of the United States and citizens of their parents' homeland, which in some cases might mean that at birth the child actually has three legitimate citizenships (if the parents were from two different countries). Meanwhile, those nations of Western Europe that were once primarily sending nations have since the second half of the twentieth century become immigrant-receiving nations—and as a consequence have had to wrestle with the issue of naturalization that since the nineteenth century has primarily preoccupied the historic settler states.

It is in this historical context that current developments in the expansion of dual citizenship need to be understood, including those related to state efforts to reconsider the principle of the Hague Convention and changes that are a consequence of the growing role of trans-state entities in shaping citizenship regimes. Stephen Legomsky (2003, 81) has pointed to the inherent instability of this approach to citizenship by noting that there are three factors shaping citizenship regimes that have the capacity to interact to yield dual or plural citizenship in spite of opposition to it in principle: (1) "each state decides who its own nationals are"; (2) "a state typically provides alternative multiple routes to nationality"; and (3) "the rules vary from state to state."

CONTEMPORARY DEVELOPMENTS

Until the last decades of the twentieth century, this instability did not lead to a dramatic escalation of dual citizenship. When it did, it would occur as a consequence of mass immigration and, to a lesser extent, of the reconfiguration of national boundaries or the willingness to embrace expatriates in nearby countries in certain parts of Central and Eastern Europe. Seyla Benhabib (2004, 1) has provided the following backdrop to recent developments:

> The modern nation-state has regulated membership in terms of one principal category: national citizenship. We have entered an era when state sovereignty has been frayed and the institution of national citizenship has been disaggregated or unbundled into diverse elements. New modalities

of membership have emerged, with the result that the boundaries of the political community, as defined by the nation-state system, are no longer adequate to membership.

In discussing the disaggregation of citizenship, Benhabib (2004, 145) distinguishes three parts: "collective identity, privileges of political membership, and social rights and claims." In a subsequent article, she observes that linked to the disaggregation of citizenship are two other developments that serve to frame the factors shaping traditional perspectives on citizenship: the rise of an international human rights regime and the expansion of cosmopolitan norms (Benhabib 2007). She points to the role of global capitalism in effecting the growing "deterritorialization of law." Though the implications and impacts of each vary by case, in combination they have undermined state sovereignty. However, undermining means that state sovereignty has been eroded or weakened, not that it has been replaced.

It is in this context that one can discuss the recasting of citizenship from being rooted in the nation-state to becoming, not unfettered from the state, but located in an expanding circle of ties that move from the locality through the region to the transnational level. Benhabib refers to this as a "citizenship of residency," contending that this shift constitutes support, in part, for the postnational thesis. Such a reconfigured citizenship is predicated on multicultural engagements in all three spatial sectors. This is, thus, nested citizenship—and as such it is evident in the nations of the EU, not in the United States. This might account in part for the greater willingness of many (though not all) European states compared to the United States to consider dual citizenship, for in Europe, there appears to be an elective affinity between dual and nested citizenship. Although Benhabib provides concrete examples of the ways that activist citizens are exemplifying the cosmopolitan sensibility underpinning a citizenship of residency, she makes clear that this is an incipient form of citizenship, far more aspiration than actualization. Indeed, her article ends by stressing that it is only possible if provided with the institutional structure to nurture and sustain it.

Dual citizenship is not her focus. However, implicitly her work offers a partial answer to why so many states have been willing in recent years to entertain the prospect of legitimizing, or barring that, tolerating dual citizenship. The simple answer is this: the erosion of the sovereignty of nation-states makes them vulnerable to pressures exerted by trans-state institutional actors and a transnational citizenry.

DUAL CITIZENSHIP AND SOLIDARITY

Peter Spiro (2007) has focused on the impact of postnationalism on dual citizenship. Like Benhabib, he is not particularly sanguine about what the erosion of state sovereignty will yield—at least in the short term, at a point characterized by "immature post-national structures." Spiro expresses concern about the lack of the institutional structures needed to insure the robustness of an international human rights regime. Not knowing precisely what will happen in the longer term, he makes the following claims about the present and near term. First, dual citizenship will continue to grow and will become part of the political landscape. Second, the prospect of dual citizenship will be perceived and pursued in largely instrumental terms. Transnational migrants can find it advantageous to possess multiple passports. While receiving states sometimes operate with the assumption that easing naturalization requirements will facilitate incorporation into the new society of residence, Spiro does not think this is a given.

He does think that one of the consequences of the cheapening of citizenship is that it "doesn't get or give much any more." Thus, while citizenship continues to speak to in-group membership, such membership is devalued as both the rights that accrue to citizenship status and the obligations flowing from it become increasingly thin. An instrumental attitude toward citizenship derives from this fact. What this suggests is that the bases for solidarity predicated on emotional ties to the political community and to fellow citizens are lacking, or at least are insufficiently powerful to be efficacious.

There is a large claim being advanced here: dual citizenship serves to undermine the state-based societal community. If this is true, the prevalence of dual citizenship represents a challenge to theorists building on the tradition of T. H. Marshall who have invested citizenship with the capacity to unite individuals in a transcendent community. The work of Parsons (1971, 2007) constitutes the primary example of such a position, arguing that modern citizenship contains the capacity of overcoming the divisiveness of religious, racial, and ethnic identities without necessitating the elimination of difference. Parsons thought that these particularistic identities could persist over time as long as their salience was tempered. Key to this happening was the emergence of cross-cutting allegiances and social ties, the likes of which would serve to tamp down the potentially incendiary character of these particularistic identities. Citizenship, in this scheme, would become the overarching identity of individual members, containing and constraining all other identities.

Parsons operated within a theoretical perspective that treated society and the nation-state as isomorphic. His theoretical framework was not conceived in terms of a recognition of transnational or globalizing forces that located nations within a larger, trans-state and global context. Moreover, although he thought difference might persist, he did so without a consideration of the potential for a multicultural perspective to emerge and to promote the idea of group rights complementing individual rights. Equipped in his later years with an evolutionary schema, Parsons's work strikes us today as naively optimistic.

Such cannot be said of the work of Jeffrey Alexander, who though deeply influenced by Parsons has also moved beyond the Parsonian imprint. In his book *The Civil Sphere* (2006), Alexander claims that multiculturalism properly understood can have a positive impact on the incorporation of marginalized groups— immigrants and others. The civil sphere becomes for him the site where both difference and solidarity are possible. Rather than being conceived as mutually exclusive, as critics of multiculturalism often claim, they are seen as having the potential to coexist. Stripped of any notion of evolutionary movement, the project of civil society is conceived in terms of possibilities, not inevitabilities. Civil society must be achieved, not once and for all, but over and over again.

Spiro does not address such theoretical projects, but his bottom-line conclusion does reflect a significant challenge. If dual citizenship undermines solidarity at the national level, those particularistic identities will fill the void, offering themselves as alternatives. This is a disturbing prospect insofar as what it can suggest is the balkanization of a nation. Douglas Hartmann and Joseph Gerteis (2005) refer to this situation as "fragmented pluralism," which occurs when the center does not hold. Given the abundant evidence we have, not from the world's existing liberal democracies, but from such failed states as Yugoslavia, Rwanda, Congo, and Iraq, fragmented pluralism can produce hell on earth. This is not to suggest that such a scenario is likely in the liberal democracies. Even those who see an erosion of such states know that they remain powerful. What Spiro seems to think the future might portend for such nations is a situation in which the capacity of the state to forge allegiances does not disappear, but national identity should be seen as increasingly competing with other identities and solidarities. No longer the overarching mode of identity containing others, it is becoming merely one among others.

Given that we are early into what will be a long process, it is impossible to provide sufficient evidence to either support or refute the assertion that dual citizenship serves to undermine the state. However, there are some clues that can be distilled from other chapters in this encyclopedia that offer a variety of concrete empirical examples to provisionally assess this thesis. Herein, we find support for Benhabib and Spiro as well as evidence that calls their claims into question, leading to an appreciation of the fundamental ambiguity of the present. These clues might be taken as key elements to consider in future research agendas aimed at ascertaining the precise impact of dual citizenship.

BEYOND 9/11

Since the events of September 11, 2001, the U.S. government has aggressively pursued policies aimed at reasserting the singular role of the state in promoting national security. In response to the tragic events of that fateful day, the Bush administration orchestrated a public relations campaign aimed at convincing the citizenry that their safety rested in the hands of government that of necessity had to operate in new ways to meet the terrorist threat. The color-coded national alerts were intended to be a device to calibrate levels of fear among the public at large. The administration acted without transparency and argued that secrecy was essential if they were to succeed in protecting the nation. At the same time, administration officials argued that their conduct had to be unilateral, that, in other words, they would not be tied to a variety of international agreements. (Thus, the attorney general described certain features of the Geneva Convention as quaint.) Not surprisingly, the United Kingdom, America's closest ally in the "War on Terror," pushed the securitization envelope close to that of the United States, especially after the London Underground suicide bombing on July 7, 2005. However, even states opposed to the U.S. approach and critical of the war in Iraq have also, in more limited ways, reasserted the power of the state in security matters.

Audrey Macklin (2007) provides a lesson in point in her discussion of how securitization affects dual citizenship. Her argument can be summarized in two words: membership counts. In examining the relationship between membership and the rights and obligations substance of citizenship, she indicates just how much it counts in her case studies of the Khadr family in Canada and Yaser Hamdi in the United States. The awesome power of the state is being asserted here and elsewhere as ideas such as revoking citizenship—as she points out, most acutely in the United Kingdom and Germany—have gained currency in some policy circles and among the public at large. While these have not always been acted on, far more consequential at the moment is the widespread resistance to the continued entry of asylum seekers and refugees.

Mackin sees these and related developments as challenging the idea of dual citizenship on the suspicion of the divided loyalties of newcomers. In this she is no doubt quite right. This suggests that we have not yet moved decisively past the old concerns that informed the Hague Convention. Given the right circumstances, state authorities can find themselves in a position to ratchet up public suspicions of foreigners and cast into doubt the wisdom of granting citizenship rights to people who might also maintain their legal attachments to their nation of origin.

This position is echoed by Triadafilos Triadafilopoulos (2007), who locates what he refers to as the current post-9/11 "security norms" in broader historical context. Three interrelated topics are discussed, beginning with the role of war in the formation of modern nation-states, moving to changes that have occurred since the middle of the twentieth century, and finally engaging the debate on postnationalism. The need to make loyal subject bodies available for the protective and expansionist activities of militaries and to be able to extract needed funds through taxation required states to forge the bonds of nationalistic solidarity. As Triadafilopoulos puts it, this amounted early on in a "revolution in loyalties." In his view, the primacy of warfare meant that the loyalty of subjects had to be sufficient to yield a willingness to make blood sacrifices on behalf of the state.

In such a situation, dual nationalities were inherently problematic and thus, from the vantage of states, were to be prevented whenever possible. This particular perspective was codified in the aforementioned 1930 Hague Convention. Writing at around the same time, German political theorist Carl Schmitt (1996) argued that states could not exist without enemies. Triadafilopoulos views the post–World War II era as a watershed in the history of the modern state insofar as war was no longer normative in the same sense and intrastate rivalries took on a new character. While this is no doubt an apt characterization of most of the world's major liberal democracies, it looks somewhat different from the vantage of the United States, where the Cold War, which stretched over four decades, quickly gave way to the new war on combating nonstate terrorists, a war the Bush regime and its British allies have frequently described as never-ending and as shaping the political agenda of the twenty-first century. Wars in various guises continue, but they no longer tend to require mass mobilization of the citizenry.

Triadafilopoulos stresses what he refers to as the reprivatization of war, by which he means the increasingly reliance on a professional military rather than conscription. The significance of such a shift is that the issue of dual loyalties ceases to have the same urgency as it did prior to World War II. This, he contends, goes some distance in explaining why so many states are today willing to entertain the prospect of dual citizenship. It is not that the states support dual nationality but, rather, that the reasons for avoiding it become less compelling. In contrast to Mackin, although not ruling out a reversal of this trend as a result of fears of terrorism and thus in the interest of state security, Triadafilopoulos sees little evidence that the trend will reverse anytime in the near future.

Jürgen Gerdes, Thomas Faist, and Beate Rieple (2007) attempt to explain why it is that Germany managed to pass a new citizenship law that was among the most liberal in Europe in terms of its *jus soli* component while at the same time was averse to passing legislation that would have legitimized dual citizenship. In this view, one might have expected liberalization in one aspect of citizenship law to be linked to liberalization in the other. If it is true that the shift from an ethnic to a civic definition of citizenship is predicated on a republican model, then despite voices of protest being registered on the extreme right, the claim can be made that "we are all republican now." To the extent that this claim was embraced on the left and elicited sufficient support on the right, the introduction of a more tolerant civic version of citizenship was possible.

However, at the same time, dual citizenship proved to be problematic insofar as it highlighted differences between the left and right over the respective weights to be accorded to rights versus obligations. The left, endorsing a liberal individualist perspective, placed an emphasis on individual rights, including the right to maintain dual citizenship. On the other hand, the right operated from what Gerdes, Faist, and Rieple (2007, 12) called a "state-communitarian standpoint" or what would commonly be seen as a republican rather than liberal perspective. The concern with dual citizenship from this perspective emanates from the conviction that citizenship must be predicated on solidarity rooted in an emotional attachment to the nation and a willingness to entertain the prospect that one might actually have to sacrifice on its behalf. From this vantage, dual citizenship is inherently suspected because it smacks of promoting an instrumental attitude toward membership.

The current German stance on dual citizenship parallels that of the United States. Of course, the United States was from its founding—at least in principle—based on a civic rather than ethnic base. National solidarity was thus conceived in voluntaristic terms rather than rooted in bloodlines. This generated a conception of national identity that allowed for considerable ethnic diversity. If there was a suspicion that any particular group's ethnic allegiances would trump national solidarity—and the suspicion arose often in the nation's history—this tended with the passage of time and generational succession to give way to the view that ethnicity could safely be subsumed within the overarching solidarity of national identity. National elites often sent mixed messages about ethnic involvements in homeland politics. At times, such involvements worked in the interests of elites, as they did for anti-Castro Cubans during the Cold War. At other times, the prospect of homeland engagements, real or perceived, were seen as threatening, with the Japanese case in World War II being the most obvious and troubling example.

In this context, dual citizenship could be problematic, though not necessarily so—which may explain why American policy for the past half century can be characterized as ambivalent. On the one hand, there has been no effort to permit naturalizing citizens to maintain their earlier citizenships. On the other hand, there has been no attempt to impose criminal sanctions on individuals who do maintain dual citizenship. This amounts to a "don't ask, don't tell" policy.

IMPACTS OF DUAL CITIZENSHIP

What do we know about the actual impacts of dual citizenship and about whether the substantive content of citizenship has been changed by cross-cutting national loyalties? Irene Bloemraad is interested in whether a state's openness to dual citizenship has an impact on the willingness of immigrants to naturalize, which she sees as a central indicator of incorporation. In *Becoming a Citizen* (2006), she enters into a comparative analysis of a select number of immigrant groups in the United States and Canada. What she discovered is that immigrants are more inclined to naturalize in Canada compared to those locating in the United States. The question is why? If the primary reason for naturalizing was instrumental, one might expect the rates to be essentially the same. Given that this is not the case, Bloemraad offers a counter-explanation. The United States still demands a renunciation of prior citizenship at naturalization proceedings. Though immigrants tend to know that this renunciation will not be acted on, the requirement does set a tone that implies dual nationality may be tolerated but is not embraced by the state. This approach stands in contrast to Canada, where dual nationality is valorized in official government statements.

Bloemraad interprets this valorization as significant at the symbolic rather than the instrumental level. In short, it defines Canada as an accepting and inclusive multicultural nation—a place, in short, sufficiently attractive for immigrants to want to forge a permanent legal attachment. In a sense, this might strike one as counterintuitive given that one's willingness to reject a previous allegiance might be taken to signal a desire to attach at an emotional level with a nation. However, what Bloemraad has identified is a manifestation of what Barbara Ballis Lal (1990, 3) has referred to as the "ethnicity paradox," which contends that in the process of seeking to remain attached to their ethnic origins, group members paradoxically prepare themselves for incorporation into the host society. Although Bloemraad does not say so in as many words, what this might suggest is that dual citizenship is in some sense a temporary phenomenon insofar as with the passage of time, the salience of the citizenship of the nation of origin progressively declines.

Such a conclusion can be drawn from José Itzigsohn's 2007 study of dual citizenship among Mexicans and Dominicans in the United States. In both instances, homeland political officials confronted the reality of well-established migratory networks and a new political climate brought about by the end of rule of entrenched political elites. Realizing the economic significance of remittances, these officials promoted dual citizenship as a mechanism designed to maintain loyalty to the homeland while simultaneously encouraging incorporation into the United States. The anticipated consequences of dual citizenship included the perpetuation of the remittance system and the willingness of the émigré population to serve a lobbying function on behalf of the homeland.

Itzigsohn has discovered that in both cases these expectations have not been realized, concluding that what he refers to as transnational citizenship has produced "paradoxical and contradictory" results. One of the findings most relevant to the assessment of the significance of dual citizenship is that for both Mexicans and Dominicans, a very small percentage of the eligible populations living in the United States have opted to participate in their respective homeland's electoral process. Although Itzigsohn is hesitant to draw broad conclusions about what this means for dual citizenship, his evidence suggests that in becoming naturalized citizens, immigrants have opted to hang their political loyalties on the receiving country's peg rather than on the homeland peg. This is not to suggest that transnational practices will cease, for this shift of political allegiances does not necessarily mean the end to transnational economic, cultural, and personal ties.

The complex character of dual citizenship is also evident in a study of Hong Kong Canadians conducted by Valerie Preston, Myer Siemiatycki, and Audrey Kobayashi (2007). If there are any recent immigrants more inclined to operate with a purely instrumental view of citizenship, it is members of Hong Kong's business community attempting to sort out the implications of the transition from British to Chinese rule. As it turns out, however, the picture is considerably more complex. Although the small sample size cautions against broad generalizations, it appears that for most immigrants, instrumental and symbolic factors are interwoven. That being said, what that might mean for the future remains unclear. Dual citizenship could conceivably be important in both ways for those economic "Argonauts" that are exemplars of economic transnationalism. However, for those Hong Kong Chinese who over time find their economic future located chiefly in North America, dual citizenship may increasingly become symbolic in the sense of Gans's concept of symbolic ethnicity—an ethnicity based primarily on nostalgia, with few behavioral consequences (1979).

DUAL CITIZENSHIP IN AN ERA OF HEIGHTENED SECURITY CONCERNS: A RESEARCH AGENDA

The proliferation of people in Europe and North America who possess dual or multiple citizenships has proven to be a path-dependent process—one that once set in motion has little chance of being effectively reversed. It is for this reason that nation-states appear to be engaged in a process of learning to adjust to this new reality. The implications of this situation for state-defined security interests are little understood. Some states will—and indeed are—resorting to the old view that questions whether dual citizenship results in divided loyalties potentially, though not necessarily, threatening to security. Others, under the influence of postnationalist thought, will contend on the contrary that since citizenship has become increasingly instrumental, involving the acquisition of various rights, it is increasingly becoming less, not more, consequential in defining individual loyalties. Between these two positions is considerable room for other potential outcomes.

It is useful to be reminded that in many respects the study of dual citizenship is in its infancy, reflective of the fact that contemporary developments have only recently begun to receive the scholarly attention they deserve. It is also useful to note that social scientists have a rather checkered record of predicting how the future is likely to unfold. It behooves us to keenly appreciate that there is much we do not know about dual citizenship and we should therefore be rather circumspect in predicting future trends. Instead, we ought to be about the business of developing comprehensive comparative research agendas. In an era of mass immigration, it can safely be assumed that levels of dual citizenship will remain high. What we know relatively little about at the moment is the larger significance and the meaning attached to dual citizenship.

One track of research ought to focus on state actors as they either embrace or resist dual citizenship. We know less than we should at the moment about the actual constellation of political forces at play in getting dual citizenship onto the legislative agenda. Why, for example, has this matter been the focus of parliamentary debate in Germany, whereas it has not received comparable attention in the United States? What is the role of political elites, and how do the divisions among elites structure discourse? Similarly, we need to know more about the role of nonelites, ranging from the impacts of organized anti-immigration social movements to the lobbying efforts of pro-immigrant forces and the immigrants themselves. Contrary to postnationalist theorists who argue that the focus of policy-related research on dual citizenship ought to be focused on the role of trans-state entities, one might argue—backed in part by a growing body of research on the post-9/11 security state—that states continue to be the central locus of decision making regarding all aspects of dual citizenship. At the same time, it is true that trans-state institutions have increasingly come to play a role in this process, particular in Europe, where the EU's significance in such matters has expanded in recent decades.

The second research locus ought to be on dual citizens themselves. How did they become dual citizens and why? Did they make a conscious choice or not? Did they opt to become dual citizens for instrumental reasons or for deeply held attachments, with similar emotional valences, to two places? Do they perceive dual citizenship as a temporary or permanent aspect of their lives? What is their understanding of the issue of divided loyalties? How do they define citizenship: in thin, but rights-bearing terms or in thicker, more republican terms involving emotional and behavioral solidarity with particular polities? At the moment, we actually know precious little about these and related questions, though some researchers have begun to redress this situation.

In short, we need to know much more about the phenomenology of dual citizenship. While true, knowing more is not in itself sufficient. Conducting research into the social psychology of dual citizens is important, but this needs to be complemented with research into the impacts of dual citizenship on the political systems of both the nation of origin and the receiving nation (Deaux 2006).

Indeed, we live in a transitional age, one where the previous international consensus about the undesirability of dual citizenship has broken down and has not been replaced by a comparable international consensus that definitely rejects that earlier consensus. Rather, we live at present in an interstitial moment, where much remains indeterminate. In such a time, research ought to be framed in a way that appreciates dual citizenship's fluid and ambiguous character and that carefully distinguishes its long-term implications from those of the short term.

FURTHER READING

Alexander, Jeffrey C. *The Civil Sphere.* New York: Oxford University Press, 2006.
Benhabib, Seyla. *The Rights of Others: Aliens, Residents, and Citizens.* Cambridge: Cambridge University Press, 2004.
Deaux, Kay. *To Be an Immigrant.* New York: Russell Sage Foundation, 2006.
Kivisto, Peter, and Thomas Faist. *Citizenship: Discourse, Theory, and Transnational Prospects.* Malden, MA: Blackwell, 2007.

REFERENCES

Alexander, Jeffrey C. 2006. *The civil sphere.* New York: Oxford University Press.
Béland, Daniel. 2005. Insecurity, citizenship, and globalization: The multiple faces of state protection. *Sociological Theory* 23: 25–41.
Benhabib, Seyla. 2004. *The rights of others: Aliens, residents, and citizens.* Cambridge: Cambridge University Press.
———. 2007. Twilight of sovereignty or the emergence of cosmopolitan norms? Rethinking citizenship in volatile times. In *Dual citizenship in global perspective,* ed. Thomas Faist and Peter Kivisto, 247–71. Basingstoke, UK: Palgrave Macmillan.
Bloemraad, Irene. 2006. *Becoming a citizen: Incorporating immigrants and refugees in the United States and Canada.* Berkeley: University of California Press.
Deaux, Kay. 2006. *To be an immigrant.* New York: Russell Sage Foundation.
Gans, Herbert. 1979. Symbolic ethnicity: The future of ethnic groups and cultures in America. *Ethnic and Racial Studies* 2: 1–20.
Gerdes, Jürgen, Thomas Faist, and Beate Rieple. 2007. We are all "Republicans" now: The politics of dual citizenship in Germany. In *Dual citizenship in Europe,* ed Thomas Faist, 45–76. Aldershot, UK: Ashgate.
Hansen, Randall, and Patrick Weil. 2002. Dual citizenship in a changed world: Immigration, gender, and social rights. In *Dual nationality, social rights, and federal citizenship in the U.S. and Europe: The reinvention of citizenship,* ed. Randall Hansen and Patrick Weil, 1–15. New York: Berghahn.
Hartmann, Douglas, and Joseph Gerteis. 2005. Dealing with diversity: Mapping multi- culturalism in sociological terms." *Sociological Theory* 23: 218–40.
Itzigsohn, José. 2007. Migration and transnational citizenship in Latin America: The cases of Mexico and the Dominican Republic." In *Dual citizenship in global perspective*, ed. Thomas Faist and Peter Kivisto, 113–34. Basingstoke, UK: Palgrave Macmillan.
Kivisto, Peter, and Thomas Faist. 2007. *Citizenship: Discourse, theory, and transnational prospects.* Malden, MA: Blackwell.
Lal, Barbara Ballis. 1990. *The romance of culture in an urban civilization: Robert E. Park on race and ethnic relations in cities.* London: Routledge.
Legomsky, Stephen. 2003. Dual nationality and military service: Strategy number two. In *Rights and duties of dual nationals: Evolution and prospects,* ed. David A. Martin and Kay Hailbronner, 79–126. The Hague: Kluwer Law International.

Macklin, Audrey. 2007. The securitisation of dual citizenship. In *Dual citizenship in global perspective*, ed. Thomas Faist and Peter Kivisto, 42–66. Basingstoke, UK: Palgrave Macmillan.

Parsons, Talcott. 1971. *The system of modern societies.* Englewood Cliffs, NJ: Prentice Hall.

———. 2007. *American society: Toward a theory of societal community,* ed. Giuseppe Sciortino. Boulder, CO: Paradigm.

Preston, Valerie, Myer Siemiatycki, and Audrey Kobayashi. 2007. Dual citizenship among Hong Kong Canadians: Convenience or commitment? In *Dual citizenship in global perspective,* ed. Thomas Faist and Peter Kivisto, 208–23. Basingstoke, UK: Palgrave Macmillan.

Schmitt, Carl. 1996. *The concept of the political.* Chicago: University of Chicago.

Soysal, Yasemin Nuhoğlu. 1994. *Limits of citizenship: Migrants and postnational membership in Europe.* Chicago: University of Chicago Press.

Spiro, Peter. 2002. Embracing dual nationality. In *Dual nationality, social rights, and federal citizenship in the U.S. and Europe: The reinvention of citizenship,* ed. Randall Hansen and Patrick Weil, 19–33. New York: Berghahn.

———. 2007. Dual citizenship: A postnational view. In *Dual citizenship in global perspective,* ed. Thomas Faist and Peter Kivisto, 189–202. Basingstoke, UK: Palgrave Macmillan.

Tilly, Charles. 1985. War making and state making as organized crime. In *Bringing the state back in,* ed. Peter B. Evans, Dietrich Rueschmeyer, and Theda Skocpol, 169–91. Cambridge: Cambridge University Press.

Triadafilopoulos, Triadafilos. 2007. Dual citizenship and security norms in historical perspective. In *Dual citizenship in global perspective,* ed. Thomas Faist and Peter Kivisto, 27–41. Basingstoke, UK: Palgrave Macmillan.

2

Democracy

Harry F. Dahms

> Democracy ... [is] a political system which seeks to steer the movement of society toward its conception of civilization. It is a way of harmonizing our relationships and groupings so that increasingly these may embody the ideas of freedom, equality, and justice. Where successfully practiced, democracy can be called that government of the people which is conducted by representatives of their choosing on their behalf and under their ultimate control. Through these institutions it aspires to become a state of humanity, directed by humanists for the realization of the humaner values. When [Woodrow] Wilson spoke of making the world safe for democracy, he had in mind the need to cultivate an environment favorable for the fruits of this civilization to ripen. (Lipson 1964, 569)

On first sight, *democracy* might appear to be a concept whose meaning and importance are quite straightforward. Yet upon closer inspection, "democracy" tends to be just as intricate and complicated an issue as the societies in whose context it is being employed. On the one hand, the ubiquity of uses of "democracy" and such related terms as "democratization" and "democratic" suggests that life in "democratic societies" is becoming an integral part of normalcy for a continuously growing number of people. On the other hand, it is neither possible to provide an agreed-upon definition of democracy that would be safe from contestation nor to circumscribe with any degree of precision its actual impact and force in the world today.[1] Even were it possible to delineate the spectrum of uses of the concept in politics, culture, and society that favor continuing efforts at democratization, in societies whose political systems embody democracy to varying degrees, its proclivity toward being employed—as well as abused—for ideological purposes makes attempts to accurately describe its practical and theoretical meanings difficult.[2] Under conditions of globalization, in particular, it is necessary to specify the larger social and political contexts in which the past, present, and future of democracy can be examined. What complicates matters further is that in many societies, the achievements of past struggles in the name of democracy, both institutional and cultural, appear less secure and reliable now than they did two decades ago—not to mention the popular commitment to continuing those struggles.[3]

Since the beginning of the modern age, efforts at illuminating issues relating to democracy, both as a political and theoretical concept and as a concrete practice, have been burdened by tensions between two sets of perspectives. On the one hand, the search for rules, procedures, and institutions that enable "the people" to govern themselves has inspired the development of a diversity of models (esp. Held 2006). To differing degrees, "actually existing democracies" resulted from efforts to implement particular models, or combined elements from different models, in societies framed by the political organization of the nation-state and an economic process based on more or less self-regulating markets.[4] In modern societies, the spread of democracy occurred within a landscape of political economy whose horizon ranges from free markets at one extreme to socialism at the other. On the other hand, the commitment to advancing a qualitatively superior form of social life and coexistence has been driving periodic renewals of conceptions of democracy that start out from limitations resulting from established rules, procedures, and institutions, which come to be viewed as impeding progress in the name of democracy, toward a truly democratic civilization (Arblaster 2002).

Perspectives on democracy have been fraught with contest, conflict, and fragmentation; and beyond a small number of basic propositions, there is little agreement about democracy's meaning. To the extent that politicians, scholars, and citizens have engaged in discussion about the *most desirable* form of democracy in society, they have little shared understanding of what democracy actually is. Democracy is a concept so open to competing interpretations and conceptualizations that in declaration and in practice, individuals and collective actors seem to be driven by common goals and values, though they may be incompatible or mutually exclusive, reflecting social, political, cultural, and economic conflicts and related contradictions. To be sure, practically speaking, both among scholars and citizens, modes of thinking about democracy tend to be delimited, if not determined, by concrete, historically formed rules, procedures, and institutions. As a consequence, a somewhat fuzzy understanding of democracy as entailing some kind of popular involvement in making laws, formulating policies, and conducting the business of government may be the necessary precondition for collective efforts at tackling or overcoming concrete structural, cultural, and systematic obstacles to the advancement of democracy beyond any particular status quo. In the present context, the status quo would be the framework of liberal democracy.

TOWARD "POST-AUTISTIC" PERSPECTIVES ON THE STUDY OF DEMOCRACY

One of the most compelling features of the debate about globalization is that it occasions opportunities to recognize that the categories developed and employed in the social sciences may not be conducive to illuminating the nature and logic of social life today. Two reasons explain this view. First, to the degree to which globalization is a new phenomenon, the proliferation of markets, intensification of trade and competition across borders, and amplification of communication are producing historically unprecedented circumstances. We require novel tools and frameworks to try to capture the consequences resulting from those processes. Second, conditions of human existence around the world will continue to change in ways that can be anticipated and predicted only to a very limited, and probably to a decreasing, extent. We have little sense of what any society will look like a decade or two from now, or especially a half century from now. Nor does there appear to be more than a vague sense of what ought to be the vanishing point of progress in the near future. Partly because of the ubiquity of uncertainties, people, but especially decision makers in government, business, and organizations, show a weakening commitment to attain identifiable goals or even to identify goals beyond the most obvious and uninspiring imperatives relating to prosperity and stability. Individuals and collective actors alike have become increasingly tepid about pursuing the goals that propelled us toward modern societies, especially after World War II. Yet despite the inevitability of continuing change, there is spreading reluctance to re-envision the future in ways that would be more consistent with the values and desires relating to human security, social justice, and a decent life that have inspired generations of social movements. This reluctance appears especially strong in the institutions of democracy, despite proclamations to the contrary.

Researchers in the social sciences have designed descriptive, explanatory, and interpretive tools and research agendas to circumscribe phenomena as well as to track transformative trends in politics, culture, economy, and society. The tools also help us determine how changes are shaping and reshaping key dimensions of social reality. A common premise for social scientists is that the history and the priorities of each social science are closely linked to the features and processes whose study, especially, is the responsibility of sociology, political science, and economics. Yet a body of literature that has been growing since the early 1990s, when globalization began to be widely recognized as a social force, stresses the need to examine whether the tools and agendas that facilitated social research during the second half of the twentieth century will continue to be useful, especially in studying the proliferating challenges faced by individual societies and human civilization as a whole. A related concern is that such key features of social life as the relationships between business, labor, and government keep changing. Expressed concerns also reflect, however, the recognition that the tools and agendas researchers relied on in the past may have been problematic even before the recent changes associated with globalization became manifest. In the early twenty-first century, the role of democracy is a particularly contested issue, such that agreement about the relevance of democracy's many meanings for research within and across disciplines, as well as societies, remains exceedingly elusive.

Since Karl Marx's critiques of political economy, a long line of critical social and political theorists within and beyond the tradition he inspired have been cautioning that the social sciences are permanently in danger of conflating the goals that provide research institutes and universities with purpose, legitimacy, and funding (and thus are anchored in and reflect concrete societal conditions) with the pursuit of issues most vital for the continued well-being and security of people in the modern age. On the one hand, to be sure, it would be impossible to explicate the multiplicity of human needs related to well-being and human security; indeed, it would be enormously difficult to reduce them to a clearly discernable and adequate set of indicators. Established approaches are more likely to stress some aspects of social reality at the expense of others rather than do justice to their range and depth. On the other hand, in the absence of ongoing efforts in each social science to ensure that the indicators and categories employed correspond to existing and emerging needs and conditions, there is a growing risk of lost opportunities to envision more compelling and effective strategies to address different needs and to increase human security. The continuing and unacknowledged neglect of issues and challenges whose pursuit might enable social scientists to amplify the relevance of research related to concrete social, political, economic, and cultural concerns and limitations also undercuts opportunities to transform the overall practice of each discipline, especially where a discipline reinforces those features of societies that rely on the persistence of needs, limitations, and human insecurities.

With regard to democracy, both its study and its promotion have been impaired by varied ideologies at many levels (Dahms 2005). While studying or promoting democracy independently of concrete social contexts may not be possible, making meaningful statements about democracy without clarifying the precise meaning of the term would likewise be impossible. Indeed, to refer to democracy without acknowledging that the term has been used in too many different contexts and in too many different ways further aggravates the fact that there is neither a widely agreed-upon definition of democracy nor any intuitively obvious way of framing related debates with any degree of coherence.[5] Whether we admit it or not, our use of the concept presupposes a shared understanding; and without our ascertaining the actual extent of such an understanding, common misconceptions, gaps, and failures in communication inevitably persist. Exchanges about democracy, as a set of institutions, mechanisms, or processes, often implicitly reflect the concrete sociohistorical conditions and challenges to which discourse about democracy may, or may not, be an effective response. In turn, where the meaning of democracy remains implied rather than defined, democracy will likely function as a means of avoiding, or distracting from, issues and challenges whose confrontation and resolution will remain ineffectual as long as they remain unaddressed.[6]

In recent years, a number of scholars have started to criticize mainstream approaches in economics as suffering from a condition comparable to autism. The main symptoms of autism relevant in this regard are the more or less pronounced inclination to focus on particular aspects of an environment at the expense of confronting and processing complex conditions and of maintaining functional relationships with other members of one's society. Applied to economics, autism has been employed to describe the proclivity of mainstream economists to reduce the undeniable complexity of dimensions of economic life in society to a small number of variables and to regard those variables as germane to the study of economic life. In addition, disciplinary practices in economics could be compared to autism inasmuch as researchers suffer from disciplinary priorities relating to professional and research success that pose obstacles to recognizing the limited and limiting nature of particular approaches within economics, as well as between economics and the other social sciences. By extension, applying autism to the study of democracy would highlight perspectives, especially in political science, that rely on rational-choice approaches and reduce the social, cultural, and economic complexities of democracy accordingly. Typically though not universally, rational-choice approaches tend to accept as given—and to hypostatize as inescapable—the boundaries of established ways of framing democracy. Such approaches are in danger of implicitly and uncritically replicating and reinforcing features, including those boundaries that appear as more or less problematic, beyond the narrow frame of autistic approaches (Fullbrook 2003, 2007).

During the Cold War, the tendency of the term "democracy" to become shorthand for, and to veil, sedimented assumptions about the desirability of certain political-legal institutional arrangements and processes, corresponding ways of life and culture, and their superiority over alternative models was especially pervasive. Within those societies, politicians and social scientists have interpreted the spread of democracy since the end of World War II as a consequence of the progress of democracy itself, both practically and theoretically. Yet the spread of democracy was to a high degree a function of the priorities and the thrust of the Cold War, which largely framed the formation of democracy as we know it today. Yet both Western capitalist societies and actually existing socialist societies laid claim to democracy, with both claiming the right of first use: communist countries claimed that Western societies undercut their legitimate use of the term in light of the prevalence of social and economic inequalities, which what used to be called bourgeois democracy is barely able to penetrate. Western societies, in turn, contended that the emphasis on political and legal equality, the rule of law, and its strategy for increasing social justice in a context of growing economic prosperity at the national level was more truly democratic than the communist system of repression and control. Yet though Western societies cannot deny or reject democracy and must proclaim related values and goals to be primary guideposts for collective decision making and public policies, given how those societies work, they also cannot truly actualize democracy. Institutionally, liberal democracy tends to be inherently static, whereas modern civilization is inherently dynamic. Yet social scientists are only slowly beginning to think and work in ways that are compatible with the prevalence of dynamic processes and conducive to understanding those processes. Recognizing the capitalist economic system's centrality to Western democracy is the necessary first step for confronting the dynamism of a continuously growing number of societies under the aegis of globalization.

THE COLD WAR, THE AMERICAN CENTURY, AND THE DEMOCRATIC METHOD

The institutional design of Western democracy after World War II—that is, liberal democracy combined with capitalist market economies—to a large extent facilitated the combination of growing social and political stability and economic prosperity experienced in Western Europe, North America, Japan, Australia, and by degree of difference a growing number of other countries, under the leadership of the United States.[7] However, liberal democracy and capitalist market economies neither were singularly responsible for nor did they simply create sociopolitical stability and economic prosperity. Rather, they provided governments, along with their public policy apparatuses (including especially the welfare state and social legislation) in concert with a myriad of other institutions and organizations, in the various areas of social life, with a set of internal and external political and policy priorities. Internally, these priorities were supported by economic, political, and social frameworks for interpreting the new era as the age of democracy. The priorities were further reinforced by old and new linkages between corresponding bureaucracies that directed political, social, and economic recovery efforts after the devastation of World War II. Externally, the priorities took the form of new international strategic alliances whose purpose, in the context of the Cold War, was the expansion of markets, especially for goods produced in the United States, and later in Europe and Japan, and the detection and containment of threats to the newly emerging international system of political economy built around the proliferation of multinational businesses as the newly dominant form of economic organization.[8]

In discussing "some contradictions of the modern welfare state," Claus Offe (1984a) contended that starting during the 1980s, the post–World War II welfare state's ability to function as part of the peace formula that facilitated postwar political and social stability increasingly appeared to have been exhausted.[9] From today's perspective, Offe's thesis could be applied more broadly to the corresponding model of democracy itself. The capacity of liberal democracy, capitalist market economies, and social welfare states to manage continuing and newly emerging political, social, cultural, and economic challenges indeed seems to be in danger of reaching a breaking point.

To be sure, the peace formula was never intended to solve social problems or to meet imminent challenges in ways conducive to the resolution of structural and systemic features of modern societies. Even though the systemic features drained public resources and increased expenditures, they also provided the scaffolding that stabilized societies and facilitated ongoing economic growth and the expansion of markets. At the time of its inception in different countries, the appeal of the peace formula to diverse social, economic, and political constituencies consisted in its ability to stabilize the existing social and political order in its specificity (e.g., with regard to the concrete distribution of wealth and income), rather than order more broadly, in ways that functioned as a buffer against the threats to stability generated on a continual basis by the dynamism of expanding capitalist market economies and concurrent international conflicts.

In analogy, regarding the spread of democracy after World War II, two distinct processes appear to have been conflated: the growing demand for increased popular participation in the political process and the need for social and political stability as a precondition for postwar economic reconstruction and expansion to prevent a relapse into the Great Depression. Democracy expanded and spread because a variety of social and political movements in industrialized, colonized, and postcolonial societies demanded more democracy—and because granting greater democracy was conducive to the kind of social and political stability that made possible postwar economic growth and development and expanding markets. Yet instead of facilitating the regeneration and renewal of such institutional frameworks of democracy as educational access, job skills training, and improved security in ways that would have enabled citizens to recognize themselves as true stakeholders, as opposed to consumers of goods and services provided by elites pursuing particular political and economic interests ever more bluntly, elites saw themselves as the true representatives of the "general interest" of society—as embodied in political institutions, social order, and economic organizations. As elites have done throughout much of human history, they more or less actively undercut their society's chances—and ultimately, the chances of civilization as a whole—to adapt to changes constructively so as to increase democracy as a mechanism for expanding the people's capacity to partake in, and take responsibility for, decisions and actions directed at increasing the rationality of political, economic, and social policies.

In his most well-known work, *Capitalism, Socialism, and Democracy* (1942, 269–83), the Austrian-born political economist Joseph A. Schumpeter (best known today for having coined the expression "creative destruction") introduced the phrase "democratic method." As the centerpiece of his theory of democracy, the democratic method served two purposes. First, it enabled Schumpeter to spell out his realist critique of the most problematic features of what he referred to as the classical doctrine of democracy, which he regarded as overly idealist: the notion that efforts at advancing the idea of democracy should be oriented toward actualizing the rule of the people—that is, government by the people, for the people, as self-government—in any meaningful sense. Second, it also provided him with a venue for conceiving of democracy narrowly, such that against those who asserted that democracy and socialism were mutually exclusive, he could contend that democracy is, in fact, as compatible with socialism as with managerial capitalism and, perhaps, even more so.

Schumpeter's formally realist take on democracy foreshadowed developments in Western industrialized societies after World War II (Kleinewefers 1985). In Schumpeter's analysis, democracy features not as a highly desirable future stage of human coexistence but, rather, as a set of claims that attempt to facilitate stable government in the modern age. Rather than putting democracy on the pedestal of past, present, and future world achievements, Schumpeter argued that by the second quarter of the twentieth century—especially during World War II, as a conflict between democracy and totalitarianism—it had become impossible for political elites in such modern societies as Great Britain and the United States to govern without a firm commitment to democracy. It was no longer possible to ignore the demands made by large factions of the population to participate in democratic government, especially if elites were concerned about social order. Assuming that the Western Allies would be victorious over fascism, Schumpeter surmised this demand would spread across the industrialized and industrializing world. He did not view democracy as the best, most rational, effective, and desirable form of government.[10]

Schumpeter contended that at the stage in human history reached during the first half of the twentieth century, societies with dynamic market economies would be unable to ensure political stability and avoid the danger of war if they ignored the demands for political participation put forth by large segments of the population. Put differently, the safest, most reliable strategy for insuring political stability, as a precondition for economic activity and growth, was the political and economic elites' proclaimed commitment to democracy, even and especially when and where their actions were only marginally conducive to democracy, if at all. In a second step, his inquiry was directed at the particular meaning of democracy to be inferred in the interest of sustaining continued economic activity.

In essence, Schumpeter suggested that adherence to the classical doctrine of democracy was secondary to the ability of a political system to maintain the appearance of being committed to democracy. Given the multiplicity of meanings of democracy, satisfying the expectations, ideas, and demands of a majority of citizens of a democratic state would never be possible. Any democratic polity would have to confront the problem of legitimacy continuously, though to differing degrees, and at varying levels of intensity. If democracy were construed as a means of selecting elites rather than as a qualitatively different way of making collective decisions, it would be better to reduce citizens' expectations of their political leaders and to limit especially the citizens' fiscal demands on the state, thus also limiting corresponding forms of social life.

The larger framework of Schumpeter's theory of political economy relates to the shift from entrepreneurial (or competitive) to managerial (or corporate) capitalism. At bottom, his primary concern pertained to the likelihood that capitalism would survive well into the future, given social, political, cultural, and organizational trends in sway before and during the 1940s. Most important, while Schumpeter was a strong advocate of entrepreneurial (or competitive) capitalism, his attitude toward managerial (or corporate) capitalism was quite different. In fact, he viewed as disingenuous the conceit that capitalism in any form was more compatible with democracy than any form of socialism, for the type of capitalism that had taken shape during the first half of the twentieth century grew less and less compatible with the idea, and especially the practice, of democracy.[11] Yet, Schumpeter's primary related interest was not the link between democracy and capitalism but the connection between democracy and socialism. He asserted that capitalism and democracy are not naturally compatible in the sense that democracy would be conducive to capitalism, or capitalism to democracy. Rather, the affinity is largely historical and certainly not characterized by necessity.[12] Corporate capitalism, moreover, as it relies on extensive bureaucratic hierarchies, could be conceived as compatible with democracy; but in the absence of sustained related efforts to make those hierarchies compatible, practically speaking, they are neither compatible with nor conducive to democracy—although maintaining the appearance of their compatibility with democracy is necessary for the continuation of both as established forms of political and economic organization.

THE CRISIS OF DEMOCRACY, THE TRILATERAL COMMISSION, AND THE COMING OF THE "END OF HISTORY": MORE DEMOCRACIES, LESS DEMOCRACY

It would be quite justified to trace the history of democracy up to the early 1970s as a history of progress and expansion.[13] Although democratic ideas and democratic institutions spread across societies in far from linear fashion, at least in terms of the quality of popular participation in the local and national politics of a continuously growing number of countries, evidence of democratization could be traced through the two centuries preceding. During the post–World War II period, the explicit commitment of democratic governments to combating social problems that impede equal opportunity for all members of society became an important component of political legitimacy. The assumption was that if institutions, organizations, and public policies converge toward the end of equalizing opportunity and advancing human security and social justice for a continuously growing number of citizens, success would be exceedingly likely. Yet, during the 1970s, in conservative circles this commitment increasingly came to be viewed as problematic. Indeed, in the history of modern democracy, the 1970s present a turning point: in all Western societies, there grew concerns that governments had become too responsive to citizens' demands for social programs to combat poverty, tackle unemployment, and deal with issues related to old age.

In *The Crisis of Democracy*, which became a classic in the then-emerging literature warning against the dangers for democracy of state institutions' inability to slow the explosion of demands, Samuel Huntington, who was responsible for the United States, wrote:

> Al Smith once remarked that "the only cure for the evils of democracy is more democracy." Our analysis suggests that applying that cure at the present time could well be adding fuel to the flames. Instead, some of the problems of governance in the United States today stem from an excess of democracy—an "excess of democracy" in … the … sense in which … the term [referred] to the consequences of the Jacksonian revolution which helped to precipitate the Civil War. Needed, instead, is a greater degree of moderation in democracy." (Crozier, Huntington, and Watanuki 1975, 113)

While critics on the left warned against the growing danger of the waning commitment to democracy in what used to be referred to as the "advanced capitalist democracies" of North America and Western Europe, critics on the right predicated an age of ungovernability.[14] In this regard, *The Crisis of Democracy* is the most important document; as the report to the Trilateral Commission, it laid out an agenda for the governability of democracies that placed the most emphasis on stability and the persistence of democratic government.[15] The commission continues to exist; and though it would not be possible to pinpoint the nature of its concrete impact, the latter may be described best as engendering a paternalistic perspective on the world's population that is more interested in preserving the status quo than in bringing about qualitative social, political, cultural, and economic change. In this regard, the Trilateral Commission's mission may best be described as a combination of alleviating imminent problems and preventing their disruptive, even destructive potential well ahead of time while observing them, as it were, from the perspective of an imagined world government (see Scott 1999; also Martin and Schumann 1997).

During the crises of the 1970s, democracy should have moved further in the direction of a civilization, yet instead the reliance on a system of procedures and institutions further supplanted the possibility for renewing what Larry Diamond (2008) refers to as the "spirit of democracy." Instead of making qualitative improvements to democracy—ever more urgently regarded at the time as a strategy for solving problems of legitimacy, related crises of democracy and the welfare state, the problem of ungovernability, and the economic crisis—the push toward further democratization was directed, not at democracy at a higher level, but at the quantitative expansion of democracy: the spread of formally democratic political systems. Although it was apparent that existing democracies were fraught with a variety of structurally and historically grounded flaws, efforts to remedy those flaws were undercut by an orientation toward the proliferation of models of liberal democracy that had been taking shape since the late eighteenth century.

Social and political theorists, along with movement activists, contended that the most desirable strategy for confronting the crisis of democracy was to tackle its flaws, with an eye toward overcoming those flaws.[16] Yet, with the support of mainstream social scientists, especially in sociology, political science, and economics, politicians preferred to work with the notion that the quantitative expansion of democracy, especially in Latin America, the Far East, and by the late 1980s the former member nations of the Warsaw Pact, would help resolve the flaws and economic burdens of democratic polities in societies that had the luxury of looking back on decades of experiences with democratic institutions and processes. Yet this stance was recognizably problematic then, and its problematic nature continues to become ever more apparent as time goes by. More specifically, while the advantages of the Cold War constellation for democracy were appreciated, its detrimental effects on democracy were neglected then and have remained under-theorized to this day. After all, the Cold War did provide an easy framework for distinguishing between desirable and undesirable forms of politics, collective behavior, and economizing that enabled politicians as well as social scientists to downplay the importance of problematic aspects of postwar industrialized societies, including especially the "seamy side of democracy" (Wolfe 1973).

While during the 1970s Western economies had begun to re-engineer themselves in the name of innovation, efficiency, and competitiveness, related momentum increased dramatically during the 1980s—the decade of conservative political revolutions and realignments in the West (Borchert 1995). At the same time, the Soviet Union's calculation that political opening and transparency (glasnost) would spark economic development misfired—a lesson the Chinese government took to heart during the 1990s, facilitating an economic opening without a corresponding political opening. By all accounts perestroika restructuring in the Soviet Union under Gorbachev increased Western-style democracy and led to the end of the Soviet Union; but in the West, the argument could be made that restructuring engendered a period that shifted democratic development from the qualitative plane to the quantitative plane. Until the 1970s, progress had been both: a continuing process of democratization was underway that was both quantitative—affecting a growing number of people around the globe—and qualitative, in the sense that democratic institutions and processes became increasingly conducive to living conditions and opportunities for more and more citizens. In the West, democratic progress engendered increasingly egalitarian public policies and produced a proliferation of new social movements and citizen initiatives. However, the conservative revolution of the 1980s slowed and ultimately stopped that progress. In the United States in particular, progressive social movements as mass movements were in clinch with conservative movements, whose ability to mass organize proved to be greater than among liberals and the left. Ironically, movement activism during the 1970s and into the 1980s rang in a period of political apathy in Western societies and, along with globalization, a growing emphasis on materialism.

Famously, and no less notoriously, Francis Fukuyama (1992) suggested that not just the end of the Cold War but the "end of history" may have arrived—the end of ideology combined with liberal democracy as the final form of human government. During the 1990s, for the first time in history, more people lived in societies with democratic systems than did not. Yet as an idea, a practice, and a civilization, democracy remains in a state of stasis. The dominant form of democratic polities—liberal democracy—remains incapable of adjusting to the increasingly dynamic nature of societal change that has been in sway since the 1980s, and especially since the 1990s. Furthermore, as U.S. foreign policy during the early twenty-first century has been demonstrating, the Cold War may not have ended in 1989 after all.

During the 1970s, crisis management had become the dominant form of governance—not merely with regard to concrete and ever more important challenges facing societies and polities but also with regard to the process of governance itself: managing crises at all levels, from global and national crises to crises of image management during electoral campaigns and party politics. Evidently, in the absence of a qualitative leap in governance, electoral politics, modes of representation, and creation of "mass loyalty," the future of democracy will become increasingly uncertain and the very possibility of its future, doubtful. Indeed, the political economy that contemporary politics is built upon evolved so as to prevent the possibility of qualitative leaps in democratic governance, and culture itself has been honed to play a critical role in making such leaps exceedingly unlikely. Both political economy and culture are neither compatible with nor conducive to qualitative leaps. Actually existing democracies look less and less like frameworks for appreciating and confronting challenges at hand, and more and more like mechanisms devised to ignore and prevent recognition of those challenges and to distract the populace from training a mindset capable of sustained attention toward those challenges (esp. Wolin 2008).

Actually existing democracies have become a key impediment to confronting imminent challenges by discouraging adjustments in the societal arrangement between business, labor, and government in ways that would engender a new, qualitatively superior peace formula for the twenty-first century. A key part of the problem may have been that a large number of Western social scientists turned their attention to the East and South, seeking opportunities to engender Western-style democracy in formerly state-socialist and authoritarian societies— at the expense of conceiving of opportunities to renew democracy in the West. To a certain degree, this reorientation toward less democratically advanced societies might have been symptomatic of the frustration experienced when efforts to renew Western-style democratic systems from within proved futile; the reorientation was indicative of the hope that democratization processes in formerly authoritarian societies might reflect back on the "advanced democracies"; yet, within the latter, the discourse about how to renew democracy has continued, variably as deliberative democracy (Habermas 1996), inclusive democracy (Fotopoulos 1997), or reflexive democracy (Olson 2006), to name just a few.

FROM THE DEMOCRATIC METHOD TO DEMOCRATIC CIVILIZATION: BEYOND THE LIMITS OF LIBERAL DEMOCRACY

It should be apparent, by now, why democracy is such a contested issue. To some, the concept's primary function relates to efforts to arrive at a realistic assessment of political possibilities and prospects. To others, it supplies the more or less abstract standards to which to compare actually existing forms of democratic practice, processes, and institutions, especially as far as claims to advance the "general interest of society" are concerned. To others still its appeal derives directly from its utility as a tool of ideology, pursuing the politics of power while projecting an image of actions and decisions inspired by genuinely democratic values and goals.

Rather than being recognized as the prime, perhaps even the sole, viable means of confronting the contradictions of the modern world, democratic processes and institutions often function as key supporters and amplifiers of those contradictions. It is the prevalence of contradictions as well as the absence of pointed and explicit strategies to tackle contradictions that undercuts the effectiveness of formal democracy; this situation, combined with efforts to advance democratic goals while ignoring the contradictions as primary impediments to success, sustains the overall crisis of democracy. Globalization is thus problematic, not of itself but in light of the defects and deficiencies of formal democracy. Indeed, formal democracy remains ill equipped to confront those defects and deficiencies and acknowledge how they burden efforts to create a more desirable, sane, and reasonable civilization. Actually existing democracies have turned into mechanisms guided primarily by self-preservation—their aim one of preserving their concrete form of existence, rather than the ideals that inspired collective actors to achieve democracy—even if in the long run, this orientation toward self-preservation, as well as a corresponding unwillingness to foster qualitative changes, may turn into the primary cause of its demise. Consequently, the crisis of democracy cannot adequately be understood in terms of democracy alone. The crisis must be viewed in the context of the diminishing efficacy of democratic governance. If we focus on the problems of democracy with an eye to solving them within the established realm of democracy yet ignore that they are symptoms of societal problems, democracy cannot be a means for qualitative change. It will, instead, be a key impediment. We must recognize the problematic nature of contemporary societies on all continents and see democracy as both an expression of its problems and a unique venue for confronting them (Dunn 2001). How we frame the link between democracy and structural societal problems will determine the opportunities for conceiving of solutions related to the nature of the problems at hand.

Democracy will have to be more actively and forcefully prepared. Movement is required in the direction of increasing the reality and efficacy of democracy as necessary preconditions. The impossibility of ignoring the need for viable strategies to solve imminent economic, environmental, energy, and population problems, to name a few, is a defining characteristic of the present age. Yet the circumstances seem to present major hurdles to conceiving of effective strategies conducive to attaining stated goals. Our societies, including especially their political systems, function in ways that do not allow for qualitative changes that might otherwise be attainable and whose attainment is becoming ever more important. In fact, our societies have evolved to effectively immunize themselves against such change. The paradox appears to be that whenever reflection focuses on strategies directed at solving imminent problems, the resulting strategies are likely to fail or to produce results other than those intended. The paradox exists, not because we lack intelligence, but because modern societies are the result of ongoing adaptation to various environments. As a result of our ongoing activities and interventions, our environments are changing in ways that undercut our efforts to conceive of effectively viable strategies. We propose strategies in ways that are supposed to be compelling to all intelligent individuals while ignoring that the constitutional principles of social order, not our lack of reasoning abilities and practical skills, are the primary obstacle. Indeed, pursuing strategies to attain set and agreed-upon goals will require a different mindset entirely. Instead, we ignore how the socially, politically, economically, and culturally constructed reality inadvertently works against collective success, against the reconciliation of facts and norms, against the actualization of shared goals. The problems of democracy to a large extent are problems that were actively constructed and are actively being maintained by identifiable interests and their representatives. What we confront is a profound discrepancy between how we think about modern democratic society and how we would have to think about it in order to take serious steps ahead.

As soon as democracy became a professional field and democratic politics a career trajectory, the essence of what democracy is supposed to be started to recede into the background: democracy is a set of institutions designed to engender modes of interaction and decision-making that facilitate our making qualitatively superior choices and finding effective strategies for confronting societies' past, present, and future challenges (Borchert 2003; Borchert and Zeiss 2003). In the context of globalization, Schumpeter's perspective on democracy introduced earlier is useful in that it goes against the grain of what he was trying to convey. The basic distinction between an abstract, theoretically oriented concept of democracy, on the one hand, and a realist concept that enables us to take into consideration the specificity of time and space—of particular societies or states in history, for example—compels us to further explicate and refine the meanings of democracy we may presuppose, employ, suggest, apply, and advocate. As a matter of principle, the word "democracy" should never be used in the singular, as it always suggests a multiplicity of ideas, concepts, models, practices, and processes. Because "democracy" is a highly malleable term we can employ in many ways, for present purposes we need to circumscribe the term, framing it within the coordinate system of globalization and human security.

Globalization is pertinent to our understanding of democracy for several reasons. Most important, globalization provides the opportunity to take account of advances that have been made with regard to democracy, both in the practical-political realm and in terms of our understanding of its meanings. Furthermore, it also provides the foil for examining how our perspectives on democracy have been deficient, especially as far as failures to advance democracy are concerned. Globalization supplies an incentive to examine whether the questions scholars have been trying to address in recent decades have been at all helpful. In this regard, globalization constitutes an unprecedented opportunity for us to determine which questions to address—indeed, whether we should ask the questions that ought to have been asked, and which should have informed our take on democracy, at the latest after World War II, when began an epoch that shaped many of the institutions that have been framing approaches to confronting the social, political, economic, and cultural problems of the last half century. It also provided a set of priorities so sedimented that for us today to relate to reality independently of those sedimentations would be difficult.

Given the present entwinement of social, political, economic, environmental, and cultural circumstances, realizing objectives integral to democratic civilization remains unlikely. Thus, in individual nations, "network states" (Castells 1996), and at the global level, efforts to realize a more democratic civilization may be more likely to lead to success if they focus on *preparing* theoretically and working practically *toward* creating the necessary preconditions for engendering such a civilization. To do so, we must ask what such a civilization would, and especially should, look like; what kind of characteristics it should have; and what kind of features would have to be in place beforehand. Predictably, those characteristics and features cannot be realized by means of prevailing politics or policy, for the simple and obvious reason that its established patterns are not favorable to the pursuit of those characteristics and features. Indeed, the problem is precisely that contemporary political and policy strategies sustain a web of problems that present obstacles to the attainment of the kind of goals that, purportedly, drive democratic progress.

We need to engage in thought experiments whose purpose it is to begin to think about democracy in ways that are not largely the product of historical contingencies and political manipulation—the latter directed at compelling individuals to fulfill functions in an economic system where the social structure, and our place within it, is itself a function. To the extent that structural conditions and systemic imperatives in societies in the age of globalization are not conducive to democratic practices nor compatible with democratic principles—in more ways than we may be able to conceive—the struggle for the realization of democracy as the most important precondition of human security may barely have begun.

NOTES

1. Among the most common distinctions are bourgeois vs. socialist democracy, representative vs. participatory democracy, formal vs. material democracy, and elite vs. popular democracy.

2. Especially since September 11, 2001, scholars have been scrutinizing how language employed after World War II, if not earlier, to support the spread of democracy by means of national and international policies has also been used to conceal actions that promote national and economic interests not conducive to the consolidation and further advancement of democracy as the self-government of people. Harvey (2003), esp. chap. 2.

3. The extent and type of popular support enjoyed by democratic institutions and procedures is an issue that has accompanied the spread of democracy since the late eighteenth century. Even in countries regarded as the cradles of modern democracy, as is the United States, individuals and institutions are not as firmly committed to the practice of democracy as political discourse would admit. See, e.g, Phillips (2006).

4. The German Democratic Republic described its social, economic, and political system as "actually existing socialism" to deflect criticisms that its society was not truly communist, since it did not make that claim to begin with. Given the organization of the world economy, it would not have been able to succeed, anyway. Nancy Fraser (1997) has applied the designation to "actually existing democracies" to highlight that just as there have not been any truly socialist societies in the modern age, there also are no truly democratic societies, though there are societies whose political systems are democratic in different ways and to differing degrees.

5. See esp. Tilly (2007). Part of the problem is also that debates about democracy are often entangled with such even less precise and procedurally specific discourses as "civil society." Cohen and Arato (1992); see also Wood (1995), Keane (1988, 1998, 2003), and Shefner (2008).

6. One prominent example is the discourse about capitalism and democracy, which often really centers on tensions between competing views of what a government's responsibilities are with regard to social inequalities, the social costs of public policies supporting capitalist market economies, and the like. Since discussing the latter will explicitly generate the organized resistance of vested interests, the confrontation of issues involved is transposed onto the level of democracy, which makes related discussions less relevant. See Prindle (2006).

7. See esp. Slater and Taylor (1999).

8. In the literature, this period has been referred to as the "golden age of capitalism." See Margin and Schor (1991) and Webber and Rigby (1996).

9. Offe (1984a) declares: "The welfare state has served as the major peace formula of advanced capitalist democracies for the period following the Second World War. This peace formula basically consists, first, in the explicit obligation

of the state apparatus to provide assistance and support (either in money or in kind) to those citizens who suffer from specific needs and risks which are characteristic of the market society; such assistance is provided as a matter of legal claims granted to the citizens. Second, the welfare state is based on the recognition of the formal role of labor unions both in collective bargaining and the formation of public policy. Both of these structural components of the welfare state are considered to limit and mitigate class conflict, to balance the asymmetrical power relation of labor and capital, and thus to overcome the condition of disruptive struggle and contradictions that was the most prominent feature of pre-welfare state, or liberal, capitalism; in sum, the welfare state has been celebrated throughout the post-war period as the political solution to societal contradictions" (147). Also Gutmann (1988).

10. Formally speaking, Schumpeter's perspective was reminiscent of Machiavelli's advocacy of the Prince's ability to stay in power over extended periods of time as a necessary precondition of political stability, which in turn was a necessary precondition for economic growth and development. In the latter regard, this concern about sociopolitical stability facilitating economic activity also inspired what C. B. MacPherson (1962, also 1977) referred to as the tradition of "possessive individualism."

11. See esp., Susan Buck-Morss's (2000) comparison of the East's and West's closely related versions of modernity.

12. This point has been made again and developed much further; see, e.g., Wood (1995).

13. As always, the real histories are far more complicated and contradictory than attempts at providing straight stories suggest. See, e.g., Markoff (1996) and Tilly (2007).

14. For example, for strongly prodemocratic critiques of state and government inertia and for related risks, see O'Connor (1972), Habermas (1975), and Wolfe (1977). For an assessment of the discourse about ungovernability, see Offe (1984b).

15. On its Web site (http://www.trilateral.org), the Trilateral Commission describes itself as having been "formed in 1973 by private citizens of Japan, Europe (European Union countries), and North America (United States and Canada) to foster closer cooperation among these core democratic industrialized areas of the world with shared leadership responsibilities in the wider international system. Originally established for three years, our work has been renewed for successive triennia (three-year periods), most recently for a triennium to be completed in 2009."

16. See esp. the new social movements literature, e.g., Social Research 52 (Winter 1985), especially Cohen (1985), Eder (1985), and Offe (1985).

FURTHER READING

Dahl, R. A. *A Preface to Economic Democracy*. Berkeley: University of California Press, 1985.

———. *Democracy and Its Critics*. New Haven, CT: Yale University Press, 1989.

Dunn, J. *Setting the People Free: The Story of Democracy.* London: Atlantic, 2005.
Eisenstadt, S. N. *Paradoxes of Democracy: Fragility, Continuity, and Change.* Washington, DC: Woodrow Wilson Center Press, 1999.
Gould, C. C. *Rethinking Democracy: Freedom and Social Cooperation in Politics, Economy, and Society.* Cambridge: Cambridge University Press, 1988.
Lijphart, A. *Thinking about Democracy: Power Sharing and Majority Rule in Theory and Practice.* New York: Routledge, 2007.
Paehlke, R. *Democracy's Dilemma: Environment, Social Equity, and the Global Economy.* Cambridge, MA: MIT Press, 2003.
Unger, R. M. *Democracy Realized: The Progressive Alternative.* London: Verso, 1998.
Weale, A. *Democracy*, 2nd ed. New York: Palgrave Macmillan, 2007.

REFERENCES

Arblaster, A. 2002. *Democracy.* 3rd ed. Philadelphia: Open University Press.
Borchert, J. 1995. *Die konservative Transformation des Wohlfahrtsstaates: Grossbritannien, Kanada, die USA und Deutschland im Vergleich* [The Conservative Transformation of the Welfare State: A Comparison of Great Britain, Canada, USA and Germany]. Frankfurt/M.: Campus.
———. 2003. *Die Professionalisierung der Politik: Zur Notwendigkeit eines Ärgernisses* [The Professionalization of Politics: On the Necessity of a Nuisance]. Frankfurt/M.: Campus.
Borchert, J., and J. Zeiss. 2003. *The political class in advanced democracies.* Oxford: Oxford University Press.
Buck-Morss, Susan. 2000. *Dreamworld and catastrophe: The passing of mass utopia in East and West.* Cambridge, MA: MIT Press.
Castells, M. 1996. *The rise of the network society.* Vol. 1 of *The information age: Economy, society and culture.* Cambridge, MA: Blackwell.
Cohen, J., and A. Arato. 1992. *Civil society and political theory.* Cambridge, MA: MIT Press.
Cohen, J. L. 1985. Strategy or identity: New theoretical paradigms and contemporary social movements. *Social Research* 52: 663–716.
Crozier, M. J., S. Huntington, and J. Watanuki. 1975. *The crisis of democracy: Report on the governability of democracies to the Trilateral Commission.* New York: New York University Press.
Dahms, H. F. 2005. Ideology. In *International encyclopedia of economic sociology*, ed. J. Beckert and M. Zafirovsky, 335–37. London: Routledge.
Diamond, L. 2008. *The spirit of democracy: The struggle to build free societies throughout the world.* New York: Times Books/Henry Holt.
Dunn, J. 2001. *The cunning of unreason: Making sense of politics.* New York: Basic Books.
Eder, K.1985. The "new social movements": Moral crusades, political pressure groups, or social movements? *Social Research* 52: 869–900.
Fotopoulos, T. 1997. *Towards an inclusive democracy: The crisis of the growth economy and the need for a new liberatory project.* London: Cassell.

Fraser, N. 1997. Rethinking the public sphere: A contribution to the critique of actually existing democracy. In *Justice Interruptus: Critical Reflections on the "Postsocialist" Condition*, 69–98. London: Routledge.
Fukuyama, F. 1992. *The end of history and the last man*. New York: Free Press.
Fullbrook, E., ed. 2003. *The crisis in economics: The post-autistic economics movement; The First 600 Days*. London: Routledge.
———, ed. 2007. *Real world economics: A post-autistic economics reader*. London: Anthem Press.
Gutmann, A., ed. 1988. *Democracy and the welfare state*. Princeton, NJ: Princeton University Press.
Habermas, J. 1975. *Legitimation crisis*. Trans. Th. McCarthy. Boston: Beacon Press.
———. 1996. *Between facts and norms: Contributions to a discourse theory of law and democracy*. Trans. W. Rehg. Cambridge, MA: MIT Press.
Harvey, D. 2003. *The new imperialism*. New York: Oxford University Press.
Held, D. 2006. *Models of democracy*. 3rd ed. Stanford, CA: Stanford University Press.
Keane, J. 1988. *Democracy and civil society: On the predicaments of European socialism, the prospects for democracy, and the problem of controlling social and political power*. London: Verso.
———. 1998. *Civil society: Old images, new visions*. Cambridge: Polity Press.
———. 2003. *Global civil society?* Cambridge: Cambridge University Press.
Kleinewefers, H. 1985. *Reformen für Wirtschaft und Gesellschaft: Utopien, Konzepte, Realitäten* [Reforms for Economics and Society: Utopias, Concepts, Realities]. Frankfurt/M.: Campus.
Lipson, L. 1964. *The democratic civilization*. New York: Oxford University Press.
MacPherson, C. B. 1962. *The political theory of possessive individualism: Hobbes to Locke*. Oxford: Clarendon Press.
———. 1977. *The life and times of liberal democracy*. Oxford: Oxford University Press.
Markoff, J. 1996. *Waves of democracy: Social movements and political change*. Thousand Oaks, CA: Pine Forge Press.
Martin, H. P., and H. Schumann. 1997. *The global trap: Globalization and the assault on prosperity and democracy*. Trans. P. Camiller. New York: St. Martin's Press.
O'Connor, J. 1972. *The fiscal crisis of the state*. New York: St. Martin's Press.
Offe, C. 1984a. Some contradictions of the modern welfare state. In *Contradictions of the modern welfare state*, 147–61. Trans. John Keane. Cambridge, MA: MIT Press.
———. 1984b. "Ungovernability": The renaissance of conservative theories of crisis. In *Contradictions of the modern welfare state*, 65–87. Cambridge, MA: MIT Press.
———. 1985. New social movements: Challenging the boundaries of institutional politics. *Social Research* 52: 817–68.
Olson, K. 2006. *Reflexive democracy: Political equality and the welfare state*. Cambridge, MA: MIT Press.

Phillips, K. 2006. *American theocracy: The peril and politics of radical religion, oil, and borrowed money in the 21st century.* New York: Viking.

Prindle, D. F. 2006. *The paradox of democratic capitalism: Politics and economics in American thought.* Baltimore: Johns Hopkins University Press.

Schumpeter, J. A. 1942. *Capitalism, socialism, and democracy.* New York: Harper.

Scott, J. C. 1999. *Seeing like a state: How certain schemes to improve the human condition have failed.* New Haven, CT: Yale University Press.

Shefner, J. 2008. *The illusion of civil society: Democratization and community mobilization in low-income Mexico.* University Park: Penn State Press.

Slater, D., and P. J. Taylor, eds. 1999. *The American century: Consensus and coercion in the projection of American power.* Malden, MA: Blackwell.

Tilly, C. 2007. *Democracy.* Cambridge: Cambridge University Press.

Webber, M. J., and D. L. Rigby. 1996. *The golden age illusion: Rethinking postwar capitalism.* New York: Guilford Press.

Wolfe, A. 1973. *The seamy side of democracy.* New York: McKay.

———. 1977. *The limits of legitimacy: Political contradictions of contemporary capitalism.* New York: Free Press.

Wolin, S. S. 2008. *Democracy incorporated: Managed democracy and the specter of inverted totalitarianism.* Princeton, NJ: Princeton University Press.

Wood, E. M. 1995. *Democracy against capitalism: Renewing historical materialism.* Cambridge: Cambridge University Press.

3

Development

Mark T. Berger

Development has a complicated historical and contemporary relationship to security. In the context of changing ideas about what development entails, the growing significance of globalization, and the subsequent end of the Cold War, development and security have been reformulated in separate and interconnected ways. Development theorists and planners have talked, or continue to talk, about national development, dependent development, and human development, along with a range of other qualifying terms that attempt to make the character or goals of development clearer. Meanwhile, security is regularly approached in terms of international security, national security, or human security, to mention only three prominent formulations. In order to better understand contemporary conceptions of development and their relationship to security, and to globalization, the first section in this chapter focuses on the theory and practice of development and on its close connection to security (what is being termed here as the development-security nexus) in the Cold War. The second section looks primarily at the post–Cold War era, by which time globalization had increasingly displaced or become equated with development, while new, or reconfigured, notions of the development-security nexus were being discussed and implemented. After September 11, 2001, this was taking place against not only the backdrop of the uneven spread and deepening of globalization but also the imperatives of the U.S.-led global War on Terror, or what is also now referred to as the Long War (Berger and Borer 2007, 197–215).

THE IDEA OF DEVELOPMENT AND THE EARLY COLD WAR

The consolidation of the idea and practice of modern development was directly connected to national liberation, decolonization, and the universalization of the nation-state system after the World War II. Against the backdrop of the security concerns that surrounded the demise of formal colonialism and the early Cold War, the nation-state became the central object of an increasingly elaborate and universal set of overlapping national and international institutions seeking to promote development and/or security. In the early Cold War era, the nation-state was increasingly presented as the constitutive element of both capitalist and socialist development. At the moment of decolonization and national independence, the nation-state was seen as embodying the promise of self-determination, development, and security. However, the promise of the nation-state was constrained by, among other things, powerful institutional and structural legacies inherited from the colonial era. Between the 1940s and the 1970s, the many contradictions and tensions of the various nationalist movements in Asia, Africa, and the Middle East were played out in the context of, and given a new unity by, the pursuit of national security and national development as an ostensibly unified project.

A key shortcoming was that the modern idea of development rested squarely on the foundations of colonial institutions, boundaries, modes of governance, and social relations. The principle of self-determination, as embodied in the UN Charter after 1946, served to legitimate the boundaries and sovereignty of nation-states as they emerged from the wreckage of colonialism to become the key vehicle for the pursuit of modern development. The distinction between states and nations is particularly relevant to understanding the way in which sovereignty, especially national sovereignty, continued to reside with the state rather than with the people that inhabited the new nation (Hardt and Negri 2000, 69–70; also see Jackson 1990).

At the same time, the idea of development also became central to the wider process through which the new nation-states were incorporated into the international order of the Cold War. The new nation-states, in what became known as the Third World, were positioned behind the First World. The dominant ideas and practices of development and security and the network of treaties, organizations, and institutions that went with them facilitated the theoretical and practical subordination of the onetime Third World. Both the First World and the Second World enshrined development or, more importantly, a lack thereof, as a constituent element in the making of national identities and the pursuit of development and security in the Third World. That is, the end of the hierarchies of formal colonialism had now been displaced by a hierarchical nation-state system comprised of three worlds of development constituting a global North–South divide (Berger 2004, 9–39; Eckl and Weber 2007, 3–23).

During the Cold War, the Soviet Union and its client nation-states, which comprised the Second World, were not the only challengers to the model of development offered by the First World. State-socialist regimes such as Yugoslavia and China, which were not allied with Moscow, promoted alternative state-socialist models of modern development as direct challenges to liberal capitalist development, as did reformist and revolutionary regimes in the Third World itself. Explicitly state-socialist development models were directly linked to concerns about national and international security, and like their liberal capitalist counterparts, they took the nation-state as the key means of achieving security and development. In fact, socialist states, as well as various reformist and revolutionary Third World states, not only embraced the nation-state but also sought from the outset to duplicate the economic results of liberal capitalism, setting goals that, as became increasingly apparent over time, they were not equipped to realize (Dirlik 1994, 44).

Despite the vagaries of the theory and practice of development and security within the Second and Third Worlds, the key dynamic of international relations for decades was the rivalry between the United States and the Soviet Union. Both superpowers presided over expanding alliance systems and increasingly disbursed large quantities of economic, as well as military, aid to the nation-states of the emerging Third World. As the Cold War deepened, the International Monetary Fund (IMF) and the International Bank for Reconstruction and Development (World Bank), as well as the United Nations, played a growing role in distributing foreign aid and promoting economic development; whereas the IMF and the World Bank were, and still are, heavily financed and influenced by the United States, before the end of the Cold War the governments of the Soviet bloc generally refused to participate in these organizations.

One of the first indications of the close link between security and development in the Cold War came with President Harry. S. Truman's (1945–1952) announcement of the Truman Doctrine on March 12, 1947. The Truman Doctrine was a response to the growing influence of communist parties in Greece and Turkey and included the extension of $400 million in economic and military aid to the Greek and Turkish governments. This was soon followed by the launch, on June 4, 1947, of the European Recovery Program, otherwise known as the Marshall Plan. The Marshall Plan was driven by a concern that a destabilized Western Europe would result in a power vacuum and provide an opportunity for the Soviet Union to expand its influence westward. The United States made clear that the Marshall Plan was aimed at preventing or containing the appearance in Europe of governments, or groupings of governments, that would threaten the security interests of the United States.

The Marshall Plan involved the disbursement of $12.5 billion toward the reconstruction of Western Europe over a four-year period. By 1952, the Marshall Plan was a key factor in increasing industrial production to 35 percent and agricultural production to 18 percent above their pre–World War II levels in Western Europe. The Marshall Plan also drew attention to the benefits of foreign aid for the U.S. economy. One of the requirements of the Marshall Plan had been that the bulk of the aid money had to be used to purchase U.S. exports. The Organisation for European Economic Co-operation (OEEC) was set up to coordinate the Marshall Plan. With the cessation of aid in the 1950s, it continued to operate as a focus of economic cooperation among the governments of Europe. In 1961, the OEEC changed its name to the Organisation for Economic Co-operation and Development (OECD). The United States and Canada joined the OECD, and it also began to act as a vehicle for the distribution of foreign aid from North America and Western Europe to promote security and development in the Third World.

From the outset, the Marshall Plan represented an important precedent for subsequent security and development initiatives in Asia, Latin America, the Middle East, and Africa. By the end of the 1940s, the Truman administration was increasingly concerned about the new nation-states in the Third World. It was hoped that an extension of U.S. foreign aid to those regions would help to undercut the influence of the Soviet Union and international communism. On January 20, 1949, at the start of his second term as president, Truman delivered his inaugural address, in which he sketched out an expanded foreign aid policy. This became known as the Point Four Program (International Development Act). Point 1 pledged continuing U.S. support for the United Nations. Point 2 emphasized U.S. support for world economic recovery. Point 3 reiterated U.S. commitment to supporting "freedom loving nations." Point 4 briefly set out a U.S. commitment to providing U.S. technical and scientific expertise, and U.S. capital, to "underdeveloped" nations in an effort to improve their living standards. The program started with a budget of $45 million. In 1953 the U.S. Congress increased the budge of the Point Four program to $155 million.

By the late 1940s, meanwhile, security and development concerns were central to the U.S. effort to turn Japan, South Korea, and Taiwan into capitalist bulwarks against the Soviet Union and Maoist China. After the Korean War the sustained U.S. economic and military aid that went to South Korea and Taiwan in the 1950s and 1960s played an important role in strengthening the capabilities of their emergent national security states. Between 1945 and 1973, U.S. economic aid to South Korea was $5.5 billion, while U.S. military aid was $7 billion. United States economic aid to South Korea was more than all the U.S. economic aid to sub-Saharan Africa and half the figure for all of Latin America over the same period. In the 1950s more than 80 percent of South Korean imports were financed by U.S. economic assistance. By the end of 1950, the United States had already also disbursed at least $133 million to the war effort in French Indochina (1946–1954). By late 1952 U.S., assistance covered 40 percent of the overall cost of the war. By the beginning of 1954, the U.S. contribution had risen to 80 percent. Between the collapse of French colonial power in 1954 and the end of Dwight D. Eisenhower's presidency at the beginning of 1961, the United States disbursed over US$2 billion worth of military and economic aid to the government of South Vietnam. For the Eisenhower administration, and its his immediate successor, the regime of Ngo Dinh Diem (1955–1963) became the site for an increasingly prominent effort at nation building—the key to the development-security nexus in the Cold War.

THE DEVELOPMENT-SECURITY NEXUS AND THE RISE AND FALL OF CLASSIC MODERNIZATION THEORY

Far more than his predecessor, the new U.S. president, John F. Kennedy (1961–1963), emphasized the need for Washington to take the initiative in the Third World through infusions of economic and military aid and national development and counterinsurgency programs. The theoretical justification for the promotion of an increasingly elaborate development-security nexus in the late 1950s and early 1960s is often described as classic modernization theory. The latter was committed to a period of tutelage and focused on the need for cultural transformation in order for the Third World to achieve modernity. History was regarded as linear, and the achievement of development and security was seen as a movement from the traditional to the modern. Classic modernization theory emphasized the totality of change and saw modernization as a process, often called diffusion, which spread throughout a society affecting economics, the type of government, social structure, values, religion, and family structure. Classic modernization theorists viewed underdevelopment in the Third World as the result of internal shortcomings specific to underdeveloped nation-states and their precolonial, rather than their colonial or postcolonial, history.

Classic modernization theory was in practice somewhat messier, of course. In South Vietnam in the early 1960s, for example, the Strategic Hamlet Program initially became the pivot of Washington's wider strategy for security and development. The United States drew on previous French colonial initiatives and earlier efforts by the Diem regime, as well as on British counterinsurgency programs in Malaya in the 1950s. The result was a development-security nexus that emphasized the removal of peasants from widely dispersed villages, placing them in concentrated settlements that could be controlled more directly by the government in Saigon. With this approach the U.S. Military Assistance Command Vietnam (MACV) and the Agency for International Development (USAID) sought to undermine the National Liberation Front's (NLF) ability to get intelligence, food, and other supplies, as well as recruits, from the southern population. The NLF quickly responded by promising the peasants that following the revolution, they would be allowed to return to their old villages. The NLF also intensified its military attacks on, and its recruitment activities in, the strategic hamlets.

Despite the apparent failure of the Strategic Hamlet Program by the end of 1963, subsequent efforts to resettle and control the rural population did little but rework the basic approach while excising the term "strategic hamlet" from the theory and practice of security and development. Meanwhile, following the overthrow and assassination of Diem and his brother Nhu Dinh Diem in a military coup in late 1963, the successor programs to the Strategic Hamlet Program were increasingly overshadowed by full-scale warfare. The United States had hoped the overthrow of the Diem regime would improve the stability of South Vietnam; however, the deterioration in the military situation following the coup paved the way for the escalation of U.S. involvement and direct military intervention by 1965. This led, in turn, to immense human, material, and environmental destruction but failed to solve the fundamental political problems of the Saigon regime and the fragile nation-state of South Vietnam. The pervasive reliance on U.S. aid generated growing possibilities for government and private corruption. With the Tet Offensive in early 1968, any idea that U.S. power could turn South Vietnam into a viable capitalist nation-state and achieve military victory against the North had disappeared.

As part of its wider emphasis on meshing security and development, the Kennedy administration also set up USAID in 1961 to coordinate government foreign aid initiatives. Established as a semi-autonomous body operating in the State Department, it was responsible for disbursing and administering aid in South Vietnam and around the world. Apart from South Vietnam, a large percentage of the aid this new body disbursed initially went to the Alliance for Progress. This was another ambitious initiative the Kennedy administration hoped would contain the communist threat to Latin America following the revolution in Cuba, where communists came to power at the beginning of 1959, in the final years of the Eisenhower era.

The Alliance for Progress began as a decade-long program of land and economic reform expected to cost $100 billion and aimed at bringing about an annual growth rate for the region of at least 2.5 percent. It also sought to achieve greater productivity in the agricultural sector, eradicate illiteracy, stimulate trade diversification, generate improvements in housing, and bring about improved income distribution in the region. However, its major, if unstated, goal was the protection of North American investments in Latin America at the same time as many of the proposed reforms of the Alliance for Progress endangered those investments. Trade diversification would undermine the monopoly of primary agricultural products and mineral extraction enjoyed by a number of U.S.-based corporations. Meanwhile, land reform threatened the power of the still largely land-based ruling elites in Latin America. This contradiction was apparent in the way that Kennedy's reformism went hand-in-hand with Washington's ever-deepening commitment to military and police aid and counterinsurgency to defeat peasant-based rebellions in the region. High rates of economic growth had been achieved in many instances by the late 1960s. However, the growth exacerbated social inequality, while politics, instead of becoming more democratic, moved increasingly toward authoritarianism. American support for counterrevolutionary military and political activity in Latin America grew in the 1960s. There were 16 military coups within eight years of the launch of the Alliance for Progress.

In the context of the escalation of the war in Vietnam and the increasingly militarized character of the Alliance for Progress, the creation of institutions and organizations that could provide order became even more important for proponents of development and security in the Third World. The concerns of the officials who carried the United States into full-scale war in Vietnam were closely connected to the revised theories of modernization and development that emerged by the late 1960s. The major concern of Samuel Huntington's influential 1968 book *Political Order in Changing Societies*, for example, was to determine what might or might not be necessary to ensure continued social order and political stability. Widely regarded as the standard revision of classic modernization theory and a key text in the burgeoning literature on military-led modernization, Huntington held up political order as the ultimate goal of any society. He argued that contrary to earlier expectations, the instability in Asia and the rest of the Third World since World War II was primarily the result of "rapid social change and the rapid mobilization of new groups into politics coupled with the slow development of political institutions." Furthermore, U.S. foreign policy since 1945 had, in his view, missed this point because Washington had placed too great an emphasis on the economic gap while overlooking the political gap. He emphasized that the political gap had been ignored because of the assumption in North America that political stability flowed from social reform stimulated by economic development. However, in his view it was actually the process of modernization that led to political instability. For Huntington, organization was the key to political power as well as the basis of development and security.

THE DEVELOPMENT-SECURITY NEXUS AND THE RISE AND FALL OF CLASSIC DEPENDENCY THEORY

Huntington's prescriptions held out the possibility that successful nation building in South Vietnam and elsewhere remained within Washington's power. However, as suggested here, with the Tet Offensive in early 1968 the elite consensus in America that U.S. power could turn South Vietnam into a stable capitalist nation-state and achieve military victory against North Vietnam had been completely undermined. As the intractability of the U.S. development-security effort in South Vietnam became increasingly apparent, the U.S.-led mission to develop the Third World more generally was also increasingly challenged. By the late 1960s, revolution and economic nationalism was on the agenda in Asia, Africa, and Latin America.

Under these circumstances, radical theories of development emerged as part of the rise of, and often commitment to, Third Worldism. At the center of the new radicalism were dependency theory and the increasingly attractive model of the Cuban Revolution. Between the late 1960s and the late 1980s, dependency theory was continually revised in the context of an ongoing debate with liberal capitalist theories of development and security and as a result of criticisms from more explicitly Marxist theorists. Dependency theory, as it came to be understood in the 1960s, developed out of Latin American historico-structuralism, which was initially associated with Raul Prebisch and the UN's Economic Commission for Latin America (ECLA), and out of the American Marxism of Paul Baran, among others (Prebisch 1950; Baran 1957). André Gunder Frank emerged in the second half of the 1960s as one of the main proponents of classic dependency theory. Walter Rodney was another important figure whose career and work reflected the linkages between the dependency debate in the Caribbean and Latin America and nationalist and radical debates in Africa; at the same time, his dependency model was also popularized in America and Western Europe (Rodney 1972).

The emphasis on external factors that characterized classic dependency theory in this period, which was linked to radical Third Worldism, contributed to a homogenized understanding of the Third World as much as modernization theory did. This was readily apparent in Frank's work. In *Capitalism and Underdevelopment in Latin America*, published in 1967, Frank outlined the concept of the development of underdevelopment and articulated a model of historical development, which directly linked underdevelopment and economic stagnation to the siphoning off of the economic surplus from the periphery to the industrialized core. Frank made a dramatic break with classical Marxism, asserting "that it is capitalism, both world and national, which produced underdevelopment in the past and which still, generates underdevelopment in the present" (Frank, 1967, xi). Frank's work rose to particular prominence, and his ideas were produced and reproduced so widely that they emerged in the late 1960s and early 1970s as the dominant radical version of dependency theory and Third Worldism.

By the second half of the 1970s, dependency theory and Third Worldism had peaked. Their demise can be traced to their failure as revolutionary prophecy and to the end of the U.S. war in Southeast Asia. Meanwhile, the rise of the newly industrializing countries (NICs) in East Asia and Latin America (specifically Mexico and Brazil) and the rise of the Organization of Petroleum Exporting Countries (OPEC) helped to undermine the subordinate image of the Third World. At the same time, by the late 1970s, an emphasis on the corruption and authoritarianism of many nation-states in the Third World shifted the blame for underdevelopment back on to the Third World. Another important factor behind the fall of dependency theory and Third Worldism was that by the mid-1970s they had been partially contained by their political and theoretical incorporation into the dominant liberal capitalist narrative on development and security (see, e.g., Evans 1978). The new approaches departed from the determinism associated with classic dependency theory while they continued to facilitate the circulation of the idea of a homogeneous Third World.

This was part of the wider shift in the 1970s toward greater influence at the UN by Third World governments. In particular, the UN launched a call for a new international economic order (NIEO) and the recognition in America and Western Europe that the North-South conflict was more important than the East-West (Cold War) conflict. This reformist agenda envisioned improving North-South relations without making any major structural changes to the international economic order. These ideas were partially reflected in the policies adopted by President Jimmy Carter's (1977–1981) administration in his first two years in office. Carter, as well as Zbigniew Brzezinski, who served as his national security advisor, and virtually all the members of the Carter administration concerned with foreign policy, were members of the Trilateral Commission. They saw U.S. relations with Japan and Western Europe as the "strategic hard core for both global stability and progress" (Brzezinski 1983, 289). The Trilateral Commission's central goal was to develop a cohesive and semipermanent alliance that embraced the world's major capitalist nation-states in order to promote stability and order and protect their interests. In the case of the Third World, Trilateralism advocated limited reform in order to maintain long-term stability. By the end of the 1970s, the Brandt Commission and its North-South report had emerged as a major initiative that reflected the attempt by a handful of industrial nation-states to manage the Third World through relatively piecemeal reforms to the theory and practice of security and development (Brandt 1980). In the United States, for example, Congress passed various reformist pieces of legislation generally grouped under the heading New Directions. These initiatives emphasized both basic needs of the poor and direct grassroots participation in the process of development. At the same time, the Foreign Assistance Act was amended to provide for an increased focus on human rights in the disbursement of foreign aid.

THE DEVELOPMENT-SECURITY NEXUS AND THE RISE AND FALL OF THE NEW COLD WAR

By the late 1970s, however, influential free market critics of New Directions were in the ascendance. Their views were consolidated during the Reagan administration (1981–1988). In the 1980s USAID's focus was the Private Enterprise Initiative (PEI), which promoted private sector development and encouraged market-oriented reform (Adams 2000, 53–54, 68–70, 75). These changes were backed up by American and West European power over the IMF and the World Bank in the context of their newfound leverage provided by the debt crisis and the international economic recession of the early 1980s. This situation also weakened the impact of the United Nations and related organizations such as the International Labor Organization (ILO), the UN Conference on Trade and Development (UNCTAD), and the UN Development Programme (UNDP), where Third World views had gained weight in the 1970s. The central prescription for the Third World that flowed from free market ideology was that underdevelopment was caused by excessive state involvement in the economy.

In a 1984 policy paper entitled "Private Enterprise Development," for example, USAID asserted that "a private enterprise economy is held to be the most efficient means of achieving broad-based economic development." Of USAID's goals, a central objective was clearly stated: "To encourage LDCs (Less Developed Countries) to open their economies to a greater reliance on competitive markets and private enterprise in order to meet the basic human needs of their poor majorities." Closely connected to this was an injunction about the need "to foster the growth of productive, self-sustaining income and job producing private enterprises in developing countries" (USAID November 9, 1984, 1). At the same time, U.S. foreign assistance policy in the 1980s, as in earlier periods, remained firmly grounded in geopolitical calculations, with the percentage of foreign assistance going to development-related programs declining and the amount spent on security-related projects rising.

This trend became readily apparent in Washington's growing involvement in Central America following the revolutionary overthrow of the Somoza regime in Nicaragua in 1979. In the 1980s, Central America became a crucial focus of the Reagan administration's new Cold War. The nation-states of Central America received more U.S. economic and military aid during Reagan's first term (1981–1984) than they had in the preceding 30 years (1950–1980). For example, between 1981 and 1984 the El Salvadoran government received $758 million in economic aid and $396 million in military aid (compared to only $6 million in military aid in 1980). By the middle of Reagan's first term, El Salvador had emerged as the recipient of more U.S. aid than any other country in Latin America. In fact, in this period El Salvador was the third-largest U.S. aid recipient worldwide, behind Israel and Egypt. Reflecting the ongoing strategic significance of the Middle East, Israel and Egypt received about one-third of all U.S. foreign aid disbursed in the 1980s. Ultimately, the level of foreign aid for El Salvador in the 1980s was on a scale reminiscent of the U.S. nation-building effort in South Vietnam in the 1960s, without direct U.S. military intervention. By the end of the 1980s the United States had disbursed upward of $3 billion in economic and military aid to El Salvador, the equivalent of about $800,000 a day for ten years (see LaFeber 1993, 353–58).

That economic aid to Central America in this period was driven by geopolitical considerations did not negate its focus on the liberalization of the economies of the region. In the 1980s the United States combined its support for the military and proxy warfare with pressure on the governments of Central America to adopt neoliberal economic policies. This led, among other things, to the dismantling of national institutions that had bolstered almost 50 years of Costa Rican social democracy. In El Salvador and Nicaragua, it threatened even the very limited popular economic and political gains made during the 1980s. This shift contributed to the rising levels of social inequality and privatized violence in the region that have continued since the electoral defeat of the Sandinistas in 1990 and the finalization of peace agreements in El Salvador in 1992 and in Guatemala in 1996.

GLOBALIZATION, THE DEVELOPMENT-SECURITY NEXUS, AND THE END OF THE COLD WAR

The end of the Cold War initially precipitated a revision of the emphasis on the connection between development and security. For example, President Bill Clinton (1993–2000) presided over a range of reforms that ostensibly sought to reduce the significance of security concerns in the disbursement of foreign aid and the promotion of development. At that time, USAID was still expected to promote economic development by encouraging trade, investment, and market-oriented reform, but it also established new programs aimed at building democratic political institutions. A greater emphasis was also placed on humanitarian assistance and sustainable development. This reorientation, however, symbolized by the passage of a new foreign aid bill by Congress in 1994, still involved a major commitment to U.S. security concerns. Thus, Israel and Egypt continued to receive over one-third of all U.S. foreign aid. In 1994 Israel received $3 billion and Egypt received $2.1 billion, while sub-Saharan Africa was allotted a total of $800 million. Foreign aid was also directed increasingly at the former Soviet bloc, again for security reasons. The long shadow of the Vietnam era also continued to shape security and development policy in the post–Cold War era.

In the post-9/11 era, however, the connection between development and security has taken on renewed significance. The post-9/11 era has seen a revitalization of state-directed security and development initiatives. This shift is embodied in the growing links between strategies of conflict resolution, social reconstruction, and foreign aid policies. At the same time, the pursuit of security and development is increasingly being shifted to new or reconfigured networks that combine national governments, military establishments, myriad private companies and contractors, and nongovernmental organizations (NGOs). The renewed merging of security and development in a distinct post–Cold War form is reminiscent, although not the same as, the anti-communist nation-building and poverty-alleviating strategies and efforts that rose and fell during the Cold War. The new, more privatized and more decentralized approach to development reflects the shift from state-guided national development and security concerns to more free market–oriented strategies that were consolidated with the rise of globalization in the 1980s.

The limited redirection of U.S. foreign aid policy after the Cold War reflected the relative continuity in U.S. strategic thinking in the 1990s. Planning documents and public pronouncements that emanated from the administration of President George Bush (1989–1992), for example, reflected a preoccupation with Russia and such other successor states as Ukraine that had emerged from the collapse of the Soviet Union. There was also a continued focus on the Middle East; at the same time, Central America and Afghanistan quickly dropped from view. In contrast to the global orientation of the Cold War era, policy makers also emphasized the regional character of strategic planning and threat assessment. The Gulf War also highlighted the continued centrality of Saudi Arabia to U.S. policy in the Middle East as well as the centrality of the Middle East to U.S. policy. Along with Israel and Egypt, Saudi Arabia remains one of the three most important U.S. allies in the region. Saudi Arabia, which along with Japan and South Korea was one of the few non-European countries to receive Marshall Plan assistance in the late 1940s, has the biggest oil reserves in the world.

Despite the high degree of continuity in U.S. foreign policy in the 1990s, Clinton emphasized that his administration's main goal was not just to "secure the peace won in the Cold War" but also to strengthen the country's "national security" by "enlarging the community of market democracies" (Office of the President of the United States 1996). Like the administration of his predecessor, however, the Clinton team understood that the immediate post–Cold War world conferred on the United States clear geopolitical and economic advantages; these they sought primarily to manage and wherever possible worked to enhance and extend U.S. preponderance. Like the Bush administration, Clinton's team remained focused on the major powers: Britain, Germany, France, Russia, Japan, and China. Clinton, like Bush before him, also attempted to maintain as high a level of defense spending as possible. Throughout the 1990s, rhetoric about humanitarian intervention to the contrary, the Clinton administration clearly viewed Europe, East Asia and the Asia-Pacific region, and the Middle East and the Southwest Asia region as the three most important areas in the world in terms of U.S. strategy and security. Meanwhile, Latin America, Africa, and South Asia were perceived as regions where no vital U.S. security interests were at stake. Europe was apparently at the top of the list, while the Middle East and Southwest Asia region came in third. In the 1990s, East Asia and the Asia-Pacific region were regarded as number 2 and rising. The interconnection between security and economic development was also particularly obvious in the thinking of defense planners in relation to East Asia. A 1995 Department of Defense document, for example, described the U.S. military operations in the Asia-Pacific region as the "foundation for economic growth" and the "oxygen" of "development" (Office of International Security Affairs February 1995, 1–2). This also highlighted the close connection between China's economic development, on the one hand, and U.S. geopolitical and security concerns, on the other. Following the collapse of the USSR and the U.S. victory in the First Gulf War (1990–1991), the search for threats to the United States increasingly shifted to East Asia. By the second half of the 1990s, if not before, Washington had clearly fastened on the geopolitical implications of the economic rise of China against the wider backdrop of the transformation of Asia.

GLOBALIZATION, THE DEVELOPMENT-SECURITY NEXUS, AND THE RISE AND FALL OF THE DEVELOPMENTAL STATE

The rise of East Asia had, in fact, been increasingly central to the wider debate about development and security since the 1970s, with Japan's reemergence as a major economic power. Japan's resurgence was complemented by the economic success of the NICs of South Korea, Taiwan, Hong Kong, Singapore, and latterly, Thailand, Malaysia, and Indonesia, and then China. The rise of East Asia provided support for the exponents of development economics, state intervention, planning, and the relative importance of industrialization. Between the 1940s and the 1960s, development economics had been the driving intellectual force behind liberal capitalist development models that sought to meet the challenge of state-socialism and dependency theory through more moderate reformist approaches to development and security. Development economics had continued, albeit decreasing, purchase in the theory and the practice of development by the 1970s and early 1980s as globalization gained in prominence.

Nevertheless, development economics retained influence in the late Cold War and early post–Cold War era in the form of theories of the developmental state, which emphasized and elaborated the central role of state-directed industrial policy in successful national development. While developmental state theorists challenged neoclassical economics, they also shared many of the key assumptions on which neoclassical economics rests. Like their neoclassical counterparts, theorists of the developmental state routinized the nation-state and the nation-state system and produced historical and technocratic explanations. The origins of the idea of the developmental state are complex. In a general fashion, it is safe to say that before 1945, moderate and radical ideas in Japanese economic thought, interacting with intellectual currents in Western Europe and North America, provided an important setting for the emergence and codification of ideas about state-guided national development.

It is Chalmers Johnson's *MITI and the Japanese Miracle* that is now regarded as the central text in English involved in the promotion of the developmental state approach to East Asian industrialization (1982). By the end of the 1980s and the early 1990s, a number of approaches to capitalist development in East Asia, which emphasized the role of a developmental state in the process of national development and were inspired directly or indirectly by Johnson's work, had emerged and gained some influence. This revisionist work became increasingly policy oriented in an effort to challenge the dominant neoclassical approach to capitalist development. This literature emerged as an important element in the wider struggle between the Japanese state-centered model and the U.S. market-oriented model of capitalist development. Most theorists were increasingly constrained by their efforts to extract policy lessons from the East Asian experience without attempting to analyze why, in historical terms, strong institutions, or a developmental state, emerged in East Asia. They collapsed space and time in their pursuit of policy lessons. Alice Amsden's *The Rise of "The Rest": Challenges to the West from Late-Industrializing Economies* (2001), for example, provides a highly selective and technocratic analysis of late-industrializing economies despite its ostensibly historical framework.

Alice Amsden's work in the late 1980s was an important example of the academic studies of the developmental state that were influenced by Johnson's work. Amsden and others focused more on South Korea and Taiwan and the NICs other than Japan. They were also generally more concerned with the significance of the rise of East Asia for the Third World. They sought to find lessons that would allow developing nation-states in Latin America and Africa to replicate the success of South Korea and Taiwan. By the early 1990s, Amsden's book *Asia's Next Giant: South Korea and Late Industrialization* (1989) emerged as a key text in developmental state theory. Amsden's overall argument that industrialization in South Korea flowed from "government initiatives and not the forces of the free market" and this is "applicable to similar countries" was a clear and explicit challenge to neoliberal interpretations of the South Korean trajectory. It was also a direct challenge to the types of lessons that neoliberalism sought to extract from the East Asian Miracle (Amsden 1989, 27). Her work, which extracted lessons from the distinctive South Korean experience and then emphasized their relevance for the Third World, also clearly embodied the technocratic and historical assumptions at the center of the developmental state tradition as it was codified and consolidated by the end of the 1980s. For proponents of the developmental state, economic development ultimately involved the subordination or containment of major social actors to state power, while complicated historical processes were regularly reinvented as technocratic and managerial practices.

Many observers saw the Asian financial crisis of 1997–1998 as an indictment of the developmental state. However, defenders of state-guided development and even some proponents of neoclassical economics argued that the crisis needed to be understood primarily in terms of unregulated financial markets, of which boom-bust cycles are a normal element, rather than as a result of excessive state intervention or "crony capitalism" (Weiss 1998, xii–xiii). In fact, the actual developmental states in East Asia were in disarray well before the crisis. For example, by the late 1980s and early 1990s, if not before, the state-guided national development project in South Korea—which emerged as a paradigmatic developmental state—was being undone by its own success and by the wider historical context in which it operated. The developmental state in South Korea was able to pursue certain developmental objectives for many years because the state was particularly well insulated from the wider social order, especially from those social classes that might have challenged or undermined its developmental goals. The relative autonomy of the state in South Korea and its ability to spearhead a particularly successful national development effort were grounded in the very particular history of the Korean peninsula in the twentieth century. The success of the developmental state in South Korea, however, led to a strengthening of various social classes whose growing political demands had dramatically weakened state autonomy by the second half of the 1980s. When this change intersected with the increasingly global, but still highly uneven, shift from national development to globalization against the backdrop of the waning of the Cold War, the result was the retreat of the developmental state in South Korea. This process was repeated, with important variations, in Taiwan and elsewhere. Furthermore, that such writers as Linda Weiss and Alice

Amsden identified South Korea as a more general model also provided implicit, if not explicit, justification for authoritarianism and militarism, highlighting the connection between theories of the developmental state and early theories of military-led modernization. While the military modernization theorists were preoccupied with security and political order, advocates of the developmental state focused on the state's capacity to bring about economic development, setting out successful development under state auspices as the best guarantee for strengthening the power of the state. But both groups emphasized that the power and capacity of the state was the basis for social and economic development.

GLOBALIZATION, THE DEVELOPMENT-SECURITY NEXUS, AND THE RETURN OF NATION BUILDING IN COLLAPSED STATES

By the 1990s, and even more so after 9/11, the question that increasingly preoccupied academics and students of the development-security nexus had less to do with explaining economic development and more to do with explicating the breakdown and collapse of nation-states, and thus with preventing or containing the breakdown. With the end of the Cold War, the focus increasingly rested on failing, failed, or collapsing and collapsed states. And after September 11, 2001, in particular came a renewed effort to explain the breakdown of nation-states and a renewed interest in the theory and practice of nation building. A central concern of this debate was whether state collapse stemmed from a scarcity of natural resources or an abundance of resources. Thomas Fraser Homer-Dixon (1999), for example, argued that resource scarcity drives elites to "capture" natural resources, thereby alienating powerless groups who respond by taking up arms. Other observers argue that it is the abundance, not the shortage, of natural resources that is the key to violent conflict and state collapse. Furthermore, according to this latter view, the civil conflict for some participants may be of more economic benefit than peace. In a detailed study of Colombia, for example, Nazih Richani (2002) has noted that under certain identifiable conditions "war systems," or "systems of violence," emerge that are self-perpetuating (3–4).

The view that civil wars and endemic political violence flow primarily from the key combatants' pursuit of economic gain by was given its most well-known and most reductive articulation in a series of World Bank studies carried out by Paul Collier, Anke Hoeffler, and a number of other collaborators (2003). As the result of a broad statistical analysis of virtually all civil wars since the mid-1960s, they concluded that variables such as regime type, economic mismanagement, political rights, and levels of ethnic homogeneity or heterogeneity were statistically irrelevant to explaining the causes of civil wars. Their study concluded that economic factors were the crucial explanatory variable. In their analysis, low economic growth rates and low incomes predisposed nation-states to civil war, but there was no strong connection between high levels of social inequality and civil conflict. They also emphasized that polities highly dependent on the export of primary commodities and populated by large numbers of young men, with limited or no education, were also highly susceptible to civil conflict and political instability. Their overall conclusions were that political grievances were not directly connected to the outbreak of civil wars. In their view, nation-states that contained significant cohorts of poorly educated youths and readily accessible natural resources were particularly susceptible to civil conflict and the emergence of rebels driven primarily by powerful economic incentives ("greed") rather than political motives ("grievance") to use violence to acquire wealth (Collier et al. 2003).

While the "greed and grievance" argument satisfied some observers, its reliance on quantitative analysis and its economic determinism were challenged in many quarters. A growing number of commentators sought to situate their analysis of civil conflict, national instability, and postconflict transitions within an historical and politico-economic context (see Reno 1998). A particularly self-conscious effort to go "beyond greed and grievance" was mapped out by Karen Ballentine and Jake Sherman (2003). At the outset they emphasize that while there is considerable agreement that the dynamics of conflict can only be understood with reference to economic factors, what remains to be clarified is why, when, and how (much) economics matters. Furthermore, the highly normative character of greed and grievance has combined with their terminological imprecision to generate considerable disagreement about their usage. Ballentine and Sherman conclude that the "greed theory of civil war," grounded as it is in statistics, generates propositions about the role of economic factors (in relation to "motive" or "opportunity") that "are probabilistic" assessments of the risk of conflict. But, most important, what Collier's approach is not is an actual description of the dynamics of civil conflict in "specific real-world instances." As a result, ascertaining the role of economics can be achieved only through comparative examination and descriptive analysis of particular examples of civil conflict. For them, moving "beyond greed and grievance" in this fashion is "essential" to any effort to devise policies for the prevention of civil conflicts, to facilitate nation building, and to enhance international security and promote development more generally (Ballentine and Sherman 2003, 4–5).

Regardless of the improvements advocated by Ballentine and Sherman, the most influential academic narratives on nation building and international security in the post–Cold War era continue to avoid or downplay issues of history, culture, and identity in favor of a quantitative and technocratic approach. That approach, in turn, is linked to an even more fundamental problem: the dominant theories of development and security, as they emerged and were revised, routinized, and continue to routinize the nation-state as their key unit, or subunit, of analysis. The growing array of theories and policy proposals seeking to explain and facilitate conflict resolution and nation building continue to be outlined and implemented on the assumption that nation-states are the basic, even the natural, units of a wider international order. This is further underpinned by the assumption that capitalism, or the currently dominant and highly romanticized neoliberal conception of capitalism, is an equally natural part of the post–Cold War order.

Such a view is readily apparent in most of the recent literature on nation building. A particular good example is Francis Fukuyama's edited book

Nation-Building: Beyond Afghanistan and Iraq (2006). The contributors to this edited book provide historically grounded examinations of nation building generally, followed by a series of chapters on Afghanistan and Iraq. Fukuyama himself provides a thorough introduction and conclusion to the book. While Fukuyama continues to rely on broad technocratic prescriptions, the key point of his introduction ("Nation-Building and the Failure of Institutional Memory") reiterated in his conclusion ("Guidelines for Future Nation-Builders"), is of considerable importance. At both the outset and the end he emphasizes "the relatively weak degree of institutional learning on the part of the U.S. government concerning approaches to nation-building." Furthermore, although in his view the United Nations "may have done a bit better in preserving institutional knowledge, it has also suffered from short memory and disorganization at the start of each new effort" (Fukuyama in Fukuyama 2006, 231–32). I take this to be one of the two most important points of the book as a whole. The second point, which is central to both Fukuyama's approach and that of a number of such contributors as Larry Goodson, is the importance of a long-term commitment to nation building. Goodson emphasizes that the "final lesson from Afghanistan's nation-building may well be the most important: successful nation-building requires sustained, determined engagement by the international community and often leadership by the United States." In his view, "A foundation for the rebuilding of Afghanistan has been laid" and "now it is time to finish the job" (Goodson in Fukuyama 2006, 167). Given the emphasis on institutional memory and long-term commitment, Fukuyama's volume effectively encapsulates the dominant paradigm on nation building as it has emerged today.

CONCLUSION: THE DEVELOPMENT-SECURITY NEXUS AND THE PATHS NOT YET TAKEN

The modern theory and practice of development has had a complicated relationship to security and more recently to globalization. As we have seen, the theory and practice of development in the Cold War established certain precedents even as the development-security nexus has undergone considerable reorientation and revision in the context of the Cold War and the post–Cold War era. After September 11, 2001, the development-security nexus continued to be rethought against the backdrop of globalization and the Long War. Despite this history, the dominant development-security nexus continues to rest on key assumptions that may well prove to be the main obstacles to realizing the goals of development and security on a global scale in an era of globalization. That is, development and security continue to be framed in national and international terms that take the post-1945 nation-state system for granted. This approach persists despite the growing number of nation-states that have clearly failed to realize the expectations for development and security they thought the nation-state and the nation-state system could deliver. It is this failure that has given rise to a wide range of alternative conceptions and approaches to development that fall outside the scope of this chapter. These approaches, which focus on social and environmental issues, as well as questions of gender inequality, and move away from a focus on the state, are reflected in the day-to-day actions of countless peoples and organizations. They hold out a wide range of paths-not-yet-taken, despite the dismal situation in many parts of the globe today, where successful development and security remain elusive.

FURTHER READING

Berger, Mark T., ed. *After the Third World?* Routledge Research in Comparative Politics Series. London: Routledge, 2010 (forthcoming).
———. *The battle for Asia: From decolonization to globalization.* London: Routledge Curzon, 2004.
———, ed. *From Nation-Building to State-Building.* Routledge Research in Comparative Politics Series. London: Routledge, 2008.
Berger, Mark T., and Douglas A. Borer, eds. *The Long War: Insurgency, Counterinsurgency and Collapsing States.* Routledge Research in Comparative Politics Series. London: Routledge, 2008.
Berger, Mark T., and Heloise Weber. *Rethinking the Third World: International Development and World Politics.* London: Palgrave Macmillan, 2010 (forthcoming).
Cooper, Frederick. *Colonialism in Question: Theory, Knowledge, History.* Berkeley: University of California Press, 2005.
McMichael, Philip. *Development and Social Change: A Global Perspective*, 3rd ed. Thousand Oaks, CA: Pine Forge Press, 2004.
Yount, Robert J. C. *Postcolonialism: An Historical Introduction.* Oxford: Blackwell, 2001.

REFERENCES

Adams, Francis. 2000. *Dollar diplomacy: United States economic assistance to Latin America.* Aldershot, UK: Ashgate.
Amsden, Alice H. 1989. *Asia's next giant: South Korea and late industrialization.* New York: Oxford University Press.
———. 2001. *The rise of "the rest": Challenges to the West from late-industrializing economies.* New York: Oxford University Press.
Ballentine, Karen, and Jake Sherman. 2003. Introduction. In *The political economy of armed conflict: Beyond greed and grievance,* ed. Karen Ballentine and Jake Sherman. Boulder, CO: Lynne Rienner, 1–23.
Baran, Paul A. 1957. *The political economy of growth.* New York: Monthly Review Press.
Berger, Mark T. 2004. After the Third World? History, destiny and the fate of Third Worldism. *Third World Quarterly* 25: 9–39.
Berger, Mark T., and Douglas A. Borer. 2007. The Long War: Insurgency, counterinsurgency and collapsing states. *Third World Quarterly* 28: 197–215.
Brandt, Willy. 1980. *North-South: A programme for survival. Report of the Independent Commission on International Development Issues.* London: Pan.
Brzezinski, Zbigniew. 1983. *Power and principle: Memoirs of the national security advisor, 1977–1981.* London: Weidenfeld and Nicolson.

Collier, Paul., V. L. Elliot, Håvard Hegre, Anke Hoeffler, Marta Reynal-Querol, and Nicholas Sambanis. 2003. *Breaking the conflict trap: Civil war and development policy.* Washington, DC: World Bank.

Dirlik, Arif. 1994. *After the revolution: Waking to global capitalism.* Hanover, OH: Wesleyan University Press.

Eckl, Julian, and Ralph Weber. 2007. North-South? Pitfalls of dividing the world by words. *Third World Quarterly* 28: 3–23.

Evans, Peter. 1978. *Dependent development: The alliance of multinational, state and foreign capital in Brazil.* Princeton, NJ: Princeton University Press.

Gunder Frank, André. 1967. *Capitalism and underdevelopment in Latin America: Historical studies of Chile and Brazil.* New York: Monthly Review Press.

Fukuyama, Francis, ed. 2006. *Nation-building: Beyond Afghanistan and Iraq.* Baltimore: Johns Hopkins University Press.

Goodson, Larry P. 2006. Lessons of nation-building in Afghanistan. In *Nation-building: Beyond Afghanistan and Iraq,* ed. Francis Fukuyama. Baltimore: Johns Hopkins University Press.

Hardt, Michael, and Antonio Negri. 2000. *Empire.* Cambridge: Harvard University Press.

Homer-Dixon, Thomas Fraser. 1999. *Environment, scarcity and violence.* Princeton, NJ: Princeton University Press.

Jackson, Robert H. 1990. *Quasi-states: Sovereignty, international relations and the Third World.* Cambridge: Cambridge University Press.

Johnson, Chalmers. 1982. *MITI and the Japanese miracle: The growth of industrial policy, 1925–1975.* Stanford, CA: Stanford University Press.

LaFeber, Walter. 1993. *Inevitable revolutions: The United States in Central America.* 2nd ed. New York: W. W. Norton.

Office of International Security Affairs. 1995. *United States security strategy for the East Asia and Pacific Region.* Washington, DC: U.S. Department of Defense. February.

Office of the President of the United States. 1996. *A national security strategy of engagement and enlargement.* Washington, DC: U.S. Government Printing Office, 1996. Available online at http://www.fas.org/spp/military/docops/national/1996stra.htm.

Prebisch, Raul. 1950. *The economic development of Latin America and its principal problems.* New York: United Nations.

Reno, William. 1998. *Warlord politics and African states.* Boulder, CO: Lynne Rienner.

Richani, Nazih. 2002. *Systems of violence: The political economy of war and peace in Colombia.* Albany: State University of New York Press.

Rodney, Walter. 1972. *How Europe underdeveloped Africa.* London: Bogle-L'Ouverture Publications.

United States Agency for International Development (USAID). 1984. *Private enterprise development.* Washington, DC: Bureau for Program and Policy Coordination, USAID. November 9. Available online at http://www.usaid.gov.

Weiss, Linda. 1998. *The myth of the powerless state: Governing the economy in a global era.* Cambridge: Polity Press.

4

Environmental Insecurity

Erika Cudworth and Stephen Hobden

WHAT IS ENVIRONMENTAL SECURITY?

Since the early 1990s, the environment has emerged as a significant element in discussions of global security (Dalby 2002c, 95). Increasing concerns about the environment have combined with changing notions of what constitutes security (as discussed elsewhere in this volume). However, environmental security is a much contested concept. As Mark Levy notes, "Both 'environment' and 'security' are flexible enough to mean almost anything one wishes" (1995, 37). There is no consensus on what is meant by the term "security" and what is included under the term "environment." In other words, what is being secured, and by and for whom, and from what?

In terms of the environment, two main views define what is included. First is a concern with the environment as a resource. Security issues are related to the possibility of either running out of resources (e.g., oil) or degrading resources (e.g., soil erosion). For these analyses, the environment is something "out there." An alternative approach is to consider the issue in systemic terms, having to do with the biosphere. No distinction is made between human activity and the environment; rather, human beings are part of a larger series of processes: the environment is not something "out there."

At the same time, the broadening of the security agenda has had implications for the ways in which the environment has been viewed. Although state-centered approaches to security have been integral to the environmental security debate, expanded notions of what constitutes security have also led to the development of analyses that focus on such substate groups as communities or the individual; such suprastate formations as international organizations; or the biosphere. Larry Swatuk (2006) draws a distinction between "environmental security studies" and "critical environmental studies." The former is concerned with traditional notions of security, related to resources degradation or resource wealth. The latter engages with much broader notions of security and, in some variants, with a less anthropocentric concept of the environment.

Although a considerable literature now exists on the issue of environmental security, the concept is not without its critics. Daniel Deudney, for example, has argued that the use of the term "security" links the environment too closely to questions of national survival. Such an association may lead to inappropriate polices, especially the prioritizing of military solutions over diplomatic methods (Deudney 1990, 465–69).

While debates have proceeded on the meaning of the terms "environment" and "security" and whether they can be meaningfully linked, the processes described as globalization have contributed to concerns regarding the pace at which Earth's resources are being depleted and the accelerated human impact on the environment. In Thomas Homer-Dixon's words, "Only in the past few decades has our impact on the natural environment become truly planetary: we're now a physical force on the scale of nature itself" (2007, 13).

Within the literature, the emphasis tends to be on broadly defined notions of security and securitization, but not on what might seem more obvious—environmental *in*security in a context of potential risks and hazards (Barnett 2001, 8). Environmental change and resource shortages and possible mass migrations and international conflicts potentially associated with such developments have led to environmental risks and problems being seen as global in scope and matters for international politics (Diehl and Gleditsch 2001). Often absent is the possible contribution of ecological thought (Hayward 1994) or ecologism (Dobson 2002). The various ecologisms indicate the desirability of radically rethinking the notion of security and suggest possible conceptions of globalization and critiques of the processes associated with globalization. Global environmental change presents an incredible international relations challenge for current approaches to security because, as Hugh Dyer (2001, 68) points out, it presents "concerns which are qualitatively different from traditional security threats."

This chapter begins by considering the traditional security agenda of international relations and political decision making, in particular addressing whether states' internal and external security is threatened by the depletion of natural resources and whether the local and regional security of people is undermined by environmental degradation. A key question is the possible relationship between environmental problems and political or military conflict. Second, the chapter considers environmental problems themselves and assesses the extent to which these can be seen as global phenomena. It focuses on the uneven effects of environmental damage and raises the idea that some groups of humans and some political formations are likely to be more insecure than others. Third, the chapter considers the different understandings of, and solutions to, environmental problems posed by the various ecologisms and the extent to which these have influenced international policy making on the environment.

RESOURCE WARS: INTERNATIONAL RELATIONS, THE ENVIRONMENT, AND CONFLICT

Issues related to the environment appear to be of direct concern to international relations theorists. The environment transcends international boundaries.

Environmental Insecurity 81

Pollution caused in one country can affect adjacent countries. Global warming affects all countries, whether or not they are major producers of carbon dioxide. Furthermore, the resolution of environmental problems requires states to cooperate. Some countries may be very effective at reducing their levels of carbon dioxide emissions, but unless the major carbon dioxide producers—especially the United States and China—are encouraged to reduce releases, then no country will be able to isolate itself from the effects of global warming.

International relations as a subject, however, has had notable difficulty in engaging with environmental questions. This is perhaps because a subject that is centred on interstate relations has difficulty in dealing with problems that refuse to be restricted to state borders. Despite a broadening of the security agenda, a more traditional approach to thinking about the ways in which environmental issues may impact global relations is apparent: environmental degradation as a cause of conflict. This concern with the environment as a source of conflict not only has been a concern to writers within international relations; it also has been an issue discussed by politicians, the popular media, and international organizations.

Box 4.1 Views of Environmental Conflict in the Media and Politics

[Climate Change] will make scarce resources, clean water, viable agricultural land, even scarcer ... Such changes make the emergence of violent conflict more rather than less likely.

John Reid, British Secretary of Defense, February 2006

Across the world, they are coming: the water wars.

The Independent, February 28, 2006

Sudan ... faces a number of challenges. Among these are critical environmental issues, including land degradation, deforestation and the impacts of climate change, that threaten the Sudanese people's prospects for long-term peace, food security and sustainable development. In addition, complex but clear linkages exist between environmental problems and the ongoing conflict in Darfur, as well as other historical and current conflicts in Sudan.

Source: United Nations Environment Programme, *Sudan: Post Conflict Environmental Assessment* (Nairobi: UNEP, 2007).

A clear example of a state-centric account of environmental security is given by Michael Klare's *Resource Wars* (2001). Klare argues that following the end of the Cold War, a conflict that centered on ideology rather that resources, interstate conflict returned to the main concerns of the nineteenth century—namely, the control of natural resources. Access to resources is "becoming an increasingly prominent feature of American security policy," Klare believes (2001, 6).

For many observers, the U.S. and British invasion of Iraq has presented a clear example of such a resource war. Although the war was justified on the grounds of the presence of weapons of mass destruction and of the claimed links between the Iraqi government and Al Qaeda, no weapons were ever found, and no evidence of links to terrorism have ever been proved. Iraq has the second largest reserves of oil, however, and comments by some members of the U.S. government appear to confirm the invasion as a clear instance of "petro-imperialism" (Jhaveri 2004).

While retaining a focus on access to resources, other authors have provided a more nuanced account of the relations between resource availability and conflict at both a state and substate level. Michael Renner (2002, 6) argues that in 2001, about one-quarter of the approximately 50 violent conflicts in the world had "a strong resources dimension." This meant that legal and illegal resource exploitation provided a cause of war, and access to wealth from resource exploitation helped perpetuate war. Renner draws attention to the point that in other wars, it is not only resource scarcity that can prompt conflict; resource wealth can also provide a significant contribution to conflict. Diamonds are a notable means by which conflict in Africa has been financed (Lujala, Gleditsch, and Gilmore 2005), whereas in Colombia, control over cocaine production has been a major source of finance for both sides in the civil war. Phillipe Le Billon (2005, 23) argues that "natural resources have become the economic mainstay of most wars in the post–Cold War context."

One of the most ambitious attempts to draw links between the environment and conflict has been carried out by Homer-Dixon and his associates (1999). Homer-Dixon pointed to a number of ways in which the environment could be linked to conflict and that "in coming decades the world will probably see a steady increase in the incidence of violent conflict that is caused at least in part by environmental scarcity" (1999, 4). He also argued that environmental conflict was more likely to affect developing countries and was more likely to result in conflict within a state rather than between states, although the possibility existed for internal disruption to overflow into the international arena. Furthermore, Homer-Dixon claimed that in most of the examples that his research had examined, environmental scarcity was a contributing factor rather than the direct cause (1999, 133–36).

Although many analysts have drawn a link between the environment and conflict, others remain sceptical of how far environmental factors contribute to instances of conflict. There is much talk of water wars, for example, yet according to Aaron Wolf (1999, 256), "there has never been a single war fought over water." Urdal argues that there is very little evidence to support the contention that the environment is emerging as a major contributor to conflict. He claims that "there is no support for claims that the post–Cold War period represents a new era of insecurity, or an erupting state of anarchy due to demographic pressure and resource scarcity" (2005, 430). For Richard Matthew, Ted Gaulin, and Bryan McDonald (2003, 875), the attempt to link conflict and the environment is an "elusive quest." They argue that there has been a tendency to underestimate the ability of states to adapt and react to environmental change. These writers share the scepticism over the utility of the term "environmental security" that was discussed in the previous section. They argue that most of those who claim that there *is* a link between the environment and conflict are asserting a future *potential* link. Attempts to analyze contemporary or past wars have found it difficult to establish a direct association. The move to include the environment under the umbrella of security is a political move that represents an attempt to shift the issue of the environment further up the political agenda, rather than representing a verifiable relationship between the environment and conflict, either between states or within them.

The link between conflict and resource shortages or wealth is a complex one and remains a subject of ongoing debate. Homer-Dixon's work suggests that environmental issues are, at most, a contributory factor to a number of conflicts, rather than a specific cause. The work on resource wars has, in general, looked at localized environmental issues, yet through the 1990s and into the early years of the twenty-first century, there has been an increasing concern about the worldwide impact of certain environmental concerns.

GLOBAL ENVIRONMENTAL CHANGE

This planet is divided politically, economically, socially, culturally, and in myriad ways. Yet radically different regions share a "global environmental commons" of air, seas and waterways, and climate (*Ecologist* 1993) characterized by a range of what are often referred to as global environmental problems. However, the causes and consequences of such problems and their regional locations raise questions about their apparently globalized qualities.

The Environment as a Site of Global Risk

Ulrich Beck (1992) has developed a highly influential analysis of risk, which suggests that we have moved from a society in which some of us are under the threat of material deprivation, to a risk society where we all live in a "community of danger" as a result of environmental threats caused by industrial production and mass prosperity and consumption. Humanity is collectively subject to similar risks from environmental catastrophe, and environmental risk, or insecurity, is now a globalized phenomenon (Beck 1999).

In countries where malnutrition and starvation may be endemic, however, material deprivation may continue to be a pertinent cause of insecurity. Many authors argue that global climate change will have greater impact on the South. Stephen Devereux and Jenny Edwards argue that the effects of global warming will be globally stratifying. Those countries where drought is already a problem are likely to become drier, since they are more dependent on agriculture where the possibilities for diversification are more limited. It is likely, they argue, that "the prevalence and depth of hunger will deteriorate in those countries and population groups where food security is already significant" (Devereux and Edwards 2004, 28).

Simon Dalby argues that the exploitation of the global South's environment commenced during the colonial period and has continued since the demise of the European empires. In this sense, the global North has exported much of its environmentally damaging industrialization, making national environmental security a nonsensical notion. According to Dalby, "Ecological security cannot be understood in the conventional parameters of territorial states" (2002a, 141), given the global exploitation of resources.

Beck (2000) further suggests there are three elements to risk that are apposite for understanding environmental risks as questions of security. He suggests that we live in a situation of real as well as imagined risk, in an age of "manufactured risk" resulting from our increased intervention in nature—through genetic modification, for example. The existence of such risk raises the political question of who is manufacturing risk. Consider pollution, for example, which illustrates both the global impact and the unequal distribution of environmental problems resulting from manufactured risk. People in one country may produce significant amounts of air-borne pollution, but countries elsewhere may bear the brunt in terms of the pollution's environmental effects. In the well-known case of the devastation of Scandinavian forests by acid rain, one of the key culprits was British electricity generation. Environmental risk, as we will see, disturbs long-settled Western assumptions about the appropriate ends of politics. But first, what are environmental problems, and in what ways do they place human communities at risk?

The Global Qualities of Environmental Problems

The term "environment" is a catch-all category that homogenizes the diversity of nonhuman life and encompasses a multiplicity of incredibly varied plant and animal species in such contexts of human and nonhuman life as climate, waterways, and oceanic systems (Cudworth 2003, 2; 2005, 42–43). Such an understanding of the environment and the distinction of the human species from it is certainly a product of Western histories and sensibilities (Soper 1995). Historically, there have been diverse formations of society-environment relations (McNeill 2000). Such complexity notwithstanding, recent decades have seen the emergence of an increasing consensus on environmental issues and problems.

In the 1970s, population expansion—overwhelmingly that associated with poorer and developing countries of the global South—was often seen as the cause of environmental threats. Well-publicized reports advocated a Malthusian perspective that assumed rapid population growth meant an inevitable crisis caused by a scarcity of natural resources available to burgeoning human populations. A group of scientists based at Massachusetts Institute of Technology (MIT), for example, produced a doomsday report in which they used computer simulation technology to predict patterns in population growth and the rates at which this would outstrip the carrying capacity of the earth (Meadows et al. 1972). This report argued that the limits of growth would be reached by 2070. The more measured sequel balanced a demand for population limitation with a clear case for limits on material consumption and more efficient deployment of resources (Meadows, Meadows, and Randers 1992). This shift was common within the literature, and from the 1990s, there was a move away from

Environmental Insecurity

Figure 4.1 The Bering Strait, July 13, 1999. A young walrus rests on a small, thin, and melting iceberg as the Greenpeace ship *Arctic Sunrise* passes by. Global warming is blamed for affecting the polar regions. Photo: © Greenpeace/Daniel Beltra.

population as key to explaining environmental problems to a focus on the impact of agricultural and industrial practices associated with Western modernization and the notion of ecological footprint.

Global warming is probably the clearest example of a global environmental problem, and evidence suggests it is accelerating (McCarthy et al. 2001). It derives from both industrial and agricultural processes. Its consequences are global, with all parts of the world likely to expect some shift in climate and therefore of the types of flora and fauna suited to the changed climatic conditions. Such effects as the melting of ice sheets and consequent rise in sea levels, however, will primarily affect certain low-lying coastal areas. Thus an irony of the effects of global climate change is that its effects are likely to be visited upon less-industrialized countries having less responsibility for the emission of greenhouse gases. The climate and greenhouse gas emissions are no respecters of national boundaries (see Figure 4.1).

The Intergovernmental Panel on Climate Change makes clear that global warming is utterly urgent and that some parts of the globe are incredibly vulnerable (McNeill 2000). James Lovelock (2000, 15) argues that the earth is a superorganism able to regulate its own temperature. However, the unprecedented impact of modern, rich, industrialized, and consumption-orientated societies on the composition of atmospheric gases is huge (Lovelock 2000, 15), and our disruption of natural systems may be so dramatic that the earth's climate will shift in a way that compromises the long-term survival of humanity and

Figure 4.2 Democatic Republic of Congo, 2007. Photo: © Greenpeace.

other higher animal species (Lovelock 1979, 107). He now argues that we are fast approaching the point of no return (Lovelock 2006). While Lovelock's apocalyptic language has raised the ire of many journalists, academics, and activists, many researchers have cautiously accepted the premises of his science.

The loss of species biodiversity, that is, the amount of genetic diversity, or how many species and varieties within a species there are,—has also come to be defined as an environmental problem (see Figure 4.2). Large animals such as tigers, rhinos, and whales have experienced severe declines in populations and face potential extinction. The blame is often locally attributed to populations of Southern regions where these species live, conveniently forgetting that in much of Europe megafauna such as wolves have been hunted to extinction (Guha 1989a). Various UN reports have documented the dramatic declines in both temperate and tropical forests with the associated dramatic losses of species and the rapid clearing of costal flora (UN Environment Programme, 1997; UN Development Programme, 1998).

Thus, all problems may have localized impacts and global effects. Most researchers in the environmental sciences see such difficulties as immediately pressing and serious. The arguments of Lovelock and others, for example, indicate that we are rapidly changing the conditions for our own existence and must act immediately, collectively, and radically to prevent environmental disaster.

ECOLOGISM AND INTERNATIONAL POLITICS

How, then, have we acted in response to such challenges? The organization most often able to act to avert environmental risk and implement an environmental security agenda is the (nation) state together with international political organizations, which are themselves usually composed of individual states. Yet, as Dalby (2002b, 5) notes, charging states with responsibility for the environment may well be a case of foxes guarding chickens. States have been drivers for modernization, putting in place an infrastructure, which so depends on carbon fuels and high levels of resource use, in large part by establishing a capitalist system of property relations (Latouche 1993). This section examines the social and political thought of ecologism and considers the extent to which any of these ideas might have influenced global policy making in reaction to environmental problems.

Different Ecologisms

Andrew Dobson (2002, 13–23) distinguishes environmentalism from ecologism. Environmentalism is usually defined by its concern with conservation through technocratic means, and environmentalists are often seen as reformers who do not consider radical change in political, social, and economic institutions and processes necessary (Benton 1994, 31). Some environmentalists, for example, believe such existing social practices as those associated with consumer capitalism can be modified in order to preserve the environment (Elkington and Burke 1987). It is a sense of environment-society relations as in crisis, however, that defines ecological perspectives (Merchant 1992, 1), although different schools of ecologism have different analyses of this problematic relationship and what might be done to address it (these are summarized in Table 4.1).

"Deep ecology" considers humanity to have damaged the environment to such a catastrophic extent that radical, drastic measures are necessary to halt such destruction. Deep ecologists argue that modern Western societies are anthropocentric, or human-centered, treating nature as a means to human ends. Rather, they argue, we should care for the environment because nature has intrinsic value. If we do not, they continue, we will endanger our own species (Devall 1990, 70). Deep ecology tends to see humans as collectively responsible for environmental destruction, rather than having differing forms of social organization and differing degrees of environmental impact.

For social ecologists, on the other hand, environmental exploitation is the direct result of intra-human domination. For Murray Bookchin, the exploitation of humans by other humans is the key to explaining the human exploitation of the natural environment, and therefore all humans are not equally responsible for environmental destruction (1980, 62; 1990, 44). Social ecology is clearly aware of the social causes of environmental destruction, understanding that "human society is fractured by race, class and sex. It is not right to hold the poor or people of the South responsible for developments by the rich white North" (Mellor 1992, 106).

Some ecosocialists have suggested that poverty was the main cause of environmental problems (Weston 1986, 4), leaving unanswered the questions raised by deep ecologists about the unsustainable nature of affluent Western consumer

Table 4.1 Varieties of Ecologism

	Ethics, Nature, and Humanity	Conception of the Relationship Between the Environment and Society	Environmental Priorities and Political Solutions
Deep Ecology	Humans are not separate from nature, but a part of nature. Ethics must not be human centered. All nature has intrinsic value. Humanity also has an interest in preserving the natural environment and its conditions for existence.	Contemporary society is anthropocentric. Humans as a species dominate the natural environment and are collectively responsible for damaging it. Anthropocentrism fails to appreciate that natural resources are finite.	Global warming is prioritized, but other concerns include pollution and decline of biodiversity. Radical cuts of greenhouse emissions sought by international agreement on industrial emissions, aviation policy, etc. Reduction of consumerism in the West. Preservation of biodiversity and wilderness.
Social Ecology	Humans are a special kind of animal because they are rational and reflective beings. Ethics is inevitably human centered because humans must attribute value to nature.	The destruction of the environment is a result of intrahuman domination or hierarchy. State oppression and exploitation of class, caste, gender, and race leads to human exploitation of natural resources.	The state and related international organizations are not vehicles for social justice and environmental change. Change comes from local or municipal democracy and social movement initiatives.
Ecosocialism	Humans and other animals have a specific nature or species life.	Capitalism commodifies nature and defines natural resources as objects for human use. The	A social democratic agenda, reducing poverty and other socials inequalities, should be

88

Table 4.1 (*Continued*)

	Ethics, Nature, and Humanity	Conception of the Relationship Between the Environment and Society	Environmental Priorities and Political Solutions
	Different species have different kinds of life needs. Therefore, different species need different treatment. Humans attribute ethical value and decide what such treatment might be.	organization of work means humans are alienated from nature. Multifaceted social deprivation contributes strongly to environmental problems.	requisite for environmental sustainability. A concern with global inequities of trade. Proponents seek to rein in transnational corporations and ensure the polluter pays.
Ecofeminism	For "social" ecofeminists, social practices and institutions shape human nature and change the "species being" of humans and other species. For "affinity" ecofeminists, patriarchal relations (i.e., of male domination) have led to the alienation of most men from their biological natures as human animals, and from nature.	Humans collectively exploit and dominate nature, but this behavior is shaped by social forces and divisions around gender, class, colonialism, etc. Patriarchal capitalism exploits women's productive and reproductive labor. For some researchers, patriarchy assigns women to caring labor because women are more likely to empathize with other species.	A wide range of concerns. Specifically ecofeminist concerns include chemical pollution of child-care and household products, genetic modification of food, and effects of new reproductive technologies. Women need to be better represented in decision making nationally and internationally. Overlaps with liberation and socialist ecologism—the West needs to "de-develop." Policy needs to take account of social inequality; e.g., population

(*Continued*)

Table 4.1 (*Continued*)

	Ethics, Nature, and Humanity	Conception of the Relationship Between the Environment and Society	Environmental Priorities and Political Solutions
			growth is linked to gender inequalities.
		Ideologies of gender crosscut those on colonialism, racism, and the domination of nature. Patriarchal culture devalues women, colonized peoples, and exploits nature.	
Liberation Ecologism	The incredible differences of cultures and forms of social organization across the globe mean that there is a plethora of ethical stances on human relations with nature.	Relations between rich and poor countries shape the use of resources. Histories of colonialism have altered the environments of both North and South. Some colonial initiatives are environmentally disastrous, e.g., dam building, plantation agriculture. A wide variety of relationships between human communities and nature shaped by history and multiple cultures.	Environmental problems are either the greatest (e.g., loss of species diversity) or are likely to have the most severe impacts (e.g., desertification or flooding as a result of global warming) in poorer countries. Poorer countries need to be more strongly represented in international decision making. Key changes needed include removal of Third World debt and rapid reduction in poverty, as well as a culturally and politically sensitive, sustainable development agenda.

Environmental Insecurity

Figure 4.3 Guiyu, China, March 9, 2005. A Chinese worker dismantles motherboards in an e-waste workshop. Photo: © Greenpeace/Natalie Behring.

societies. Peter Dickens (1996) addresses this by suggesting that capitalism, as a system of economic production and social relations, encourages us to see the natural world as a series of commodities and is organized around the production of goods for the market on the basis of increased production and consumption to satisfy the profit motive. An ecosocialist mode of production would produce and distribute goods and resources according to need, not the demands of capitalist consumerism (Pepper 1993, 146). Thus a socialist system of production and, one assumes, a socialist or social democratic state, might be better placed to operate within natural limits (Benton 1989).

Ecofeminism considers that social exclusion, particularly the gendered division of labor, structures relations between society and the environment, and that ideologies suggesting the domination of nature are interwoven with those that marginalize certain social groups. Carolyn Merchant (1980) argues that the ideas associated with seventeenth-century European modernization involved the objectification of the natural world as a prerequisite for the commercial exploitation of natural resources and the social exclusion of women. Vandana Shiva (1988) argues that the West has imposed its ecologically destructive and gender dichotomous model of modernity on the rest of the globe. Maria Mies (1986; Benolt-Thompsen and Mies 1999) considers that the gendered division of labor is at the core of the linked exploitations of women by men, Southern countries by the wealthy Northern states of the globe, and the natural environment by human society (see Figures 4.3 and 4.4).

Figure 4.4 Guiyu, China, March 8. A family of migrant workers from Henan Province strip wires and e-trash in Guangzhou Province. Photo: © Greenpeace/ Natalie Behring.

   Liberation ecologism also sees environmental difficulties as embedded in the political and economic relations between rich and poor countries (Chatterjee and Finger 1994). The legacy of colonialism has shaped the natural and social forms of colonized regions. Guha (1989b) has suggested that such colonial institutions as dams, canals, and plantations functioned to disrupt local ecologies as well as to control and exploit human populations. Environmental issues and problems differ across the regional formations of the global South and differ much from those experienced in the North (Peet and Watts 1996, 14); thus, liberation ecologism has stressed the need for Western-dominated environmental movements and international organizations to avoid the temptation to engage in conservation imperialism (Guha 1997).
   So all ecologisms see human communities, varied as they are, in a complex network of relationships with nonhuman nature—relationships characterized by reciprocity and interdependency, as well as by exploitation and domination. That inter-complexity suggests matters of social inequality and injustice are bound up with attempts to promote sustainable ways of living. Ecologism has put the environment and the risks associated with its destruction on the political agenda, but the solutions suggested by this analysis are radical and, as we will see later in this chapter, have, perhaps as a consequence, had less influence on global-level policy making than they might otherwise have had.

International Politics and the Environment

Since 1945, much of the development of international environmental policy has taken place under the auspices of the United Nations. The convention regulating international whaling was signed in 1946, and some regulations on nuclear and other toxic waste disposal, in addition to some forms of habitat protection, were agreed in the 1950s and 1960s. The first significant initiative was the 1972 Stockholm Intergovernmental Conference on the Human Environment (Miller 1995, 8). Over a decade later, the UN Commission on Environment and Development produced the Bruntland Report, *Our Common Future* (see Box 4.2), the findings and general arguments of which have been echoed in much of the subsequent academic work on environmental security (Matthew 2002, 112).

Box 4.2 Sustainable Development: The Bruntland Agenda

In 1983, in the context of increased concern around environmental security, the then UN secretary general commissioned the former prime minister of Norway, Go-Harlem Bruntland, to establish and chair an independent commission (World Commission on Environment and Development, WCED) to assess environmental risks and threats. The so-called Bruntland Report, *Our Common Future*, was presented to the UN General Assembly in 1987. The report recommended the following principles as a guide to policy making:

- Economic development should be sustainable to "meets the needs of the present without compromising the ability of future generations to meet their own needs" (43).
- All countries should integrate environment and development policies.
- Continued economic growth is essential to environmental protection.
- Sustainable levels of population must be ensured.
- Conservation and enhancement of natural resources must be pursued.
- International economic relations and practices centering on trade, finance, and aid should be reformed.

The report made the notion of sustainable development mainstream, and its understandings and recommendations continue to influence environmental policy at the global level. It was criticized, however, for a commitment to such ecological modernization as a commitment to environmental sustainability alongside development within the context of free market capitalism.

Divisions between North and South have been apparent in negotiations about environmental protection (see Payne 2005, chap. 8). Many countries in the South have been concerned that environmental protection measures not restrict their potential for development. For some countries, the calls for environmental protection are a new form of neo-imperialism—a means of placing restrictions on the sovereignty of developing countries to exploit their natural resources, such as rain forests, and limit industrialization (Miller 1995). Yet the right of developing countries to exploit their developing resources and prioritize economic development has been a cornerstone of UN-negotiated agreements (Williams 2005, 56).

Box 4.3 The Rio Declaration and Agenda 21

In 1989, the UN General Assembly launched the United Nations Conference on Environment and Development (UNCED). The agenda for the main conference took two years and a number of preparatory conferences to establish. The UNCED was held in Rio de Janeiro in June 1992. Attendance and participation and media coverage were unprecedented for an environmental event. Five agreements were signed, including the Convention on Climate Change, the Convention on Biological Diversity, and the Declaration of Forest Principles. Most important were the following points:

- **The Rio Declaration**—a set of guiding principles for national and international behavior, including the precautionary principle and the polluter pays principle. It advocated better information on environmental matters, increased public involvement in environmental decision making, and environmental impact assessments prior to development. Importantly, it acknowledged the responsibility of states of the global North for environmental degradation.
- **Agenda 21**—specifies what actions are necessary at national and international levels to reconcile development with environmental concern; was adopted by all the states represented at UNCED. It emphasized the importance of democratic decision making and the full integration of environmental issues into all areas of policy.

The UNCED was strongly criticized by environmental and developmental NGOs and social movement organizations, as well as many governments in developing countries of the Southern Hemisphere. While tackling Third World debt, reducing poverty, curtailing Western consumption levels, and reducing use of fossil fuels were all part of Agenda 21, no targets were set and the proposals were not binding on signatories. Sustainable development in Agenda 21 is based on a model of free market capitalist development. It also emphasized that the sovereignty of nation-states and did little to question the established international order (see Chatterjee and Finger 1994; Porter and Brown 1996).

In a belated follow up to the Stockholm conference of 1972 came the First Earth Summit, an intergovernmental conference held in Rio de Janeiro in 1992.

Environmental Insecurity 95

Figure 4.5 Montreal, Canada, December 2005. Campaigners for action on climate change. Canada hosted the United Nations Climate Change Conference (COP11 and COP/MOP1), the largest talks since those at Kyoto, Japan, in 1997. Photo: © Friends of the Earth/Philip McMaster.

Conducted under UN auspices and with almost every member state represented, Rio sought to establish a far-reaching set of global agreements and targets on environmental protection (see Box 4.3). It included conventions on the rainforest, climate change and greenhouse gases, and biodiversity. One of the undercurrents of the Rio conference, however, was the dissatisfaction of governments of poorer countries with the Western domination of the issues debated and the decisions made.

The fundamental question is whether states, and the international organizations of which they are members, can construct new physical and institutional infrastructures that move us away from an ever-expanding use of resources. Much of what we have seen in terms of the internationalization of environmental policy involves an assumption that economic growth can be compatible with ecological sustainability and that "there is a techno-institutional fix for the present problems" (Hajer 1995, 32). The politics of ecologism implies radical departures from our currently normative economic, political, and social practices in wealthy Western and Northern states and has been extremely pessimistic concerning the ability of states to deliver change (Sachs, Loske, and Linz 1998). Many adherents, like Robert Goodin (1992), are skeptical of statist reform, which tends to be seen as a process in which environmental questions are subsumed under a bureaucratic rationality of resource managerialism (Luke 1999). (See Figures 4.5 and 4.6.)

Figure 4.6 Montreal, Canada, December 2005. Protest signs. Photo: © Friends of the Earth/Philip McMaster.

The state remains the prime arena wherein forms of representation concerning the impacts of ecological degradation are articulated; thus, some observers suggest practical political engagement is both inevitable and imperative (Patterson, Doran, and Barry 2006, 138, 153). Robyn Eckersely (2004, 241) is confident that a decline in territorially based governance accompanying globalization, coupled with a radical institutional reform, will make possible the consideration of ecological concern. She suggests a move from liberal democracies to "ecological democracies," where those collectivities subject to ecological risk must be involved in or represented in decision-making that may involve or generate ecological risk. Yet we are still left with a system of states with functions of security defined in military terms and with sustainable economic development understood in the context of market capitalism.

CONCLUSION: CAN A SECURITY AGENDA GO GREEN?

Some observers consider that the development of environmental security as an academic project and a policy agenda has been a boon for the environmental movement, and has been pioneering in developing our understanding of changing security contexts and has contributed in important ways to the broader debates around the social and political effects of change beyond and across the boundaries of nation-states (Matthew 2002, 109). Critics, however, consider that there is no "good reason to think that ecological matters can be usefully understood in terms of security from some external threat at all" (Dalby 2002b, 2). Indeed, certainly for those of us in the wealthier parts of the globe, the threat is embedded in our way of life and everyday practices.

The idea of ecological security, as opposed to environmental security, does not necessarily fare much better, implying, as it does, an agenda of deep ecologism. We argue here for a radical social ecologism that takes account our imperative need to care for the biosphere, together with an understanding of the ways in which multiple and complex inequalities shape the securities of different populations. Ultimately, however, Dalby is probably right to jettison the term "security." The environmental security literature tends to reproduce a dualistic understanding of human relations to the environment in which we humans are either threatened by or pose a threat to nature (Barnett 2001, 67). We are in a complex situation of risk as a result of human modifications of our habitat, but those modifications are shaped by histories of social relations, economic practices, and formations of political power.

The politics of social ecologism, broadly defined and including insights from Marxist, feminist, and postcolonial approaches, suggests that the way to face hazard may be to take concrete steps to regulate the uneven flow of resources from poor to rich, institutionalize and normativize the practices and ideals of social justice. In addition, those developments should take account of the complex relationships of interdependency between human communities and the natural environment. Carboniferous consumer capitalism may be what needs to become less secure, and this would entail a re-conceptualization of dominant economic relations and social practices and a reinvention of our political world.

FURTHER READING

Cudworth, Erika. *Developing Eco-feminist Theory*. Basingstoke, UK: Palgrave, 2005. A comprehensive discussion of ecologism, with a focus on feminist approaches.

Dalby, Simon. *Environmental Security*. Minneapolis: University of Minnesota Press, 2002. A broad-ranging critique of the environmental security concept.

Homer-Dixon, Thomas. *Environment, Scarcity and Violence*. Princeton, NJ: Princeton University Press, 1999. Based on over a decade of research, an in-depth examination of the links between environmental degradation and violence.

Klare, Michael T. *Resource Wars: The New Landscape of Global Conflict*. New York: Metropolitan Books, 2001. A realist account of the role of resource shortages in international relations.

Lovelock, James. *The Revenge of Gaia*. London: Allen Lane, 2006. A gloomy prognosis of the future impacts of climate change.

REFERENCES

Barnett, Jon. 2001 *The meaning of environmental security: Ecological politics and politics and policy in the new security era*. London: Zed.

Beck, Ulrich. 1992. *The risk society: Towards a new modernity*. London: Sage.
———. 1999. *World risk society*. Cambridge: Polity.
———. 2000. Risk society revisited. In *The risk society and beyond: Critical issues for social theory*, ed. Barbara Adam, Ulrich Beck, and Joost Van Loon, 211–29. London: Sage.
Benolt-Thompsen, Victoria, and Maria Mies. 1999. *The subsistence perspective: Beyond the globalised economy*. London: Zed Books.
Benton, Ted. 1989. Marxism and natural limits: An ecological critique and reconstruction. *New Left Review* 178: 51–86.
———. 1994. Biology and social theory in the environment debate. In *Social theory and the global environment*, ed. Ted Benton and Michael Redclift, 28–50. London: Routledge.
Bookchin, Murray. 1980. *Towards an ecological society*. Montreal: Black Rose Books.
———. 1990. *The philosophy of social ecology*. Montreal: Black Rose Books.
Chatterjee, Pratap, and Matthias Finger. 1994. *The earth brokers: Power, politics and world development*. London: Routledge.
Cudworth, Erika. 2003. *Environment and society*. London: Routledge.
———. 2005. *Developing eco-feminist theory: The complexity of difference*. Basingstoke, UK: Palgrave.
Dalbeko, Geoffrey. 1997. Environmental security: Core ideas and U.S. government initiatives. *SAIS Review* 17: 127–46.
Dalby, Simon. 2002a. *Environmental security*. University of Minnesota Press.
———. 2002b. Environmental security: Ecology or international relations. Paper presented at the annual convention of the International Studies Association, March, in New Orleans, LA.
———. 2002c. Security and ecology in the age of globalization. *Environmental Change and Security Report* 8: 95–108.
Deudney, Daniel. 1990. The case against linking environmental degradation and national security. *Millenium* 19: 461–76.
Devall, Bill. 1990. *Simple in means, rich in ends*. London: Greenprint.
Devereux, Stephen, and Jenny Edwards. 2004. Climate change and food security. *IDS Bulletin* 35: 22–30.
Dickens, Peter. 1996. *Reconstructing nature: Alienation, emancipation and the division of labour*. London: Routledge.
Diehl, Paul F., and Nils Petter Gleditsch, eds. *Environmental conflict*. Boulder, CO: Westview Press.
Dobson, Andrew. 2002. *Green political thought*. 2nd ed. London: Unwin Hyman.
Dyer, Hugh. 2001. Theoretical aspects of environmental security. In *Responding to environmental conflicts: Implications for theory and practice*, ed. Ellen Petzold-Bradley, Alexander Carius, and Arpad Vincze, 67–82. Dordrecht, Neth.: Kulwer Academic Publishers.
Eckersley, Robyn. 2004. *The green state: Re-thinking democracy and sovereignty*. Cambridge, MA: MIT Press.
Ecologist, The. 1993. *Whose common future? Reclaiming the commons*. London: Earthscan.
Elkington, John, and Tom Burke. 1987. *The green capitalists: Industry's search for environmental excellence*. London: Gollancz.

Goodin, Robert. 1992. *Green political theory*. Cambridge: Polity.
Guha, Ramachandra. 1989a. Radical American environmentalists and wilderness protection: A Third World critique. *Environmental Ethics* 11: 71–83.
———. 1989b. *The unquiet woods: Ecological change and peasant resistance in the Himalayas*. Oxford and Berkeley: University of California Press.
———. 1997. The environmentalism of the poor. In *Varieties of Environmentalism*, ed. Ramachandra Guha and Juan Martinez-Alier, 3–21. London: Earthscan.
Hajer, Martin. 1995. *The politics of environmental discourse: Ecological modernization and the policy process*. Oxford: Clarendon.
Hayward, Tim. 1994. *Ecological thought: An introduction*. Cambridge: Polity Press.
Homer-Dixon, Thomas. 1999. *Environment, scarcity and violence*. Princeton, NJ: Princeton University Press.
———. 2007. *The upside of down: Catastrophe, creativity and the renewal of civilisation*. London: Souvenir Press.
Jhaveri, Nayna J. 2004. Petroimperialism: U.S. oil interests and the Iraq War. *Antipode* 36: 2–11.
Klare, Michael T. 2001. *Resource wars: The new landscape of global conflict*. New York: Metropolitan Books.
Latouche, Serge. 1993. *In the wake of the affluent society: An exploration of post-development*. London: Zed Books.
Le Billon, Phillipe. 2005. The geopolitical economy of "resource wars." In *The geopolitics of resource wars*, ed. Philippe Le Billon, 1–28. London: Frank Cass.
Levy, Mark. 1995. Is the environment a national security issue? *International Security* 20: 35–62.
Lohmann, Larry. 1999. Forests: Myths and reality in violent conflicts. In *Ecology, politics and violent conflict*, ed. Mohammed Suliman, 158–80. London: Zed.
Lovelock, James. 1979. *Gaia: A new look at life on earth*. Oxford University Press.
———. 2000. *Ages of Gaia: A biography of our living earth*, 2nd ed. Oxford University Press.
———. 2006. *The revenge of Gaia*. London: Allen Lane.
Lujala, Päivi, Nils Petter Gleditsch, and Elizabeth Gilmore. 2005. A diamond curse? Civil war and a lootable resource. *Journal of Conflict Research* 49: 538–62.
Luke, Tim W. 1999. *Capitalism, democracy and ecology: Departing from Marx*. Champaign: University of Illinois Press.
Matthew, Richard A. 2002. In defense of environment and security research. *Environmental Change and Security Report* 8: 109–24.
Matthew, Richard A., Ted Gaulin, and Bryan McDonald. 2003. The elusive quest: Linking environmental change and conflict. *Canadian Journal of Political Science*, 36: 857–78.
McCarthy, James., Osvaldo F. Canzian:, Neil A. Leary, David J. Dokken, and Kasey S. White, eds. 2001. *Climate change 2001: Impacts, adaptation and vulnerability*. Cambridge: Cambridge University Press.
McNeill, John R. 2000. *Something new under the sun: An environmental history of the twentieth century*. New York: W. W. Norton.
Meadows, Donella H., Dennis L. Meadows, and Jørgen Randers. 1992. *Beyond the limits: Global collapse or a sustainable future*. London: Earthscan.

Meadows, Donella H., Dennis L. Meadows, Jørgen Randers, and William W. Behrens III. 1972. *The limits to growth: A report for the Club of Rome's project on the predicament of mankind*. London: Earth Island.

Mellor, Mary. 1992. *Breaking the boundaries: Towards a feminist green socialism*. London: Virago.

Merchant, Carolyn. 1980. *The death of nature: Women, ecology and the scientific revolution*. San Francisco: Harper and Row.

———. 1992. *Radical ecology: The search for a livable world*. London: Routledge.

Mies, Maria. 1986. *Patriarchy and accumulation on a world scale*. London: Zed Books.

Miller, Marion A. L. 1995. *The Third World in global environmental politics*. Buckingham, UK: Open University Press.

Patterson, Matthew, Peter Doran, and John Barry. 2006. Green theory. In *The state: Theories and issues*, ed. Colin Hay, Michael Lister, and David Marsh, 135–54. Basingstoke, UK: Palgrave.

Payne, Anthony. 2005. *The global politics of unequal development*. Basingstoke, UK: Palgrave.

Peet, Richard, and Michael Watts, eds. 1996. *Liberation ecologies: Environment, development, social movements*. London: Routledge.

Pepper, David. 1993. *Eco-socialism: From deep ecology to social justice*. London: Routledge.

Redclift, Michael. 1996. *Wasted: Counting the costs of global consumption*. London: Earthscan.

Renner, Michael. 2002. *The anatomy of resource wars*. Washington, DC: World Watch Institute.

Sachs, Wolfgang, Reinhard Loske, and Manfred Linz. 1998. *Greening the North: A post-industrial blueprint for ecology and equity*. London: Zed Books.

Shiva, Vandana. 1988. *Staying alive: Women, ecology and development*. London: Zed Books.

———. 1998. *Biopiracy: The plunder of nature and knowledge*. Cambridge, MA: South End Press.

Soper, Kate. 1995. *What is nature?* Oxford: Blackwell.

Swatuk, Larry A. 2006. Environmental security. In *Palgrave advance in international environmental politics*, ed. Michele M. Betsill, Kathryn Hochstetler, and Dimitris Stevis, 203–36. Basingstoke, UK: Palgrave.

UN Development Programme. 1998. *Human development report, 1998*. Oxford and New York: Oxford University Press.

UN Environment Programme. 1997. *Global environment outlook, 1997*. Oxford and New York: Oxford University Press.

Urdal, Henrik. 2005. People vs. Malthus: Population pressure, environmental degradation, and armed conflict revisited. *Journal of Peace Research* 42: 417–34.

Weston, Joe, ed. 1986. *Red and green: A new politics of the environment*. London: Pluto.

Williams, Marc. 2005. The Third World and global environmental negotiations: Interests, institutions and ideas. *Global Environmental Politics* 5: 48–69.

Wolf, Aaron T. 1999. "Water wars" and water reality: Conflict and co-operation along international waterways. In *Environmental change, adaptation and security*, ed. Steve Lonergan, 251–68. Dordercht, Neth.: Kluwer Academic Publishers.

5

Finance

Eleni Tsingou

GLOBALIZATION AND FINANCE: ANALYZING TRENDS AND DEVELOPMENTS

Global financial markets are transnational and complex. Several factors have contributed to this, including technological and communication innovations and the liberalization of markets through public policy, for example, the phasing-out of exchange and capital controls. In addition, such new and ever-evolving products and instruments as derivatives are changing the nature of financial transactions, as the so-called subprime crisis of 2007–2008 demonstrates. Global finance has arguably become transnational faster and more comprehensively than other aspects of the economy; so has its governance.

In parallel, several developments have taken place. First, global finance has come to be overwhelmingly understood in technical and specialist terms, making it often difficult to address in traditional public policy debates. Second, financial activities and their oversight have become increasingly harmonized at the transnational level through the proliferation of widely accepted standards and best-practice codes.

Multiple layers of institutions and a wide range of public and private actors can be seen to be in charge of global financial governance. On the one hand, international organizations such as the Bretton Woods institutions of the World Bank Group and the IMF have, in conjunction with national governments, been instrumental in setting global public policy parameters with respect to economic and monetary policy, including a more limited economic role for the state (through privatization and the introduction of the private sector as provider of public goods) and participation in the processes of economic globalization (through liberalized capital markets and global supply chains).

At the same time, the institutional framework at the global level is one of coordinated standard setting. The Basel Committee on Banking Supervision (Basel Committee), the International Organization of Securities Commissions (IOSCO), and the International Association of Insurers Supervisors (IAIS) act as formal coordination mechanisms while less formally, governance is generated through the interaction of the regulators and supervisors of core (G10) countries, the private sector (private financial institutions and transnational business associations), and a community of experts (primarily economists). This setup corresponds to the framework built by Martin Hewson and Timothy Sinclair (1999) to explain emerging global governance patterns, which focuses on marketized institutions, professional or specialized knowledge, and the structural element of complex infrastructural technologies.

In a framework of multiple actors, authority shifts occur and the relative role and input of different actors varies. How, then, do we conceptualize how these actors relate to each other? The international political economy (IPE) literature has dealt with these issues through debates on states and markets. At the core of these analyses is the reassessment of the role of the state and a realization of the importance of exploratory devices employed in political economy. Some research has concentrated on economic issues in terms of interaction between states (Gilpin 1987). Concurrently, economic developments in the 1970s—the collapse of the Bretton Woods system, the oil crises—invited frameworks of analysis to enhance our understanding of transnational ties and account for the growing importance of nonstate actors in international politics. Complex interdependence refers to international relations operating through "multiple channels of contact" and "transnational, transgovernmental and interstate relations" (Keohane and Nye 1987). Krasner sought to further nuance the scope for transnational cooperation and coordination by introducing the concept of international regimes, defined as "sets of implicit or explicit principles, norms, rules and decision-making procedures around which actors' expectations converge in a given issue-area" (1983, 2). It is understood that "within [a] multilayered system, a major function of international regimes is to facilitate the making of specific agreements on matters of substantive significance within the issue-area covered by the regime" (Keohane 1983, 150). These approaches, however, remained state centered and thus did not effectively address the politics or the economics of changing governance patterns. Most important, they were not fully "political economy" approaches.

Susan Strange's approach to IPE takes us closer to conceptualizing relations among different types of actors. Strange defined IPE as the study that "concerns the social, political and economic arrangements affecting the global systems of production, exchange and distribution, and the mix of values reflected wherein. Those arrangements are not divinely ordained, nor are they the fortuitous outcome if blind chance. Rather they are the result of human decisions taken in the context of man-made institutions and sets of rules and customs" (Strange 1988, 18). Yet, in her analysis of the retreat of the state in the latter part of the twentieth century, she encourages a confrontation and separation between state and market actors, declaring that "where states were once the masters of markets, now it is markets which, on many crucial issues, are the masters of states" (Strange 1996, 4). This stark analytical dichotomy of states and markets might not, however, adequately explain global financial governance because it misses out the growing interaction of public and private actors and limits accounts of authority diffusion to zero-sum considerations. Instead, global financial governance might be better explained through an integrative analysis of economic and financial activity that includes a range of actors that exercise varying degrees of authority; we need to view the state and the market "as part of the same integrated ensemble of governance, a state-market *condominium*" (Underhill 2000, 821).

FINANCE AND SECURITY: LINKAGES AND INTERACTIONS

While topics relating to global finance often appear esoteric and detached from everyday political debates and preoccupations, the activities of financial actors are important and closely interlinked to other aspects of policy activity at the national and global levels. In particular, global finance matters to global security in several significant ways:

- With respect to traditional security analyses, global finance provides the framework for the movement of money across borders. This has significant implications for the financing of criminal activities and the regularization of funds generated by crime, as global policy issues such as arms control, terrorism, and trafficking indicate.
- Global finance is at the core of debates and discourses on human security, which emphasize poverty, famine, economic crises, and environmental degradation.

ACTORS: INTERNATIONAL FINANCIAL INSTITUTIONS, STATES, PRIVATE ACTORS

The study of global finance and analyses of global financial activities and governance frameworks call for an examination of multiple actors, operating at the global, regional, and national levels.

Key among the actors, and often most prominent in the discourse of global finance in general and the global financial architecture in particular, are the international financial institutions (IFIs), the IMF, and the World Bank. Established following the July 1944 UN Monetary and Financial Conference (Bretton Woods) on the basis that international cooperation on monetary affairs would contribute to prosperity and order in the postwar period, the IFIs were created with the specific aims of regulating international monetary (including exchange rate movements) and financial order after the Great Depression and World War II and preventing economic nationalism. They both have 185 member countries.

The World Bank is comprised of four different organizations: the International Bank for Reconstruction and Development, most commonly known as the World Bank; the International Financial Corporation, which provides investment lending through the private sector: the Multilateral Investment Guarantee Agency, and the International Development Agency. Altogether, the World Bank employs over 10.000 people, many in its Washington, D.C., headquarters but also in country offices around the world. Its main formal objectives are reconstruction, developments, and, more implicitly, economic growth. It operates primarily through the provision of technical advice as well as project and program lending. The IMF, also headquartered in Washington, D.C., comprises approximately 3,000 employees and deals with such issues as balance of payments, macroeconomic stability, and economic growth. Over time, the organization has also evolved to be in charge of macroeconomic surveillance, as well as technical advice and financial assistance. The two institutions undertake assessments on member country financial sectors through the Financial Sector Assessment Program and the Reports on the Observance of Standards and Codes.

Much of the attention, scholarly and otherwise, on the IFIs has focused on the so-called Washington Consensus policies advocated as a strategy to economic growth and in line with their lending practices (Woods 2006). The Washington Consensus promoted economic liberalization, privatization, and structural adjustment along with a reduced role for the state both as economic actor and, to a certain degree, as a welfare provider. These policies were put in the spotlight following a series of crises to affect emerging market countries: Mexico in 1994, East Asia in 1997–1998, and Argentina in 2001. Though for many commentators, the sources of these crises lay in underdeveloped domestic financial systems, the focus has been readjusted and IFI policies appear more nuanced and less ideological in their commitment to neoliberal economic theory. In the late 2000s, debates, especially with respect to the IMF, have concentrated on (1) institutional reforms as attempts are made to change the governance structure so as to reduce the dominance of bigger states and ensure a better representation for emerging markets, and (2) reassessment of the relevance of the institution, in particular as East Asian countries, following the 1997–1998 crisis, have accumulated reserves in order to be less reliant on the institution.

Also at the global level, a series of more specialist and less inclusive institutions can be found that also play a significant part in the governance of global finance. One such body is the Organization for Economic Cooperation and Development, which counts 30 members among the most developed nations and addresses corporate governance issues and tax, including in the context of targeting the harmful tax practices of offshore financial centers (Sharman 2006). Another, the Basel Committee, comprised of the banking regulators and supervisors of countries with the most developed financial systems, proposes rules and standards for global banking and finance (Tsingou 2008).

The regional dimension is also important in exploring significant actors in global finance. While the European Union is by far the most active regional governance arrangement for financial issues, especially in securities regulation, the majority of regional cooperation institutions include an emphasis on finance. Moving on to the state level, it is important to note the various transgovernmental mechanisms through which states manage global finance, such as the Group of Seven (G7) countries (Baker 2006), as well as the extent to which financial arrangements are guided by the domestic preferences of the most influential states in the system (Seabrooke 2006).

Finally, no analysis of global finance is complete without an understanding of the role of private actors and private authority in global finance. As discussed in the opening section of this chapter, a thorough conceptualization of the influence of private actors and their governance functions is important in order to highlight the ways in which interests and ideas are shaped and represented in global financial governance arrangements. These actors may be banks or advocacy groups (Tsingou 2008), but they may also be such more specialized institutions as credit rating agencies (Sinclair 2005).

KEY DEBATES AND ISSUES IN THE TWENTY-FIRST CENTURY

As global economic and financial integration continues to intensify, a number of issues come to the fore and are likely to be important for the policy and academic communities in coming years. In the first place, the role of international financial institutions is being reassessed and more attention is placed on the twin development goals of economic development and poverty reduction (Vetterlein 2007). Talk of reform of the institutions, so as to improve representation and plurality of ideas and approaches, both internally and at the membership and governance structure levels, is expected to continue (Underhill 2007).

Another set of debates concerns the nature of financial regulation and the gaps in the regulation and supervision of some financial activities as exemplified by the subprime crisis of 2007–2008. While far from global in character, the crisis affected many of the large financial conglomerates and has highlighted that some financial institutions were deemed "too big to fail" because of fears of systemic contagion, possibly increasing moral hazard, since irresponsible risk taking appears not to be penalized. The crisis, through its links to mortgage provision, also drew attention to the links between finance and the real economy. Discussions on unregulated entities, such off-balance-sheet activities as those involving derivatives instruments, the role of credit rating agencies, risk management, and banking staff remuneration will continue; it remains to be seen, the extent to which the crisis might lead to significant changes in the governance of global finance.

Finally, academic focus is turning to the so-called everyday politics of the world economy (Hobson and Seabrooke 2007). This academic work moves beyond the elite or powerful actor emphasis often associated with studies of IPE and global finance to explore the ways in which everyday actions can ultimately be significant. Debates about pension funds, access to funds and mortgages, or a more balanced gender representation may also be addressed through these approaches.

GLOBAL FINANCE AND SECURITY INTERLINKED: THE FIGHT AGAINST MONEY LAUNDERING AND TERRORIST FINANCING: A CASE STUDY

Why Tackle Money Laundering?

The Financial Action Task Force (FATF), the international organization responsible for standard setting in anti–money laundering (AML) offers the following definition: "The goal of a large number of criminal acts is to generate profit for the individual or group that carries out the act. Money laundering is the processing of these criminal proceeds to disguise their illegal origin." However, international harmonization about which crimes are relevant under the above definition has only recently started to take place. Traditionally, rules and laws evolved from regulation and legislation attempts at curtailing the trade in illegal drugs, but a diverse array of crimes have since been added to the list in different jurisdictions.

It is extremely difficult to assess how much money is actually being laundered: the most often quoted figure comes from research by the IMF and estimates the total as a figure equal to between 2 and 5 percent of the world's GDP. This amounts to anything up to $2 trillion. Another set of figures puts the amount of drug money laundering at 2 percent of total financial flows. The methodology used for such estimates is, however, widely challenged and FATF's effort to calculate estimates, made between 1996 and 2000, failed. These limitations are important because it is difficult to know the significance of the money-laundering problem, but also because they make an objective assessment of the effectiveness of the emerging regime particularly challenging. Furthermore, there is no clear benchmark of what would constitute success or what an acceptable figure for globally laundered funds might be.

Why Is Money Laundering a Concern?

Ever since policy makers embarked on targeting money laundering in the 1980s, official explanations have focused on a political preoccupation with regards to the crimes that might eventually lead to money laundering. Public officials have consistently presented the AML regime as a way of (1) tackling the drugs trade, the arms trade, people trafficking, and other organized crime activities; (2) supporting the integrity of the financial system, including supporting good governance and transparency; (3) combating corruption and its economic and political consequences, especially in the developing world; (4) promoting economic development and ensuring that funds are channeled to appropriate economic endeavors and allowing for adequate levels of tax revenue; and most recently, (5) combating terrorist financing (CFT).

It is difficult to separate thejust-mentioned concerns, however, from less touted yet significant reasons why money laundering matters to the policy community. The lines between money laundering and tax havens or banking secrecy are often blurred even though publicly, they are separate and distinct concerns, since money laundering is unequivocally illegal. The drive toward building an AML regime is nevertheless connected with questions of competitive pressure and establishing a regulatory level playing field. With the introduction of an officially sanctioned focus on problem countries and politically exposed persons, AML measures are also fast becoming a potent foreign policy tool.

While the concerns noted are all relevant, how they are prioritized over time and which actors care most about what makes for a diverse set of interests that illuminates developments in the AML regime. In recent years, combating terrorist financing has appeared as the primary preoccupation.

The AML Framework

The AML regime is developing on two fronts, prevention and enforcement, and at three levels: national, regional, and international or global (see Table 5.1).

Table 5.1 The Global Anti-money-laundering Regime: Key Measures and Initiatives

	Global level	USA	Europe	Private Sector
1970		Bank Secrecy Act		
1980	Offshore Group of Banking Supervisors		Council of Europe's measures against the transfer and safekeeping of funds of criminal origin	
1986		Money Laundering Control Act	UK Drug Trafficking Offenses Act	
1988	UN Convention against Illicit Traffic in Narcotic Drugs and Psychotropic Substances			
1989	Financial Action Task Force (FATF)			
1990	FATF recommendations; Caribbean FATF			
1991			European Commission's first money-laundering directive Europol	
1995	Egmont Group of Financial Intelligence Units			
1996	Revised FATF recommendations			
1997	OECD Convention on Combating Bribery of Foreign Officials in International Business Transactions			
1998	OECD report on harmful tax practices			
1999	Eastern and Southern Africa Anti-Money-Laundering Group			
2000	FATF list of noncooperative countries and territories; OECD list of tax			Wolfsberg Principles

(*Continued*)

Table 5.1 (*Continued*)

	Global level	USA	Europe	Private Sector
	havens with harmful tax practices; Regional Anti-Money-Laundering Task Force, Latin America; UN Convention Against Transnational Organized Crime			
2001	FATF special recommendations on combating the financing of terrorism; Basel Committee's Customer Due Diligence	USA Patriot Act, Title III: International Money Laundering Abatement and Anti-Terrorist Financing Act	European Commission's second money-laundering directive	
2002	FATF, IMF, and World Bank agreement on Anti-Money-Laundering Pilot Project		Europol mandate expanded; UK Proceeds of Crime Act	Wolfsberg Principles on Combating Terrorist Financing
2003	Revised FATF recommendations; UN Convention against Corruption			
2004	IMF and World Bank include FATF standards in their financial sector assessment programs; Eurasia Group; North Africa and Middle East Group			
2005	UN Security Council Resolution 1617		European Commission's third money-laundering directive	
2006	Last countries removed from NCCT list	USA Patriot Act renewed		International Association of Money Transfer Networks

Source: Author.

Prevention is a regulatory tool and focuses mostly on sanctions, regulatory and supervisory rules and standards, reporting, and customer due diligence. Enforcement is a legal tool, concentrating on investigation, confiscation, prosecution, and punishment. In essence, however, despite the criminalization of money laundering and the recent prominent and public role of enforcement agencies in the AML regime, the regulatory process is far more comprehensive and developed.

The Global Level

Money laundering became a pertinent global issue in the 1980s, culminating in the establishment of the FATF in 1989. Comprised of 16 members in the early days, it reached a membership of 28 by 1992 and now counts 34 members. FATF's role is to issue AML recommendations that aim to set legislative and regulatory standards; these are regularly updated. The 40 recommendations are addressed to countries and deal with an extensive range of themes: the adoption of background policies that facilitate the fight against money laundering, ensuring banking secrecy laws do not impede detection, and participating in multilateral initiatives and solutions; the criminalization of money laundering; the establishment of laws that allow for the seizure and confiscation of funds generated from criminal activity; the implementation of customer identification and record-keeping rules; the adoption of increased diligence of financial institutions, including the development of internal policies and controls; the strengthening of international cooperation, including the exchange of information and the legal facilitation of mutual assistance. The recommendations were most recently reviewed and revised in 2003 to create a "comprehensive, consistent and substantially strengthened international framework for combating money laundering and terrorist financing." Changes included tougher provisions for high-risk customers, the extension of anti–money-laundering measures to several nonfinancial businesses, the explicit extension to existing requirements to cover terrorist financing, and the prohibition of shell banks. Following the terrorist attacks of September 11, 2001, FATF issued a further nine recommendations focusing on the combating of terrorist financing.

Monitoring of the implementation of the recommendations takes two forms. All member countries carry out a self-assessment exercise, and FATF has a mutual evaluation procedure in place, whereby on-site visits by legal, financial, and law enforcement experts from other member governments are conducted. Also, FATF has provisions for dealing with noncompliant members, though to this date only Austria and Turkey have been in any way reprimanded. In 1999, the FATF took a further step, engaging in a "naming and shaming" campaign beyond the scopes of its membership and identifying countries guilty of noncooperation. The first non-cooperative countries and territories (NCCTs) report was made public in 2000 and was was subsequently regularly reviewed, though the program currently lies dormant.

A variety of groups and policies supplement FATF efforts. Among those supplemental programs are regional task forces; the Egmont Group of Financial Intelligence Units, which annually brings together representatives of the relevant national agencies; and the UN Global Program Against Money Laundering. Most important, the IMF, as part of its work on financial integrity, is now examining AML standards in its financial sector reviews and, where appropriate, offers technical assistance; FATF, the IMF, and the World Bank use similar assessment processes, documentation, and procedures in their AML evaluations.

Against this highly ambitious global regime of standard setting and prevention, international coordination in law enforcement is a relatively underdeveloped and slow process. Limited interstate cooperation is taking place in the context of Interpol (and Europol), and FATF is involved in some of those activities. It remains unclear, however, whether actual changes in the practices of law enforcement agencies have occurred as a result of the AML regime or whether effective communication channels are being established.

The Regional Level

There is extensive regional support of the AML regime both in regulatory terms and with respect to technical assistance. In the first place, interest on the European continent has long been strong in these issues, with an early initiative by the Council of Europe (1980). Through three money-laundering directives (1991, 2001, and 2005), the European Union (EU) has also brought a certain degree of harmonization to practice and standards in member countries. This has been a topic of some tension among member states, and there are several discerning trends in the EU AML drive: (1) the linkage with FATF standards and discussions is both strong and, in many ways, binding; (2) such G7 members as the United Kingdom and France are at the forefront of proposals and more eager to push for comprehensive regional standards, and (3) countries with long-established offshore status, most notably Luxembourg, are experiencing intense pressure (at the political and regulatory levels but also in the media) to address potential weaknesses.

The regional level is also where much monitoring and promotion work is taking place, as manifested by the plethora of regional groupings that have formed over the past decade to provide discussion and learning for a larger number of countries as well as technical expertise and a framework for assessment. Aside from FATF members EC and GCC (Gulf Cooperation Council), regional bodies include the Eastern and Southern Africa Anti–Money Laundering Group, The Regional Anti–Money Laundering Task Force–Latin America, the Eurasia Group, the North Africa and Middle East Group, the Asia-Pacific Group, the West African Group, and the Caribbean Financial Action Task Force, as well as the Offshore Group of Banking Supervisors.

The National Level

The main actor and initiator at the national level is the United States, which first led the way in the criminalization of money laundering in the 1980s (Andreas and Nadelmann 2006). There are apparently good reasons for this early and sustained interest: a 2001 report by the Federal Bureau of Investigation (FBI) claims that approximately 50 percent of total money laundered goes through the U.S. financial system while the U.S. Treasury estimates that 99.9 percent of such funds are laundered successfully (Mitchell 2003). The criminalization of money laundering in the 1980s and a series of high-profile scandals brought attention to the issue, but there was little interest in pursuing matters beyond the FATF framework or in a way that would lead to additional legislation or reinforced AML functions for regulators. Following the terrorist attacks of September 11, 2001, however, an AML package was produced for speedy inclusion in the USA Patriot Act, Title III. The U.S. approach remains far from uniform; indeed, a plethora of agencies, including the Financial Crimes Enforcement Network (FinCEN), the dedicated Treasury Department authority, and the new Department of Homeland Security, have been trying to determine both who does what and who should be doing what, with financial regulators and supervisors rather unenthusiastic participants. The United States remains the source of most AML initiatives, and, as will subsequently be discussed, it is where the inclusion of terrorist financing in the regime was instigated.

Staying in the world of developed financial systems, a very different national environment is observed in Switzerland, where a tradition of self-regulation has been challenged in the context of a strengthening AML regime. Because of its banking secrecy provisions, Switzerland is particularly exposed and closely watched by competitors and the AML community as a whole. As a result, financial market actors in both the private and the public sector are keen to set the example and following UBS's reprimand for dealing with funds suspected to have links to Sani Abacha, the former Nigerian dictator, have been at the forefront of the adoption of global standards. It is important to note, however, that though Switzerland has been involved in the FATF process from the outset, and while it has thus far withstood pressures to link money laundering to banking secrecy issues in ways that would significantly affect the financial industry, while not simply reacting, it is essentially following global trends in AML.

Yet another set of issues emerges when examining offshore centers that are not members of FATF. As the FATF focus on NCCTs has shown, an important part of the global strategy against money laundering has revolved around improving practices and promoting transparency in offshore centers. Offshore centers are traditionally seen as having the following characteristics: "minimal or no personal or corporate taxation; effective bank secrecy laws; few, preferably no, restrictions or regulations concerning financial transactions; and protection of the secrecy of transactions" (Palan 2002, 155). In the case of developing nations, they may also be reluctant to adopt strict anti–money laundering rules as they might consider them damaging to their development strategy. As a result, some countries have few incentives to enthusiastically join the fight against money laundering, and only strong leadership from other countries and the embarrassment of being blacklisted may persuade them otherwise (Simmons 2001, 605–7).

The preceding schematic overview of the global, regional, and national levels of the emerging AML regime indicates that while the global and institutional character of the regime encourages regulatory diffusion, the priorities of certain actors in the G7 are predominantly defining these standards; offshore centers and the many developing countries who are members of the regional anti–money laundering bodies, on the other hand, are mostly downloading regulation.

Policy Priorities

Much of the political drive in building a robust AML regime stems, at least in public discourse, from the importance of dealing with a series of crucial public policy issues. The first set of reasons put forward in support of addressing money laundering relate to the effects of money laundering on the economy and the financial system. Involvement in money-laundering activities can affect public confidence in the financial system as well as impinge on legitimate entities in the private sector. Launderers regularly use front operations such as shops and restaurants, which primarily rely on illegal activities for profit. In this context, legitimate businesses often find themselves undercut and find it difficult to compete. Another consequence is the distortion of financial market operations, since large sums of money may enter and leave the system suddenly, thus affecting the liquidity of financial institutions. A more drastic set of effects could lead to loss of control of economic policy, for in some developing countries, the sums laundered may correspond to a substantial part of national wealth. Money-laundering activities can also alter investment patterns as funds are allocated to sectors where the risk of detection is lower (e.g., construction) and not necessarily to ones that are profitable or in need of investment. Developing countries may also see their privatization policies hampered should launderers become the main beneficiaries of such schemes; further, the countries may suffer reputation damage if they are seen to tolerate such activities on their territory. Finally, states everywhere are affected through loss of tax revenue.

The second set of concerns focuses on corruption in the developing world, whereby criminal groups can use laundered funds to consolidate their position in the political system and further contaminate the local private sector. In some cases, such criminal organizations can use their position to exercise coercive power and intimidate through violent activities; they can also damage the institutions of the state by utilizing their organization's wealth to corrupt public and private officials. It is understood that the long-term development of such states is harmed by these corruptive elements.

The third set of incentives for targeting money-laundering activities is defined in terms of social costs, from policing and health costs in the countries that deal with the effects of drug use, to the wider implications of the payoffs of crime for corruption in the public and private spheres. In these cases, the focus is on law enforcement and public policy, dealing with the consequences of money laundering and of the activities that generate the illicit funds.

The fourth set of motives in the fight against money laundering deal with the eradication of the activities that produce the funds in the first place. Organized crime is most commonly manifested in drug trafficking, but illegal alien smuggling is also on the rise. At the same time, human trafficking, predominantly the trafficking of women and children for the purposes of the sex trade, though increasingly for organ trade, is a source of substantial financial rewards for criminals, with most developed countries acting as recipients. Other activities that can lead to money being laundered include illegal business deals on cars, antiques, endangered species, or arms.

The final driving force for attacking money-laundering practices is the extent to which the funds thus cleaned are used in ways that affect global stability. In the early years of the regime, such concerns concentrated on the political situation in countries in the developing world; drug-trafficking centers such as Colombia and Afghanistan have also been politically unstable and violent, whereas "blood diamonds" in Angola and Sierra Leone have helped finance civil wars. The events of September 11, 2001, have, however, shifted the focus to a much more global scale, firmly linking the fight against money laundering to the "economic war on terror."

The incentives for attacking money-laundering are all crucial public policy issues that legitimately require attention. It is unclear, however, that the AML regime is an efficient way in which to address them and whether they constitute more that political rhetoric; while doing the right thing by making it more difficult for criminals to benefit financially from their crimes is a worthwhile pursuit, widespread concerns about the costs of the regime, especially for non-OECD countries, point to the severe shortcomings in the regime's potential with respect to these goals. Moreover, the less official reasons behind the AML regime—competitive pressures and foreign policy—are never far behind in the reasoning underlying ongoing AML developments.

The Principal Actors

At the core of the regime, FATF promotes global standards but is essentially a political organization in its membership and practices; while its scope is de facto global, in order to qualify for membership, a country has to be "strategically important," as is boldly stated in the organization's Web site. Indicatively, Russia joined FATF soon after being delisted from the NCCT list, and this can be seen as symptomatic of the political character of FATF, as well as of the organization's emphasis on form rather than practice. That insistence is not unjustified; recent work on the scale and impacts of money laundering confirms that "giants wash more" (Unger 2007). Yet the effects and spread of the actual AML regime are felt, perhaps in a disproportionate manner, by a much wider number of countries, for which applying the recommendations may be a less than necessary investment.

Attempts to broaden participation in the AML regime have been restricted to the proliferation of regional agencies. The narrow membership, but also the peer review procedures and, to this date, limited reprimands, means that FATF's legitimacy can and has been questioned. Within FATF, the NCCT process has also been criticized, both for being wound down despite its effectiveness in changing regulatory and legislative frameworks and, most important, for being arbitrary and lacking a consistent methodology. For many commentators on the AML regime, it reinforced the political character of FATF and highlighted the influence of core G7 countries. That some countries removed from the list following thorough reviews of their regulatory and legislative frameworks have not seen a marked improvement in perceived reputation and market access adds further credibility to these views.

The role of the IMF in the process has not been without controversy either. In the first place, the IMF started as a reluctant participant, succumbing to U.S. and G7 campaigning, and piggy-backing money-laundering issues on top of the extending emphasis on its financial integrity work. Endorsement of the FATF recommendations was based on a narrow compromise that included winding down the NCCT list and emphasizing consensus, cooperation, and a fair and transparent methodology instead. The inclusion of the IMF in the regime addressed some of the membership shortcomings of FATF; however, it also raised the question of whether financial assessments can efficiently and legitimately deal with standards closely linked to criminal justice.

The Structure

As the nature of regulation generation indicates, the structure of the AML regime is defined by asymmetries of influence and standard formulation. The structure, however, is also characterized by an unbalanced process of coordination and cooperation between regulators and supervisors, on the one hand, and law enforcement agencies, on the other. Regulators and the financial institutions of which they are in charge have a patchy, often adversarial, or inconsequential relationship with law enforcement. Tensions can arise not only from the lack of established procedures but also from different interpretations of the results of anti-money-laundering efforts; while the financial sector assesses success in terms of lack of problematic instances, law enforcement bodies concentrate on quantifiable confiscated sums and convictions. The strategies of regulators and law enforcement agents are indeed rather different: whereas the first group focuses on the process, including persuasion, cooperation, self-regulation, risk-based discretion and, sometimes, the second stresses prosecution, external regulation, and public justice and punishment. In essence, the AML regime is trying to reconcile two rather different goals: compliance and results. This brings about contradictions and further hampers the effectiveness and, by extension, the legitimacy of the emerging regime.

Introducing Terrorism

Another dimension of the AML regime, and a controversial one, at least in academic circles, is the inclusion, post-9/11, of provisions for the combating of terrorist financing. Indeed, fighting terrorist financing was an uncontroversial early measure by the international community and brought about immediate effects with the freezing of assets (Navias 2002, 58–59). The response from FATF came in the form of eight Special Recommendations on Terrorist Financing, which included the criminalization of the financing of terrorism, the creation of provisions for freezing and confiscating assets, the requirement to report suspicious transactions with potential criminal links, the imposition of anti-money-laundering requirements on alternative remittance systems, and the review of laws dealing with nonprofit organizations. These efforts were mirrored in the adoption of related standards at the regional level and were further consolidated through national regulation and legislation, most notably the USA Patriot Act.

In practice, however, these measures can have only limited effect and are not guaranteed to achieve the aim of reducing the financing of terrorism. When the FBI attempted to design a profile of the way terrorists may use banks, it highlighted the practice of making a large deposit and withdrawing small amounts of cash at frequent intervals; yet practitioners say that this profile is consistent with that of approximately one-quarter of a bank's customers. Forensic work by FinCEN on the 9/11 terrorists has also shown that money-laundering tools cannot proactively spot the financing of terrorism. An additional problem is one of methodology: the funding of terrorism is often based on resources that are clean and legitimate, essentially requiring banks to make value judgments about future use of money, as well as about the potential of a customer who has not to this day acted unlawfully to do so in the future. That is a subjective and time-consuming strategy that can also lead to discrimination on the basis of ethnic background and create biases linked to personal characteristics; it is also one that requires consistent, forthcoming, and up-to-date intelligence information. Charities are also put in the spotlight, and though many have been targeted with regards to their knowing or unknowing support of Al Qaeda terrorists, other than encouraging charity verification field trips, standards remain vague and cannot produce a comprehensive approach. Furthermore, alternative remittance systems have been targeted, most notably *hawala*, which avoids wire transfers, paper trails, and formal banking (de Goede 2003). Regular remittance systems are also being increasingly marginalized, with money service businesses (MSBs) finding it difficult to maintain relationships with the formal banking sector; a growing number of banking institutions in the United States, for instance, are finding that compliance costs are not justified by the relatively narrow profit margins that business with MSBs are offering, and remittance accounts are closing. Finally, the sums involved in the financing of terrorism are relatively small, even in comparison with other activities related to money laundering. It is often commented that the attacks of September 11, 2001, may have cost less than $500,000; this amount could be raised with relative ease, as transactions not exceeding $10,000 do not require the same level of scrutiny.

It is still early to assess the terrorist attacks' impact on long-term money-laundering measures and practices. Nevertheless, a renewed impetus put anti–money laundering firmly on policy and regulatory agendas, and public authorities in developed financial centers have been taking the subject very seriously. The pattern of incentives for the private sector has also been adapted, and the shift reflects the patriotic element of the "economic war on terror." It also remains unclear whether the AML regime is the appropriate setting for dealing with terrorist financing. This debate at the policy level may be closed; but whereas in the United States the link between money laundering, terrorist financing, and national security has been widely adopted by policy makers, elsewhere it has often been grudgingly accepted as a political decision that everyone is learning to live with.

The Role of the Private Sector

Financial institutions have some straightforward incentives to take AML measures seriously, mainly to do with reputational and legal issues. Indeed, they have long adopted a series of procedures to combat money laundering and comply with regulatory requirements. These include special identification measures, the know-your-customer mantra applied to all financial services; monitoring processes based on internal systems and a comprehensive system of dealing with suspicious activity; up-to-date training programs; the implementation of evaluations, auditing procedures, and such accountability measures as signed attestations of knowledge of anti-money-laundering measures; the setting-up of specialized AML units; and the full participation and commitment of senior management.

Major banks have gone further and taken the initiative to create appropriate standards by establishing the Wolfsberg Group of Banks. Created in 2000, the group issues global AML and CFT guidelines for international private banks, focusing on correspondent banking relationships. The reasoning behind such a voluntary code of conduct is the harmonization of principles and the strengthening of private-sector reputation and credibility (Pieth and Aiolfi 2003). While membership of the group remains restricted, the initiative now includes an annual Wolfsberg Forum, which brings together a wider spectrum of financial institutions (50 of the world's largest banks), as well as representatives from regulatory and supervisory agencies at the national and global level (e.g., the Basel Committee) and FATF. Despite these efforts, some real problems remain because the costs of compliance are particularly high. A 2007 international survey of 224 banks in 55 countries provides further evidence of the mounting (and unexpected) costs of AML compliance, mostly a consequence of transaction monitoring and staff training, especially for smaller financial institutions (KPMG 2007).

THE POLITICS OF THE AML/CFT REGIME: WHAT LESSONS FOR IPE?

With few exceptions, and despite accepting the inevitability of the AML/CFT regime, most participants remain puzzled at the need to deal with issues related to terrorist financing; this is a potent reminder that politics in the international economy matters. Can the regime, however, still find effectiveness and legitimacy?

On a technical level, analysis of whether the AML/CFT regime works is welcome, and success and effectiveness indicators need to be further developed, both on the regulatory and the detection and law enforcement sides. At the same time, however, it is important to reach a better understanding of the figures and relative shares of AML activity. More broadly, the question of whether money laundering is indeed a genuine threat to the financial system needs to be addressed. In this context, it may be important to acknowledge that including dirty money in the system may be an acceptable price to pay for efficient and adaptable financial markets as promoted by regulators and private sector alike.

This goes to the heart of long-established principles and practices of what is appropriate in global financial governance, for the elimination of money laundering will require an extensive reworking of the system and affect how we understand the concept of free movement of money.

The roles of respective participants in the regime are being blurred: are regulators and banks being turned into law enforcers? How can law enforcement best be integrated in the institutional framework, and at which level does policing best work? Guidance, feedback, and cooperation are to be encouraged, but the differing objectives of regulators and law enforcers need to be reconciled. Such reconciliation is proving challenging at the national level—even more so when international cooperation and collaboration are being sought.

The links between the AML/CFT regime and the much-heralded public policy goals also call for reassessment. Beyond the political rhetoric, studies have shown that money laundering and corruption, especially in the developing world, are often linked with detrimental results. Are the political will and its associated incentives strong enough to bring about lasting changes in practice? In using the AML as part of a development strategy, might there be, for example, political space for a discussion on capital controls and tax evasion and avoidance?

Not easily addressed in a cost-benefit analysis framework, the marginalization and financial exclusion of such distinct groups of individuals as students, migrants, and black market participants through know-your-customer banking practices and the increasing criminalization of cash remain outside the scope of official concerns. Can the AML/CFT still be redefined in less technologically deterministic terms? Indeed, how long term are such consequences?

Finally, if, despite the shortcomings of the approach, the link between the AML and the CFT is no longer questioned, could the opportunity to deal comprehensively with financial crime be grabbed? Initial agreement on the establishment of FATF was reached on the basis that it would not address tax issues; could tax evasion, however, be considered as an associated issue in meaningful information-sharing processes? The policy community at all levels and in most jurisdictions has appeared reluctant to make this linkage and explore the possibility.

FURTHER READING

Cutler, A. Claire, Virginia Haufler, and Tony Porter, eds. *Private Authority and International Affairs*. Albany: State University of New York, 1999.

Hobson, John, and Leonard Seabrooke, eds. *Everyday Politics of the World Economy*. Cambridge: Cambridge University Press, 2007.

Sinclair, Timothy. *The New Masters of Capital*. Ithaca: Cornell University Press, 2005.

Strange, Susan. *States and Markets*, 2nd ed. London: Pinter, 1994.

Woods, Ngaire. *The Globalizers: The IMF, the World Bank and Their Borrowers*. Ithaca, NY: Cornell University Press, 2006.

REFERENCES

Andreas, Peter, and Ethan Nadelmann. 2006. *Policing the globe: criminalization and crime control in international relations*. New York: Oxford University Press.

Baker, Andrew. 2006. *The group of seven: Finance ministries, central banks and global financial governance*. London: Routledge.

Cutler, A. Claire, Virginia Haufler, and Tony Porter, eds. 1999. *Private authority and international affairs*, Albany: State University of New York.

De Goede, Marieke. 2003. Hawala discourses and the war on terrorist finance. *Environment and Planning D: Society and Space* 21: 513–32.

Gilpin, Robert. 1987. *The political economy of international relations*, Princeton, NJ: Princeton University Press.

Helleiner, Eric. 1994. *States and the reemergence of global finance: From Bretton Woods to the 1990s*. Ithaca, NY: Cornell University Press.

Hewson, Martin, and Timothy J. Sinclair, eds. 1999. *Approaches to global governance theory*, Albany: State University of New York Press.

Hobson, John, and Leonard Seabrooke, eds. 2007. *Everyday politics of the world economy*, Cambridge: Cambridge University Press.

Keohane, Robert O., and Joseph S. Nye Jr. 1987. Power and interdependence revisited. *International Organization* 41: 725–53.

KPMG. 2007. *Global anti-money laundering survey*.

Krasner, Stephen D. 1983. Structural causes and regime consequences: Regimes as intervening variables. In *International Regimes*, ed. Stephen D. Krasner, 1–21. Ithaca, NY: Cornell University Press.

Mitchell, Daniel. 2003. U.S. government agencies confirm that low-tax jurisdictions are not money laundering havens. *Journal of Financial Crime* 11: 127–33.

Mooslechner, Peter, Helene Schuberth, and Beat Weber, eds. 2006. *The political economy of financial market regulation*. Cheltenham, UK: Edward Elgar.

Navias, Martin. 2002. Finance warfare and international terrorism. In *Superterrorism: Policy responses*, ed. Lawrence Freedman, 57–79. Oxford: Blackwell.

Palan, Ronen. 2002. Tax havens and the commercialization of state sovereignty. *International Organization* 56: 151–76.

Pieth, Mark, and Gemma Aiolfi. 2003. The private sector becomes active: The Wolfsberg process. *Journal of Financial Crime* 10: 359–65.

Seabrooke, Leonard. 2006. *The social sources of financial power*. Ithaca, NY: Cornell University Press.

Sharman, Jason. 2006. *Havens in a storm: The struggle for global tax regulation*. Ithaca, NY: Cornell University Press.

Simmons, Beth A. 2001. The international politics of harmonization: The case of capital market regulation. *International Organization* 55: 589–620.

Sinclair, Timothy. 2005. *The new masters of capital*. Ithaca, NY: Cornell University Press.

Strange, Susan. 1988. *States and markets*. 2nd ed. London: Pinter.

Strange, Susan. 1996. *The retreat of the state*. Cambridge: Cambridge University Press.

Tsingou, Eleni. 2008. Transnational private governance and the Basel process: Banking regulation, private interests and Basel II. In *Transnational private governance and its limits*, ed. Andreas Nölke and Jean-Christophe Graz, 58–68. London: Routledge.
Underhill, Geoffrey R. D. 2000. State, market, and global political economy: Genealogy of an (inter-?) discipline. *International Affairs* 76: 805–24.
———. 2007. Global financial architecture, legitimacy and representation: A voice for emerging markets. Garnet Policy Brief 3.
Unger, Brigitte. 2007 *The scale and impacts of money laundering*. Cheltenham, UK: Edward Elgar.
Vetterlein, Antje. 2007. Economic growth, poverty reduction and the role of social policies; The evolution of the World Bank's social development approach. *Global Governance* 13: 513–33.
Woods, Ngaire. 2006. *The globalizers: The IMF, the World Bank and their borrowers*. Ithaca, NY: Cornell University Press.

WEB SITES OF PUBLIC BODIES

Basel Committee: http://www.bis.org
Financial Action Task Force: http://www.fatf-gafi.org
International Monetary Fund: http://www.imf.org
Organization for Economic Cooperation and Development: http://www.oecd.org
World Bank: http://www.worldbank.org

WEB SITES OF PRIVATE GROUPS

Group of Thirty: http://www.group30.org
Institute of International Finance: http://www.iif.com
Wolfsberg Group: http://www.wolfsberg-principles.com

6

Food Security/Fisheries

Liza Griffin

FISHERIES SECURITY: A HISTORICAL PROBLEM

Food security can be defined as "secure access to enough food at all times" (Kent 1997). This chapter is concerned with the problems of securing access to enough fish. Fisheries security has historically been a problem for many maritime nation-states. The chapter will describe how this problem has re-emerged in the twenty-first century in the face of a potential fisheries crisis. In the process, fisheries security, traditionally regarded as a problem of national and regional scope, has become recognized as a globalizing issue. Like globalization itself, overfishing and fisheries security are concerns that demand that we think in terms of the interdependence of localities, regions, and nation-states across the world.

Fisheries security, then, is not a new problem. The first act regulating fishing was passed in Britain in the thirteenth century, to counter overfishing. But it was not until the early twentieth-century development of European economies, with accompanying capitalization and mechanization of fishing fleets and the widespread use of steam trawlers, that overfishing became a structural issue. In the North Sea it led to collapse of the Great North Whale Fishery in 1880, and the once booming herring and tuna fisheries in the early twentieth century. However, after respite from fishing activity during the world wars, the North Sea again became a rich, productive fishing ground.

For the nascent European Community of the 1950s, food security in general was high on the political agenda, following the blockades and depredations of World War II. Fisheries were important in this context as an important source of food and a shared resource demanding international collaboration if security of supply was to be maintained. By and large, the security issue was about *secure access* to *spaces* in which there existed a resource thought fundamentally plentiful. At that time, fish stocks were treated as limitless, and any warnings from scientists about diminishing stocks were largely ignored. Today, however, the fisheries security issue is also, and increasingly, a concern about security over *time*, or ensuring that stocks are maintained at a level where they can replace themselves indefinitely into the future and not become extinct. Thus the issue is one of *sustainable* exploitation of fisheries.

PROBLEMS OF MANAGING FISH STOCKS

Being surrounded by many nation-states, the North Sea well illustrates many of the problems of maintaining fisheries security. Although fishing here contributes only a small percentage of national incomes, total catch value exceeds 1.5 million euros, and the North Sea's fishing industries directly employ around 138,000 people (Mardle and Pascoe 2002). There are several interconnected multispecies fisheries here, exploited mainly by Belgium, Denmark, France, Germany, Netherlands, Norway, Sweden, and the United Kingdom. In the past it has been a major battleground for fishers, involved in various attempts by nations to maintain their own secure supplies of fish in competition with other nations.

Resolving such battles has been fraught with difficulties partly because of the fugitive nature of this mobile resource, with its constantly changing location and straddling of international boundaries. Spawning areas and nursery grounds are dynamic features of fish life histories: they are rarely in a fixed place from year to year (Rogers and Stocks 2001). Hence, prudent stewardship will be unrewarded when one nation or region carefully manages a vulnerable stock in its jurisdiction only to find that the same fish then move, in their natural cycle, to another, less regulated province to feed—and are promptly fished to oblivion.

This problem is compounded by the diverse nature of stocks often found in the same fishery. In the North Sea, for instance, prawns and flat fish live alongside cod, and between 5 and 15 percent of the catch of fishers targeting prawns will also invariably comprise cod (this is known as bycatch). The diversity of fish sizes is also problematic (see Figure 6.1). Because cod is larger than haddock, for instance, a net mesh size designed to catch mature haddock will also catch juvenile cod that has not yet spawned, thus threatening future supplies of this fish.

Substantial amounts of ocean are now territorialized by the extension of exclusive economic zones (EEZs), areas in which a coastal state has sovereign rights over all economic resources of the sea, seabed, and subsoil, rights established in the 1970s through the UN Convention on the Law of the Sea. Many more marine resources still form part of the global commons, however, and while access to EU fisheries is not technically open to all, the fisheries might effectively be considered archetypal common pool resources (CPR)—that is, under some kind of common ownership—because of the difficulties of excluding would-be users (Pomeroy and Berkes 1997). It is this common-property condition that has been blamed for the overfishing threat to fisheries security in the EU.

Here, the problem of open access affected most nineteenth- and twentieth-century fisheries, and in the wake of conflicts it became largely accepted that national governments could not achieve fisheries security by acting alone. Hence, an EU Common Fisheries Policy (CFP) was established under article 38 of the first Communities treaty, the 1957 Treaty of Rome. The CFP's objective was defined as enabling stock exploitation through equal access to nonterritorial waters for each member state. Access was to be controlled by measures to limit

Figure 6.1 North Sea Cod.

total fishing effort and the size of national catches, so that the future security of supply would not be prejudiced and marine ecosystems would not be damaged. However, it was another 45 years before CFP legislation was amended to make conservation one of the main pillars on which the policy is supposed to rest, establishing conservation as equally important as other pillars.

THE CFP's FAILINGS AND THE FISHERIES CRISIS IN EUROPE

Despite the relative importance of conservation today, the CFP continues to share the aims of Europe's Common Agricultural Policy, which include increasing productivity by promoting technical progress and optimizing factors of production, including labor. Those aims are in place although it is often said that there are too many fishers and fishing boats for the size of stocks. Such goals tend to inhibit the economic pillar's compatibility with the conservation pillar. Thus tensions between the two regularly surface at the annual December negotiations of the EU's Council of Ministers, where, after protracted negotiations, all-important quotas for the next year are allocated to each member state. It is then that the total allowable catch (TAC) in EU waters is determined—that is, the negotiators specify the total number of fish allowed to be caught from a particular stock by all resource users over a particular period of time. The outcome of this exercise usually satisfies neither the fishing industry nor the environmentalists, nor even the scientists on whose recommendations the council is meant to base its decisions. The industry is often frustrated by scientific arguments that fishing effort across Europe should be reduced to ecologically sound limits to stave off the collapse of vulnerable but economically important species like North Sea cod. The arguments persist even though North Sea cod TACs have already been cut almost by half since 2001. But each year the industry applies considerable political pressure to fix quotas at higher quantities than advised by scientists. That, in turn, incurs disapproval from environmentalists, who think the fishing effort is too high for effective conservation. The spectre of overfishing has again appeared, blamed on a failure to enforce existing regulations governing fishing effort and the technologies used and on fishers' reluctance to comply with these regulations.

The decline in stocks of North Sea cod, in particular, has become a proxy for the general deterioration of marine biodiversity in Europe. There is widespread concern that cod numbers are well below the levels needed to maintain the stocks, which scientists and environmentalists think are on the verge of collapse. The same scientists have suggested that the North Sea's total stock of fish has dropped from 26 million metric tons to 10 million in just over a century (ICES 2004). During the boom in the North Sea white fish fishery in the 1970s and 1980s, over 60 percent of the entire biomass of cod and haddock was removed annually (Mardle and Pascoe 2002). Now, "the state of the stocks in the seas surrounding the UK is, for the most part, in a seriously over-exploited condition with most of the stocks of commercially important species outside or at least close to their safe biological limits" (Symes 1998).

A multitude of practical and theoretical problems contribute to this crisis. They include the CFP's use of quotas as a principal method of fisheries management. Quotas may be effective in sharing a resource, but not necessarily in conserving it. All depends on the levels at which quotas are set. Further, as already noted, after annual haggling and horse trading between member states at the fisheries Council of Ministers meeting, TAC levels are frequently set higher than scientists advise. Fisheries decisions made in this forum are overwhelmingly political ones, born of bureaucratic incentives and economic pressures, so the numbers and distribution of fish caught in Europe's waters are an indirect expression of political power.

It is also estimated that the actual number of fish caught has exceeded TACs for many species. The situation results partly from the practice of high-grading, that is, of discarding from the catch fish of lower value in order to increase the proportion of higher-value fish in the allowed quota. It is thought that between one-quarter and one-third of the weight of catch is made up of bycatch (Symes 1998). Over 55,000 metric tons of edible fish is discarded annually in the North Sea, while the figure for the North East Atlantic is 3.7 million metric tons per year (Todd and Ritchie 2000). The unintended effect of CFP rules is that if fishers catch fish for which they have no quota allocation, they must discard the fish regardless of their market value—or land and sell their catch on the black market, further undercutting quotas. The situation is exacerbated by poor enforcement of policy decisions, noncompliance, and lack of policing of quotas.

Yet the realm of fisheries is an area over which the EU appears to possess considerable power, since the CFP gave it "exclusive competence" to make decisions over this sector of the economy. This means ostensibly that the EU institutions, namely the EU Council, the EU Commission, and the EU Parliament, have ultimate authority over fisheries—at the expense, if needs be, of the national interests of member states. In practice, such an approach to fisheries management proved, according to many critics, top-down, centralized, inflexible, and cumbersome. Consequently, the EU has been unable to respond quickly or adequately enough to sharp reductions in fish stocks. Responses have usually been reactive, managing crisis and "fire fighting," rather than dealing with long-term issues, because the basic policy framework has been able to make only small, incremental changes. Eventually, after years of mere tinkering the CFP became immensely complicated. All this also led to mistrust between fisheries stakeholders and inhibited their meaningful participation in the policy process. Fishers, for example, felt policy makers took their knowledge and expertise insufficiently into account.

Eventually, widespread dissatisfaction with the CFP led to its reform from 2002 onwards. A set of principles intended to embody good governance was applied. The new terms included a clear definition of responsibilities at Community, national, and local levels; decision making based on sound scientific advice; broad involvement of stakeholders at all stages of policy formulation and implementation; and consistence with environmental, social, regional, and other Community policies. As part of the reform, regional advisory councils (RACs) were established to facilitate a new process in which stakeholders could openly and democratically discuss and formulate advice to the EU Council, albeit that ultimately the principle of EU exclusive competence was retained. It was also intended that the CFP reforms would secure application of such principles as the polluter pays, wherein those responsible for the damage should pay, and would maintain the precautionary approach, which states that where there are threats of serious or irreversible damage, lack of scientific certainty should not be used as a reason for postponing measures to prevent environmental degradation.

The precautionary approach, however, has been undermined by the CFP's stated objective referred to earlier: "to increase productivity by promoting technical progress," ensuring optimal utilization of labor. Here, the fishing sector has been a victim of its own success (Porritt 2005). The strategy of making fisheries more productive has backfired, for the fishing capacity of the community fleets is now 40 percent too large for the available fish resources (CEC 2001). In short, the capacity far exceeds that required to harvest fish stocks sustainably. Too many fishers are chasing too few fish, too effectively.

Thus, for example, despite the trends toward overfishing and stock collapse, the EU has been subsidizing vessel construction and capitalization of the fishing industry for much of the past 30 years. There were, until 2004, socioeconomic funds that supported the introduction of new boats in peripheral, economically deprived regions. Absurdly, at the same time, through decommissioning schemes fishers were and are being paid not to use their boats (see Figure 6.2). The decommissioning effort has been largely unsuccessful, however, partly because it has been under-funded by governments wishing to support shipbuilding as a declining industry, and partly because decommissioning schemes have often ended up providing the collaterals that banks require to underwrite fleet modernizations (Pauly, Christensen, et al. 2002).

Food Security/Fisheries   125

Figure 6.2 Policy Contradiction in the Common Fisheries Policy. *Source:* McLachlan Associates.

IS THERE AN EU FISHERIES CRISIS?

Despite growing concerns about fisheries security, as noted in the preceding section, stakeholders have not unanimously agreed that the European situation could be described as a crisis, or what the nature of that crisis might be. In the past, there has been fundamental disagreement on the matter, especially between fishing industry representatives and environmentalists. Whereas the former alleged that any crisis might be because the sector is not *economically* and *socially* sustainable, the latter argued that levels of fishing are not *environmentally* sustainable. Environmentalists claimed that fishers are happy to pillage, and "sod the cod", whereas fishers maintained that "for greens, cod is god."

Whatever the case, there is no doubt that through their campaigns over the past 30 years, European environmentalists have helped to make fisheries security a major political issue. Often supported by recreational fishers, as well as some scientists, they have argued that overfishing has destroyed delicate, diverse, sensitive, and productive marine ecosystems and has brought some species to the verge of extinction. Greenpeace, especially, regularly uses charismatic species like seals to lever public support, much to the chagrin of fishers, who argue that burgeoning populations of protected seals are eating up much of the cod. Some fishers deny overfishing, proclaiming that it is possible to "walk to Norway on the backs of haddock," despite haddock being classified as a potentially vulnerable stock. Or, they suggest, stocks have not so much diminished as migrated northward in reaction to the effects of global warming.

One impediment to the accurate assessment of whether there is a crisis lies in the way stock levels are assessed. Most government fisheries laboratories still work in such traditional ways as performing assessments for single-species fisheries in order to estimate their TAC. This puts government labs at odds with more holistic conservationist perspectives, which insist that fisheries affect numerous bycatch species and, in fact, serially destroy their supporting ecosystems (Pauly, Watson, et al. 2005). Now, however, there appears to be a significant emerging view that single-species stock assessments are deficient and that they should be complemented by ecosystems-based management, assessing trophic interactions between species and their habitats (Pauly, Christensen, et al. 2002).

Reasoning from such a perspective, some fisheries scientists and other academics strongly support the establishment of marine protected areas (MPAs), where there is no take of catch. It is argued that such marine reserves can significantly contribute to fisheries security through enhancing the biological diversity of both target and nontarget species in a relatively short time. Although profits cannot be made from fishing in such areas, MPAs could nonetheless prove to be cost-effective security measures because they create regions where stock recovery and endangered species protection could occur for less than the present cost of subsidies to industrial fisheries. Conserving 20–30 percent of the world's oceans might cost between $5 billion and $19 billion annually but could create about a million new jobs to manage and protect them (Ovetz 2006).

Most EU fishers tend to oppose such measures. Many of them, nowadays, no longer deny the possibility of overfishing but argue that the problem is caused by someone else, usually fishers from another country using different types of gear or refusing to obey the rules. Such nationalist discourse is offered, for example, by a vocal minority of fishers as the answer to Britain's fisheries security problems. With quasi-religious fervor, one group argues for withdrawal from the CFP, an act that might automatically entail withdrawal from the EU, and touts the campaign slogan Save Britain's Fish. Nationalism is bound up with the fisheries security issue in other regions also, notably Basque Spain, where the cod has considerable cultural significance. And in countries bordering the North Sea, the North Atlantic, and the Baltic states, sometimes rhetoric associated with national claims on ocean resources is warlike and pervaded by the language of militarism and invasion.

However powerful such rhetoric may be, historically there has been no such thing as, for example, "British" fish. Fish around the United Kingdom's coast have always been fished by other nations, just as British fishermen have always fished far from UK shores (Nadel-Klein 2003). Yet national claims to ocean resources are not new. Ocean territorial rights were first recognized and contested in the twelfth century, when sea resources were seen as extension of land rights and not as common property. There is, though, a new breed of fisher operating in European waters for whom the nationalist discourse is irrelevant. These are the owners of multiple or super trawlers, who are emerging global capitalists of the ocean.

Just like other successful modern entrepreneurs, they are not as dedicated to nation as they are to profit. Indeed, they see Save Britain's Fish supporters adversarially, given their and other dissidents' espousal of nationalist rhetoric hindering the lobby to remove residual national barriers to their fishing prospects.

SPREAD OF INDUSTRIAL-SCALE FISHING AND GLOBAL FISH MARKETS

In Europe, the decommissioning policy discussed earlier has coincided with a phenomenon known as "capital stuffing". This means that although boats are taken out of service, the overall catching power of fleets remains the same or increases because of the use of more sophisticated fishing gear and technologies like fish-finding devices. It is estimated that if EU fleets were cut by 40 percent, they could still catch the same number of fish (*Economist* 1994). Capital intensiveness has reduced the number of people employed in the sector, but this is often offset by the use of financial aid—intended to sustain vulnerable fishing communities—to buy more boats. Attempts to counter the effects of this greater technological efficiency—through such strategies as limiting boat size, engine power, mesh sizes, days at sea, and the like—do not seem to have gone far enough to avert potential crisis.

A major reason for this is that fleets now travel greater distances in search of fewer fish. That increase in distant-water fishing has become possible through such improved technology as factory freezer trawlers, which can remain at sea for months. The global impact on stock sustainability of such distant-water fishing is, some say, potentially immense; for whatever management solutions may be attempted, it is ultimately the *inaccessibility* of fisheries that is likely to offer greatest protection from overexploitation. But now that distance and depth refuges are vulnerable to industrial-scale techniques, fishing is increasingly likely to resemble old wars of species extermination carried out in Australia and North America by newly arrived hunters thousands of years ago (Pauly, Watson, et al. 2005).

However, trawler fishing, which can be as destructive of ecosystems as is the clear felling of forests, is not the only industrial-scale fishing technique to threaten fisheries security in regions hitherto unthreatened. Industrial long-lining—again, a highly unselective technique—uses thousands of baited hooks. It involves large vessels from the United States; Spain; Japan, Taiwan, and other Asian countries; and Latin American countries—all primarily exporting their catches to the United States, Japan, and the European Union. Long-lining targets migratory predatory fish species including tuna and swordfish, but it also catches or kills large numbers of sea turtles, billfish, sharks, marine mammals, and seabirds. The technique has caused a decline in the population of large pelagic fish species—those that live in the upper layers of the ocean and traverse huge distances—including billfish, sharks, and tuna, in the order of 60 to 99 percent in the Atlantic and Gulf of Mexico since the 1950s (Ovetz 2006). Aquaculture is another industrial-scale fishery. Like long-lining, it is environmentally threatening. It not only requires many high energy inputs but also destroys or degrades whole ecosystems, such areas as coastal mangrove swamps converted to fish and shrimp ponds (York and Hill-Gossard 2004).

Globally, industrial-scale fishing since the late 1980s has created a damaging feedback loop both for the marine ecosystem and the societies that rely on pelagic species for their livelihoods. It has allowed rapid expansion of fishing capacity far exceeding the reproductive capacity of the targeted fish stocks. Such overfishing has driven industrial fleets farther from shore to catch dwindling stocks. At the same time, decreasing catches have forced small-scale fishers to try to increase vessel size and fish farther from shore. Encouraged by a wide range of subsidies and access to lucrative foreign export markets, many of these fleets have descended deeper into debt to finance an expansion of capacity in order to chase fewer and fewer fish farther and farther from shore (Ovetz 2006).

The resulting feedback loop is driven by the increasingly competitive environment surrounding the quest for more commercially viable stocks. Skippers want to invest profits in new and more efficient technology so they can compete with other vessel owners who will be doing the same. They are targeting part of an expanding global market in which demand for fish has doubled in less than 30 years (UNFAO 2004). It is generally assumed that the driver for this expansion is spreading economic modernization, with corresponding increase in some nations' affluence levels and demand for superior foods like meat and fish. The relationship between increasing income and changing food taste is not simple, however, and cultural traditions and ecological conditions also strongly influence the latter (York and Hill-Gossard 2004).

Nonetheless, some fishers are increasingly tempted to contribute to exhaustion of the shared ocean in order to generate commodities for export to wealthy global markets. Indeed, the share of world catch going to international trade in the 1980s rose from 32 percent to 38 percent (FAO figure), with the international trade in fisheries up by 10 percent per year in that decade. By the end of the 1980s, the wealthy developed nations of the global North imported 76 percent of the food fish by weight—that is, fish for consumption, not for fishmeal or oils—which was traded internationally. Poorer nations in the developing countries of the global South now export more fish than they import, so there is a net flow from them to wealthy nations in the North (Kent 1997). And overfishing of local fisheries in the Northern Hemisphere, the result of increased recognition of the benefits of eating seafood and of increased affluence, has been masked by this expansion of imports from new fishing grounds, especially in the Southern Hemisphere. The general trend toward declining catch of bigger, more valuable species has, then, affected poorer countries more than wealthy ones, since the latter have been able to meet their shortfall by increasing imports from the global South. This masking has been made possible by an increasingly integrated but unregulated global market, facilitated by the relaxation of investment regulations, the opening up of international banking, and further advances in telecommunications (Pauly, Watson, et al. 2005). The changes are all part of a move away from governance founded in state control toward reliance on private firms operating in free markets.

A GLOBAL CRISIS OF FISHERIES SECURITY

With globalization of fisheries markets and fishing grounds has come globalization of the fisheries crisis. For it now appears that the masking effect from global extension of fisheries has met its natural limits; catches from newly accessed stocks have ceased to compensate for the collapse in catches in areas accessed earlier. Hence, there is now a gradual decline in global landings. For some time this did not seem to be the message coming from official catch statistics, which showed global catches apparently continuing to *increase* through the 1990s. The true situation was revealed recently, however, when massive overreporting of marine fisheries catches by one single country, the People's Republic of China, was uncovered. Correcting for this showed that reported world fisheries landings have, in fact, been *declining* slowly since the late 1980s, by about 0.7 million metric tons per year (Pauly, Christensen, et al. 2002). Various reports all point in this direction, suggesting that production from marine fisheries has peaked at 100 million tons and is now flattening off or is in decline, and that aquaculture production, which doubled between 1984 and 1992, will increase at a slower rate between 1990 and 2020 (Pinstrup-Andersen and Pandya-Lorch 1998). The UN has suggested that more than two-thirds of the world's commercial fish species are now fully exploited, overexploited, or depleted (1992), and FAO statistics show that a rapidly increasing proportion of world catches originates from depleted or collapsed stocks. One of the most alarming forecasts claims that all the world's commercial fish and seafood species could collapse by the middle of this century if present trends continue (Worm et al. 2006). Bycatch and overfishing would contribute significantly to this collapse, for it is estimated that global commercial fisheries generate roughly 44 billion pounds of wasted catch each year, including over 3 billion pounds by U.S. fishers alone (Ovetz 2006). And because worldwide fishing and fishing-related industries employ approximately 400 million people and another 1 billion rely on fish for a significant source of protein, wasteful fishing practices can have significant multiplier effects (Ovetz 2006).

Another manifestation of the trends in global fisheries lies in the phenomenon known as the "fishing down" of marine food webs. This relates to the trophic level (TL) of global marine landings. (The TL indicates position in the food chain, with plankton and detritus, for example, at TL 1, while such small pelagics as herring, sardine, and anchovy are at TL 3, with larger fish at higher TLs.) What is happening over time is that although technological advances make fleets increasingly capable of more valuable catches at high TLs (e.g., cod), in practice there are increasing landings of fish at lower TLs, which are less valuable (Pauly, Watson, et al. 2005).

The observed decline of 0.05–0.10 trophic levels per decade in global fisheries landings implies the gradual removal of large, long-lived fish from the ecosystems of the world oceans. As R. Myers and B. Worm (2003, 280) estimate, as a result of industrialized fishing, "large predatory fish biomass today is only about 10% of pre-industrial levels." Global fisheries were operating, on average, at a TL of 3.37 in the early 1950s; now their mean TL is around 3.29. These broad trends have been documented through mapping changes in the sizes of fish caught (Pauly, Watson, et al. 2005). The characteristic declines in size and value appeared first in the nearshore waters of industrialized countries of the Northern Hemisphere; then they spread offshore and to the Southern Hemisphere. The maps also show how widespread the fishing down phenomenon has become. Of particular concern must be the shelf areas, where 90 percent of fish live. Here, TLs have strongly declined, for these areas contribute a large proportion of the world's fisheries catches. The declining fecundity of the shelves is also reflected in the mean depth of global fishing, which has increased over the past 50 years, along with the spread of industrial fishing techniques.

IMPACT ON THE GLOBAL SOUTH

The global extension of industrial fishing is partly a result of the response of the North's fishing industry to conservation efforts in their home countries. For when such efforts succeed in closing off large areas of such territorial waters as the Shetland box in order to stimulate recovery of dwindling stocks, the same vessels that caused the overfishing crisis have often relocated, perhaps with the aid of government subsidies, to fisheries in the waters of the global South. The process shifts the problem abroad to somewhere out of public oversight and scrutiny (Ovetz 2006). It happens partly because poorer countries sell licenses allowing the purchasers access to their extended EEZs—something they themselves cannot fully exploit because of insufficient funds. For the benefit of large industrial vessels, local laws are often changed to commercialize previously publicly owned fisheries. In addition to the many EU access agreements signed in recent years, a 1987 treaty between 16 Pacific island nations and the United States granted access to their EEZs to as many as 50 vessels. The U.S. government subsidizes $14 million of the annual $18 million payment (Ovetz 2006). One-third of fish caught off West Africa's coast is now taken by foreign fleets, and in the Western and Central Pacific, only an estimated 10 percent of the total tuna catch is taken by vessels based in the region (Ovetz 2006).

The meager fees obtained thus constitute only a short-term payoff because of the ecological damage the industrial-scale fishing licensees cause. In 2001, the European Council recognized that the access of foreign fleets to the waters of poorer coastal and island nations also threatened widespread social and economic harm to the employment and food security of local populations—harm that often exceeded the value of fees paid by the foreign users. The European Council explicitly noted "concern that many developing countries are experiencing problems related to decreasing catches, while supply of fish is vital for their food security and their economic development" (Earle 2002, 3).

In such manner, some of the globe's fish resources, as well as jobs in fisheries, are effectively reallocated from developing to wealthy nations. This outflow is consonant with contemporary globalization processes whereby sites of production and consumption may become increasingly separated and levels of consumption of food and other resources within a nation may not necessarily reflect the absolute availability of its resources. The adverse effects of access agreements are reinforced by the way poorer countries are encouraged to earn currency by selling fish from their own fleets into the global market. Doing so tends to decrease the effort they invest in catching fish for their own subsistence while it may, incidentally, undercut the prices fishers from the North can get for their catches.

But economic globalization's impacts seem, on balance, to be particularly detrimental to small-scale artisan fishers in the global South, who represent 90 percent of the world's fishermen and women and are responsible for almost 50 percent of total world landings (Ovetz 2006). They lose some of their traditional fishing grounds and their catch, and seafood consumers in the global South may face rising prices and shortages. When the foreign industrial fishers have exhausted an area and moved on, the main beneficiaries have been the consumers in wealthy European, American, and Japanese markets, but the social and environmental externalities are borne by the communities, who have to subsist on the remaining resources of damaged marine ecosystems.

Yet, as R. Ovetz (2006) observes, in many parts of the Pacific, indigenous people rely on seafood for their livelihoods and as important sources of protein. In parts of the U.S. Pacific islands, for example, 80 to 95 percent of the coastal marine harvests have traditionally been collected for home consumption. Now the area contains hugely valuable commercial fisheries, exporting and transhipping such valuable species as tuna to the United States. And in Chile, artisan fisheries received only 2 percent of the quota in the horse mackerel fishery, too little to maintain current fishing effort, when individual nontransferable quotas were created in 2001. The impact on food security, says Ovetz (2006), was severe, since horse mackerel is an important source of food in Chile. But it also has value to industrial fisheries as fishmeal for animals exported abroad as meat.

It may be that such other businesses as ecotourism, recreational fishing, and whale watching could bring in steady revenue to coastal communities of the global South, outstripping the value of access agreements with industrial fishers. Unfortunately, though, most ocean-related recreation depends on maintaining the integrity of the marine ecosystems now being degraded as a result of the agreements.

It appears, then, that aspects of the crisis in fisheries security have been fended off by the North by transference to the global South. The transfer is illustrated by nutritional trends of recent years, which clearly suggest that most of the increased supply from poorer countries' fisheries is going to the North. In many countries of Europe, Asia, and North and Central America in the 1980s, for instance, fish consumption per capita rose by about 25 percent. In African and South American nations, by contrast, it fell by up to 25 percent. Again, in 1988–1990, people in poorer nations had a yearly fish supply of 9.3 kg per capita, whereas the figure for wealthy nations was 25.8—a ratio of nearly 1–3 (Kent 1997). This ratio has not improved. Meanwhile, 9 of the top 40 fish-exporting countries globally are considered to have a low-income food deficit; that is, they have low food security.

Some observers argue that this is not particularly problematic. Poorer nations are paid for their fish exports, and, it is argued, they would drop the trade if they did not benefit from what is a substantial foreign exchange earner. They can use this revenue to buy other food of high nutrition. And since exported fish are high value, they are not of interest to the poor. The argument here, however, is purely an economic one that neglects the fact that fish for people in the global South comes mostly from small-scale fisheries. Such fisheries yield more nutritional benefits and more employment, and they are better for the environment. The possibility that they are not efficient when assessed in conventional economic terms is outweighed by their considerable efficiency by social and ecological criteria (Kent 1997). It needs also to be remembered that the cultural survival of local communities is threatened by the loss of the marine biodiversity that is at the center of many of their worldviews and spiritual beliefs (Ovetz 2006).

SECURITY ISSUES AND THE POTENTIAL FOR CONFLICT

Food security in general is again a pressing issue at a time when more than 800 million people, or 20 percent of the global South's population, are food insecure—that is, they lack economic and physical access to the food required to lead healthy and productive lives (Pinstrup-Andersen and Pandya-Lorch 1998). With the global reallocation of fish resources and jobs, as described here, the problem for some fish consumers is increasingly one of uneven spatial and social distribution of fish availability in relation to demand. In addition, fisheries security over time is problematic because the enterprise of global fisheries is so severely affecting its own resources base that if present trends continue, it will collapse in the next decades and drag down with it many of the fish species it exploits, together with their supporting ecosystems (Pauly, Watson, et al. 2005). This is, in short, the problem of sustainability, which fisheries scientists and environmentalists increasingly believe can be solved only by setting large areas aside from all fishing while, at the same time, eliminating fleet over-capacity.

The prospect of averting the crisis by developing aquaculture is not good, it seems, for the rapid growth in farming carnivorous fish species, which consume other fish suited for human consumption, has led to serious food security issues. Where such farming requires fishmeal and fish oil, as in salmon farming, for instance, this means that small pelagics, perfectly good for direct human consumption, effectively lose nutritive value as they pass through the gut of a carnivore on their way to humans (Pauly, Watson, et al. 2005). Also, there are a number of pollution problems associated with aquaculture.

Such developing fisheries security problems have given rise to emerging conflicts in which nearshore waters long used for subsistence fishing are becoming an increasingly contested terrain. Increasing are such international disputes over fish stocks as that between the EU and Chile caused by Spanish vessels overfishing swordfish off Chile's coast. Such conflict, often between parties that have legal access to fisheries, is compounded by the growth in illegal, or pirate, fishing.

Pirate fishing, known by the less colorful name of illegal, unreported, and unregulated (IUU) fishing, is fast becoming the scourge of the oceans, from the islands of the South Pacific to the coasts of West Africa. It leaves communities that can least afford to be robbed without much needed food and income, and the marine environment smashed and empty. In 2001, Greenpeace estimated there were at least 1,300 industrial-scale pirate fishing ships at sea. The United Nations estimates that Somalia loses $300 million a year to the pirates; Guinea loses $100 million. Globally more than $4 billion is lost each year.

While the fluttering skull-and-crossbones flag easily identifies fictional pirates, those in real life hide their identity and origin, often flying the flags of countries that ask no questions about their fishing. With the click of a computer mouse, for as little as $500, flags can be bought over the Internet from countries like Malta, Panama, Belize, Honduras, St Vincent, and the Grenadines. Far from policing the rogue traders, governments around the world do little to check their activities or what is landed in their own ports despite the various international commitments and plans. The pirate booty is often illegally transferred to factory ships, mixed with legally caught stocks, and then knowingly sold in legitimate ports like Las Palmas and Suva. The countries that are the biggest victims of this wholesale robbery are usually those least able to enforce the laws in their own waters. But the owners and operators are not impossible to track down. Playing host to the pirates are around 80 different countries, including Taiwan, Panama, Belize, Honduras, and some EU countries.

Pirate fishing compounds the global environmental damage from other destructive fisheries. Because pirate fishers operate, quite literally, off the radar of any enforcement, the fishing techniques they use are destroying ocean life. Tuna fisheries around Tanzania, Somalia, Papua New Guinea, and Tuvalu, for example, are targeted each year with giant nets that scoop up entire shoals, including the young fish vital for breeding and future stock growth. The bycatch fish, which will not make money on the market but could still provide food and income for others, are thrown back dead. It is estimated that for every kilo of shrimp landed, over three kilos of tropical marine life are caught and die. Shrimp fishing accounts for between 3 and 4 percent of the world fishing industry but is responsible for over 27 percent of the unnecessary destruction of marine life.

THE NEED FOR NEW FISHERIES SECURITY GOVERNANCE

Yet pirate fishing could be stopped and shut down by international enforcement, backed by such technologies as satellite monitoring of fisheries vessels. Governments could outlaw flags of convenience and refuse entry to fishing and supply vessels sailing under such flags. Such measures are a matter of political will: to create and participate in governance arrangements appropriate to delivering the enforcement needed to protect the marine environment and the communities depending upon it; and to achieve greater compliance with regulations, agreements, and such codes as the FAO Code of Conduct for Responsible Fisheries. Governance for sustainable fisheries needs both new policies and institutional change because sustainable development, where the use of resources for present development does not detract from their value to future generations, requires social, economic, and environmental factors of policy making to be addressed *together*.

Generally speaking, global fisheries governance is a mishmash of codes of conduct, conventions, and agreements, but there are influential UN frameworks covering such things as biodiversity or the management of straddling or migratory fish stocks. One of the most significant documents is the UN's 1998 Aarhus Convention on public participation in decision making and access to environmental information. This encompasses the idea that a greater degree of more informed stakeholder participation in decisions ultimately secures better management of, and compliance with, those decisions.

In Europe, such ideas strongly underwrite recent changes in governance procedures and institutions, including changes in fisheries management. Here, following some of the failures and deficiencies discussed earlier, CFP reform has, at least ostensibly, now taken on the task of instituting a set of "principles of good governance." The principles are about securing more transparent, flexible, and consensual decision-making political arrangements at various scales—supranational, national, regional, and local. Policies are to be coherent with each other, which is especially important when trying to resolve the overfishing problem. The ultimate aim of the governance reforms might be a more deliberative democracy among fisheries stakeholders. This, it is believed, will enable them to participate meaningfully in environmental decisions and bring their diverse environmental knowledge to the table. It should also enable fisheries stakeholders who were previously antagonistic to each other to empathize more and to reach shared understandings.

The EU is trying to implement such governance reforms alongside various environmentally-based management perspectives. The perspectives include the polluter paid principle, the precautionary principle, and the ecosystem approach. This last is founded on the belief that problems of overexploitation stem from a mismatch between ecological and management boundaries, and so it involves treating fish stocks as part of complicated ecologies, rather than as isolated components of marine systems. Its application is meant to produce more holistic policies, involving all activities in the marine environment, and it lends itself to the creation of marine reserves and closed-off areas.

Another strong theme in EU governance reforms is that of decentralized stakeholder consultation, in observance of the widely applied principle of subsidiary, which means that matters should be handled by the lowest-scale competent authority. In EU fisheries, this reform has meant the establishment of Regional Advisory Councils, notwithstanding EU exclusive competence, noted earlier. Each RAC has a brief for a specific geographical marine region (North Sea, Mediterranean, etc.), or fisheries sector (e.g., pelagic), and a major remit is systematically to gather and articulate opinion from stakeholders that operate regionally and have a better idea than does the European Commission about local conditions. The overriding ethos behind these deliberative forums is that they will enable the fishing industry to share a sense of ownership of fisheries management rules. The assumption is that this will instill a desire to implement and uphold existing legislation. And, it is argued, the improved application of rules should produce more effective measures that sustain fisheries environmentally and economically. The RACs are also meant to improve mutual understanding among the stakeholder representatives and others making up their membership: fishers, environmentalists, scientists, and community groups (Griffin 2007). Such a double commitment to democratization and environmental improvement follows a long tradition in green thinking that says that democratic politics is more likely to engender environmentally benign outcomes (Dobson 2000).

In the early years of the twenty-first century, it remains to be seen if the EU's attempts to procure sustainable fisheries through good governance arrangements will get results. Whether the global diffusion of such arrangements is appropriate is a moot point. Commentators such as R. L. Paarlberg (2002) argue that in these globalization-obsessed times, the problems of hunger and food insecurity still mainly require what would be primarily a national, rather than global or regional, focus. For many national governments in poorer countries still do not provide such essential public goods as civil peace, rule of law, transport infrastructure, clean water, electrical power, and public research to generate new agricultural and fisheries productivity—all essential ingredients in the effort to boost incomes. Of course, in areas such as open-ocean fisheries protection, global governance arrangements would be most appropriate. But for Paarlberg, the main governance challenge as far as food security is concerned is to persuade sovereign governments to provide the necessary public goods to ensure access to adequate food. Global governance institutions have at times tried to step in and fill such national governance deficits in the global South. Most of these attempts have ended in frustration, however, since the traditional norm of state sovereignty continues to stand in the way.

FURTHER READING

Clover, C. *The End of the Line: How Overfishing Is Changing the World and What We Eat.* London: Ebury, 2005.
Griffin, L. "The North Sea Fisheries Crisis and Good Governance." *Geography Compass* 2 (2008): 452–75.
Paarlberg, R. L. "Governance and Food Security in an Age of Globalization." Food, Agriculture, and the Environment Discussion Paper 36. International Food Policy Research Institute, 2002.
Pauly, D., R. Watson, and J. Alder. "Global Trends in World Fisheries: Impacts on Marine Ecosystems and Food Security." *Philosophical Transactions of the Royal Society* B (2005): 512.
Pinstrup-Andersen, P., and R. Pandya-Lorch. "Food Security and Sustainable Use of Natural Resources: A 2020 Vision." *Ecological Economics* 26 (1998): 1–10.

REFERENCES

CEC. 2001. Commission communication on elements of a strategy for the integration of environmental protection requirements into the Common Fisheries Policy 143. Brussels: CEC.
Dobson, A. 2000. *Green political thought.* London: Routledge.
Earle, M. 2002. *Comments on the EU-Senegal fisheries agreement, 2002–2006.* Report to the European Parliament. Brussells: European Commission.
Economist, The. 1994. The tragedy of the oceans. *The Economist,* March 19.
Griffin, L. 2007. All aboard: Power, participation and governance in the North Sea Regional Advisory Council. *International Journal of Green Economics* 1, 314: 478–493.
ICES. 2004. International Council for the Exploration of the Oceans: Introduction. *ICES.* http://www.ices.dk/ (accessed August 2006).

Kent, G. 1997. Fisheries, food security, and the poor. *Food Policy* 22: 393–404.

Mardle, S., and S. Pascoe. 2002. Modeling the effects of trade-offs between long- and short-term objectives in fisheries management. *Journal of Environmental Management* 65: 49–62.

Myers, R., and B. Worm. 2003. Rapid worldwide depletion of predatory fish communities. *Nature* 423: 280–83.

Nadel-Klein, J. 2003. *Fishing for heritage.* Oxford: Berg.

Ovetz, R. 2006. The bottom line: An investigation of the economic, cultural and social costs of high seas industrial longline fishing in the Pacific and the benefits of conservation. *Marine Policy* 30: 809–20.

Paarlberg, R. L. 2002. *Governance and food security in an age of globalization: Food, agriculture, and the environment.* International Food Policy Research Institute Discussion Paper 36.

Pauly, D., V. Christensen, S. Guénette, T. J. Pitcher, U. R. Sumaila, C. J. Walters, R. Watson, and D. Zeller. 2002. Towards sustainability in world fisheries. *Nature* 418: 689–95.

Pauly, D., R. Watson, and J. Alder. 2005. Global trends in world fisheries: Impacts on marine ecosystems and food security. *Philosophical Transactions of the Royal Society* B: 5–12.

Pinstrup-Andersen, P., and R. Pandya-Lorch. 1998. Food security and sustainable use of natural resources: A 2020 vision. *Ecological Economics* 26: 1–10.

Pomeroy, R. S., and F. Berkes. 1997. Two to tango: The role of government in fisheries co-management. *Marine Policy* 21: 465–80.

Porritt, J. 2005. Fishing for good. *London: Forum for the Future.*

Rogers, S., and R. Stocks. 2001. *North Sea fish and fisheries.* Technical report produced for strategic environmental assessment. London: CEFAS.

Symes, D. 1998. The integration of fisheries management and marine wildlife conservation. Joint Nature Conservation Committee Report 287.

Todd, E., and E. Ritchie. 2000. Environmental non-governmental organizations and the common fisheries policy. *Aquatic Conservation: Marine and Freshwater Ecosystems* 10: 141–49.

UN Environment Programme. 1992. Rio declaration on environment and development. Made at the United Nations Conference on Environment and Development, Rio de Janeiro, Brazil.

UNFAO. 2004. *The state of world fisheries and aquaculture.* Rome: FAO.

Worm, B., et al. 2006. Impacts of biodiversity loss on ocean ecosystem services. *Science* 314: 787–90.

York, R., and M. Hill-Gossard. 2004. Cross-national meat and fish consumption: Exploring the effects of modernization and ecological context. *Ecological Economics* 48: 293–302.

7

Geopolitics

Klaus Dodds

Geopolitics has had a controversial intellectual history ever since a Swedish law professor, Rudolf Kjellen, first coined the term in the late 1890s. At the heart of geopolitical thinking lies a concern for the intersection of territory, power, resources, and the physical geographies of the earth. Following Robert Cox (1981), one might make a distinction between two types of geopolitical theorizing—*orthodox* and *critical*. With regards to the former, geopolitical scholars prioritize as objects of study the state, national security, and, of course, territory. For much of the last century, intellectual energies were devoted to developing a problem-solving dimension to this orthodox tradition. As a consequence, many writers subsequently expressed an interest in advising and informing elite and popular audiences about particular dangers and threats facing specific countries, empires, and even civilizations. In contemporary America, such academics and journalists as Thomas Barnett (2003), Samuel Huntington (1996), Robert Kagan (2002), and Robert Kaplan (1994) have become particularly well known in this regard for contributing to what has been dubbed a "tabloid geopolitical culture" because of the evocative, often simplistic, and highly visual nature, usually in the form of maps, of their collective pronouncements about the United States and the wider world (Dalby 2006; Debrix 2007).

The alternative form of geopolitics, of a more critical variety, does not fundamentally prioritize those aforementioned objects of study. In parallel with the emergence of critical security studies (Krause and Williams 1997), the emphasis is shifted toward a more discursive turn, which considers how security is constructed and geographically imagined. As one leading geographical scholar has noted:

> The world is actively "spatialized," divided up, labelled, sorted out into a hierarchy of places of greater or lesser "importance" by political geographers, other academics and political leaders. This process provides the geographical framing within which political elites and mass publics act in the world in pursuit of their own identities and interests. (Agnew 2003, 3)

Figure 7.1 The Natural Seats of Power. *Source:* Halford MacKinder (1904).

As a form of critical theory, this more recent variant of geopolitical scholarship does not necessarily seek to inform or advise elite audiences about foreign and security policies. As a form of critique, attention is devoted to how the physical and political geographies of the earth are described and with what consequences. Categories such as states, regions, blocs, continents, and resources are critically evaluated rather than simply assumed (O Tuathail 1996; Dalby 2007). Arguably, this task has taken on an added urgency in post-9/11 America and the associated War on Terror. As Francois Debrix (2007) has concluded, "Crucial to most popular discourses of geopolitics since the mid-1990s is a desire to mobilise strategies and techniques of power that have chosen global life—or the question of who must stay alive or who must die, of which way of life is to be privileged and which one has to be destroyed—as their primary object of concern." Since September 2001, the Pentagon has devoted considerable energies to investing in additional defense-related spending, including surveillance that encapsulates the entire earth in the form of global command structures.

For much of the formal intellectual history of geopolitics, the problem-solving variant has been dominant. Founding figures such as the British geographer, Member of Parliament, and former director of the London School of Economics Sir Halford Mackinder (1861–1947) was instrumental in drawing attention to the existence of land- and sea-based powers ever eager to dominate such vast physical spaces as the Euro-Asian landmass, which he labeled the Heartland Mackinder (1904, 1919; see Figure 7.1). Early geopolitical writers shared similar concerns with their colleagues within the scholarly discipline of international relations, which emerged in the early decades of the twentieth century. Both approaches devote a great deal of concern to the security of the territorial state and conceive the international system as anarchic. Without any form of world government, states are thus forced into behaving in a self-interested manner in order to survive in a world made insecure in part by the behavior of other states. Controversially, geopolitical theorizing in interwar Europe conceptualized the state as a living organism and placed a renewed emphasis on the state's acquiring territory and resources for the purpose of securing itself and the population therein. Postwar scholars in North America and elsewhere later saw such a theorization of the state and society as instrumental in informing the more extreme expressions of militant nationalism, notably National Socialism in Germany. Although the connections between geopolitics and Nazism are not as clear-cut as some observers might have thought, the American geographer Richard Hartshorne was not alone when he condemned geopolitics as an intellectual poison. He offered that judgement in 1954 and, as a consequence, helped to demonize geopolitics, at least in the Anglophone world (Hartshorne 1954; Hepple 1986; Dodds and Atkinson 2000).

The revival of geopolitics in the Anglophone world owes a great deal not only to eminent individuals but also to changing world events. Former Secretary of State Henry Kissinger is often credited with helping to restore the intellectual status of geopolitics. As a German Jewish émigré and historian armed with a doctorate on nineteenth-century European rivalries, he used the term "geopolitics" to signal a renewed interest in American foreign and security policy in Great Power relations, territorial influence, and power projection (Kissinger 1979). Writing in the early 1970s, Kissinger believed the Cold War was taking a new turn; America was preparing to leave Vietnam in an ignominious manner, U.S.-Sino relations were entering a new phase, the 1973–1974 oil crisis was placing new pressures on the global economic system, and the dangers of nuclear annihilation had receded somewhat from earlier crises over Berlin (1961) and Cuba (1962). Kissinger, as with a new generation of such orthodox geopolitical scholars as Colin Gray (1977), turned to geopolitics as a shorthand term for analyzing new international political realities, which placed due emphasis on such earthly features as the global distribution of natural resources, shipping lanes, and such strategic landscapes like the Middle East. As the Cold War worsened in the early to mid-1980s, policy-related and scholarly interest in geopolitics was further rejuvenated in and beyond the English-speaking world (Taylor 1983).

While geopolitical thinking has been accused of being nationalistic, militaristic, and even, as acknowledged earlier, noxious, more critical strains emerged in the late 1980s. In one sense, these more critical geopolitical expressions were not novel. Ever since the invention of the term, such writers as the Russian anarchist Peter Kropotkin and later the French geographer Yves Lacoste (1973) have demonstrated that it is possible to resist the more orthodox and problem-solving variants of geopolitics. In the English-speaking world, a new generation of geographers and other scholars sought to reconceptualize geopolitics as a discourse and practice, which actively imagined and represented earthly realities (O Tuathail and Agnew 1992). If places and environments were judged to be strategic, then it was imperative that scholars examined on what basis such an assessment was made. In other words, any attempt to naturalize such concepts as security, territory, and resources was resisted.

The apparent ending of the Cold War in 1989, however, placed the relevance of geopolitics under pressure as the Iron Curtain collapsed and old territorial divisions in Europe were upended. While other scholars were tempted to dismiss the significance of territory in an age of apparent post–Cold War stability and intense globalization, a new generation of such critical geopolitical writers as John Agnew (2003), Simon Dalby (1990), and Gearoid O Tuathail (1996) were contending that territorial factors had not diminished in significance. If anything, the conclusion being reached was quite the opposite. Old territorial divisions were collapsing, but in their place were emerging such new configurations of territories and flows as the expansion of the European Union and the North Atlantic Treaty Organization. New regional agreements in the global South changed the political and economic geographies of Asia, Latin America, and Africa. A bipolar world was being replaced by a more complex, multipolar world, and flows of people, money, goods, and ideas were contributing to the decentralizing of global politics.

Former President George H. W. Bush, on the back of the successful United Nations–sanctioned military intervention in Kuwait in January 1991, mused that a new world order might actually be emerging. International law, interstate cooperation, and the hegemonic presence of the United States were central to this presidential vision. As events were to prove later, this optimism diminished; the military debacle in Somalia (1992), the genocide in Rwanda (1994), and the breakup of the former Yugoslavia (1992–1995) revealed the continued if problematic significance of territory, resources, and competing definitions of national, regional, and global security. As the 1990s were to demonstrate, the ending of the Cold War initiated a great deal of reflection on the geopolitics of the post–Cold War era and how that might or might not coexist with a neoliberal discourse of globalization, which placed emphasis on emerging markets, regional cooperation, global trading, and macroeconomic stability (see, for a review, Steger 2005). Some writers even predicted the replacement of geopolitics with geoeconomics in terms of the key driver of future global change (Luttwak 1993; Friedman 1999).

By the start of the new century, few commentators expressed any confidence that a new world order would prevail, but critically no one suspected that this uncertainty and instability would affect the United States directly. All this was to change on the basis of one dramatic day in early autumn. On September 11, 2001, the American cities of New York and Washington, D.C., bore the brunt of an airborne attack that left nearly 3,000 people dead. The hijackers singled out the twin pillars of American-led neoliberal globalization (the World Trade Center) and military power (the Pentagon). A fourth plane, had it not crashed into a field in Pennsylvania, might have hit either the White House or Congress. Stung by the worst losses on American soil, President George W. Bush launched a War on Terror and extended America's extraterritorial reach so that military personnel were dispatched into Afghanistan and later Iraq. In other areas of foreign and security policy, the administration articulated a doctrine of preemption and warned that U.S. military power would be used against those who harbored terrorists and terror groups judged to be threatening to the United States (for a critical review, see Cox 2004). Whereas in the recent past, flows of people, money, and goods were judged, on the whole, to be beneficial to the American economy, the attacks of September 11 had highlighted the apparent dangers of such movement. Equipped with mobile phones, flight school training, and box cutters, 19 hijackers had entered the United States and carried out a murderous plot.

International terrorism has propelled discussions of geopolitics to the top of the global agenda as such other states as China, Pakistan, and Russia also engage in their own, highly opportunistic, wars on terror. As C-P. Chung noted:

> In the wake of the September 11 attacks on the United States, China has launched its own "war on terror." Beijing now labels as terrorists those who are fighting for an independent state in the northwestern province of Xinjiang, which the separatists call "Eastern Turkestan." The government considers these activists part of a network of international Islamic terror, with funding from the Middle East, training in Pakistan, and combat experience in Chechnya and Afghanistan. (2002)

In the case of Pakistan, the military government quickly sided with the United States and committed itself to pursuing terror bases and insurgents in or just beyond the Pakistani-Afghan border.

The Bush administration continues to prioritize national security both within the United States and beyond. such new institutions as the Department of Homeland Security spend millions of dollars on assessing security threats within the territory of the United States. Surveillance has expanded, and as any visitor to the United States would have noticed, a new generation of biometric security measures has been introduced at all airports (Amoore 2007). Externally, military and intelligence-based agencies such as the Central Intelligence Agency (CIA) continue to operate in Central Asia, the Middle East, and in other parts of the world either judged to be threatening and or conducive to operations including the interrogation and rendition terror suspects. For the purpose of this chapter, it is noteworthy that American citizens emphatically turned to President Bush as their commander in chief for guidance and protection following the September 11 attacks. The president, in turn, appealed to allies such as the United Kingdom and NATO, but not the United Nations, Interpol, and or humanitarian agencies such as the International Committee of the Red Cross. In other words, 9/11 and the War on Terror revealed how important the state remains not only in defining security but also in choosing preferred institutions to help implement programs designed to enhance particular understandings of national and global security. As Michael Cox concluded, "If we have learnt anything over the last couple of years, it is that one very special state with an enormous amount of power continues to play a central role in international relations" (2007, 4).

GEOPOLITICS AND SECURITY: LEARNING FROM LATIN AMERICA?

In order to explore some of the claims embedded in the introduction of this chapter, it is necessary to consider a little further the concept of security and its relationship to geopolitics and to highlight some of the pre-9/11 discussion regarding the apparent limits of national security. In doing so, attention is centered on events in Latin America in the 1970s and 1980s, rather than the Cold War experiences of Europe and United States. Geopolitics, for much of its intellectual history, has been concerned with the security of the state and the physical geographies of the earth. As with the realist tradition of international relations (IR), a premium continues to be placed on territorial security as defined and defended by the state and its political and military elites.

In Latin America and especially in the Southern Cone, such geopolitical writers as General Pinochet had the opportunity to put into practice some of the ideas taught at Chilean military academies in the 1950s and 1960s. Just as many North American scholars were shunning the scholarly terrain occupied by geopolitics, so others were embracing its concepts and intellectual history. As a former professor of geopolitics, Pinochet was convinced that the state, if conceptualized as a living organism, had to consider foremost the question of national security. As Pinochet noted:

> Geopolitics tries to give a scientific and reasoned explanation of the life of these super-beings who, with unrelenting activity on earth, are born, develop, and die, a cycle during which they show all kinds of appetites and a powerful instinct of conservation. They are as sensible and rational beings as men. (1981, 25)

His writings on geopolitical theory and practice place needed emphasis on the life cycle of the state and its birth, expansion, and eventual demise. Such other contemporary writers as J. Von Chrismar (1968) expanded upon this premise and placed further emphasis on territorial security and frontier regions like Antarctica and the Southern Ocean. Without a doubt, the organic theory prioritized the survival and growth of the state and the role of the military. While this concern for frontiers and territory may strike European and American observers as odd, given the prevailing Cold War, it is entirely understandable in the context of Latin America's postcolonial trajectory. Since the beginning of the nineteenth century, territorial boundaries have been the subject of disputes and deadly conflicts like the War of the Triple Alliance, which decimated the population of Paraguay. Alongside the losses endured as a consequence of interstate conflict, indigenous Indian populations also suffered great losses in the same period.

When Pinochet and other military officers seized power on September 11, 1973, the militarization of Chilean society was initiated. As part of that transformation, the organic theory of the state was changed from a concern for external threats to internal subversion. As Leslie Hepple (1992, 147–48) noted, this shift was significant because it led to the articulation of a national security doctrine (NSD). Spending priorities favored defense-related activities, and individuals and communities judged to be "threatening" were targeted. The country was divided into security zones, and terror suspects were rounded up and interrogated in police and military detention centres scattered around the country. The definition of national security was not merely an academic matter. For those judged to be a security threat, the implications could be severe it not fatal, as thousands simply disappeared. As David Pion-Berlin reflected:

> The organic metaphor is saved by visualising "uncooperative" individuals as cancerous cells, which must be excised by the state so that the entire organism may endure. This view provides a strong sanction and

justification for dictatorship. The Chilean junta took this metaphor seriously in eliminating some 10,000 sympathizers of the Salvador Allende government in the first year after the 1973 coup. (1989, 411–12)

This unedifying pattern was to be repeated in Argentina, Brazil, and Uruguay in the 1970s and early 1980s.

In Argentina, the application of the NSD by three successive military regimes was to have tragic consequences for at least 30,000 people. Under the rubric of the Dirty War, military leaders used the armed forces and intelligence personnel to target individuals and such sections of society as trade unionists and church leaders judged to be threatening. As with neighbouring Chile, a strong anticommunist worldview became an essential element in legitimating and justifying imprisonment, torture, and state-sanctioned murder. Those targeted were frequently described as leftwing subversives, hell-bent on overthrowing the state and eager to promote a socialist revolution. For the United States, the presence of military regimes with impeccable anti-communist credentials was judged to be of greater importance when compared to the human rights abuses committed within those countries. As in other parts of the global South, such military and developmental aid as provided by the Alliance for Progress in the 1960s was targeted in favor of regimes judged politically loyal and anticommunist.

Human rights activists and such external events as the 1982 Falklands-Malvinas conflict and the demise of the Cold War in part precipitated the ending of military rule in the 1980s. In Argentina, groups such as the so-called Mothers of the Plaza de Mayo were active in highlighting the disappearances of male relatives in particular. By gathering and protesting in public spaces in such major cities as Buenos Aires, they drew attention to the violent consequences of the NSD and the organic theory of the state. They also highlighted the varied consequences of so-called national security depending on gender and ethnicity in the case of other parts of Latin America (Radcliffe and Westwood 1993, 66). In order to secure the control and surveillance of Argentine territory and its population, men and women were victims of different forms of violence. Women were raped, and in some cases mothers had their babies and small children taken away from them and given to childless military officers and their families. Both women and men were tortured and killed, and their bodies were dumped in either mass graves or the South Atlantic.

As later feminist writers such as Cynthia Enloe (1989) have noted, the definition and implementation of security has different consequences for men and women across the world. Latin American regimes demonstrated only too clearly that state-sanctioned policies like the NSD did not provide citizens with physical and psychological safety, let alone material security. Furthermore, as Simon Dalby has noted, "In rethinking international relations in these terms [i.e., gender], feminist analyses raise perhaps most directly the crucial point that is so often silenced in the conventional neorealist premises in contemporary security studies. They ask the simple question of who and what is precisely being rendered secure by the provision of national and international security" (1997, 8). The resources devoted to maintaining the national security state in Latin America were substantial and ultimately ensured that vital funding for education, health, and welfare was diminished. As with other military regimes in Latin America, Asia, and Africa, women and children were often the worst affected and thus the most likely to be without adequate food, shelter, and health care.

The geopolitical formulations of security need to be critically considered, and the conventional definitions of security with due reference to territory, political community, resources, and external threats deserve further critical reflection (see Sempa 2002). A new body of geopolitical scholarship in the 1980s and 1990s has not only challenged such specific theories of the states as the organic variety but also questioned the manner in which security was conceived in the first place. On the one hand, this has involved challenging the manner in which security discourses secured particular geopolitical orders and political identities. On the other hand, traditional notions of security have been challenged by a range of other issues, including climate change and massive human rights abuses, which call into question the ability of any one state to protect and secure its territory in the face of challenges intrinsically transboundary in scope.

GEOPOLITICS AND SECURITY IN AN ERA OF INTENSE GLOBALIZATION

For some observers, the 1990s were characterized by ever more intense forms of globalization, which further challenged traditional notions of state-centric security and sovereignty. In the more extreme versions of this contention, it was asserted that globalization had replaced geopolitics as territorial boundaries and geographical space diminished in significance. Richard O'Brien (1992), for example, proclaimed the "end of geography" in a manner reminiscent of Francis Fukuyama's (1989) claims regarding the "end of history." Such a reading of the contemporary epoch, as John Agnew (2003, 2005) has noted, is a fundamental mistake in the sense that it underplays the geopolitical roots and biases of the current global economic and political order. From World War II onward, U.S.-led globalization has been instrumental in shaping the global capitalist economy and the geopolitics of the Cold War. The creation of international institutions such as the World Bank and the International Monetary Fund, alongside American promotion of free trade, international investment, and currency convertibility, was instrumental in producing and expanding an embedded liberalism. With this foundation, American-led investment was critical in reviving European and Asian economies and paved the way for the promotion of development in the Third World. Geopolitical priorities, informed by a keen sense of anti-communism, meant that such regions as Latin America, the Middle East, and Southeast Asia received a disproportionate share of such investment as compared to sub-Saharan Africa.

Although the international economic system underwent fundamental changes following the oil crisis of 1973–1974, the role of the United States remains considerable even if other such actors as transnational corporations and global financial and technological networks have created a more complex mosaic of states, regions, city-states, and localities. The realist worldview of state sovereignty and an accompanying international system composed of nearly 200 states is only one element of this changing landscape as new forms of globalization continue to alter the relationship between these different entities. The ending of the Cold War did not, therefore, disconnect geopolitics from neoliberal forms of economic globalization; rather, it highlighted how the demise of the Cold War facilitated new debates and controversies over the meaning and material significance of development, human rights, security, and governance (for a brief overview, see Steger 2005).

According to Robert Kaplan (1994), the ending of the Cold War would not provide much comfort to those concerned with the contemporary state of the world. His article and later book titled *The Coming Anarchy* deployed a form of descriptive geopolitical reasoning in order to convince readers that the United States faced new dangers, which required it to think well beyond its national boundaries. He also provided a stark warning at the end of the original article:

> When the Berlin Wall was falling, in November of 1989, I happened to be in Kosovo, covering a riot between Serbs and Albanians. The future was in Kosovo, I told myself that night, not in Berlin. The same day that Yitzhak Rabin and Yasser Arafat clasped hands on the White House lawn, my Air Afrique plane was approaching Bamako, Mali, revealing corrugated-zinc shacks at the edge of an expanding desert. The real news wasn't at the White House, I realized. It was right below. (1994, 76)

Along with other popular scholars, Samuel Huntington (1993, 1996) deemed the post–Cold War world to be more unstable and prone to potential seismic conflict involving not only the United States but also entire civilizations, as, for example, the conflicts between the West and Islam. As he noted in his original article published in *Foreign Affairs*:

> It is my hypothesis that the fundamental source of conflict in this new world will not be primarily ideological or primarily economic. The great divisions among humankind and the dominating source of conflict will be cultural. Nation states will remain the most powerful actors in world affairs, but the principal conflicts of global politics will occur between nations and groups of different civilizations. The clash of civilizations will dominate global politics. The fault lines between civilizations will be the battle lines of the future. (Huntington 1993, 22)

As political realists would acknowledge, Huntington's predictions about civilizations did not in any way undermine his conviction that the state will remain "the most powerful act in world affairs" and, as a consequence, continue to mold ideas and practices associated with national security, especially American.

This apparent unease about the ending of the Cold War and future global incarnations coexisted with belated attempts to reposition discussion about international order, national boundaries, states, and security. In April 1999, former British prime minister Tony Blair articulated his doctrine of the international community in a speech given at the Economic Club in Chicago in 1999.

With reference to the NATO-led assault on Serbian forces and infrastructure in Kosovo and Serbia, he noted:

> No one in the West who has seen what is happening in Kosovo can doubt that NATO's military action is justified. Bismarck famously said the Balkans were not worth the bones of one Pomeranian Grenadier. *Anyone who has seen the tear stained faces of the hundreds of thousands of refugees streaming across the border*, heard their heart-rending tales of cruelty or contemplated the unknown fates of those left behind, knows that Bismarck was wrong.
>
> This is a just war, based not on any territorial ambitions but on values. We cannot let the evil of ethnic cleansing stand. We must not rest until it is reversed. We have learned twice before in this century that appeasement does not work. If we let an evil dictator range unchallenged, we will have to spill infinitely more blood and treasure to stop him later. (Available online at http://www.pm.gov.uk/output/Page1297.asp [accessed June 20, 2007, emphasis added by author].)

While reference to the suffering of others and the responsibility of the international community to address war-affected societies and associated human rights violations is significant, the reference to "streaming across the border" was also significant. If the geopolitical situation in Kosovo could not be contained, European and American political leaders worried, it would compromise the national security of other states as thousands of people sought refuge from ethnic cleansing.

While the 1999 NATO-led intervention in Kosovo continues to be mired in controversy, it did highlight a different if limited alternative conception of security based on a broader sense of international obligation, human security, and the United Nations Declaration of Human Rights. American intervention proved decisive even if the Clinton administration was initially unwilling to commit itself to any military operation in Southeast Europe. If anything, the administration was more concerned with such so-called rogue states as Iran, Syria, and North Korea and their capacity to disrupt the global economic and political order. Five years earlier, in January 1994, in an important speech made in Brussels to a multinational audience and future leaders of Europe, President Clinton linked economic globalization to the dangers posed by rogue states:

> The danger is clear and present. Growing missile capabilities are bringing more of Europe into the range of rogue states such as Iran and Libya. There are disturbing reports of efforts to smuggle nuclear materials into and out of Eastern Europe. And this eastward-looking summit will give us the chance to begin to address the threat on our own territory.
>
> The second element of the new security we are building must be greater economic vitality, the issue which I would imagine is of most immediate concern to most of you. We must build it on vibrant and open market economies, the engines that have given us the greatest prosperity in human history over the last several decades in Europe and in the United States. (Available online at http://usa.usembassy.de/etexts/ga6-940109.htm [accessed June 25, 2007].)

For the Clinton administration, therefore, national security was linked not only to the activities of the rogue states—a term dropped in 2000 and replaced with "states of concern"—but also to the extent of integration and "economic vitality" in Europe, the United States, and elsewhere.

"THE DARK SIDE OF GLOBALIZATION": GEOPOLITICS, INSECURITY, AND THE WAR ON TERROR

While the September 11, 2001, attacks on the United States helped to ensure the return of more militaristic understandings of security, the purported connection between neoliberal globalization, global security, and economic integration was not neglected by the new Bush administration. Indeed, former secretary of state Colin Powell referred to the "dark side of globalization" in the aftermath of September 11 (for another view, albeit pre-9/11, see Barber 1996). Given the scale of the human losses and the shock felt by many Americans on that day, it is unsurprising that national security defined the contemporary zeitgeist. Global flows of people, ideas, and money were now shown to be anything but benign as official investigations into the planning and implementation of the airborne assaults revealed that the hijackers had deployed and depended upon a complex array of financial and material flows in and out of the United States, Central Asia, Europe, and the Middle East. Subsequent scares involving anthrax and suspect mail packages containing white powder (some scares perpetrated as hoaxes by U.S. citizens) seemed to amplify further anxieties about the circulation of substances and objects often apparently mundane (Kellner 2003).

Besides, it became clear that Cold War legacies were also critical in shaping the eventual implementation of this assault. The 1979 Soviet invasion of Afghanistan and subsequent U.S. support for the anti-Soviet resistance movement were shown to be crucial in recasting not only the security situation in Central Asia but also, 20 years later, in the United States itself. With the help of U.S.-supplied weapons, Osama Bin Laden, the leader of the Al Qaeda network, had fought against the Soviet armed forces while deeply resenting the American military presence in Saudi Arabia and the wider Middle East. As Chalmers Johnson (2000, 8) noted:

> The term "blowback," which officials of the Central Intelligence Agency first invented for their own internal use, is starting to circulate among students of international relations. It refers to the unintended consequences of policies that were kept secret from the American people. What the daily press reports as the malign acts of "terrorists" or "drug lords" or "rogue states" or "illegal arms merchants" often turn out to be blowback from earlier American operations.

Recasting national security in explicitly military terms has had practical implications for the American-led War on Terror. Once the September 11 attacks were conceptualized as an act of terror rather than an international crime, the event became "securitized," and the military and intelligence agencies of the United

States became more significant than either Interpol and or the United Nations. Domestically, unprecedented amounts of money have now been devoted to homeland security and the 2002 National Security Strategy of the United States, which maps a new global geography of danger. Rogue states, along with the axis of evil states of Iran and North Korea, are held to be particularly threatening because of their ability and willingness to harbor terrorists, develop weapons of mass destruction (WMD), and violate human rights. Moreover, weak or failed states adjacent to ungoverned areas in the global South—parts of sub-Saharan Africa such as the Congo, for example—are highlighted as further areas of insecurity to the United States and the global economic order. As the National Security Strategy concluded in the opening section:

> Finally, the United States will use this moment of opportunity to extend the benefits of freedom across the globe. We will actively work to bring the hope of democracy, development, free markets, and free trade to every corner of the world. The events of September 11, 2001, taught us that weak states, like Afghanistan, can pose as great a danger to our national interests as strong states. Poverty does not make poor people into terrorists and murderers. Yet poverty, weak institutions, and corruption can make weak states vulnerable to terrorist networks and drug cartels within their borders. (National Security Strategy 2002)

Economic globalization and technology transfer has not only enabled this all-reaching threat of Islamic radicalism coupled with international terrorism to exist but also encouraged additional activities by nonstate and terrorist actors across the world. Rather than contain these pockets of terror, the United States committed itself to use military force along withe the active promotion of neoliberal forms of economic integration in order to neutralize potential threats.

International terror networks and nonstate actors have, therefore, played their part in strengthening the emergence of a national security state in the United States. If the Ford Falcon was the car of choice of Argentine regimes in the 1970s, then the Gulf Stream V Executive jet was the plane of choice for the George W. Bush administration because it has flown terror suspects all over the world in order to extract intelligence about potential threats (Danchev 2006). Such domestic legislation as the USA Patriot Act (2001) and the Enhanced U.S. Border Security and Visa Entry Reform Act (2002) greatly extended federal authority to survey and control the flow of information, money, and people inside and outside the United States. Passed in the immediate aftermath of September 11, such legislation paved the way for national security considerations to prevail, with associated concerns expressed over border controls, territorial integrity, internal surveillance, and sovereign rights. As President Bush reflected with regard to the USA Patriot Act in April 2004 in conversation at Kleinshans Music Hall in Buffalo, New York:

> The point is, is that—what he's telling you is, is that we needed to share this information throughout our government, which we couldn't do before. And it just doesn't make any sense. We got people working hard

overseas that are collecting information to better help us protect ourselves. And what 9/11 was, is that—said—is that a threat overseas now must be taken seriously here at home. It's one thing to protect our embassies, and we work hard to do so. But now a threat overseas could end up being a threat to the homeland. And in order to protect the homeland, these good people have got to be able to share information.

Those who criticize the Patriot Act must listen to those folks on the front line of defending America. The Patriot Act defends our liberty, is what it does, under the Constitution of the United States. (Available online at http://www.whitehouse.gov/news/releases/2004/04/20040420-2.html [accessed 20th June 2007].)

The remapping of global geopolitics has continued with some gusto following the publication of the 2002 National Security Strategy of the United States. In his 2002 State of the Union address, President Bush noted, "States like these, and their terrorist allies, constitute an axis of evil, arming to threaten the peace of the world." Iraq, Iran, and North Korea were identified as particularly odious on the basis of human rights abuses, development of WMD, and threatening behavior. In a return to the binary logic of the Cold War, the American leader also made clear that other governments faced a stark choice: "You are either with us, or you are with the terrorists." As with the all-encompassing threat posed by the Soviet Union and global communism, international terrorism, and Islamic radicalism were deemed to occupy a similar interpretative space. Critically, however, it is believed that these nonstate organizations will use the interconnected global economic and political order to their advantage and, unlike such Cold War foes as the Soviet Union, will not need to deploy conventional armed forces. Cold War strategy is thus moribund.

The consequences of the American-led War on Terror on understandings of sovereignty and the international system have been considerable. Two areas need to be briefly highlighted here: America's challenge to the role of the UN and American global strategy.

First, the status of international law and the role of the United Nations have been challenged by recent American strategic pronouncements. The Anglo-American invasion of Iraq in March 2003 was condemned by many observers as illegal and predicated on the false premise that Iraq's possession of WMD posed an immediate danger to the United States and regional neighbors. While the American overthrow of the Taliban regime in Afghanistan was widely conceived as just and largely proportionate, the question of Iraq was somewhat different. Having been initially justified on the basis of disarming the Iraqi regime, the failure to find WMD led to a shift in Anglo-American security discourse in favor of the invasion as motivated by humanitarian concerns in light of the long-term brutality of Saddam Hussein. While the subsequent occupation of Iraq has not delivered stability, U.S.-led military operations in Iraq and Afghanistan are now being recast as part of a broader project to promote both countries as democratic and stable.

Second, the 2003 invasion of Iraq has been interpreted by critical scholars as only one element in an imperial project designed to secure American political-economic hegemony. The widespread deployment of American forces coupled with a renewed interest in other regions judged to be strategically significant and resource rich have also been implicated in this global strategy. In sub-Saharan Africa, Nigeria and other oil-exporting states are deemed to be important because of their contribution to broadening American energy supplies. In contrast, less significant are such regions as West Africa, judged to be disease prone, vulnerable to Islamic extremism, and poorly connected to the prevailing neoliberal economic order. Such policy initiatives as the 2005 Trans-Saharan Counter-Terrorism Initiative and the 2004 Millennium Challenge Account are part of an American process that explicitly ties the national security of the United States to broader regional and even global agendas surrounding governance, development, health, and globalization.

As the populist strategist Thomas Barnett (2003, 2004) warned in his much-cited *Esquire* article "The Pentagon's New Map" and subsequent book:

> Show me where globalization is thick with network connectivity, financial transactions, liberal media flows, and collective security, and I will show you regions featuring stable governments, rising standards of living, and more deaths by suicide than murder. These parts of the world I call the Functioning Core, or Core. But show me where globalization is thinning or just plain absent, and I will show you regions plagued by politically repressive regimes, widespread poverty and disease, routine mass murder, and—most important—the chronic conflicts that incubate the next generation of global terrorists. These parts of the world I call the Non-Integrating Gap, or Gap. (See http://www.thomaspmbarnett.com/published/pentagonsnewmap.htm [accessed June 24, 2007].)

Yet such critical geopolitical scholars as Dalby (2007) and Sparke (2005) have noted that the extension of neoliberal forms of globalization has operated hand-in-hand with the Bush administration's national security strategies post-9/11. Barnett's populist arguments further support the promotion of economic globalization and associated interdependencies as an obligatory precondition for America's longer-term national security. The 2006 National Security Strategy of the United States makes its goals clear:

> The first pillar is promoting freedom, justice, and human dignity – working to end tyranny, to promote effective democracies, and to extend prosperity through free and fair trade and wise development policies. Free governments are accountable to their people, govern their territory effectively, and pursue economic and political policies that benefit their citizens. Free governments do not oppress their people or attack other free nations. Peace and international stability are most reliably built on a foundation of freedom. (Available at http://www.whitehouse.gov/nsc/nss/2006/intro.html [accessed June 26, 2007].)

As many critics have noted, however, whether the contemporary Bush administration is best placed to comment and reflect on these apparent necessities must indeed be something of a moot point.

CONCLUSIONS

According to Mark Duffield, "International danger now equates with the unsecured circulatory flows and networked connections associated with the social, economic and political life of global population. Geopolitics, the security of states, and bio-politics, the security of population, are not mutually exclusive; they are complementary, interdependent and work together to lesser or greater degrees" (2005, 143). Whereas for the United States this approach may appear a novel departure from some of the associated geopolitical patterns established during the Cold War, the national security strategies of 1970s Latin America were adept at combining an interest in territory, economic stability, and the regulation of national population. Within the confines of national territory, Argentine and other Southern Cone citizens were monitored, surveyed, classified, all in the name of national security and development. In the name of national security, it appears that the same thing is now happening to citizens in the United States, the United Kingdom, Australia, and elsewhere.

However, in the context of the United States and the post–September 11 era, the interconnection between the geopolitical and the biopolitical have become all the more apparent such as terms as "security" are invoked both to justify internal order and to legitimate truly global operations, including the War on Terror, poverty reduction, energy security, good governance, and debt cancellation. Again as Duffield (2005, 157) opined, "In this respect, it is part of a wider security mentality that is interconnecting the policing of international migration, the strengthening of homeland social cohesion and the development of fragile states … Escaping this architecture involves seeking a new formula for living in the world with others; a formula that focuses beyond the divisive bio-evolutionary categories of development to acknowledge a world of competing truths and rights to existence." In more general terms, the terms used to defend the current American-led War on Terror—such terms as "freedom," "globalization," and "civilization"—seem remarkably insensitive to the way in which people, regions, and flows are not only interrelated with one another but also disconnected from such recent events as the Cold War.

In the post–September 11 epoch, the connections made by the Bush administration between neoliberal globalization and military security have implications for other possible understandings of the contemporary condition. While attention is devoted toward so-called weak states, nonstate organizations, and even entire regions of the global South, the reemergence of the traditional security agenda insures that such other challenges as global climate change, environmental degradation, and criminal activities are either shaped by the securitizing practices of the state and or marginalized, as in the case of the Bush administration's early rejection of the Kyoto Protocol, in 2001, and such global institutions as the International Criminal Court. Critical geopolitical writers face the challenge not only to assess the contemporary geographical framings of national governments and their associated militaries but also to explore further the resulting implications by imagining alternative human futures (Dalby 2007). Given the potential impact of global climate change, for instance, these debates are by no means of purely academic interest. A new U.S. president in January,

2009, may help to re-position American strategy away from previously unilateral tendencies towards a more multi-national and global outlook.

FURTHER READING

Agnew, J. *Hegemony*. Philadelphia: Temple University Press, 2005.
Dodds, K. *Geopolitics: A Very Short Introduction*. Oxford: Oxford University Press, 2007.
Grygiel, J. *Great Powers and Geopolitical Change*. Baltimore: Johns Hopkins University Press, 2006.
O Tuathail, G. *Critical Geopolitics*. London: Routledge, 1996.
O Tuathail G., S. Dalby, and P. Routledge, eds. *The Geopolitics Reader*. London: Routledge, 2006.

REFERENCES

Agnew, J. 2003. *Geopolitics* London: Routledge.
———. 2005. *Hegemony* Philadelphia: Temple University Press.
Amoore, L. 2007. Vigilant visualities: The watchful politics of the War on Terror. *Security Dialogue* 38: 215–32.
Barber, B. 1996. *Jihad vs. McWorld*. New York: Times Books.
Barnett, T. 2003. The Pentagon's new map. *Esquire Magazine,* March, 1–10.
———. 2004. *The Pentagon's new map.* New York: Putnam's.
Chung, C-P. 2002. China's war on terror: September 11th and Uighur separatism. *Foreign Affairs* 81. Available online at http://www.foreignaffairs.org/20020701facomment8515/chien-peng-chung/china-s-war-on-terror-september-11-and-uighur-separatism.html.
Cox, M. 2004. Empire, imperialism and the Bush Doctrine. *Review of International Studies* 30: 585–608.
———. 2007. The empire's back in town: Or America's imperial temptation—again. *Millennium* 32: 1–27.
Cox, R. 1981. Social forces, states and world orders. *Millennium* 10: 126–55.
Dalby, S. 1990. *Creating the second Cold War.* London: Frances Pinter.
———. 1997. Contesting a contested concept. In *Critical Security Studies,* ed. K. Krause and M. Williams, 1–37. London: UCL Press.
———. 2006. The Pentagon's new imperial cartography: Tabloid realism and the war on terror. In *Violent Geographies,* ed. D. Gregory and A. Pred. London: Routledge, 295–308.
———. 2007. Anthropocene geopolitics: Globalisation, empire, environment and critique *Geography Compass* 1: 103–18.
Danchev, A. 2006 Accomplicity: Britain, torture and terror. *British Journal of Politics and International Relations* 8: 587–601.
Debrix, F. 2007. Tabloid imperialism: American geopolitical anxieties and the War on Terror. *Geography Compass*. http://www.blackwell.comapss.com/Doi:10.111/j.1749-8198.2007.00042.x (online early articles, May 27, 2007).

Dodds, K. 2007. *Geopolitics: A very short introduction.* Oxford: Oxford University Press.
Dodds, K., and D. Atkinson, eds. 2000. *Geopolitical traditions.* London: Routledge.
Duffield, M. 2005. Getting savages to fight barbarians: Development, security and the colonial present. *Conflict, Security and Development* 5: 141–59.
Enloe, C. 1989. *Bananas, beaches and bases.* Berkeley: University of California Press.
Friedman T. 1999. *The Lexus and the olive tree* New York: Anchor.
Fukuyama F. 1989. The end of history. *National Interest* 16: 1–8.
Gray, C. 1977. *The geopolitics of the nuclear era.* New York: Crane and Russak.
Hartshorne, R. 1954. Political geography. In *American geography,* ed. P. James and C. Jones. Syracuse, NY: Syracuse University Press, 167–225.
Hepple, L. 1986. The revival of geopolitics. *Political Geography Quarterly Supplement* 5: 21–36.
———. 1992. Metaphor, geopolitical discourse and the military in South America. In *Writing worlds,* ed. T. Barnes and J. Duncan, 136–54. London: Routledge.
Huntington S. 1993. The clash of civilizations? *Foreign Affairs* 72: 22–50.
———. 1996. *The clash of civilizations and the remaking of world order.* New York: Global Vision.
Johnson C. 2000. *Blowback.* New York: Times Warner.
Kagan, R. 2002. Power and weakness. *Policy Review* 113. Available online at http://www.hoover.org/publications/policyreview/3460246.html.
Kaplan, R. 1994. The coming anarchy. *Atlantic Monthly* 273: 1–8.
Kellner, D. 2003. *From September 11th to terror war.* Lanham, MD: Rowman and Littlefield.
Kissinger, H. 1979. *The White House years* London: Weidenfeld and Nicolson.
Krause, K., and M. Williams, eds. *Critical security studies.* London: UCL Press.
Lacoste, Y. 1973. An illustration of geographical warfare: Bombing of the dikes on the Red River, North Vietnam. *Antipode* 5: 1–13.
Luttwak, E. 1993. From geopolitics to geo-economics. *National Interest* 20: 17–23.
Mackinder, H. 1904. The geographical pivot of history. *Geographical Journal* 23: 421–42.
———. 1919. *Democratic ideals and reality.* London: Constable.
National Security Strategy of the United States, 2002. Available online at http://www.whitehouse.gov/nsc/nssintro.html (accessed June 25, 2007).
O'Brien, R. 1992. *The end of geography.* London: Routledge.
O Tuathail, G. 1996. *Critical geopolitics.* London: Routledge.
O Tuathail, G., and J. Agnew. 1992. Geopolitics and discourse: Practical geopolitical reasoning and American foreign policy. *Political Geography* 11: 190–204.
Pinochet, A. 1968. *Geopolitica.* Santiago: Biblioteca del Oficial.
Pion-Berlin, D. 1989. Latin American national security doctrine: hard- and soft-line themes. *Armed Forces and Society* 15: 411–29.
Radcliffe, S., and S. Westwood. 1993. *Remaking the nation.* London: Routledge.
Sempa, F. 2002. *Geopolitics: From Cold War to 21st century.* London: Transaction.

Sparke, M. 2005. *In Space of Theory*. Minneapolis: University of Minnesota Press.

Steger, M. 2005. *Globalisation: A very short introduction*. Oxford: Oxford University Press.

Taylor, P. 1983. The question of theory in political geography. In *Pluralism and political geography*, ed. N. Kliot and S. Waterman, 117–32. Beckenham, UK: Croom Helm.

Von Chrismar, J. 1968. *Geopolitica*. Santiago: Biblioteca del Oficial.

Wallerstein, I. 2004. Soft mulitlateralism. *The Nation* (February 2): 14–20.

8

Global Ethics and Human Security

Des Gasper

A FRAMEWORK FOR GLOBALIZATION OF ETHICAL THINKING

Global or world ethics is the study of ethical claims made on human beings—individually or in groups, not only grouped as states—in their relations with individuals and groups (again, not only states) throughout the world, in the standard definition by Nigel Dower (1998). The topics within global ethics include whether individuals and states have any morally justified obligations across national boundaries other than obligations they have already explicitly agreed to. The obligations under discussion include those that are or would be embedded within rules and institutions.

Thomas Pogge's influential work uses terms differently to make a particular claim within global ethics as defined by Dower. For Pogge, following John Rawls, the term "ethics" refers to assessment of actions by agents, whether individuals or organizations, including states, whereas the term "justice" refers to assessment of social rules and institutional structures. Rawls considered such issues of justice only for within states. For him and other social contract theorists, like Thomas Hobbes, people ensure security by accepting the authority of a power center, a contract enforcer, which in their view could only be the nation-state. That assumption is now partly obsolete. Pogge uses the term "global justice," in order to distance himself from Rawls's nationalism and to assert that the globe should be seen as an arena for justice, not an arena where each agent is justified to seek only its own interest or where we assess agents' individual actions (as, for example, in many discussions in business ethics) but take as given whatever structures exist (like the legal and institutional setup within which businesses operate). We should normatively assess the rules and structures that govern the world economy and world society. While I will not adopt Pogge's terms, we should recognize and acknowledge this global justice agenda that he and others investigate (e.g., in Follesdal and Pogge, 2005). It represents one type of cosmopolitanism. As in any form of cosmopolitanism, the whole world is taken as the ethical universe, the space in which we have to ethically locate and justify ourselves.

Prior to entry into any of the detailed debates in global ethics comes a series of interrelated choices about how we see ourselves and the world. First, how far do we see shared interests between people, thanks to a perception of causal interdependence, so that appeals to self-interest are also appeals to mutual interest. Second, how far do we value other people's interests, so that appeals to sympathy can be influential because of interconnections in emotion. Third, how far do we see ourselves and others fundamentally as members of a common humanity, or as members of a national or other limited social community—with, for example, an ethnic, religious, ideological, or economic basis of identity—or as pure individuals; in other words, what is our primary self-identification—as interconnected beings or as separate individuals. This prior set of perspectives determines our response to proposed reasoning about ethics and justice.

A human security perspective is likely to reflect, and generate, particular sorts of stance on these issues. Adoption of a human security perspective may influence, even reconfigure, how we see ourselves and others and our interconnectedness, and it may thereby reconfigure how we think about both ethics and security. According to its advocates, such a framework can contribute to ethical globalization: to globalization of ethical thinking and to doing globalization ethically.

The framework has been emergent for at least a generation in various versions and under various names, for example, in 1970s conflict and peace research and on basic human needs work by such figures as Kenneth Boulding, John Burton, and Johan Galtung and in the 1980s work of the Brandt Commission, the Palme Commission, and the South American Peace Commission. In the 1990s, it became prominent under the "human security" name, especially through the *Human Development Report 1994* (UNDP 1994).

Terms like "human security" try to catch the attention of an audience, and also to catch the user's own attention; in other words, they aim to stimulate and motivate. Having caught attention, they try to organize it: they link to a perspective, a direction for and way of looking. Having caught and organized attention, they aspire to influence or even to organize activity: they provide frames for work. Such terms, and the frameworks that they mark, very often seem, though, to come and then quickly go, to rise and fall in international usage. A few terms become established, but, in the process, they often change or lose much meaning. How important, persuasive, and durable is a so-called human security framework likely to be?

The idea and framework have been subject to much debate and dispute, and different versions compete. But significantly, they have spread into and within many areas of analysis and policy, including conflict, climate, migration, public health, socioeconomic security, and well-being. They seem to be fulfilling their roles to stimulate, to motivate, to organize attention and activity. The idea of human security has also spread more widely outside the UN system than has its elder sibling and partner, human development. Why? What is its significance for discussions of global ethics?

Consider a possible analogy. South Africa has long described itself as "a world in one country." Coming together in this land have been African, European, and Asian peoples, as well as people from much of the rest of the world. Responding to this diversity, the Europeans, in power nationally for most of the twentieth century, enforced division into racially defined groups, later further subdivided ad hoc into supposed national communities that were to relate to each other as politically separate nations. Of course, Europeans were not divided for political purposes into separate national groups (e.g., according to language background—Afrikaans, English, Portuguese, etc.), for this would have weakened their ability to control power. Although the Europeans had intermingled to a large degree, as had the African groups upon whom separation was enforced, long, bitter, and brutal attempts were made to separate Europeans from other groups, residentially, socially, and politically even while economic development and mass culture increasingly pulled them together. Eventually, the African National Congress (ANC) project for a politically unified South African people won against the apartheid system that had denied a shared political and ethical community. The post-apartheid order's ethic of unification is reflected in the central role given to human rights in South Africa's constitution, stronger than in any other country. The ANC's "one people" project won, not by military conquest, but in part by a conquest of ideas and feeling: an increased acceptance of sharing environments and predicaments and of shared humanity.

The world as a whole seems organized as a system of global apartheid—dramatically illustrated by the barriers and patrols that separate the United States from Mexico, or Spain from North Africa, and the daily attempts by thousands of people to evade those barriers and patrols to find employment in Northern economies hungry for services and workers. As the world pulls together through such migrations, societies can respond in diverse ways: by trying to enforce separations, as did the apartheid regime in South Africa, or by rethinking global systems to reflect a growing ideal and the reality of one world. Human security frameworks contribute to rethinking the meanings of such terms as "security," "we," "self," "interests," "self-interest," and "common interest." Evolution away from global apartheid will be extremely difficult, complex, contingent, and uncertain, even more than was the move away from apartheid in South Africa. Unlike in the South Africa case, as yet no big outside powers exert pressure on the insecure rich fearfully barricaded into their laager. Globalization often undermines psychological security. Yet, it also establishes bases for potential real human security by building interconnections that can give shared interests, richer identities, and mutual respect.

CHARACTERISTICS OF A HUMAN SECURITY PERSPECTIVE

Central in security matters are certain paradoxes. First, security forces can make people insecure and prey on them. State military security is not identical to human security. Second, steps to increase my security in isolation from that of other people will often fail. In a military context, the reduced vulnerability of one player can make all the others feel more under threat. In nonmilitary contexts too, we must remember that "no man is an island, entire of itself; every man is a piece of the continent, a part of the main" (from Meditation XVII by John Donne, 1573–1631). This principle of common security reflects a reality of pervasive interconnection. Psychologically, as well as in almost every other way, people are parts of bigger systems–indeed, of global systems. Self-engrossed nest building may not win the friendship and cooperation of other persons, who do not form an insentient environment but are sensitive and proud potential actors and reactors. In these two paradoxes, the posited means of security fail to achieve the ends because human systems are misunderstood.

A further paradox concerns the nature of the ends. Felt security correlates very weakly with more objective measures of security. The more the fearful barricade themselves, the more fearful they may feel. The more they have, the more they fear losing it, even if the risks they face are objectively far less than those faced by people less fortunate. We need to consider both felt security and objective security. A human security perspective does this, looking hard at the human meanings of security. We cannot talk sensibly about security without asking whose security; and we cannot think clearly about *human* security without reflecting on the nature of being human. We will see how this line of reflection links to a certain type of perspective on issues of global ethics.

Definitions of the Concept

Human security means, in a broad formulation, the security of human persons against important threats to their basic needs. It refers to the security of all people, not just the security of the security forces, or of the state, or of the rich. A second, but common narrow formulation refers only to the physical, bodily security of persons. More narrowly still, a third formulation refers to bodily security against intentional physical threats. Less narrow is a fourth view, Robert Picciotto's definition: security in terms of quantity of years lived (adjusted for life quality, as done in health planning, and with the normative benchmark of a normal human lifespan of, say, 70 years), against all threats to life, whether physical or not and intentional or not (see, e.g., Picciotto, Olonisakin, and Clarke 2007). Intermediate between the latter and the broad first formulation lies, fifthly, the widely used phrase "freedom from fear and freedom from want." (For a fuller examination of definitions, see Gasper 2005.)

This chapter largely refers to the broader formulations—the first, fourth, and fifth—because these have more implications for thinking about global ethics. Even the narrower formulations of human security are radical, though, in relation to traditional security studies thinking. The term "human" is inherently global in coverage and contains, for humans, a moral appeal. Combined with "human," the term "security" too makes a normative appeal, for priority; human security thus conveys a message about basic life quality and a claim for its priority in policy. Since overwhelmingly most victims of violent conflicts are now not members of armed forces, and since most violent conflicts are now not between states, security studies must look at the security of persons, not only at the security of national boundaries, as the International Commission on Intervention and State Sovereignty underlined (ICISS 2001).

The broad formulation we will mostly consider here, security against threats to fulfillment of basic human needs, closely corresponds to that introduced in the UNDP human development reports and followed up in many national human development reports (Jolly and BasuRay 2007). It does not go quite as far as the UN's advisory commission on human security as reported in their study *Human Security Now* (CHS 2003), which refers to threats against core values. The core values of apartheid South Africa were threatened by majority rule, but this was not a threat to human security as understood here. Even so, human security as a framework of analysis, not merely an isolated definition, encourages us to give close attention to the subjective insecurity of apartheid's proponents for purposes both of understanding and of constructive response.

A Human Security Perspective or Framework

Human security language conveys more than did the older language of basic human needs alone. Security language adds a number of important themes. One is the significance of stability in fulfilling basic needs and of avoiding certain types of loss. Second is a sense of danger, the danger of triggering fundamental damage when we lapse below certain thresholds; in other words, it is a sense of the limits to safety in pervasively interconnected systems that contain maximum tolerance levels beyond which ramifying harm can ensue. Third is the importance of attention to feelings and subjectivity as well as to objective life circumstances; losses can mean not only the loss of things but also the loss of major meanings and even identity.

Wendy Harcourt shows how these three issues impact on Nepal, and how they have affected women in particular. They form the backdrop to its long civil war, which was equally long forewarned (e.g., Blaikie, Cameron, and Seddon 1980): the combination and interaction of an oppressive social system, extremely limited economic opportunities, and intensifying environmental pressures contributed to the emergence of a Maoist insurgency, open armed conflict, and large-scale population displacement. These have harmed women, especially, through rape, robbery, and other forms of physical and psychic violation, which add to and exacerbate very high levels of domestic violence, trauma, and anger. Hurt is thus not only physical; there is damage to psyches, to trust, and to communities. The civil war led to revival of child marriage as an attempt to avoid the danger of abduction by the Maoists. Health services, which had already neglected mental health and women's reproductive health, deteriorated. (In a rather similar case, that of Afghanistan, the 2004 national human development report, which focused on human security, found self-reported mental health problems among 35 percent of women questioned.) Desperation and disruption have fueled large-scale human trafficking and prostitution (Harcourt 2004).

A human security perspective thus involves a system of ideas, not just a single definition. That system includes a focus on individual human persons and on stability in fulfillment of their basic needs. It further includes attention and emphasis on causal interconnections and tipping points, as well as to felt insecurities. For ease of reference, let us organize the aspects of the approach to human security found in the work led by UNDP and the Commission on Human Security, and much similar research, under the following headings, though in reality they interweave: first, strong attention to the contents of individual persons' lives and to provision of human depth in understanding of security; second, a synthesis of features from the normative languages of human needs, human rights, and human development; and third, a framework for situation-specific wide-ranging explanatory syntheses.

First, human security thinking directs us to look at ordinary people's daily lives and at the vulnerabilities, contingencies, and consequent possible sequences of disadvantage that can arise. The concentration on the contents and fluctuations of daily life, and on specific threats and misfortunes—including ill-health, disability, displacement, and death—gives a more intense, realistic awareness of the meanings of the term "human." We can call this a holistic perspective at the level of the individual. As in the work of John Burton (1990) and his basic needs school in conflict studies, we see how people seek security of various types, physical, economic, and psychological. Human security thinking has thus often a stronger concern with felt experience than has been found in some of the legal-led work on human rights and economics-led work on human development. It adds to them not just a supplementary interest in the stability of people's basic rights and capabilities but also a foundational concern with the priority capacities and vulnerabilities that form the grounds for basic rights.

Second, as in the other "human" languages—human needs, human rights, and human development—normative importance is given to all living as well as future persons; everyone matters. Using and advocating this human perspective means that we adopt "joined-up feeling"; that is, we give weight to others, not only to ourselves (Gasper and Truong 2005). Human security thinking adds to more individualistic human rights thinking an emphasis on the human species as a whole and its shared security, insecurity, and fragility.

Within the family of "human" languages, the human security language links the other three (Gasper 2005, 2007; see also Held 2004). The "security" label highlights basic priorities—that is, basic needs, seen as justifying human rights and expressed in the human development language of capabilities, or abilities to achieve, as part of a commitment to freedoms (Sen 1999). The stresses on shared fragility, basic requirements, and felt experience give a foundation for solidarity, for the joined-up feeling. By encouraging thinking deeply about individuals, all individuals, human rights language can thus be grounded in a way that helps to counter dangers that can otherwise arise in the use of rights language.

Third, human security thinking extends the holistic perspective of explanation from individual daily lives to social, national, and global systems. We saw this in Harcourt's review of the crisis in Nepal: how national- and local-level insecurities and conflicts affect and hurt individuals, and how individual level insecurities and conflicts contribute to local and national level pathologies. Also contributing to the national economic pressures and political conflicts are international economic structures and ideas: Maoism is one external model; and human trafficking, an international business, another. "Significant in this new endeavor [human security thinking] is the ability to comprehend and respond to threats to human life and dignity as outcomes of interplay between global forces and those forces embedded in national and local structures" (Truong 2005). For vividness we can call this joined-up thinking. It can reinforce joined-up feeling through a greater awareness of interconnection. Awareness of the actual, probable, or possible effects of one's actions on others might generate feelings of sympathy, even responsibility, whereas awareness of actual, probable, or possible boomerang effects on oneself can generate feelings of fear and precaution. Awareness of the impossibility of full knowledge in any one center of all the relevant factors and connections could bring a more consultative learning style in policy (Truong 2005).

Much ink has been spilled on whether to define human security in relation to a broad or narrow range of threats and possible types of damage. Once we enter a perspective of joined-up thinking, in which environmental insecurity, health insecurity, economic insecurity, military insecurity, psychological insecurity, and more, all sometimes strongly affect each other, the definitional dispute declines in significance. Broad attention to types of threat and damage does fit with a broad causal analysis, but even those users of a narrow physical violence definition of human security who adopt a transdisciplinary causal perspective will be led to engage with many other types of insecurity and harm, as well as with how people value and react to them.

Which connections are strong and considered most important in a particular case remains a matter for investigation and evaluation, case-by-case. Richard Jolly and Deepayar BasuRay show this from the different national human development reports that have taken human security as their theme. A human security perspective is a frame for work, differently elaborated each time, not an instruction to study the effect of everything on everything or a fixed blueprint of research design. In the language of the sociology of science, the type of work involved here is boundary work, and the effect of the perspective is to help us break from the fixed habits of the traditional scientific disciplines concerning which factors should be analyzed in relation to which others. Boundary work takes place at and across a boundary between such varied mental worlds as different disciplines, between different organizational cultures and bureaucratic empires like security forces and development departments, and between the worlds of research, on the one hand, and policy and politics, on the other.

Academic disciplines typically go deep by thinking in a sustained way about the interaction of a restricted number of factors; and they still use some of the forms of organization and socialization inherited from the religious traditions out of which the European university grew: exclusive affiliations and loyalties created through long induction of trainees at an impressionable stage of their lives. The disciplinary groups are marked by much mutual ignorance and suspicion; disciplines train disciples. The Gulbenkian Commission on the future of the social sciences warned that this existing organization of social science, which had taken shape in Europe in the nineteenth century as a series of distinct and disconnected disciplines, was shaped by a number of historical and political circumstances that in many ways no longer apply. In particular, each of the disciplines was molded by and within a nation-state framework, which is now to an important degree superseded (Wallerstein et al. 1995). We need types of boundary work for connecting the deep but often narrow and unbalanced disciplinary knowledges to each other and to everyday knowledge not captured within formal sciences, as required for many types of explanatory and policy task. Conceptual frameworks are required that can bridge the boundaries and can motivate as well as permit cooperation. Human security thinking may be one productive framework for doing this, including for thinking about global ethics. Let us examine how after first looking at a fuller case study.

Rwanda

Conduct of economic analysis and formulation of economic policy without reference to the social and physical effects, thanks to assumptions of social and natural environments able to comfortably absorb all external effects, are always dangerous. They can become calamitous as interconnections increase in strength and thresholds are crossed. Even affluent core societies will be profoundly shaken by, for example, climate change. Fragile dependent peripheral societies can spiral into disaster.

Rwanda provides a grim forewarning. Tensions grew within the country during the 1970s and 1980s, stemming from increasing population pressure, heavy reliance on unstable agricultural export markets, especially for coffee, loss of access to land by many people in a quickly commercializing society, and extreme and rising inequality (Ballet, Mahieu, and Radja 2007; Gasper 2007; Prunier 1997). A severe slump in the world coffee market in the late 1980s led to a massive fall in real national per capita income, estimated at around 40 percent. The IMF piled financial shock therapy on top of this in the early 1990s, seeking rapid reduction of the trade and public sector deficits. To mobilize or retain support, politicians increasingly emphasized ascribed ethnic affiliations, uncovering the wounds from earlier conflicts and the fears aroused by recent interethnic conflict in neighboring Burundi. Ethic confrontation escalated. Identities became simplified and reformed as the socioeconomic crisis became a political crisis. Some groups were "othered," identified as dangerous, evil, subhuman, alien. The international community, which had rigorously imposed financial discipline, ignored UN officials' warnings of imminent disaster in Rwanda and then long ignored and minimized reports of the genocide in which between 0.5 million and 1.0 million people—around 10 percent of the population—were massacred. But with modern media coverage and other means of communication, this genocide could not remain largely ignored, unlike some earlier ones.

The Rwanda disaster illustrates themes highlighted by human security thinking: the interconnection of economic issues, identity issues, and physical security; and the interconnections of countries linked through global markets, global tastes and trends, the arms trade, and global media. Like the Nepal crisis, the Rwanda disaster did not directly damage rich countries. Even so, the costs of the subsequent chaotic humanitarian relief efforts dwarfed what would have been the costs of timely preventive assistance (e.g., see Gasper 1999). A human security framework suggests, further, that the effects of such disintegration—the anger and recourse to violence, state collapse, drugs exports (as in Afghanistan or Colombia), disease, and traumatized refugees—do not stay for ever off-screen. They spread and can have impacts anywhere in the world.

Armed conflicts leave scars that lead to further violence. Violence violates people emotionally, not only bodily; it can undermine positive capabilities and build negative ones (Dubois and Trabelsi 2007). Potentially, though, the response to crises can include favorable reforming of identities, as we have seen in South Africa. But the requirements of building and sustaining a life in common are several: sufficient elements of shared identity, of accepted mutual responsibilities; and of common vision for the future, as well as corresponding life skills. Learning to live together is on UNESCO's agenda for education: included are understanding interdependence and gaining skills of cooperation and codetermination, skills that have, unfortunately, typically been ignored in secondary and tertiary education. Similar education is required for national and international decision makers too, not only for combatants or potential combatants. National decision makers in a country like Rwanda still face extreme pressures and constraints, and thus international decision makers have the obligation, as well as a prudential interest, to offer conflict-prone countries broad economic and educational support, rather than government-assisted export of arms and landmines (Gasper 2007).

HOW A HUMAN SECURITY PERSPECTIVE MIGHT RECONFIGURE DISCUSSION OF GLOBAL ETHICS

Issues in Global Ethics

A broad conception of human security opens up questions about global justice, that is, the justice of the basic global institutional structure. In the present IMF structure, for example, insufficiently informed and unaccountable decision makers and main stakeholders can sometimes enforce disastrous courses of action on weak clients. We noted already that before engaging in detailed debate about ethics in global relations we must consider a number of perspective issues: How far do we see shared interests between people, thanks to a perception of causal two-way interdependence? How far do we value other people's interests? How do we identify self and other, and what is our primary self-identification, as interconnected or separate beings? Unless there is significant globalization of thought on at least one of these dimensions, detailed debates about global ethics will get little audience. Nobody will be paying attention. Human security thinking might influence each of those fundamental perspectives.

Appeals to Self-interest and Mutual Interest

Human security thinking brings, as noted, a transdisciplinary approach to tracing interconnections across conventional intellectual divisions and across the world. In terms of connections across nations, we saw the paradox of military security—namely, that states that pursue security solely by self-strengthening are unlikely to achieve it, for they make others insecure. Similar logics apply in other important arenas. Human interaction in general involves feedback, since the players are intelligent, proud, and resourceful. Rich countries are unlikely, then, to obtain security by building Fortress America, Fortress Europe, or Fortress Japan, all largely sealed behind barriers not only to migration from poor countries but to much of the agricultural produce, textiles and labor-intensive manufactures those countries could readily and advantageously supply. Poor countries, struggling and vulnerable in a disequalizing global system, with policy dictated to them from underinformed metropolitan centers, with rising expectations promoted through global marketing, and with their best-trained workers attracted and even deliberately recruited by rich countries, will not sleep quietly in their poverty. They are at risk of violent conflict; they will turn to profits from other forms of trade, including trade in drugs and people; and they will emit streams of migrants, some of whom fall into the hands of the traders in people but who will thereby often find their way into the rich countries.

Two further types of logic require emphasis: the logic of global public goods (Kaul, Grunberg, and Stern 1999), and the special case of the logic of global public health. In public health affairs, each person, the rich included, lacks health security if each has sanitized his or her own private space but the neighbors' yards and public spaces remain unsanitized. Not only must people travel through the public spaces and even sometimes visit their neighbors, but the carriers of health threats respect no paper boundaries. They are nonexcludable "bads." Further, such nonmedical factors as peace, food, and clean water often have more influence on health threats and their impact than do medical services. Assuring one's own health requires assuring decent life conditions for one's neighbors, not undermining them by the indirect effects of one's other actions. Health impact assessments of alternative international trading arrangements and other international nonhealth policies are now recognized as central for global public health (special issue of *Bulletin of the World Health Organization* 2007).

Consider health impact more broadly. Certain major "bads," as perceived by the intake country, that emanate from one's neighbors, other countries, can largely not be kept out: pollution, weapons, people, drugs, diseases, and criminal networks may not be restrained. There cannot be security in one country alone, just as there as cannot be health in one house alone. In nineteenth-century Europe and North America, the middle classes in the new industrial cities gradually decided their fate was indissolubly connected to the industrial working classes with respect to public health and other public goods such as physical security. The alternatives of seeking security through enclave systems for the well-off or through physically distancing the poor, as attempted in apartheid South Africa, would be neither feasible nor effective. It seems to remain an open issue in South Asia, for example, whether the growing middle classes there will make a similar such calculation or instead seek to establish secure enclaves (Wood and Newton 2005). Globally, the issue certainly remains open: will rich nations and rich groups conclude that they cannot sustain health and security in one part of town alone?

In some respects, the human security perspective is a generalization of the public health perspective in which disease anywhere and the conditions that breed disease form a threat everywhere. A human security policy approach can perhaps be called global civic health. In the case of climate change, though, powerful groups in some rich countries have until lately calculated that global warming would bring them no net harm, and it might even result in net benefits, since agricultural growing seasons, for example, would extend (e.g., Nordhaus). Problems for other countries were their problems alone. It is now evident that global warming will bring, not modest marginal variations in climate, but massive system-breaking impacts within countries and, when more fragile countries disintegrate, across countries. Fortunately, in one sense, the past generation of inaction on climate change has meant there is now much less room for debate. The delay and the acceleration of deterioration mean that even if only for the benefit of people presently alive, it is imperative to stabilize and reduce greenhouse gas emissions regardless of whichever ethical theory one subscribes to, according to the Climate Ethics group at Pennsylvania State University (www.climateethics.org). Arguments about the claims of future generations are no longer critical; they simply add to the necessity for structural adjustment in the high-emissions countries.

Appeals to Sympathy and the Evolution of Identity

Public goods provision cannot, however, be merely a matter of calculation of self-interest. Even though provision is to the benefit of all participants, as compared to its absence, free-riding by self-interested participants can destroy a system. Ironically, people's self-interest can be reliably promoted only if individuals think in a way other than direct self-interest. The growth and maintenance of civic facilities in Europe, while requiring compatibility with middle classes' perceived overall interests, also rested on a growth of civic spirit and feelings of wider solidarity, perhaps partly supplied by the growth of nationalism. Similar points apply now for global security: only shared norms, institutions, and regulatory activities can bring security.

Energy for moving toward and sustaining norms of solidarity comes especially from looking at real cases that evoke understanding of shared humanity, awareness of human fragility, and feelings of unfairness. Sympathy is fostered by cases highlighting the personal, the individual, the imaginable, and the tangible, which touches. K. Schaffer and S. Smith (2004) argue that the enormous growth in the use and authority of human rights language over the last 60 years has come less through the work of lawyers and philosophers than through the reporting worldwide of real cases. Its sister, the human security perspective, shares this intense attention to individuals, often in a particularly vivid and realistic way because it focuses on priority requirements of physical security, food security, physical and mental health, and community membership. The stress on these human specifics provides a conceptualization of what is indeed common in our common humanity. A human security perspective thus adds or strengthens attention to humanity as a whole, the human species, a community of fate that shares a fragile life support system—the perception brought home to humankind since the 1968 *Apollo 8* flight by looking back at the terrestrial globe from the moon. In summary to an awareness of and respect for individuals it adds an understanding of *human* individuals, the category of human *species*, humankind, and sensitivity to the specifics of human need, vulnerability, and shared *insecurity*, wherein each affects all. Discussions in international relations contrast the human security concept to state security and stress security of individual persons. But a concern for other individuals and a concern for humankind rely on each other and need to go hand-in-hand.

A more intense awareness of others and of interconnectedness contributes to rethinking the identities of me, you, and us. A sustainable concern for others, and a sense of subjective security, may both depend on change in the perception of us. For feelings of sympathy to be more than fleeting, and to have influence against the lifestyle pressures built into consumer societies, the feelings need to generate something more—perhaps lifestyle change movements, political movements, and modified self-identifications, which in turn lead to modified institutions and systems that embody norms of sympathy and solidarity.

Given the dangers of free-riding, to an important degree cooperation to secure global public goods relies on the presence of a sense of common good: a sense of living in common and of mutual concern. To rely only on enlightened self-interest is dangerous because of the uncertainties in global-scale cause-effect chains. *Human Security Now*, the report of the Commission on Human Security, chaired by Sadako Ogata and Amartya Sen (CHS 2003), addressed how to promote a common global ethic and eloquently expressed the necessity of such elements as a sense of common good.

Appeals to Rational Comparison

A human security approach may add little directly to philosophical work on global ethics. It instead adds before and after such exercises. First, it influences the type of vision—the attitudes, scope of consideration, and range of evidence—brought into ethical discussion. It changes the data used in reasoning on mutual advantage and sharing of costs; it can affect the habitual framing, the conception of we, and the other attitudinal starting blocks that instrumental reason is required to serve; and it affects the attention to risk and uncertainty.

Second, it influences the concrete agenda of policy alternatives and comparisons and value weightings in policy design and evaluation. Some writers argue that a broad human security discourse makes prioritization too difficult and thus diverts us from real priorities, typically military (e.g., MacFarlane and Khong 2006). Human security analysis shows in practice an intense and creative concentration on matters of prioritization. The Millennium Development Goals are one area of expression of a human security agenda and include prioritization of areas and especially within areas. Breadth is shown in the range of areas covered, but priority goes, not to securing a whole issue area per se, but to ensuring basic levels of achievement in each such area.

Human security analysis also enters the lion's den of comparisons between policy areas, engaging in textbook logic that clashes with political logic, namely, the power and convenience of established interests that do not wish to have existing allocations queried (Lodgaard 2000). A broad-scope human security concept encourages fundamental comparisons: can we better promote security through more military spending or, for example, through democracy education or women's education, given that mothers educate everyone else? Looking back in the 1970s at his previous decade as U.S. secretary of defense, Robert MacNamara concluded that the United States had reached a level of military capability wherein further military expenditure would do nothing to increase the country's security but could even undermine it, and where far better security returns could be obtained from nonsecurity expenditures. Smallpox, for example, was eradicated in the late 1960s and 1970s at a cost equal to that of three fighter-bombers: $300 million. What, we must ask, would be the impact on achieved human life-years of diverting military spending to spending on health issues, bearing in mind the possible impacts of economic adjustments on political conflict and health conditions? Just as, for example, gender-budgeting frameworks require us to routinely thoroughly examine the implications for women of budgetary allocations and tax arrangements, so a human security perspective helps to institutionalize habits of reasoned comparison, of looking at evidence and of debating, rather than bowing automatically to established power.

Some commentators fear that human security language subordinates human development concerns to conventional thinking on military security. In reality human security analysis is a reaction to such a danger, not its cause. In addition to its key concerns with matters of environment, public health, and financial and economic instability, it encourages us to ask, in a sustained fashion, whose security is in question, and what really increases security? Human security analyses have argued in detail that major reductions of military expenditures can often increase security by redirecting efforts to building democratic peace (e.g., Haq 1999). Let us consider one such effort, the Human Security Network, led by Canada and Norway, which has organized to reduce parts of the international arms trade.

The Human Security Network mainly follows a narrower version of the approach, centered on the impacts of physical conflict on persons. We might call it a human safety perspective. The vivid narrow focus has led to successful campaigns and concrete action in important areas: the anti-landmines campaign, the International Criminal Court, and the small arms trade. It deals with the immediate causes and immediate damage from violent conflict, but not with underlying causes and long-run damage. This matches the short-run convenience of powerful interest groups in rich countries, who do not want evaluation of the global basic institutional structure they have established, dominated, and gained from. They prefer to avoid analyses that may indicate required reforms and new responsibilities. Failure to look at deeper system interconnections means that fleeting pangs of sympathy will not be converted into the required institutions to embody norms of solidarity and enlightened self-interest.

Along with campaigns like the Human Security Network's, we need attention to the longer-term agenda. The bigger long-term gains for humankind's security will come through a broader version of the perspective and through rethinking of frameworks and self-perceptions. The longer-term agenda involves studying underlying causes and acting on the demonstrated vastly greater cost-effectiveness of prevention rather than first aid. The narrower and broader versions of human security work can, however, be partners; they need not be treated as competitors.

Any language can be diversely used and misused. Some observers see human security language, together with human rights language, used to justify imperial interference in poor countries. Others see it used instead to justify disengagement from a developing world perceived as generating threats to human security in rich countries. These criticisms concern human security language users who merely put a fashionable label on what they were going to do anyway and who ignore the central principles of interconnection and feedback effects. The criticisms miss the heart of the issue. The relevant comparison to use in evaluation is not against perfection but against what would happen otherwise. In the case of human rights language too, one can see much lip-service and even misuse, but also massive favorable impacts, achieved despite massive resistance. The human rights perspective has been variously dismissed as theoretically ungrounded, financially unaffordable, Eurocentric, individualistic, the path to socialism or the shield of the bourgeoisie, and the Trojan horse for Great Power intervention. Yet it contains powerful and inspiring insights as well as a potential for refinement, adaptation, and deepening. The same applies for the human security perspective; further, it adds to and compensates for limitations in human rights thinking in several ways.

CONCLUSIONS: WHAT A HUMAN SECURITY PERSPECTIVE ADDS

Just a few years after the arrival of majority rule in South Africa, the preceding era of apartheid—an era of a security-obsessed minority regime that spent enormous sums on security that in reality reduced security for everyone, even the privileged—looked, in retrospect, like a bizarre nightmare to nearly all those concerned. After 50 years of moving against the trend symbolized by the 1948 Universal Declaration of Human Rights and trying to seal themselves into a morally isolated realm of white European privilege, the apartheid regime lacked sufficient self-belief to continue in its direction and concluded its constituency's interests were better reconceived and pursued along another path. In the same way we now look back at other past attempts to separate races, castes, slaves, and free men and women as if they were different species. Will humankind be able to look back similarly, after a generation, 50 years, a century, or more, at a transition from the fundamentally unequal and unbalanced world order in which we presently live?

Will future humankind be able also to look back at a transition from the extraordinarily wasteful, thoughtless, unsustainable style of resource use now present in rich countries, with its presumption that Mother Earth will tidy up after them? How such a transition could happen is examined in the Great Transition project that originated in the Stockholm Environment Institute (Raskin et al. 2002; Raskin 2006). The project identifies three required value shifts if we are to move to social and environmental sustainability: first, from a preoccupation with the acquisition and consumption of commodities to a broader and deeper picture of what gives quality of life; second, from an overwhelming individualism to a human solidarity based on respect for individuals; and third, from an attitude of mastery and domination of nature to an attitude of stewardship for Mother Earth.

Any transition needs a language or languages of transition that make vivid and meaningful what is at stake, that unite and motivate groups committed to change, and that persuade enough of those groups who could otherwise block change. Given the existing language and global ethic of human rights and that of human development as the expansion of human freedoms, what does a human security perspective add? If we look at the value shifts identified as necessary by the Great Transition work (see also Kates et al. 2006), we see that human rights language and the idea of development as freedom, though important, are not sufficient. By themselves they are too potentially individualistic and compatible with visions of self-fulfillment through unlimited consumption and exploitation of nature. The emphases required—on human solidarity, stability, and prioritization; on prudence and enlightened self-interest; on sources of richer quality of life, felt security, and fulfillment; and on ecological interconnection that demands careful stewardship—are more fully present in human security thinking. A human security perspective helps to appropriately ground the human rights and human development approaches in attention to the nature of being and well-being, and to appropriately focus them on priorities. It conveys interdependence more than does human rights language; it adds a synthesizing approach in explanation and diagnosis; it alerts us to a realization of dangers, vulnerability, and fragility; and it connects strongly to human subjectivity, which increases its explanatory force and motivating potential.

FURTHER READING

Commission on Human Security (CHS). *Human Security Now*. New York: Commission on Human Security, 2003. http://www.humansecurity-chs.org/finalreport/index.html.

Gasper, D. "Human Rights, Human Needs, Human Development, Human Security: Relationships between Four International 'Human' Discourses." *Forum for Development Studies* (Norwegian Institute of International Affairs), 2007: 1, 9–43. Available online at http://biblio.iss.nl/opac/uploads/wp/wp445.pdf.

Held, D. *Global Covenant*. Cambridge: Polity Press, 2004.

Kaul, I., I. Grunberg, and M. Stern, eds. *Global Public Goods*. New York: Oxford University Press, 1999.

Raskin, P., T. Banuri, G. Gallopin, P. Gutman, A. Kammind, R. Kates, and R. Swart. *Great Transition*. 2002. http://www.tellus.org/Publications/Great_Transitions.pdf.

Nussbaum, M. *Frontiers of Justice*. Cambridge, MA: Harvard University Press, 2006.

REFERENCES

Ballet, J., F-R. Mahieu, and K. Radja. 2007. Destabilising identity structures: The impacts of domestic and international policy in the 1994 Rwanda genocide. *International Journal of Social Economics* 34: 37–52.

Blaikie, P., J. Cameron, and D. Seddon. 1980. *Nepal in crisis*. Oxford: Clarendon.
Burton, J. W. 1990. *Conflict: Basic human needs*. New York: St. Martin's Press.
Commission on Human Security (CHS). 2003. *Human security now*. New York: Commission on Human Security. http://www.humansecurity-chs.org/finalreport/index.html.
Dower, N. 1998. *World ethics: The new agenda*. Edinburgh: Edinburgh University Press.
Dubois, J-L., and M. Trabelsi. 2007. Education in pre- and post-conflict situations: Relating capability and life-skill approaches. *International Journal of Social Economics* 34: 53–65.
Follesdal, A., and T. Pogge, eds. 2005. *Real world justice*. Dordrecht, Neth.: Springer.
Gasper, D. 1999. Drawing a line: Ethical and political strategies in complex emergency assistance. *European Journal of Development Research* 11: 87–115.
———. 2005. Securing humanity. *Journal of Human Development* 6: 221–45.
———. 2007. Goods and persons, reasons and responsibilities. *International Journal of Social Economics* 34: 6–18.
Gasper, D., and T-D. Truong. 2005. Deepening development ethics: From economism to human development to human security. *European Journal of Development Research* 17: 372–84.
Harcourt, W. 2004. Women, human security and well-being in South Asia. Paper presented at the conference of the Human Development and Capability Association, University of Pavia, September.
Held, D. 2004. *Global covenant*. Cambridge, UK: Polity Press.
ICISS. 2001. *The responsibility to protect*. http://www.iciss.ca.
Jolly, R., and D. BasuRay. 2007. Human security: National perspectives and global agendas. *Journal of International Development* 19: 457–72.
Kates, Robert, A. Leiserowitz, and T. M. Parris. 2006. *Great transition values: Present attitudes, future changes*. Great Transition Initiative. http://www.gtinitiative.org/documents/PDFFINALS/9Values.pdf.
Kaul, I., I. Grunberg, and M. Stern, eds. 1999. *Global public goods*. New York: Oxford University Press.
Lodgaard, S. 2000. Human security: Concept and operationalization. Paper for the UN University for Peace. http://www.upeace.org/documents/resources%5Creport_lodgaard.doc.
MacFarlane, N., and Khong Y-F. 2006. *Human security and the UN: A critical history*. Bloomington: University of Indiana Press.
Nordhaus, W. 1994. *Managing the global commons*. Cambridge, MA: MIT Press.
Picciotto, R., F. Olonisakin, and M. Clarke. 2007. *Global development and human security*. New York: Transaction Publishers.
Prunier, G. 1997. *The Rwanda crisis: History of a genocide*. 2nd ed. London: Hurst & Co.
Raskin, P. 2006. World lines: Pathways, pivots and the global future. Great Transition Initiative. http://www.gtinitiative.org/.
Raskin, P., T. Banuri, G. Gallopin, P. Gutman, A. Kammind, R. Kates, and R. Swart. 2002. *Great Transition*. http://www.tellus.org/Publications/Great_Transitions.pdf.

Schaffer, K., and S. Smith. 2004. *Human rights and narrated lives: The ethics of recognition.* London: Palgrave.
Sen, A. K. 1999. *Development as freedom.* New York: Oxford University Press.
Truong, T-D. 2005. Human security and human rights. In *The essentials of human rights*, ed. R. Smith and C. van den Anker, 172–75. London: Hodder Arnold.
UN Development Programme (UNDP). 1994. *Human Development Report 1994.* New York: Human Development Report Office, UNDP.
———. 2005. Security with a human face. *Afghanistan Human Development Report 2004.* Kabul: UNDP. http://www.cphd.af/nhdr/nhdr04/nhdr04.html.
Wallerstein, I., et al. 1995. *Open the social sciences: Report of the Gulbenkian Commission on the Restructuring of the Social Sciences.* Stanford, CA: Stanford University Press.
Wood, G., and J. Newton. 2005. From welfare to well-being regimes. http://siteresources.worldbank.org/INTRANETSOCIALDEVELOPMENT/Resources/fromwelfaretowellbeing.pdf.

9

Human Rights

Chiara Certomà

Human rights are a set of rights considered as innate and natural rights of every human being purely because he or she is human. Their provision has been traditionally regarded by the international regime as pertaining to nation-states, so violation and remediation are interpreted as a matter between the state and its citizens. However, globalization challenges this regime. The global world is characterized by a time-space compression producing a growing internationalization and an increasing instability. The defense of such categories as citizenship, closed places, and coherent cultural community is now difficult to sustain. Cosmopolitan systems, even if they constitute a means to pursue individual freedom and rights and increase the flow of information and the economic opportunities for a large number of people, at the same time either represent a source of new threats or do not change at all the repression and conditions of violence people are suffering. Together with the flow of goods in the international market, an uncountable flow of migrants presents new the possibilities of new violations that are not amenable to state-based human rights regimes but do call for a revision of conventional political categories and new forms of control. Such transnational social movement networks and unelected global institutions as the World Bank and the peacekeeper and environmental organizations have a stronger control over the life of citizens than weak state institutions. At the same time, they have the potential to address human rights challenges, especially by increasing consciousness. Together with the institutional forms of humanitarian intervention and transnational legal accountability, promoting universal norms, and enforcement of state power, new forms of advocacy and control have been organized by local and global group for rights violation monitoring (Brysk 2002). Nevertheless, the access to justice is unevenly distributed, and long-standing state repression and rights violations assume new forms and require more complicate mechanism of redress. Along with the fulfilment of old rights, the need to define and protect new rights emerges from the integration of markets, shrinking states, new powerful global actors, and increasing material and nonmaterial flows. Such is the case for environmental rights and the right to development, to peace, to solidarity, and to bioethics. Lots of them do not yet represent a well-defined right to be protected, but they do represent a claim for new needs that, through the language of rights, seek international acknowledgment and guarantees. To better understand the relationship between the human rights regime and globalization, it is necessary to understand where the idea of human rights comes from and what kind of theoretical bases sustain it.

The modern conception of human rights is rooted in the seventeenth-century Western contractualist and natural law theory and represents the base of modern constitutional charts. Three processes accompanied the evolution of human rights. The first process pertains to the codification and inclusion of such rights in the national constitutions (legal protection under domestic jurisdiction); the second process implies the extension of such rights to all citizens of every single nation (universalization of rights provisions); the third process consists in considering the particular instances deriving from the concrete application of such rights to diverse classes of subjects (rights multiplication or specification).

Inclusion in the modern constitutional charts is indeed the first concrete guarantee of human rights, even though the philosophical debate on what is to be considered fundamental and natural for human beings has a long tradition and some very ancient documents are often presented as the very first human rights declarations. The universalization process started during the twentieth century when the Universal Declaration of Human Rights (UDHR) was adopted by the General Assembly of the United Nations. Rights in this declaration are described as *universal* because every human being is entitled to them, and *inalienable* because one cannot be other than human. They seek to realize a particular and nowadays often contested conception of human nature, dignity, and well-being and to consider every human being, not as bearers of defined social rules, but as inherently valuable per se. Everybody is entitled to equal respect from the state and to the opportunity of freely making fundamental choices about what he or she considers a good life (Donnelly 2002).

Beyond abstract principles and theoretical assumptions, however, the widespread fulfillment of human rights has proven to be much more difficult. Many states systematically violate them not only in the poorest areas of the world but also in the richest areas. The concrete implementation of human rights in our globalized world is highly problematic, and their philosophical justification is highly contested.

ORIGIN OF THE HUMAN RIGHTS CONCEPT

Several ancient documents have been considered relevant in the evolution of human rights. Among such documents are the cylinder of citizens' rights by Cyrus of Babylon (539 BC); the principles of civil rights by Ashoka in India (third century BC); the Magna *Charta Libertatum* (1215), issued in England during the reign of John Lackland; the *Manden Chart* (1222), issued in Mali by Emperor Sundjata Keita; the writ of *Habeas corpus* (1305), issued under the reign of Edward I in England. (The *Habeas Corpus Wit* has been codified in the *Habeas Corpus Act* in 1679.)

However, the conception of human rights as currently referred to derives from the modern consideration of the individual as elaborated by natural law and contractualist philosophies in the seventeenth-century Europe. They provide a bourgeois answer to the political power of aristocracy, under the influx of the rising free market capitalism. In this period, Thomas Hobbes's philosophy of individualism and social contract constituted an important source of inspiration for the constitution of modern Western states (1991). Hobbes affirms that human beings exist free in the state of nature and are able to determine their actions in conditions of equality. In the original state of nature, however, their individualistic behavior produces a permanent and generalized war. The only way to escape this is through the constitution of society that emerges from the free subscription of a contract between citizens and political authority. This "social contract" allows the transfer of natural rights from the single individual to the ruler. As a consequence, natural law in Hobbes's theory derives its validity only by the state authority legitimization. At the same time, English philosopher John Locke (1988) presented a natural rights theory according to which every man has a natural right to life, liberty, and estates deriving from the divine will and not limited by any cultural, ethnic, or religious belongingness. Locke's theory, despite the apparent universality is exclusively concerned with the protection of European males' property rights. Locke's natural state, contrary to Hobbes's, is not an *amoral* but a *premoral* state where people are conducted in good practices according to the natural law, directly emanating from God. This is the basis of morality that commands that others' life, health, liberty, or possessions should not be harmed. Ideals such as natural rights, moral autonomy, and human dignity provided a normative background for the constitution of modern political systems. The concept of rights becomes the vehicle for effective political claims. The principal purpose of the investiture of political authority in a sovereign state is the protection of an individual's basic natural rights.

Natural law philosophers deeply influenced the making of modern constitutions and supported the revolt against absolutism at the beginning of the modern age. The U.S. Declaration of Independence (1776) states that "all men are created equal, that they are endowed by their Creator with certain unalienable rights, that among these are life, liberty and the pursuit of happiness" (Library of Congress 2008). In the same spirit a few years later and with a deep acknowledgment of the first, the Declaration of the Rights of Men and of the Citizen (HRCR 2008) was adopted by the National Constituent Assembly during the French Revolution. It states in the first article that "men are born and remain free and equal in rights. Social distinctions can be founded only on the common utility" (HRCR 2008, art. 1). Equality before the law, the rights of property, security, and rejection of oppression are guaranteed, as well as the presumption of innocence and the freedom of speech and press. No rights are specifically granted to women, and neither is the abolition of slavery mentioned. One of the main inspirations for the National Constituent Assembly was the Swiss philosopher Jean-Jacques Rousseau (1987). He explained how the state derives from a voluntary claim to the unlimited individual's freedom enjoyed in a natural state. Every single member of the society decides to submit himself to the authority of a general will, an assembly that everybody is part of. This represents a guarantee to preserving himself and his freedom.

Even if natural law theory is the doctrine most closely associated with the modern concept of human rights, another important source is juridical positivism, which emphasizes the normative power of the political community in the definition of rights (Shestack 2002). As against natural law theory, juridical positivism states that all authority derives from what the state and the officials have prescribed. Thus, it poses a great emphasis on national sovereignty and hardly accepts any influence above the state. The philosopher Jeremy Bentham argued that there cannot be something like human rights existing prior to or independently from legal codification (1843). Moral rights are, in a strict sense, not rights but moral claims that may or may not be assimilated in national or international law. The only rights that can legitimately be said to exist are legal rights derived from a legal system. According to positivism, human rights may be considered moral rights that have been codified in juridical declarations and thus recognized as legitimate and authoritative.

THE UNIVERSAL DECLARATION OF HUMAN RIGHTS

Even if many cultures throughout history shared and declared such values as brotherhood, compassion, and respect for the other human beings, the conception of these values as truly universal and the effort to realize them without any discrimination was absent, and differences of sex, birth, occupation, and language always maintained a crucial role.

The first Universal Declaration of Human Rights that referred to every single human being without distinction was adopted on December 10, 1948, by the UN General Assembly (1948b). After the experience of the World War II and the Holocaust, traditional international law was interpreted as being too weak to protect citizens from being massacred by their own state. There was a genuine belief that the United Nation should become the international protector of individual rights. The first action undertaken to face the legacy of the war was the institution of the Nuremberg War Crimes Tribunal, in 1945, charged with judging Nazi officials for the crime of genocide, considered a gross violation of human rights. Such violations as genocide, torture, death squad murders, involuntary disappearances, abductions, slavery, mass rape, and ethnic cleansing demand humanitarian intervention, as later made explicit by the UN General Assembly in its *Convention on the Prevention and Punishment of the Crime of Genocide* (1948a, Res. 60 A[3]).

The Charter of the United Nations came into force on October 24, 1945, explicitly reaffirming faith in human rights and providing the normative basis for their protection. With the adoption of the UN Charter, the idea of human rights protection exceeding national borders and the idea of single human beings as the subject of rights that governments have the duty to guarantee revolutionized the international law domain. Whereas traditional international law had mainly been concerned with relations between states, now with the UN Charter and later UDHR it would protect individuals, who would be entitled to special consideration wherever their rights are violated. In viewing the creation of well-being and stable conditions for peaceful and friendly relations among nations, the UN Charter calls for the "respect for Human Rights and fundamental freedom for all without distinctions as to race, sex, language or religion" (UN General Assembly 1945, art. 1[3]).

The UDHR proclaimed in 1948 was adopted as a nonbinding resolution in the "recognition of the inherent dignity and of the equal and inalienable rights of all the members of the human family" (UN General Assembly 1948b, preamble), defined as free and equal, and endowed with reason and conscience. The Declaration is presented as a "common understanding" not only for all nations but also for all people, after the "barbarous acts which have outraged the conscience of mankind" (UN General Assembly 1948b, preamble).

In the meantime it became clear that despite the moral authority of the UDHR in international law, the document's nonbinding status constituted a point of weakness. To convert it into a binding instrument, it was necessary to overcome the resistances of a large number of states concerned about possible international interference in their domestic affair should the UDHR have a binding status. A long debate on the elaboration of a binding instrument and the transformation of UDHR into hard law led to the adoption of two covenants: the International Covenant on Civil and Political Rights, or ICCPR (UN General Assembly 1966a); and the International Covenant on Economic, Social and Cultural Rights, or ICESCR (UN General Assembly 1966b). The UN General Assembly adopted both covenants. To the covenants were then added two optional protocols. The first, the Optional Protocol to the International Covenant on Civil and Political Rights, allows individuals to submit complaints directly to the ad hoc Human Rights Committee (UN General Assembly 1966a, Res. 2200 A[21]). The Second Optional Protocol to the International Covenant on Civil and Political Rights, aiming at the abolition of the death penalty, was adopted later (UN General Assembly 1989, Res. 44/128).

The necessity for two separate covenants was motivated by an active debate on some fundamental issues: the relationship between the individual and the society and the state, the role of member states' sovereignty, the link between rights and responsibilities, but mostly the Cold War between the United States and the Soviet-bloc countries. While the United States frequently used the language of freedom and democracy in public speeches, the Soviets accused them of human rights violations like colonialism, racism, and unemployment (Donnelly 1982b). This conflict determined the separation of human rights into two blocs: civil and political rights, as preferred by the Western bloc; and economic, social, and cultural rights, as preferred by the Eastern bloc. The U.S.-Soviet antagonism was partly responsible for the long-lasting block on the implementation of an effective mechanism of human rights protection.

The following period saw much consolidation in universal and regional treaty-based institutions for the protection of human rights. In 1978, the American Convention on Human Rights entered into force. The European Convention for the Protection of Human Rights and Fundamental Freedoms entered into force in 1953 (Council of Europe 1950) and was empowered in the 1970s through implementation by the European Court of Human Right. The ratification of the African Charter of Humans and Peoples' Rights occurred in 1986 (OAU 1981). (The African Charter is the only regional instrument to include so-called solidarity rights. To date, Asian states have not developed such a binding regional treaty for the protection of human rights.)

The end of the colonial era saw the entry to the UN of newly independent states of Africa and Asia, which tended to view internal violation of human rights as an aftereffect of colonialism. Their first initiatives led to the 1965 International Convention on the Elimination of All Forms of Racial Discrimination (UN General Assembly 1965). At the same time, several related institutions contributed to the emergence of nongovernmental human rights organizations. Significantly, in 1977 one such organization, Amnesty International, won the Nobel Price for Peace. The post–Cold War period was characterized by an increasing number of multilateral procedures, a great emphasis in international response to politicide and genocide (Burundi in 1972; East Pakistan in 1971; Cambodia in 1975–1979) and on peace-keeping operations (Namibia in 1989; El Salvador in 1991; Mozambique in 1992; Bosnia in 2002). It became clear that some countries have serious difficulties in protecting their citizens from the violations committed by powerful groups in their own territory. This has been interpreted by the international community as a reason to introduce new organizations to offer protection and to restore justice after the crimes (Donnelly 1982b). Examples of such internationally sanctioned bodies are the 1993 International Tribunal for the Former Yugoslavia (UN Security Council 1993) and the 1994 International Tribunal for Rwanda (UN Security Council 1994), both with jurisdiction for crimes against humanity, genocide, and war crimes.

UCHR, ICCPR, ICESCR AND VULNERABLE GROUP'S RIGHTS

The UN Declaration of Human Rights is composed of 30 articles in which all the rights considered fundamental for human beings are stated and the basic principles are in international law considered *jus cogens*. The document was compared with a Greek temple by Rene Cassin, one of its main drafters (Micheline 2004, 359). According to Cassin, the foundations are constituted by the declaration's preamble, in which human rights are defined as the common standard of achievement. Articles 1 and 2 declare that all human beings are born (that is, "by nature are") free and equal. They represent the base of the temple. Articles 3 to 11 define individual freedoms; they are the first column of the temple. The second column is represented by articles 12 to 17, where the rights of single human beings in respect of the community are described. The third column is composed of articles 18 to 21, in which the freedom of thought and association is stated. The last column is represented by articles 22 to 27, which declare economic, social, and cultural rights. Articles 28 to 30 define general dispositions for rights implementation and are symbolically associated with the pediment of the temple.

The UDHR is characterized by a state-centric approach that appeared with the liberal social contract theory in which the state is seen as an instrument for the protection, implementation, and effective realization of natural rights (Donnelly 1982a, 303). As a consequence, human rights are explicitly concerned with the prevention of state wrongs and also require the state to provide certain goods, services, and opportunities. This distinction defines negative and positive rights. Negative rights ask the state to refrain from certain harmful actions (such as from discrimination) (UN General Assembly 1966a, art. 2). These are mainly associated with civil and political rights, currently defined as "first-generation rights," which derive from the constitution of modern states and realize individual autonomy.

Positive rights are usually associated with "second-generation rights" and consist in actively creating the conditions for the enjoyment of the rights (such as the right to education) (UN General Assembly 1966b, art. 13). These are economic, social, and cultural rights that need the state's active intervention to guarantee substantial equality. The separation of human rights into two different bodies is the consequence of a widespread legal tradition to establish a hierarchy that places civil rights at the top. Such a strategy, however, often masks the simple fact that a common standard of rights cannot derive from the general development of human rights as a whole. The Vienna Declaration states that "all Human Rights are universal, indivisible and interdependent and interrelated" (UN World Conference 1993, art. 1[5]). However, second-generation rights, mainly for the poorest countries, are interpreted as subject to progressive implementation when an immediate fulfillment is not possible. The distinction is questionable, though, because some negative rights may appear positive in creating the condition to properly exercise them. This argument is proposed by several countries of the global South, who argue that without the enjoyment of an adequate standard of life—which means satisfying basic needs as stated in the ICESCR—any right to vote or participate in elections as proclaimed in ICCPR is meaningless.

The ICCPR's control mechanism consists of the examination of periodical reports all states send to the UN Human Rights Committee (UN General Assembly 1966a, art. 25–40), which has the power to comment on their efforts to reach the covenant's defined standards. Moreover, states may agree that the committee examine the complaints put forward by other states. In the case where the committee has ratified the first optional protocol, it will also accept individual complaints for violation of every right stated in the covenant, such complaints being receivable only after all internal jurisdictional procedures have been attempted. In contrast, the ICESCR control mechanism consists only in the periodical transmission of reports to the Committee on Economic Social and Cultural Rights (UN General Assembly 1966b, art. 17) provided by the individual states.

Political and civil rights are based on the rationalistic doctrine of natural law and are the expression of two different concepts of freedom.[1] One is the ancient democratic concept of collective freedom derived from active participation in political life; the other is the modern liberal concept of individual freedom derived by the protection of a private sphere against public interference. Thus, such political rights as the right to vote, the right to take part in government, and the right to equal access to public services are the individualistic expression of democratic values, whereas civil rights are the expression of liberal values. Some political freedoms can be considered democratic and liberal at the same time and constitute a link between political rights and such civil rights as the right to expression and the freedom of media, arts, assembly, and association. Civil rights range from the protection of the individual's physical, spiritual, legal, and economic existence—that is, rights to life, physical integrity, privacy, dignity, freedom of thought, conscience, religion and opinion, and recognition as a person before the law—to such classical notions of liberty as freedom of movement and expression, as well as freedom from slavery, and to such procedural safeguards as fair trial and the rule of law. With the exception of only a few rights, such as torture, considered as *jus cogens*, states can restrict the exercise of rights in the interest of public safety, public order, and moral or national security if such limitations are provided by domestic law and are proportional, reasonable, and nonarbitrary (Nowak 2002).

Economic, social, and cultural rights refer to specific conditions of life—for example, an adequate standard of life, food, housing, care, work and working conditions, health, education, and social security—that require different measures to become effective. States are requested to take "the measures likely to contribute to the effective progressive implementation" (UN General Assembly 1966b, art. 23). Unlike the ICCPR, the ICESCR includes rights that imply a collective dimension and are therefore not amenable to becoming individual rights. Especially such cultural rights as cultural identity, participation in cultural life, education, information, enjoyment of scientific progress, and cultural heritage are rights to which human beings are entitled "in community with the other members of their groups" (UN General Assembly 1966b, art. 27). The relevance of the collective dimension is evident in vulnerable group rights. In 1992, the UN General Assembly adopted a resolution that formulates states' obligation to protect the existence and the identity of minorities within their respective territories. States have largely adopted the rhetoric of one people, one state, but contemporary society's growing heterogeneity calls for special consideration of the different ties of identity between several cultures living on the same territory. Minorities distinguish themselves from the rest of society by such characteristics as language, religion, ethnicity, and culture. The Declaration on the Rights of Person Belonging to National or Ethnic, Religious and Linguistic Minorities states that "states shall take measures to create favorable conditions to enable person belonging to minorities to express their characteristic and to develop their culture, language, religion, tradition and custom, except where specific practices are in violation of national law and contrary to international standards" (UN General Assembly 1992, art. 4).

For a long time, indigenous people were regarded as a minority group, but today most governments tend to agree that they represent a distinct category in international human rights regimes. They demand legal equality as individuals but exercise their identity as groups; thus, they claim self-determination and self-government. In June 2006, the Human Rights Council, which replaced the Commission on Human Rights from 2006 onward (see UN General Assembly 2006, Res. 60/251), adopted the Declaration on the Rights of Indigenous People to promote harmonious relations and mutual respect between indigenous peoples and States (UN General Assembly 2006).

Another important issue concerns the struggle against the discrimination toward women. In the UDHR the term "gender" mostly denotes discrimination on the grounds of sex that can victimize both men and women, whereas gender discrimination in real life currently deprives women of recognition and the exercise of their rights. This is made quite evident by the large number of reservations in many countries, even in the Western world, that have presented covenants dealing with women's issues. In the early 1990s, the UN promoted several conferences, including the Fourth Conference on Women in Beijing in 1995, to increase the awareness of women's rights under international conventions and national law. The conferences especially championed such women's rights as women having control over their own bodies; it addressed the conditions faced by migrant and refugee women and women in war situations, and it declared the need to further support women belonging to minority groups. The Convention on the Elimination of All Forms of Discrimination against Women too often remained, de facto, unattended (UN General Assembly 1979).

A further group has been considered as deserving special protection: the children. Adopted by the UN General Assembly in 1989, the Convention on the Rights of the Child considers childhood as the most sensitive part of the life of every individual. The convention addresses the specific rights of children in difficult circumstances: for example, children separated from their parents; abused and neglected children; adopted children; refugee, disabled, or exploited children; and children in armed conflict. The cardinal concept is the recognition of the child as an active subject of right, rather than as property of the family.

GLOBALIZATION AND HUMAN RIGHTS

From a human rights perspective, the process of globalization leads us to the consideration of migrant workers as a new subject for human rights; to such new possible threats as nonstate violations; and to such new interpretations of human rights as the statement of Asian values, affecting the very base of the human rights foundation. International initiatives document constant and increasing attention toward changing world issues, with the ad hoc creation of commissions and declarations. The 1999 UN Human Development Report declares that globalization is "shrinking space, shrinking time and disappearing borders" and "linking people's lives more deeply, more intensely, more immediately than ever before" (1). In the resolution Globalization and Its Impact on the Full Enjoyment of All Human Rights, the UN General Assembly recognized" that globalization affects all countries differently and makes them more susceptible to external developments, positive as well as negative, including in the field of Human Rights, ... that globalization is not merely an economic process, but also has social, political, environmental, cultural and legal dimensions which have an impact on the full enjoyment of all Human Rights" (UN 2000, preamble). Such elements as structural adjustment, effects of high foreign debt, inequitable income distribution, misguided visions of development, lack of political will, environmental degradation, and armed conflict may affect the realization of Human Rights. The new global society is seen as a society at risk of human rights violation resulting from the rise of authoritarian government, civil wars, strong ethnic cleavages, weakening of civil society, power vacuums, and military dominances. In newly democratized countries with weak institutions, the growth of the global market tends to destabilize the political institutions and to increase crime and corruption. The weakening of the central state through globalization processes implies the strengthening of other actors operating at the international level, particularly in the economic sector. There is no reason that corporations could not be considered duty-bearers of obligation correlative to human rights. They are private entities over which individual citizens lack even the limited control provided by electoral participation (Donnelly 1982b).

Globalization can be a threat for human rights regimes, but it is also a powerful tool to spread the idea of human rights even if contested, reinterpreted, or questioned. The rising force of global civil society can be particularly effective in controlling and denouncing the crimes of transnational actors and nation-states (Brysk 2000). Notwithstanding globalization's very important material effect on people's daily lives, the theoretical challenges affecting the classic definition of human rights can be considered the core problem of the global world, where a plurality of voices emerge, together with a plurality of needs and beliefs.

THIRD- AND FOURTH-GENERATION RIGHTS

A "third generation" of rights has been defined as including rights not directly stated in the UDHR. They are defined as solidarity rights and include the right to self-determination, the right to development, the right to life in an unpolluted environment, and the right to peace or to humanitarian help in the case of catastrophes. Such rights are mainly related to the community. A further generation of rights, the fourth, has been proposed to answer the risks deriving from technological development. Such rights include the right not to be controlled in daily life without permission and the right to genetic integrity.

Anyway, the definitions of the third and fourth generations of rights remain unclear. Furthermore, such rights are difficult to implement. They are often claimed by the mediation of NGOs and civil society forums but represent a contested terrain. Following Norberto Bobbio (1996), it may be better to be careful in formulating new rights because the third-generation rights—such rights relating to the environment, peace, and genetic property—are still too unspecific and heterogeneous to constitute a rule of law. On the contrary, they can be considered a claim for limiting the concentration of power in order to protect social freedoms. They represent ideals, aspirations, and wishes for a future regulation of behaviors deemed incorrect.

The case for environmental right is an interesting example. Considering environmental claims as a rights matter might lead to several technical problems. Someone argues that mobilizing existing rights is sufficient to foster an environmentally friendly political and social order (Boyle and Anderson 1996). Others argue that at least a reinterpretation of existing rights would be necessary, particularly, the right to life, to equal opportunities, to health, and the like (Sachs 2003). Yet others assert that new rights to protect the environment should be elaborated *ex novo*, and they wonder if this new right should be a procedural right (concerning information, participation, legal redress, etc.) or a substantive right (defining what should be interpreted as environmental quality) (Hayward 2005).

One of the rights claimed as third-generation rights is the right to development, affirmed in the UN's 1986 Declaration on the Right to Development as "an alienable human right by virtue of which every human person and all people are entitled to participate in, contribute to, and enjoy economic, social, cultural and political development" (art. 1). Furthermore, the declaration makes clear, "States shall take resolute steps to eliminate the massive and flagrant violations of the Human Rights of peoples and human beings affected by situations such as those resulting from apartheid, all forms of racism and racial discrimination, colonialism, foreign domination and occupation, aggression, foreign interference and threats against national sovereignty, national unity and territorial integrity, threats of war and refusal to recognize the fundamental right of peoples to self-determination" (UN General Assembly 1986, art. 5). The declaration can thus be interpreted as an explicit condemnation of the violence affecting the security of people and national sovereignty.

An example of fourth-generation rights concerning new biotechnologies is provided in UNESCO's 2005 Universal Declaration on Bioethics and Human Rights. The declaration states that "ethical issues raised by the rapid advances in science and their technological applications should be examined with due respect to the dignity of the human person" but at the same time it recognizes that when biotechnologies are "based on the freedom of science and research, scientific and technological developments have been, and can be, of great benefit to humankind" (UNESCO 2005, preamble). Thus, the declaration tends to balance the interest of science with the welfare of the individuals by arguing that the scientific research "should only be carried out with the prior, free, express and informed consent of the person concerned" (UNESCO 2005, art. 6).

UNIVERSALISM VERSUS RELATIVISM

Despite the huge debate on the definition of new generations of rights, the main theoretical issue raised by globalization concerns the debate around the true universality of human rights. Even if binding only for the states that explicitly accepted the declarations through ratification or accession, UDHR, ICCPR, and ICESCR provide a unified view of humanity. They have been created by referring to universal parameters of behavior, but countries are left free to adopt the arrangements they find most congenial (Cassese 1994). The text asks for the respect of only certain minimal standards concerning relations between citizens and the state. Even if one adopts such a minimalist view of human rights, great differences and divergences still exist between the states. According to the universalist approach, human rights are universal and reflect the autonomous, individual nature of human beings. Immanuel Kant's philosophy provides a basis for arguing that a minimum absolute of any just and universal system of rights must include the recognition of the value of individual freedom and autonomy (1949). Kant argued for the universal community of rational individuals that autonomously determines the moral principles for securing equality of condition. The capacity of reason is the distinguishing characteristic of humanity and the basis for justifying human dignity. Personal integrity and the principle of nondiscrimination may be derived from the core values of fundamental freedom and autonomy. Thus human rights are based, not on religious belief, but on the moral autonomy of rational human beings. There are particular grounds upon which the right-holders can justify their claim. The liberal universalist view is one of these grounds, and it states that morality exists by virtue of our common, built-in humanity (Donnelly 1982a, 391). Therefore, human rights, even if applied to the individual members of particular communities, do not depend for their own existence on the communities' legal and moral practices. Irrespective of cultural difference, there is a certain unity among all peoples of the world based on the transcultural faculty of reason.

As against universalism, there is also the relativistic position. Relativists state that there is simply no such thing as a universally valid moral doctrine: the notion is merely a social and historical phenomenon. This relativism implies respect for differences and, in its more extreme form, produces an abstention from moral judgment. It does not reject the validity of human rights doctrine but only the claim that its validity has a foundation deeper than the cultural beliefs and values of human rights supporters. The principles used for judging behaviors are relative to the society—that is, they are culturally variable—and all cultures are morally equal. The philosopher Richard Rorty (1993), argues that our beliefs are no more than contingent preferences. He considers himself a liberal and affirms that the liberals, as creators of the human rights story, have the responsibility of nurturing and strengthening human rights. In addition, according to Rorty, the foundation for human rights resides not in human rationality but in the manipulation of sentiments based on the belief that our differences with others are less important than our shared capacity to experience pain and suffering. This implies that we can feel, or at least understand, the pain suffered by another human being. People who choose to conceive of and treat other people as if they were subhumans are not morally wrong, for this notion implies the existence of a universal human nature; such people have, however, been deprived of the condition in which to develop feelings of human solidarity. They thus have to be considered as deprived, not of truth or moral knowledge, as universalists think, but of security and sympathy. Security is the condition of life sufficiently risk free; sympathy is the possibility to immediately experience another human's feeling. Rorty argues that in the post-Enlightenment European culture, relatively secure and safe people have manipulated each other's sentiments for two centuries, whereas in other parts of the world such sentimental education has had no place. Thus, some people canot comprehend why membership in a biological species should be considered a sufficient basis for membership in a moral community. In their world, to let one's sense of moral community stretch beyond one's familiar relations would be too risky.

There is another path, one situated between moral relativism and universalism: it is the path of *minimum universalism,* which recognizes the fact of moral diversity but insists that there should be a universally valid body of values. Sheyla Behnabib (2004) calls that third path *dialogic universalism.* She proposes that when one moves beyond one's own culture, it is necessary to choose the values that amplify respect for others. Indeed, one should not tolerate anything that contradicts the tolerance principle itself. This view recognizes the relevance of the political dialogical dimension, the role of conversation with the other, and the openness toward different narratives. This position calls for a transcultural consensus and has been proposed by John Rawls (1999), who affirms that each person possesses an inviolability founded on the idea of justice. Rawls sees the liberal idea of justice as dealing with three fundamental elements: a list of certain basic rights and opportunities, a high priority for fundamental freedoms, and measures assuring for all citizens adequate all–purpose means to make effective use of their freedoms. In Rawls's theory, however, human rights are conceived as the rights of citizens rather than as the rights of human beings. His theory is elaborated based on the concept of a body of people forming a political society rather than on the human race forming a moral community. The problem with this approach is its ineffectiveness in categorizing such groups of citizens as migrant peoples or refugees in the globalized world.

INTERPRETATIONS OF HUMAN RIGHTS

Human rights are observed in distinct ways in different parts of the world, but they are also conceived in distinct ways. Western countries consider human rights as innate and individual, intrinsic to the quality of human life. Scandinavian countries, especially, affirm that the modern state should be a *glass house* so that everyone can look inside to establish that it conforms to international standards. There is no distinction, in this case, between accepting international obligations and implementing them at a national level. For socialist countries, rights existed only in a state community. For according to the Marxist view, rights exist only if they are guaranteed by the state, and their exercise is contingent on the fulfillment of obligations to society and state. Individual freedom can be realized only in a society without a capitalist class system, so everybody can fully participate in the life of the community. The Marxist concept goes back to Jean-Jacques Rousseau, who stated that the central power was an expression of the community, so freedom means creating the proper condition of integration between individuals and community. According to socialist countries, it is not for other states or the international community to inquire into the observance of human rights in another country because doing so would contravene a fundamental principle of international law, namely, the prohibition of interference in internal affairs. Consequently, the only acceptable international supervisory mechanism is a state's periodic reports, but no criticism or condemnations are accepted from the international community.

In the socialist countries and the global South, the causes of breaches of human rights are frequently attributed to underdevelopment and the lack of economic means. Such causes could explain the historical conditions that render compliance with human rights standards more difficult. The Western world charges that these arguments are often an excuse to justify serious departures from international standards. Ironically, given this charge, severe violations of human rights take place in Western countries that often look at themselves as defenders of justice and freedom. In the case of the U.S. prison in Guantanamo, for example, UN inspectors had difficulty in accessing the prison and several NGOs, Amnesty International among them, denounced worrisome breaches of every standard of human dignity.

The concern for human rights is interpreted in various ways in non-Western cultures, religions, and philosophies. Even if the differences are not always definitive obstacles to the pursuit of a common understanding, they represent s major challenge to globalization of human rights. In some African traditions, for instance, self-realization implies a deep involvement in the community, headed by a leader whose authority everybody must recognize. Today, the African Charter recognizes the social dimension of human beings and defines the rights of peoples as well as the specific rights of individuals (OAU 1981). In the Islamic tradition, numerous authors assert that human rights have an important place: Muslims are constantly engaged in reassuring each other over what Western parliaments call human rights (Islamic Council 1981). Liberal Muslims demand a courageous criticism of the Islamic Sharia, not by dismembering it but, rather, by revisiting its main sources, the Qur'an and the Sunna. They think that human rights can be connected with the spirit of the Sharia, but the main problem is that even liberal Muslims are reluctant to endorse secularist concepts lying at the very base of human rights because they often associate them with an antireligious ideology (Bielefeldt 2000, 90).

Asian countries declared themselves societies in which freedom consists in harmonizing as far as possible the individual's action with the leader's in duty and obedience (Donnelly, 1982a, 303). During the 1980s the prime minister of Singapore Lee Kuan Yew elaborated the concept of Asian values to criticize the individualistic approach to human rights by focusing on differences between Western and Eastern traditions. These are, according to Kwan Yew, based primarily on differences in the authority of traditional family and state and on the importance of collective actions in Asian cultures. Amartya Sen (1991) contests the position of Asian values because, he argues, there is no evidence that Asian values are any less supportive of freedom and more concerned with order and discipline than are Western values. The presentation of Asia as a single entity dominated by the Confucian culture is the product of an essentialist and Eurocentric perspective, as is the tendency of America and Europe to assume freedom and democracy as fundamental and ancient features of their own civilization only. Both traditions have had non-freedom-oriented and freedom-oriented perspectives. The dichotomy is only the sign of oversimplified generalization.

Charles Taylor (1996), a contemporary communitarian philosopher, has explored the conditions for a possible *overlapping consensus*.[2] He asks what kind of consensus we are talking about. Rights primacy is something related to Western culture. The legal tradition is Western, and Western peoples consider it the proper candidate for universalization of values, arguing that these can, however, be justified in more than one way, such that legal culture would define the norms around which every culture should build its own justification. This language of rights involves both a legal form of respect for immunities and liberties of the person and a philosophical understanding of the relationship between the individual and society. According to some voices in the non-Western tradition, the basic notion of the individual as possessor of rights, given the consequent, sometimes aggressive actions enabled by those rights, leads to a weakening of solidarity and an increase in social conflict. This interpretation finds an echo in the Western communitarian philosophy, which has likewise interpreted the danger of any form of individualism that undermines trust in a common allegiance as citizens of a state. According to Taylor, one of the main obstacles to mutual understanding derives from the unwillingness of some Western cultures to see themselves as one among many possible cultures. Overlapping consensus would fare better if every culture contributed on equal terms to the common dialogue, rather than if a unique right way were imposed to achieve human rights goals.

CONCLUSION

Globalization presents a dual challenge to human rights: the challenge is a theoretical one that presents an increasing debate between supporters of diverse interpretations; and it has a practical aspect, which refers to the concrete threats to human dignity. The huge debate on the universalistic character of human rights is far from being merely an academic exercise, for it represents the outcome of the opening of international political arena. Several voices from very different traditions advance alternative concepts of what a human being is and what elements constitute human dignity, that is, what is good and highly valuable in life. The attacks on the core of human right doctrine are at the same time a sign of vital public interests and an attempt to delegitimize the authority of the Universal Declaration of Human Rights. The attack is often moved in an instrumental way by non-Western countries, which consider the human rights regime a further form of Western hegemony in the moral, political, and juridical spheres. In order to obtain the public's consensus, maintain traditional powers, and preserve the state from international control, spiritual, religious, ideological, and historical reasons are often adduced, some of them really reflecting the feelings of non-Western cultures.

In the case of a noninstrumental claim to other values, the international debate is enriched with further suggestions, as in the case of indigenous people's rights or solidarity rights that emphasize the community's role and the collective will. At the opposite end of the spectrum, where contestation of human rights is used only instrumentally to protect elite privileges and despotic powers, the lack of international juridical accountability gives way to the empowerment of military groups, leads to internal disputes, and encourages violence. At the same time, global economic mechanisms often reduce weak states to exploiting territories under the control of transnational companies, which are not subject to any form of international public control.

From another perspective, the globalization of information and action makes it possible for many international campaigns, grassroots movements, and humanitarian organizations to directly intervene in critical situations and to raise forgotten cases to public knowledge. In the struggle for the fulfillment of old rights and the identification of new rights, human rights activists constantly face claims for state sovereignty, cultural autonomy, group rights, limitation of non-state powers, and guarantees of physical and psychological integrity in regard to new biotechnologies. Despite all the critiques and the concrete difficulties, the human rights regime remains the only actor able to face global challenges. Even if globalization requires a rethinking of the contents, the means, and the enforcement structure of the human rights regime, the current regime nonetheless remains the international community's only means of guaranteeing human dignity throughout the world.

NOTES

1. For a historical analysis, see Benjamin Constant, *The Liberty of Ancients Compared with That of Moderns* (1816).

2. According to the definition, provided by John Rawls, radically different groups, countries, and religions come to an agreement in order to govern human behavior even if they have different backgrounds to justify how they behave.

FURTHER READING

Bobbio, Norberto. *The Age of Rights*. Cambridge: Polity Press, 1996.
Brysk, Alison, ed. *Human Rights and Globalization*. Berkeley: University of California Press, 2002.
Cassese, Antonio. *Human Rights in a Changing World*. Oxford: Polity Press, 1994.
Mahoney, Jack. *The Challenge of Human Rights: Origin, Development, and Significance.* Malden, MA: Blackwell, 2007.
Parekh, Bhiku. *Rethinking Multiculturalism: Cultural Diversity and Political Theory.* Basingstoke, UK: Palgrave, 2000.

REFERENCES

Benhabib, Sheyla. 2004. *The rights of others: Aliens, residents, and citizens*. Cambridge: Cambridge University Press.
Bentham, Jeremy. 1843. Anarchical fallacies. In *The works of Jeremy Bentham*. Ed. John Bowring. Vol. 2. Edinburgh: Simpkin, Marshall & Co.
Bielefeldt, Heiner. 2000. "Western" versus "Islamic" human rights conceptions? A critique of cultural essentialism in the discussion of human rights. *Political Theory* 28: 90–121.
Bobbio, Norberto. 1996. *The age of rights*. Cambridge: Polity Press.
Boyle., Alan E., and Michael R. Anderson, eds. 1996. *Human rights approaches to environmental protection*. Oxford: Clarendon Paperbacks.
Brysk, Alison, ed. 2002. *Human rights and globalization.* Berkeley: University of California Press.
Cassese, Antonio. 1994. *Human rights in a changing world*. Oxford: Polity Press.

Council of Europe. 1950. *Convention for the Protection of Human Rights and Fundamental Freedoms.* November 4, 1950 (entry into force September 3, 1953).

Donnelly, Jack. 1982a. Human rights and human dignity: An analytic critique of non-Western conceptions of human rights. *American Political Science Review* 76: 303–16.

———. 1982b. Human rights as natural rights. *Human Rights Quarterly* 4: 391–405.

———. 2002. The social construction of international human rights. In *Human rights in global politics,* ed. Tim Dunne and Nicholas J. Wheeler, 71–102. Cambridge: Cambridge University Press.

Hayward, Tim. 2005. *Constitutional environmental rights.* Oxford: Oxford University Press.

Hobbes, Thomas. 1991. *Leviathan.* Ed. Richard Tuck. Cambridge: Cambridge University Press. (This edition orig. pub. 1961.)

Ishay, Micheline R. 2004. What are human rights? Six historical controversies. *Journal of Human Rights* 3: 359–71.

Islamic Council. 1981. *Universal Islamic Declaration of Human Rights,* 21 Dhul Qaidah 1401.

Kant, Immanuel. 1949. *Fundamental principles of the metaphysic of morals.* Indianapolis: Bobbs Merrill. (Orig. pub. 1785.)

Locke, John. 1988. *Two treatises on government.* Ed. Peter Laslett. Cambridge: Cambridge University Press. (Orig. pub. 1690.)

National Constituent Assembly. 1789. *Declaration of the Rights of Men and of the Citizen.* Available online at http://www.hrcr.org/docs/frenchdec.html (accessed May 1, 2008). (Orig. pub. 1789.)

Nowak, Manfred. 2002. Civil and political rights. In *Human rights: Concept and standards,* ed. Janusz Symonides, 69L107. Paris: UNESCO.

OAU. 1981. *African Charter on Human and Peoples' Rights.* Doc. CAB/LEG/67/3 rev. 5, 21 I.L.M. 58 (entry into force October 21, 1986).

Rawls, John. 1999. *The law of peoples.* Cambridge MA: Harvard University Press.

Rorty, Richard. 1993. Human rights, rationality, and sentimentality. In *On human rights: The Oxford Amnesty Lectures, 1993,* ed. Stephen Shute and Susan Hurley, 111–34. New York: Basic Books.

Rousseau, Jean-Jacques. 1987. *The social contract.* Ed. Maurice Cranston. Harmondsworth, Middlesex, UK: Penguin. (Orig. pub. 1762.)

Sachs, Wolfagang. 2003. Environment and human rights. In *Wuppertal Paper* 137. Wuppertal: Wuppertal Institute for Climate, Environment, Energy.

Second Continental Congress. 1776. *Declaration of Independence of United States of America.* Available online at http://www.loc.gov/rr/program/bib/ourdocs/DeclarInd.html (accessed May 1, 2008).

Sen, Amartya. 1991. Human rights and Asian values. *The New Republic,* July 14–21. Available online at http://www.mtholyoke.edu/acad/intrel/sen.htm.

Shestack, Jerome J. 2002. The philosophical foundation of human rights. In *Human rights: Concept and standards,* ed. Janusz Symonides, 31–67. Paris: UNESCO.

Taylor, Charles. 1996. Conditions of an unforced consensus on human rights. *Belgrade Circle Journal,* no. 3–4 (1995) and no. 1–2 (1996). Available online at http://www.usm.maine.edu/~bcj/issues/three/taylor.html.

UN Development Programme (UNDP). 1999. *Human development report.* New York: Oxford University Press.

UN Economic and Social Council. 2000 Globalization and its impact on the full enjoyment of human rights. E/CNN/Sub2/2000/13.

UN General Assembly. 1945. *Charter of the United Nations* (entry into force October 24, 1945).

———. 1948a. *Convention on the Prevention and Punishment of the Crime of Genocide.* Res. 60 A(3).

———. 1948b. *Universal Declaration of Human Rights.* Res. 217 A(3).

———. 1965. *International Convention on the Elimination of All Forms of Racial Discrimination.* Res. 2106(20) (entry into force 4 January 4, 1969).

———. 1966a. *International Covenant on Civil and Political Right.* Res. 2200 A(21) (entry into force March 23, 1976).

———. 1966b. *International Covenant on Economic, Social and Cultural Rights* Res. 2200 A(21) (entry into force January 3, 1976).

———. 1979. *Convention on the Elimination of All Forms of Discrimination against Women,* Res. 34/180 (entry into force September 3, 1981).

———. 1986. *Declaration on the Right to Development,* Res. 41/128.

———. 1989. *Convention on the Rights of the Child.* Res. 44/25 (entry into force September 2, 1990).

———. 1992. *Declaration on the Rights of Person Belonging to National or Ethnic, Religious and Linguistic Minorities.* Res. 47/135.

UN Human Rights Council. 2006. *Declaration on the Rights of Indigenous People,* Res. 2006/2.

UN Security Council. 1993. Res. 808.

———. 1994. Res. 955.

UN World Conference on Human Rights. 1993. *Vienna Declaration and Programme of Action.*

UNESCO. 2005. *Universal Declaration on Bioethics and Human Rights.*

10

Imperialism

Radhika Desai

IMPERIALISM IN THE TWENTY-FIRST CENTURY

The twenty-first century opened with the world's sole superpower fighting terrorism in Afghanistan and Iraq and threatening war against several other states in a new unilaterally aggressive and militarist mode. Only a decade before, having triumphed over communism, the United States had attempted a combination of multilateralism and commercialism, festooned with themes of human rights and democracy, in the discourse and practices of globalization. Although many had legitimately criticized globalization and its military interventions in the name of human rights and democracy as imperial, the brazen swagger of the new imperialism of the twenty-first century seemed a dramatic reversal. The tide of literature on globalization, which had risen so high so fast during the 1990s, now ebbed just as rapidly, and the waters of a new wave of writing on imperialism rushed in.

While critics of the new U.S. imperialism pointed to its contradictions, advocates enjoined imperialism on the United States as a historic duty,[1] often portraying it as characteristic, if not of human civilization, at least of its peaks. For such advocates, the United States was a New Rome (Ferguson 2004; Johnson 2004; Maier 2006) with "the classical architecture of its capital and the republican structure of its constitution" (Ferguson 2004, 14) and empire was displacing civil society (so soon after its triumph over communism) as the relevant fin-de-siècle concept (Maier 2006, 8).[2] Critics of America's new imperialism, meanwhile, recalled how imperium unraveled the republic in Rome: the Euphrates and the Tigris were the modern Rubicons (Johnson 2004, 15–17; 2007). However, most advocates and critics agreed that, for good or ill, the new U.S. imperialism was here to stay.

Undoubtedly, twenty-first-century events opened a new chapter in the long history of imperialism, as reflection on them opened another in the literature on imperialism. Remarkably, however, although this literature had already reached something of an intellectual peak already by the early twentieth century, twenty-first-century discourses about imperialism seemed to bear little relation to it. They harked back, instead, to more antique and less rigorous modes of reflection. Three interrelated discontinuities could be detected.

Rooted in communism, socialism, and nationalism, twentieth-century accounts overturned imperialism's positive connotation hitherto, replacing talk of "the white man's burden" and "civilizing missions" with the realities of genocide, slavery, plunder, poverty, exploitation, famine, racism, underdevelopment, and inequality.[3] Given such discourse, it became impossible to openly advocate imperialism. Many twenty-first-century discourses reverted to a positive view of imperialism. All that remained of intellectual and ideological labors in the early twenty-first century was the need to portray imperialism as reluctant (e.g., Mallaby 2002) just as Caesar had to appear reluctant in still-republican Rome. Denigrating the developmental record of ex-colonial nations, invoking the dangers for democracy of failed and rogue states, human rights and stability advocates claimed that only the United States could stabilize and police the world effectively. Whereas globalization discourse had merely consigned Third World nation-states to irrelevance, the discourse of new imperialism made many of them out to be outright dangers.

Second, where the chief twentieth-century theories attempted rigorous analyses of *modern* imperialism and its relationship to capitalism, twenty-first-century reflections eschewed such ambitions, relying on suggestive but none-too-theoretical transhistorical analogies. V. I. Lenin had been clear about the difference.

> Colonial policy and imperialism existed before the latest stage of capitalism and even before capitalism. Rome, founded on slavery, pursued a colonial policy and practised imperialism. But "general" disquisitions on imperialism which ignore, or put into the background, the fundamental difference between socio-economic formations, inevitably turn into the most vapid banality or bragging, like the comparison: "Greater Rome and Greater Britain." (Lenin 1970, 731)

Bernard Semmel had noted, "There had been comparatively little theorising concerning earlier empires" (1993, 2). Perhaps plain brute conquest and appropriation required none. *Theorizations* of imperialism became possible *and* necessary in a new type of society with a new type of imperialism, resting on a separation of politics from the economy, a self-regulating, self-expanding, and self-justifying realm with its own laws to be discovered and obeyed: capitalist society. Of course, as Karl Marx saw clearly, the separation between politics and the economy was merely formal; it was also ideologically and politically fundamental to capitalism and imperialism. It made the deployment of force and command, including against other societies, for economic gain appear anomalous: as interfering with the economy, preventing its proper expansion, and detracting from its benefits while being critical to its emergence and reproduction.

Finally, where twentieth-century theories focused on such developments in capitalism as the growth of monopoly or the new role of the nation-states through concepts such as finance capital, twenty-first-century writings overlooked the one major development of the latter twentieth century–the generalization of the nation-states system and the dissolution of formal imperialism–in favor of untheoretical accounts of military actions, capabilities, and strategies and particular economic or financial advantages or difficulties of the United States.

Such theoretical atavism testified that the task of accounting for the geopolitics of capitalism, attempted in the twentieth century, had been abandoned. It needs to be taken up again. In the next section are outlined the classical early-twentieth-century theorizations of imperialism that immediately preceded or accompanied the Great War–their theoretical gains and faults. The third section outlines the U.S.-dominated world order of the mid-twentieth century, which ended the chaos of the three decades of crisis inaugurated by that war. The end of formal imperialism in that order made the relevance of earlier accounts of imperialism unclear, and many observers, particularly modernization theorists, eschewed the term. However, before the theoretical contestation between modernization theory, on the one hand, and critical theoretical traditions that attempted to retheorize imperialism, on the other—dependency and world system theories and political Marxism—could be resolved, the new imperialism of the United States diverted attention. The fourth section outlines its contradictions and shows how important it is to understand the workings and limitations of imperialism in a world of independent nation-states if we are to steer clear of the meaningless transhistorical accounts currently on offer (e.g., "empire is the historical norm and, contrary to naïve assumptions of progress, our age is no different").

CAPITALIST IMPERIALISM AND ITS CLASSICAL THEORIZATION

For most of the nineteenth-century, imperialism was England's expansion; and thanks to the dominant ideology of free trading classical political economy, it appeared to contemporaries as no more than a largely pacific expansion of the world market. At century's end, however, the Boer War, the scramble for Africa, Japan's forays into Manchuria and Korea, and America's into the Philippines inaugurated that earlier form of new imperialism—more violent, aggressive, and competitive – and placed imperialism on the theoretical agenda as never before. New theories emerged. Known as classical theories of imperialism, they were primarily Marxist. Marxism's sophisticated understanding of the double-sided, that is, merely formal but politically critical, character of the separation of the economic and the political in capitalism could problematize and account for their combination in imperialism. The main non-Marxist theorists were John A. Hobson and Joseph Schumpeter—the one absorbed into Marxism; the other, a response to it.

In addition to imperialism's core meaning of the formal or informal subordination of one society by another, interimperialist competition was critical in such theories. It as an aspect of wider changes in capitalism: higher concentration of capital, forms of monopoly and cartelization, and the close intertwining of state and capital, all of which were tied to the "second industrial revolution" of heavy industry. Less explicitly theorized were the changes that brought politics and geopolitics to the fore as never before. Britain's industrial dominance was now challenged by such newly industrializing countries as the United

States, Germany, and Japan, who were conscious of the colonies' centrality to Britain's industrial development and competed for them. These states also industrialized by rejecting the doctrine of free trade, directing their industrializations, and protecting their industries with quasi-mercantilist policies. Nationhood was critical: Britain's loss of her industrial supremacy began precisely at the end of the 1860s when all the three nations that challenged Britain completed their nation-formation: the U.S. Civil War ended with the victory of the industrial North; the Meiji Restoration laid the basis for a modern, centralized Japanese state; and Germany was unified. The world created and dominated by the capitalist imperial expansion of the first industrial capitalist country under the guise of free trade had ceased to exist.[4] It was replaced by one of competing national capitalisms and imperialisms. The nation-state, as much as imperialism, lay at the heart of the events that closed the nineteenth century. The attention of observers remained fixed, however, on the latter alone, and this one-sidedness continued to plague the analysis of imperialism in the twentieth century.

Writing as a new liberal moving leftward at the turn-of-the-century and sceptical of capitalism's ability to deliver on liberal principles and values (Clarke 1978), Hobson outlined a critical analysis of capitalist imperialism that Marxists would draw on. Capitalism created underconsumption, and imperialism was the external efflux of this problem. The all-too-small share of wages in the economy led to the "divorcement of the desire to consume and the power to consume" (Hobson 1965, 87). It constrained demand and, in turn, constrained opportunities for investment. Capitalists' consequent search for external investment outlets led to imperialism and imperialist rivalry.

> Every improvement of methods of production, every concentration of ownership and control, seems to accentuate the tendency. As one nation after another enters the machine economy and adopts advanced industrial methods, it becomes more difficult for its manufacturers, merchants and financiers to dispose profitably of their economic resources, and they are tempted more and more to use their Governments in order to secure for their particular use some distant undeveloped territory by annexation and protection. The process, we are told, is inevitable, and so it seems upon a superficial inspection. Everywhere excessive powers of production, excessive capital in search of investment. It is admitted by all business men that the growth of the powers of production in their country exceeds the growth in consumption, that more goods can be produced than can be sold at a profit, and that more capital exists than can find remunerative investment. It is this economic condition of affairs that forms the taproot of Imperialism. (Hobson 1965, 80–81)

As a new liberal Hobson shunted the old liberal argument about imperialism being unnecessary on a new basis: it was no longer unnecessary because capitalism spontaneously increased wealth and welfare, which it did not. It was unnecessary because government action could overcome the problem of overproduction and underconsumption in better, universally beneficial ways through social reforms and the redistribution of income. If Hobson found the resolution of the imperialist problem in social reform, Marxists radicalized the argument to propose that only revolution and socialism constituted adequate resolutions to the problems of imperialism.

The chief Marxist works of this era were *Finance Capital* (1910) by the Austro-Marxist Rudolf Hilferding, *The Accumulation of Capital on a World Scale* (1913) by Rosa Luxemburg, and *Imperialism and the World Economy* by Nikolai Bukharin, written in 1915 but not published until 1918. However, it was Lenin's 1917 pamphlet *Imperialism: The Highest Stage of Capitalism*, which relied on Hobson's, Hilferding's, and Bukharin's analyses to support the Bolshevik stance against the "imperialist" war, that most popularized the Marxist analysis. Its main interest lies in the strong and, in hindsight, dubious contention that imperialism made war inevitable and that only socialism would create peace.

Hilferding focused on the forms capitalism took in the second industrial revolution—concentration through joint-stock companies, monopoly and cartelization, and new articulations between financial and productive capital required by the higher capital intensity, primarily in Germany. Finance capital, which he defined as bank capital, transformed through industrial investment into industrial capital (Hilferding 1981, 225), referred specifically to the German relationship between banks and industry. Everywhere, however, capital massed in competing national blocs and protection, "from being a defence against the conquest of the domestic market by foreign industries . . . has become a means for the conquest of foreign markets by domestic industry" (Hilferding 1981, 310). Finally, like Hobson, he considered the export of capital for higher returns and to overcome protectionist barriers critical. Though his focus was finance capital, not imperialism. Hilferding linked the era's expansionist, militarist, and colonial policies and competition clearly to the new form of capital.

Rosa Luxemburg took an altogether different approach, for she was less concerned with new forms of capitalism than with its congenital tendencies. Imperialism was endemic to capitalism because capitalists could not realize surplus value without trade with noncapitalist formations in imperialist relationships. While her necessitarian argument is generally held to be wrong (Robinson 2004, xxx–xxxi), Patnaik's recent defense and restatement are likely to revise this view. And, certainly, *The Accumulation of Capital* is Universally admired for its account of capitalist imperialism breaking up the old social relations of production in subject territories. While following Marx on colonialism and primitive accumulation, she also showed more clearly that these processes, based on political and military manipulation and force, were relevant to understanding not only the beginnings of capitalism but also its whole course.[5]

Observing many of the same processes as Hilferding, Bukharin went further, pointing to a "process of 'nationalization' of capital, i.e. the creation of homogenous economic organisms included within state boundaries and sharply opposing each other" (2003, 81), a process driven by competition for markets, raw materials, and avenues for investment. Formerly competition took place within national boundaries, and to Bukharin and Lenin its new international character of inter-imperialist rivalry necessarily meant war. This was not a prediction: both were writing after war had already broken out. The purpose of this insistence was political; they were contesting Karl Kautsky's position on "ultra-imperialism"—

namely, that while competition between national concentrations of finance capital could lead to war, it could also lead to peace if the powers were able to settle their differences and make accommodations. In contrast, Lenin insisted that war was necessary to imperialism to direct popular anger against the war in revolutionary directions. Socialism was the only answer, since capitalism inevitably led to war and its immediate dangers for the working classes.

Given the centrality accorded to Lenin's position in later decades by both orthodox Marxists and their critics, intent on proving it wrong, it is noteworthy that the analytical differences between Lenin and Kautsky had diminished by 1918, when Lenin came to fear that Europe's enthusiastic response to Wilson's proposals for a community of nation-states after the war, ironically a response to the Bolsheviks' own anti-imperialist demands, could result in an "imperialist peace." In "A Turn in World Politics," Lenin "pointed to a shift 'from imperialist war, which brought the people utter misery and the great betrayal of Socialism . . . toward an *imperialist peace*, which will bring the people the greatest deception in the form of nice phrases, semi-reforms, semi-concessions, etc.'" (quoted in Mayer 1964, 161–62), disagreeing still with Kautsky's view that it could be a democratic peace. He feared a pacification of the European masses and its implications for the fledgling Soviet regime.

In addition to the intertwining of fast-changing wartime political positions and analysis that proved so confusing in later decades, three other problems accompanied the Marxist accounts of imperialism. *Analytically*, while Hilferding focused on Germany, regarding Great Britain as a laggard, Lenin, also relying on Hobson, spoke of the relationships between financial and productive capital in Germany and Britain as though they were the same. However, seen through contemporary understandings as a rising catch-up industrializer, Germany had *subordinated* finance to the long-term needs of productive capital. Britain fit the description of the hegemony of finance over, and often to the detriment of, industrial capital more closely, but it formed no part of Hilferding's analysis.[6] The late 20th century dominance of Anglo-Saxon financial capital is the opposite of its namesake. *Historically*, developments overtook the question of imperialism or revolution. The Great War turned out not to be the terminal crisis of capitalism, as the title of Lenin's 1917 pamphlet implied. It merely inaugurated a 30 years' crisis, a period of transition (not normality), of war and economic dislocation; and at its end, a very different capitalist world order emerged. *Theoretically*, the catch-up industrialization of the second-tier of capitalist industrializers demonstrated more clearly than before the close nexus between capitalism and the nation-state, but the attention of then-contemporary Marxist theorists of imperialism remained fixed on that between capitalism and imperialism. Industrial capitalism had gone from being a matter of the imperial expansion of a single nation, Great Britain, to being an international and, necessarily at the time, an inter- imperial affair. From this time on, however, the geopolitics of capitalism featured both imperialism and nation-states. While anticolonial nationalist movements and the fledgling USSR's own nationalities problem led, in Lenin's writings, to a far more complex understanding of the role of the nation-state in capitalism and its geopolitics than is generally appreciated, it tended to be eclipsed by his more popular work on imperialism.[7] Theorization remained split between a critical analysis of imperialism and a mainstream analysis of national development when the dust of the 30 years' crisis finally settled.

TWENTIETH-CENTURY U.S. IMPERIALISM AND THE NATION-STATE

When the dust did settle, the United States emerged as the most militarily powerful of the victorious Allies, the world's largest economy, accounting for fully half of the world's total production, and the world's leading financial power. Although analogies between Great Britain's dominance in the nineteenth century and America's in the twentieth became widespread, the post–World War II world order was distinctive in three interrelated ways. First, the capitalist world was truncated by the Russian Revolution and U. S. power compromised by the USSR's indispensability to the Allied victory, the spread of communism into Eastern Europe and China, and the communist bloc's new weight in world affairs. Second, U.S. interest in diminishing the power of its potential capitalist rivals and Soviet support for nationalist movements initiated decolonization, thus ending the era of formal empires. Membership in the United Nations expanded from 51 in 1945 to 99 in 1960, the high point of decolonization. The newly independent nations became the key stake in the Cold War between the United States and the Soviet Union. Third, national development, not unadulterated free trade, was the reigning ideology of the world order thanks to high popular expectations of Third World peoples mobilized for national liberation and others mobilized for war. What could theories of imperialism have to say about this radically new scenario?

Decolonization notwithstanding, communist and left discourses still saw imperialism in the actions of Western countries. Imperialism was evident, for example, in U.S. maneuvers to subordinate new countries in its ring of alliances to contain the communist bloc, in the wars in Korea and Vietnam, and in the interventions of all Western powers in former colonies and spheres of influence—as the United States' stand against Iran's Mossadegh government, Great Britain's opposition to Nasser's nationalization of the Suez canal, and France's resistance to nationalist forces in Algeria and Vietnam. After all, imperialism had always been informal as well as formal. Western discourses replied in kind, accusing the USSR of imperialism toward its own allies and sundry Third World countries, and they were reinforced by the Chinese after the Sino-Soviet split in 1964. Cold War mudslinging apart, however, a theoretically interesting dialogue also emerged on the condition and future of ex-colonial nations.

American attempts to woo new nations from communism centered on development and modernization,[8] aspirations shared by the leaders and people of newly independent states. The new Bretton Woods institutions, which sought to rebuild capitalism after the disasters of the preceding three decades by providing institutions of international economic governance, were, revealingly, designed to support to ideas and institutions of national development rather than free trade.

These arrangements permitted national governments to manage their economies so as to maximize growth and employment. Capital was not allowed to cross frontiers without government approval, which meant governments could determine domestic interest rates, fix the exchange rate of the national currency, and tax and spend as they saw fit to secure national economic objectives. National economic planning was seen as a natural extension of such thinking, as were domestic and international arrangements to stabilize commodity prices (Leys 1996, 6–7).

Such institutional support was theoretically buttressed. Originally, Keynesian development economics sought to accelerate growth rates by injecting capital and appropriate macroeconomic policies. By the late 1950s, however, social and political factors tended to defeat these economic strategies and modernization theory supplemented bare economics with sociology and political science in a more encompassing modernization of traditional societies through a diffusion of modern values, institutions, and technology, in addition to capital, from the formerly imperial to the ex-colonial countries. Crucially, these U.S.-led ideas and practices of national development simply assumed away the history of capitalist imperialism, designating the ex-colonial countries as merely traditional—that is, existing in a condition before capitalist development through capital injection or diffusion. They also assumed that increasingly close economic, social, political, and cultural contact between the former colonial and former imperial countries would foster development.

Bretton Woods institutions and U.S. facilitation of Western European and Japanese recovery contributed to unprecedented world growth in the 1950s and 1960s. Ex-colonial countries benefited, though their performance fell short of expectations. That growth ended in the late 1960s, however, producing new stresses and strains. First, the keystone of Bretton Woods, the dollar's peg to gold, was broken, bringing down the financial order of other currencies pegged to the dollar. Bretton Woods institutions now acquired a new vocation as brazen instruments of U.S. and more generally Western policies. Second, modernization theory veered off in more authoritarian directions, signaling a harsher regime for the Third World.[9] Third, such opposing discourses claiming allegiance to Marxism as underdevelopment or dependency theory[10] and later world system[11] theory challenged modernization theory. They theorized a largely *informal* imperialism, giving rise to terms like "neocolonialism." Thus were carried forward classical theorizations in the dialogue about the condition and future of the ex-colonial world.

Fittingly, perhaps, for a theory stressing the continuing salience of imperialism despite formal decolonization, dependency theory originated in Latin America, where national independence had, in most cases, come more than a century before. Politically, dependency theorists ranged from "organic intellectuals" of their own national bourgeoisies (Brazil's former president, Fernando Henrique Cardoso, comes to mind here), chafing at their subordination to the interests of foreign companies and the influence of the U.S. state in domestic politics, to sympathizers of the working class and radical currents (Leys 1996, 12). Some observers merely pointed to obstacles to development; others argued for delinking national economies from the world capitalist economy dominated by advanced and imperial capitalist country to foster real, autonomous national development; and yet others claimed that only socialism would produce real development.

Dependency theory's focus on economic mechanisms of imperialist subjection and exploitation was critical. After all, Marx's theory of exploitation was unrelated to these forms of surplus extraction, and they affected more working people than those he so brilliantly uncovered. The wealth of writing on the operation of unequal trade (Emmanuel 1969), multinational capital (Hymer 1972), and aid and official development organizations (George 1988; Hayter 1985; Payer 1991) is too vast to summarize here. The literature confirmed, though through quite different means, the classical Marxist conclusion that imperialism and dependency were endemic to capitalism and that socialist revolution must end them together.

On the question of national development, dependency proved a mirror image of modernization theory: the one inevitabilist, the other impossibilist. While Dependency Theory aimed to contest the idea of national autonomous development amid imperialism and revived that concept to theorize the reality of nominally independent Third World nation-states, in many cases still struggling, after two decades of independence, to foster development, the very vehemence of its critique ironically reinforced the ideal of national autonomous development. For dependency theorists shared with modernization theorists the idea that there was an *alternative* (capitalist or socialist) autonomous national development path, thus rescuing the core of development (Leys 1996).

Meanwhile, though the analogy between America's twentieth-century dominance and Great Britain's nineteenth-century dominance was widely made, in world system theory (WST) it was the object of a far greater theoretical ambition. Based on Fernand Braudel's vast and rambling *ouvre* (1992), Immanuel Wallerstein original theorization of the modern world system was an account of 500-year world capitalism anchored successively to hegemonic powers that organized its productive expansion, protection, and money on a world scale. The latest in the succession was U.S. hegemony, the Genoese, the Dutch, and the English having preceded the United States. For Braudel, hegemonies began with vigorous material expansion and ended in an "autumn" in which financial expansion overtook productive expansion and laid the foundation for the emergence of its successor. Giovanni Arrighi (1994) streamlined and codified the main propositions of WST in his impressive and rich *The Long Twentieth Century*.

While dependency and WST served to powerfully contest the evasion of issues of imperialism in modernization theory, their positions on key issues were challenged by other Marxists, contesting their claim to be based on Marxist theory. One question, which became particularly vexing, was whether inserting hitherto excluded lands into the world market could lead to the development of capitalism in those lands. Dependency and WST claimed, simply, that such inclusion was tantamount to the establishment of capitalism. Further, if the results differed from, or were even opposite to, those in the core lands of capitalist accumulation, well, that was imperialism and dependency for you. Other Marxists, however, answered the question very differently, enabling theorization of the limits of imperialism, emphasising the power of nation-states in the development of capitalism that can, one must argue, counterbalance the tendency to collapse the geopolitics of capitalism into imperialism alone.

Drawing from Marx's writings on colonialism, Rosa Luxemburg's on imperialism, Robert Brenner's historically and theoretically impressive critique of the neo-Smithian character of dependency and WST, and the subsequent modes-of-production debate, one can outline another view that defines capitalism in terms of social relations of production (and not only exchange) and argues that a variety of noncapitalist forms of incorporation into the world market have been historically observed—like, for example, Latin American *latifundia* or Eastern Europe's second serfdom, not to mention the still-numerous peasantries of the world. Such forms of world market incorporation did not immediately or easily lead to the development of capitalist relations of production; they accounted for the symptoms of underdevelopment, but they could also yield capitalist development in certain circumstances.

Recently dubbed political Marxism (Teschke 2003), such a critique of dependency and WST revealed the historical and, indeed, moral and political ambiguity about whether it was the development of capitalism or its absence that brought more exploitation, oppression, or suffering (Kay 1975). Since political Marxists could envisage the possibility, if not probability, of an end to dependency and, therefore, imperialism in at least some parts of the ex-colonial world, they were criticized for underestimating the problems engendered by dependency (Lipietz 1982). They countered that they were not dismissing the dependency account, only its impossibility in practice and pointed to counterindications in the Third World's evolution through the postwar period (Leys and Saul 2006). Bill Warren's inconoclastic account of Third World industrialization in the twentieth century, invoking Marx's image of imperialism as a pioneer of capitalism (1973, 1980), was a roster of such counterindications.

The miraculous rise of the East Asian economies in the 1970s, and the less spectacular but more widespread industrialization of a great number of Third World countries in the 1970s and 1980s, focused attention on the types of policies and states that facilitated capitalist development.[12] The resulting literature on developmental states converged with political Marxism in emphasizing social relations of production, the political character of the states to which they give rise, the policy options available to them, and the circumstances in which the developmental ones could be exercised. In turn, this literature revived older traditions of theorizing the "late developer" industrial catchup such as that of Henry Carey and Friedrich List. This literature, recently dubbed "the other canon" by Erik Reinert, attempted to apply "late developer" lessons to developing countries (Carey 1848; List 1977; see also Chang 2004; Gerschenkron 1962; Reinert and Daastøl 2007). Finally, with political Marxism concentrating on the developmental history of the First World, and the literature on the developmental state on that of the Third, one can envisage a single account of the development of the world order of capitalism—imperialism, nation-states, and all—without eternalizing dependency and imperialism. Benno Teschke's view of the system of sovereign states as the geopolitical counterpart of capitalism, maturing in tandem with it, combining the economics and politics of capitalism, may well provide a viable link between the two literatures, though it would need to be further specified and theorized.

Contra Marx and Engels in *The Communist Manifesto*, the expansion of capitalism was not an *economic* process in which the trans-nationalising forces of the market or civil society surreptitiously penetrated pre-capitalist states, driven by the logic of cheap commodities that eventually perfected a universal world market. It was a *political* and, *a fortiori, geopolitical* process in which pre-capitalist state classes had to design counterstrategies of reproduction to defend their position in an international environment which put them at an economic *and* coercive disadvantage. More often than not, it was heavy artillery that battered down pre-capitalist walls, and the construction and reconstruction of these walls required new state strategies of modernization. (Teschke 2004, 265)

However, further development of such thought on retheorizing the geopolitics of capitalism in a way that theorizes the roles of imperialism and the nation-states has recently been drowned in the tumult of the maturing crisis of U.S. hegemony and the din of discourse about the new imperialism it has set in motion.

ANOTHER "NEW IMPERIALISM"?

The new imperialism of the United States is another in a succession of attempts to manage or overcome the crisis of U.S. hegemony, which began in the late 1960s—and quite possibly the crisis is a terminal one (Desai 2007). The substance of that crisis has been the diminution of America's *relative* economic strength, the inevitable outcome of the recovery of its capitalist rivals, Western Europe and Japan—a recovery the United States was forced to facilitate as a consequence of the Cold War. As Great Britain had done in the nineteenth century, when it was the workshop of the world, the United States too, so recently accounting for half the world's economy, has had to accept and accommodate to relative economic decline. Today America accounts for one-fourth to one-fifth of world production.

However, contrary to the claims of WST and other theories that see analogies between the hegemony of nineteenth-century Britain and the twentieth-century United States, there are reasons to doubt that this is just another historical moment when one hegemony succeeds another. The overwhelming productive superiority enjoyed respectively by the United Kingdom and the United States in their time, to which their hegemonies were anchored, were products of exceptional circumstances. Whereas Great Britain was the first industrial capitalist country facing no competition from other industrial capitalist powers (Leys 1989), the United States benefited from its continental size and natural protection, as well as from the unprecedented destruction to its competitors caused by two world wars. Unsurprisingly, then, as soon as other capitalist manufacturing nations emerged, in the 1870s, Great Britain lost its competitive edge and its dominance; likewise, as soon as America's capitalist rivals recovered from the destruction of war, in the 1960s, U.S. dominance also entered its critical period.[13] Interestingly, writing in 2005, world system theorist Giovanni Arrighi came to believe that in contrast to previous hegemonies, U.S. hegemony was never successful. Indeed, he declared that "the new imperialism of the Project for a New American Century probably marks the inglorious end of the sixty-year-long struggle of the United States to become the organizing centre of a world state. The struggle changed the world but even in its most triumphant moments, the U.S. never succeeded in its endeavour" (Arrighi 2005). Arrighi did not explore how this view relates to WST theory—namely, that imperialism is endemic to capitalism or that there remains a continuous succession of hegemonies—perhaps because he was unsure of China's real prospects of emerging as the new hegemony. However, that China will emerge as a world power is a doubtful proposition—on the one hand, because the extent to which China's spectacular growth of recent decades has been correctly estimated or is sustainable is unclear and, on the other, because the relative size, power, and wealth of Europe and the United States remain substantial; in addition, ecological limits to growth may limit China's ability to move farther ahead of the Western nations. Even if we accept that China will emerge as a hegemonic power, any world order centered on China will have to accommodate itself to the existence of nation-states to an even greater extent than did the United States in the twentieth century.

Such observations have implications for the further development of world capitalism. In particular, we can legitimately doubt whether the continuation of the world capitalist system can be seen in terms of the succession of another hegemony. Without some exceptional occurrence, it seems unlikely that any power will achieve the same productive superiority that Great Britain and the United States enjoyed in their time. No doubt various forms of imperial and colonial subjection and exploitation will continue, and no doubt the income gaps between the rich nations and the poor nations of the world will widen. As Branko Milanovich has shown, however, in purchasing power terms at least, thus far they have widened *less precipitously* than they did during the century or more of formal colonialism before the mid-twentieth century (2005, 144). Though that is perhaps not much, the report does indicate the need for a more balanced account of the geopolitics of capitalism than the one-sided emphasis on imperialism dominating the critical currents of the last third of the twentieth century and reinforced today from unexpectedly conservative and rightwing quarters (Ferguson 2004).

NOTES

1. Among those who have warned of the dangers of contemporary U.S. imperialism are Bacevich (2002), Harvey (2003), Johnson (2004), Leys and Panitch (2005), Mann (2005), and Smith (2003, 2005). Among its advocates are Boot (2003), Ferguson (2004), and Maier (2006). See also various writings of Michael Ignatieff, Robert Kaplan, Sebastian Malaby, and Daniel DeSouza and, of course, the Project for the New American Century.

2. Indeed, Hardt and Negri's avowedly critical work (2000) blended "empire" and "globalization," inviting readers to knowingly revel in the cosmopolitan "new Rome" even as one opposed it, indeed, only as one opposed it, in correspondingly cosmopolitan ways.

3. Mike Davis (2001) testifies to the continuity of this tradition while adding to it a new political ecology.

4. And free trade was only a guise: in reality, Britain's industrial development benefited from precisely the sort of state-led, protectionist, and quasi-mercantilist policies that characterized the industrial ascent of other countries (see Chang 2002). That said, the financial sector's—that is, the City of London's—political dominance over manufacturing systematically worked to the detriment of British manufacturing, at least after 1870. On this see Ingham (1984), Gamble (1994), and Leys (1989).

5. Harvey (2003) rests on this insight.

6. In pointing out this problem, Giovanni Arrighi sees England's conformity with the model of finance capitalism as a matter of its declining position in the world order (1978). However, the English configuration of capital was of longer standing. See Ingham (1984) and Leys (1990).

7. Key works on Lenin's and the Bolsheviks' understanding of nation-states and national self-determination are Mayer (1964), Suny (1993 and 1998), and Martin (2001). See also Desai (2008).

8. For the connection between modernization theory and theorists and the Cold War, see Gendzier (1985).

9. See Leys (1996, 45–63) and O'Brien (1971). The key text of this rightward shift is Huntington (1969).

10. The most prominent among dependency theorists were Andre Gunder Frank and Samir Amin.

11. Immanuel Wallerstein is the key figure here; Wallerstein (1983) provides a convenient overview of his argument.

12. The spectacular capitalist growth in South Korea and Taiwan may not be the best examples to hold up to the rest of the Third World, since their development enjoyed exceptionally benign international conditions thanks to their position as frontline states against communism. In that sense, more modest instances of industrialization in an India or a Brazil seem more worthy of study.

13. This is the true significance of Robert Brenner's (1998) analysis of the "long downturn."

FURTHER READING

Brewer, Anthony. *Marxist Theories of Imperialism*, 2nd ed. London: Routledge, 1990.

Desai, Radhika. "The Last Empire? From Nation-Building Compulsion to Nation-Wrecking Futility and Beyond," *Third World Quarterly* 28 (2007).

Hobsbawm, Eric. *On Empire: America, War and Global Supremacy*. New York: Pantheon Books, 2008.

Hobson, J. A. *Imperialism: A Study*. Ann Arbor: University of Michigan Press, 1965.

Patniak, Utsa. "The Free Lunch: Transfers from Tropical Countries and Their Role in Capital Formation in Britain during the Industrial Revolution." In *Globalization under Hegemony: The Changing World Economy*, edited by K. S. Jomo. New Delhi: Oxford University Press, 2006.

Semmel, Bernard. *The Liberal Ideal and the Demons of Empire: Theories of Imperialism from Adam Smith to Lenin*. Baltimore: Johns Hopkins University Press, 1993.

REFERENCES

Ahmad, Aijaz. 1992. Marx on India. *In theory: Nations, classes, literatures*. London: Verso.
Anderson, Perry. 1978. *Lineages of the absolutist state*. London: Verso.
Arrighi, Giovanni. 1978. *The geometry of imperialism: The limits of Hobson's paradigm*. Trans. P. Camiller. London: New Left Books.
———. 1994. *The long twentieth century*. London: Verso.
———. 2005. *Hegemony unravelling*. Pts. 1 and 2. *New Left Review* 2 (May–June), 33.
Avineri, Shlomo. ed. 1968. *Marx on colonialism and modernization*. Garden City: Doubleday.
Bacevich, Andrew. 2002. *American empire*. Cambridge, MA: MIT Press.
Barratt-Brown, Michael. 1963. *After imperialism*. London: Heinemann.
Boot, Max. 2003. *Savage wars of peace: Small wars and the rise of American power*. New York: Basic Books.
Braudel, Fernand. 1992. *Civilization and capitalism*. 3 vols. Berkeley: University of California Press.
Brenner, Robert. 1977. The origins of capitalist development. *New Left Review* I/104 (July–August), 25–92.
———. 1998. The economics of global turbulence. *New Left Review* I/229 (May–June), 1–265.
Brewer, Anthony. 1977. *Marxist theories of imperialism: A critical survey*. 2nd ed. London: Routledge.
Bukharin, Nikolai. 2003. *Imperialism and the world economy*. London: Bookmarks.
Carey, Henry. 1848. *The past, the present and the future*. Philadelphia: Carey and Hart.
Chang, Ha-Joon. 2002. *Kicking away the ladder*. London: Anthem.
Clarke, Peter. 1978. *Liberals and Social Democrats*. Cambridge: Cambridge University Press.
Davis, Mike. 2001. *Late Victorian holocausts: El Niño famines and the making of the Third World*. London: Verso.
Desai, Radhika. 2007. The last empire? From nation-building compulsion to nation-wrecking futility and beyond. *Third World Quarterly* 28.
———. 2008. The political economy and cultural politics of nationalisms in historical perspective. Introduction to *Developmental and cultural nationalisms*. Special Issue of *Third World Quarterly* 29. Guest editor, Radhika Desai.
Emmanuel, Arghiri. 1969. *Unequal trade: A study in the imperialism of trade*. London: New Left Books.
Ferguson, Niall. 2004. *Colossus: The rise and fall of the American empire*. New York: Penguin.
Gallagher, John, and Ronald Robinson. 1953. The imperialism of free trade. *Economic History Review* New Series 6.
Gamble, Andrew. 1994. *Britain in decline*. London: St. Martin's Press.
Gendzier, Irene. 1985. *Managing political change: Social scientists and the Third World*. Boulder, CO: Westview.
George, Susan. 1988. *A fate worse than debt*. New York: Grove Press.

———. 1994. *Faith and credit: The World Bank's secular empire*. Boulder, CO: Westview.
Gerschenkron, Alexander. 1962. *Economic backwardness in historical perspective*, Cambridge, MA: Belknap Press.
Hardt, Michael, and Antony Negri. 2000. *Empire*. Cambridge, MA: Harvard University Press.
Harvey, David. 2003. *The new imperialism*. Oxford: Oxford University Press.
Hayter, Teresa. 1985. *Aid: rhetoric and reality*. London: Pluto.
Hilferding, Rudolf. 1981. *Finance capital: A study of the latest phase of capitalist development*. Ed. with intro. Tom Bottomore. London: Routledge and Kegan Paul.
Hobson, J. A. 1965. *Imperialism: A study*. Ann Arbor: University of Michigan Press.
Huntington, Samuel. 1969. *Political order in changing societies*. New Haven, CT: Yale University Press.
Hymer, Stephen. 1972. The multinational corporation and the law of uneven development. In *Economics and the world order from the 1970s to the 1990s*, ed. Jagdish Bhagwati. New York: Collier-Macmillan.
Ingham, Geoffrey. 1984. *Capitalism divided? The city and industry in British social development*. Basingstoke, UK: Macmillan.
Johnson, Chalmers. 2004 *The sorrows of empire*. New York: Metropolitan Books.
———. 2007 *Nemesis: The last days of the American republic*. New York: Metropolitan.
Kay, Geoffrey. 1975. *Development and underdevelopment: A Marxist analysis*. New York: St. Martin's Press.
Keynes, J. M. 1967. *General theory of employment, interest and money*. London: Macmillan.
Lenin, V. I. 1970. Imperialism: The highest stage of capitalism. *Selected works*. Vol. 1. Moscow: Progress Publishers.
Leys, Colin. 1989. *Politics in Britain*. London: Verso.
———. 1990. Still a question of hegemony? *New Left Review* I/81 (May–June), 119–128.
———. 1996. *The Rise and fall of development theory*. Oxford: James Currey.
Leys, Colin, and John Saul. 2006. Dependency. In *The Elgar companion to development studies*, ed. D. A. Clark. Cheltenham, UK: Edward Elgar.
Lipietz, Alain. 1982. Marx or Rostow? *New Left Review* I/132 (March–April), 43–58.
List, Friedrich. 1977. *The national system of political economy*. Fairfield, NJ: AM Kelly.
Maier, Charles. 2006. *Among empires: American ascendancy and its predecessors*. Cambridge, MA: Harvard University Press.
Mallaby, Sebastian. 2002. The reluctant imperialist: Terrorism, failed states and the case for American empire. *Foreign Affairs*, March–April.
Mann, Michael. 2005. *Incoherent empire*. London: Verso.
Martin, Terry. 2001. *The affirmative action empire: Nations and nationalism in the Soviet Union, 1923–1939*. Ithaca, NY: Cornell University Press.
Marx, Karl. 1969. *Theories of surplus value*. Vol. 2. London: Lawrence and Wishart.
Marx, Karl. 1974. *Political writings II: Surveys from exile*. New York: Vintage.

———. 1977. *Capital*. Vol. 1. London: Vintage.
Mayer, Arno. 1964. *Wilson vs Lenin: Political origins of the new diplomacy*. Cleveland: World Publishing.
Milanovich, Branko. 2005. *Worlds apart: Measuring international and global inequality*. Princeton, NJ: Princeton University Press.
Momsen, Wolfgang. 1977. *Theories of Imperialism*. Trans. P. S. Falla. London: Weidenfeld and Nicholson.
O'Brien, Conor Cruise. 1971. Modernization, order and the erosion of a democratic ideal. *Journal of Development Studies* 7.
Panitch, Leo, and Colin Leys, eds. 2005. *The empire reloaded: Socialist register 2005*. London: Merlin Press.
Patniak, Utsa. 2005. Ricardo's fallacy. In *Pioneers of development economics*, ed. K. S. Jomo. New Delhi: Tulika.
———. 2006. The free lunch: Transfers from tropical countries and their role in capital formation in Britain during the Industrial Revolution. In *Globalization under hegemony: The changing world economy*, ed. K. S. Jomo. New Delhi: Oxford University Press.
Payer, Cheryl. 1991. *Lent and lost: Foreign credit and Third World development*. London: Zed Books.
Reinert, Erik, and Arno Daastøl. 2007. The other canon: The history of Renaissance economics. In *Globalization, economic development and inequality: An alternative perspective*, ed. Erik Reinert. Cheltenham, UK: Edward Elgar.
Robinson, Joan. 2004. Rosa Luxemburg. Introduction to *The accumulation of capital*. London: Routledge Classics.
Rosenberg, Justin. 1994. *The empire of civil society*. London: Verso.
Seeley, J. R. 1890. *The expansion of England*. London: Macmillan.
Semmel, Bernard. 1960. *Imperialism and social reform: English social imperial thought, 1895–1914*. London: G. Allen and Unwin.
———. 1993. *The liberal ideal and the demons of empire: Theories of imperialism from Adam Smith to Lenin*. Baltimore: Johns Hopkins University Press.
Smith, Adam. *The wealth of nations*. Bks. 1–2. London: Penguin.
Smith, Neil. 2003. *American empire: Roosevelt's geographer and the prelude to globalization*. Berkeley: University of California Press.
———. 2005. *The endgame of globalization*. New York: Routledge.
Suny, Ronald. 1993. *The revenge of the past: Nationalism, revolution and the collapse of the Soviet Union*. Stanford, CA: Stanford University Press.
———. 1998. *The Soviet experiment: Russia, USSR and the successor states*. New York: Oxford University Press.
Stavrianos, L. S. 1981. *Global rift: The Third World comes of age*. New York: William Morrow.
Teschke, Benno. 2003. *The myth of 1648*. London: Verso.
Wallerstein, Immanuel. 1983. *Historical capitalism*. London: Verso.
Warren, Bill. 1973. Imperialism and capitalist industrialization. *New Left Review* I/81 (September–October), 3–44.
———. 1980. *Imperialism: Pioneer of capitalism*. London: New Left Books.
Wood, Ellen. 1981. The separation of the economic and the political in capitalism, *New Left Review* I/127 (May–June), 66–95.

11

Information Wars

John Arquilla

TECHNOLOGY AND WARFARE

All the major technological advances of the Industrial Revolution, which began some two centuries ago, while initially aimed at improving commerce and society, quickly found their way into battle. Starting with the decades immediately after Waterloo (1815), steam engines came to power mass production and the ships and railroads that moved about large numbers of people and goods at hitherto unimagined sustained speeds. Soon thereafter, the electric telegraph completely replaced its optical predecessor, and vast amounts of information flowed by Morse code wherever the wires were set in place. These developments all had tremendous effects on commercial and social development. They also revolutionized warfare.

Weapons production soared during these years, as did the size of armies, and railroads made it possible to mobilize and swiftly deploy huge numbers of troops, while the telegraph, the "Victorian Internet,"[1] insured that such undertakings could be properly choreographed and controlled. The American Civil War (1861–1865) and the German wars of unification (1866 and 1870–1871) showed how profoundly the realm of conflict had been influenced by these advances in weapons manufacturing, mass movement, and information systems.

By the turn of the twentieth century, another pattern was added to the Industrial Age mix, as in the case of powered flight, where in this instance the *first use* of the new technology was primarily for war making, with civil aviation services trailing decades behind in the wake of such notions as close support and strategic bombing. In particular, the allure of being able to make war without first having to engage enemy land and naval forces exercised a powerful hold on the military imagination. And when nuclear power was harnessed late in World War II, it was immediately used against Japan; the first two atomic bombs, which destroyed two major cities in moments, were quickly joined by many more, then married to the concept of strategic aerial bombardment.

THE INFORMATION REVOLUTION AND WAR

A similar, though not identical, pattern of development seems to have taken hold in more recent years with the onset of the information revolution. While the virtual world of cyberspace seems ideally suited to social and commercial networking, it must be remembered that the origins of the Internet lie to some extent in security concerns (dating back to the 1960s) over maintaining connectivity despite the havoc that would be wrought by nuclear war. At the same time, well before the emergence of cyberspace as it is known today—and so named by novelist William Gibson in his classic cyber punk novel *Neuromancer* (1984)—some theorists, keenly aware of the growing dependence of societies and their militaries on swift, secure information flows, were speculating about the possibility of a new form of war aimed at breaking such connections. Air power advocates, in much the same way, had been thinking about strategic bombardment half a century earlier. The seminal study of this newer notion was the late Thomas Rona's monograph "Weapons Systems and Information War," written for his employers at Boeing in 1976.

While Rona implicitly anticipated cyberspace-based attack and defense at both the tactical and strategic levels, his major purpose was to depict a landscape of conflict in which advanced militaries and their societies would see their functions seriously degraded by a wide range of attacks of all sorts on their information systems—from bits and bytes to bombs and precisely directed electronic beams. Rona's ideas profoundly influenced an international community of engineers, soldiers, and scholars who were working at the juncture of technology and strategy—so much so that by the mid-1980s, high-tech militaries were focusing heavily on what came to be called radio electronic combat (REC),[2] a lineal descendant of the electronic warfare concepts pioneered by radar-jammers and their foes in the night-bombing campaigns of the Blitz against Britain and the later air offensive against Germany during World War II.[3] Related concerns of Rona and others interested in the functioning of information systems in battle—and, conversely, the effects of battle on information systems—were the practical questions about how well or poorly computers would function in the field. Would they meet the needs of soldiers, parsing bits of data in time to inform decision makers? More prosaically, would they crash if jostled, clog up with sand, or break down from other causes?[4]

Answers soon came, and the advocates in favor of fully integrating advanced information systems in battle saw in the lop-sided victory over Iraq during the fight for Kuwait (1991) the first true fruits of this form of information warfare. Saddam Hussein's large field forces were virtually paralyzed by precise attacks on their communications, while coalition information systems functioned smoothly and guided friendly forces with timely, targeted information.[5] Ever since the existence proof provided by Operation Desert Storm, the world's more advanced militaries have been striving to develop their own capacities for crippling an enemy's information systems, or for defending against such attacks, so as to retain the secure ability to manage their own information flows.

CYBERWARS

In the years immediately following the war for Kuwait, the explosive growth of cyberspace and the increasing dependency of societies and their security forces on the Net and the Web prompted several strategists to raise the general level of consciousness regarding the vulnerabilities that would come along with such connectivity. Their concerns may at first have seemed undue, but the simultaneous rise of a hacker culture whose occasional exploits highlighted these worries ensured high-level attention to the problem.[6] Then during the 1990s, fueled by such official studies as the RAND Corporation's *Strategic Information Warfare* (1996), as well as by presidential commissions, the pace of development of thinking about "cyberwar" quickened.[7] It was during those years that the similarities and differences between information warfare and strategic bombing were debated, the balance between offense and defense explored, and the ethics of engaging in this new mode of conflict considered.[8]

The greatest similarity with aerial bombing that was noted was being able to strike at an enemy's "homeland" without first having to engage and defeat opposing military forces. The biggest difference between cyber attack and strategic aerial assault was that the former would focus on disruption—largely in the form of causing power outages—while the latter was a fundamentally and traditionally destructive exercise in the use of force. That is, it delivered iron bombs, which blew things up, rather than logic bombs, which confused and corrupted computer operating systems.

Beneath these surface differences, though, lay the fundamental point that the "entry costs" for developing a cyber warfare capability were almost nil compared to the requirements for mounting bombardment campaigns with attack aircraft or long-range ballistic missiles. Whereas air and space power remain in the dominant hands of a few leading nation-states, cyber power is almost universally available. In this important respect, the information revolution has granted strategic war-making capabilities to the level of the determined small band or even the individual. Indeed, the entry costs for waging information wars are even lower than those associated with the formation of terror cells.

BALANCE BETWEEN OFFENSE AND DEFENSE

Awareness of the whole problem of ease of entry has been and remains keen, and concerns about the proliferation of cyber threats have sparked a great deal of study of issues that bear upon the balance between offense and defense, a longstanding strategic construct[9] that also applies to the cyber realm. Briefly, in the early twentieth century, advances in firepower (machine guns, mortars, artillery) gave a great advantage to defenders, and so wars should not have started so easily, since aggressors' chances were limited. Sadly, most militaries failed to appreciate the technological state of play, and the offensive disasters of World War I ensued (Snyder 1984). Two decades later, mechanization gave birth to maneuver doctrines that conjured visions of short, sharp wars and fed fascist aggressiveness. The problem, however, was that such developments were easily replicated, giving others the same offensive capabilities and proving that mobile defenses could be more than adequate against the blitzkrieg. This latter point was particularly emphasized at the decisive World War II Battle of Kursk, where the largest tank battle in history was fought and won by Soviet defenders.

The balance between offense and defense became a somewhat blurrier concept during the Cold War. Intercontinental ballistic missiles were invented, and no way of intercepting them existed—nor is there one today, several decades after their creation. But this hasn't conveyed a great advantage to the offense, because even nuclear-tipped missiles are unusable. When both sides have such weapons, mutual deterrence puts down iron constraints on action. And the normative inhibitions are so great that a nuclear power could almost certainly not even threaten to use such weapons against a non-nuclear state—the American nuclear bombing of Japan in 1945 being the exception that proves the rule. Thus, despite the offense having a technological edge, the real situation in this realm is one of defense dominance (Jervis 1978, 167–214).

But the Cold War also saw the rise of other modes of conflict, highly irregular in nature, in which very slight material capabilities, used creatively, could give fits to much larger opponents. Thus the period from the 1950s to the 1970s became the heyday of modern guerrilla warfare, with people's liberation and insurgent movements winning a wide array of wars, across a swath of the world from Africa to East Asia, against colonial masters and others (including the United States in Vietnam) who sought to shore up the old order. Throughout this period, the offensive capacity of insurgents came at very low entry cost, and the returns on investing in this form of irregular warfare were quite high (Taber 1970).

By the early 1970s, anticolonial insurgencies had spawned darker manifestations of themselves in the form of terrorism: the deliberate targeting of innocents in the hope of gaining coercive leverage over one's adversaries. The start-up costs for engaging in terrorism were even lower than for insurgency, and such groups quickly proliferated. As they were shadowy networks rather than nations, they were hard to extirpate, and their power has grown to the point where, accentuated by the 9/11 attacks on America and the continued resilience of the Al Qaeda organization, they have taken center stage in strategic affairs today. Yet, it is hard to point to terrorist campaigns that have achieved their goals.[10] From the Irish Republican Army to the Palestinians, and on to Al Qaeda itself, the various quests for independence, separatism, or even the establishment of a new caliphate have remained out of reach. So, in the case of terrorism, offense may be easy, in a tactical sense, but the strategic defenses of those who oppose terror have remained robust.

CYBERWAR OFFENSE AND LOW ENTRY COSTS

Information wars have now waded into this mix, and thinking about the balance between offense and defense in the cyber realm relates in many ways to the foregoing discussion. For example, intercontinental ballistic missiles (ICBMs) were and still are unstoppable, mechanistically, but deterrence was and still is robust. By way of contrast, cyber weapons, mostly consisting of malicious types of software, can often be defended against—ultimately if not immediately—but deterring such attacks from a wide range of small actors is well nigh impossible. Very simply, it is hard to make credible retaliatory threats against small groups, or even individuals, who may never even be identified. Indeed, one of the most distinguishing aspects of information wars is that, at least in the cyber realm, the identity of one or more of the protagonists may remain "cloaked." This point was nicely illuminated by Frederik Pohl in his dystopian novel *The Cool War* (1979), in which nations, fearful of fighting each other openly due to the risk of nuclear escalation, were encouraged to engage small covert bands of saboteurs with which to wage war against each other, all the while trying to retain "plausible deniability" about the source of such attacks.

The similarities between cyber warfare and the insurgency model are also quite considerable, given the low entry costs of both and the generally shared purpose of winning "liberation" from some form of unwanted control. If one adds to this a willingness to focus on persuasive content issues rather than just on the disruption of conduits, then it is possible to see the ways in which advanced information technologies, the Web and the Net in particular, have fueled a series of insurgent "netwars"[11] that have made life very difficult for many authoritarian regimes. Indeed, the *Otpor* insurgency in Serbia, which overthrew Milosevic, and the "color revolutions" in Ukraine and Georgia, along with a range of other democratizing movements, have all been greatly empowered by cyberspace. In these cases, though, the role of the cyber realm has largely been to put out persuasive messages that can win "the battle of the story" and also help to coordinate insurgent activities in the physical world.

MISINFORMATION IN CYBERWARS

The "war of ideas" waged over the past several years against terrorism falls into the category of netwar as well, given its goal of creating and sustaining a global anti-terror coalition. It is also a classic, content-based type of information war, the kind that has been quite evident over the past century, visible in the rise of modern propaganda during World War I, its refinement during World War II, and the central role played by competing ideas during the Cold War.[12] While initially a creature of print, propaganda quickly adapted to radio and visual media, its influence growing with the expansion of these new realms (McLuhan and Fiore 1968). But something odd happened when propaganda moved into cyberspace: its twisting and untruthfulness had somehow become more apparent, more likely to be "outed" by the scrutiny of vast virtual communities.

If the color revolutions of the past decade were greatly aided by information wars that spoke truth to authoritarian power, both the War on Terror and terror's war on the world have suffered, in the realm of such influence operations, because of their disrespect for truth. The terrorists' exaggerations and misrepresentations have been routinely debunked by diligent observers but so have many of the assertions of nations like the United States. This is best exemplified by the virtual groundswell of self-appointed investigators and critics who refuted notions of an Iraqi role in 9/11, and of Saddam Hussein being in possession of, or pursuing the development of, weapons of mass destruction. However American strategists have labeled this form of information war, variously calling it "perception management," "strategic influence," "soft power," "strategic communications," and most recently, "smart power," such operations have tended to get traction to the extent to which they have been unabashedly truthful. On this point, perhaps it would be useful for information warriors engaged in battles of the story to be reminded of Thomas Jefferson's sage advice about information strategy: "Tell the naked truth always, whether favorable or unfavorable. For they will believe the good, if we tell them the bad also."[13] Lies, twisting, and selected omissions may prevail briefly at some times and in some situations. But the real lesson for this mode of information war is that in a many-to-many world where the mass public provides an unrelenting audit function, the false will generally have a short shelf-life.

HACKTIVISM: THE NEW THREAT

Beyond wars of ideas, another area of information conflict is one wherein cyber insurgents have limited themselves to disruptive attacks on government information systems in acts of what many call "hacktivism." The results of such actions have generally been poor. Perhaps the greatest failure of this type has been the Palestinian "cyber jihad" against Israel, which has done very little over the past decade to disrupt the Israeli economy, critical infrastructure, or the operations of the military. Viewed through the lens of insurgency, then, the conclusion may be that when it comes to cyberspace, it is the message, especially the truthful message that matters most in this new medium. A focus on targeting conduits may prove far less productive than a careful effort to craft persuasive content.

Does the foregoing imply that terrorists are going to have a hard time "militarizing" cyberspace? Many thoughtful studies have suggested this, beginning with Martin Libicki's seminal *What Is Information Warfare?* (1995). Here he made the argument that such attacks might enjoy a short run of success, but adequate defenses would be mounted soon after the reality of the threat was made manifest. More recently, Gabriel Weimann's *Terror on the Internet* (2006) affirms the notion of there being sharp limits to the potential for such attacks to grow in seriousness. In this respect, cyber terror has also been viewed as a kind of "wasting asset"; that is, it exists conditionally, having a "use it and lose it" dynamic. In the years since Libicki first wrote on this topic, the lack of a major cyber attack—a "digital Pearl Harbor" mounted by either a nation or a terror network—has seemed to confirm the general judgment that cyber warfare is a lesser-included mode of conflict.

Against this argument and the course of nonevents that seems to support it, others have thoughtfully, sometimes dramatically, pointed out the real vulnerabilities to cyber attack that exist in commercial, governmental, and military information systems.[14] Their views have been supported in three ways. First, rigorously crafted exercises conducted since the late 1990s have repeatedly demonstrated the ease with which cyber disruptions can be caused, often with grave and costly consequences. The process began with an American a military exercise in 1998, Eligible Receiver, the results of which remain highly classified today. However, it has been publicly reported that a hacker team, using tools downloaded from open sources on the Web, managed to cripple significant U.S. military elements for the duration of the exercise (Verton 2003, 31–34). Going beyond the purely military realm to include defense of the civil infrastructure, other test exercises such as Blue Cascades and Black Ice, and such more recent ones as Silent Horizon and Cyber Storm—almost all of which remain classified—have confirmed beyond doubt that huge vulnerabilities to cyber disruption do exist.

The second and third elements that support the view of growing danger emanating from cyberspace are firmly grounded in real events. One is the trend in insured losses paid out to indemnify businesses for the attacks inflicted on them by hackers. This figure has grown steadily over the past decade to amounts well over $40 billion annually in the United States alone, that figure being roughly the amount of insured loss payouts related to the attacks on the World Trade Center in 2001. If dispersed, uncoordinated hackers can inflict something of a virtual 9/11 each year, and it does not take much imagination to see that a deliberate cyber terror campaign could make things far worse.

The other real-world events that suggest the potential of cyber attack have to do with sustained intrusions into very sensitive defense information systems. Around the same time as Eligible Receiver, hackers began making their ways into Pentagon computers, and they continued to do so for a period of years. Little can be said openly about this, save for the admission that despite vigorous defense measures and a "back hacking" investigation, dubbed Moonlight Maze, that led to computers in Russia, the intrusions continued. More recently, a similar set of cyber infiltration and spying incidents, given the name Titan Rain, has been underway. This episode, which appears to involve Chinese hackers, is even more sensitive than Moonlight Maze.

Taken together, such systematic, deeply penetrating, aggressive intrusion campaigns—even though so far limited to information gathering—are viewed as powerful proofs that a determined attacker could do serious harm to American national security. For they are "observationally equivalent" to cyber attacks that aim at creating serious disruptions, given that the same techniques of entry and movement are employed, whether one is simply observing and absconding with information or attacking one or more of the highly automated defense systems that govern, for example, the time-phased deployment of U.S. forces and their weapons or the conduct of aerial bombardment campaigns.

The United States, though offering perhaps the richest set of targets to cyber attack, is hardly the only country with serious concerns. The Russian military, still reconstituting itself in the wake of the Cold War, is also deeply concerned about cyber disruption—so much so, that in an apparent effort to deter such attacks on military or civilian systems, the Russians have from time to time articulated the view that it would be justifiable to respond to cyber attacks with any and all means, including, as one leading Russian defense analyst put it, "the nuclear response."[15] No other nations have emulated this punitive Russian declaratory stance. Instead, most have focused trying to deter attacks by demonstrating their ability to defend themselves,[16] thereby denying the "cyboteurs" their aims. In this regard, the swift, successful Estonian response to a series of cyber attacks in 2007—apparently (and if so, somewhat ironically) perpetrated by Russian hackers in the wake of the removal of a statue of a Soviet World War II soldier from a prominent place in Tallinn—might well be viewed as a possible model of "denial deterrence" for the virtual realm. In the Estonian case, the attacks were quickly contained and died out almost immediately, suggesting the possibility that good defenses might indeed have shored up some form of denial deterrence and caused the malefactors to call off further attacks.[17]

Perhaps the most effective tool of denial deterrence would be the widespread employment of very strong encryption. Today, for the first time in the long historical competition between code makers and code breakers, the advantage lies, seemingly unalterably, with the former. Advanced mathematics, high-performance computing, and very advanced software make unbreakable codes a reality. This means, in practical terms, that even if a master hacker intrudes into a system, little damage can be done because the interloper will be unable to parse any of the data found. In terms of the benefits of strong encryption, transnational criminal organizations were among the first to appreciate this and have secured many of their communications in this manner.

Terrorists, a bit slower off the mark, also appear to be in the process of adopting very strong encryption. Curiously, nation-states have been reluctant to go down this path to securing their own vital data and systems; indeed, many—including, until recently, the United States—have even gone to the point of outlawing their citizens' use of strong encryption.[18] This is a policy no longer in force in the United States, but it has been replaced by an official attitude of benign neglect. That is, though doing so would almost surely make Americans far more secure and would unquestionably shore up a policy of denial deterrence against cyber attacks, officialdom does not vigorously call for giving "crypto to the people."

There are, of course, reasons for the reluctance of governments and their commercial sectors to secure themselves with strong "crypto," none of them very good. The most prominent are the twin beliefs that the security gained by widespread adoption of strong encryption comes only with a significant cost—in time and effort—and at reduced levels of efficiency. Such reasoning may have had some validity two decades ago but has long since been superseded by advances in computer and software engineering. Even so, the mantra of efficiency loss continues to be intoned and, coupled with affirmations that the cyber threat is overblown, has proven sufficient to keep the existing, firewall-based approach to security in place. This means that most electronic data around the world remain at risk. For as even mid-level hackers know, firewalls can defend only against things they recognize. And so hackers make it their business to employ tools that they know will not be recognized. There is more nuance to governmental resistance to allowing citizens to secure their own communications and databases. Most prominent has been the opposition of intelligence and law enforcement entities that worry about their surveillance capabilities being unduly curtailed by crypto. From a regulation-and-taxation perspective, others in government have grown concerned that completely secure individual communications might further facilitate the growth of the world's subterranean economy; that is, the portion of commercial activity that lies outside official awareness and control. These are all reasonable concerns. But the simple fact is that criminals and terrorists already have access to such technology. Keeping it from average citizens only guarantees their continued vulnerability in a world where cyber security matters more each day.

With the foregoing in mind, along with awareness of the few real-world events that have sparked at least some interest in cyber defense and deterrence, the greater question concerning cyber warfare today is perhaps less about these matters and more about why, if the real vulnerabilities to attack are so great, has so little actual disruption actually been done? There are two interrelated answers to this question: the world's master hackers, those capable of pulling off such feats of disruption, are not yet sufficiently radicalized; and terrorists, who would love to conduct such strikes, are not sufficiently "informatized." That is, those who can do not want to, and those who want to cannot.

A further complicating factor is that master hackers, those who range freely throughout the virtual wilderness of cyberspace, even into its most preclusive places, and command vast armies of "slave computers," "zombies," and robot networks ("botnets") still number in just the few dozens worldwide. Not all are men, and it appears that less than half are Americans.[19] Drawn to the beauty and complexity of cyberspace, none seem particularly interested in launching a self-destructive war that would despoil this domain. Even so, the generally hostile relations that prevail between master hackers and governmental authorities suggest at least the possibility that one or more of them will be sufficiently antagonized so as to reach out and help radicals, militants, and terrorists to develop their cyber warfare capabilities.

Were this to happen, a tremendous upswing in cyber terror would no doubt result. Because even one or a few master hackers would quickly be able to bring up the skill levels of the much larger group—measured in the several thousands—of already very good hackers. This is the layer of cyber operators that lies below the masters and above the multitude of "script kiddies" (numbering in the millions, worldwide), who are largely limited to downloading attack tools off the Web and deploying them with little understanding of their nature or how to exploit the effects they generate.

But would the radicalization of master hackers lead them to assist terror groups like Al Qaeda, Hezbollah, or others? Perhaps they would be willing to do so; but out of security concerns, such terrorist groups would likely be reluctant to employ one of the masters. The terrorists would worry that the hacker was a plant who, once inside their systems, might illuminate them so as to facilitate detection and tracking by their enemies. Or the hacker might leave backdoors in their systems that would allow disruptive intrusions, intensive mapping of new changes in the organization, and perhaps the laying of delayed-action viruses and logic bombs. Given all these concerns, the greater likelihood is that terror networks will strive to develop their own master hackers, selecting candidates from within their ranks and sending them off to study computer science and related disciplines at leading universities. There is some slight evidence that Al Qaeda has pursued this path. But growing one's own master hacker takes a lot of time—at least a decade, and likely a few years more—and runs its own risks of the operative either being discovered and tracked or, even worse, turned and used against them. Seen in this light, the lack of serious cyber warfare capabilities in terrorist organizations seems less mysterious.

NATION-STATES AND HACKING

Mystery still reigns among nation-states. Nations have larger pools of talent upon which to draw, and many countries have excellent higher-education systems, supplemented later on by willing military and intelligence services fully capable of developing hacking skills to the highest levels. Given that serious national-level thinking has been going on about cyber warfare since the early 1990s, it seems quite puzzling that beyond the information-gathering and mapping intrusions highlighted by Moonlight Maze and Titan Rain (which may have some connection to Russia and China), so little may actually have occurred under the aegis of nation-state sponsorship. This absence of serious cyber warfare at the national level, despite there being significant, persistent, large vulnerabilities to such modes of attack—and thus good prospects for successful offensives—suggests the need to revisit the concept of deterrence, with punitive rather than denial deterrence in mind. It is very likely that nations prefer not to start waging cyber warfare because if the veil of anonymity were ever pierced, such behavior would invite retaliatory strikes from others. Or, more generally, engaging in systematic cyber warfare campaigns might signal the start of an arms race in the virtual realm, since the implication would be that this was an acceptable mode of warfare. Indeed, during the Kosovo War (1999), one reason mentioned for the lack of U.S. cyber attacks on Serbia is that President Clinton did not want to set an example for others or suggest to the world that permissive conditions existed for mounting such attacks. This position has both ethical and practical implications, for trying to tamp down the ardor for cyber warfare serves both to stand in favor of having a less, rather than more, conflict-prone global environment and at the same time, in the American case, perhaps makes it less likely that a society that offers an immense, rich set of targets will be struck in this manner. It may well be a case of doing good and also doing well.

Thus, information wars may be deterrable at the national level by means of punitive retaliatory threats. Nevertheless, all indications are that many leading nations are vigorously cultivating both offensive and defensive cyber warfare capabilities. So much so that even if deterrence is generally strong, the temptation to use such means, especially in the course of an ongoing general war, is sure to be great. Indeed, it would be hard to think of a major shooting war going on, with all the attendant destruction that comes with such conflicts, in which combatants tacitly agreed to refrain from attacks on each others' information systems. Both military and civilian information targets would be hit to maximize effects both on the tactical battlefield, where loss of connectivity could be catastrophic for high-tech militaries, and in this new form of strategic warfare against adversary "homelands." Besides, many militaries rely on civilian infrastructures for much, sometimes most, of their connectivity, and so these civilian links would have to be hit in order to generate battlefield effects.

DETERRING CYBER WARFARE?

While an outbreak of cyber warfare between nations will be unlikely in a period of peace in the physical world, the foregoing analysis suggests that in a hard, close-fought general conflict, the incentives for fighting from and in cyberspace will be great. But this restriction, the perceived preference for integrating virtual operations with military field operations, simply does not obtain for hackers and cyber terrorists, who may always have strong incentives for mounting such attacks, whether or not a larger war is under way. Although even these incentives for nonstate actors might rise along with a desire to influence an ongoing general war with cyber attacks, much as piracy and privateering have flourished in previous centuries during periods of extended great power conflict. The key point here is that those who have invested in crafting offensive cyber warfare capabilities are likely to limit their use to system mapping and intelligence gathering in peacetime and to achieve tactical battlefield and strategic homeland effects only in the context of general conflicts. But those individuals and networks, particularly terror networks, that have no worries about retaliatory cyber strikes will not be very susceptible to punitive deterrence. And once they come seriously into cyber attack capabilities, they are sure to use them. All of which leads back to the urgent need to craft the most robust defenses and hope that they can afford a modicum of denial deterrence. But, as discussed earlier, poor habits of mind and old-fashioned institutional interests have in many countries conspired to sustain the faith in firewalls rather than encourage a shift to strong encryption. This mindset guarantees that when the cyber terrorists are at last ready, they will still have a rich, inviting set of targets upon which to inflict their "digital Pearl Harbor." Barring sudden governmental epiphanies, it is unlikely that this state of affairs will change anytime soon. Thus an information-age clock, analogous to the nuclear doomsday clock, is ticking; but right now the minute hand for cyber attack is probably much closer to midnight than the more famous one for nuclear warfare. And as close as the nuclear minute hand has ever been to midnight, few anywhere take seriously the notion that there will be a general nuclear war. Conversely, a general cyber war is highly thinkable. So it is crucial to identify other measures that might be taken to mitigate this risk.

Perhaps the single, most important initiative that could be undertaken to deter cyber attacks by either nations or nonstate networks would be one that greatly improved the capacity for "back hacking"—that is, using a system for tracking cyber attackers and achieving ultimate user identification. If either nations or networks knew that whatever disruption they caused, the victim would be able to track them down virtually, punitive deterrence might well be shored up. To be sure, this is a daunting task, given the vastness and complexity of cyberspace. But this would be an undertaking no greater in scope than the World War II-era effort to break the codes of the Axis powers with Ultra and Magic, an initiative that succeeded on a grand scale, playing a decisive role in the war's outcome. So it would be with a similar-scaled breakthrough today in cyber tracking. Indeed, it is hard to see how a global terror network like Al Qaeda could survive in the face of such a tracking capability.

For such an undertaking, it would be imperative to reach out to some in the master hacker community, whose collective skills would greatly advance such an effort. In this respect, hackers are analogous to the German rocket scientists of the early postwar period, who were vigorously sought after by both sides in the Cold War. They greatly accelerated both sides' missile development and space programs, for their knowledge shaved many years off the time it would have taken to make progress in these areas without their help. So it is with master hackers today, and there are a few signs that some nations are exploring the idea of employing them, even to a small extent in the United States, where official hostility to hackers runs very high.[20]

Still, far more can and should be done, perhaps in the context of a United Nations or other transnational cyber defense initiative (CDI), a latter-day successor to the nuclear-age strategic defense initiative (SDI) first advanced by Ronald Reagan in 1983. But whereas prospects for defending against missile attack have advanced little in the past three decades, chances are that a concerted cyber effort of the kind just outlined would achieve resounding success in relatively short order. To the objection that recruiting master hackers for cyber defensive purposes is a case of seeking protection from a principal predatory element, the response is that these hackers have not as yet been radicalized, and a CDI would be a good way to channel their energies in more productive ways. Needless to say, those recruited would be carefully monitored, 24/7, to insure that the sensitive knowledge shared with them would be used only for appropriate purposes.

Finally, it is important to think in cool-headed ways about the appropriate uses of information wars. First impulses may lead one to think such conflicts should be tamped down. But when an information war, particularly one of ideas, serves to empower civil society actors in their efforts to free themselves from authoritarian rule, is this not a good cause? Is not an information war of this sort a less costly and relatively bloodless way to achieve regime change? Certainly, it seems more attractive than effecting such change by means of armed civil insurrection or outside military intervention. Even on the traditional battlefield, the skillful employment of information warfare techniques might lead to a much swifter victory, as modern militaries can hardly function without secure, available connectivity. Therefore, war as we have known it may change for the better, thanks to the impact of information operations. In at least these respects, the information revolution offers a sharp contrast to the Industrial Revolution, which fostered and sustained larger, bloodier, and more costly wars. Properly employed, information wars may reverse the trend permanently.

NOTES

1. On the social and strategic consequences of the telegraph, see Tom Standage (1998).

2. A good survey of this concept of operations was provided by Munro (1991).

3. On the early days of radio electronic warfare, see Jones (1978).

4. See, e.g., Bellin and Chapman (1987).

5. An insightful assessment of the role of information management in this conflict can be found in Allard (1994).

6. On the rise of hacking, see Bruce Sterling (1992).

7. "Cyberwar" is a term first popularized in Arquilla and Ronfeldt (1993).

8. For an outstanding overview of these developments and debates, as well as the policy struggles that accompanied them, see Rattray (2001). His second chapter explores the analogies between strategic aerial bombing and cyberwar, a theme introduced earlier in Arquilla and Ronfeldt (1997).

9. A classic study of this issue is Quester's *Offense and Defense in the International System* (1973).

10. On this point, see Carr (2002). Interesting counterpoint is offered in Dershowitz's *Why Terrorism Works* (2002).

11. This concept was first described in Arquilla and Ronfeldt, "Cyberwar Is Coming!" But it was elaborated further in their *Advent of Netwar and Networks and Netwars* (Santa Monica, CA: RAND, 1996 and 2001).

12. An outstanding history of such modern influence operations can be found in Ellul (1965).

13. From a letter Jefferson wrote to James Monroe, dated January 1, 1815. See Ford (1898). Frankfurt (2006) also offers a profound meditation on the importance of refraining from twisting information or engaging in outright lies.

14. An important early study of this issue was provided by Schwartau (1994). For a more recent assessment, see Verton (2003).

15. Anonymous Russian official, cited in Thomas (1997), 77.

16. The notion of using robust defensive capabilities as a basis for deterrence, rather than just punitive threats, is thoroughly considered in Morgan (1977) and Mearsheimer (1984).

17. Of course, the hackers may have had no intention of conducting a longer cyber campaign, so one must draw conclusions about cyber deterrence with care. Nevertheless, the attacks stopped almost immediately when the strong defensive responses were mounted, suggesting that something more than a coincidence of timing was at work.

18. On the muddled U.S. policy toward encryption and on citizen responses to it, see Levy (2002).

19. The assertions here about the master hacker community reflect the author's personal assessment based on his field research in this issue area over the past two decades. The author can confirm that remote-controlled armies of slaves, zombies, and botnets under a single master hacker's control often number in the several hundreds of thousands of computers. A common use is to assist in code-breaking endeavors.

20. The author's assessment, based on his experiences, is that a master hacker in service to some government has been a rarity over the past two decades. However, many second-tier cyber operators have indeed been recruited by many nations.

FURTHER READING

Libicki, Martin. *What Is Information Warfare?* Washington, DC: National Defense University, 1995.

Rattray, Gregory. *Strategic Warfare in Cyberspace.* Cambridge, MA: MIT Press, 2001.

Verton, Dan. *Black Ice: The Invisible Threat of Cyber-Terrorism.* New York: McGraw-Hill, 2003.

Weimann, Gabriel. *Terror on the Internet.* Washington, DC: U.S. Institute of Peace Press, 2006.

REFERENCES

Allard, C. Kenneth. 1994. The future of command and control: Toward a paradigm of information warfare. In *Turning point: The Gulf War and U.S. military strategy,* ed. L. B. Ederington and M. J. Mazarr, 161–92. Boulder, CO: Westview Press.

Arquilla, John, and David Ronfeldt. 1993. Cyberwar is coming! *Comparative Strategy* 12: 141–65.

———. 1997. *In Athena's camp: Preparing for conflict in the Information Age.* Santa Monica, CA: RAND.

Bellin, David, and Gary Chapman, eds. 1987. *Computers in battle: Will they work?* New York: Harcourt, Brace Jovanovich.

Carr, Caleb. 2002. *The lessons of terror.* New York: Random House.

Dershowitz, Alan. 2002. *Why terrorism works.* New Haven, CT: Yale University Press.

Ellul, Jacques. 1965. *Propaganda: The formation of men's attitudes.* Trans. Konrad Kellen and Jean Lerner. New York: Random House.

Ford, Paul Leicester, ed. 1898. *The writings of Thomas Jefferson.* New York.

Frankfurt, Harry G. 2006. *On truth.* New York: Alfred A. Knopf.

Jervis, Robert. 1978. Cooperation under the security dilemma. *World Politics* 30: 167–214.

Jones, R. V. 1978. *The wizard war: British scientific intelligence, 1939–1945.* New York: Coward, McCann & Geoghegan.

Levy, Steven. 2002. *Crypto: How the rebels beat the government, saving privacy in the digital age.* New York: Penguin.

McLuhan, Marshall, and Quentin Fiore. 1997. *War and peace in the global village.* San Francisco: Wired. (Originally published in 1968.)

Mearsheimer, John. 1984. *Conventional deterrence.* Ithaca, NY: Cornell University Press.

Morgan, Patrick. 1977. *Deterrence: A conceptual analysis.* Beverly Hills, CA: Sage Publications.

Munro, Neil. 1991. *The quick and the dead: Electronic combat and modern warfare.* New York: St. Martin's Press.

Quester, George. 1973. *Offense and defense in the international system.* New York: Wiley.

Rattray, Gregory J. 2001. *Strategic warfare in cyberspace.* Cambridge, MA: MIT Press.
Schwartau, Winn. 1994. *Information warfare: Chaos on the electronic superhighway.* New York: Thunder's Mouth Press.
Snyder, Jack. 1984. *The ideology of the offensive: Military decision making and the disasters of 1914.* Ithaca, NY: Cornell University Press.
Standage, Tom. 1998. *The Victorian internet.* New York: Walker and Company.
Sterling, Bruce. 1992. *The hacker crackdown: Law and disorder on the electronic frontier.* New York: Bantam.
Taber, Robert. 1970. *The war of the flea.* New York: Citadel Press.
Thomas, Timothy L. 1997. The threat of information operations: A Russian perspective. In *War in the Information Age: New challenges for U.S. security,* ed. R. Pfaltzgraff and R. H. Shultz. London: Brassey's.
Verton, Dan. 2003. *Black ice: The invisible threat of cyber-terrorism.* New York: McGraw-Hill.

12

Nation-State

Cory Blad

The modern era of human history has been organized and defined by the sociopolitical institution of the nation-state. Our geography is ordered by its territorial boundaries, our identities are shaped by our relationships to its cultural norms, our wars are fought between them, and our societies are shaped by its organizational structure. Any discussion of contemporary or modern historical social, political, economic, and cultural order *must* focus on this institution. The problem, however, is that any social institution designed to provide security, order, stability, and protection in heterogeneous societies is by definition multifaceted. How are we to understand the nation-state? How are we even to define it?

This chapter briefly chronicles the historical development of the nation-state, illustrates theories of its functions and dynamics, and finally discusses the recent changes that have impacted the nation-state in our contemporary era of globalization. These three categories are designed to offer an introductory look at where the nation-state came from, how we study it, and what its future might hold.

HISTORY OF THE NATION-STATE

The early state system in Europe developed in the wake of the Roman Empire as a means to manage the populations and territory formerly governed by Rome. The steady decline of the Roman Empire in the fourth and fifth centuries CE created a series of political opportunities that enabled several Germanic tribes to coalesce their power into territorial kingdoms. Notable examples of these Germanic kingdoms were the Saxons in Britain, Gothic tribes throughout Southern Europe and into Spain, and arguably the most successful kingdom, the Franks, in what would become France.

The evolution of these early imperial states ultimately centered on agricultural production and the requisite land for such productive activities. The emergence of the political economic system known as *feudalism* was based on a hierarchical political system (local lords acting as political emissaries for regional dukes, barons, or counts, who in turn served monarchical leadership) that relied on control over land, and subsequent agricultural resources produced, for state power.[1] In other words, the more productive the land controlled by a respective state, the more power the state possessed.

Feudal conflict over land and resources was perpetually violent. This condition of persistent violence was exacerbated by emergent cultural conflict between Catholic and Protestant adherents during the Thirty Years' War (1618–1648). While a significant motivation for this brutal war was over religious dominance, numerous political forces were at work in creating this extended period of violent conflict, including territorial rivalries between such states as France and the Hapsburg dynastic states of Spain, Flanders (included in the contemporary Netherlands), and Austria. In fact, a major outcome of the war was the realization that state affiliation, and not cultural affinity, was becoming increasingly important.

In 1648, the treaties of Münster and Osnabrück, better known as the Peace of Westphalia, were signed, ending the Thirty Years' War. The signatories (the Holy Roman Empire, numerous German principalities, France, Spain, the Dutch Republic, and Sweden) agreed on a series of territorial and political boundaries that would come to define the modern concept of *sovereignty*. In short, the Peace of Westphalia codified territorial sovereignty by establishing international laws that forbade one political entity from interfering in the affairs of another. This was particularly important in the transformation from a regional mode of governance based primarily on a supranational cultural authority, Catholicism, to a set of legally distinct autonomous and sovereign states responsible for managing internal political, economic, social, and cultural affairs. State institutions and increasingly important national populations determined local means of social organization. Increasingly, *local* or *national* culture—such as religious adherence, vernacular language, and local norms—became more important in defining territorial association and geographic limits of respective sovereignty.

The combination of territorial sovereignty and national cultural identity facilitated the rise of the modern nation-state. It can be argued, however, that the primary motivation for this political development was largely economic. The emergence of *capitalism* as the dominant social and economic structure in European society motivated the protection of local production and markets. The political structure of the nation-state system made it much easier to create a system privileging sovereignty and protecting capitalist production and consumption within a specifically defined territory. The development of *mercantile capitalism* would reflect this emphasis on national protection. The expansion of European exploration and colonialism was directly motivated by the desire to acquire new sources of material wealth (either in the form of precious metals or, more commonly, natural resources) that could be used to fuel increased manufacturing activities in home countries. Mercantile colonies produced solely for the parent (home) country, and therefore the relationship between home country and colony, from an economic perspective, could only be understood as purely exploitative. (For a Marxist perspective, see Lenin 1939 and Luxemburg 1951; for a liberal perspective, see Paine 1953.)

As capitalism matured, technological improvements in both agricultural and industrial production ushered in a new era of socioeconomic organization that would both strengthen and challenge the nation-state and define the political economic era in which we live (see Table 12.1).

INDUSTRIAL CAPITALISM AND THE MODERN STATE

The industrial manufacturing economy that developed in England and quickly spread to the rest of the developed world allowed production to expand more quickly and at higher volume than ever before. The result was a surplus of manufactured goods that needed to be sold. Industrial capitalism also required an expansion of markets in which surplus goods could be sold. The existing mercantile order, in which international trade occurred under heavy nationalist protections that discouraged or eliminated foreign competition, soon came to be resented by industrial capitalists because of its restrictions on liberal, "free" trade between nation-states. In order for capital interests to be unfettered, the ideology of liberalism and limited state interference was required.

State institutions could not easily promote freedoms and liberties for economic interests while denying them to the whole of the citizenry—at least not

Table 12.1 Important Dates in the Early Development of Nation-States

Important Dates in the Early Development of Nation-States	
476	Fall of the Western Roman Empire
843	Treaty of Verdun partitions the Frankish Kingdom and creates the Holy Roman Empire
1337–1453	Hundred Years' War, significant because of the transition of military salaries from land to gold (or other capital)
1517	Beginnings of the Protestant Reformation and the further division of international cultural authority
1618–1648	Thirty Years' War, fought primarily between Protestant and Catholic adherents over territorial control and cultural authority
1648	Peace of Westphalia, comprising the Treaties of Münster and Osnabrück, is signed by the Holy Roman Empire, numerous German principalities, France, Spain, the Dutch Republic, and Sweden. The Peace of Westphalia established an international standard of territorial sovereignty that effectively outlawed warfare between states over territory. The concept of territorial sovereignty, and the right to autonomous government within respective territories, is the foundation for the modern nation-state.
1776	American Revolution begins an antimercantilist effort to expand liberalism in political and economic forms
1789	French Revolution, arguably the first truly liberal revolutionary movement that sought a complete overthrow of the traditional socioeconomic order on mainland Europe

Source: Author.

for sustained periods of time. The solution was found in the marriage of liberalism and capitalism in the eighteenth and nineteenth centuries that enabled capitalist operation and growth to occur in a free and unrestrained fashion. Economic liberals championed limited state interference in matters of economics and argued that such laws of the market as supply and demand were more than sufficient to manage liberal market economic systemic operation. Ironically, historical examinations of liberal capitalism cannot identify any instance of capital accumulation and growth without the support of state institutions, resources, or legislation (see Polanyi 2001; Barrow 2005).

The state was necessary for a number of reasons. The first was that national economic markets that were vulnerable to foreign competition continued to demand protection. Monetary policy, including taxation on imported goods (tariffs) and national currency valuation, continued to be utilized to encourage national economic growth by hindering external competition. This fiscal strategy ran counter to liberal economic theory; however, national capital interests and national populations often supported this derivation from theoretical orthodoxy. In summary, liberal capitalism never emerged as an exclusive economic strategy for any industrial capitalist nation-state because of the threat of foreign competition to national economic interests.

The modern state must manage dual requirements: to create conditions of unrestrained capitalist growth as well as meeting national protectionist demands. The latter is primarily important to the state because of the necessity of maintaining social order. States have utilized social welfare strategies to meet national social protectionist demands largely for the purpose of ensuring social order. These welfare strategies have generally proven effective in ensuring desired order, although they are consistently attacked by proponents of liberal capitalism as creating unnecessary restraints on capitalist operation and therefore limiting growth.

This brief historical overview of nation-state emergence and development ends in the nineteenth century. The large-scale social transformations that created massive upheaval in the 1800s were the result of the ubiquitous transition of state institutions to a model of liberal democracy and capitalism. The freedoms granted to common citizens were decried by such social conservatives who bemoaned the loss of traditional social order as Edmund Burke and Gustave LeBon. In turn, the freedoms grants to capitalist operation were summarily criticized by such others who viewed the new social order as destroying stabilizing structures of traditional society as Karl Marx and Robert Owen.

The struggle to understand the dynamics of the modern nation-state, particularly the relationship between liberal democracy and liberal capitalism, would consume political scientists and political sociologists for years to come. In fact, by examining several competing theories of the nation-state developed in the twentieth century, we can better understand the problematic conflict between these two defining features of the modern nation-state. The following section continues the historical development of the nation-state but also embeds this historical narrative in a larger discussion of the theoretical debates that center on the precarious role of the state in an era of increased global political economic integration (i.e., globalization).

GLOBALIZATION, SECURITY, AND THE CRISIS OF THE STATE

In 1990, Kenichi Ohmae presented the view that territorial sovereignty was being qualitatively eroded by the increased financial mobility and trade occurring on a global scale. This was hardly a new claim (see Burton 1972; Keohane and Nye 1972); however, the large-scale increases in financial mobility and global trade that would come to define the decade of the 1990s would lead Ohmae in 1995 to more forcefully proclaim the "end of the nation-state" in favor of more efficient regional economic agreements that would facilitate the new era of globalization.

The popularity of Ohmae's position and the emergence of a massive volume of literature on globalization as a new era (see Robinson 2004, 1996; Weinstein 2005), one in which the state is either dead or dying (see later section on state decline), has generated a strong defense of the concept and reality of the nation-state. The work of Clyde Barrow (2005), Peter Evans (1997), Eric Helleiner (1994), and Linda Weiss (2003, 1998), to name a few, offers a substantial defense of the nation-state as an institution of continued importance. From this perspective, the nation-state remains a necessary social, political, and economic institution that has adapted to changing conditions, largely motivated by increased global economic integration. This represents not a decline or death of the nation-state but, rather, an adaptation.

The two conclusions are exclusive to a degree. On the one hand, globalization (specifically, the global economy) has become the driving force behind social change throughout the world in our contemporary era. On the other hand, the nation-state is a required institution, without which globalization could not function. How did this debate emerge? More to the point, what changed to motivate globalization theorists to proclaim the "end of the nation-state"?

EMBEDDED LIBERALISM AND THE RESURGENCE OF GLOBAL CAPITALISM

The post–World War II era has been defined by two seemingly contradictory patterns with respect to the state: expansion and decline. The first period, from approximately 1945 through the mid-1970s, has been variously described as a period of "welfare capitalism," the era of "welfare state expansion," and the era of "embedded liberalism." In brief, this period is characterized by a nearly universal expansion of social welfare spending by Western state institutions while at the same time increasing liberal trade reforms that facilitated international trade. John Ruggie (1982) popularized the term "embedded liberalism" to define this period in which national social spending and welfare state expansion occurred (and was encouraged) at the same time as nation-states supported the resumption of global trade liberalization (i.e., the reduction of protectionist tariffs and national subsidies). This was, in fact, a period of political economic compromise in which the economic liberalism promoted by capitalist elites and national social protectionism coexisted. This compromise managed by empowered state institutions that were responsible for supplying social welfare provisions demanded by national constituencies, at the same time enabling trade liberalization and limiting national economic protectionism with respect to international trade.

The end of this period of strong states and class compromise began in the early 1970s. For a series of monetary and political reasons, Richard Nixon took the dollar off of its established valuation mechanism of gold (then pegged at $35 per ounce) in 1971 and effectively ended the system of managed international trade that was established at the Bretton Woods Conference in 1944 (see Frieden 2006; Gilpin 1987). The end of the Bretton Woods system of managed liberal international trade, coupled with successive oil price increases in 1973 and 1979, created conditions that made social welfare spending much more expensive for state institutions.

Between 1944 and 1971, national currency values were fixed in relation to the U.S. dollar, which was essentially the official currency for the international economic system. When the dollar was taken off gold, national currency values were based on a series of floating exchange rates determined through private market means or a value determined by such market mechanisms as supply and demand. The result was a massive increase in global financial trading of national currencies that has led to an exponential increase in global financial market activity (in 2004, foreign exchange market activity totaled over $1.8 *billion a day*). Some analysts have understood this historical period as being defined by the "liberation" of financial capital from national economic controls (see Robinson 2004). As the value of a national currency became more and more determined by private market speculation and private valuation, the less and less the nation-state could utilize monetary policy as an effective means to enforce national economic and social protections. The state still had the ability to influence the value of its own currency, of course, but at the risk of adversely affecting the global currency exchange market—which, nation-states actively supported after 1973.[2]

The globalization of financial capital was soon coupled with a specific political economic ideology intended to resolve the lingering fiscal crises facing Western nation-states. *Neoliberalism* emerged in the late 1970s as a political economic project championing private capital and market capitalism over the embedded liberalism of the early postwar period. In simplest terms, neoliberal ideology states that private business could more efficiently provide social and economic services than could the state. Governments in the United States, Great Britain, and Chile were the first to begin implementing these neoliberal reforms that generally reduced the scale, expenditures, and regulatory power of state institutions. Privatization, or the shift from public to private control, of transportation, health care, education, and even social welfare provision soon came to define the 1980s throughout the Western world.

In the early 1990s, neoliberalism was also used as a strategy to integrate former communist nation-states into the global capitalist economy by championing the liberal market economic system as well as devaluing the influence of nascent democratic states in Eastern Europe. For structural and ideological reasons, the state was deemed by many to be in decline because of the globalization of political ideology (neoliberalism), economics (liberal market capitalism), and even culture (material consumption). Several theorists began to openly question the claim that the nation-state remained the primary political force within the international political economic system. Predictably, many analysts disagree and remain convinced that the nation-state retains its primary position of power.

THEORIES OF THE STATE

This section offers a brief overview of theoretical perspectives in an effort to better understand the state. The section then returns to the previous question of state decline to offer a more detailed explanation of the theoretical perspectives purported to explain the challenges to the nation-state in an era of globalization and increased interconnectivity.

Society-Centered: Elite and Pluralist Theories of the State

Elite and pluralist theories are polar opposites: The former understands the state as being controlled and managed by small, oligarchic groups of powerful individuals. The latter views the state as being explicitly democratic with equal opportunity for political participation regardless of class, status, or other inhibiting factors. The conflict between these perspectives is reflective of the difficulties in reconciling capitalism, which is inherently unequal in the distribution of capital resources, and democracy, which professes a foundation of equality.

Elite theory was popularized in the 1950s with the work of C. Wright Mills (1956); more recent contributions were made by G. William Domhoff (1990) and Thomas Dye (2001), who continue to define contemporary elite theory. Mills's work was largely inspired by the political theory of Karl Marx as well as by members of the "Italian School of Elitists" such as Robert Michaels (1956), Gaetano Mosca (1939), and Vilfredo Pareto (1935). While the nuances of each theorist differ, the contemporary work of Mills, Domhoff, and others is linked by a central belief that political power is controlled by a specific group that is comprised of economic elites in any respective society. In short, the economic elite of any respective state will always control the political processes and institutions of contemporary democratic nation-states. There is very little distinction between economic power and political power in elite theory. In fact, political power is viewed as somewhat ancillary to economic power simply because one cannot hope to have any substantial political influence without first having the economic resources necessary to become a member of the ruling elite.

Pluralism, on the other hand, makes a clear demarcation between economic and political power. Pluralist theory is a specifically political theory of the democratic state in which the economic power of capitalist interests does not adversely affect the mechanical functions of democratic (read: egalitarian) governance. This perspective is founded on classical works by Frederic Maitland (2003) and Harold Laski (1935), with Robert Dahl (1967), Charles Lindblom (1965), and Nelson Polsby (1965) offering a mid-twentieth-century perspective. Pluralists dismiss claims by elite theorists that there is a single dominant group in any democratic nation-state. Instead, they argue that the bureaucratic mechanisms of the modern state create a condition of political equality as the result of an established hierarchy of political process. When a problem or concern arises, local groups form voluntarily in support or opposition to any particular issue. These groups then approach state bureaucratic institutions or representatives, which then pass on these concerns up the appropriate chain of command until action can be taken.

From this perspective, all groups in a respective nation-state have access to the state bureaucracy, thus creating equal access opportunities for political participation. While socioeconomic inequality undoubtedly exists in all nation-states, pluralists argue that this inequality does not inhibit political participation nor does it enable power to be located in a single group of economic elites. Even members of a specific elite class have divergent interests and rivalries, which makes any form of group collusion difficult if not impossible.

Both theories claim to explain how the state is organized and functions, but clearly, both differ in their conclusions. Elite theory has proven more lasting; however, its linear focus on a single elite group has led to numerous challenges. Many argue that this explanation is overly simplistic and often not supported by empirical evidence. The ability to combine economic and political power within a single theoretical framework has proven to be one of the most effective contributions of elite theory in its attempts to explain the operation of the capitalist democratic nation-state.

Conversely, pluralism does not engage capitalism in the same manner and has been criticized for its limited scope by focusing solely on the political processes of democratic bureaucracy. Pluralist theory is often criticized for its inherent belief in equal access to democratic political processes, which either ignores or minimizes the role of socioeconomic inequality in defining access to the state and other political resources.

Marxian State Theory: Instrumentalist and Structuralist Perspectives

Marxian state theory (re)emerged in the 1960s and 1970s as a theoretical challenge to both structural-functionalist theories of social cohesion and perceived weaknesses inherent in elite theory. Two main perspectives, instrumentalist and structuralist, dominate Marxian theories of the state and will be discussed in turn. While there are significant differences between the instrumentalist and structuralist theories of the state, both are based on the central Marxist tenet of class domination based on power derived through economic means. In fact, the basic theoretical foundation for Marxian state theory is similar to that utilized by Mills in support of his version of elite theory. The main difference is in the Marxian development of specific class interests. In other words, it is not simply an oligarchical group of elite individuals that have control over the state (as in elite theory), but an entire class of individuals operating in a cohesive and unified fashion.

Instrumentalist state theory was promoted by Ralph Miliband in his 1969 *The State in Capitalist Society*. The basic premise of this perspective is similar to that of elite theory: that a "ruling class" of capitalist elites is able to "use the state as its instrument for the domination of society" (1969, 23). Miliband offered a direct challenge to pluralist perspectives by studying common class interests and defining the capitalist class as the large-scale owners of established corporations and associated interests. In short, this dominant capitalist class manipulates the state much as a cellist manipulates the cello.

The similarities between instrumentalist state theory and elite theory are obvious. Both understand state institutional bureaucracy to be controlled by a small group of economic elites. The major difference, however, is that elite theory (after Mills) moved away from its Marxian foundations by marginalizing class. For instrumentalist state theorists, class is the primary unit of analysis when studying the modern state. The elites in control of state agendas and actions have specific class interests—that is, they act in relative unison to support their dominance as a capitalist elite. Instrumentalists commonly argue that the state does not exist as an institutional entity; rather, it is merely the organizational manifestation of the capitalist class. This is a significant departure from pluralist theories that argue that no unified class cooperation exists within the democratic (capitalist) system. Miliband and others disagree and cite specific evidence of interlocking leaderships positions within the state and corporations (see Sweezy 1970). In other words, those in control of major corporate interests are also in control of positions of power within state institutions.

Within Marxian state theory, however, there were those that disagreed with the instrumentalist understanding of the state. Nicos Poulantzas (1978), inspired by the work of Louis Althusser (1970), specifically questioned the instrumentalist understanding that the state did not exist outside of its function as a tool for capitalist class power retention. Poulantzas promoted a *structuralist* understanding of the state that specifically separated state *structure* from state *power*. In short, the structure of the state (its bureaucratic organization and particularly the individual bureaucratic agents of the state) exists in a real sense and provides structural support for the capitalist socioeconomic system. That is, the state provides the structure that maintains social order necessary for capitalist operation. State power, on the other hand, can be defined (and quantified) as the capacity of a specific class to control the agendas and actions of the state. State structure is constant and exists for the purpose of supporting capitalist development and growth; however, state power can ebb and flow, given specific conditions. Given the static nature of the state (structure) and the variable nature of (state) power, Poulantzas concluded, the state can at times be relatively autonomous of capitalist class interests.

In the early 1970s, Miliband (1970, 1973) and Poulantzas (1969, 1973, 1976) engaged in a substantial debate over the methodological differences between their respective positions. The debate was steeped in Marxist theoretical disagreements, but it succeeded in bringing Marxian state theory into the academic limelight once again. While instrumentalists and structuralists disagree over certain aspects of state operation and composition, they are united in the belief that specific class interests drive the primary responsibility of the contemporary state. Marxian state theory highlights this central role of the state and the inherent class inequality of the capitalist system. Thus, the primary purpose of state analysis from a Marxian perspective is to illustrate and examine the relationship of capitalism and the institutions of the contemporary nation-state. The prevailing finding of this research agenda is that the capitalist (or "bourgeois," to use the traditional Marxist term) class dominates political institutions in respective nation-states and utilizes the state to maintain this position of dominance.

State-Centered Theory: State Autonomy, Embedded Autonomy, and Social Embedded Approaches

Soon after Marxian state theory gained in notoriety (largely as a consequence of the prestige of the Miliband-Poulantzas debate) many political sociologists and political scientists questioned the class-based conclusions generated by both instrumentalists and structuralists. The lack of institutional autonomy from capitalist class interests struck many as a primary flaw in Marxian state theory. How, for example, could action taken by the state, in contradiction to prevailing capitalist class interests, be explained using existing Marxian perspectives? In 1979, Theda Skocpol articulated a theory of the state that directly critiqued existing pluralist, elite, and Marxian theories as being too "society-centered." For Skocpol, state action taken contrary to capitalist class interests was reflective of full, not relative, autonomy of state bureaucracy and institutions. That is, the state was not beholden to capitalist class demands, nor was it required to adhere to other class-based demands on its agenda and actions. Rather, the state exists in *isolated autonomy* from the remainder of any respective society. The state, as a result of the development of a rational bureaucratic structure, insulates itself from society so that it functions without large-scale interference by class factions and/or popular resistance to agendas and actions (Skocpol 1979; Evans, Rueschemeyer, and Skocpol 1985; see also Nettl 1968). This state-centered theory provided a popular, but soon-challenged corrective to existing society-centered theories of the state.

As the idea of "isolated" or "full" state autonomy gained in utility and application, it was increasingly critiqued by Marxian, elite, and pluralist state theorists. Even more interesting was the critique coming from one of the early proponents of the "isolated autonomy approach." Peter Evans promoted a less isolated approach to understanding the state, termed *embedded autonomy*. This is a limited autonomy, for the role of the state in Evans's work is closely tied to the desires and interests of economic (capitalist) interest groups. For Evans, the state is embedded in society, but only to the extent that it satisfies national economic interests. In an ironic nod to elite or instrumentalist Marxian theory, he predicts that ultimately the embedded autonomy of states will succumb to the power and interests of economic elites (see Evans 1995).

The work of Linda Weiss (2003, 1998), while generally falling into the embedded autonomy perspective, does not share Evans's pessimistic outlook. Weiss argues that the autonomy of states offers the ability to adjust strategic agendas and actions in support of economic (industrial) growth, thus allowing the state to manage socioeconomic conditions to benefit national economic interests. While Evans and Weiss differ in their conclusions, both agree that the state is autonomous from larger social structures, but it is also embedded in certain social structures; namely, the economic interests of dominant elite groups.

Embedded autonomous states are limited in their autonomy because specific social interests guide state actions. The nature of state embeddedness is also limited to the economic interests of the dominant capital-industrial private sector. While the embedded autonomy approach shares the emphasis on autonomous state bureaucratic institutions, the work of Evans and Weiss has much in common with Marxian and elite theorists of the state in their emphasis on the disproportionate political power inherent in private capitalist interests.

The final state-centered theoretical perspective is generally termed *social embeddedness*. In short, this perspective moves even further from Skocpol's original isolated autonomy approach to allocate much more agency to national populations, regardless of class. John Hobson's work is most indicative of this approach and argues that popular interest groups actively and successfully influence the agendas and actions of respective state bureaucratic institutions (see Hobson 2000, 1997; Hobson and Seabrooke 2001). This perspective questions the theoretical limitations imposed by simply viewing state power and capacity as being determined by a dominant capitalist class. Proponents of social embeddedness offer evidence that such class reductionism ignores an obvious and important relationship between the state and inclusive nation populations. Social embeddedness theory argues that states require a level of social legitimacy in order to operate. Without national popular approval, long-term social stability and state legitimacy is threatened. This legitimacy implies a constant relationship between state institutions and national populations, not simply a relationship between state institutions and the dominant economic interests of any respective nation-state (see Table 12.2).

In all, theories of the state—be they elite, pluralist, Marxian, or state-centered—focus exclusively on the operation, structure, and dynamics of the

Table 12.2 Notable Theories of the State

Notable Theories of the State	
Elite Theory	**Pluralist Theory**
C. Wright Mills	Robert Dahl
Thomas Dye	Charles Lindblom
G. William Domhoff	Nelson Polsby
State-centered Theory	**Marxian State Theory**
Isolated Autonomy	*Instrumentalist*
Charles Tilly	Ralph Miliband
Theda Skocpol	Paul Sweezy
Embedded Autonomy	*Structuralist*
Peter Evans	Nicos Poulantzas
Linda Weiss	Robert Cox
Social Embeddedness	
Fred Block	
John Hobson	

Source: Author.

nation-state. This unit of analysis was logical given that the primary locus of political power had always been the institutional bureaucracy inherent in the nation-state. Beginning in the 1970s, though, global political economic conditions began to change. By the 1980s and 1990s, many theorists actively questioned whether the nation-state remained the primary location for political economic power.

STATE DECLINE

Many scholars have observed the phenomenon of state decline since the 1970s (see Habermas 1975; O'Connor 1973; Touraine 1977). Only recently though, has a consensus developed that has enabled the globalist perspective to claim the demise or even the death of the nation-state as a result of increasing global socioeconomic interconnectedness known as globalization. The main claims of the globalist perspective range from those who view the nation-state as having lost control of a specific group of economic elites, the Transnational Capitalist Class, who have no specific national economic agenda and answer to no state authority (see Dicken 1998; Robinson 2004; Sklair 2002); to those who view the fiscal crises of the state in the 1970s as having long-term effects on the legitimacy of state authority in general, particularly with respect a perceived loss of authority over national populations (see Habermas 2001; Held 1995; Giddens 1990); to explanations of state decline being the result of advanced telecommunications technologies and the emergence of a new information society (see Castells 1996–1998; Wriston 1992). These samples of a large and growing literature point the global mobility of financial capital, information, and even production (i.e., outsourcing or offshoring) as the main culprits in the decreasing power of the state. While these analysts generally agree that the state has declined in its relative power, they are cautious in concluding anything more than a general decline.

Other notable examples of globalization or globalism theory are less willing to grant any political economic power to the contemporary nation-state. Some of these "hyperglobalists" have argued that given advances in information technologies and developments in economic globalization, the state is an outdated institution (see Camilleri and Falk 1992; Guéhenno 1995; Horsman and Marshall 1994; Ohmae 1995). Kenichi Ohmae offers a particularly specific assessment of the nation-state that is indicative of this perspective: "The nation state has become an unnatural, even dysfunctional, unit for organizing human activity and managing economic endeavor in a borderless world" (1993, 78).

This wide-raging dismissal of the nation-state as a primary political economic unit of analysis has led many to respond in defense of the state as retaining its primary position of political economic power. The development of embedded autonomy and social embeddedness theories of the state (previously discussed) have provided many opportunities for theorists to argue that the state remains a significant player in shaping political economic strategies. Linda Weiss (1998), for example, argues that globalization affects nation-states unevenly and elicits varying responses based on the political economic capacity of any respective state. Examining state ability to adapt to changing global economic conditions is therefore a valuable analytical endeavor. Others, including Marxian state theorists, have argued for a return to society-centered theory in viewing the state as managing an arena of conflict between liberal market forces and national population demands (Barrow 2005; Hobson and Ramesh 2002; Yeates 2002).

The debate over state decline or state adaptation continues to produce substantial scholarship on both sides. While the debate over the contemporary utility and power of state institutions has generally concluded that the development of a truly global economic system (globalization) has hindered the traditional capacities of the nation-state to meet national economic protectionist demands or fund large-scale social welfare programs, for example, the question of the *nation* has become increasingly important, particularly in the post-2001 global system.

RESURGENT NATIONALISM

The post–World War II era has seen the rise of ethnic nationalism around the globe. From efforts to achieve political sovereignty in Quebec, Scotland, and Catalonia to the explosion of violent ethnocultural conflicts in Rwanda, the former Yugoslavia, Thailand, and elsewhere, the past 60-plus years have seen a precipitous increase in political conflict predicated on cultural and ethnic affiliation. It seems that as globalization has reduced the traditional power of state institutions, the intensity of ethnocultural conflict has increased.

Several theorists have commented on this phenomenon. Most argue that this increase in nationalist sentiment, ethnocultural conflict, and even the emergence of fundamentalist religiosity is the result of declining state authority. Anthony Giddens provides a particularly direct summary:

> Globalisation is the reason for the revival of local cultural identities in different parts of the world. If one asks, for example, why the Scots want more independence in the UK, or why there is a strong separatist movement in Quebec, the answer is not to be found only in their cultural history. Local nationalisms spring up as a response to globalizing tendencies, as the hold of older nation-states weakens. (2003, 13)

Other analysts point to similar political opportunities for long-repressed ethnocultural minority populations (Castells 2004; Guibernau 1999; Riggs 1994). Legitimate authority weakens as a result of privatization, declining capacity to provide social services, and decreased ability to protect national economic interests. The result is a dual condition in which states are increasingly unable to pacify national populations through traditional protectionist means and the turn is toward such national cultural groups as those based on religion, language, ethnicity or race. As Manuel Castells has observed, a primary analytical problem is "to explain the simultaneous rise of postmodern nationalism and decline of the modern state" (2004, 34).

Michael Keating addresses this problem of state decline as a function of a loss in the "capacity for territorial management" (1996, 221). Various fiscal and legitimation crises around the world have reduced the ability of state institutions to control ethnocultural nationalism. The traditional strategy was for state institutions to circumvent ethnic and cultural rivalries by promoting an official ideology centered on such civic conceptualization of nationalism as ethnoculturally neutral symbols and traditions basically invented by state institutions. As states are downsized and subjugated by the ideology of neoliberalism, are financially challenged by structural changes in the global economic system, and as a result lose national popular legitimacy, they are increasingly unable to maintain control over these civic symbols and traditions. Concurrently, the state may be replaced by national popular groups espousing group membership and spouting protectionist rhetoric couched in ethnically and culturally specific terms.

A QUESTION OF SECURITY

While strong evidence points to the decline, if not forced strategic adaptation, of state power, most analyses conclude that the state retains a significant role within the global political economic system. Capitalism relies on conditions of stability; therefore, the primary role of the contemporary state in the era of globalization is to ensure local stability. Each state is tasked with ensuring labor complicity, sociopolitical stability, and protection of conditions favorable to large-scale profit through capital accumulation (see Panitch 1994; Wallerstein 1974). Although neoliberal ideology advocates the reduction of state bureaucratic infrastructure, it does not advocate the elimination of the state, primarily for the aforementioned specific reasons.

The challenge unforeseen by neoliberal architects and transnational capitalist interests was the emergence of strong, nationally based cultural challenges to the weakened state and to the global political economic system itself. Proponents and enablers of the modern global political economic system failed to appreciate the strength of national protectionist demands. As the welfare state compromises of the embedded liberalism era eroded, liberal market capitalism began to become more and more unfettered in its operation. Deindustrialization and urban decline led to increased financial burdens for state institutions already unable to meet traditional fiscal responsibilities. In the developing world, the dominance of neoliberal ideology and the involvement of international financial institutions such as the IMF and World Bank, which generally operate on neoliberal political economic principles, has created conditions in which state institutions have little control over foreign capital investment and even less ability to draw taxable revenue from the operation of foreign-owned manufacturing facilities.

The weakened state is unable, in many cases, to meet the traditional protectionist demands of its national populations. As a result, populist and nationalist groups based on cultural affinity have increased their power within, and in some cases over, states. The contemporary challenge facing both nation-states and the global system is how to meet national protectionist demands within the rational-legal framework of the modern state structure while facilitating positive liberal economic conditions. Without a viable international political alternative, state institutions are still needed to ensure local stability; however, the emasculated nature of many state institutions has opened the door to grassroots national groups offering social protectionism in the form of religious fundamentalism, ethnic nationalism, nativism, and isolationism.

Security can be defined in numerous ways. With respect to the contemporary nation-state, the security of national populations and proponents of global liberal market capitalism—transnational capitalists, if you will—have clashed to the point where the state may not be strong enough to adequately pacify all groups. The mediation-role that has generally defined the state is increasingly challenged as institutional capacity to enforce past comprise measures is reduced. As a result, the state must either be strengthened to adequately resume its role as mediator or alternative political institutions must be constructed to meet national protectionist demands and ensure local stability. The alternative is that further deterioration of the state could result in a deterioration of secure conditions for national populations and global economic systemic health.

NOTES

1. The concept of feudalism is often challenged by those who argue that the term and its use in historical studies is varied and inconsistent. The diversity of medieval political structures and social systems makes it difficult, if not impossible, to generally conclude that one system of sociopolitical organization defined this era; however, for the ease of presentation and in the interest of brevity, the term "feudalism" is used in its conventional sense: to describe a particular historical period in which social and political life was ordered along the aforementioned hierarchical lines. For more on this debate, see Brown (1978), Reynolds (1994), and Morillo (2003).

2. President Nixon took the U.S. dollar off gold in 1971, but the system of market-determined floating exchange rates was not formally established until 1973.

FURTHER READING

Barrow, Clyde W. *Critical Theories of the State: Marxist, Neo-Marxist, Post-Marxist*. Madison: University of Wisconsin Press, 1993.
Evans, Peter B. *Embedded Autonomy: States and Industrial Transformation*. Princeton, NJ: Princeton University Press, 1995.
McGrew, Anthony G., and Paul G. Lewis. *Global Politics: Globalization and the Nation-State*. Oxford: Polity Press, 1992.
Opello, Walter C., and Stephen J. Rostow. *The Nation-State and Global Order: A Historical Introduction to Contemporary Politics*. Boulder, CO: Lynne Rienner, 1999.
White, George W. *Nation, State, and Territory: Origins, Evolutions, and Relationships*. Lanham, MD: Rowman & Littlefield, 2004.

REFERENCES

Althusser, Louis. 1970. *Reading capital*. New York: Parthenon Books.
Anderson, Benedict. 1983. *Imagined communities: Reflections on the origins and spread of nationalism*. London: Verso Press.
Barrow, Clyde. 2005. The return of the state: Globalization, state theory, and the new imperialism. *New Political Science* 27: 123–45.
Brown, E. A. R. 1978. The tyranny of a construct: Feudalism and historians of medieval Europe. *American Historical Review* 79: 1063–88.
Burton, John. 1972. *World society*. Cambridge: Cambridge University Press.
Camilleri, Joseph A., and James Falk. 1992. *The end of sovereignty?* London: Aldershot.
Castells, Manuel. 1996–1998. *The Information Age: Economy, society and culture*. Vols. 1–3. Oxford: Blackwell.
———. 2004. *The power of identity*. 2nd ed. Oxford: Blackwell.
Dahl, Robert. 1967. *Pluralist democracy in the United States: Conflict and consent*. Chicago: Rand-McNally.
Dicken, Peter. 1998. *Global shift*. 3rd ed. New York: Guilford Press.
Domhoff, G. William. 1990. *The power elite and the state: How policy is made in America*. New York: A. de Gruyter.
Dye, Thomas R. 2001. *Who's running America? The Bush restoration*. Englewood Cliffs, NJ: Prentice-Hall.
Evans, Peter. 1995. *Embedded autonomy: States and industrial transformation*. Princeton, NJ: Princeton University Press.
———. 1997. The eclipse of the state? Reflections on stateness in an era of globalization. *World Politics* 50: 62–87.
Evans, Peter, Dietrich Rueschemeyer, and Theda Skocpol, eds. 1985. *Bringing the state back in*. New York: Cambridge University Press.
Frieden, Jeffry A. 2006. *Global capitalism: Its fall and rise in the twentieth century*. New York: W. W. Norton.
Gellner, Ernest. 1983. *Nations and nationalism*. Oxford: Blackwell Publishers.
Giddens, Anthony. 1990. *The consequences of modernity*. Stanford, CA: Stanford University Press.
———. 2003. *Runaway world: How globalization is reshaping our lives*. New York: Routledge.
Gilpin, Robert. 1987. *The political economy of international relations*. Princeton, NJ: Princeton University Press.
Guéhenno, Jean-Marie. 1995. *The end of the nation-state*. Minneapolis: University of Minnesota Press.
Guibernau, Montserrat. 1999. *Nations without states: Political communities in a global age*. Cambridge: Polity Press.
Habermas, Jürgen. 1975. *Legitimation crisis*. Boston: Beacon Press
———. 2001. *The postnational constellation*. Cambridge: MIT Press.
Held, David. 1995. *Democracy and the global order: From the modern state to cosmopolitan governance*. Stanford, CA: Stanford University Press.
Helleiner, Eric. 1994. *States and the reemergence of global finance: From Bretton Woods to the 1990s*. Ithaca, NY: Cornell University Press.

Hobsbawm, Eric. 1990. *Nations and nationalism since 1780*. Cambridge: Cambridge University Press.
Hobson, John M. 1997. *The wealth of states: A comparative sociology of international economic and political change*. Cambridge: Cambridge University Press.
———. 2000. *The state and international relations*. Cambridge: Cambridge University Press.
Hobson, John M., and M. Ramesh. 2002. Globalisation makes of states what states make of it: Between agency and structure in the state/globalisation debate. *New Political Economy* 7: 5–22.
Hobson, John M., and Leonard Seabrooke. 2001. Reimagining Weber: Constructing international society and the social balance of power. *European Journal of International Relations* 7: 239–74.
Horsman, Matthew, and Andres Marshall. 1994. *After the nation-state*. London: Macmillan.
Keating, Michael. 1996. *Nations against the state: The new politics of nationalism in Quebec, Catalonia, and Scotland*. London: Macmillan Press.
Keohane, Robert, and Joseph Nye, eds. 1972. *Transnational relations and world politics*. Cambridge, MA: Harvard University Press.
Laski, Harold J. 1935. *The state in theory and practice*. New York: Viking Press.
Lenin, V. I. 1939. *Imperialism, the highest state of capitalism: A popular outline*. New York: International Publishers.
Lindblom, Charles E. 1965. *The intelligence of democracy: Decision-making through mutual adjustment*. New York: Free Press.
Luxemburg, Rosa. 1951. *The accumulation of capital*. New Haven, CT: Yale University Press. (Orig. pub. 1913.)
Madden, Thomas. 1999. *A concise history of the Crusades*. Lanham, MD: Rowman & Littlefield.
Maitland, Frederic William. 2003. *State, trust, and corporation*. Cambridge: Cambridge University Press. (Orig. pub. 1904.)
Marx, Karl. 1964. *The economic & philosophic manuscripts of 1844*. New York: International Publishers.
Michels, Robert. 1956. *Political parties: A sociological study of the oligarchical tendencies of modern democracy*. New York: Dover Publications.
Miliband, Ralph. 1969. *The state in capitalist society*. New York: Basic Books.
———. 1970. The capitalist state: A reply to Poulantzas. *New Left Review* 59: 53–60.
———. 1973. Poulantzas and the capitalist state. *New Left Review* 82: 83–92.
Mills, C. Wright. 1956. *The power elite*. New York: Oxford University Press.
Morillo, Stephen. 2003. A "feudal mutation"? Conceptual tools and historical patterns in world history. *Journal of World History* 14: 531–50.
Mosca, Gaetano. 1939. *The ruling class*. New York: McGraw-Hill.
Nettl, J. P. 1968. The state as a conceptual variable. *World Politics* 20:559–92.
O'Connor, James. 1973. *The fiscal crisis of the state*. New York: St. Martin's Press.
Ohmae, Kenichi. 1990. *The borderless world: Power and strategy in the interlinked economy*. New York: Harper Business.
———. 1993. The rise of the region state. *Foreign Affairs* 72: 78–87.
———. 1995. *The end of the nation-state: The rise of regional economies*. New York: Free Press.

Paine, Thomas. 1953 [1776]. *Common Sense, and other political writings*. New York: Liberal Arts Press.

Panitch, Leo. 1994. Globalisation and the state. In *Socialist Register 1994: Between globalism and nationalism*, ed. Ralph Miliband and Leo Panitch. London: Merlin Press, 60–93.

Pareto, Vilfredo. 1935. *The mind and society: A treatise on general sociology*. New York: Dover Publications.

Polanyi, Karl. 2001. *The great transformation: The political and economic origins of our time*. Boston: Beacon Press. (Orig. pub. 1944.)

Polsby, Nelson W. 1963. *Community power and political theory*. New Haven, CT: Yale University Press.

Poulantzas, Nicos. 1969. The problem of the capitalist state. *New Left Review* 58: 67–78.

———. 1973. On social classes. *New Left Review* 78: 27–54.

———. 1976. The capitalist state: A reply to Miliband and Laclau. *New Left Review* 95: 63–83.

———. 1978. *Political power and social classes*. London: Verso Books.

———. 1980. *State, power, socialism*. London: Verso Books.

Reynolds, Susan. 1994. *Fiefs and vassals: The medieval evidence reinterpreted*. Oxford: Oxford University Press.

Riggs, Fred W. 1994. Ethnonationalism, industrialism, and the modern state. *Third World Quarterly* 15: 583–610.

Riley-Smith, Jonathan. 1986. *The First Crusade and the idea of crusading*. Philadelphia: University of Pennsylvania Press.

Robinson, William. 1996. *Promoting polyarchy: Globalization, U.S. intervention, and hegemony*. Cambridge: Cambridge University Press.

———. 2004. *A theory of global capitalism: Production, class, and state in a transnational world*. Baltimore: Johns Hopkins University Press.

Ruggie, John G. 1982. International regimes, transactions, and change: Embedded liberalism in the postwar economic order. *International Organization* 36: 379–415.

Sklair, Leslie. 2002. *Globalization: Capitalism & its alternatives*, 3rd ed. New York: Oxford University Press.

Skocpol, Theda. 1979. *States and social revolutions: A comparative analysis of France, Russia, and China*. New York: Cambridge University Press.

Sweezy, Paul. 1970. *The theory of capitalist development: Principles of Marxian political economy*. New York: Modern Reader Paperbacks.

Touraine, Alain. 1977. *The self production of society*. Chicago: University of Chicago Press.

Weinstein, Michael, ed. 2005. *Globalization: What's new?* New York: Columbia University Press.

Weiss, Linda. 1998. *The myth of the powerless state*. Ithaca, NY: Cornell University Press.

———, ed. 2003. *States in the global economy: Bringing domestic institutions back in*. Cambridge: Cambridge University Press.

Wriston, Walter. 1992. *The twilight of sovereignty*. New York: MacMillan.

Yeates, Nicola. 2002. Globalization and social policy: From global neoliberal hegemony to global political pluralism. *Global Social Policy* 2: 69–91.

13

Natural Resources: Diamonds and Human Security

Ian Smillie

Natural resources have always been closely related to issues of security: security of the individual, the family, entire nations. Wars have been fought for millennia over land and water, and access to timber, oil, fisheries, and minerals. Growing awareness of global warming has heightened the debate about natural resources, raising it to global and sometimes apocalyptic levels. The diamond wars that began in the late twentieth century demonstrate what can happen when the demand for a natural resource outstrips the ethical and human costs of obtaining it. Efforts to resolve the problem demonstrate how a completely unregulated, globalized industry was brought into an international regulatory framework to solve the human security problem without impinging on national sovereignty or damaging commercial profitability.

Diamonds, symbols of wealth and, if you accept the advertising, glamor, loyalty, and love, became in the late twentieth century an alternative to the fast-evaporating Cold War cash that had for 40 years sustained countless repressive African regimes and rebel armies. By the end of the century, diamonds were fueling regional instability across large swathes of Africa, paying for some of the continent's most horrific wars and their consequent human suffering and death. This chapter describes how a globalized industry, its civil society antagonists, and the governments of five continents dealt with a stone that had come to represent one of the greatest security threats in Africa.

The international diamond industry is in many ways representative of globalization in both its historical and its modern manifestations, as the following paragraphs will show. The diamond industry includes producers on almost every continent, including Australia. The most important trading centers are located in London, Antwerp, Israel, and Dubai. Cutting and polishing is dominated by India, with growing hubs in China and Thailand, and the $60 billion retail trade is strongest in North America. When diamond miners, buyers, and sellers meet at bourses and sales across the world, national boundaries disappear; racial, religious, and historical antagonisms vanish. Although the diamond industry is a highly competitive business, most of the senior players, whether they are from Russia, Namibia, or India, know each other on a first name basis.

Historically, one company, De Beers, dominated the production and sale of as much as 90 percent of the world's rough diamonds for the better part of the twentieth century.[1] Unlike almost any other company one can think of, it survived more or less intact through World War I, World War II, and the Cold War. A South African enterprise, it thrived throughout independent Africa, though usually under different corporate identities, during the darkest days of apartheid. As much a symbol of nineteenth-century cartel as twentieth-century capitalism, De Beers embraced the discovery of diamonds in the Soviet Union in the 1950s, and soon thereafter embraced most Soviet diamonds, just as it had embraced most African diamonds.

Large as De Beers and some of its new twenty-first-century competitors are, however, much of the industry is populated by small firms: family-owned trading companies, small cutting and polishing factories, one-off retail shops. More than 10 percent of the world's rough diamonds emerge from the informal sector, mined by more than a million "self-employed" diggers in Africa and South America.

Geologically speaking, the distribution of diamonds is nothing if not democratic. In ancient times, all diamonds originated in India. As Indian diamond mines were depleted in the nineteenth century, diamonds were discovered in Brazil and then in South Africa. Today there are a dozen African producing countries, but two of the world's top three producers by value are Russia and Canada, and the largest producer by volume—largely industrial diamonds—is Australia. Antwerp has long been the world center for diamond trading, although Israel has been a major player for 40 years, and Dubai is emerging as an important hub. Diamond manufacturing—the conversion of rough stones into polished goods for the retail market—has come to be dominated by India, where more than a million people earn a living from the industry. Although diamonds are no longer mined in India, they remain the country's largest export. Other polishing centers are in places as far afield as China, Armenia, Mauritius, and Thailand.

The retail trade, which sees $10 billion worth of rough diamonds turned into $60 billion worth of diamond jewelry, is immense. Half the world's gem diamonds are sold in the United States alone.

In addition to the diamond industry's symbolic possibilities where globalization is concerned, diamonds became one of the greatest contributors to war, death, and destruction in Africa during the 1990s. As many as 4 million people died directly and indirectly in wars fueled almost entirely by diamonds in Sierra Leone, the Democratic Republic of the Congo, and Angola; and they contributed to political destabilization throughout much of western and central Africa. The efforts to halt what came to be known as "conflict diamonds" or "blood diamonds" adds to the representative value of diamonds in a discussion about globalization and security.

THE DIAMOND WARS

During the 1990s and into the 2000s, rebel armies in Angola, Sierra Leone, and the Democratic Republic of the Congo exploited the alluvial diamond fields of these countries in order to finance wars of insurgency. Alluvial diamonds, unlike those mined in the deep kimberlite "pipes" of Canada, Russia, and Botswana, are scattered over vast areas, often only a few inches or feet below the surface of the earth. Alluvial diamonds have, from colonial times, proven difficult to manage and to regulate. Because of their high weight-to-value ratio, the ease with which they can be mined, and endemic corruption in the global diamond market, alluvial diamonds became a ready target for rebel armies.

The trade in conflict diamonds began in the early 1990s with Jonas Savimbi's União Nacional para a Independência Total de Angola (UNITA) in Angola but was quickly copied by the Revolutionary United Front (RUF) in Sierra Leone, with assistance from a Liberian warlord who eventually became president, Charles Taylor. It was then taken up by rebel armies in the Democratic Republic of the Congo and has affected the diamond industries of Guinea, Liberia, and Côte d'Ivoire as well. By 1997, as much as 14 percent of the world's $10 billion annual diamond production fell into the category of conflict diamonds. Hundreds of thousands of people died as a direct result of these wars, and millions died of indirect causes (Coughlan et al. 2006, 44–51).

In considering how and whether rough diamonds might be regulated, several problems had to be confronted. First, while diamonds have different characteristics from one mine or one country to the next, the differences are minuscule; and when diamonds are mixed, it is impossible even for the best "diamantaire" to distinguish one from the other. Scientific experiments to fingerprint diamonds based on trace elements have not yet advanced to the stage of practical application. Marking or coating diamonds at the production site is a possibility, but available techniques are expensive and logistically prohibitive, and there is no mark or coating that cannot be removed from a rough diamond.

A further complication in developing a tracking system is that the diamond industry had always operated in an opaque and secretive manner. Historically, effective regulation has proven almost impossible, whether in Africa, Europe, Israel, or North America. This is partly because of secrecy and security issues around such a valuable commodity, but it is also because the trade in diamonds, after mining, has traditionally been in the hands of very small, close-knit family enterprises, the kind of enterprise that defies effective governmental regulation. Historically, for example, high taxes have only served to drive diamonds underground, and most governments long ago stopped trying to impose more than minimal duties on rough diamond imports and exports (Oomes and Vocke 2003). Even so, a parallel diamond economy, operating in grey and black markets, has always existed.

Diamonds have thus proven useful in money laundering and have long been used to finance drugs and other illicit goods. In Africa, where more than 70 percent of the world's gem diamonds (by value) were produced throughout most of the twentieth century, diamonds were used to hide and export profits and capital, and, as an alternative hard currency, to finance imports in weak economies. Corrupt and predatory governments in Sierra Leone, the DRC, and Angola drove the diamond business even further underground. In addition, much of the legitimate diamond trade operated largely on a cash basis, without formal contracts or auditable paper trails. Diamonds were almost ideally suited to the purpose for which rebel armies came to use them.

THE PROCESS: GETTING TO KIMBERLEY

Before there could be an effort to control diamonds, there had to be a willingness to do so. Conflict diamonds were first identified as such in Angola by a British NGO, Global Witness, at the end of 1998. The issue was important to the UN Security Council, which had withdrawn a peacekeeping force from the country that year because of its inability to prevail in a war that had lasted off and on since independence 25 years earlier. At the beginning of 2000, a Canadian NGO, Partnership Africa Canada, published a report on the role diamonds were playing in fuelling Sierra Leone's nine-year-old war (Smillie, Gberie, and Hazleton 2000). Later in 2000, the UN Security Council issued its own report on Angola, confirming what the NGOs had written about diamonds and the industry's complicity in the conflicts (United Nations 2000b).

Until then, the diamond industry had largely ignored the problem; however, by mid-2000 denial had turned into engagement. Several factors contributed to the change. A large proportion of the world's gem-quality rough diamonds passed through two narrow funnels. One was De Beers. Although the company had divested itself of all alluvial diamond sources by 2000, De Beers had much to lose from a sustained generic campaign against a luxury consumer product. Gem diamonds have little intrinsic value beyond decoration and sentiment, and high market prices had been manipulated for years by withholding supply and devoting hundreds of millions of dollars to advertising. De Beers understood the vulnerability of diamonds. The wider industry had much to lose as well.

The second funnel was Antwerp. Center of the world's diamond trade for more than two centuries, Antwerp serves as a crossroads for as much as 90 percent of the world's rough diamonds. It is also a major trading center for polished diamonds. Collectively, the Antwerp diamond business, Antwerp itself, and the Belgian economy as a whole had much to lose if a consumer campaign were to erupt.

The government of South Africa was another player with high stakes in the diamond industry. In May 2000, South Africa's then-minister of minerals and energy Phumzile Mlambo-Ngcuka, who in June 2005 became the country's deputy president, called a meeting to discuss the issue. The meeting was held in Kimberley, where South African diamonds were first discovered, giving its name to the process that ensued. The meeting brought together industry leaders, governments, and NGOs. So important had the issue become for Belgium that its foreign minister, Louis Michel, attended, rubbing shoulders with NGO antagonists, industry leaders, and other government representatives. Concerned southern African governments with significant diamond industries were there in force—South Africa, Botswana, and Namibia—as were such other governments as Canada's (with its own burgeoning diamond industry) and Britain's, which was beginning to take a lead on the conflict prevention side of the issue.

The meeting took its cue from a system that had been initiated in Angola in mid-1998. Under a UN Security Council arrangement, no diamonds could be purchased from Angola unless the government of Angola issued a certificate saying they were conflict free. The certification system was largely ineffective because conflict diamonds from Angola were simply smuggled to other countries and exported from there. Liberia, for example, was given as the origin of *billions* of dollars worth of diamonds during the 1990s, and many other countries with no diamond resources at all were being recorded as the country of origin or provenance in Belgian customs data (Smillie, Gberie, Hazleton 2000). Alone, the Angolan certificate was ineffective, but if *all* countries were to become part of a system of certification, and if this system were based on good internal controls in each country, including producing, trading, and polishing countries, something might be done.

The broad outlines of such a system were articulated at that first Kimberley Process (KP) meeting in South Africa. A further technical meeting was proposed to elaborate the issue, and it was assumed that a workable system could be developed in a matter of months. It would actually take 40 months—something of a speed record in such matters, but still much longer than was originally imagined. The issue was not so much the technicalities of the system, although these were complex; it was politics. Many countries came to the table with more than a little ambivalence to the entire concept of controls. The United States (the biggest consumer of gem diamonds), Russia (the second-largest diamond-producing country), and China (an up-and-coming polishing country) were at first hostile to the idea. For them, the problem was a combination of workload, cost, and issues around the regulation of trade. Others were late in coming to the table; and as the meetings grew bigger, momentum slowed.

By 2001, however, the NGO coalition had grown to more than 200 organizations, including large brand-name organizations like Oxfam, World Vision, and Amnesty International. Nongovernmental organizations continued to generate media attention: articles appeared around the world in every major newspaper and newsmagazine, and blood diamonds became a frequent topic on television news programs. The NGOs took part in every KP meeting as full participants, and their vociferous media campaign sustained pressure. For its part, the industry created a new body, the World Diamond Council (WDC), in 2000. A coalition of mining firms, trading companies, and jewelry industry representatives, the WDC was created to engage exclusively on the issue of conflict diamonds and to represent industry interests at KP meetings.[2]

Additional pressure came from the objective fact of conflict diamonds and the horrific wars that continued to blaze across Africa. A second UN Security Council expert panel confirmed the diamond connection in Sierra Leone at the end of 2000 (United Nations, 2000a), and later UN reports on Angola, the DRC, and Liberia continued to document the problem.

In all, there were a dozen KP meetings, held in various African and European capitals and in Ottawa, before a final agreement was hammered out at Interlaken in November 2002. Although not a formal part of the process, a dozen other meetings in various locales helped the parties to rehearse the issues and to grow more familiar with the challenges and each other. A UN General Assembly resolution in December 2000 endorsed the KP and urged "the implementation of the certification scheme as soon as possible, recognizing the urgency of the situation from a humanitarian and security standpoint" (United Nations 2000c). Also, two G8 meetings, in Okinawa in July 2000 and at Kananaskis in Canada in July 2002, referred to the KP in their final communiqués.

Important as the endorsements engineered by concerned governments and NGOs may seem, they did little to deflect some governments from technical and procedural concerns. The United States wanted the system to be open to any government, whereas NGOs argued that some governments had demonstrated enough criminal behavior where diamonds were concerned to be excluded.[3] China agreed that there should be a credentials committee, but this was because it wanted to exclude Taiwan, though it never explicitly said so. Some governments worried that they might be forced to implement new laws and regulations, and so they wanted a system that could be based as much as possible on existing national laws. The industry wanted the least intrusive and least costly system possible, and NGOs wanted a water-tight agreement with independent monitoring.

As agreement neared, Canada and a small number of other governments felt that the Kimberly Process Certification Scheme (KPCS) should seek a WTO waiver, as the proposed system might be interpreted as an infringement on trade. In February 2003, the WTO Council for Trade in Goods agreed to recommend that the UN General Council grant requesting members a waiver for trade measures taken under the KPCS through December 2006. The decision recognized "the extraordinary humanitarian nature of this issue and the devastating impact of conflicts fuelled by trade in conflict diamonds on the peace, safety and security of people in affected countries and the systematic and gross human rights violations that have been perpetrated in such conflicts" (Kimberley Process).

THE AGREEMENT

The agreement reached at Interlaken defined such terms as, the three customs codes covering the types of rough diamonds of interest to the KPCS, spelled out the minimum standards required of participants, and provided details on some additional optional standards. It reflected many of the concerns expressed during the negotiations by various governments, and at face value it appears rather weak. The KPCS is not a treaty—it is not legally binding as a formal international treaty might be—and no government signed any document. The KPCS preamble recalls the UN General Assembly resolution, cleverly worded by anonymous officials, that said the KPCS should be "a simple and workable international certification scheme based on national certification schemes and on internationally agreed minimum standards" (Kimberley Process). It recognized "the differences in production methods and trading practices" that might require "different approaches." It recognized the importance of state sovereignty and said that everything would be agreed by consensus.

Consensus means that if one government dissents from a proposed position, the position cannot go forward, a provision that would test the KPCS on more than one occasion in the months ahead. The arrangement for monitoring was weak in the extreme, with no provision for sanctions in the unlikely event that a review mission ever took place. Reviews would occur only if a participant *agreed* to be reviewed, and only if there were "significant indications" of noncompliance. What "significant indications" meant was not spelled out. Further, the entire scheme was to be open to any government "willing and able to fulfill the requirements of [the] scheme," with no credentials review of any kind. Nongovernmental organizations and industry, which had participated in all the discussions as equals up to that point, were now relegated to "observer" status. There would be no secretariat, no staff, and no budget. Plenary meetings would be held once a year in the country of the KP chair. The chair was to be elected annually.

None of the aforementioned weaknesses were lost on those who wanted a tough, binding agreement with strong admission and verification standards. For NGOs, the question at Interlaken was whether to accept a weak agreement and to work later to strengthen it from the inside or to leave the table entirely and for good. Given the obvious inability of the process to move beyond what was agreed at Interlaken, the latter would probably have destroyed the entire process, culminating in the consumer war that the industry feared, but that NGOs knew would hurt hundreds of thousands of innocent diamond miners and polishers in many developing countries.

STRENGTHS

The agreement has several strengths, however, that were not obvious at first. One is that although the KPCS is completely voluntary, those countries that are members undertake not to trade with those that are not.[4] Countries that "voluntarily" stay out of the KPCS, therefore, cannot trade diamonds with countries that are in the organization. This creates a situation where virtually any country with a rough diamond business, whether production, trade, or consumption, *must* be a member. The scheme is voluntary, but in real commercial terms it is compulsory.

The KPCS minimum standards are not minimal standards, and some are set quite high. More important, they are de facto compulsory for all participants—something that is not true of many ratified international treaties. It was necessary for almost every serious participant to pass new laws in order to enforce the KPCS at home. New Kimberley-specific laws were passed in the European Community, Canada, the United States and virtually every one of the more than 40 countries that joined. These laws spell out how rough diamonds will be handled prior to export and after import (internal controls). They state the need for tamper-proof packaging, the requirement for a government-controlled certificate testifying to the diamonds' bona fides. They spell out penalties for infractions, which in most cases include fines and prison terms plus forfeiture of any diamonds seized. So while the KPCS is not a legally binding international treaty, each participating country has made its provisions legally binding within its own borders. Where an international treaty might have been difficult to enforce, laws in each participating country are much less so.

Within the first six months of operation, several countries were dropped from the participant list: Norway was dropped because it had no laws or certificate (although it did produce these later and was able to rejoin). Burkina Faso was dropped for the same reason (it never came back); Brazil, as well as a number of others, took several months before they could comply and were dropped from the system until they did.

Box 13.1 The KPCS: A Snapshot

The Kimberley Process Certification Scheme, or KPCS, for rough diamonds came into effect on January 1, 2003. Over 45 countries, as well as all those represented by the European Community, participate. Under the terms of this agreement, each participant agrees to issue a certificate to accompany any rough diamonds being exported from its territory, certifying that the diamonds are conflict free. Each country must, therefore, be able to track the diamonds being offered for export back to the place where they were mined or to the point of import, and each country must meet a set of standards for these internal controls. All importing countries agree not to allow any rough diamonds into their territory without an approved KPCS certificate.

Given the large volume of diamonds being traded across borders, it was deemed necessary to produce trade and production statistics to be compared from time to time in order to ensure that the diamonds leaving one country match by volume and by value those entering another. Working groups comprising representatives of governments, industry, and NGOs deal with statistics, monitoring, technical issues, and membership in the KP. A peer review mechanism has also been created, and more than 30 country reviews had been undertaken by October 2006. During 2006, a review of the overall KPCS was carried out, examining its impact and the effectiveness of its various systems and processes.

Many of the improvements in the KPCS have been, and continue to be, worked out among participants and observers behind closed doors and then brought to the annual plenary discussion for wider endorsement. One improvement has been the development of a monitoring system through a complex sequence of events that has brought about significant and fairly quick change. The first event was a complaint of noncompliance lodged against the Central African Republic (CAR) following a coup early in 2003. Several participants, supported by industry and NGOs, demanded a review under the noncompliance provision, and the CAR agreed.

The two primary NGO players, Partnership Africa Canada and Global Witness, continued to press for a broader, more comprehensive monitoring system, however, submitting background papers on monitoring provisions in other agreements.[5] Just before the plenary of October 2003, the NGOs, the World Diamond Council, and the Israeli government worked out an understanding, which in essence paved the way for industry and Israeli support for a "voluntary peer review mechanism." Under this proposal, only countries that *volunteered* for a review visit would actually receive one. Review teams would comprise representatives of three other governments and one each from NGOs and industry. In the event, this bland arrangement was almost impossible to resist. A monitoring working group was struck, and when several countries began to request review visits, it became harder for others not to volunteer. By mid-2007, more than 40 such voluntary reviews had been carried out, there was almost no country left in the KPCS that had not requested one, and a second round was scheduled to begin.

Some reviews have been tougher than others. The review of the Republic of Congo (Brazzaville) was carried out in June 2003. This was not a voluntary review, and the KP chair—Canada at the time—had to press the government to agree. At issue were voluminous diamond exports from a country with no known diamond mining and no documented imports. The review resulted in the ROC being "dropped from the list," a KP euphemism for expulsion. This was a defining moment for the KP, one with few precedents in the multilateral system. A separate issue arose in the case of Lebanon. Here, the issue was not expulsion but admission. Lebanon had been slow to pass the requisite KP-related laws, and there were allegations about illicit trade between Africa and Lebanon. Before Lebanon was considered for admission in 2005, a review visit was required. This, too, was a first. Neither the Congo's expulsion nor Lebanon's admission happened without a great amount of behind-the-scenes debate, some of it quite strident. But that, too, was part of the KP maturation process.

If NGOs and industry representatives worried at Interlaken about being downgraded to passive "observers," they need not have. Nothing, in fact, changed. For NGOs and industry representatives continued to attend all meetings and to be recognized by the chair every time they wished to make an intervention. Nongovernmental organizations and industry representatives are members of every working group, and serious comments from their side are taken as much into consideration where consensus is concerned as those of anyone else. This may be without precedent in organizations with the effective power to exclude a country from the trade in an important commodity. But it is one of the factors that allowed the KP to make so much progress so fast. The NGO and industry representatives have participated on almost every review team. The June 2005 review of the United States, for example, was chaired by Russia, with government team members from the EC and South Africa, an Israeli industry representative, and one from a Canadian NGO. Each review examines a participant's compliance with the KPCS minimum standards and makes recommendations, where appropriate, for improvement. The participant is expected to report on action taken.

Despite early misgivings by some, the provision on consensus decision making has proven in many ways to be a strength. In the early days of the agreement, a voting arrangement would have had the effect of ganging up on members that held contrary and often very strong views. The possibility of an important participant walking away from the table was real, and this could have proven very destructive. While some decisions may represent the lowest common denominator, there are at least, as a result, few major ructions. Many of the individuals involved have been with the process from the beginning, and this has helped to leaven the confusion and mistrust that newcomers sometimes bring to the table. Reaching consensus has become easier with time.

The lack of a formal secretariat has stretched the KPCS in several ways; but again, this may not have been a bad thing for the early years. Some feared that an office with staff and a budget could take on a life of its own, usurping prerogatives of the plenary. South Africa was the self-appointed chair of the KP from May 2000 until December 2003, serving as unofficial champion of the overall process. Canada took over the chair during 2004, and later estimated that it expended something like $250,000 in the process. Russia took the chair in 2005, Botswana in 2006, and the European Community in 2007. This rotational system has worked reasonably well, but the frequent changes work against continuity, and there are a limit to the number of countries willing and able to take on the position.

The secretariat function, however, is not as onerous as it might be because the KPCS has developed a system of "working groups."[6] The working groups on monitoring and participation have been described herein, but there is also a working group on statistics and a technical working group of "diamond experts" dealing with issues such as harmonized customs codes, problems relating to diamond powder, and how to deal with core samples from exploration projects. All working groups have members drawn from a cross-section of participating countries—with efforts at geographic balance—as well as representatives of industry and NGOs. The working groups "meet" as often as required, by teleconference. During 2006, the statistics working group, for example, held about 10 conference calls, most lasting about two hours. The committees are chaired by participants who volunteer to do so, knowing there will inevitably be considerable time and cost involved. In addition to dealing with the work of the KPCS and laying the groundwork for eventual consensus-based decisions at the annual plenary, the working groups help to build and maintain solidarity through the system and through the year. The annual plenary meeting draws about 200 people or more.

Some conclusions can be made about the impact of the KPCS. Diamond shipments operating outside the KPCS have now been seized by most major trading countries, a sign to anyone with an interest that the KPCS is serious. The fact of the KP negotiations alone helped choke diamond supplies to rebel movements in Angola and Sierra Leone and contributed to the end of hostilities. And the KPCS is credited by several countries as having a direct impact on the growth in legitimate diamond exports (and thus of tax revenue). In 2005, Sierra Leone exported $142 million worth of diamonds, up from $26 million in 2001 (Partnership Africa Canada 2006). In 2005, the DRC had its best diamond-export year in history. As important, the KPCS has helped to formalize and clean up an industry that had operated for a century with little transparency and few paper trails, making it a fertile playground for all manner of illicit activity, including for some of the world's most ruthless predators.

WEAKNESSES

By the end of 2006, a number of weaknesses in the Kimberley Process had become evident. A UN report found that diamonds from Côte d'Ivoire, under UN embargo because the country's diamond mines were located in rebel-held areas, were being laundered through Accra as Ghanaian diamonds (United

Nations 2006). Ghana, a charter member of the KPCS, was allegedly providing Ivorian diamonds with certificates of legitimacy. Partnership Africa Canada produced reports on Brazil, Guyana, and Venezuela showing that cross-border smuggling was rampant.[7] More than one-third of Brazil's KP certificates between 2003 and 2006 turned out to be fraudulent, and Venezuela's entire production of diamonds was being exported without any reference to the country's KPCS controls. In other words, all of Venezuela's diamonds were being smuggled. Clearly, the system was far from leak-proof. The governments in question were failing to enforce regulations they had enacted. But they were not alone. If Venezuela's diamonds were being smuggled *out* of Venezuela, they were being smuggled *into* other countries where controls were also lax.

By mid 2009, the KP was showing severe signs of stress. Action had been taken on Ghanaian diamonds, and Brazil suspended shipments for six months while its regulations were reinforced. The KPCS had demonstrated that it could act fairly quickly and decisively, especially when pressed by NGOs and their allies in the media. But the Venezuelan issue was only solved by sleight of hand: Venezuela said it would suspend all diamond shipments until its house was in order. In fact, diamond miners and dealers continued to be registered and diamonds continued to be smuggled out. By accepting this arrangement in 2008, the KP effectively endorsed Venezuelan diamond smuggling. More cracks appeared in Africa, where internal controls in Angola, the Democratic Republic of Congo and others proved to be so weak that nobody could guarantee with any assurance the origin of the diamonds being exported. In Zimbabwe, the 2008 killing of as many as 200 artisanal miners by government forces became a human rights issue, but a KP review team sent to the country in 2009 was no more able to deal with this issue than Zimbabwean smuggling, corruption and mismanagement.

More, obviously, remains to be done. Clearly the KPCS needs its own investigative capacity. Triennial review visits and unrequited "recommendations" are not enough to detect and deter illicit trafficking in a commodity as valuable as diamonds. Most Western governments conduct no audits – periodic or otherwise – of the companies that buy and sell rough diamonds. And clearly, the KP as an institution run completely on voluntary labor – with a handful of countries doing the donkey work and many others doing little or nothing – was becoming inadequate to the task of regulating a complex and variegated industry.

REMAINING ISSUES: CONFLICT DIAMONDS VERSUS ILLICIT DIAMONDS

The term "illicit diamonds" covers a lot of territory. Diamonds have always been stolen, and they probably always will be. Historically, diamonds have long been used for money laundering, for tax evasion, and for a variety of other illicit purposes, including as barter for drugs, arms, and other banned or controlled goods. *Conflict* diamonds are more specific. There had to be a definition for KP purposes, and the one adopted is as follows:

> Conflict Diamonds means rough diamonds used by rebel movements or their allies to finance conflict aimed at undermining legitimate governments,

as described in relevant United Nations Security Council (UNSC) resolutions insofar as they remain in effect, or in other similar UNSC resolutions which may be adopted in the future, and as understood and recognized in United Nations General Assembly (UNGA) Resolution 55/56, or in other similar UNGA resolutions which may be adopted in future. (Kimberley Process)

Using this definition, the volume of conflict diamonds has changed dramatically in recent years. The KP and the diamond industry have consistently used a figure of 4 percent as the total volume of conflict diamonds when the KP began negotiations. This was based on an estimate in 1999 of $150 million worth of diamonds from Angola, $70 million from Sierra Leone, and $35 million from the Democratic Republic of the Congo. Assuming these estimates were correct (and there is no reason to doubt them), this represented a percentage of rough production value that year ($6.8 billion) of 3.7 percent.

Earlier, however, UNITA controlled much more of Angola's diamond-mining areas than it did by 1999 and represented an estimated 10 percent of world production. Even if the figure was half this number, it would have brought the global total to $400 million, or about 7 percent. If the larger UN figure was accurate, the total would have been closer, with Sierra Leone and DRC included, to $800 million, representing 12–14 percent of rough production value at the time. At its worst, therefore, and using consistent definitions and figures, conflict diamonds represented between 7 percent and 14 percent of total world diamond production during the mid-1990s.

At the end of 2006, the UN estimate of conflict diamonds emerging from Côte d'Ivoire that year was something between $9 and $23 million. The only country apart from Côte d'Ivoire under UN embargo at the time, Liberia, has never been a major producer of quality diamonds; and although there was likely some smuggling, it probably did not amount to more than $10 million. Using the high estimates, as a percentage of rough production value (estimated in 2005 at $12.67 billion), this would have represented something less than 0.3 percent of world production. This was a significant achievement.

The definitional issue will be addressed again subsequently because with an end to the bloodiest aspects of conflict diamonds, some campaigners began to argue that violence in alluvial diamond-mining areas, environmental destruction, and child labor should also be included in the definition. But first, it is important to understand that the KPCS could never single out one kind of smuggled diamond from another. It was always understood that *all* countries producing, trading, and processing diamonds would have to be members of the Kimberley Process, even if they were continents removed from Africa's diamond wars. Like water, conflict diamonds will always find their way to and through the available cracks. In 2006, one of Brazil's largest diamond exporters was arrested after it was discovered that the diamonds he was exporting did not come from the mines he had listed in his KP documentation. The exporter was a Sierra Leonean of Lebanese extraction with direct family links to companies with bad reputations in the DRC, Sierra Leone, and Antwerp. Were his exports conflict diamonds? Perhaps not, but they were certainly illicit, and the point is that if Brazilian KP systems are weak, smugglers will use them. So while the KPCS was established to deal only with conflict diamonds, it had to deal as well with the larger illicit trade. That is why the Venezuelan government's apathy toward its diamond exports in 2006 was so worrisome. After the clampdown on Ghanaian exports, Venezuela would have been an excellent place to drop genuine conflict diamonds into the stream—at a point where nobody was watching.

The de facto inclusion of illicit diamonds in the KPCS coverage was good, in fact, for an industry that had, for generations, been infected by illegality. Four years into its application, however, the difficulties of the challenge were still being revealed. The challenge was not only to ensure that countries like Brazil and Venezuela enforce their KPCS regulations effectively; there was something else. Some exporters were not bothering to find corrupt officials or neighboring countries where their diamonds could enter a sloppy KP certification regime. They were being smuggled straight to cutting and polishing factories in KP member countries where this part of the business, falling outside KPCS standards, was ignored. As long as these loopholes exist, diamond smuggling remains a possibility everywhere, and an attractive possibility at that, where duties and taxes are a significant part of the cost of business. Estimates of diamond smuggling in 2007 from Sierra Leone, for example, ran between 10 and 25 percent of total production. As long as diamond smuggling continues to exist at this level, as long as the diamond industry at large shelters criminality, as long as there is no KPCS or national government examination of the cutting and polishing side of the business, the potential for a revival of conflict diamonds remains real.

DIAMONDS AND DEVELOPMENT

Nongovernmental organizations involved in the campaign against conflict diamonds were often asked about other diamond-related issues: the environment, labor standards, fair wages, and children. While all these were real issues, the campaign's single-minded focus on war was perhaps its greatest strength. Other issues would have diluted the campaign and might have made the KPCS impossible. It can be argued that the vast array of agendas around better-controlled logging, for example, has worked against the achievement of a comprehensive agreement on timber. Diamond campaigners had no interest in damaging the diamond industry, which provides good jobs for many people in developing countries far from conflict. But if the diamond-fueled wars could not be stopped, it would be better to end the diamond trade completely than to work at the periphery—in the middle of war zones, perhaps—on issues that might have no future.

With the advent of the KPCS, however, that changed. The KPCS helped to consolidate the peace in several African countries, but it is a *regulatory* system; it is not a tool for development. In the rush to congratulation, there was a danger of forgetting some of those who suffered most in the diamond wars—namely, the diggers, their families, and their communities.

Conflict diamonds were a product of vast alluvial diamond areas in Africa where diamonds are mined by artisans, that is, diggers. There are as many as

120,000 diggers in Sierra Leone, 700,000 in the DRC, and many tens of thousands in Angola, Liberia, Brazil, and elsewhere. Research by Partnership Africa Canada and Global Witness in 2004 detailed the desperate nature of alluvial diamond digging. It is a hard, dangerous casino economy in which diggers remain poor while buyers, exporters, processors, and retailers make healthy profits.

The 2004 report *Rich Man, Poor Man* (Partnership Africa Canada and Global Witness 2004) called on governments, NGOs, and the private sector to come together to find ways in which some of the poorest people in Africa—people who produce great wealth for others—could obtain a fairer share. This was and remains a human security issue; it is about development at its most basic, and it is about justice. Diggers, many of them children, face appalling working conditions. Residents of mining areas complain of environmental degradation, water pollution, and the influx of migrant labor, with high rates of prostitution and HIV/AIDS. Family and societal violence follow. Most diamond diggers lead hard, insecure, dangerous, and unhealthy lives. With average earnings of less than a dollar a day, they fall squarely into the broad category of absolute poverty. Until such problems are addressed, diamonds will continue to be a source of insecurity; conversely, change could produce significantly better lives for diggers and their communities.

After a year of preliminary discussions among NGOs, governments, labor groups, academics, and industry representatives, the Diamond Development Initiative (DDI) was formally launched at a meeting in Accra in October 2005 (Diamond Development Initiative 2005). The DDI's basic challenge is to encourage better work environments and better prices for diggers. This will involve education for miners, access to credit and artisanal mining equipment, training in diamond valuation, government intervention to help streamline marketing, and improved labor laws. The initial group of NGOs and companies involved in the DDI, including the industry leader, De Beers, gave way to a larger network of NGOs and companies and to the incorporation of DDI International as a nonprofit organization registered in the United States, with affiliates or potential affiliates in a range of other countries.

Although by 2007 the DDI had begun some interesting projects and was widely supported by the diamond industry and the governments of the countries in question, the future will tell whether it can have the impact it seeks on a form of mining that has defied regulation for a half century and that has remains largely outside the formal sector because of its inherent lack of profitability.

LESSONS

Some basic lessons emerge from the KP experience:

- The humanitarian imperative was an important driver of the process during the negotiating period. As the KPCS has matured, however, it is understood to be as much about prevention as about cure. Early calls for a sunset clause are no longer voiced.

- The vulnerability of diamonds to consumer action helped to bring the industry and several reluctant governments to the negotiating table.
- Heavy media pressure fostered by NGOs helped to keep the momentum going.
- A government champion was important to the organization of meetings; it is unlikely that NGOs or industry could have played the role that South Africa did.
- United Nations expert panels, the UN General Assembly resolution, and positive references to the KP at two G8 meetings, for example, helped with momentum and legitimacy.
- The KPCS could never have been meaningful without strong industry participation. Had governments or NGOs attempted to design a certification system, the outcome would likely have been unworkable. The industry knew where the problems lay, and it knew best how they could be addressed effectively.
- An important lesson in the Kimberley Process is the process itself. Governments, industry and NGOs participated on an equal basis. Set speeches were discouraged; there was real and sometimes protracted debate; and although it took time, government delegations eventually came to meetings with enough authority to bargain.
- The relative informality of the process and the nonbureaucratic nature of decision making helped advance issues during negotiation and after implementation.
- While the KPCS is voluntary, diamond-producing and -trading countries *needed* to be members, making membership virtually compulsory.
- The idea that a WTO waiver might be necessary came late in the negotiations. Had it failed, the KPCS would likely have failed as well. Having the application made by a cross-section of 11 governments helped.
- To have made the KPCS an international treaty might have added years but little substance to the process—although this was not clear in the early stages of discussion; each country having its own KPCS-specific laws makes it as legally binding as it needs to be as long as there are strong provisions for monitoring and an understanding, even implicit, that serious noncompliance may result in expulsion.
- A weak agreement may be better than none at all if there is enough goodwill in the system to allow for change and adaptation. Many of the worst fears of NGOs, industry representatives, and governments turned out to be unfounded. Adaptation of the agreement, however, was not easy and required good and constant communication.
- Had the KP not been able to move forward on monitoring and statistics, NGOs would probably have been unable to stay on the inside for long. Acceptance of the initial weak agreement by NGOs was reluctant and (privately) conditional on forward movement.
- Despite early misgivings by NGOs and a few others, the consensus decision-making system is probably better than one based on votes. Consensus, no matter how grudging, is better than having some participants feel they have lost something important. The weakness of consensus, however, is that one or

two participants can block the rest. Fortunately, such stalemates have not lasted long in the KP.
- A secretariat, budget, and staff were not required to make the KPCS work. How long this can last, however, is uncertain.
- The system of working groups spreads the workload, eases the financial burden on individual participants, and helps build trust and solidarity. For working groups to work, however, governments must volunteer to chair and participate in them. This requires time, effort, and a budget. In the case of the KPCS, the contributions of South Africa, Canada, Russia, Botswana, the European Community, and Belgium's Diamond High Council have been significant. How long the KPCS can depend on only a few countries remains uncertain.
- Implementation problems were reduced significantly over the first four years of KPCS operation, but many issues remain. Some are the result of capacity weaknesses in some countries. Continuing NGO research and media pressure have helped to keep unresolved issues alive.
- Where the diamond industry is concerned, there are always receptions and cocktail parties; this has helped enormously. Insiders often refer to the "Kimberley family," and some of those who were antagonists have become friends and genuine allies.

Over the medium term, better self-regulation by the industry is required to weed out those who still trade in smuggled diamonds. The 2006–2007 clampdown in Ghana demonstrates that the excuse of porous borders is not good enough to absolve African governments from their responsibility to develop better internal controls over the mining and movement of diamonds. Nor does an emphasis on Africa absolve the governments of major trading, processing, and retailing countries from the need for similarly effective internal controls. The long-term challenge, however, remains developmental—and whether initiatives like the Diamond Development Initiative and other investments can turn diamonds from the curse they have been in some of Africa's poorest countries into the engine of development that so many hope they can be.

NOTES

1. Many books have been written about the diamond industry and about De Beers. See, e.g., Edward Jay Epstein, *The Rise and Fall of Diamonds: The Shattering of a Brilliant Illusion* (New York: Simon & Schuster, 1982); Stefan Kanfer, *The Last Empire: De Beers, Diamonds and the World* (New York: Farrar Straus Giroux, 1993); Matthew Hart, *Diamond: A Journey to the Heart of an Obsession* (New York: Viking, 2001).

2. Information on the World Diamond Council can be found at http://www.worlddiamondcouncil.com/.

3. The heads of state of Burkina Faso, Togo, and Liberia had been named in UN expert panel reports for their direct involvement in trafficking conflict diamonds and breaking UN sanctions on weapons.

4. Apart from Chapter VII instruments of the UN Security Council, all international agreements are, in any case, voluntary. In this regard, the KPCS was not different from other arrangements.

5. Global Witness, "Conflict Diamonds: Possibilities for the Identification, Certification and Control of Diamonds" (London: June 2000); Ian Smillie, "The Kimberley Process: The Case for Proper Monitoring" (Ottawa: Partnership Africa Canada, September 2002); Partnership Africa Canada and Global Witness, "The Key to Kimberley: Internal Diamond Controls, Seven Case Studies" (Ottawa: November 2004).

6. A description of the KPCS structure is available online at http//www.kimberleyprocess.com:8080/site/?name=structure.

7. Four reports by Partnership Africa Canada: *The Failure of Good Intentions: Theft, Fraud and Murder in the Brazilian Diamond Industry* (Ottawa: May 2005); *Fugitives and Phantoms: The Diamond Exporters of Brazil* (Ottawa: March 2006); *Triple Jeopardy-Triplicate Forms and Triple Borders: Controlling Diamond Exports from Guyana* (Ottawa: April 2006); *The Lost World: Diamond Mining and Smuggling in Venezuela* (Ottawa: November 2006).

FURTHER READING

Campbell, Greg. *Blood Diamonds: Tracing the Deadly Path of the World's Most Precious Stones.* Boulder, CO: Westview Press, 2002.

Diamond Development Initiative, The. http//www.ddiglobal.org/.

Farah, Douglas. *Blood from Stones: The Secret Financial Network of Terror.* New York: Broadway Books, 2004.

Global Witness. http://www.globalwitness.org/.

Hart, Matthew. *Diamond: A Journey to the Heart of an Obsession.* New York: Viking, 2001.

Partnership Africa Canada. http://www.pacweb.org/.

Zoellner, Tom. *The Heartless Stone: A Journey Through the World of Diamonds, Deceit and Desire.* New York: St. Martin's Press, 2006.

REFERENCES

Coghlan, Benjamin, P. N. Goy, and F. Muluma. 2006. Mortality in the Democratic republic of Congo: A nationwide survey. *Lancet* 367: 44–51.

Diamond Development Initiative. 2005. *Report of the proceedings of the DDI Conference, Accra, 2005.* http://www.pacweb.org/e/images/stories/documents/accra%20report-engl.pdf.

Global Witness. 1998. *A rough trade: The role of diamond companies and governments in the Angolan conflict.* London: Global Witness.

Kimberley Process. http://www.google.com/search?q=kimberley+process+workshop+on+WTO+conformity&hl=en&lr=&rls=com.microsoft:en-US&start=0&sa=N.

Oomes, Nienke, and Matthias Vocke. 2003. *Diamond smuggling and taxation in sub-Saharan Africa.* IMF Working Paper 03/167. Washington, DC: International Monetary Fund.

Partnership Africa Canada. 2006. *Diamond industry annual review: Sierra Leone 2006.* Ottawa: Partnership Africa Canada.

Partnership Africa Canada and Global Witness. 2004. *Rich man, poor man—development diamonds and poverty diamonds: The potential for change in the artisanal alluvial diamond fields of Africa.* Ottawa: Partnership Africa Canada and Global Witness.

Smillie, Ian, Lansana Gberie, and Ralph Hazleton. 2000. *The heart of the matter: Sierra Leone, diamonds & human security.* Ottawa: Partnership Africa Canada.

United Nations. 2000a. Report of the panel of experts appointed pursuant to UN Security Council Resolution 1306 (2000), para. 19 in relation to Sierra Leone. S/2000/1195. New York.

United Nations. 2000b. Report of the panel of experts on violations of Security Council sanctions against UNITA. S/2000/203. New York.

United Nations. 2000c. UN General Assembly res. A/RES55/56, Dec. 1. New York. http://daccessdds.un.org/doc/UNDOC/GEN/N00/562/75/PDF/N0056275.pdf?OpenElement.

United Nations. 2006. Report of the group of experts submitted in accordance with para. 2 of res. 1708. S/2006/964. New York.

World Diamond Council. http://www.worlddiamondcouncil.com/.

14

New Economy

Neil Lee

The term "new economy" describes several related concepts that share an emphasis on the impact of recent improvements in information and communications technology (ICT) on the economy and society. The narrowest use of the term is by U.S. economists who have used it to refer to a period of productivity growth in the economy that was associated with the effect of advances in computing technology. A more common use, often in the popular media, is to describe the growth and, often, decline of Internet start-up companies in the late 1990s. But the impact of technology on the global economy has been far wider than this, and some academic commentators have used the term "the new economy" to describe a process of restructuring of the economy and labor market that involved privatization, deregulation of industries, and technological change.

The new economy is linked closely to globalization, with the same improvements in technology that led to the new economy being among the key drivers of global economic integration (Perrons 2005). Moreover, the new economy became a popular phrase at around the same time as globalization increased in popularity. Some influential commentators argued that the new economy was a global economy, with advances in ICT allowing companies to order goods from many countries and so intensifying the process of competition between firms. High-profile relocations of firms and outsourcing of employment from high- to low-wage nations gave an impression of a global labor market. This led to concerns about risk and insecurity, with changes in technology allowing new organizational forms based on subcontracting and instability, the cost of which was a loss of security of employment. Rather than the burden of risk being shared within the structure of a large corporation, individuals working in the new economy faced the burden of risk on their own.

The impact of the new economy, however it is defined, tends to be geographically and socially uneven. The salience of the concept applies unevenly within and across countries, regions, and local communities. The impact has been diverse for different social groups, but it often tends to reinforce existing patterns of social stratification. There are concerns that new technology may be entrenching dependency in less developed countries, with a reliance on inappropriate technology produced in the developed world. Such issues contrast with suggestions that new technology can be a powerful tool in development. Because the new economy is diverse, it is difficult to establish its impact in each place. There is thus a tendency in the literature to generalize from relatively unique situations.

This chapter attempts to address some of those issues. First, it addresses the varying meanings of the new economy. These meanings differ in their emphasis but rely on a shared subject of the impact of technology on the economy. Second, the impact of the new economy on work is discussed; although these changes are clear in some places, they do not apply everywhere. Third, and related, the ways in which the new economy relates to inequality are discussed. One of these is the digital divide, which is discussed fourth, before the uses of ICT for development, discussed fifth. The chapter conclude by noting that problems with the concept of the new economy should not disguise very real concerns that the costs and benefits of new technology may be distributed unequally.

WHAT IS THE NEW ECONOMY?

Given the wide range of uses to which the appellation "new economy" has been put, it has been suggested that it is a "slippery term" (Pratt 2007, 77). One use is to describe the period of high productivity growth in the U.S. economy in the late 1990s, culminating in the dot-com boom. Other commentators have used the term more broadly to imply the wider restructuring of the economy in the wake of technological change and globalization. Such uses are not entirely distinct, and together they rely on many shared assumptions about the nature of economic change.

The U.S. "New Economy" and the Dot-Com Boom

Much discussion of the new economy focuses on a period of productivity growth in the United States in the 1990s. Following decades of relatively stagnant productivity growth, the productivity of the U.S. economy began to increase in 1995. Much of this success was attributed to the impact of technology, with optimistic commentators viewing this as a seminal change in the structure of the economy (Perrons 2005). Moreover, there were few more urgent issues to distract media attention, and so it became a popular agenda, with the term associated particularly with the economic policy of the Clinton administration (Henwood 2003). Clinton himself was responsible for an early use of the term, referring to a hopeful new economy during his 1992 campaign for election as U.S. president (Amman, Carpenter, and Neff 2007).

Business magazines propagated the idea of economic growth based on high technology and the use of the Internet. In *Business Week* magazine, Stephen Sheppard (November 17, 1997) argued that the new economy derived from two interlinked trends: globalization and digitization. Globalization implied "capitalism ... spreading around the world—if not full blown capitalism, at least the introduction of market forces freer trade and widespread deregulation" (1997, 1). This was linked to improvements in information technology, which allowed the "digitization of all information—words, pictures, data and so on. This digital technology is creating new companies and new industries before our eyes" (Sheppard 1997, 1). When linked together, these two factors were having profound implications for business, "transforming Corporate America," as information technology allowed long-term growth with little inflation while simultaneously increasing the productivity of other industries.

One of the most visible aspects of the new economy was the rapid growth of a series of Internet-based businesses. These were both highly publicized and plentiful, and many investors believed these companies, with "dot-com" at the end of their Web addresses, were likely to achieve considerable growth. Initially, valuations grew rapidly. The total value of prices on the NASDAQ, the U.S. stock market on which high-technology firms were listed, showed the valuation placed on these high-technology companies. Between 1996 and the middle of 1998, the value of these shares increased steadily. But in the second half of 1998, their values increased steeply, reaching a peak in the first few months of 2000, at which point the shares were worth five times their 1996 total value. Then came a sharp crash and slower decline over the subsequent three years.

The index has seen only modest growth since 2003. Speculative purchases of these shares had created a bubble, with investors attracted by growth rather than dividend profit (DeLong and Magin 2006). Company strategy had been based on the need to quickly build market share (the proportion of total spending in a given market that the firm could accrue), rather than any necessity of producing dividends for shareholders. Rather than being based on sound economic principals, the sector had become based on speculation and a desire not to miss out on anticipated profits in the future. In many cases, the profits never came. With time, investors became reluctant to fund companies making losses and began to withdraw, leading to the closure of many firms (Henwood 2003). Other events, such as the terrorist attacks of 2001, alongside a more general scepticism about the health of this market, exacerbated the decline. Meanwhile, accounting scandals in such new economy firms as the telecommunications company WorldCom meant that better standards of accounting were increasingly demanded to restrict the possibility for the financial maneuverings that had led to the bubble.

Productivity Growth and ICT

The dot-com boom was followed by an economic postmortem, with economists questioning the causes and sustainability of the increases in productivity. A cluster of U.S. economists began to dissect the productivity growth that underlay the dot-com boom. For these economists, the term "new economy" was used more narrowly to describe the productivity growth alone. The source of this growth was highly significant, since it had apparently addressed wider problems in the U.S. economy. But the source was not entirely clear. Growth economist Robert Solow had famously suggested that "we can see computers everywhere except in the productivity statistics" (1987, 36). The late 1990s had seen both productivity growth and computerization; it was important to assess whether Solow was wrong.

First was required an understanding of where in the economy the productivity growth had occurred. Writing at the height of the boom, Robert Gordon (1999) found that productivity growth in the U.S. economy in the period 1994–1999 was almost entirely attributable to growth in productivity in the sector of the economy that produced computers; in fact, the new economy of productivity growth had been restricted to a relatively small and high-technology part of the economy. Other economists found more of an impact. William Nordhaus (2002), for example, found that while new economy high-technology sectors have performed well, the productivity growth is not isolated in these sectors. Furthermore, looking at the role of ICT within sectors, Kevin Stiroh (2002) finds that those sectors that *use* ICT, in addition to those that produce it, experienced significant gains in productivity.

In short, while the evidence on the impact of ICT on productivity in the United States was not conclusive, there was considerable evidence of productivity gains in those few sectors that produce computers. This led to beneficial suggestions about the use of ICT. But these studies did little to address the question of who gained and who lost from ICT's impact in the economy.

The Information Society and the New Economy

Using the new economy to refer exclusively to the U.S. situation ignores broader questions about the impact of ICT at global and local levels. Other commentators have taken a broader perspective. Manuel Castells (2001, 150) defines the new economy as an "economy in which companies—or firms or entrepreneurs—around the world are working on the basis of the internet and in which their organizational and innovation logic is embedded in the Internet or related information technologies." For Castells, the important question is not so much what the technology is but how it changes the methods of production for firms and the way everyday life is lived. His analogy is the introduction of electricity. The economy did not just work through electricity but worked with it, for it enabled new forms of production and consumption.

For Castells, this new economy is about more than productivity growth (although productivity growth is important). He argues that the new economy has three main features:

- *Productivity Growth.* Such growth is achieved through the use of knowledge in the production process, with the aim of innovation, or through the introduction of new products and processes.
- *"Global Environment for Competitiveness."* By this term, Castells means the increasingly interdependent global economic system.
- *New Organizational Forms.* These are established through networks that are adaptable, decentralized systems of economic relationships that outperform older hierarchical organizational forms.

Castells includes productivity growth as just one aspect of the impact of ICT, but he highlights the changing organization of firms. This has considerable implications for economic restructuring at a local level.

The New Economy as Economic Restructuring

Wider and less technology-focused views of the new economy have also been suggested. Building on work by Castells, Diane Perrons and her colleagues (2002) use the term to refer to the broader aspects of socioeconomic change and the nature of economic change in modern, usually Western economies. These include liberalization of the economy and economic deregulation and privatization, which may, in turn, have changed much paid work, the structure of families, and feminization and flexibilization of paid work and inequality. They also link the new economy to patterns of government in the West, with the response to globalization of the economy being neoliberal policies resulting in the introduction of intensified competition in many sectors of the economy. Such changes have particular consequences for the nature of paid employment.

Thus, for Perrons (2003, 271), "in general, the new economy is characterised by globalisation and the increasing use of communication and information technologies, but also deregulation, polarisation and feminisation of employment and new, more flexible patterns and hours of work." The new economy cannot be removed from these wider social and economic changes that moderate and alter the impact of these technologies on the economy.

By arguing that the new economy is part of wider social and economic change, it makes it more difficult to assess the extent to which it is a discrete change or a continuation of past trends. While academics are clear that there have been significant changes as a result of technology, most are unclear about exactly what has happened (Pratt 2007). Indeed, technological change is embedded in existing structures of social and economic organization, and there are many other social and economic changes operate concurrently. This means that to consider the new economy as the impact of technology alone would be to lose much of the nuance of theories of contemporary economic restructuring.

THE NEW ECONOMY AND WORK

One of the key areas where the new economy has been felt is in the workplace. In some countries, technology has led to substantial changes in the structure of the labor market—that is, technology has affected which jobs are available to be done, the tasks performed within these occupations, and the way in which people engage with the labor market. Changes might include increased flexible, casual, or part-time employment, as well as the changing of the burden of risk or changes in labor demand increasing the demand for the highly skilled. The nature of these changes, and the extent to which they are widespread across the economy, are contested.

The End of Work?

Several commentators took new technology to imply profound changes in the nature of employment. One of the more extreme views came from journalist Jeremy Rifkin (1995) in his book *The End of Work*. Rifkin argued that the introduction of computers across all sectors of the economy was increasingly displacing human labor. Previously, as sectors that had experienced new technology (through the impact of new machinery) shed labor, the surplus workers had been taken up by such sectors as retail, which had expanded. But the advent of computerization had bleaker consequences, Rifkin argued:

> Now, for the first time, human labor is being systematically eliminated from the production process. Within less than a century, "mass" work in the market sector is likely to be phased out in virtually all of the industrialized nations of the world. A new generation of sophisticated information and communications technologies is being hurried into a wide variety of work situations. Intelligent machines are replacing human beings in countless tasks, forcing millions of blue and white collar workers into unemployment lines, or worse still, breadlines. (1995, 3)

There was, according to Rifkin, a small group of highly educated people who were exceptions to this wave of computerized redundancies: these people could perform tasks involving mental processes that could not be automated by computers and so would remain in "knowledge employment."

Rifkin is a journalist and so presents a pessimistic and polemical view. Other authors have viewed similar changes as leading to more optimistic outcomes. One such author is Charles Leadbeater (2000), who in his book *Living on Thin Air* also took changes in the labor market as a starting point but used his own employment history as an example. Noting that he had difficulty explaining his occupation to his children, he argued that employment patterns were changing. In contrast to traditional occupations such as being a teacher, nurse, or farmer, the new employment types were more amorphous and harder to place within traditional working categories. Instead, using his individual skills, Leadbeater worked as a freelance consultant, employed by a range of different organizations and functioning as a specialist or subcontractor for each one, rather than remaining in post at a single organization. He was removed from hierarchical corporate structures and fixed employment contracts, and by placing himself at the mercy of a network, he received better pay, more interesting employment, and flexibility. But he was also aware of the risk he was taking: in working flexibly and independently, he had placed the consequences of this risk specifically on himself.

Characteristics of Work in the New Economy

It has proved difficult for commentators to assess the actual changes in the workplace. Some of the supposed characteristics of this change are described in Table 14.1. These characteristics are open to question, however, and they may describe changes that apply to small groups of people in employment rather than widespread changes across the whole of the economy.

A caricature of employment in the old economy looks something like this: employees worked for large companies that conduct many different tasks within the same organization. They have permanent and stable employment contracts, with employees working for a single employer for a large part, if not

Table 14.1 Employment Characteristics of the Old and New Economies

"Old Economy" Employment	"New Economy" Employment
• Stable Employment Contracts	• Flexibility
• Narrative	• Subcontracting
• Hierarchies	• Networks
• National Demand	• Contract work
• Shared Risk	• Global Networks
• Unionization	• Individualized Risk
• Loyalty and Length of Service	• Individualization
• Slow Communications	• Instantaneous Communications
	• Work Fragmentation

Source: Author.

all of their careers. Promotion is relatively routine, with pay raises based on length of service and loyalty rather than short-term performance. This structure allowed the development of a career narrative, encompassing entry at a relatively basic level and steady progression to management.

In contrast, the new economy worker develops a portfolio career. Rather than serving a single large employer, the worker works for a series of employers, often performing small and specialized tasks. Contracts are short term and fragmented, with reward given for recent performance and up-to-date knowledge rather than long-term work performance. The loss of the stable employer means flexibility and some degree of autonomy over working times and work location. But it also places the burden of risk on individuals, without the support that a mass organization depends on.

There is some truth to these changes, and there is little doubt that they apply to certain people. But other authors have questioned the extent to which these changes are generalizable across the economy as a whole. Neither of the two scenarios presented here was ever universal; conditions have always changed within the workforce, according to the particular industry, location, job role, and employer for whom individuals work.

A key theme in the literature on work in the new economy is risk. The key theorist on risk and employment was Ulrich Beck (1992), who argues that risk is increasingly a feature of the modern economy. In the labor market, risk is developed through the fragmentation of working lives as stable employment for a single firm is replaced by networked forms of work organization. The risk of unemployment was previously offset by the welfare state or the ability to move sideways within the organization. The new economy, with the emphasis on decentralization of productive forms and network organization, removes the worker from such constraints.

This has been exacerbated in some countries by the contracting out of service industries from the state sector to private firms, which are supposed to perform the work more cheaply. This process removes employees from well-protected government jobs and places their employment in the private sector, with the worst conditions and the highest risk of unemployment greatest for those who are already the worst paid (Allen and Henry 1997). The new organizational forms associated with the new economy prioritize flexibility through new networked productive forms, with firms aiming to subcontract, rather than maintain, stable employment relations. This flexibilization of employment relations shifts the emphasis on risk, with some commentators arguing that "if flexibility is the language of the firm, perhaps risk is more appropriately the language of the workforce" (Allen and Henry 1997, 183). In this way, it is argued, the shift to a network form of employment has removed employees from the security of the large firm, where risk is shared within the corporation; as a result, the employees become individually responsible for managing the burden of this risk.

Risk Across the Economy?

While the theory of work in the new economy appears anecdotally appropriate, some commentators have expressed doubts about how generalizable they are across the economy. In particular, the notion of the portfolio worker has been criticized. Polemic accounts of work in the new economy predict that employees will work for many different organizations for short periods of time. One way of testing this notion is through the average length of time each employee spends with a particular organization. In the United Kingdom, at least, there has been an increase in job tenures. In the period 1992–2000, job tenure had increased by an average of six years with two months to seven years and four months (Nolan and Wood 2003).

Similarly, the labor market in the United Kingdom, for example, appears to be shifting toward permanent employment, rather than flexible work or self-employment. These flexible trends were apparent in the labor market from 1986 to 1996. Employment growth was dominated in this period by self-employment and temporary employment. In the period 1996–2006, however, most of the growth was in full-time employment (Brinkley, Coats, and Overell 2007). These figures are different for 1996–2006, when the growth was in full-time employment; during that same period, self-employment grew slowly while temporary employment fell. So this new economy period was marked by an apparent increase in old economy employment.

The trends do not mean, of course, that the labor market has not changed or that the changes have not affected large numbers of people. There has been considerable change in some sectors, particularly those that have been subject to deregulation (Perrons 2003). Case studies of employment change can illuminate aspects of changing employment relations. Diane Perrons (2003) compares workers in different sectors in the seaside town of Brighton in the United Kingdom. The "new media" sector is indisputably a new economy sector. Work in this sector is characterized by long working hours, relative insecurity, and small firm size. Consequently, workers with childcare or caring responsibilities are unable to continue into management; thus, the management and ownership of such firms tend to be male. In contrast, childcare workers tend to be female and relatively low paid. In a single location, the new economy has affected different employees in different ways.

NEW ECONOMIC INEQUALITIES

The impact of ICT technology was felt concurrent with large increases in inequality both globally and within many nations. This led to considerable concerns that new technology might in some way be responsible. Two of the most prominent explanations for this rise in inequality are the impact of technology on the labor market within countries and the winner-takes-all effects that technology may make possible.

Technology and the Labor Market

There have long been concerns about the impact of technology on the distribution of employment. The classic theory that seeks to explain the impact of computers on the labor market is Skills Biased Technological Change (SBTC). Theories such as this see employment as being distributed along a spectrum. At the top of the spectrum are the highest-skilled jobs, with skill decreasing until the bottom of the distribution, where the lowest-skilled jobs are located. In general, the ideas of skills is often a proxy for the qualifications required for employment, and higher-skilled jobs are seen as better paid.

The SBTC theory suggests that the technology will lead to reductions in the number of jobs at the bottom of this spectrum. Computers and other technology will replace jobs that do not need high skills, since tasks are increasingly automated. This will tend to reduce employment at the bottom of the distribution and lead to unemployment because those who have low skills will be unable to find suitable employment. This may, in turn, lead to inequality, for those workers with low skills will no longer be included in the formal labor market, whereas the highly-skilled workers will gain employment.

A more subtle version of this hypothesis is the Autor-Levy-Murnane (ALM) hypothesis. David Autor, Frank Levy, and Richard Murnane (2003) believe that workers at the bottom of the distribution will not simply be replaced. Instead, they argue, in the new economy, "computer capital substitutes for workers in carrying out a limited and well-defined set of cognitive and manual activities, those that can be accomplished by following explicitly rules," or routine tasks. These routine tasks are primarily concentrated at the bottom of the distribution. Simultaneously, they argue, "computer capital complements workers in carrying out problem-solving and complex communication activities." These latter tasks are primarily performed by those workers at the top of the distribution, and so this model predicts that an hour-glass job market will develop.

Autor, Levy, and Murnane (2003) tested their theory with data for the United States, where they found the predicted trends to hold broadly. In fact, the U.S. economy saw that employment declined in those areas they termed routine, whereas employment in the nonroutine tasks increased. As their theory predicts, these changes were most acute in industries that were also investing in computers. These trends were relatively weak in the 1960s, when computers were still rare, but increased in importance subsequently as computers became widespread. The nature of people's jobs also changed as they began to perform more nonroutine tasks. In short, across industries, within industries, and in specific jobs, increasing numbers of computers shifted the nature of demand for labor. Evidence for other countries suggests that the ALM hypothesis holds, albeit often to a less extreme level. For example, Goos and Manning tested a similar model for the UK labor market between 1975 and 1999 and found a u-shaped change in the employment distribution: increases in jobs at the top and the bottom of the distribution (Goos and Manning 2007).

The Winner-takes-all Effect

A second explanaion for increased inequality is the winner-takes-all effect. The new economy is related to a change in the nature of production from physical, manufactured goods to such intangible or dematerialized products as digital music. One way to link this change to inequality is the work of Danny Quah (1999), who argues that there is an increasingly weightless economy. Digitized or weightless goods can be transported with relatively little cost. They are infinitely expansible, meaning they can be replicated at low cost. They are also nonrival; that is, they may be used over and over, so use by one person does not diminish another person's the ability to use them.

But nonrival goods may lead to inequality through what Quah (1999) terms a "superstar" effect. In the first place, people prefer goods that are famous, of which they have heard, rather than niche products. Because these products can be reproduced cheaply, they may capture the market, thereby becoming superstars.

Quah's premise has proved difficult to test, however. But Ian Dew Becker and Robert J. Gordon (2005) have looked at the distribution of U.S. productivity growth, which forms a large part of some narratives of the new economy. They find considerable polarization of income inequality, specifically finding that "only the top 10% of the income distribution enjoyed a growth rate of real wages and salary income equal to or above the average rate of economy wide productivity growth." In the United Kingdom, Anthony Atkinson (2002) has shown that the very rich have seen their proportion of income increase disproportionately. Net of tax, the top 1 percent of the population saw their share of national income increase from 7.1 percent in 1989 to 9.1 percent in 1989. This was particularly acute for those at the very top. The income share of the top 0.1 percent grew from 0.66 percent in 1977 to 1.81 percent in 1989 before a rise of an additional 1.4 percent by 2000 (Atkinson 2002).

THE DIGITAL DIVIDE

An important facet of the new economy is the diffusion of information and communications technology. Access to ICT remains highly differentiated, however, a situation referred to as the digital divide. The term "digital divide" serves as a summary for a complex set of interlinked processes about uneven international access to computers and information technology (IT). Many commentators have divided this complicated set of interconnections into several different processes. The first digital divide—the meaning most often implied by users of the term—refers to direct access to computers or new technology. This

Table 14.2 The Digital Divide

Causes of the Digital Divide

- Cost: Perceived or actual cost of equipment and subscriptions
- Access: Particularly lack of public facilities or facilities at work
- Skills: Lack of skills in ICT, general literacy, or numeracy or lack of knowledge of the Internet
- Cultural Issues: Lack of family or friends online or other cultural barriers
- Personal Factors:
  - Lack of confidence
  - Lack of credit card or bank account
  - Fear of technology
  - Lack of interest
  - A feeling that it is "too late" to learn
  - Physical reasons (e.g., poor eyesight)

Source: Scottish Executive, *Digital Inclusion: Connecting Scotland's People* (Edinburgh: Scottish Executive, 2001).

may relate to actual technology or access to the Internet. In much of the world, access to the Internet depends on the provision of physical infrastructure, which tends to be predominantly urban or concentrated in more affluent areas. However, within most developed nations almost the entire population has high-speed linkages available, so access is largely dependent on a user's finances—can the user afford the connection and the necessary equipment—rather than physical access (Craig and Greenhill 2005).

But several commentators have suggested that the second digital divide may be equally important: do people have the skills or ability to use computers if they have access to them?[1] One of the key factors is education, with the higher educated more likely to have the skills to operate ICT, but older people likely to have worse skills and so be less able to use it. This is a dynamic process. People who are less affluent are also less likely to be able to use ICT and likely to have less access to equipment. But because ICT skills are increasingly important in the labor market, individuals without ICT skills are less marketable and therefore more likely to remain less affluent.[2] A wider range of barriers is set out in Table 14.2.

The consequences of such divides may be widespread. Without access to computers or the ability to use them, individuals will find a range of marketplaces inaccessible, including online trading or auction sites such as e-Bay, and they may also thereby be prevented from accessing online information about which services are cheaper, for example, or from paying bills online and so gaining discounts. Lack of access or computer skills may also prevent individuals access to online employment activities. The digital divide can be particularly severe for people with disabilities, who might otherwise be able to use the Internet to stay connected, or for people living in rural areas.

The digital divide has been exacerbated in those areas where the Internet is necessary to use other services (Pratt 2007). The Internet is primarily used for such consumption-based activities as shopping, but individuals on low incomes may be excluded from this online use simply because low incomes exclude them from similar activities in everyday life. But the prominence of the Internet now serves as justification, for example, to remove a commercial business's physical facilities in particular areas or to close a bank's local branch, where the customer base is reduced because some people bank online. Such closures most likely take place in low-income areas where operation of the business or bank may be less profitable anyway.

Because processes of access tend to reflect income, the digital divide tends to reinforce existing patterns of social stratification (Mansell 2002). In one study, for example, which looked at Internet use in the United Kingdom, males and the highly educated were seen to use the Internet disproportionately (Losh 2004). Women were less likely to use the Internet at work. Studies such as this do not, however, manage to differentiate between the productive and nonproductive use of computers.

The Global Digital Divide

The digital divide may also have implications at a global level. In general, use of the Internet or telecoms reflects the distribution of national income, since richer countries will have higher levels of Internet use (Perrons 2005). The countries with the highest Internet penetration are Sweden, with 762 users per 1,000 inhabitants, and the Netherlands, with 740 per 1,000. The United States and Japan have 663 and 666 users per 1,000 respectively (International Telecommunications Union 2007).

Some observers have suggested that the digital divide may impede economic development in the developing world. The World Bank publishes figures on cellphone subscribers and Internet users. Although such data are difficult to collect and need to be treated with caution, they do indicate considerable growth and considerable international diversity. The data are divided into regions in only low- and middle-income economies. In 2000, telephones were most widespread in Europe and Central Asia and in Latin America and the Caribbean, with 315 and 267 subscribers per 1,000 people respectively. By 2004, these figures had increased significantly: Europe and Central Asia now had 730 subscribers per 1,000, while Latin America and the Caribbean had almost doubled to 507 per 1,000. This growth was widespread, although the smallest growth was in South Asia and sub-Saharan Africa. South Asia increased from 31 subscribers per 1,000 people in 2000 to only 87 per 1,000; sub-Saharan Africa saw a higher increase in subscribers from 32 per 1,000 people to 103 per 1,000. Growth in these two regions was considerably lower than in any others.

Data on Internet use reveal similar patterns. Internet use is most widespread in Europe and Central Asia and in Latin America and the Caribbean, and these two regions saw the greatest absolute growth: growing from 29 to 117 and 34 to 104 subscribers per 1,000 respectively. There was also substantial growth in East Asia and the Pacific, from 18 per 1,000 to 76 per 1,000. South Asia and sub-Saharan Africa again had the lowest subscriptions, with growth from only 5 subscribers per 1,000 to 21 per 1,000 in South Asia and from 5 per 1,000 to

Table 14.3 Telephone and Internet Access by Region, 2000 and 2004, per 1,000 People

	Fixed and Mobile Subscribers 2000	2004	Internet Users 2000	2004
East Asia and Pacific	148	450	18	76
Europe and Central Asia	315	730	29	117
Latin America and the Caribbean	267	507	34	104
Middle East and North Africa	119	206	10	47
South Asia	31	87	5	21
Sub-Saharan Africa	32	103	5	15

Source: World Bank, *Information and Communications for Development: Global Trends and Policies* (Washington, DC: World Bank, 2006).

15 per 1,000 in sub-Saharan Africa. Table 14.3 shows figures for telephone and Internet access in 2000 and 2004.

There remains, therefore, a clear digital divide in access to ICT across regions of the world. This is perhaps more concerning given the substantial growth—those regions that began with high usage of technology grew disproportionately. But these figures do not account for considerable variation of use within developing countries, with some countries displaying considerable internal disparities. Authors discussing China, for example, are caught in the peculiar situation of discussing the economic impact of high-technology industry in the east of the country but still needing to discuss the penetration of landline telephones in the West (Meng and Li 2002). Similarly, statistics like these do not account for differences in the way people use the Internet. A single access point in the south of China may be used by a wider range of users than one in the north, with the result that access to ICT is undercounted (Heeks 2005). Note that the figures given here are for subscribers, where this might clearly be the case, and for users, where the arguments might be more opaque.

ICT AND DEVELOPMENT

There have been suggestions, then, that ICT can be a powerful tool in development. But the links between ICT and development are not entirely clear; they are dependent on a wide range of intervening variables. Two main ways of using ICT to address uneven development are the use of high-technology industries in developing countries and the use of technology in development projects.

National Economies and New Economy Industries

Such development organizations as the World Bank have highlighted the importance of ICT industries for the wider economies of developing countries. One way ICT might spread to developing countries is through facilitating the shift of some employment from high-cost countries among the developing countries to countries with lower costs, a trend known as offshoring. Previously, outsourcing was seen as a threat only to those jobs that revolved around tradable manufacturing processes and limited service employment. Advances in ICT, however, increased the potential of offshoring to a wider range of services industries. This combined with such other globalization initiatives as China's entry into the WTO extended the trend. Particularly in countries with significant groups of low-wage but well-educated workers, as in India and China, offshoring has been seen as a benefit for development; but it is also perceived as a threat to jobs in the West.

Offshored employment tends to be relatively low value, with concentrations of employment in labor-intensive but low-skilled industries such as call centers. Wages for workers in these industries in the developing world are considerably lower than those of workers in the developed. A call center operator in India will earn only between 13 and 20 percent of the salary of a similar U.K. or U.S. worker. But comparable wage rates are also available for higher-skilled occupations: accountants earn around 12 percent of the U.S. or U.K. average (Work Foundation 2004).

Given that it is also substantially cheaper to employ skilled labor as well as unskilled labor, it is unsurprising that some developing economies have developed increasingly highly skilled industrial bases. This extends to high-technology industries, although this trend is far from widespread. China is an exemplar in this sense, for it now hosts many foreign ICT firms while also having a sizable industry subcontracting technology manufacturing for Western firms. In 2004, China became the world's largest exporter of ICT goods (OECD 2006).

But the Chinese experience remains an exception rather than a rule, for computing sectors in developing countries tend to be based around adapting imported products for internal demand rather than producing for export. One survey of Nigerian computer firms, conducted between 1998 and 2001, suggested they were focused on technical support for imported rather than locally produced software, altering and supporting local firms in their use of foreign software rather than producing software individually (Soriyan and Heeks 2004).

ICT and Economic Development

ICT has wider purposes than just its role as an industry. Many of the uses of ICT revolve around the use of mobile-phone technology to exchange information. Mobile phones have features that may make them appropriate in developing countries: mobile-phone systems have lower requirements for infrastructure than do landline telephone systems, and mobile-phone networks are often of higher quality or greater reliability. For the user, there are such advantages as portability and the status of owning a mobile phone; in addition, prepaid phone cards mean users are in control of the amount they are spending and do not have to pass a credit check (Panos Institute 2004). Such factors mean that mobile phones are increasingly important in the developing world, particularly in rural areas.

Mobile phones have a range of economic uses. For example, for farmers mobiles phones can allow rapid and relatively cheap access to information about market prices. Having mobile phones can enable farmers who have to travel to market to assess whether the prices are sufficient to justify the cost of their journey. Development organizations have designed projects to address this possibility. In Burkina Faso and Mali, for example, the UN has sponsored the Trade at Hand project, which provides up to date prices to farmers (see http:www.tradeathand.info).

Such problems are, of course, predicated on full coverage of telecoms. In many countries, coverage remains patchy. Where the telecom sector has been privatized, providers may lack incentives to provide coverage in rural areas because they are less profitable than urban areas. This has led to concerns about inequality of access within countries. To address the issue, some countries have used "smart subsidies," where a proportion of the revenues is charged to the private sector and used to subsidize provision in the rural areas (Panos Institute 2004).

Critical Views

Despite high expectations for ICT's role in development, as well as some successful projects, such projects have been far from revolutionary. Indeed, Robert Wade (2002) argues there has been a high "aspiration-to-evidence ratio" in the literature on ICT and development. Such development organizations as the World Bank continue to push ICT projects. Wade has highlighted the problems in these projects. In some cases, there has been insufficient funding for more basic supplies, including even pencils or pens, while aid money has been spent on development projects involving computers. In other situations, projects impose computers in situations without a reorganization of the productive process. Introducing computers inappropriately in such situations can actually reduce productivity.

Instead, Wade argues, the asymmetries in the global economy may be leading to dependency, with developing countries reliant on software and hardware produced in the developed world. One way this may happen is through commercial issues around the continual expansion of computing power. It is in the interest of computer and software manufacturers to continually upgrade the capacity of their products. As computing becomes more powerful, software is expanded to fill the available capacity, often with clever marketing or branding developed to improve it. In developing countries, this increases the cost of adoption, particular for firms who want their product to be compatible with firms in the developed world.

There are other reasons to suspect that the economies of developing countries will find less benefit from ICT than developed counties. Reasons for this might include the relatively small sector of the economy that is equipped to take advantage of the equipment, higher relative costs of introducing the new technology, and the general population's low levels of education, and in particular ICT skills (Kenny 2006). Such barriers imply that suggestions that ICT will revolutionize development need to be viewed sceptically.

CONCLUSION

The new economy is used in diverse ways to describe broad, complex, and changing situations that are broadly related to the impact of computers and ICT on the economy and society. It is no surprise that the result is a somewhat confused literature on the topic. The nature of the changes implied in the new economy means that opinions are often polarized, with some commentators optimistic, but others using very similar arguments pessimistically. As presented in this chapter, these authors have commented on the new economy's impact on work and employment, inequality, the digital divide, and development.

Clearly, the impact of the new economy has been diverse. Within different countries and regions the new economy has had a highly varied impact, and generalizations often appear to overstate the new economy's effects. There is a real concern that in generalizing, analyses will miss groups whose experiences have been different. In the United Kingdom, for example, the overall trend has been toward increasing job tenure, yet for some groups there has been an increase in insecurity. In short, the impact has been diverse.

Of particular concern is the evidence that the costs and benefits of technological change may be distributed unequally, with the costs disproportionately borne by the relatively poor. At a local level, changing patterns of skills demand and the digital divide may lead to inequality. At an international level, there are concerns that technological changes will lead to productivity growth in some developed countries at the same time that ICT projects in the developed world will be failing. Along with these concerns comes considerable evidence that the very rich are increasing their share of income, helped by the changing nature of economic production and ownership. Such phenomena have highly differential patterns within and across different places. Affluent nations, for example, are most likely to have widespread Internet access, and the highly skilled are likely to see their employment options increase. While representing the processes of economic change clearly and consistently is difficult, these processes remain important objects of study.

NOTES

1. Both Losh (2004) and Hargatti (2002) use this term.
2. See, e.g., EU Taskforce on ICT Competitiveness and ICT Up-Take, "Skills and Employability," European Union (2006). http://eskills.cedefop.europa.eu/conference2006/download/ICT_Taskforce_WG5.pdf.

FURTHER READING

Amman, J., T. Carpenter, and G. Neff. *Surviving the New Economy.* Boulder, CO: Paradigm, 2007.
Henwood, D. *After the New Economy: The Binge and the Hangover That Won't Go Away.* New York: New Press, 2003.
Perrons, D. *Globalization and Social Change: People and Places in a Divided World.* London: Routledge, 2005.
Peter, W. D., J. Beaverstock, M. Bradshaw, and A. Leyshon. *Geographies of the New Economy: Critical Reflections.* London: Routledge, 2007.
Wade, R. H. "Bridging the Digital Divide: New Route to Development or New Form of Dependency." *Global Governance* 8 (2002): 443–66.

REFERENCES

Allen, J., and N. Henry. 1997. Ulrich Beck's "risk society" at work: Labour and employment in the contract service industries. *Transactions of the Institute of British Geographers* 22: 180–96.

Amman, J., T. Carpenter, and G. Neff. 2007. *Surviving the new economy.* Boulder, CO: Paradigm.

Atkinson, A. B. 2002. Top incomes in the United Kingdom over the twentieth century. University of Oxford Discussion Papers in Economic and Social History 23: 1–58.

Autor, D., F. Levy, and R. Murnane. 2003. The skill content of recent technological change: An empirical exploration. *Quarterly Journal of Economics* 118: 1279–1333.

Beck, U. 1992. *Risk society: Towards a new modernity.* London: Sage.

Brinkley, I., D. Coats, and S. Overell. 2007. *7 out of 10: Labour under Labour, 1997–2007.* London: Work Foundation.

Castells, M. 2001. The information society, the new economy and the network society. In *The information society reader,* Frank Webster ed., 150–64. London: Routledge.

Craig, J., and B. Greenhill. 2005. *Beyond digital divides? The future for ICT in rural areas,* Wetherby, UK: Countryside Agency.

DeLong, J. B., and K. Magin. 2006. A short note on the size of the dot-com bubble. NBER Working Paper 12011.

Dew Becker, I., and R. J. Gordon. 2005. Where did the productivity growth go? Inflation dynamics and the distribution of income. NBER Working Paper 11842.

Goos, M., and A. Manning. 2007. Lousy and lovely jobs: The rising polarization of work in Britain. *Review of Economics and Statistics* 89: 118–33.

Gordon, R. J. 1999. Has the "new economy" rendered the productivity slowdown obsolete ? Northwestern University Working Paper. http://faculty-web.at.northwestern.edu/economics/gordon/334.html (accessed June 15, 2007).

Hargittai, E.. 2002. The second level digital divide: Differences in people's online skills. *First Monday* 7.

Heeks, R. 2005. Overestimating the global digital divide. eDevelopment Briefing 7. Manchester, UK: University of Manchester.

Henwood, D. 2003. *After the new economy: The binge and the hangover that won't go away.* New York: New Press.

International Telecommunications Union. 2007. Key statistics. http://www.itu.int (accessed May 27, 2007).

Kenny, C. 2006. The internet and economic growth in LDCs: A case of managing expectations. In *The new economy in development: ICT challenges and opportunities,* ed. Anthony P. D'Costa, 67–89. Basingstoke, UK: Palgrave MacMillan.

Leadbeater, C. 2000. *Living on thin air: The new economy.* London: Penguin.

Losh, S. C. 2004. Gender, educational and occupational digital gaps, 1983–2002. *Social Science Computer Review* 22: 152–66.

Mansell, R. 2002. From eigital divides to digital entitlements in knowledge societies. *Current Sociology* 50: 407–26.

Meng, Q., and M. Li. 2002. New economy and ICT development in China. *Information Economics and Policy* 14: 275–95.

Nolan, P., and S. Wood. 2003. Mapping the future of work. *British Journal of Industrial Relations* 41: 165–74.

Nordhaus, W. D. 2002. Productivity growth and the new economy. *Brookings Papers in Economic Activity* 2: 211–44.

OECD. 2006. *Information Technology Outlook.* Paris: OECD.

Panos Institute. 2004. Completing the revolution: The challenge of rural telephony in Africa. Panos Report 48. London: Panos.

Perrons, D. 2002. Gendered divisions in the new economy: Risks and opportunities. *GeoJournal* 56: 271–80.

———. 2003. The new economy and the work life balance: Conceptual explorations and a case study of new media. *Gender, Work and Organisation* 67: 65–93.

———. 2005. *Globalization and social change: People and places in a divided world.* London: Routledge.

Perrons, D., L. McDowell, C. Fagan, K. Ray, and K. Ward, eds. 2002. Work, life and time in the new economy. Introduction to *Gender Divisions and Working Time in the New Economy,* ed. D. Perrons, L. McDowell, C. Fagan, K. Ray, and K. Ward, 1–15. Cheltenham, UK: Edward Elgar.

Pratt, A. 2007. The new economy, or the emperor's new clothes. In *Geographies of the New Economy,* ed. P. W. Daniels, J. Beaverstock, M. Bradshaw, and A. Leyshon, 71–86. London: Routledge.

Quah, D. 1999. The weightless economy in growth, *Business Economist* 30: 40–53.

Rifkin, J. 1995. *The end of work: The decline of the global labor force and the dawn of the post-market era.* New York: Putnam.

Solow, R. 1987. We'd better watch out. *New York Times Book Review,* July 12, 36.

Soriyan, H. A., and R. Heeks. 2004. A profile of Nigeria's software industry. Development Informatics Working Paper 21. Manchester, UK: Institute for Development Policy and Management, University of Manchester.

Stiroh, K. 2002. Information technology and the U.S. productivity revival: What do the industry data say? *American Economic Review* 92: 1559–76.

Wade, R. H. 2002. Bridging the digital divide: New route to development or new form of dependency. *Global Governance* 8: 443–66.

Work Foundation, The. 2004. *Outsourcing and offshoring: Implications for organisational capacity.* London: Work Foundation.

15

New Wars

Helen Dexter

The idea that the warfare witnessed in the post–Cold War era is something new or novel has been cited as "perhaps the most influential academic narrative of contemporary war" (Jackson forthcoming, 25). The new war thesis has, David Chandler believes, "become the new ideological template for current international security regimes" (2006, 484). In the immediate aftermath of the Cold War, many hoped that the world would become a more peaceful place. Instead, as the superpower rivalry came to an end, there seemed to be a growing sense of insecurity. Although the chance of war *between* states was reduced, the collapse of bipolarity appeared to result in an increase of brutal wars *within* states. Since 1989 an estimated 5 million lives have been lost and 50 million people displaced through war (Murshed 2003). In February 2004, the then British foreign secretary Jack Straw described the new post–Cold War security environment: "The end of the Cold War brought liberty and democracy to millions, and lifted the threat of global nuclear confrontation. But as the superpower stand-off came to an end, the world also became more complex, and new threats to our security emerged" (2004).

The end of the Cold War and superpower patronage created a power vacuum in some states. The effect of globalization on these weak states has resulted in political and social transformations characterized by violent identity politics, criminalization, and the privatization of violence (Newman 2004, 175). New wars take place within the context of the erosion of the state as a result of the processes of globalization. The violence that was witnessed in Africa and the Balkans in the 1990s, for example, was far removed from our traditional Western conception of warfare. Civilians rather than soldiers bore the brunt of the violence, targeted because of their ethnic or religious identity. The violence carried out against them included such horrific atrocities as amputation, mutilation, or rape. Criminality was rife and sustained by a complex network of local and global markets. The characteristics of such contemporary intrastate warfare since the end of the Cold War—the conflicts that have been labeled as the "new war"—are the focus of this chapter. First, the chapter sets out what we consider old war to be. Next, the chapter discusses the relationship between globalization—particularly neoliberal economics—weak states, and violence in an attempt to understand the underlying structural characteristics of new war. The chapter then briefly describes the nature of the violence exhibited in contemporary intrastate war, focusing on the actors, economics, political aims, and methods said to distinguish the new war from the old. The chapter concludes by addressing some of the challenges made against the new war theory, highlighting the Nigerian civil war as an example of an old "new" war.

OLD WAR

Before we can understand the nature of contemporary intrastate war and why it is thought to be something new, we must first consider what *old* war looks like. The conventional view of warfare in the West is formed in large part from our experiences in World War I and World War II. When we think of warfare, we tend to picture those early scenes from *Saving Private Ryan*: patriotic soldiers fighting on the battlefield, airplanes flying overhead, bombs falling, and artillery firing in all directions. In these scenes, we know which men (for women are seldom in this picture) are soldiers because they are wearing uniforms. We know they are on a battlefield because beyond it lies something else—houses, farmland, *civilians*. The soldiers arriving on the beach know what they want to achieve there; they have a strategy. We know that these men are fighting for a purpose, fighting for victory, and that when they achieve their aims, there will be peace again. Modern warfare in this image employs conventional weaponry—in other words, tanks, heavy artillery, massive firepower, and air power. This is the prevailing conception of warfare. It is based on a set of binaries: war and peace; friend and foe; soldier and civilian; public and private. Within this dominant image, war is a conflict between states. It is a rational and well-organized social activity fought for a national or ideological cause. At the center of it all is the state, which maintains the legitimate monopoly over the use of force. Warfare is governed by hierarchical authority that stems from the state and runs to a disciplined armed force. This, our dominant image of warfare, is influenced by the work of Carl von Clausewitz, the most widely taught theorist in military academies and whose writing on the art of war still heavily influences strategic studies. Clausewitz began his seminal work *On War* in 1816 in the aftermath of the Napoleonic Wars. He taught war is an instrument of policy, an act of violence intended to compel our opponent to fulfil our will. War is "political discourse with the addition of other means."

NEW WARS

The warfare witnessed after the end of the Cold War in such places as the Balkans, Sierra Leone, Somalia, Burundi, Democratic Republic of Congo (DRC), Liberia, Angola, and Chechnya was nothing like the dominant Clausewitz-inspired image of war in the West. These were wars where civilians were targeted because of their religion or ethnicity, where ordinary people attacked their neighbors; these were sometimes genocidal wars, wars where it was claimed there were rape camps, where there was looting and crime, and where children carried guns. We did not see organized, disciplined soldiers fighting according to the rules of war. We saw massacre. New wars are considered unconventional and to "exist beyond the Clausewitzian paradigm" (Møller 1999, 15). It is now often stated that the very nature of modern internal war, the disparate actors involved, the avoidance of pitched battles, and the targeting of civilians makes modern war "hardly what [Clausewitz] had in mind" (Shaw 2001, online).

Mary Kaldor's definition of a new war recognizes three characteristics of new wars that distinguish them from old wars (2001). The first characteristic involves a blurring of the distinctions between war (usually defined as violence between states or organized political groups for political motives), organized crime (violence undertaken by privately organized groups for private purposes, usually financial gain), and large-scale violations of human rights (violence undertaken by states or politically organized groups against individuals) (Kaldor 2001, 2). The second characteristic of contemporary armed conflict is a changed mode of warfare. New wars avoid pitched battles and aim to control territory through the political control of populations. Rather than aiming to capture the "hearts and minds" of the people, as does the guerrilla warfare espoused by Mao Tse-tung or Che Guevara, new warfare borrows from the counterinsurgency techniques of destabilization, which is aimed at sowing "hatred and fear." The third way in which new wars are contrasted with old is what Kaldor refers to as the "globalized" war economy. The war economy of the two world wars was centralized and totalizing, yet in the new war it is decentralized and fragmented. War damages domestic production, involves physical destruction, and interrupts trade and tax collection. In such conditions, the new globalized war economy relies heavily on outside funding through either the taxation of humanitarian supplies, illegal trade, or funding from neighboring governments or diaspora (people who now live outside what they consider their homeland). Fighters fund themselves through plunder and organized crime. Violence sustains the war economy, and, therefore, war is built into the logic of the economy.

Authors such as Hans Magnus Enzensberger (1994), Robert Kaplan (1994), and Michael Ignatieff (1998) also argue that the nature of warfare has changed, their analysis spurred by the onset of war in the former Yugoslavia. The new war argument was soon taken up by scholars working within the disciplines of international relations, security studies and even political economy (see Duffield 1998; Holsti 1996; Keen 1998). Donald Snow's *Uncivil Wars* (1996) is a similar exploration of modern internal warfare to Kaldor's. For Snow, four characteristics distinguish new war from conventional insurgencies. First, new wars have no clear military objects to translate into clear tactics or strategies; second, the forces involved are irregular, unlike regular forces, for they are organized differently, fight differently, and wear no uniform; third, there is a distinct lack of military order or discipline among combatants; and finally, there is a striking level of ferocity and atrocity regularly committed in the new war (Snow 1996, 109–10). The defining characteristic of this new type of internal warfare is, for

Table 15.1 New and Old Wars

	Old War	New War
Actors	States or blocs: regular, organized armed forces	Mix of state and nonstate actors: paramilitary groups, militia, international criminal groups, child-soldiers.
Economy	Formal centralized; mobilizing the population, mostly self-sufficient.	Decentralized, fragmented; relies on outside assistants, control of natural resources, and illegal trade.
Politics/Aims	National security, territorial gain, succession, revolution, ideological goals	Identity politics. Sometimes considered irrational or for private economic gain.
Methods	Strategic, decisive battles. Mechanized, technological warfare.	Collaboration between warring parties. Avoidance of pitched battles. Targeting of civilians.

Source: Adapted from Kaldor (2001, 14).

Snow as well as for Kaldor, the systematic targeting of civilians. For Snow, new "uncivil" wars are "curiously non-military ... what passes for military action was more or less systematic murder and terrorising of civilian populations" (Snow 1996, xi).

In military circles, what is referred to as new war is known as "Fourth-Generation warfare." The United Kingdom's Center for Defense Information describes Fourth-Generation warfare thus:

> This primarily involves land forces—irregular or guerrilla warfare carried out by groups motivated by ideology, revenge, lust for power, ethnicity, religion or some other unifying bond. Such irregulars often are associated with or supported by regular military forces, but in the late 20th century this was less often the case. In fact there are countervailing trends. There are more small groups of very loosely knit organisations that employ terror by threatening or actually attacking civilian populations. (2002, online)

Thus, new wars are irregular, more violent, and more threatening to civilians than were the old wars. For a comparison of old and new wars, see Table 15.1.

GLOBALIZATION, THE STATE, AND NEW WAR

New wars are said to take place within the context of a failed state or weak state. Weak states often suffer from unstable political regimes and experience coups, plots, riots, and rebellions. Weak states, as such, are not considered legitimate by some or all of their population and are often forced to rely on coercion

Table 15.2 Strong and Weak States

Strong States	Weak States
Maintain control over society	Have unstable politics, governmental crises
Ensure compliance with the law	Rely on coercion
Act decisively	Are unable to secure desired outcomes
Provide basic services	Cannot provide basic services
Control a productive national economy	Suffer severe social cleavages
Have a strong national identity	Centralize power
Show significant levels of participation in the political process	Demonstrate economic weakness, danger of collapse
	Show institutional incapacity
Have legitimacy	Are vulnerable to external actors and forces
	Have serious problems of legitimacy

Source: Adapted from Jackson (2002, 38–41).

and violence in order to act. Weak states are also characterized by a lack of sociopolitical cohesion; rather than having a strong national identity, society is spilt along ethnic, religious, or class lines. Weak states have unconsolidated or nonexistent democracies, power is centralized to a ruling elite, and ordinary people participate little if at all in the political process. Existing state institutions are not able to carry out their roles. Weak states cannot impose the rule of law and often fail or are simply unable to provide their populations with many basic services such as electricity, water and sanitation, food, or useable roads. Weak states are often the product of a weak or failing economy (Jackson 2002, 38–41). For a comparison of strong and weak states, see Table 15.2.

The weakness of the state in the post–Cold War world is attributed in large part to the forces of globalization, particularly liberal economic reforms that undermine the state's capacity. The pressures of globalization on weak states have been attributed to continuing instability and violence, particularly in Africa. There, policies to establish market economies and liberal democratic states have underpinned development policies since the 1990s. The spread of stable liberal democracies in the image of Western states is now viewed as a prerequisite for both developing states and global security (Duffield 2001). However, according to Richard Jackson, liberalization policies as prescribed by international financial institutions (IFIs), particularly the IMF and the World Bank, have "undercut the ability of African Leaders to maintain their regimes without resorting to war or reinventing patrimonialism in new and innovate forms" (2002, 44).

All but 1 of Africa's 47 sub-Saharan states borrows from the World Bank and is therefore obliged to follow its prescriptions. Creditors have failed to recognize the domestic constraints placed on weak state rulers in such countries as Sierra Leone, Nigeria, Liberia, and Democratic Republic of Congo (Zaire). Rigid orthodox reforms have had detrimental effects on weak states such as these. Based on a neoliberal conception that an ideal state is a minimalist organization, IFIs have sought to reduce state administration of the economy. The IFIs' neoliberal policies recommended closer alliances between the state and external firms so that private companies could supply state services and allow for civil service cuts. Privatization was promoted to improve efficiency and subject the state's economy to the discipline of the market. Cuts in state bureaucracies were prescribed to remove corrupt officials and those who may have blocked reform.

Liberal economic reforms have had a number of unintended consequences in weak states and have helped create the structural conditions to promote and sustain new wars. Weak state rulers have found in manipulating liberal reforms new sources of wealth and forms of coercion. Privatization has placed valuable assets in the hands of the weak state ruler and their supporters. Rather than forcing rulers of weak states to seek support from their state's citizens by providing services and security, liberalization has given the rulers the incentive and opportunity to follow private interests without having to provide for their own people (Bienen and Herbst 1996; Reno 1998; Sessay 1995).

In a state unable or unwilling to provide for its people's basic needs, insurgency is more likely; at the same time, economic crises make the state less able to deal effectively with unrest. Leaders can use violence to maintain their positions of power within a weak or failed state. Indeed, a way of controlling rival strong leaders has been by maintaining instability and violence, often through funding. Thus, for example, when rivalry between the United States and the Soviet Union came to an end, external funding for states as well as rebel groups was generally withdrawn. With the withdrawal of such superpower support, leaders of weak states lost their means of patronage—that is, they lost their ability to buy support. The structural characteristics of weak states turn politics into a continual process of what Jackson refers to as "crisis management" (2002, 41). Ethnic politics, violence, and instability are thus the strategies leaders of weak states use for political survival.

Another aspect of globalization, the intensification of transnational commerce, also plays an important role in new wars. Being able to buy arms or sell natural resources in order to fight and fund wars relies on relatively easy access to global markets. In Sierra Leone and Angola, for example, war has been sustained through the sale of diamonds. In Cambodia, both the Thai government and the Khmer Rouge funded their military operations through the sale of timber and precious gems.

New wars are also said to arise from erosion of the state's monopoly of legitimate violence. This monopoly is eroded from above by the transnationalization of military forces, including treaties and agreements that prevent states from using force unilaterally, and from below by the growing privatization of violence. The latter is seen, for instance, in the growth in organized crime, paramilitary groups, and private militias. In strong states the only legitimate violence is that which is employed by the state, namely, the army, security forces, and judiciary or the police. In weak states the government does not control legitimate violence; rather, violence is privatized, being used by both state and nonstate actors. When such large multinational corporations, or MNCs, as mining or engineering firms operate in weak states, they often bring with them their own security firms. Because rulers of weak states may be unable to rely on their own military's loyalty, private security organizations (PSOs) or private military corporations (PMCs) offer an alternative solution. The availability of cheap, light weaponry has also contributed to the privatization of violence by enabling nonstate actors to obtain arms easily.

Box 15.1 Case Study 1. Sierra Leone: Liberalization and New War

The civil war in Sierra Leone began in March 1991 when the rebel group the Revolutionary United Front (RUF), backed by Liberian warlord Charles Taylor, began a guerrilla-style campaign against the then president Joseph Momoh's government.

Between 20,000 and 50,000 people died in this vicious war. When the rebels first reached the capital city, Freetown, the BBC reported that in only a matter of days they had amputated the limbs of around 1,500 people (BBC 1999, online). In all, an estimated 30,000 civilians, including many children, had limbs amputated or suffered other forms of mutilation and terror. Between 215,000 and 275,000 women were subjected to sexual violence (Project Ploughshare 2002, online). In July 1999, the Lome Peace Accord was signed, although there was still much violence through 2000. In 2001, the government and the RUF agreed to a ceasefire and the process of disarmament began, led by the newly created UN Mission in Sierra Leone (UNAMSIL). In January 2002, when the last rebel leader had been disarmed, the UN peacekeeping force declared the conflict a success.

David Keen (2005) argues that liberalization policies encouraged by IFIs in the 1970s and 1980s both created the conditions for war in Sierra Leone and shaped the character of the conflict. Privatization as stressed by the World Bank was high-jacked by powerful elites who corrupted the process in order to gain personal wealth. IFIs encouraged moving state-led enterprises into private hands. Consequently, Lebanese diamond traders gained control of most of the state's valuable diamond mines. These diamond traders brought with them their own private military companies to provide security. Allied to the then president Siaha Stevens (who preceded Joseph Momoh) the diamond traders gained significant political influence. Any profits gained by a rise in prices on the world diamond market were not passed on to local miners, who instead turned to smuggling diamonds through Liberia. By the late 1980s, it was estimated, 95 percent of Sierra Leone's diamonds were being smuggled out of the country, thereby significantly damaging government revenue.

> Reduction in state services caused social unrest and resentment. An economic crisis in the 1980s saw many families reduced to poverty as gasoline and food subsidies were cut. Education and health services suffered greatly. A lack of education opportunities resulted in large numbers disaffected youths who had turned to looting and drugs even before war broke out. When civil war did happen, many of these young people were easily recruited to rebel forces. Cuts in civil service wages meant that underpaid state officials turned to illegal activities to supplement their income. As pay and conditions deteriorated for the armed forces, demoralized soldiers had little reason to stay loyal to the state. Where economic gains could be made, the largely self-funded Kamajors militia and other state soldiers abused and exploited civilians and collaborated with the rebels they were supposed to defeat. By the end of the civil war in 2002, an estimated 18–35 percent of the population were unemployed and the average wage for state employees was just a dollar a day. Since the end of the war, the World Bank has conceded that the state and its institutions must be strengthened. Privatization remains a priority for the bank, though, in its postwar policies in Sierra Leone (Keen 2005, 73–89).

ACTORS: WHO FIGHTS IN NEW WARS?

In our traditional image, war is fought between two states employing regular armed forces identifiable by their uniforms. This is not the case in contemporary intrastate warfare. Since the end of the Cold War, commentators have suggested that we are witnessing the end of interstate war. The recent wars in Afghanistan in 2001, Iraq in 2003, and Lebanon in 2006 are, in fact, an anomaly. Byman and van Evera report that 60 percent of wars in the nineteenth century were international; 51 percent of wars between 1900 and 1960 were international; the number of international wars then dropped significantly to 36 percent of all wars in the 1960s, continuing to fall to 26 percent in the 1970s, 17 percent in the 1980s, and only 10 percent in the 1990s (Byman and Van Evera 1998, 24). Kalevi Holsti's study concludes that only 18–20 percent of all wars since 1945 can be accurately classified as interstate war (Smith 2003, 30). The dominant form of warfare is now *within* states, what is sometimes referred to as civil war or low-intensity warfare, the name given to guerrilla warfare during the Cold War. Civil war tends to denote a war within a state between two sides, usually a rebel group (insurgency) and state forces (counterinsurgency). This description may have been adequate for the colonial and revolutionary wars that took place between the 1950s and 1980s. Today's wars, however, involve a host of different actors and aims and tend now to be referred to as *intrastate* wars. New wars involve a disparate group of actors from both the state and private sources. In fact, it is argued, the distinction between what is done in the name of the state and what is done for private or economic gain has become blurred such that the labels state and nonstate are no longer accurate descriptions. Actors in new wars include regular armed forces, breakaway units from state forces, paramilitary units, militia (both government and private that can be based on religious, ethnic, clan, and community groups), criminal gangs (from local groups to large-scale international criminal organizations), warlords, mercenaries, police forces, and terrorist organizations. There are often a number of different insurgent groups with changing short- and long-term aims and shifting alliances. Combatants tend not to wear uniforms, and groups are not hierarchically organized but are dispersed and decentralized, sometimes splintering into new groups.

Although warfare tends to be within rather than between states, intrastate wars involve a myriad international actors and are not contained within a state's borders. The international actors involved in warfare either directly or indirectly are, among others, neighboring countries, supportive states supplying either arms or finance, peacekeeping forces, mercenaries, international aid organizations and other NGOs, diaspora, journalists, and multinational corporations.

The use of child-soldiers is also considered a striking characteristic of the new war. Today, approximately 300,000 children are involved in warfare in over 30 countries, including Angola, Colombia, Liberia, Sri Lanka, Sudan, Sierra Leone, and Uganda (Amnesty International, online). Some 7,000 children were forced to fight for the RUF in Sierra Leone, and some 20,000 children were forced to take part in conflict in Liberia, where warlord Charles Taylor used combat units made up entirely of child-soldiers known as the Small Boys Unit (Jackson forthcoming). Often abducted and forced to join armed groups, children are made to fight or to carry equipment and loot, cook, or help in a variety of other ways. Girls are regularly raped. Children are thus used by armed groups for a number of reasons. Easy to intimidate, children ask few questions about what they are doing. They are cheap, asking for little money or food. Having children take part in killing or terrorizing is also a psychological tactic used against an enemy, and the result can have severe long-term effects on communities.

Box 15.2 Child-Soldiers in Uganda

In Uganda, the Lord's Resistance Army (LRA) forces children to join them in their attempt to overthrow the Ugandan government. Susan was 16 when she told this story about a boy who tried to escape from the RUF:

"One boy tried to escape, but he was caught. They made him eat a mouthful of red pepper, and five people were beating him. His hands were tied, and then they made us, the other new captives, kill him with a stick. I felt sick. I knew this boy from before. We were from the same village. I refused to kill him, and they told me they would shoot me. They pointed a gun at me, so I had to do it. The boy was asking me, 'Why are you doing this?' I said I had no choice. After we killed him, they made us smear his blood on our arms. I felt dizzy. There was another dead body nearby, and I could smell the body. I felt so sick. They said we had to do this so we would not fear death, and so we would not try to escape."

> Source: Human Rights Watch, "The Scars of Death: Children Abducted by the Lord's Resistance Army in Uganda," Human Rights Watch Report 1997, http://www.hrw.org/en/reports/1997/09/18/scars-death.

ECONOMY: FINANCING NEW WARS

New wars are characterized by the collapse of a formal economy. Whereas conventional wars were funded by a formal, centralized economy, the "globalized war economy" of the new war is decentralized, informal, and fragmented. As noted, new wars take place in the context of failing states and globalization in the aftermath of the Cold War. One characteristic of a failed state is a lack of legitimacy. If a population does not view its government as a legitimate authority, the state may be unable to raise taxes, thereby denying government a vital source of income. With unemployment and inflation high and domestic production low, states are forced to finance war efforts through other means. Financing of new wars comes from a variety of sources, including looting, robbery, illegal trade, and hostage taking. By restricting and controlling trade, paramilitary groups are often able to control market prices, thereby forcing civilians to sell their goods at very low prices and pay very high prices for such essential items as food or clothes. In new wars, governments in Angola, Ethiopia, Liberia, Sierra Leone, and Zaire, as well as others, used unpaid or underpaid soldiers. Soldiers were instead rewarded with the impunity to extract whatever rents they could from the war. In Sierra Leone in 1992, the military was granted the legal right to raid private houses (Keen 1998, 26). The war effort also often relies heavily on outside funding from other governments, trade with private firms, money from diaspora, or international aid from NGOs.

A lack of resources may lead to violence, but an abundance of resources can also create the conditions for violence, particularly in weak states. The latter case is known as a resource curse. Warfare in order to control natural resources is associated with countries that have a natural resource that is easy to access without sophisticated technology and can easily be sold; such resources are, for example, oil, drugs, diamonds, and timber. Diamonds have played a part in instigating and maintaining violence in Angola, Liberia, and Sierra Leone. Preferable to money as a means of wealth, diamonds are easier to store, easier to transport, and harder to trace than cash. Consider the situation in Angola, the fifteenth most underdeveloped country in the world. It has the second worst level of under-five child mortality. Yet Angola is the second largest sub-Saharan oil producer and the world's fourth biggest diamond producer by value (Billon 2001, 67). The National Union for the Total Independence of Angola (UNITA), one of the two competing armed factions in Angola, has been funding its activities through the control of diamond mines since the early 1970s. By the late 1980s, it had trained men and was operating on a small industrial scale that significantly undermined government revenue.

David Keen (1998) argues that studying the economic functions of warfare helps to explain their characteristics. In order to better appreciate intrastate war we must not view it as a traditional war with two sides vying for victory, nor should it be considered irrational violence. Instead of focusing on the negative aspects of violence, we should ask ourselves, who benefits from war? Keen argues that elites and ordinary people can both benefit from warfare to the extent that they perpetuate violence rather than seek to eliminate it. Many people are forced to take part in violence; however, we should acknowledge that many choose to, and we should understand why they make that choice. Paul Collier suggests that greed, more than grievances, may motivate violence. Violence can have short-term benefits. It can provide rent-seeking opportunities to help meet an individual's basic needs, whether it be through stealing or illegal trade. Violence can also provide a sense of worth and status, particularly for young men who feel that there are no other opportunities for them.

Keen (1998) recognizes seven economic benefits from warfare:

- *Pillage.* Pillage is carried out by individuals as well as by organized groups on a large scale, often clearing whole villages. An example is what happened in Bosnia during its civil war.
- *Protection money.* Paramilitaries, warlords, strong men, or others who can control violence may offer protection in return for payment. An example is the Irish Republican Army (IRA) in Northern Ireland.
- *Trade.* Controlling the distribution of resources creates forced markets rather than market forces. Examples are evident in the civil wars in Africa, Asia, and Latin America.
- *Labor exploitation.* Forcing individuals to work cheaply or for free is characteristic of the ongoing warfare in Sudan.
- *Land.* Clearing land allows for access to water or other valuable resources, as evident in events in Somalia.
- *Stealing aid.* Appropriating aid is a way of controlling its distribution and a means of taxing it.
- *Securing funding for the military.* After the Cold War ended, many countries reduced the amount of funding given to their armed forces. Violence and instability ensure that the military continues to have high levels of funding; therefore, conflict may actually be beneficial for the military.

AIMS: THE POLITICS OF NEW WARS

Clausewitz argued that war should be considered the continuation of politics by other means. Traditionally, wars have been fought for such state interests as national security (protecting national borders and territory or furthering the nation's economic interest), regime change, wars of independence or succession, or revolutions. Commentators believe the instances of post–Cold War wars have disproved Clausewitz's central argument that war is "an instrument of policy," (1993, 371), an argument summed up by Kalevi Holsti in a interview when he commented: "Our implicit understanding of war as a Clausewitzian enterprise needs re-examination. Many wars today are not politics pursued by other means" (Jones 2002, 627). New wars are sometimes thought to be fought for "less noble" purposes than traditional wars (Jackson forthcoming). Some new wars have been described as "irrational," others as criminal, for private economic gain or in the name of religion or ethnicity. Identity politics is thought to be at the heart of the new war. Civilians are targeted because of their ethnicity or their religion. Rather than being about geopolitical or ideological goals, Kaldor argues, "the politics of the new wars are about the claim to power based on seemingly traditional identities—nation, tribe, religion." Kaldor does not believe, though, that the new wars have been caused by ancient hatreds between groups or by historic grievances. Rather, she believes that these traditional labels have been reinvented by elites seeking political power in order to appeal to certain sections of the population (Kaldor 2001, 6–7). During the Bosnian war, the political goals of the Bosnian Serbs and the Bosnian Croats was ethnic cleansing, aimed at creating ethnically homogenous areas that would eventually be incorporated into Croatia and Serbia and dividing the ethnically diverse Bosnia-Herzegovina into a Serbian part and a Croat part (Kaldor 2001, 33).

METHODS: HOW ARE NEW WARS FOUGHT?

The economic functions of intrastate war may go some way to explaining the methods undertaken in contemporary warfare, many of which seem counterproductive when applied to the dominant image of warfare. One of the most striking methods of contemporary war is the distinct lack of battles. Opposing armed groups rarely fight each other directly. Instead, warring factions will cooperate with each other. In Sierra Leone government troops avoided direct confrontation with the RUF and actually sold them arms, ammunition, and uniforms. Both government and rebel forces would cooperate to depopulate resource-rich areas and share the rewards. During the Bosnian war Croats, Bosnians, and Serbs would cooperate in different combinations throughout the many phases of the conflict.

Violence in the new wars, instead of attacking opposing factions, is targeted against civilians. Indeed, it is the victimization of civilians that perhaps best defines the new wars. Civilian victims are no longer considered collateral damage, that is, unintended targets. Instead, they are the primary target in warfare either through killing and terrorizing or through forced displacement. R efugees are no longer considered a side effect of war. Rather, the vast resettlement of peoples is often a primary motive to gain access to valuable land. (For a comparison of civilian to combatant deaths in war, see Table 15.3.)

It is not simply the targeting of civilians that has characterized the new war but also the nature of the violence that is undertaken. Atrocity is commonplace. New wars deploy a mix of tactics, including conventional war fighting methods and those associated with guerrilla warfare or asymmetric war. Whereas guerrilla groups may have aimed to capture the hearts and minds of civilian populations in order to secure their support, forces in contemporary intrastate wars terrorize in order to control civilians. Tactics in new wars often involve murder,

Table 15.3 Ratio of Civilian Deaths to Combatant Deaths in War

	ca. 1900	World War II	Late 1990s
Civilian Deaths	10%–15%	50%	80%
Combatant Deaths	85%–90%	50%	20%

Source: Data taken from Kaldor (2001, 100).

mutilation, terrorism, limb amputation, rape, torture, abduction, hostage taking, ethnic cleansing, and slavery, as well as sieges and destruction of societal infrastructure and historical or religious sites. As noted, easy access to light weapons has shaped the nature of violence undertaken. Light weapons are easy to use, even by children, and easily transported. Although new wars are characterized by low-technology, some conventional larger weapons are also used. In May 1999, for example, indiscriminate attacks by RUF gunships in Sierra Leone saw the mass displacement of approximately 330,000 people behind enemy lines (Human Rights Watch 2001, online). The literature written about new wars has bought to the forefront of debate the terrible human cost that warfare brings.

Box 15.3 The Human Cost of War

This is how Abu described the ordeal he went through in June 2001 when Civil Defense Force (CDF) militia units, who are part of the government's forces, attacked the village of Yiraia in Sierra Leone:

> When we heard the gunshots my children yelled, "Father, they're going to kill us." I had all my family stand behind me and cracked the door open to make sure it was safe for us to run. But as I did, I saw three Kamajors [the largest an most powerful militia in the CDF] standing in front of our door and just seconds later they opened fire. I fell down and, together with my young son, slithered on my back into the bedroom and under the bed. As I did I saw my mother and sister lying there struggling to die. I heard my father, who is blind, yelling, "They're killing me." We hid there for almost an hour listening to the gunfire and the sounds of them singing and clapping. Then one yelled "ceasefire," and shortly after I heard footsteps coming into the house. My son, who had been shot through the knee, was crying from the pain, but I told him if he didn't be silent they'd kill us. Thank God they didn't find us. Some time later my brother came into the house and pulled us out, but a few metres from the house I found my father's body. I guess he'd tried to find his way out of the house and was caught. My brother and I cried as we passed his body; he was lying on his back and it looked like his stomach had been cut open.

Source: Human Rights Watch, "Sierra Leone: Worst Attacks in Months." 2001, http://www.hrw.org/en/news/2001/07/24/sierra-leone-most-serious-attacks-months#_Interviews_with_Victims.

CHALLENGES TO THE NEW WAR THEORY: ARE NEW WARS REALLY NEW?

There have been a number of challenges to the idea of new war, and in response it has been argued that all the characteristics of the new war can, in fact, be found throughout the history of warfare. In reality, warfare has never matched our stylized, traditional image of it. Today, could it be that we are merely more aware of the horrific realities of warfare? Here are some arguments that suggest we may not be witnessing a new type of warfare at all.

Globalization does not affect all states in the same way. One could find many examples of states where involvement in the global economy has strengthened the state as, for example, in Malaysia, Singapore, Barbados, Indonesia, Lesotho, and South Korea. One of the apparent visible signs of globalization in new wars, the involvement of outsiders in intrastate wars is nothing new. International churches, charities, mercenary troops, foreign adventurers, volunteers, international reporters, neighboring countries, and strong state patrons were all visible during the Nigerian civil war, which began in 1967, yet few critics would argue that this war was best understood by framing it within the global processes that affected it.

Warfare has also always involved a wide range of actors. In fact, it is only relatively recently that warfare has been the prerogative of the state and fought by professional armies. Spanish guerrillas fought against the French in the Napoleonic Wars (Clausewitz himself wrote about guerrilla warfare). For hundreds of years, mercenaries have been employed in warfare: paid foreign forces have ranged from the predominantly mercenary armies of the European monarchs to such newly independent states as Zaire, who employed private military companies (PMCs) to quell rebellions. Child-soldiers have been a historic feature of such rebel movements as, for example, the Shining Path in Peru, the Khmer Rouge in Cambodia, and even the Chinese Cultural Revolution. Internationally, a child-soldier is recognized as being under the age of 18, yet the British army recruits from the age of 16, and, therefore, child-soldiers should not necessarily be associated just with weak states and new wars.

There have always been economic gains from warfare. Historically, soldiers have been entitled to the spoils of war. Nonstate forces have always sought finance from a variety of sources, particularly external patronage and illegal trade. Warfare has also always involved a criminal element. The armies of the French Revolution, for example, were known as robbers and highwaymen.

Although the end of the Cold War seems to have ushered in an increase in ethnically and religiously fueled violence, identity politics has always been used to garner support for warfare. Nationalism and racism helped to fuel World War II. In terms of whether identity-fueled violence represents a depoliticization of war and therefore a change in the nature of warfare, it could be argued that engineering ethnic loyalties to secure support fits entirely with the Clausewitzian argument that warfare is an extension of politics by other means. The role of identity as a cause of warfare is sometimes overemphasized, of course. Rebel movements are often more politically motivated than is reported. Analysts pay little attention to the rebels' own reasons for engaging in violence.

As noted, the targeting of civilians characterizes the new wars. However, the distinction between combatants and civilians has never been maintained in warfare. The deliberate targeting of civilians was a feature of both world wars, for example, and was carried out by both sides of the conflict. The bombing of German, British, and Japanese cities and the use of two atomic bombs saw warfare reduced to the mass slaughter of entire nations. Atrocity is a part of all warfare.

Extreme violence was used in such old wars such the Russian Revolution and the Spanish Civil War. It is also important to note that killing is culturally defined. In the West, killing by machete tends to be viewed as more horrific than dropping bombs.

Box 15.4 Case Study 2. The Nigerian Civil War: An Old "New" War

The Nigerian civil war, or the Biafran War of 1967–1970, was in almost all respects a new war. The war began after the eastern region of the Nigerian Federation, home primarily to the Ibo people, declared itself independent and the Biafran state was born. After two and a half years of bitter warfare, the Biafran government finally surrendered to federal forces. In its politics, its methods of warfare, and the actors involved, this war fits perfectly the description of the new post–Cold War organized violence. For those old enough, the Biafran conflict will be remembered primarily by the shocking photos that hit the newspapers and TV screens in 1968, photos of starving babies with sticklike frames and shameful potbellies. The war was reported from the outset, in Britain at least, as a futile war that needlessly caused immense human suffering. The conflict demonstrated to the world just how cheaply human life was valued in an unnecessary war. At the time the *Manchester Guardian* reported, "As they stand now, the aims of both Nigerians and Biafrans can apparently be achieved only through death and destruction on a scale that would make even victory hollow" (Schwarz 1968, 8).

Fighting took place between Biafran and federal forces; but as in the new wars, a wide variety of actors were involved in the conflict. The Biafran forces had an army, a small air force, and an equally small navy, and there was also a heavy militia involvement. Not directly under the control of the regular armed forces, the militia was an entirely civilian organization made up of intellectuals, businesspeople, and professionals. Another force in the war, the Biafran Organization of Freedom Fighters (BOFF), conducted guerrilla warfare with limited success against the Nigerian forces. Mercenaries were used more widely on the Biafran side, but nonetheless by both parties to the conflict, again a prominent feature of new wars. Although perhaps not extreme in comparison to other historical conflicts, it was the brutality of the conflict, the bloodshed, and the disrespect for human life that brought this war to the world's attention (*Manchester Guardian* 1968, 12). But even in 1967, in witnessing this war, was the world witnessing anything new? Was this the emergence of a new type of violence, or was it just the first time pictures of mutilated soldiers, executions, and starving children had made it onto our TV screens? Compared to the Nigerian conflict, we must ask ourselves, in our modern-day conflicts, what are we witnessing that is truly new?

> John De St Jorre sums up the Nigerian civil war and our reaction to it:
>
> The Nigerian struggle, like other similar internecine conflicts was a dirty war: a war in which human life was often worth less than a bottle of beer or a packet of cigarettes; a war in which both sides were terrified of each other, and sometimes killed as much from nervousness as from premeditation or hatred; a war in which most of the fighting troops, officers and NCOs [noncommissioned officers] included, had virtually no military training worth the name; a war where uneducated or semi-literate men easily went on the rampage in the anarchical, sanctionless desert of the battlefield. It was, in short, a war not very different from any other and it is disturbing that we Westerners should have been so shocked, so blind, so patronising and so remarkably devious in our interpretation of its manifestations (1972, 287).

CONCLUSION

Within academia there are now significant critiques of the argument that the end of the Cold War and the pressures of globalization have resulted in a new kind of war. Nevertheless, analysis of the new war has starkly described to us the complex and disturbing nature of contemporary intrastate conflict and has provoked a much-needed shift in research and discussion. Without a clear understanding of the logic of contemporary warfare, states, international organizations, and NGOs will continue to struggle in their response to them. We cannot halt or prevent violence if we do not understand its rationale. This is particularly important for Western military forces. The wars they are likely to be involved with in the future will not resemble the traditional, stylized notion of war between states. The recent wars in Afghanistan and Iraq have highlighted the difficulties faced by militaries when they apply old conceptions of warfare to conflicts that simply do not fit this model. In 2006, a new edition of Kaldor's book *New and Old Wars* was published with an additional chapter. This chapter addressed the war in Iraq as a similar new war: "In a way, the war in Iraq could be treated as a test case of the central argument developed in this book—the danger of not adjusting our conceptions of war to the new global context" (Kaldor 2006, 151).

The study of weak states, globalization, and warfare after the end of the Cold War suggests that war should not always be considered the breakdown or collapse of normal relations. The complex relationship between development policies, external aid, economic and political liberalization, and global trade and the crisis management strategies of weak state rulers creates new networks of power. According to Mark Duffield, when faced with new wars, "instead of complex political emergencies, global governance is encountering emerging political complexes" (2002, 14). Whether you believe that the armed conflicts witnessed since the end of the Cold War are a new type of war or not, the new war debate continues to address very real and very urgent political, military, and ethical challenges. Indeed, the new war debate has marked an important step toward a better understanding of our modern security dilemmas.

FURTHER READING

Duffield, Mark. *Global Governance and the New Wars*. London: Zed Books, 2001.
Kaldor, Mary. *New and Old Wars*. Cambridge: Polity Press, 2006.
Kaldor, Mary, and Basker Vashee, eds. *New Wars*. Vol. 1 of *Restructuring the Global Military Sector*. London: Pinter, 1997.
Kalyvas, Stathis N. "'New' and 'Old' Civil Wars: A Valid Distinction?" *World Politics* 54 (2001): 99–118.
Snow, Donald M. *Uncivil Wars, International Security and the New Internal Conflicts*. London: Lynne Rienner, 1996.

REFERENCES

Amnesty International. 2007. Coalition to stop the use of child soldiers. Available online at http://news.amnesty.org/pages/childsoldiers (accessed May 18, 2007).
BBC. 1999. Special report: Civil war in Sierra Leone. Available online at http://news.bbc.co.uk/1/hi/special_report/1999/01/99/sierra_leone/251251.stm (accessed May 18, 2007).
Bienen, Henry, and Jeffry Herbst. 1996. The relationship between political and economic reform in Africa. *Comparative Politics* 29: 23–42.
Billon, Philleppe. 2001. Angola's political economy of war: The role of oil and diamonds, 1975–2000. *African Affairs* 100: 55–80.
Byman, Daniel, and Stephen Van Evera. 1998. Why they fight: Hypotheses on the causes of contemporary deadly conflict. *Security Studies* 7: 1–50.
Center for Defense Information. 2002. Reshaping the military for asymmetric warfare. Press release, October 5. Available online at http://www.cdi.org/friendlyversion/printversion.cfm?documentID=218 [18/05/07].
Chandler, David. 2006. Back to the future? The limits of neo-Wilsonian ideals of exporting democracy. *Review of International Studies* 32: 475–97.
Clausewitz, Carl von. 1993. *On war*. Ed. and trans. Michael Howard and Peter Paret. London: Everyman's Library.
Collier, Paul. 2000. Doing well out of war: An economic perspective. In *Greed and grievance: Economic agendas in civil wars*, ed. Matts Berdal and D. M. Malone. Boulder, CO: Lynne Rienner. 91–112.
Duffield, Mark. 1998. Post-modern conflict: Warlords, post-adjustment states and private protection. *Civil Wars* 1: 65–102.
———. 2001. *Global governance and the new wars*. London: Zed Books.
Enzensberger, Hans Magnus. 1994. *Civil wars: From L.A. to Bosnia*. New York: New Press.
Holsti, Kalevi. 1996. *The state, war and the state of war*. Cambridge: Cambridge University Press.

Human Rights Watch. 2001. Sierra Leone: Worst Attacks in Months Available online at http://www.hrw.org/en/news/2001/07/24/sierra-leone-most-serious-attacks-months#_Interviews_with_Victims (accessed May 17, 2007).
———. 2007. The Scars of Death: Children abducted by the Lord's Resistance Army in Uganda. Human Rights Watch Report, 1997. Available online at http://www.hrw.org/en/reports/1997/09/18/scars-death (accessed May 18, 2007).
If not "genocide," still bloody. 1968. *Manchester Guardian*, Friday October 11, p. 12.
Ignatieff, Michael. 1998. *The warrior's honor: Ethnic war and the modern conscience.* New York: Henry Holt.
Jackson, Richard. 2002. Violent internal conflict and the African state: Towards a framework for analysis. *Journal of Contemporary African Studies* 20: 29–52.
———. Forthcoming. *What causes intrastate war? Towards an understanding of organised civil violence.* Manchester, UK: Manchester University Press.
Jones, Adam. 2002. Interview with Kal Holsti. *Review of International Studies* 28: 619–33.
Kaldor, Mary. 2001. *New and old wars.* Cambridge: Polity Press.
———. 2006. *New and old wars.* Cambridge: Polity Press.
Kaplan, Robert D. 1994. *Balkan ghosts: A journey through history.* New York: Vintage.
Keen, David. 1998. The economic functions of violence in civil wars. Adelphi Papers 320.
———. 2005. Liberalisation and conflict. *International Political Science Review* 26: 73–89.
Møller, Bjørn. 1999. Faces of war. In *Ethnicity and Intra-state Conflict: Types, causes and peace strategies,* ed. Håkan Wiberg and Chritian P. Scherrer. Aldershot, UK: Ashgate.
Murshed, S. Mansoob. 2003. Old and New Wars. Bonn International Center for Conversion Bulletin 26, 1 January. Available online at http://www.bicc.de/publications/bulletin/bulletin.php (accessed May 18, 2007).
Newman, Edward. 2004. The "new wars" debate: A historical perspective is needed. *Security Dialogue* 35: 173–89.
Project Ploughshare. 2002. Armed conflict reports: Sierra Leone. Available online at http://www.ploughshares.ca/libraries/ACRText/ACR-Sierra-Leone.html#Deaths (accessed May 18, 2007).
Reno, William. 1998. *Warlord politics and African states.* Boulder, CO: Lynne Rienner.
Schwarz, Walter. 1968. How many years of devastation? *Manchester Guardian*, Wednesday, October 2, p. 8.
Sessay, Max. 1995. State capacity and the politics of economic reforms in Sierra Leone. *Journal of Contemporary African Studies* 13: 165–89.
Shaw, Martin. 2001. Return of the good war? Available online at http://www.theglobalsite.ac.uk/press/104shaw.htm (accessed May 18, 2007).
Smith, M. L. R. 2003. Guerrillas in the mist: Reassessing strategy and low intensity warfare. *Review of International Studies* 29: 19–37.
Snow, Donald M. 1996. *Uncivil wars international security and new internal conflicts.* Boulder, CO: Lynne Rienner.
Straw, Jack. 2004. A new era for foreign policy. Speech given at the Royal Institute of International Affairs, Chatham House, London, 12 February.

16

Nongovernmental Organizations

Shamima Ahmed

CONCEPTUALIZING NONGOVERNMENTAL ORGANIZATIONS

The world is seeing an unprecedented growth in nongovernmental organizations, or NGOs, and a corresponding increase in NGO activism. "The existence of an organized and effective civil society, including nongovernmental organizations (NGOs), is the greatest social phenomenon in the latter part of the twentieth century, and certainly, in this new millennium" (Sfeir-Younis 2004, 29). Nongovernmental organizations have occupied a prominent place in international politics and are viewed as powerful and influential nonstate actors. As Jonathan Doh and Hildey Teegan (2003, xv) explain, "The events surrounding the effort to launch a new round of multilateral trade negotiations in Seattle in December 1999, the protests at the World Bank meetings in the spring of 2000, and the ongoing demonstrations by nongovernmental organizations (NGOs) at the meetings of the World Economic Forum and elsewhere underscore the increasing activism and visibility of nongovernmental organizations." One author (Eizenstat 2004) even refers this group as the "fifth estate."

So, what are NGOs? Arriving at a single definition of NGOs that comprehends all the varieties of this entity is anything but easy. Scholars and practitioners have defined it in many different ways, thereby making a single definition a much more challenging task. Some tend to use the term "nongovernmental organization" interchangeably with "nonstate actor." The latter term, however, includes multinational corporations, international producer cartels like OPEC, a variety of transnational citizen groups, and such organizations as the Palestine Liberation Organization (PLO) that are neither states nor private groups. It is important to understand that NGOs are nonstate actors, but not all nonstate actors are NGOs.

One popular international relations textbook notes two types of NGOs: religious organizations and multinational corporations (Rourke 1998, 66–68), neither of which would be considered NGOs in other circles. Some also use it interchangeably with the term "civil society." The term "civil society," however, refers to the broad sphere of public activity that lies between the individual, the state, and the corporations. "One of the problems with using the term today is that 'civil society' traditionally encompassed everything from the family to the church to the business corporation" (Frumkin 2002, 13). The broad usage is also reflected in the United Nations' definition, in which transnational actors may be accepted as NGOs. According to the UN Economic and Social Council's (ECOSOC) definition, "Any international organization which is not established by inter-governmental agreement shall be considered as an NGO." The only constraints are that an NGO cannot be profit making; it cannot advocate the use of violence; it cannot be a school, a university, or a political party; and any concern with human rights must be general, rather than restricted to a particular communal group, nationality, or country.

Following are some other definitions offered by scholars:

1. Robert Gorman (1984, 2) defines NGOs as "non-governmental (private), tax-exempt, nonprofit agencies engaged in overseas provision of services for relief and development purposes. They also derive at least a portion of their funds from private, charitable donations."
2. Historian Akira Iriye (1999, 422) defines NGOs as "voluntary and open associations of individuals outside of the formal apparatus of the state that are neither for profit nor engage in political activities as their primary objective."
3. Political scientist Gerald Clarke (1998) defines NGOs as "private, non-profit, professional organizations, with a distinctive legal character, concerned with public welfare goals."
4. The World Bank's operational directive on NGOs (no. 14.70, 1989) defines them as groups and institutions that are entirely or largely independent of government and characterized primarily or largely by humanitarian or cooperative, rather than commercial objectives.

Salamon (2001), one of the prominent scholars on nonprofits, uses the following six characteristics to define nonprofit organizations:

1. *Formal*—they have formal structures.
2. *Private*—they are institutionally separate from government organizations.
3. *Nonprofit distributing*—they do not generate profits to their owners.
4. *Self-governing*—they are equipped to control their own operations.
5. *Voluntary*—their work involves a degree of meaningful voluntary participation.
6. *Public interest*—they serve some kind of pubic purpose or good.

No matter how NGOs are defined, Salamon's six characteristics capture the essence of NGOs. They are formally organized, usually following the relevant laws of the respective country; they are not owned by the government; they can earn profits, but such profits are not distributed to managers, board members, or staff but go back into the operations of the agencies; they have volunteers involved in different ways with the operations of the agencies; and they promote some type of interest or mission that promotes one or more groups' interest.

In terms of focus and locus, NGOs can be categorized as international, Northern (i.e., the global North), or Southern (i.e., the global South). International NGOs (INGOs) are those that have operations in two or more countries. Oxfam, Amnesty International, and Save the Children are examples of INGOs.

BOX 16.1 AMNESTY INTERNATIONAL

Amnesty International (AI) has clearly publicized its mission thus:

"AI's vision is of a world in which every person enjoys all of the human rights enshrined in the Universal Declaration of Human Rights and other international human rights standards. In pursuit of this vision, AI's mission is to undertake research and action focused on preventing and ending grave abuses of the rights to physical and mental integrity, freedom of conscience and expression, and freedom from discrimination, within the context of its work to promote all human rights" (http://web.amnesty.org). Currently, AI has over 2.2 million members and subscribers in more than 150 countries.

In order to remain independent, AI does not accept money from any government or any political party. The organization's major policies are made by elected representatives, from different countries, serving on the AI International Council. The elected International Executive Committee, all its members volunteers, implements AI policies and decisions. Amnesty International sends volunteers and researchers to different parts of the world to investigate reports of human rights violations and to verify those reports from different sources, among them prisoners, family members of prisoners, lawyers, journalists, and human rights agencies. Often, the organization will send fact-finding missions to assess and verify extent of such abuses. Violations of human rights include torture of prisoners, governments' inhumane policies and practices, violation of individual rights, and violence against particular groups like women.

Following are examples of AI's campaigns and activities in one month in the year 2007:

1. AI made an urgent appeal to the Iranian government's head of the judiciary to prevent the execution, by stoning, of two individuals convicted of adultery. The execution was scheduled for June 21, 2007.
2. On June 7, AI, along with other well-known human rights organizations, published a report that along with their names, provided detailed information about 39 people believed to be in U.S. custody but whose whereabouts were not known to anyone, including their family members.

3. On June 3, AI members from different parts of Europe joined a march to show solidarity and support to Latvian gays, lesbians, and bisexual and transgender people.

Source: Amnesty International, http://web.amnesty.org.

Northern NGOs (NNGOs) are those that have headquarters in one of the industrialized countries. Thee three cited INGOs—Oxfam, Amnesty International, and Save the Children—are also NNGOs.

Box 16.2 Oxfam International

Oxfam International's goal is to find "lasting solutions to poverty and injustices' (www.oxfam.org). The organization is a confederation of 13 organizations and have operations in more than 100 countries. Oxfam has three major programs: development, emergencies, and campaigns.

In its *development* work, Oxfam focuses on diverse issues, including gender, HIV/AIDS, and human rights. Some examples of Oxfam's recent development work include making a donation to the Aspeca Orphanage Center in Kampot Town, Cambodia, and developing partnership with Costa Rica and other nearby communities in designing programs and plans to prevent future earthquakes and other disasters from becoming full scale.

In its *emergencies* work, Oxfam not only provides relief to emergency situations but also engages in activities that include advocacy, prevention, and preparedness for different disasters. Examples of Oxfam's recent emergency work include providing aid to more than 30,000 people after Hurricane Felix hit Nicaragua and supplying plastic sheeting to 1,000 families for temporary shelter for people affected by the Sumatra earthquake in Indonesia.

In its *campaign* work, Oxfam joins with different partners to advocate on behalf of the poor. Its staff in Washington, D.C., Geneva, New York, and Brussels campaign for advocacy in different international organizations like the Work Bank, United Nations, World Trade Organization, and European Commission. Examples of recent Oxfam advocacy work include campaigning for fair trade, providing debt relief to poor countries, and regulating the supply of weapons.

Source: http://www.oxfam.org.

Southern NGOs (SNGOs) are those that operate in developing countries and provide a variety of social, development, and economic services. A prominent SNGO in Bangladesh, for example, is Grameen Bank.

Box 16.3 Grameen Bank

In 1971, Muhammad Yunus, a professor of economics at a university in Bangladesh, founded the Grameen Bank—"Grameen" meaning "village" in Bengali.

Grameen Bank provides credit, without requiring collateral, to the poorest of the poor in rural Bangladesh. These are poor people who cannot obtain loans from other financial institutions because they have no property or income. Professor Yunus's microcredit program provides small loans against no collateral to members of bank-organized groups of five or six people. Members of each group then decide who among its members should receive loans. Repayment responsibility rests solely on the individual borrower, while the group and the center oversee that everyone behaves in a responsible way and none gets into repayment problem. There is no form of joint liability; that is, group members are not responsible for paying on behalf of a defaulting member. The loan recovery rate is 98.28 percent (http://www.grameen-info.org).

As of May, 2007, Grameen Bank has 7.16 million borrowers, 97 percent of whom are women. With 2,422 branches, the bank provides services in 78,101 villages, covering more than 93 percent of all villages in Bangladesh. In 1983, Grameen was transformed into a formal bank under a special law passed for its creation. It is now owned by the poor borrowers of the bank, who are mostly women. Grameen Bank works exclusively for them. Borrowers at present own 94 percent of the total equity of the bank. The remaining 6 percent is owned by the government. Its success emulated in other countries, Grameen has become the model for microlending programs in 30 countries all over the world, including Africa, Asia, and the United States. Grameen Bank and its founder, Professor Muhammad Yunus, were awarded the 2006 Nobel Peace Prize.

GROWTH IN NGOS

The answer to "how many NGOs are there?" is next to impossible to provide. There is no comprehensive directory that contains a list of all NGOs worldwide. Some estimates are available, but these are incomplete. According to the Union of International Associations (2002), there are 45,674 INGOs. However, they include only NGOs known to the Union of International Associations. The estimates made by specific countries are also incomplete as a result of poor or less-than-formal record-keeping systems and processes. Such incomplete estimates, nonetheless, give observers some sense of the scope of NGOs. India, for example, is estimated to have between 1 and 2 million NGOs (www.

indianngos.com). According to a 2006 World Bank Report, there are approximately 45,000 NGOs in Bangladesh registered with the Ministry of Social Welfare, and another 1,882 NGOs, those receiving foreign fund, are registered with the NGO Affairs Bureau. According to reports published by the Yale Center for the Study of Globalization, there were 280,000 NGOs registered in China. In Russia, one estimate puts the NGO number at 450,000 (www.workers.or/2006/worold/ngos-0216).

Though INGOs are often more well known than simple NGOs, most NGOs actually operate within a single country. Nongovernmental groups are usually financed by a combination of sources, including membership dues, grants and contracts from governments and international institutions, and funding from private foundations, corporations, and wealthy individuals. However, in most underdeveloped and developing countries in, for example, Asia and Africa, NGOs are heavily funded by foreign governments, international governmental organizations, and INGOs.

Nongovernmental organizations have been in existence since the nineteenth century, at least. As Stuart Eizenstat (2004) points out, "Private networks with political, humanitarian, moral, or religious components were well-established by mid nineteenth century." Examples of such networks include groups associated with the antislavery movement and the women's suffrage movement. During the past four decades, however, the world has observed an unprecedented growth of NGOs. Different reasons are attributed to such growth.

Salamon (1994) provides three broad reasons for such growth:

1. *Global Communications Revolution*. The developments in transportation and e-communication have made it easy for different parties to come together to work on a common goal. As an example, because of e-communication, it is now easy for individuals in different parts of the world to become members of different NGOs and to participate in their different activities and deliberations.
2. *State Retreat Worldwide*. As a consequence of political, financial, and practical necessities, NGOs in different countries are stepping in to deliver services previously deemed appropriate only for states to deliver.
3. *General Economic Growth*. Economic growth has been followed by postmaterial values that have led to greater emphasis on introducing better social equity and quality of life.

Several other reasons, in addition to those provided by Salamon, explain the phenomenal growth of NGOs. Increased political globalization emerges as another reason for growth. "Rather than simply emerging as a result of bottom-up sociological and technological forces, INGOs and NGOs have also emerged and grown in large part because of top-down processes of *political* globalization, i.e., the globalization of political structures, institutions, and Western liberal democratic values" (Reimann 2006, 46). Citing "political opportunity structure" (POS), Reimann makes the claim that the two components of POS—expanding opportunities for resource mobilization and political access—are crucial variables that have spurred the growth of NGOs. As international institutions and regimes have expanded to handle new global issues, they have increasingly promoted NGOs as their service providers and advocates. He argues that in the past two decades an explosion of new international opportunities for funding and participation of NGOs has created a structural environment highly conducive to NGO growth. The increasingly diverse population in different countries also explains some of this growth. A homogenous population may have less need for NGOs, since homogeneous needs are more easily catered for and so will require fewer NGOs. In contrast, more NGOs are required in heterogeneous populations as a result of the heterogeneity and complexity of different groups' needs.

The rise of such intergovernmental organizations as the World Bank and the WTO has also stimulated the growth of NGOs by providing new political opportunities at the international level, namely, such opportunities as access to new arenas for political action, international elite allies, and such other resources as legitimacy and international media attention (Smith 2000; Passy 1999). John Boli and George Thomas (1999) found a correlation between the growth of INGOs and their formation in general. The researchers explain that the creation of new international institutions and their rapid growth in the postwar period have stimulated NGO growth worldwide by providing new political opportunities and incentives to organize. "More specifically, as the international system has expanded over time it has increasingly offered two types of international opportunities that are also crucial factors for the growth of citizen groups at the national level: (1) resources in the form of grants, contracts and other kinds of institutional support (food aid, transportation costs, technical assistance, etc.) and (2) political access to decision-making bodies and agenda-setting arenas" (Boli and Thomas 1999, 48).

NGO ROLES IN INTERNATIONAL POLITICS

The roles of NGOs in the international realm are multifaceted and are still evolving. The major roles of NGOs can be categorized as supporting relief and social and economic development, political advocacy, lobbying and agenda setting, public education, monitoring, and international security.

Relief and Social and Economic Development

Some of the traditional roles of NGOs lie in relief and social economic development. Indeed, INGOs have roots in Christian missionary organizations that date back to the sixteenth century. To this day, providing relief and emergency services are functions of such major NGOs as the Red Cross, Save the Children, Oxfam, and Medecins Sans Frontiers. Increasingly, different governments are channeling foreign aid through NGOs. As Brian Smith notes, "One reason for this increase in private involvement in foreign aid has been the growing reputation of nonprofit institutions in the United States, Canada, and Europe for being efficient and cost-effective channels of help in disasters" (1990, 3). He points out that by the early 1990s, 75 percent of British food aid was being channeled through NGOs, and 40 percent of Swedish spending on emergencies and refugees was going through Swedish NGOs. The United States has channeled as much as 30 percent of its bilateral aid to NGOs. In 2003, Japan's foreign ministry distributed approximately $63.2 million in foreign aid to different NGOs (Large 2003).

The relief function of nongovernmental organizations has increasingly been coupled with different social, economic, and development functions. This came with the realization that relief and charity work in themselves address only short-term needs; they are not effective in dealing with long-term issues of development. Along with providing relief, several NGOs are thus also incorporating various economic and development projects, including assisting in building infrastructure (e.g., transportation), offering loans, and providing training.

Box 16.4 Medecins Sans Frontiers

Medecins Sans Frontiers (MSF), or Doctors without Borders, is an "international medical humanitarian organization that delivers emergency aid to people affected by armed conflict, epidemics, natural or man-made disasters, or exclusion from heath care in more than 70 countries" (http://www.doctorswithoutborders.org). It has an international network with sections in 19 countries.

Their members include doctors, nurses, water and sanitation experts, and members of various other medical and nonmedical professionals. In addition to providing emergency services, the organization also provides such long-term programs as treating individuals with infectious diseases like HIV and providing psychological care to affected groups. Often MSF's volunteers work in remote, dangerous, and conflict-ridden places like Darfur (Sudan) and Mogadishu (Somalia). The organization also campaigns to promote international humanitarian law, in doing so seeking the support of governments, international organizations, and the general public. Through its Campaign for Access to Essential Medicines, for example, MSF is advocating to lower drug prices and to remove trade and other barriers to accessing treatments. The organization's members also educate the public by participating in speaking engagements in diverse national and international conferences.

Following are two examples of MSF activities across the globe:

1. After the 2004 Tsunami disaster, MSF was the first international organization that provided medical aid to people in Aceh, Indonesia, a region devastated by the earthquake.

2. For more than 16 years, MSF has been working in the conflict-ridden southern and central parts of Somalia. Currently, there are some 60 MSF international staff and more than 800 MSF national staff working in Somalia. In 2006, they performed more than 300,000 outpatient consultations, with another 10,000 inpatients admitted to MSF-supported hospitals.

Because of the location of their work activity, NGOs like MSF are prone to face violent act themselves. As one example, on June 2, 2004, five MSF staff members were shot and killed in Afghanistan, which prompted the agency to stop all its services in that country and to leave Afghanistan for good.

The Political Role of NGOs

Although religious, social, and economic development functions are the traditional functions of NGOs, what made NGOs gain more power and prominence in the international realm is their increasing participation in international politics.

Advocacy may be one of the most explicit roles that NGOs engage in. Margaret Keck and Kathryn Sikkink (1998) explain that advocacy networks engage in four kinds of politics: (1) information politics, in which networks provide and reinterpret information on issues of concerns; (2) symbolic politics, involving the use of symbols to raise awareness of issues; (3) leverage politics, in which networks attempt to gain moral or material leverage over more powerful actors like states and NGOs; and (4) accountability politics, in which networks try to compel states to live up to norms to which they formally agreed. The NGOs' advocacy work on environmental protection, human rights, and international security are widely known. Indeed, there are a number of high-profile examples of broad NGO advocacy within the late 1990s alone. These include efforts to discourage the purchase of non-dolphin-safe tuna, to ban textiles or clothing made in countries with inadequate health and safety conditions, to incorporate environment and labor provisions in the North American Free Trade Agreement (NAFTA) and WTO negotiations, to compel the World Bank and the IMF to forgive the debt of developing countries (Doh and Teegan 2003).

Closely related to NGOs' advocacy role is their lobbying one. It is a common role for advocacy NGOs to lobby their governments, other governments, and different international organizations on a variety of issues. In the realm of international security, NGOs regularly lobby governments to limit or eliminate certain weapons system. The nuclear freeze movement in the United States during the 1980s is an example of the advocay role. Also, NGOs are well-known activists for environmental protection. Various prominent INGOs, including Greenpeace, World Wildlife Fund, and Friends of the Earth, actively lobby governments to protect the environment.

> **Box 16.5 Greenpeace**
>
> Greenpeace acts to change attitudes and behaviors, to protect and conserve the environment, and to promote peace by
>
> a. catalyzing an energy revolution by addressing climate change
> b. defending the oceans by challenging wasteful and destructive fishing and creating a global network of marine reserves
> c. protecting the world's ancient forests
> d. working for disarmament by advocating the elimination of all nuclear weapons
> e. creating a toxic-free future by advocating safer alternatives to current use of hazardous chemicals in different products
> f. campaigning for sustainable agriculture by rejecting genetically engineered organisms, protecting biodiversity, and encouraging socially responsible farming (http://www.greenpeace.org/international)
>
> Greenpeace has offices in 40 countries across the world. Following are some recent contributions made by Greenpeace:
>
> 1. On May 2, 2007 Apple announced a phaseout of the most dangerous chemicals in its product line—brominated fire retardants (BFRs) and polyvinyl chloride (PVC)—by the year 2008 in response to an award-winning online campaign by Greenpeace.
> 2. On March 7, 2007, the New Zealand government announced cancellation of a proposed coal-burning power plant, Marsden B. Local residents, Greenpeace, and many other local and national environmental groups had been fighting the proposed station for over two years. Greenpeace and local activists had embarked on a variety of strategies, including a nine-day occupation, high court challenges, protest marches, and pubic meetings.
> 3. On May 31, 2006, Spain confirmed that it would phase out its eight operating nuclear plants and start the process of finding a solution to dispose of existing radioactive waste. Greenpeace was part of a national coalition of environmental and civic groups that on May 20, 2006, unanimously petitioned the government to deliver on election promises of "safer, cleaner, cheaper" energy.
>
> *Source:* http://greenpeace.org/international.

The participation of NGOs in the agenda-setting process, which is closely related to their lobbying function, is increasingly growing in importance. "Defining the problems of society and suggesting alternative solutions—agenda setting—is the most important stage of the policy making process"

(Dye 2002, 36). Agendas are problems and issues that get policy makers' attention. At times, major societal issues do not get to the agenda-setting process because they lack the backing of powerful groups in society. In a way, agenda setters play the role of gatekeepers. Nonetheless, NGOs are increasingly powerful in setting agendas at the international level, particularly at the United Nations, where UN Charter article 71, issued in 1945, empowers the UN's ECOSOC to "make suitable arrangements for consultation with nongovernmental organizations which are concerned with matters within their competence." The process of admission to consultative status is supervised by the UN Committee on Non-Governmental Organizations, which is a 19-member permanent standing committee of the UN Council. The number of NGOs formally accredited to ECOSOC has grown significantly over time. In 1998, there were 1,350 NGOs accredited to the council; in 2005 the number increased to 2,719.

There are another approximately 400 NGOs accredited to the Commission on Sustainable Development, a subsidiary body of the council. As part of their consultative status, NGOs can attend ECOSOC meetings, submit written statements, and in limited cases also propose items for the agenda. They also have security passes giving them access to all the buildings, including lounges and restaurants where they can meet diplomats. As well, NGOs have access to all UN documents once these are officially released. Such access gives NGOs power and opportunity to influence the agenda-setting process at the United Nations. In fact, NGOs have played a significant role in bringing such different policy areas and issues as human rights, women's rights, and environmental protection to the UN's agenda-setting process.

Public Education

Nongovernmental organizations regularly engage in public education. Greenpeace plays an educational role by bringing examples of environmental abuse to the attention of people throughout the world. A specific example of an NGO playing a public education role is the World Wild Life's (WWF) work on developing the Global 200 agenda. World Wild Life scientists have identified more than 200 outstanding terrestrial, freshwater, and marine habitats. The central concept of the Global 200 is to conserve the broadest variety of the world's habitats. Using the Global 200 as a guide, WWF believes that the broadest varieties of the world's species can be saved. The organization has used its network relationships with the conservation science community to publish a variety of research articles and has partnered with *National Geographic* and the Ford Foundation to put a map of the Global 200 in every primary school in the United States (Deslauriers and Kotschwa 2003, 74). Another example is the work of Amnesty International. One of the best-known NGOs in the field of human rights, it regularly disseminates information in defense of political prisoners. There is another group of NGOs, known as private think tanks, whose specialty lies in collecting information, conducting research, and publicizing the findings for public education and advocacy. Some private think tanks also provide input to international conferences and expertise to different projects developed by international organizations like the World Bank. Various international organizations, like the United Nations and the World Bank, regularly contract think tanks to provide expert evaluations of their programs. Examples of private think tanks include the Ford Foundation (USA), the Centre for Economic Policy Research (UK), and the Globalization Institute in Brussels.

Monitoring Agents

In various areas, NGOs monitor the situation and work as watchdogs. The International Union for the Conservation of Nature and Natural Resources (IUCN) oversees the implementation of the World Heritage Convention. There are several NGOs that specifically monitor transnational corporations. Examples include the Corporate Watch in the United Kingdom and the Multinational Resource Center in the United States. There are a growing numbers of cases where NGOs' actions have directly influenced corporations. Examples include the 1980s boycotting of Nestle by groups protesting the alleged exploitation of women in developing countries, who were misled about the benefits and proper use of infant formula, and the more recent boycotts of Nike, Walmart, and other retailers for allegedly manufacturing or purchasing goods produced under exploitative working conditions in developing countries. The campaign against Nike sweatshops in Asia was initiated in 1989 by a coalition of union and non-union NGOs (Manheim 2001). At times, NGOs have also taken a more cooperative approach. One of the most significant agreements between NGOs and industry occurred in the area of forest products, where the Forest Stewardship Council (FSC), an independent organization that monitors forestry practices, developed a global program that combined public awareness, business collaboration, and green marketing. Through such means, the NGOs convinced Home Depot, Ikea, and other retailers to sell FSC-certified products. Thus, NGOs also act as intermediaries (Doh and Teegan 2003).

Joseph Domask (2003) uses NGOs' responses to environmental degradation as an example of NGO partnerships with the private sector. Nongovernmental organizations have actively participated and responded to the crisis of global deforestation. In the mid-1980s, rates of deforestation worldwide, particularly in the tropics, reached new heights at an alarming rate. Approximately 500 million acres of tropical forests, an area equivalent to 7–8 percent of the world total, or roughly the size of Mexico, were lost just from 1980 to 1995 (FAO, 1993, 2001). The NGOs aggressively circulated information on global deforestation to different stakeholders, including the media. In addition, they put strong pressures on governments, multinational banks, and private industry to advocate the ban on the use of tropical timber. As Domask explains, NGO activism was a major reason why 400 municipalities in Germany issued guidelines prohibiting the use of tropical timber in government-funded projects. "With regard to promoting the creation of protected areas, NGO initiatives were quite successful. With prodding from NGOs, governments around the world increased the global amount

Table 16.1 NGOs Awarded the Nobel Prize for Peace

Organization/Person	Year of Award
Henri Dunant	1901
Institute of International Law	1904
Permanent International Peace Bureau	1910
International Committee of the Red Cross	1917
International Committee of the Red Cross	1944
Friends Service Committee (UK)	1947
American Friends Service Committee	1947
International Committee of the Red Cross	1963
Amnesty International	1977
International Physicians for the Prevention of Nuclear War	1985
International Campaign to Ban Landmines / Jody Williams	1997
Medecins Sans Frontieres	1999
Grameen Bank / Professor Yunus	2006

Source: Excerpt from Ahmed and Potter (2006).

of protected areas from about 500 acres in 1960 to about 3.2 billion acres in the year 2000" (Domask 2003, 164).

International Security

As Shamima Ahmed and David Potter explain, "International security is perhaps the litmus test of NGO influence in international politics" (2006, 153). Several well-known NGOs were born immediately after armed conflict. CARE, Red Cross, and Oxfam are examples of NGOs conceived in response to wars and the crisis following armed conflict. There are numerous NGOs that work to provide different types of relief to war-affected communities. One example would be Medicins Sans Frontiers, which provides medical relief to communities in war-affected areas. During the Rwanda conflict in 1994, within a few days NGOs built several camps in Zaire for 750,000 refugees (Aall, Miltenberger, and Weiss 2000). The International Campaign to Ban Landmines (ICBL), a coalition of several renowned NGOs, was the prime mover in the Mine Ban Treaty of 1997. Often NGOs are the main valid sources of information on civil wars and refugee conditions. They are frequently at the scene before any other government's delegation or IGO. The awarding of the Nobel Peace Prize to the ICBL in 1997 and to MSF in 1999 points to the significant role NGOs play in international security.

Recognition at the International Level

Over the years, several NGOs have received the Nobel Peace Prize. Table 16.1 lists those NGOs awarded the prestigious prize.

The Nobel peace awards demonstrate recognition of the positive role some NGOs have played in international politics.

CHALLENGES AND THE FUTURE

With NGOs' increasing prominence throughout the world and their increased activism, one sees a concomitant increase in pubic discourse over the roles such organizations play. Recent discourse has raised questions about NGO legitimacy and accountability. There is no doubt that the issue of NGO legitimacy is much more complex than it is for government or for-profit agencies, for NGOs operate in a context of multiple stakeholders and multiple donors, some of which are foreign donors; this contextual difference makes NGO legitimacy highly complex. However, it is clear that the bottom line for NGO legitimacy lies in trust and transparency. Core questions for NGOs to address are whether stakeholders know what they are doing and whether what they are doing is considered legitimate. As Michael Edwards succinctly puts it, "There are two ways in which NGOs can claim legitimacy—their right to do what they do and say what they say. The first is legitimacy through representation, the second is legitimacy through results, and accountability for delivering the terms of the contract" (1998, 4).

Recently, NGO legitimacy has been questioned on several grounds. Among these, the followings have received serious attention by different stakeholders: (1) questionable strategies that some have used to make their points, (2) the issue of representation, and (3) accountability. The following section explains these concerns.

Strategy Challenges

Recent criticisms focusing on NGO strategies are mounting. The 1999 protests in Seattle and against the World Bank and the IMF in Washington were criticized as the work of scattered activists with no focus (Klein 2000). The reality here is that numerous NGOs are involved in the anticorporate movement, and they share a common belief that the wide disparity between the rich and the poor results from global regulation and the concentration of power among a few elites. However, there is no common strategy for the NGOs to pursue. What their mission is or whether they might have any common mission is not at all clear. Another criticism or concern is that some well-known NGOs are "far too cozy" with the government. During the G8 summit in Scotland, for example, when organizers were protesting in a rally, Oxfam was severely criticized for being "far too cozy" with the Labour Party in the sense that its message was "virtually indistinguishable from that of its government" (Quarmby 2005).

Sebastian Mallaby's (2004) account of the ill-fated World Bank project of promoting a dam in Bujagali, Uganda, speaks of another emerging problem in the transnational networking of NGOs. In this case, we see NGO activists joining hands with each other and forming formidable blocks against projects that are otherwise supported by local residents. Information sharing and dissemination is also of concern to NGO stakeholders. The One World Trust, itself an NGO, studied the accountability mechanisms of NGOs, international businesses, and intergovernmental organizations. In its study, the One World Trust found that intergovernmental organizations such as the World Bank and the WTO scored highly in respect to online information sharing, whereas NGOs like the World Wild Fund for Nature and CARE scored much lower. The study also revealed that many NGOs fail to furnish relevant information useful to stakeholders (www.oneworldtrust.org).

Representation Challenges

The issue of NGO representation has more recently emerged: whom do NGOs actually represent? Ultimately, NGOs are accountable to their donors, but those donors do not necessarily represent the public interest. There are several NGOs promoting agendas most observers would consider as going against public interest. As an example, the Greening Earth Society, which heavily funded by the coal industry in the United States, argues that global warming is good because it enhances vegetation growth. Some observers also see an imperialistic attitude in the relationship between Northern NGOs and Southern NGOs. Most international NGOs are Northern; they are more powerful and have more resources than their Southern counterparts. Thus, in such global crises as AIDS, global warming, and sustainable development, Northern-sponsored NGOs are the ones who influence transnational NGO policy agenda. "For some in developing countries, this is a new and subtle form of imperialism, as if the ability to raise thousands of dollars at New York fundraisers gives pressure groups the right to define the problems of poor people better than they can themselves" (Elliott 2001).

Representation also concerns NGOs' political responsibilities in advocacy activities. Lisa Jordan and Peter Van Tuijl (2000) define political responsibility as "a commitment to embrace not only the goals in a campaign but to conduct the campaign with democratic principles foremost in the process" (2000). This does not necessarily always happen in practice. Mallaby's account of the World Bank's dam project in Uganda is one such example.

Accountability Challenges

The main challenge raised here is "to whom are these NGOs accountable?" It is understood that NGOs have diverse stakeholders, including donors, clients, staff, governments, and the general public. It is also expected that NGOs remain accountable to each of these stakeholders, and there are good reasons for such expectations. Donors supply funds to the NGOs; clients expect effective services; staff have certain expectations from their agencies; because NGOs operate within the boundaries of state laws, they are required to abide by the state laws; and last, the public also expects NGOs to be accountable for their performances and operations, since in most countries such agencies enjoy such privileges as tax breaks. In practice, however, in most countries NGO accountability is highly convoluted. The process or the mechanisms of accountability are less than clear.

Also, different stakeholders use different criteria for NGO accountability, and that creates a very challenging context. As J. Koppel explains, by trying to be too accountable to all its stakeholders about too many ill-defined issues, an NGO's ability to be accountable to anyone is reduced (2004).

Security Challenges

Along with the issues of legitimacy and accountability, globalization also poses some specific challenges to NGOs, especially in regard to security. Globalization provides the opportunities for individuals and groups to form new collective processes and institutions to address issues that cut across different nations and geographical boundaries. As mentioned before, globalization has thereby helped the growth of NGOs. At the same time, though, globalization has also contributed to the rise and spread of several new problems, including insecurity throughout the world. As Victor Cha explains, globalization is not just about linkages but about interpenetration. "Globalization is a spatial reorganization of production, industry, finance, and other areas which cause local decisions to have global repercussions and daily life to be affected by global events" (Cha 2000, 392). The ease of transportation, communication, and networking has made weapons more accessible to different groups all across the hemispheres and has supported the development of international terrorism networks, the illegal drug trade, smuggling, and organized crime.

The technologies for creating weapons of mass destruction are now more easily available.

The globalization of technologies and information has enabled political groups to form transnational networks of operation. Now agents of threat are thus not only states but also nonstate groups and individuals. "Globalized transportation networks make it possible for rogue states or transnational terrorists to cause destruction in strong states that previously would have been unimaginable" (Allison 1999, 81). Such threats include not only global violence but also other dangerous sources of human insecurity, including, for example, the transmission of viruses and pollution. The easy mobility of humans across states and continents has also made it possible for such diseases and viruses as tuberculosis and bird flu to spread worldwide. While globalization has thus assisted organizations in forming international networks to address a variety of security issues effectively (e.g., land mines, refugees), it has also added new security issues to international relations, thereby making NGO and INGO responsibilities and roles more challenging.

CONCLUSION

Clearly, nongovernmental organizations have significant influence and play an important role in many areas of our interconnected social, political, cultural, and environmental life around the globe. As Doh and Teegan so aptly state,

> Among the many important areas of activity, NGOs have emerged as important stakeholders in discussions over the terms and conditions under

which business, government, and multilateral institutions manage the process of globalization, one of the most vexing issues facing public policy makers, corporate executives, and broader societal interests around the world. (2003, xv)

Globalization is without doubt a major contemporary driver of the growth of NGOs. However, globalization does bring challenges for NGOs, including new global refugee flows, secession of certain ethnic groups for autonomy, new dimension of global poverty, and more competition for funding (Lindenberg 1999). Nongovernmental organizations are thus faced with several challenges at the beginning of this twenty-first century, among them globalization, legitimacy, and accountability. Unless NGOs can pose themselves as trustworthy agents, garner legitimacy, develop mechanism of cooperative workings with different state and nonstate actors, and ensure valid processes of accountability, their effectiveness in the long run is, undoubtedly, at stake.

FURTHER READING

Ahmed, Shamima, and David Potter. *NGOs in International Politics*. Bloomfield, CT: Kumarian Press, 2006.
Boli, John, and George Thomas, eds. *Constructing World Culture: International Nongovernmental Organizations Since 1875*. Stanford, CA: Stanford University Press, 1999.
Keck, Margaret E., and Kathryn Sikkink. *Activists Beyond Borders*. Ithaca, NY: Cornell University Press, 1998.
Lewis, D., and T. Wallace, eds. *New Roles and Relevance: Development NGOs and the Challenge of Change*. West Hartford, CT: Kumarian Press, 2000.
Nye, Joseph S., Jr., Mark H. Moore, and Peter Frumkin. *Governance in a Globalizing World*. Washington, DC: Brookings Institution, 1999.

REFERENCES

Aall, Pamela, Daniel T. Miltenberger, and Thomas G. Weiss. 2000. *Guide to IGOs, NGOs, and the military in peace and relief operations*. Washington, DC: U.S. Institute of Peace.
Ahmed, Shamima, and David Potter. 2006. *NGOs in international politics*. Bloomfield, CT: Kumarian Press.
Allison, Graham. 1999. The impact of globalization on national and international security. In *Governance in a globalized world*, ed. Joseph S. Nye Jr. and John D. Donahue, 72–85. Washington, DC: Brookings Institution Press.
Boli, John, and George Thomas, eds. 1999. *Constructing world culture: International nongovernmental organizations since 1875*. Stanford, CA: Stanford University Press.
Cha, Victor D. 2000. Globalization and the study of international security. *Journal of Peace Research* 37: 391–403.

Clarke, Gerald. 1998. Non-governmental organizations (NGOs) and politics in the developing world. *Political Studies* 47: 36–52.
Deslauriers, Jacqueline, and Barbara Kotschwar. 2003. How NGOs are transforming the global trade and finance agenda. In *Globalization and NGOs*, ed. Doh and Teegan, 34–64.
Doh, Jonathan P., and Hildey Teegan, eds. 2003. *Globalization and NGOs: Transforming business, government, and society.* Westport, CN: Praeger.
Domask, Joseph. 2003. From boycotts to global partnership: NGOs, the private sector, and the struggle to protect the world's forests. In *Globalization and NGOs*, ed. Doh and Teegan, 157–85.
Dye, Thomas R. 2002. *Understanding public policy.* Upper Saddle River, NJ: Prentice Hall.
Edwards, Michael. 1998. Are NGOs overrated? Why and how to say "no." *Current Issues in Comparative Education.* http://www.cice.org.
Eizenstat, Stuart E. 2004. Nongovernmental organizations as the fifth estate. *Seton Hall Journal of Diplomacy & International Relations* 5: 15–28.
Elliott, Michael, 2001. NGOs: The good, the bad and the illegitimate. http://www.msnbc.com/news/521719.asp.
Food & Agriculture Organization of the United Nations (FAO). 1993. *1990, Forest resources assessment: Tropical countries.* Rome: FAO.
———. 2001. *2001, Forests resource assessments.* Rome: FAO.
Frumkin, Peter. 2002. *On being nonprofit: A conceptual & policy primer.* Cambridge, MA: Harvard University Press.
Gorman, Robert, ed. 1984. *Private voluntary organizations as agents of development.* Boulder, CO: Westview Press.
Iriye, Akira. 1999. A century of NGOs. *Diplomatic History* 23: 421–35.
Jordan, Lisa, and Peter Van Tuijl. 2000. Political responsibility in transnational NGO advocacy. *World Development* 28: 2051–65.
Keck, Margaret E., and Kathryn Sikkink. 1998. *Activists beyond borders.* Ithaca, NY: Cornell University Press.
Klein, Naomi. 2000. Does protests need a vision? *New Statesman*, July 3: 23–25.
Koppel, J. 2004. Pathologies of accountability: ICANN and the challenge of "multiple accountability disorder." Unpublished manuscript referred by Stuart E. Eizenstat. In Nongovernmental organizations as the fifth estate. *Seton Hall Journal of Diplomacy & International Relations.*
Large, Tim. 2003. Cash-stripped Japan re-thinks foreign aid. Reuters. AlertNet Foundation. http//www.alertnet.org.
Lindenberg, Marc, and J. Patrick Dobel. 1999. The challenges of globalization for Northern international relief and development NGOs. *Nonprofit & Voluntary Sector Quarterly* 28: 4–24.
Mallaby, Sebastian. 2004. Fighting poverty, hurting the poor. *Foreign Policy* September/October: 50–58.
Manheim, Jaron B. 2001. *The death of a thousand cuts: Corporate campaigns and the attack on the corporation.* Mahwah, NJ: Lawrence Erlbaum Associates.
Passy, Florence. 1999. Supranational political opportunities as a channel of globalization of political conflicts: The case of the rights of indigenous peoples. In *Social movements in a globalizing world*, ed. D. della Porta, H. Kriesi, and D. Rucht, 148–69. London: Macmillan Press.

Reimann, Kim D. 2006. A view from the top: International politics, norms and the worldwide growth of NGOs. *International Studies Quarterly* 50: 45–67.
Rourke, John, and Mark Boyer. 1998. *World politics: International politics on the world stage, brief.* 2nd ed. New York: Dushkin/McGraw-Hill.
Salamon, Lester. 1994. The rise of the nonprofit sector. *Foreign Affairs* 73: 109–22.
———. 2001. What is the nonprofit sector and why do we have it? In *The nature of the nonprofit sector*, ed. J. Stephen Ott, 162–66. Boulder, CO: Westview Press.
Sfeir-Younis, Stuart. 2004. The role of civil society in foreign policy: A new conceptual framework. *Journal of Diplomacy & International Relations* 5: 29–32.
Smith, Brian. 1990. *More than altruism: The politics of private foreign aid.* Princeton, NJ: Princeton University Press.
Smith, Jackie. 2000. Social movements, international institutions and local empowerment. In *Global institutions and local empowerment: Competing theoretical perspective*, ed. K. Stiles. London: McMillan.

17

Regionalism in the Americas

Rosalba Icaza

REGIONALISM AND REGIONALIZATION

Numerous expressions of regionalism are now part of our daily lives: from products and services produced and provided by firms with regional outlets to environmental and security concerns about border zones in given regions. In fact, during the last decade so many regional agreements and partnerships have been in place that academics have characterized regionalism in the Americas as a "spaghetti bowl" (De Lombaerde and Garay 2006, 10). One commentator describes this complexity as follows: "Country A may have a regional agreement with countries B and C; but country B may have a completely different agreement with country C and D but not with A. Yet, A, B, C and D could be members of scheme Z" (see Table 17.1) (Caballero 2007, 18).

In part, this complexity explains why different experiences of regionalism have produced different explanations about its benefits and costs. While some explanations emphasize efficiency benefits resulting from coordinating and harmonizing trade and monetary policies, others might consider social changes taking place within regional cultures and in regional discourses. These different emphases have informed the making and remaking of regional institutions, mechanisms, forums, and agreements in the Americas. For example, for some business and government circles, the North American Free Trade Agreement (NAFTA)[1] represents a driving force of trade expansion and jobs creation (see Box 17.1). For others, regionalism as framed by MERCOSUR, the Common Market of the South,[2] is endangering Uruguay's river basin from the pulp mill production that is taking place there. Outside the Americas, the harmonization of postgraduate curricula among higher-education and research centers across Europe have inspired heated debates among pro-EU and Euro skeptics.

Table 17.1 Examples of Regionalism in the Americas

Subregion or Coverage	Type	Mechanism	Members	Objectives	Status
Hemispheric	NAFTA style FTA	FTAA/ALCA (launched in 1992)	Almost all countries with the exception of Cuba [i]	Create a hemispheric free trade area	Stalled
Latin American and Caribbean Countries	Cooperation Frameworks	ALBA (2005) and TCP (People's Commercial Agreement)	Caribbean countries, including Cuba, Bolivia, Nicaragua, Venezuela	Achieve political and economic integration	Active
North America	Free trade and non-trade issues agreement	NAFTA (signed in 1994)	Canada, Mexico, the United States	Establish a regional market	Active
	High level Partnership	SPP or NAFTA plus	Canada, Mexico, the United States	Improve ability to compete commercially and increase regional security	Active
Central America	NAFTA style FTA	DR-CAFTA	Central America, the Dominican Republic	Free trade area	Active
Caribbean	Association	ACS/AEC	CARICOM members, Mexico, Colombia,	Trade liberalization for	Active

(*Continued*)

Subregion or Coverage	Type	Mechanism	Members	Objectives	Status
			Venezuela, Central American states, Cuba, Dominican Republic, Panama	integration of the Caribbean	
	Customs Union	CARICOM 1973	Antigua and Barbuda, Barbados, Belize, Dominica, Guyana, Haiti, Jamaica, Montserrat, Saint Lucia, St. Kitts and Nevis, St. Vincent and the Grenadines, Suriname, Trinidad and Tobago	Economic cooperation, harmonization, and integration	Active

[i] Countries participating in the FTAA include Antigua and Barbuda, Argentina, Bahamas, Barbados, Belize, Bolivia, Brazil, Canada, Colombia, Chile, Costa Rica, Dominica, Dominican Republic, Ecuador, El Salvador, Grenada, Guatemala, Guyana, Haiti, Honduras, Jamaica, Mexico, Nicaragua, Panama, Paraguay, Peru, St. Kitts and Nevis, Saint Lucia, St. Vincent & Grenadines, Suriname, Trinidad & Tobago, Uruguay, United States, and Venezuela. *Source:* Author

Box 17.1 Effects of the North American Free Trade Agreement

- NAFTA has produced a disappointingly small net gain in jobs in Mexico. Data limitations preclude an exact tally, but it is clear that jobs created in export manufacturing have barely kept pace with jobs lost in agriculture because of imports. There has also been a decline in domestic manufacturing employment, related in part to import competition and perhaps also to the substitution of foreign inputs in assembly operations. About 30 percent of the jobs that were created in *maquiladoras* (export assembly plants) in the 1990s have since disappeared. Many of these operations were relocated to lower-wage countries in Asia, particularly China.
- Income inequality has been on the rise in Mexico since NAFTA took effect, reversing a brief declining trend in the early 1990s. Compared to the period before NAFTA, the top 10 percent of households have increased their share of national income, whereas the other 90 percent have lost income share or seen no change. Regional inequality within Mexico has also increased, reversing a long-term trend toward convergence in regional incomes.
- The experience of each of the NAFTA countries confirms the prediction of trade theory, that there will be winners and losers from trade. The losers may be as numerous as, or even more numerous than, the winners, especially in the short-to-medium term. In Canada, it took a decade for manufacturing employment to recover from the initial displacements caused by Canada–United States Free Trade Agrement (CUFTA). In Mexico, farmers are still struggling to adapt to NAFTA-induced changes.
- The short-to-medium term adjustment costs faced by the losers from trade can be severe, and the losers are often those segments of society least able to cope with adjustment because of their insufficient skills, meager savings, and limited mobility. It must also be recognized that there may be permanent losers from trade as a result of these limitations.

Source: Demetrious Papademetriou, John Audley, Sandra Polaski, and Scott Vaughan, "NAFTA's Promise and Reality: Lessons from Mexico for the Hemisphere" (Canergie Endowment Report, 2003). Available at http://www.carnegieendowment.org/.

For some academics, such different views highlight what regionalisms are: contested political projects driven by state and market actors but also by communities around the world that are transforming regional units located in particular geographic areas. In other words, regionalisms are also being carried out by "ordinary people and their daily activities," which are often "beyond the formal expressions of state-led regionalism," for example, criminal networks, social mobilizations, or daily cross-border activity (Marchand, Boas, and Shaw 1999,

904). Accordingly, commentators emphasize that regionalism "is the non material aspect of regionalization as it concerns the ideas, identities and ideologies related to a regional project" (Marchand, Boas, and Shaw 1999, 904).

Therefore, different regionalisms might prescribe different steps for pursuing particular forms of economic and political integration, coordination, and harmonization among countries in a given region or regions. For example, neoliberal regionalism prescribes free trade to turning national markets into economic units. The rationale behind this type of regionalism is that a fully integrated global market renders more benefits than does "middle step" regional liberalization or integration (Mittelman 2000). From this perspective, a fully integrated market among the North American nations of Canada, the United States, and Mexico would indicate a better insertion of the three countries' export sectors into other regions.

Regionalisms as "highly complex, fluid, multidimensional, multiactor and multileveled" political projects differ from globalization and regionalization processes (Soderbaum 2003, 1). For some academics, regionalization represents an intermediate level of global restructuring but with a spatial articulation in the form of regions (Marchand, Boas, and Shaw 1999). Besides geographical proximity, regions may share cultural ties or an historical past, as in the case of Spanish and Portuguese colonialism among Latin American and Caribbean countries. Regions might be located within countries—as are, for example, the Amazonian and Andean regions—but they can also include such areas as North America, Central America, South America, or the Caribbean.

For some others, multiple and complex regionalization trends in the political economy are pushing forward the interconnection, formation, expansion, and transformation of regions; and in the process, markets, states, and civil societies are been redefined (Cameron and Grinspun 1994). In the last two decades, neoliberal regionalism has been a dominant perspective for steering formal region-building processes; nonetheless, in open conflict or coexisting with this perspective are other views and aspirations. An example of this is the creation of hemispheric networks of civil society groups and social movements in the Americas that have overcome their national identities and concerns to build up common agendas and strategies to oppose the U.S. initiative of a single market as framed by Free Trade Area of the Americas (FTAA) (see Box 17.2).[3]

Box 17.2 Hemispheric Social Alliance

The Hemispheric Social Alliance (HSA) is a network of trade unions and civil society networks from the Americas formed in 1997 in opposition to the proposed FTAA and in support of alternative approaches to integration. Their consensus document "Alternatives for the Americas" supports many of the elements of the EU approach, including resource transfers to reduce disparities and enforceable social standards. It conflicts with the EU's emphasis on market liberalization, instead calling for countries to have the authority to channel trade and investment to support social goals.

> # Yes to life
> # N⊘ FTAA
> ## Another America is possible
>
> Source: Sara Anderson and John Cavanagh, "Lessons of European Integration for the Americas" (Washington, DC: Institute for Policy Studies, 2004), 5. Document available at http://www.ipc-dc.org. Image available at http://www.movimientos.org/noalca/activ-alca-en.phtml.

In summary, the processes of regional integration and the institutions, agreements, and interactions described here comprehend both aspects: the political agencies, discourses, and identities that forge through different regionalisms and the dynamism of regionalization interactions. Together, both aspects are creating and transforming regions around the world.

STRUGGLING OVER REGIONALISM IN THE AMERICAS

Regionalism as political projects in the Americas has had a long, complex, patchy, but nonetheless resilient history. In various forms and to differing extents, it has been linked to different notions of security and sustainability. The image of the Americas as a single political and economic unity from Alaska to Tierra del Fuego in Argentina has inspired opposition and support, as well as periods of activity and phases of stagnation.

For some observers, the economic and political integration of the Americas is impossible given cultural, institutional, political, economic, and historical diversity among countries. For others, integration seems possible if geographical proximity and increasing common environmental, security, and economic concerns are considered. The particular geography of such border zones as San Diego–Tijuana or the triangle formed by Argentina, Brazil, and Paraguay provides good examples of the security challenges facing national governments and local authorities and of the necessity of coordinated actions to deal with criminal and terrorist networks, environmental problems, and, migration flows (Morales 1999; Pastor 2001).

Contested views over regionalism in the Americas are loaded with political meanings and deeply anchored to political contexts, which over time attach to to the concept different meanings, objectives, and actors. For example, after the independence of American territories from European monarchies in the early nineteenth century, Spanish and Portuguese political elites embraced Simon Bolivar's regionalism as synonymous with a deepening unity to forge a new regional identity different from that of the former colonizers (Caballero 2007). A common military, mutual defense pacts, and even supranational parliamentary assemblies were part of this project. Alternatively, U.S. president James Monroe launched the so-called Monroe Doctrine as a step forward into a U.S. regionalist framework for the Western Hemisphere. This doctrine elaborates on the idea that the Americas as the New World should be free of former European colonial powers' interference.

Such competing views of regionalism in the Americas resonated strongly in examples of regionalism in the Cold War context. A pan-American view of regionalism was, for example, a security option to preserve U.S. interests in the region as a counterweight to communism. A good example of this position was Cuba's exclusion, in 1962, from the Organization of American States (OAS).[4] Cuba was excluded using the argument that Marxism-Leninism was incompatible with the inter-American system, for its ideas would break the unity and solidarity of the hemisphere. Meanwhile, a "Bolivarian" regionalism of that time was meant to promote security and peace too, but in this case, related to the preservation of national self-determination. A good example of the latter was the creation of the Contadora Group (Colombia, Mexico, Panama, and Venezuela) in 1983 to promote peace among Central American countries on the basis of self-determination and noninterference, particularly from the United States.

More recently, the Free Trade Area of the Americas (FTAA) is built upon a "Pan-American" perspective on regionalism and calls for the economic unity of *all* the countries located in the Western Hemisphere, with the exception of Cuba, under the leadership of the United States. Meanwhile, the Bolivarian Alternative for the Americas (ALBA)[5] supports a Bolivarian perspective by promoting unity for those countries in the region that share patterns of financial and political dependency on the United States. Accordingly, one of ALBA's main objectives is to counterweigh U.S. hegemony in the region and gain financial independence from such mainstream financial institutions as the World Bank, the IMF, and the Inter-American Development Bank.

OLD AND NEW REGIONALISMS IN THE AMERICAS

Differing expressions of regionalism in the Americas have also been identified as *old* and *new* regionalism. Although both overlap in different ways and their boundaries could be blurred in some areas, key characteristics can be identified (see Table 17.2). For example, in terms of context, *old* regionalism mechanisms and commitments clearly express the post–World War II's hopes for peace but

Table 17.2 Old and New Regionalism

Elements	Old Regionalism	New Regionalism
Context	Bipolar Cold War	Multipolar World Order
Key Drivers	From above, mainly by states	Multiple actors and driving forces
Economic Integration	Protectionist and inward orientation	Open and compatible with WTO rules
Scope	Specific concerns and focus	Comprehensive and multidimensional agreements

Source: De Lombaerde and Garay (2006, 3–4).

also the ideological division of the time between opposing poles of influence: capitalism and socialism. As for *new* regionalism schemes, which proliferated from the mid-1980s onward, these reflect the multiplicity of power centers that emerged with the end of the world's bipolarity at a time when market economics and liberal democratic principles converged, resulting from rising patterns of economic interdependence. A key example of new regionalism was the Enterprise for the Americas Initiative (EAI), launched in the 1990s by the U.S. government as a program designed to strengthen Latin American and Caribbean economies through increased trade and investment and the reduction of official debt to the United States. The EAI has been characterized as "the first comprehensive framework of cooperation with Latin America after the Alliance for Progress promoted by President Kennedy in the sixties" (De Lombaerde and Gary 2006).

As for economic integration, old regionalism in the Americas was heavily influenced by EU developments on policy coordination and harmonization measures and to a large extent worked under the assumption of linearity and progressive stages regarding the process of economic integration. For example, Béla Balassa's theory on economic integration applied to the Americas prescribed certain policy steps for pursuing integration according to the experience of the European Community. An underlying assumption was that progressive stages aimed at decreasing trade barriers could eventually lead to political integration. These stages start with a preferential trading area, followed by a free trade area, then a custom union, a common market, and finally economic and monetary unions.

For Latin American countries involved in the processes of national industrialization (1930–1960s) through the import-substitution industrialization (ISI) model of development,[6] economic integration was an alternative for domestic market expansion. The Economic Commission for Latin America and the Caribbean (ECLAC) would play a strong and influential leadership role in linking an inward-looking, supply-side view of economic growth to regionalism.[7] In particular, ECLAC's view on regionalism promoted controls on foreign direct investment flows (FDI), preferential access to the markets of developed countries, and integration between developing countries.

With ECLAC's support, a considerable number of regional groupings, forums, and schemes proliferated to secure preferential access to partners' products and cheap imports. However, few of these have preserved their original objectives, structures, and members. For example, the Latin American Free Trade Association (LAFTA), created in the 1960s to promote the formation of a common market in Latin America, was replaced in the 1980s by the Latin American Integration Association (LAIA), which has, since then, pursued the more limited goal of encouraging free trade but with no timetable for achieving it.[8] For Robert Devlin and Antoni Estevadeordal, the Andean Group (AG) was "the fullest expression of old integration's instrumental support of Latin America's ISI development model" (2001). Created in 1969 by Bolivia, Chile, Ecuador, Colombia, and Peru, the Andean Group sought the creation of an Andean common market after dissatisfaction with LAFTA outcomes.

Important transformations for economic integration in the Americas and for regionalism took place from the mid-1980s onward, a result of the rising of neoliberalism and the so-called Washington Consensus.[9] The changes took place in a context characterized by regional grouping formation in East Asia and Western Europe and a decrease in the U.S. world competitive rate that incited U.S. firms to move toward Latin American and the Caribbean. Therefore, ECLAC's views on regionalism based on the ISI model started to be rejected as an exclusionary policy option for development because only the members of particular regional schemes had received benefits from regional cooperation and integration (ECALC/CEPAL 1994). Moreover, ECLAC's 1950s–1980s regionalism was labeled *closed* regionalism and criticized for causing trade diversion and for promoting rather limited trade liberalization. Accordingly, such mainstream financial institutions as the Inter-American Development Bank (IADB) started to cherish *open* frameworks as nondiscriminatory to third parties and compatible with the WTO's multilateral goals.[10]

Open regionalism became a part of neoliberal restructuring policies implemented in the region. The restructuring meant the abandonment of the ISI model and a shift toward an export-oriented, demand-side strategy of development. Thus, private capital, not the state, became the driving force of regionalism. Trade liberalization, the privatization of state assets, and financial deregulation policies were seen as central steps to achieving economic growth, attracting fresh capital, and financing national development. An emphasis on coordinating policy toward deepening economic liberalization policies became paramount, and numerous bilateral, trilateral, and multilateral trade liberalization agreements were signed as a means to address risk and opportunities opened by globalization (Grugel 2004).

Since then, open regionalism has explicitly encouraged market integration among countries with different levels of development (North-South regionalism), but it has rejected differential and preferential treatment for market access to the weakest counterparts. A key example of this approach to regionalism, with deep repercussions for the subsequent integrationist trends in the Americas, is NAFTA, which came into effect January 1, 1994. At that time, it created the largest trade bloc in the world; and by 2006, trilateral trade was about $883 billion (Carlsen 2007; Grugel 2004, 9).

Absent a common external tariff, NAFTA works through complex rules of origin. In contrast to a common market, NAFTA excludes the free transit of people but allows that of goods, services, and capital. It has often been assessed as having the EU model as a point of reference. Accordingly, NAFTA is characterised as a *negative* form of integration; thus, "instead of focusing on what can be done the orientation is towards what should be avoided" (Cooper 2004, 68). Moreover, as this agreement excludes the formation of suprastate political institutions, it has been seen as a "superficial institutionalisation of a solid base of trade and investment flows" that preceded it (Bailey 2003, 21).

Furthermore, NAFTA investment provisions have established the de facto power of private actors on the development of administrative law in nonpublic (*non open*) tribunals (Cooper 2004, 68). In NAFTA, none of the arbitration systems allows public access to oral hearings. Whether to disclose documents containing substantive evidence and legal argument is a decision left to the discretion of each tribunal and the parties to the cases (Barenberg and Evans 2004). As such, NAFTA dispute resolutions frameworks empower private arbitrators under Chapter 11 regulations, which are the mechanisms responsible for sanctioning a state in question in a process that is not public. The trade organization "calls for unrestricted rights of repatriation of investment capital, payments, profits, and royalties, along with a guarantee of 'fair' compensation for expropriation. All of these are greater than the obligations under the WTO's Financial Services Agreement" (Salden 2003, 21–22). This is why NAFTA is "a WTO plus" agreement. Furthermore, at the same time that Chapter 11 gives authority to private arbitrator panels, none of the resolutions of the institutions created in NAFTA to address environmental and labor concerns are binding (Barenberg and Evans 2004).

In summary, NAFTA is not simply a trade agreement, for it covers investment rules, the liberalization of the service sector, and intellectual property rights. It also establishes dispute settlement procedures and parallel agreements on labor and environment. Because it goes far beyond WTO rules, NAFTA is much more than an agreement on trade liberalization. The organization includes, for example, rules on the entire agricultural sector, which no developed country has ever completely liberalized. In the 2000 WTO Doha Development Round, a group of Northern countries led by the United States and EU representatives attempted to include these contentious issues in the negotiations. This provoked a fierce dispute with the representatives from developing countries, which in turn eventually provoked the collapse of the round.

Overall, NAFTA as a North-South U.S.-led view on regionalism is not exempt from controversy, especially if the agreement's net benefits on development for the weakest partner (Mexico) and marginal sectors within the three countries (peasants, women) are carefully assessed (see Box 17.1). Despite this, the U.S. government has sought to replicate NAFTA—at first at the hemispheric level, by launching the Free Trade Area of the Americas (FTAA), but after this attempt failed, through bilateral and trilateral trade liberalization agreements.

According to a document produced by the Council of the Americas in 2001, the FTAA should be built upon NAFTA's success: "The continually-increasing benefits of NAFTA to the U.S. economy demonstrate the wisdom of proceeding along a similar path with other FTAA countries. U.S. trade with NAFTA partners is growing more strongly than trade with the rest of the world."[11] Since then, the FTAA has been promoted as an effort to unite the region's economies into a single free trade area by the year 2005, doing so by eliminating "barriers to trade and investment."[12] However, the FTAA has been dependent on a contentious and difficult process: the consolidation of the reforms started in Latin American and the Caribbean countries in the late 1980s (De Lombaerde and Garay, 10). To date, for different social sectors across the Americas, this process has been the main source for the financial crises in Mexico, Brazil, and Argentina, which have left many jobless and have contributed to the worsening of welfare and to increasing levels of income disparity in the region since the mid-1990s.

In view of this, it is not a surprise that the FTAA generated strong social opposition and unrest in the hemisphere, just as NAFTA had previously done in Canada, Mexico, and to lesser extent the United States. The so-called leftist turn in South America that brought into power governments with strong support from popular and marginal sectors in Argentina, Brazil, Bolivia, Ecuador, Nicaragua, and Venezuela also paved the way for the emergence of a coordinated leadership opposing U.S. pressures to agree to the FTAA in 2005. Nonetheless, a stagnant FTAA process hasn't meant U.S. abandonment of an open market–led regionalist project for the Americas. In fact, since the FTTA collapse bilateral NAFTA-style agreements have been signed between the United States and Chile; the United States and Central America (CAFTA); and the United States and the Andean countries of Colombia, Ecuador, and Peru.

REGIONALISM FOR WHOM?

Trade liberalization emphasis on regionalism continues to be a prime concern for wider sectors of civil society in the Americas. For some such groups, if regionalism aims to benefit marginalized sectors of society in the region, then trade and services liberalization policies need to be abandoned in favor of gender-sensitive, community-based, and environmentally sustainable regionalisms. In fact, some critics have called for the democratization of regional trade policy to open it to a plurality of participants, interests, and agendas and to revisit the basic question of who is benefiting from regionalism. The voices of social opposition to open regionalism in the Americas share a critical stand regarding the extent to which regional integration as framed through NAFTA, FTAA, CAFTA, or MERCOSUR is compatible with democratization.

More specifically, these critical voices point, for example, at the negative socioeconomic costs for the peasantry in Mexico associated with implementing NAFTA. As import taxes will be cut off from crops imports from January 1, 2008, it is expected that cheap U.S. seeds will flood Mexican markets and jobless-landless peasants will migrate to urban centers and to the United States.[13] In the same critical tone, feminist and women's organizations across the Americas have also expressed their concerns over the gendered nature of U.S.-led regionalism framed through FTAs: they are not neutral but framed on the basis of particular gendered conceptions of the market and the economy that determines, for example, whose labor counts and what different sectors of the economy are worth.[14] In Canada, the multisectoral working group Common Frontiers has criticized the enforcement and procedural structures proposed by governments to manage U.S.-led regionalism as these escape from wider and effective public control.[15]

Although room has been made for citizens to participate in regionalism's intergovernmental process in the Americas, ordinary citizen involvement in regional governance has been constrained by socioeconomic polarization that affects broad participation and effective democratic representation.[16] It has been observed in MERCOSUR's Foro Consultivo Económico y Social, for example, that moderate and pro–free trade civil society groups are included in the negotiations while radical groups opposed to the frameworks on regionalism have remained excluded or are simply unable to participate (Hogenboom 1998, 267).

FINAL THOUGHTS: DEMOCRACY AND REGIONALISM IN THE AMERICAS

After a short but dominant period of trade centrism in U.S.-led regionalism, focus has shifted, in the current post-9/11 era, to national security concerns, which are regaining centrality to the extent that U.S. homeland security has, for some commentators, become a major player (Carlsen 2007). However, this shift has not meant that security concerns were absent before either the open or the neoliberal version of regionalism was abandoned. The 2005 Security and Prosperity Partnership for North America (SPP) is a good example of this because it reflects the centrality of security concerns but also shows that "corporate demands for fewer obstacles to border-hopping production and sales" are as resilient as ever (Carlsen 2007). As did NAFTA 10 years before and the FTTA later on, the SPP's twofold agenda, namely, security and prosperity, is challenging democracy in various ways.

The SPP as a regional partnership aims at improving not only regional commercial competitiveness but also regional security. Together with the Smart Border Agreements signed between the United States and Canada and the United States and Mexico, the SPP represents one step toward the creation of the North American Securing Perimeter announced by President George W. Bush after September 11, 2001. The SPP has granted the United States extraterritorial rights over natural resources in Canada and Mexico (water and oil respectively) and extended the Bush administration's counterterrorism agenda to both countries.

Ten years before, civil society groups in Canada, Mexico, and the United States voiced their opposition to NAFTA, arguing that its negotiation process had been closed to regional and local citizens' engagements. This time, the SPP has taken this closure one step further. The SPP's decisions are made by *executive partnership* and hence do not need to be ratified by the legislatures in any of the three countries involved, as does such a treaty as NAFTA. Access to and participation in the SPP process has been granted to the usual suspects: trade negotiators with high levels of technical expertise in trade policy, energy sectors, financial markets, and the like. This time, however, security strategists, including the high-ranking military officials of the three countries, have had a say too.

Once more, Mexican, Canadian, and U.S. networks and organizations critical to open regionalism have been actively opposing the Security and Prosperity Partnership for North America. This time, however, citizens' access to national legislatures for the making and remaking of SPP seems to be limited. Furthermore, civil society groups are confronted by the urgency of finding ways to bring security strategists' contributions to SPP into wider public visibility and accountability.

Interestingly, at the region's other extreme are such South American regionalist projects as the Community of South American Nations (CSAN).[17] Here, the call is for deeper cooperation and integration in such highly strategic areas as energy, water, and infrastructure through the Initiative on Regional Infrastructure of South America (IIRSA).[18] The CSAN is planned upon the convergence of two large commercial blocs: MERCOSUR, with Venezuela as its newest member; and the Andean Community, along with Chile, Guyana, and Surinam. Although the proposed integration is essentially economic, greater interconnection through highway, energy, and communication systems is contemplated as a strategic regional issue.

The IIRSA portfolio projects includes highways, bridges, waterways, and interconnections in energy and communications throughout the continent, all financed by the Inter-American Bank, the Andean Promotion Corporation, the Plata Basin Financial Fund, and Brazilian governmental agencies. However, IIRSA is not exempted of controversy. For example, IIRSA's planned highways in the Brazilian Amazon are expected to increase environmental damage to the zone (Gudynas 2005). For some observers, IIRSA projects planned to "create production chains connected to global markets, mainly in North America and Europe" will work as the FTAA infrastructure.[19] Others remark that despite IIRSA's pursuit of integration born of the global South, such an approach is actually driven by Southern elites and sectors already inserted in the global market (Zibechi 2006). In these critiques, as in the ones of the SPP, the lack of ordinary citizens' involvement remains a common concern.

NOTES

1. In Spanish, Tratado de Libre Comercio de America del Norte (TLCAN).
2. In Spanish, Mercado Común del Sur.
3. In Spanish, Aérea de Libre Comercio de las Américas (ALCA). On hemispheric multisectoral coalitions opposing FTAA, see Marcelo Saguier, "Hemispheric Social Alliance and the Free Trade Area of the Americas Process: The Challenges and Opportunities of Transnational Coalitions against Neoliberalism," *Globalizations* 4 (2007): 251–65.
4. In Spanish, Organización de Estados Americanos (OEA).
5. In Spanish, Alternativa Bolivariana para Nuestra America.
6. Import Substitution Industrialization (ISI) encourages countries to substitute what they import with their own locally produced goods. It was meant to be a

core mechanism to promote industrialization by using domestic markets as its engine and hence diminish the long-term dependency of developed countries.

7. In Spanish, Comisión Económica para América Latina (CEPAL). Ensuring ISI linkages to regional integration was the task of Argentinean economist Raul Prébish, who in 1948 was director of ECLAC and from 1964 to 1969 general secretary of the UNCTAD.

8. In Spanish, LAFTAis Asociación Latinoamericana de Libre Comercio (ALALC), and LAIA is Asociación Latinoamericana de Integración (ALADI).

9. The core underpinnings of the Washington Consensus established that economic growth could be achieved through sound macroeconomic management, deregulation, liberalization, and privatization policies, since these would help end market distortions produced by states' interventions.

10. IADB Third EU-LAC Summit. See IADB's special issue on Latin American and Caribbean economic relations with the European Union, "Integration and Trade in the Americas" (Washington, DC: IADB, 2004), available at www.iadb.org/trade.

11. Council of the Americas, *FTAA: Blueprint for Prosperity; Building on the Success of NAFTA* (Washington, DC: Council of the Americas and U.S. Council of the Mexico-U.S. Business Committee, 2001), document available online at http://www.americas-society.org/coa/events/pdf.d/FTAAblueprint2001.pdf.

12. See the FTAA official Web site: http://www.ftaa-alca.org/View_e.asp.

13. "México: Ignorantes los que negociaron el maíz en TLC, acusa especialista" [Mexico: Those who negotiate corn in NAFTA are ignorant, a specialist argues], e-article available online at: www.bilateral.org.

14. For gender-informed critical analyzes on regionalism in the Americas visit www.ignt.org. See also A. Spieldoch, "NAFTA through a Gender Lens: What Free Trade Pacts Mean for Women" (2004), document available at http://www.igtn.org/page/567/1.

15. Official Web site: www.commonfrontiers.ca.

16. E.g., the FTAA opened a consultation mechanism in its official Web site (e-drop box) and sponsored consultations with NGOs on economic growth with equity, social development, and democratic governance through the institutional framework of the Organization of American States (OAS).

17. In Spanish, Comunidad Sudamericana de Naciones. Official Web site: http://www.comunidadsudamericana.com/.

18. In Spanish, Iniciativa para la Integración de la Infraestructura Regional Suramericana. Official Web site: http://www.iirsa.org/.

19. "IIRSA: Infrastructure for the FTAA?" Document available at www.choike.org.

FURTHER READING

Farrell, Mary, Bjorn Hettne, and Luk Langenhove, eds. *Global Politics of Regionalism*. London: Pluto Press, 2005.

Fawcett, Louise, and Monica Serrano, eds. *Regionalism and Governance in the Americas: Continental Drift*. London: Palgrave Macmillan, 2005.

Grugel, Jean, and Wil Hout, eds. *Regionalism across the North-South Divide: State Strategies and Globalization.* London: Routledge, 1999.

Hettne, Bjorn, Andras Inotai, and Osvaldo Sunkel, eds. *Comparing Regionalisms*, vols. 1–6. UNU-WIDER Series. London: Palgrave, 2000.

Icaza, Rosalba. "To Be and Not to Be: The Question of Transborder Civic Activism and Regionalization in Mexico: A Critical Account of Neo-Gramscian Perspectives." *Globalizations* 3 (2006): 485–506.

REFERENCES

Bailey, John, comp. 2003. *Impactos del TLC en México y Estados Unidos: Efectos subregionales del comercio y la integración económica* [Impact of the FTA in Mexico and the U.S.: Subregional effects of commerce and economic integration]. Mexico: Miguel Angel Porrua.

Barenberg, M., and P. Evans. 2004. The FTAA's impact on democratic governance. In *Integrating the Americas: FTAA and beyond,* ed. A Estevadeordal, D. Rodrik, A. M. Taylor, and A. Velasco. Cambridge, MA: Harvard University Press.

Caballero, José. 2007. Problematising regional integration in Latin America: Regional identity and the enmeshed state: The Central American case. UNU-CRIS Working Paper.

Cameron, Maxwell, and Ricardo Grinspun, eds. 1994. *The political economy of North American free trade.* New York: St. Martin's Press.

Carlsen, Laura. 2007. Deep integration: The anti-democratic expansion of NAFTA. IRC Americas. Available online at http://www.americas.ir-online.org.

Cooper, Andrew F. 2004. NAFTA a decade on. In *Trade politic,* ed. Brian Hocking and Steven McGuire, 68. 2nd ed. London: Routledge.

Council of the Americas. 2001. *FTAA: Blueprint for prosperity: Building on the success of NAFTA.* Washington, DC: Council of the Americas and the U.S. Council of the Mexico-U.S. Business Committee. Available online at http://www.americas-society.org/coa/events/pdf.d/FTAAblueprint2001.pdf.

De Lombaerde, P., and L. J. Garay. 2006. The new regionalism in Latin America and the role of the U.S. UNU-CRIS Occasional Papers, 02006/10.

Devlin, Robert, and Antoni Estevadeordal. 2001. What is new in the new regionalism in the Americas. INTAL Working Paper 6.

ECALC/CEPAL. 1994. *El regionalismo abierto en América Latina y el Caribe: La integración al servicio de la transformación productiva con equidad.* Santiago, Chile: ECLAC.

FTAA official Web site. http://www.ftaa-alca.org/View_e.asp.

Grugel, Jean. 2004. New regionalism and models of governance: Comparing U.S. and EU strategies in Latin America. *European Journal of International Relations* 10: 603–26.

Gudynas, Eduardo. 2005. The paths of the South American community of nations. Document available online at http://ww.americaspolicy.org.

Hogenboom, Barbara. 1998. *Mexico and the NAFTA environment debate: The transnational politics of economic integration.* Utrecht, Neth.: International Books.

IADB. 2004. Integration and trade in the Americas. Third EU-LAC Summit. Special issue, *Latin American and Caribbean economic relations with the European Union.* Washington, DC: IADB. Available online at http://www.iadb.org/trade.

Marchand, M. H., Martin Boas, and Tim Shaw. 1999. The political economy of new regionalisms. *Third World Quarterly* 20: 904.

Mittelman, J. H. 2000. *The globalization syndrome: Transformation and resistance.* Princeton, NJ: Princeton University Press.

Morales, Isidro. 1999. NAFTA: The institutionalisation of economic openness and the configuration of Mexican geo-economic spaces. *Third World Quarterly* 20: 971–93.

Pastor, Robert. 2001. *Towards North American community: Lessons from the old world for the new.* Washington, DC: Institute for International Economics.

Saguier, Marcelo. 2007. Hemispheric social alliance and the free trade area of the Americas process: The challenges and opportunities of transnational coalitions against neo-liberalism. *Globalizations* 4: 251–65.

Shadlen, Ken. 2003. Regional vs. multilateral strategies for economic integration: NAFTA in the context of the WTO. Paper presented at the seminar "Mexico changing place in the world: Features of contemporary world politics affecting Mexico," University of Oxford. Center for Mexican Studies, February 21–22. Document available online at http://www.areadevstudies.ox.ac.uk/.

Soderbaum, Fredrik. 2003. Theories of new regionalism. Introduction to *Theories of new regionalism: A Palgrave reader*, ed. Fredrik Soderbaum and Timothy M. Shaw. New York: Palgrave, 1–21.

South American Refund Infrastructure. 2006. IIRSA: Infrastructure for the FTAA? Document available online at http://www.choike.org.

Spieldoch, A. 2004. NAFTA through a gender lens: What free trade pacts mean for women. Document available online at http://www.igtn.org/page/567/1.

Tussi, Diana, and Peter Newell, eds. 2006. Civil society participation in trade policy-making in Latin America: Reflections and lessons, IDS Working Paper 267.

Zibechi, Raúl. 2006. IIRSA: Integration custom-made for international markets. Document available online at http://www.americaspolicy.org.

18
Regionalism in Eurasia

Mikhail A. Molchanov

Regionalism is an ideology and practice of international affairs specifically motivated by the goal of a joint construction of a "region"—that is, a territorially defined entity consisting of several adjacent states that have collectively decided to hold certain political and economic structures in common. It has become customary to distinguish between "new" and "old," "open" and "closed" regionalisms, as well as between security regionalism and development regionalism (Hettne 1999, 2001). Eurasian regionalism's uniqueness is precisely in its eclectic combination of the opposites. It is new in the sense of going beyond a purely economic model of integration and invoking numerous political, cultural, ecological, and traditional and nontraditional security motifs. However, it is also old in the sense of building upon remnants of the demised ties of former Soviet unity, on the infrastructure inherited from the collapsed communist superpower, and on the relentless Russian ambition to reconstitute itself as a regional, if not global, power of some lasting significance.

In Björn Hettne's (1999, xviii) characterization, Eurasian regionalism is peripheral, since these states clearly cannot pretend to any leadership, "core" role with regards to international markets, international politics, or the international community, which is led by the democratic, prosperous states of the global North. In this view, "peripheral regions are peripheral because they are economically stagnant, politically turbulent and war-prone, and the only way for them to become less peripheral is to become more regionalized: that is, to increase their level of regionness." True enough. However, some of the Eurasian countries are also among the fastest growing in the world, with GDP growth in 2000–2006 averaging 10 percent in Kazakhstan, 9 percent in Belarus, 8 percent in Tajikistan, 7 percent in Russia, and nearly 6 percent in Uzbekistan. With authoritarian governments entrenched across the region, its political turbulence is a thing of the past. Ethnic wars and conflicts no longer threaten the stability of the regimes, such as they are. Moreover, whatever else can be said of Vladimir Putin's Russia, decision making in the Kremlin is, once again, internationally consequential.

No longer an international periphery, but clearly not a core, Eurasia seeks to position itself as a bridge between the East and the West. The region is thus "open" to global financial, economic, migratory, and informational flows.

However, its leaders also oppose the declining hegemony of the United States and advance the idea of multipolarity in direct opposition to what, in their view, is failing U.S. unilateralism. The mostly rhetorical "closure" of the region symbolically targets one country only—the United States of America—and, then again, specifically its attempts at political and cultural diktat over the post-Soviet states. In doing so, participating states advance both security-driven and development-oriented agendas. While seeking to pursue their respective national interests, these states agree to the creation of regional institutions that do not serve any one of them exclusively or even predominantly.

Eurasian regionalism is not a code word for Russia's resurgent neo-imperialism. While Moscow could have been interested in reconstitution of its lost sphere of influence in the first decade after the end of the Soviet Union, new economic imperatives have changed its strategic calculus. Russia has learned to select its friends on the basis of economic, rather than purely geopolitical, interests. Meanwhile, other post-Soviet states sought to preserve Russian credit and trade subsidies, negotiate preferential tariffs and free trade zones with neighbors, pool resources, or take advantage of integrated industrial and transportation links. All of these states required a regional acceptance and affiliation to no lesser extent than memberships in such global clubs as the UN, the IMF, or the WTO. New economic challenges and security dilemmas propelled desire to be formally embedded in a neighborhood of allied states. Securing a reliable energy supply had soon enough appeared as one of the key issues that required regional solutions.

Over the last decade and a half, there have been several attempts to institutionalize various regional groupings on the Eurasian continent (see Table 18.1). The Commonwealth of Independent States (created in 1991) was followed by the Eurasian Economic Community (since 2000), the Shanghai Cooperation Organization (since 2001), and the announcement of the Single Economic Space agreement between Belarus, Kazakhstan, Russia, and Ukraine in 2003. Meanwhile, the Baltic states had joined the EU, while Ukraine spearheaded an implicitly anti-Russian GUAM (Georgia-Ukraine-Azerbaijan-Moldova) grouping (since 1999). The Central Asian states produced the whole string of solidarity organizations, from the Central Asian Commonwealth in 1991 to the Organization of Central Asian Cooperation (OCAC) in 2002.

Eurasian regionalism grew out of fear to be left alone in the increasingly globalized world. The end of the bipolar world brought back bandwagoning and politics of alliances. Regionalization was called forth to address political and economic insecurity while opening a new conduit for the procurement of resources that nation building required (Molchanov 2000, 263–88). Regionalization, understood as institutionalization and formalization of economic, political, and social interactions between several states constituting a larger geographic region, appeared to answer the whole host of questions that these states were ill prepared to face on their own.

EXPLAINING REGIONALISM

Regionalization today is characterized by the global spread and diversification of regionalist arrangements, institutions, and agreements. This diversification grows in parallel to the progressive decline of the American hegemony and

Table 18.1 Post-Soviet Attempts at Regional Political and Economic Integration

Date	Participants	Agreements and institutions
Commonwealth of Independent States		
12/8/1991	Belarus, Russia, Ukraine	Belovezhe Agreements on the dissolution of the USSR and creation of the Commonwealth of Independent States, 1991
12/21/1991	Azerbaijan, Armenia, Belarus, Kazakhstan, Kyrgyzstan, Moldova, Russia, Tajikistan, Turkmenistan, Ukraine, Uzbekistan	Alma-Ata Declaration
01/22/1993	Azerbaijan, Armenia, Belarus, Georgia, Kazakhstan, Kyrgyzstan, Moldova, Russia, Tajikistan, Turkmenistan, Ukraine, Uzbekistan	Charter of the Commonwealth of Independent States
09/24/1993	As above	Economic Union Treaty
April 1994	As above	Agreement on Free Trade Zone of the CIS
Oct. 1994		Agreements on the Customs Union of the CIS and the Monetary Union of the CIS
Collective Security		
05/15/1992	Armenia, Kazakhstan, Kyrgyzstan, Russia, Tajikistan, Uzbekistan	Treaty on Collective Security (TCS).
07/6/1992	As above	Creation of the Collective Security Council.
Sept.-Dec. 1993	Armenia, Azerbaijan, Belarus, Georgia, Kazakhstan, Kyrgyzstan, Russia, Tajikistan, Uzbekistan	Azerbaijan, Belarus, and Georgia join the TCS.
02/10/1995	As above	Collective Security Council adopts the Concept of Collective Security of TCS Member States.
04/2/1999	Armenia, Belarus, Kazakhstan, Kyrgyzstan, Russia and Tajikistan.	TCS is renewed for another five-year term. Participants adopt plan of main activities for second stage in formation of the Collective Security System (until 2001).

Date	Participants	Agreements and institutions
10/7/2002	Uzbekistan withdraws from the Treaty. Armenia, Belarus, Kazakhstan, Kyrgyzstan, Russia, Tajikistan	Creation of Collective Security Treaty Organization (CSTO). Charter of the CSTO and Agreement on CSTO's legal status signed by member states.
04/28/2004	Armenia, Belarus, Kazakhstan, Kyrgyzstan, Russia, Tajikistan	Creation of CSTO Joint Chiefs of Staff.
06/23/2006	Armenia, Belarus, Kazakhstan, Kyrgyzstan, Russia, Tajikistan, Uzbekistan	Uzbekistan rejoins CSTO. Declaration on further development and improvements in efficiency of CSTO activities.
Central Asian Cooperation		
12/13/1991	Kazakhstan, Kyrgyzstan, Tajikistan, Turkmenistan, Uzbekistan	Agreement on creation of Central Asian Commonwealth.
02/17/1992	Azerbaijan, Kazakhstan, Kyrgyzstan, Tajikistan, Turkmenistan, Uzbekistan	Creation of Economic Cooperation Organization. Tehran Declaration of First ECO Summit.
Jan 1993	Kazakhstan, Kyrgyzstan, Uzbekistan	Formation of Coordination Council of Central Asian States.
04/30/1994	Kazakhstan, Kyrgyzstan, Uzbekistan	Treaty on creation of Single Economic Space of the Commonwealth of Central Asian States.
July 1994	As above	Agreement on establishment of Interstate Council and Executive Committee of the Central Asian Economic Union.
1997	Azerbaijan, Afghanistan, Kazakhstan, China, Kyrgyzstan, Mongolia, Tajikistan, Uzbekistan	Central Asia regional economic. cooperation mechanism. Initiated by Asian Development Bank and China.
03/26/1998	Kazakhstan, Kyrgyzstan, Tajikistan, Turkmenistan, Uzbekistan	UN special project for economies of Central Asia. Initiated by president of Kazakhstan and the UN ECE/ESCAP.

(*Continued*)

Table 18.1 (*Continued*)

Date	Participants	Agreements and institutions
04/21/2000	Kazakhstan, Kyrgyzstan, Tajikistan, Uzbekistan	Treaty on mutual actions in fight against terrorism, political and religious extremism, and other threats to stability and security.
02/28/2002	Kazakhstan, Kyrgyzstan, Tajikistan, Uzbekistan	Treaty on foundation of Organization of Central Asian Cooperation (OCAC).
10/16/2004	Kazakhstan, Kyrgyzstan, Tajikistan, Uzbekistan, Russia	Russia becomes a member of the OCAC.
02/17/2005	China, Kazakhstan, Kyrgyzstan, Tajikistan, Uzbekistan	Launch of Silk Road Initiative, Beijing
Russia-Belarus Union and CIS Customs Union		
01/6/1995	Belarus, Russia	Agreement on formation of Customs Union of Russia and Belarus.
03/29/1996	Belarus, Russia, Kazakhstan, Kyrgyzstan	Customs Union Agreement; Treaty on deepening of integration in economic and humanitarian areas; Agreements on establishment of Interstate Council and Integration Committee.
04/02 1996	Belarus, Russia	Treaty on formation of Community of Russia and Belarus.
April 1997	Belarus, Russia	Treaty on union of Russia and Belarus.
02/26/1999	Belarus, Kazakhstan, Kyrgyzstan, Russia, Tajikistan	Treaty on Customs Union and Single Economic Space.
12/8/1999	Russia, Belarus	Treaty on formation of Union State of Russia and Belarus.
GUAM-ODED		
10/10/1997	Azerbaijan, Georgia, Moldova, Ukraine.	GUAM Consultative Forum. Established on the margins of the Strasbourg summit of the Council of Europe.

Table 18.1 (*Continued*)

Date	Participants	Agreements and institutions
06/7/2001	Uzbekistan participated in 1999–2005. Azerbaijan, Georgia, Moldova, Ukraine, Uzbekistan	Charter of the GUUAM. Establishment of GUUAM Organization.
12/2/2005	Ukraine, Georgia, Moldova, Estonia, Latvia, Lithuania, Slovenia, Romania, Macedonia	Formation of Community of Democratic Choice.
05/23/2006	Azerbaijan, Georgia, Moldova, Ukraine	Formation of GUAM Organization for Democracy and Economic Development. Charter of GUAM-ODED.
Eurasian Integration		
10/10/2000	EurAsEC: Belarus, Kazakhstan, Kyrgyzstan, Russia, Tajikistan	Treaty on creation of Eurasian Economic Community
06/15/2001	SCO: China, Kazakhstan, Kyrgyzstan, Russia, Tajikistan, Uzbekistan	Declaration on creation of Shanghai Cooperation Organization (SCO). Shanghai Convention.
07/7/2002	As above	Charter of the Shanghai Cooperation Organization.
09/19/2003	Belarus, Kazakhstan, Russia, Ukraine	Agreement and conception on formation of Single Economic Space (SES).
09/23/2003	SCO: China, Kazakhstan, Kyrgyzstan, Russia, Tajikistan, Uzbekistan	Session of prime ministers of SCO member states adopts the Program on Multilateral Trade and Economic Cooperation.
01/15/2004	As above	Establishment of Shanghai Cooperation Organization Secretariat.
07/5/2005	As above	Astana SCO summit grants observer status to India, Iran, and Pakistan.

(*Continued*)

Table 18.1 (Continued)

Date	Participants	Agreements and institutions
10/6/2005	EurAsEC: Kazakhstan, Kyrgyzstan, Russia, Tajikistan, Uzbekistan	OCAC and EurAsEC unification.
06/15/2006	SCO: China, Kazakhstan, Kyrgyzstan, Russia, Tajikistan, Uzbekistan	Sixth SCO Summit in Shanghai approved a program on combating terrorism, separatism, extremism from 2007 to 2009, and an developing an action plan of SCO Interbank Association member banks on supporting regional economic. Cooperation.
08/16/2007	As above	Seventh SCO Summit in Bishkek calls to deepen cooperation with Commonwealth of Independent States (CIS), Eurasian Economic Community (EEC), and Association of Southeast Asian Nations (ASEAN).

Source: Author.

factual pluralization of the regional centers of power. China's growing might and Russia's newly found assertiveness in Eurasia are paralleled by the impressive strengthening of the economies of India and Brazil. In all these cases, clusters of smaller neighboring states increasingly focus their economic activities on economic hubs found within a region. New regional developments are not subject to the political will of a single hegemon and do not necessarily reflect systemic distribution of power capabilities in a single international system.

Not infrequently, regionalization implies regulating access to a particular region in order to "protect it against the process of globalization" (Väyrynen 2003, 43). The "underdog" regions are tempted to use local integration movements to tilt the global economic balance, albeit slightly, to their own benefit. Moreover, regional drives in the global South are as much about identity and culture as they are about democracy. Resistance to the imposition of Western values and norms intensifies as local fights against peripheralization of developing economies at the hands of richer nations of the North acquire regional dimensions.

International relations realists may argue that the new international order is not that different from what we've seen before: it is still characterized by "several regional powers dominating their geographical areas" (Rosecrance 1991, 373, 375). Neorealists see regionalism as an epiphenomenon of such other processes of strategic interaction among states as alliance formation "to counter the power of another state or group of states within or outside the region" (Söderbaum 2005, 224). Thus, regionalism becomes a predominantly geopolitical development defined by the systemic distribution of material capabilities and power maximization strategies of the states (Walt 1990).

International relations liberals prefer to speak of regional cooperation rooted in common economic interests or similar preferences of societies (Doyle 1997). Liberalism provides more room to account for the activities of interest groups, corporations, industrial sectors, bureaucracies, and civil societies. This body of thought draws heavily on the pioneering works of the early students of European integration: David Mitrany, Ernst Haas, Leon Lindberg, and Philippe Schmitter. The "neofunctionalist" approach to European integration that these scholars developed represented regional integration as a product of trial and error interactions across the national borders where participating states and nonstate actors equally "exploit the inevitable 'spill-overs' and 'unintended consequences' that occur" as a result of earlier interactions (Schmitter 2004, 46).

Regions could be understood as primarily cultural entities. Culturalist and constructivist interpretations, ranging from Samuel Huntington's "clash of civilizations" to the so-called third-generation works on strategic culture, insist on the importance of cultural values that bind states together (Huntington 1996). Students of international alliance politics observe that cultural values affect evolution and functioning of strategic alliances (Katzenstein 1996; Kumar and Nti 2004). Constructivists emphasize "polity formation through rules and norms, the transformation of identities, the role of ideas and the uses of language" (Christiansen, Jorgensen, and Wiener 1999, 528). Some of the most influential studies of regionalism follow this route, tracing the impact of positive norms on institutionalization of regional structures and behaviors, as well as formation of transnational identities (Acharya 1998, 2000).

Finally, there have been attempts to combine insights from the economic and political theories of regional integration. In such analyses, the political science side is usually presented through reference to institution building and intraregional leadership, whereas economic reasoning enters through the examination of intraregional trade and financial flows. A political-economic region is therefore seen as juxtaposition of political and business markets, each with its own supply and demand characteristics. For the integration to succeed, it is argued, there must be robust demand "from below," from the national business actors advancing demands for regionwide rules and regulations, as well as political willingness and ability to accommodate such demands—the whole set of the "supply" conditions for integration that would result in at least some pooling of sovereignty of the participating countries. The supply conditions range from the presence of a benevolent leading country, to the establishment of the "commitment institutions" in the region, to the expectation of domestic payoffs to political leaders who pursue prointegrationist agendas (Mattli 1999, 42–43).

Thus, international regions are variously understood as mostly political-economic entities created to facilitate intraregional trade and welfare, mostly security arrangements united by common defence interests, mostly cultural communities, or mostly products of discursive practices that bind both states and nonstate actors together by "inter-subjective understandings that affect their behavior" (Ruggie 1998, 12). The understanding of the core functions performed by regional entities varies, too. Some perceive regionalism as a defense mechanism against globalization, suggesting that through a new regionalism, there "may emerge a political will to halt or to reverse the process of globalization in order to safeguard a degree of territorial control and diversity of cultures" (Hettne 1999, xx). Others contend that globalization does not necessarily elicit regionalist reactions, and when it does, regionalism does not necessarily conflict with the movement to a more open economy. From this perspective, regions should be seen as stepping stones, rather than stumbling blocks, on the way to a globally more open market economy. A middle-of-the road position maintains "a mutual interdependence or dialectic between globalization and regionalization" (Väyrynen 2003, 32), which, of course, immediately begs the question of which side in this interactive dyad will eventually prevail.

Competing regionalist projects do not exist in a political vacuum and cannot be seen as unaffected by power politics. Political pressures may either accelerate regional integration or impede it. Societies may play a larger or a more limited role in regional integration drives. Regionalization "from below" may complement or conflict with regionalization "from above." These debates and opposing arguments fully apply to regionalist processes in Eurasia.

THE EURASIAN ECONOMIC COMMUNITY

The Belovezhe agreements on the dissolution of the Soviet Union resulted in creation of the largely ceremonial Commonwealth of Independent States (CIS). The CIS was supposed to serve as an instrument of a "civilized divorce," in Ukraine's President Kravchuk memorable phrase. Since most ex-Soviet states were neither expected nor welcome in Europe, the CIS offered an interstate community of belonging. It also promised preservation of essential economic ties. However, only 12 of the 15 ex-Soviet states agreed to join. Half of those faced wars and depended on the good will of Russian military forces (Moldova, Georgia, Azerbaijan, Armenia, and Tajikistan). Others took membership as a formality while shirking active participation to the point of a virtual boycott of the organization (Uzbekistan, Turkmenistan). The member states' skepticism could not but show itself in the activities and overall effectiveness of the newly born organization. By the end of 2004, the CIS had 1,417 documents under its belt, yet none of those had been either enforced or implemented in full (Kreml 2004).

Some of the newly independent states were ill prepared for sovereignty. The Central Asian nations had no previous experience of modern statehood. Regionalization appeared as a natural answer to these states' predicament. In 1993, the CIS countries signed an Economic Union Treaty, which envisaged creation of a free trade area. Four years later, a multilateral Concept of Economic Integration and Development projected creation of a single economic space by 2005 (Nezavisimaya 1997). Finally, in October 2000, the Eurasian Economic Community (EurAsEC) came into being.

Poverty has limited cooperation. Diplomacy focused on the idea of courting international donors. There was a hope that participation in various regional integration projects could draw attention of foreign sponsors. The Central Asian states, in particular, were paralyzed by relative political and economic deprivation. With the exception of Kazakhstan, none of these states had a previously developed industrial base of any significance beyond food industry and extraction of raw materials.

Even while competing for international attention, these states could not but band together. The Organization of Central Asian Cooperation was formed soon after the collapse of the Soviet Union as the Central Asian Commonwealth. The name mutated to the Central Asian Economic Union in 1994, the Central Asian Economic Cooperation in 1998, and to its current name in 2002. On April 30, 1994, Kazakhstan, Kyrgyzstan, and Uzbekistan announced creation of a Single Economic Space. The presidents of the three states formed the Inter-state Council and its standing committee, vested with the task to supervise its several working groups. They also launched the Central Asian Bank of Cooperation and Development with its own capital based on budgetary transfers from the members. Tajikistan's entry in 1998 was delayed by a prolonged civil war, while neosultanistic Turkmenistan showed no interest in joining. Russia joined the grouping in 2004 and facilitated its merger with EurAsEC in 2006.

Russia's interest in the post-Soviet regionalist projects has evolved considerably over time. The first-generation Yeltsinites were preoccupied with the idea of getting rid of the "imperial burden" for the sake of "normal" national development. Anticipation of lavish Western aid was implicit in the "Atlanticist" orientation of Foreign Minister Kozyrev and Vice Prime Minister Gaidar. When high hopes of a "Marshall Plan for Russia" were undercut by reality, Moscow's blanket repudiation of all attempts at meaningful reintegration gave place to the more cautious strategy of preservation of the essential economic and strategic interests in the "near abroad." Originally, these interests shaped around the fate of the strategic nuclear forces and former federal property that found itself in newly independent states. A largely rhetorical concern about the plight of ethnic Russian "compatriots" stranded on the wrong side of the border soon entered into the picture. Most recently, the country's fight for a market share in international energy trade has prompted reinvention of post-Soviet regionalism. The contours of the proposed regional groupings are now shaped to coincide with the existing energy routes that link Eurasian producers with European and Asian customers.

The EurAsEC is one such grouping. It was designed as a step toward creation of a regionally tight economic association that would unite energy producers (Kazakhstan, Russia, Uzbekistan), transit countries (Belarus, Ukraine), and affiliates. By 2006, it included Belarus, Kazakhstan, Kyrgyzstan, Russia, Tajikistan, and Uzbekistan. Armenia, Moldova, and Ukraine each had an observer status. The EurAsEC promised to boost cooperation in trade, economic, social, humanitarian, and legal spheres, with the idea of finding an optimal balance between the national and common interests of participating countries (*People's Daily* 2001). The organization, which has become successor to the CIS Customs Union, is now vested with the task of completing formation of a free trade area among member states. Furthermore, it aims at establishing common external tariffs and common external customs boundaries; creating a full-fledged customs union; unifying foreign economic policies; and creating a common market for transportation services, a common energy market, and other components of the common market for trade in goods and services (EurAsEc).

Energy cooperation has been declared a mainstay of regional cooperation in Central Asia. Nonetheless, most energy cooperation projects so far have been conceived as bilateral undertakings. The Central Asian Commonwealth had little say over the scope and direction of energy deals between, say, Kazakhstan and the European Union, or Uzbekistan and China. Equally, the EurAsEC is not consulted in the bilateral negotiations between the Russian energy companies and their Central Asian counterparts. Thus, in June 2004, during President Hu Jintao's official visit to Uzbekistan, China's largest oil refiner, Sinopec, concluded a cooperation agreement with Uzbekistan's national oil and gas company. Details of the agreement were neither publicized nor disclosed to Uzbekistan's regional partners (Jiang 2005). In 2006, Russia and Kazakhstan signed an agreement envisioning a significant boost in oil exports through the jointly owned Tenghiz-Novorossiisk pipeline—from 33 million tons to 67 million tons a year. Parallel to that, it has been agreed that up to 15 billion cubic meters of Kazakh gas will be shipped annually to Russia's Gazprom refinery in the city of Orenburg (Amirov 2006). The EurAsEC bodies are not involved in these cooperative projects.

THE SINGLE ECONOMIC SPACE

For a variety of reasons, Russia, Ukraine, Belarus, Kazakhstan, and Kyrgyzstan stand apart from the rest of the CIS. Belarus and Ukraine are intimately connected to Russia by a kindred language, culture, and ethnicity and a common history, not to mention significant economic ties. Kazakhstan and Kyrgyzstan, both Russianized to a substantially higher degree than the rest of Central Asia, host significant Russian communities and are most enthusiastic about integration for reasons of economic expediency. Russia, Ukraine, and Belarus were the founders of the former Soviet Union and also formed its industrial, economic, and political core. The Ukrainian and Belarusian ethnicities remained submerged into the undifferentiated "Russian Orthodox" people of the Romanov Empire until the early modern era, which gives certain credibility to the Russian nationalist discourse of a "free tri-unity" of these nations. Moreover, the idea of the East Slavic Union was echoed in the creation of the Russia-Belarus Union in 1998 (Molchanov 2002).

In spite of such apparent closeness, political elites of newly independent states feared that Russia might use reintegration as a tool of regional power politics. Ukraine, in particular, refused to participate in the CIS Inter-Parliamentary Assembly until 1999 and has avoided committing itself to a customs union with Russia, arguing for a free trade area instead. Ukraine's customs czar warned that integration could only succeed if all member states were to be treated as equals, just "as in Europe, where there is no such thing as someone dictating one's terms for the rest to comply" (Kievskie vedomosti 1995). In Kazakhstan, a decision was made to move the national capital from the predominantly Kazakh Almaty to the predominantly Russian Astana for fears of the resurgent Russian separatism in the north. Belarus has steered clear of the infusion of any real institutional or economic meaning into the freshly minted union with Russia, preferring old-fashioned subsidies to full-fledged cooperation and economic reform.

Nonetheless, economic rationality born of the complex interdependence between the energy-producing nations (Russia and Kazakhstan) and energy-consuming owners of the transit infrastructure (Ukraine and Belarus) led to the agreement to form a Single Economic Space (SES). The September 2003 agreement saw the three East Slavic states plus Kazakhstan, where Russians constitute one-third of the population, committing themselves to the creation of a customs union and, eventually, a common regional market. Article 1 of the agreement sought to ensure the free movement of goods, services, capital, and labor internally. Participants agreed to obey by the uniform trade regulations and tax policies, and to work toward the creation of a common financial system. They planned to introduce uniform technical standards, including public health and environmental norms. They also sought harmonization of their macroeconomic policies and national legislation in the areas of international trade, competition, and regulation of natural monopolies. In short, the underlying rationale behind the SES coming into existence was to create an integrated economic bloc that would provide for free movement of all factors of production and for the effective policy coordination across the range of macroeconomic issues (Eurasia Heritage).

Next year, the SES agreement was ratified by the parliaments of all signing countries. The September 2004 summit in Astana (Kazakhstan) produced an agreement to levy the value-added tax (VAT) on a destination-country principle. A High-Level Group (HLG) was vested with the task of easing border crossings for citizens of member states. More than two dozen documents that lay the legal foundation for SES, including institution building, governance, and policy coordination, had been prepared for the planned July 2005 meeting.

However, the integration process ran aground because of Ukraine's unwillingness to fully cooperate with its partners. By May 2005, Ukraine insisted on reducing the agreed-upon package of 29 documents to 16, and later, 14 (the so-called 14 + 1 format). A year later, the HLG experts had 95 documents developed and ready for discussion as a proposed foundation of the SES legal base. Upon Ukraine's insistence, this package was trimmed to 38 documents, yet Kiev was still hesitant to extend its approval. Apart from fears that Russia might use regionalization initiatives to reassert its influence in the area, especially worrisome for Ukraine were implications of the SES agreements for the country's European integration bid. As if responding to this, Andrei Kokoshin, the chair of the Committee on the Commonwealth of Independent States in the Russian parliament, noted: "Participation in the SES by four countries in no way prevents them from integration in the world and European economies. However, if we want to participate in this process decently, we first need to make our economies competitive" (RIA Novosti 2004).

While Ukraine remained hesitant, Russian logic resonated well with Kazakhstan. Kazakh's President Nursultan Nazarbayev's repeated advocacy of a "Eurasian economic cooperation" has been influential in advancing regionalist projects in Central Asia. Kazakh diplomacy was instrumental in the establishment of the EurAsEC. It has, importantly, facilitated the creation of the Shanghai Cooperation Organization, where both Russia and China participate, and the launch of the Conference on Security and Confidence-Building Measures in Asia with 15 other countries. Nazarbayev, seeing the twenty-first century as "the century of Eurasia's blooming development," has sought to advance Eurasian regionalism as a way to "construct new bridges of mutual understanding and cooperation between states and nations" (2002).

By the end of 2005, Kazakhstan emerged as the strongest supporter of the SES, which contributed to the Eurasian overtones in Russia's foreign policy. Speaking at an international conference at the Lev Gumilev University in Kazakhstan, Putin once again claimed Russia's Eurasian inheritance, noting that "Russia is the very centre of Eurasia" (2004). Putin's annual address to the Federal Assembly in 2005 referred to Russia as "a major European power" with a "civilising mission on the Eurasian continent" (2005). The ties between the two countries grew stronger in response to the intensification of Anglo-American oil and gas interests in and around the Caspian, as well as the growing U.S. military presence in Central Asia and Transcaucasia. Energy collaboration has been the key to bilateral as well as regional cooperation. In Nazarbayev's words, "Our attention must be focused now on diversification and maintenance of reliable export channels for the delivery of Kazakhstan's energy resources to the world markets, and on the speedy development of the refining capacities that are directly tied with our oil and gas complex" (2006).

Belarus is another strong supporter of the project; yet, the motifs behind this support remain suspect because of the authoritarian nature of the Lukashenko regime. In 1996, Belarus and Russia established the Community of Sovereign Republics, which, apart from Russia's continued energy subsidies to the cash-strapped regime in Minsk, remained a mostly rhetorical formation for all practical purposes. In 1997, Russia's "Community" with Belarus was upgraded to the status of a "Union." In spite of this gesture, the substance of the bilateral relations did not change much. Moscow has not been keen on absorbing a client that had managed to preserve a stagnant version of the command and control economy, together with a political system painfully reminiscent of the bygone Soviet era. Nonetheless, Belarus maintains its strategic value for Russia as one of the main oil and gas transportation corridors to Europe and a key supporter of all regional integration plans spearheaded by Moscow. In the opinion of most enthusiasts of the Eurasian developmental projects, the Eurasian Community with both Russia and Belarus as its members maintains enough of a European identity to serve as an example for a recalcitrant Ukraine.

The move from the CIS to the SES reflected mutual disappointments with the CIS's effectiveness (Olcott, Aslund, and Garnett 1999). In the first decade of the CIS's existence, the organization's role as a facilitator of intraregional trade remained minimal. Ukraine's exports to the CIS countries declined from 53 percent in 1995 to 33 percent in 2006; Belarus's exports went down from 63 to 44 percent over the same period (Interstate Statistical Committee of the CIS 2006, 2007). By 2008, only 18 percent of the CIS total exports went out to other members of the Commonwealth, and only 28 percent of its imports were CIS in origin (Interstate Statistical Committee of the CIS 2009). had 1,417 documents under its belt, yet none of those had been either enforced or implemented in full. Only 803 of the documents had been formally enacted by the end of 2003 (Kreml 2004).

On the face of it, the SES creation could be seen as a logical step toward a free trade agreement and a customs union among the countries disadvantaged by West-led globalization. The energy links that tie Russia, Ukraine, Belarus, and Kazakhstan together provide a sufficient basis—in the form of an energy-producing and -exporting cartel—for securing a firm footing in international energy markets for all SES members. The cash thus derived can then be used for developmental purposes. In Nazarbayev's words, Eurasian regionalism aims to resolve the "contradiction between globalization and national statehood," rectify a "structural imbalance of the world," and restore the proper "ratio between liberalization and security" (2004).

All this may sound like a sermon of regional protectionism. However, current attempts to create a trade bloc centered on Russia proceed against the backdrop of the continuing engagement of the same countries with the WTO, European Union, Shanghai Cooperation Organization, and other international organizations that gravitate elsewhere. Russia has complied with a number of requirements advanced by the WTO as a condition for Russia's entry. In Russia and other post-Soviet states, voices are being raised in defense of the mutual complementarity of the EU and the nascent SES. As the chair of the Russian Federation Council's Committee on Foreign Affairs Mikhail Margelov has said, Russia is "committed to all-European values and is an organic part of a single European space" (*Belorusskaya gazeta* 2005). Thus, Eurasian regionalism is not an antidote to globalization. It seeks, rather, to complement it.

THE SHANGHAI COOPERATION ORGANIZATION

The Shanghai Cooperation Organization (SCO) was established by Russia, China, Kazakhstan, Kyrgyzstan, Tajikistan, and Uzbekistan in 2001. The SCO grew out of negotiations over the border demarcation issues. Conceived as a regional security organization, the SCO uniquely brings together a posthegemonic state (Russia), an ascendant hegemony (China), and several resource-rich states in between—most notably, Kazakhstan and Uzbekistan. The organization's joint activities now extend from antiterrorism and joint military exercises to cooperation in education, economy, trade, and finance. With the help of a credit fund of $900 million provided by China, the SCO member states agreed to speed up cooperation in the fields of energy, information technology, and transportation.

Sino-Russian relations are the mainstay of the SCO activities. Energy trade is of particular interest in considering the SCO objectives. Part of the impetus motivating China's desire for peace and stability in Central Asia is the hope that stability will mean a greater ability to exploit oil reserves in the area. Russia and Kazakhstan both want a stake in a booming Chinese market for energy imports. All Central Asian states have vested interests in protecting the existing and planned pipeline routes along the western leg of the old Great Silk Road. Thus, the stated goal of the elimination of regional instability serves an underlying economic imperative. Participation in regionwide projects provides additional incentives for the maintenance of peace and good-neighbourly relations in the region.

The talk of energy security that Moscow chose to flag at its G8 presidency in 2006 has been echoed in several statements of the SCO leaders. Energy security, in this context, is about Russia's right to sell its oil and gas on its own terms, rather than on the terms dictated by the West, as reflected in the European Energy Charter or the U.S. insistence on its "rights" to participate in oil exploration and development across Eurasia and on the Russian shelf. For China, energy security acquires a new meaning of unimpeded access to the oil and gas wells of the Eurasian continent, which must provide additional guarantees against potential disruptions of oil deliveries through the sea lanes. For all SCO states, energy security is seen as a necessary precondition and motor of regional development based on one's own resources.

That the SCO's geographic stretch essentially coincides with the trajectories of major oil and gas pipelines that traverse Eurasia from the Caspian, Kazakh, and West Siberian oil fields to the consumer markets in China is not totally accidental. The eastern "vector" of Eurasian oil politics is largely dictated by China's insatiable demand for hydrocarbons. China's need for oil doubled from 1994 to 2005; and it will double again, to 12 million barrels per day, by 2020. At the same time, domestic oil output has remained relatively flat (Klare 2005, 30). Because of that, the country imports over half its oil supply, most of it from the unstable Middle East. Diversification of China's energy supply is imperative. China's growing need thus tremendously boosts the importance of reliable energy imports from the SCO partner countries.

In October 2005, China beat American and Russian competitors with a $4.18 billion takeover of PetroKazakhstan. Two months later, China National Petroleum Corporation (CNPC) opened an oil pipeline running from Kazakhstan to China's Xinjiang Uygur Province. Interestingly enough, the use of the Kazakh pipeline also strengthens Russia-China political and economies ties, since roughly half of the 200 000 barrels per day currently pumped through the

Atasu-Alashankou pipeline originates in Russia. The pipeline's capacity is projected to grow up to 20 million tons of oil a year. The next stage of the project will link it to the Kashagan and Tenghiz oil fields in western Kazakhstan, thus completing the construction of the 3,000-km Kazakhstan-China Transnational Pipeline network. As oil analysts note, Russia may well continue using the Kazakh pipeline to deliver its oil to China: "Most importantly, this is not a single Kazakh-Chinese project, but the beginning of a policy of creating a new pipeline system in which not only Russia, but also several Central Asian states, will participate in one way or another" (Tiratsoo 2006). Vladimir Putin's proposal to increase the supply of Russian hydrocarbons using existing and planned Kazakh-Chinese networks gives substance to closer economic cooperation in the region.

In March 2006, Russia signed four bilateral energy agreements with China. Two of those covered Russia's own oil and gas pipelines. First, the construction of China's offshoot of the East Siberia–Pacific Ocean (Taishet-Nakhodka) oil pipeline to supply China's Daqing has been officially confirmed. Second, Gazprom signed a memorandum of understanding with CNPC in regards to the construction of two pipelines that will allow Russia to supply 30 billion to 40 billion cubic meters of natural gas to China annually. The first gas pipeline from Russia to China, estimated at $10 billion, can become operational as early as 2011 (RIA Novosti 2006). Agreements on supply of Kazakh hydrocarbons to Russia's refineries and the use of Russian transportation networks make Kazakhstan a de facto third participant in these agreements.

As noted by a Russian journalist, "China will continue searching for ways to access Russian energy resources. Russia in its turn needs to use China's potential to spur up the development of East Siberia and Far East" (*Pravda*). What this journalist failed to note is that Russia will have to rely increasingly on the potential of such Central Asian states as Kazakhstan, Uzbekistan, and Turkmenistan to ensure a steady supply of energy to China. Two of these states are current SCO members, and it is reasonable to expect that the third one, Turkmenistan, will not stay away for much longer. The SCO framework may be productively used to facilitate multilateral energy cooperation in the region.

Eurasian regionalism, as exemplified by the Shanghai Cooperation Organization, is clearly about many things. Economy is one of them, security is another, and joint opposition to U.S. unilateralism is the third one. The so-called colored revolutions of 2003–2005 have underscored the vulnerability of the Central Asian regimes to the West's behind-the-scenes manipulations. In the words of Uzbek's President Karimov, "the events of the recent years have shed some light on true and fake friends of the region. We are determined to decisively counteract all attempts to impose Western views of democracy and development to our countries" (Artyukov 2006). All members of the SCO oppose the idea of socioeconomic or sociopolitical engineering imposed from outside. All of them seek to replace neoliberal globalization catering exclusively to the interests of West with the alternative models of economic development.

Eurasian regionalism is also about values. Just as the European Union insists on its eastern neighbours' commitment to shared values, Eurasianists proclaim the spiritual closeness of the Russian and the East Asian civilizations, both of which value collectivity and equity over individual achievement and private property. In Russia, Eurasianism is about balancing against the West and sharing a common economic, geographic, and cultural space with other similar-minded nations. For Kazakhstan, Eurasia is a unique region where Islam and Christianity can coexist peacefully through the "centuries of mutual enrichment of Slav and Turkic peoples" (Nazarbayev 2002). For Beijing, Eurasianism is the identity claim that ensures the country's "peaceful rise," as Chinese traditional values of Confucianism are uncannily echoed in the Eurasian values of collectivism, statism, equity, and community (Xiang 2004, 109–21). Thus, the SCO can boast a certain degree of value congruence that participants to the more Euro-centered SES have not yet achieved.

CONCLUSION

What is Eurasian regionalism? Is it predominantly an attempt by Russia to resurrect its former hegemony in the former Soviet space? Many people would probably agree with Richard Falk's (1999, 245) assertion that "the trend toward reactivation of spheres of influence is clearly evident in Russia's effort to provide leadership and exert control over the new states that were formerly Soviet republics." As this chapter shows, however, regionalist developments in the post-Soviet area and Eurasia are, generally speaking, driven by more than one country. Kazakhstan is another pole of gravity for SES and EurAsEc. China is clearly as important as Russia, if not more, for the Shanghai Cooperation Organization.

Regionalism in Eurasia combines developmental and security elements (see Hettne 1999). In its apparent resistance to Western-led globalization, it may appear backward-looking, but it is not. In fact, Eurasian regionalism paves the way to a new type of international relations in Eurasia, to a community that combines traditional respect for the Westphalian conception of sovereignty with an understanding of increased economic and social interconnectedness of the world and regional interdependence in particular.

At the moment, the process is driven by the national elites of the participating countries. When these elites succeed, they do so because of a strategic confluence of interests, and not so much because of functional or political spillovers that students of European integration would expect. Nonetheless, the European Union's example is an important model. The EU's active neighborhood policies, as well as Russia's economic revival and persistence in reconstruction of its broken economic ties with its former Soviet partners, are among the principal factors contributing to the resurgence of regionalism in Eastern Europe and Eurasia.

China's continental policy and the successful evolution of the Shanghai Cooperation Organization give yet another impetus. China increasingly accepts the role of a "benevolent leading country within the region seeking integration" (Mattli 1999, 42). Some countries (Kazakhstan) are more enthusiastic about the prospect, whereas some others (Ukraine) are less so. Russia is uneasily sitting on the fence, seeking benefits from regional cooperation, but unwilling to relinquish to a new leader its former mantle of regional champion. What we see is, therefore, the emergence of a Eurasia that combines polycentricity with the idea of "concentric circles," an idea borrowed straight from the EU policy arsenal.

The early phase in the evolution of the post-Soviet regionalism could not but be influenced by the idea of preservation of the essential economic ties inherited from the old regime. In contradistinction to other known examples of regional integration, market actors initially played a subordinate role, while most regionalist initiatives were led by the political elites of the participating countries. As a state most heavily endowed with an institutional memory of the past, Russia, in particular, attempted to spearhead a drive to restore cross-border economic ties. Because of that, regionalization efforts became contaminated with suspicions of Russia's using economic instruments to reimpose itself politically on its former satellites.

However, economic imperatives of defense against the pressures of neoliberal globalization suggest a different logic of analysis. While geopolitical perspectives represent the economic integration of the ex-Soviet countries as little more than a reassertion of Russia's regional dominance, the "new regionalism" reading of such a phenomenon as the formation of the Single Economic Space or the Shanghai Cooperation Organization suggests that the politics of oil in Eurasia and these countries' efforts at regionalization from above are mutually complementary and represent a natural reaction to globalization propelled by the corporate interests of the West.

Eurasian regionalism is of a state-led, top-down, intergovernmental variety. The main concern of the participating actors is that of achieving economic development and preventing further backsliding into the ranks of the world's peripheral and semiperipheral countries. It is new regionalism par excellence precisely in its idea of using regionalist ties to adapt to the imperatives of globalization. While isolation is certainly not an option, containing "negative globalism" through a joint regional effort certainly is (see Falk 1999). The SES is premised on the belief that the global capitalist core has little interest in pulling post-Soviet countries out of their economic conundrum. Globalization, as conceived and implemented in the West, does not and cannot provide either the economic aid or the social support necessary for the successful modernization of former Soviet states. On the contrary, premature opening of these states' economies to competition with more advanced industrialized nations of the world will spell economic and social disaster. However, regionalization and emulation of the Chinese model of state-led development may well help in turning the economy around. Thus, Eurasion regionalism is called upon to provide a cushion against globalization's negative effect, while helping to achieve economies of scale and provide a sustained engine of growth on a regional basis.

FURTHER READING

Acharya, Amitav. "Geopolitical Challenges in the Asia-Eurasian Region: Some Thoughts." *Futureworldaffairs*, May 21, 2007. http://www.futureworldaffairs.blogspot.com/.

Allison, Roy. "Regionalism, regional structures and security management in Central Asia." *International Affairs* 80 (2004): 463–83.
Gleason, Gregory. "Inter-state Cooperation in Central Asia from the CIS to the Shanghai Forum." *Europe-Asia Studies* 53 (2001): 1077–95.
Gleason, Gregory, and Marat E. Shaihutdinov. "Collective Security and Non-state Actors in Eurasia." *International Studies Perspectives* 6 (2005): 274–84.
Norling, Nicklas, and Niklas Swanström. "The Virtues and Potential Gains of Continental Trade in Eurasia." *Asian Survey* 47 (2007): 351–73.
Shuja, Sharif. "China, Iran and Central Asia: The Dawning of a New Partnership." *Contemporary Review* 287 (2005): 145–51.
Sun, Zhuangzhi. "New and Old Regionalism: The Shanghai Cooperation Organization and Sino-Central Asian Relations." *Review of International Affairs* 3 (2004): 600–612.
Xiang, Lanxin. "China's Eurasian Experiment." *Survival* 46 (2004): 109–21.

REFERENCES

Amirov, V. 2006. Sovremennoe sostoianie dvustoronnikh otnoshenii stran tsentralnoaziatskogo regiona v oblasti energoresursov. Problemy i puti ikh resheniia. [The present state of the bilateral relations between the countries of the Central Asian region: Problems and the ways to solve them] (September 8). http://www.analitika.org/a08092006_russia_ca.doc (accessed October 25, 2006).
Acharya, Amitav. 1998. Culture, security, multilateralism: The "ASEAN way" and regional order. *Contemporary Security Policy* 19: 55–84.
———. 2000. *The quest for identity: International relations of Southeast Asia*. Singapore: Oxford University Press.
———. 2007. Geopolitical challenges in the Asia-Eurasian region: Some thoughts. *Futureworldaffairs*, May 21. http://www.futureworldaffairs.blogspot.com/.
Artyukov, Oleg. 2006. Shanghai Cooperation Organization to become a serious concern for the USA. *Pravda,* June 16.
Belorusskaya delovaya gazeta. 2005. May 20.
Christiansen, Thomas., Knud Erik Jorgensen, and Antje Wiener. 1999. The social construction of Europe. *Journal of European Public Policy* 6: 528–44.
Doyle, Michael W. 1997. *Ways of war and peace*. New York: W. W. Norton.
EurAsEC. *The goals of the community*. Unofficial translation from Russian. http://www.evrazes.com/files/bpage/1/e_evrazes.pdf.
Eurasia Heritage. *Single economic space*. London: London School of Economics. http://www.eurasianhome.org/doc_files/lse_ses.pdf.
Falk, Richard. 1999. Regionalism and world order after the Cold War. In *Globalism and the new regionalism,* ed. Björn Hettne, Andras Inotai, and Osvaldo Sunkel, 228–49. Houndmills, Basingstoke, UK: Macmillan.
Hettne, Björn. 1999. The new regionalism: A prologue. In *Globalism and the new regionalism,* ed. Björn Hettne, Andras Inotai, and Osvaldo Sunkel, xv–xxix. Houndmills, Basingstoke, UK: Macmillan.

———. 2001. Regionalism, security, and development: A comparative perspective. In *Comparing regionalisms: Implications for global development,* ed. Björn Hettne, Andras Inotai, and Osvaldo Sunkel, 1–53. Houndmills, Basingstoke, UK: Palgrave.
Huntington, Samuel P. 1996. *The clash of civilizations and the remaking of world order.* New York: Simon & Schuster.
Jamestown Foundation Monitor. 1999. October 7.
Jiang, Wenran. 2005. Fueling the dragon: China's quest for energy security and Canada's opportunities. http://www.uofaweb.ualberta.ca/chinainstitute//pdfs/FUELINGTHEDRAGON.pdf (accessed April 3, 2007).
Katzenstein, Peter, ed. 1996. *The culture of national security: Norms and identity in world politics.* New York: Columbia University Press.
Kievskie vedomosti. 1995. May 23.
Klare, Michael T. 2005. Revving up the China threat. *The Nation* 281: 28–32.
Kreml. 2004. Sozdanie polnomasshtabnoi zony svobodnoi torgovli iavliaetsia prioritetnoi zadachei dlia SNG [Creation of a full-fledged free trade zone is a priority for the CIS]. http://www.kreml.org/opinions/64034025 (accessed September 12, 2006).
Kumar, Rajesh, and Kofi O. Nti. 2004. National cultural values and the evolution of process and outcome discrepancies in international strategic alliances. *Journal of Applied Behavioral Science* 40: 344–61.
Mattli, Walter. 1999. *The logic of regional integration.* New York: Cambridge University Press.
Molchanov, Mikhail A. 2002. *Political culture and national identity in Russian-Ukrainian relations.* Chap. 3. College Station: Texas A&M University Press.
Nazarbayev, Nursultan. 2002. The first Eurasian media forum speech, Almaty, Kazakhstan, April 25–27. http://www.eamedia.org/prezident.php.
———. 2004. Four dilemmas of the changing world. Welcome address by the president of the Republic of Kazakhstan at the Third Eurasian Media Forum, Almaty, Khazakhstan, April 22. http://www.eamedia.org /kns04/01.php.
———. 2006. Address of the president of the Republic of Kazakhstan to the people of Kazakhstan, Almaty, Kazakhstan, March 1. http://www.akorda.kz/page.php?page_id=32&lang=1&article_id=1426.
Nezavisimaya gazeta. 1997. March 28.
Olcott, Cf. Martha Brill, Anders Aslund, and Sherman W. Garnett. 1999. *Getting it wrong: Regional cooperation and the Commonwealth of Independent States.* Washington, DC: Carnegie Endowment for International Peace.
OMRI Daily Digest. 1995. February 13.
People's Daily. 2001. Five CIS countries create Eurasian economic community. June 1. http://english.people.com.cn/english/200106/01/eng20010601_71524.html.
Pravda. 2006. Russia and China determined to join forces to establish new grand union. March 22. http://english.pravda.ru/russia/economics/77669-1/.
Putin, Vladimir. 2004. Speaking June 18 at Lev Gumilev University in Kazakhstan. *RFE/RL Newsline.*
———. 2005. Annual address to the Federal Assembly, Moscow, Russia, April 25. http://www.kremlin.ru/eng/speeches/2005/04/25/2031_type70029_87086.shtml.

RIA Novosti. 2004. May 24.

———. 2006. March 21.

Rosecrance, Richard. 1991. Regionalism and the post–Cold War era. *International Journal* 46: 373–93.

Ruggie, John Gerard. 1998. *Constructing the world polity: Essays on international institutionalization.* New York: Routledge.

Schmitter, Philippe C. 2004. Neo-neofunctionalism. In *European integration theory,* ed. Antje.

Wiener and Thomas Diez, 45–74. Oxford: Oxford University Press.

Söderbaum, Fredrik. 2005. The international political economy of regionalism. In *Globalizing international political economy,* ed. Nicola Phillips, 221–45. Basingstoke, UK: Palgrave Macmillan.

Tiratsoo, John. 2006. Kazakhstan: Oil pipeline to China a new reality of global politics. *Global Pipeline Monthly* 2. http://www.gasandoil.com/GPM/samples/detail.asp?key=659.

Väyrynen, Raimo. 2003. Regionalism: Old and new. *International Studies Review* 5: 25–51.

Walt, Stephen M. 1990. *The Origins of Alliances.* Ithaca, NY: Cornell University Press.

Xiang, Lanxin. 2004. China's Eurasian experiment. *Survival* 46: 109–21.

19

Regulation

Celine Tan

REGULATORY CHALLENGES FOR GLOBAL SECURITY

Regulation is central to the notion of security, whether it is defined conventionally to refer to state-centric territorial security or broadly to encompass aspects of universal human security. The behavior of individuals, organizations, or states must be regulated in order to dispel or manage threats to mutual survival and safety.

Transformations in the international political order and the world economy in the past 20 years have altered the ways in which societies are organized, reshaping the structures through which regulatory norms are negotiated and implemented. Globalization has meant greater interconnectedness between states, meaning that the chain of causality in the globalized era extends beyond territorial boundaries, causing local decisions and events to have global repercussions.

Globalization has been an uneven and polarizing process, widening rather than narrowing resource gaps and reinforcing existing hierarchies between countries, community groups, and individuals (Khor 2000, 9–10; Scholte 2000, 236). The fallout from such inequity has been the creation of such economic insecurity as unemployment and wage disparities and the lack of access to such resources as land or water and such essential services as health care and education. These economic dislocations, among others, have contributed to rising civil conflict and environmental degradation, instigated the increase in migration and refugee flows, and precipitated international criminal activity (Davis 2003, 4).

At the same time, polarization in the global economy has created disparities in the capacity of states to regulate against these new threats to security. While industrialized countries possess both the technological know-how and the economic capabilities of responding to conventional and novel security concerns, most countries in the developing world do not have adequate resources to address such threats to human, environmental, and territorial security.

The disparities are compounded by the unequal participation of different state and nonstate actors in international regulatory regimes. Asymmetrical governance structures privileging powerful states in global political and economic institutions and the exclusion of developing countries from such other international regulatory processes as informal regulatory networks and business practice has meant that there are significant differences in how global regulation is conceived, negotiated, and implemented. Global regulation has thus contributed toward the unequal distribution of benefits and losses in the process of globalization.

Unequal globalization has generated insecurity in terms of employment, social entitlements, land use, food availability, and agricultural sustainability, leading to competition for resources between individuals and communities within nation-states. This situation has precipitated cross-border economic migration, as people move in search for better job opportunities, and refugee movement, as individuals and communities become displaced through ensuing social or political conflict.

Migration is, in turn, increasingly becoming a source of tension in host countries as competition for resources is transferred to the host communities. It has also resulted in the brain drain of such professionals as doctors, nurses, and teachers, who migrate from developing countries to the industrialized nations, worsening access to essential services in the countries they leave behind. Insecurity resulting from poverty has also created the opportunities for criminal activity as international drug and people smugglers take advantage of the desperation of impoverished individuals and the cross-border access facilitated by globalization.

Globalization has therefore redefined the scope, nature, and scale of security threats. The challenge for regulation today is not just in examining the efficacy of regulatory regimes to manage such threats but also in identifying how existing regulatory structures may have contributed to the emergence of new security concerns.

Box 19.1 Key Points in Globalization

- Regulation of globalization is necessary to dispel or manage threats to security by controlling the behavior of individuals, organizations, or states.
- Globalization has redefined the nature of security by changing the geographical spread and substance of security threats and by introducing new sources of security threats.
- Globalized security threats require new forms of regulation, necessitating greater regulatory cooperation among states, intensifying cross-border regulation, and accelerating the rise of transnational and supranational regulatory regimes.
- States are no longer primary actors setting and enforcing regulatory norms. Such new actors as transnational corporations, business associations, and civil society groups increasingly influence the design and enforcement of global regulatory policy.
- The uneven process of globalization has created asymmetries in regulatory capacities of state and nonstate actors, leading to the unequal distribution of gains and losses and the unbalanced nature of global regulation.

- Asymmetrical regulation increases global insecurity by (1) privileging one set of actors over others and perpetuating social and economic disparities and (2) leading to loss of confidence in regulatory cooperation because of the existence of nonrepresentative regimes.
- The challenge for global security is to ensure that regulation is effective, representative, and accountable to all state and nonstate actors; that it is coherent and consistent with wider efforts to tackle such old and new global security concerns as poverty, inequality, cross-border crime, financial contagion, environmental degradation, and military arms proliferation.

WHAT IS REGULATION?

"Regulation," in the broader sense of the word, refers to the set of principles, rules, or laws designed to control or govern conduct of individuals, organizations, or states in different areas. It also refers to the institutional structures, formal or informal, that have been established to steer social, economic, and political activity and practice. Regulation occurs at the local, national, regional, or international level, but regulatory structures can be influenced by factors outside their jurisdictional control.

Formal regulatory norms can be legally binding (e.g., domestic laws or treaty or contractual obligations), which means compliance is mandatory, or they can be voluntary (e.g., codes of conduct or best-practice guidelines), which means that parties choose to abide by specific norms. The term "regulation" can also refer to such informal social conventions or epistemological rules as the laws of physics or the rules of the market, which guide behavior or thinking on particular issues. In this chapter, the term "regulation" is used to denote the former.

The objective of any regulatory regime is to establish a disciplinary framework for entities subject to its control. Such a framework not only prescribes the rules for conduct and expected outcomes but also sets standards against which compliance with the rules is measured; it also provides sanctions for failure to comply with these rules.

The objects of regulation and the processes and mechanisms of regulation are often dependent on how the subjects of regulatory regimes perceive order and, correspondingly, how they perceive threats to that order. The design of regulatory regimes is consequently influenced by decisions on how societies wish to be organized as well as by prevailing sociopolitical and economic circumstances, including changes in the external environment.

REGULATION, GLOBALIZATION, AND SECURITY

The temporal and spatial reorganization brought about by the processes of economic, sociocultural, and technological globalization have led not only to greater integration between local communities, states, and regions, but also to faster and deeper interpenetration of ideas, resources, markets, and social processes (Cha 2000, 392–93; De Sousa Santos 2002, 178–79).

A significant outcome of globalization has been the dismantling of regulatory barriers to physical and financial mobility. The liberalization of economic and social policy has led to the relaxation or removal of entry and exit restrictions on international trade, finance, and to a limited extent, labor flows. This, coupled with advances in technology, has facilitated the faster and freer movement of goods and services, finance capital, and people across national borders.

Box 19.2 Trade and Finance Regulation

Trade and Investment	• Bilateral trade agreements, e.g., U.S.-Australia Free Trade Agreement (FTA), U.S.-Chile FTA
	• Bilateral investment treaties, e.g., U.S.-Panama, U.S.-Turkey
	• Regional trade agreements, e.g., North American Free Trade Agreement (NAFTA), ASEAN Free Trade Agreement (AFTA)
	• Multilateral trade agreements under the World Trade Organization (WTO), e.g., the General Agreement on Tariffs and Trade (GATT), the General Agreement on Trade in Services (GATS), the Agreement on Agriculture
Finance	• Bilateral investment treaties
	• Bilateral taxation agreements
	• WTO General Agreement on Trade in Services International Monetary Fund (IMF)
	• Basel Committee on Banking Supervision (under the Bank for International Settlements)
	• Financial Stability Forum (FSF)
	• International Accounting Standards Committee (IASC)
	• OECD Paris Declaration on Aid Effectiveness
Intellectual Property	• Bilateral trade agreements
	• Bilateral investment agreements
	• WTO Agreement on Trade-related Intellectual Property Rights (TRIPS)
	• Treaties under the World Intellectual Property Organization (WIPO), e.g., Patent Law Treaty, Copyright Treaty, Trademark Law Treaty

---

Such changes have led to a reconceptualization of traditional notions of security, redefining both the scope and the agency of security threats. Globalization has broadened the definition of what constitutes a security threat, going beyond militarization and armed territorial threats to addressing the risks posed by the rapid global mobility of such previously localized phenomena as infectious disease, financial crisis, and environmental contamination (Cha 2000, 393–94; Scholte 2000, 207–8).

The closer integration of local and national economic activity in a globalized economy also means that domestic economic policies, particularly in economically significant countries, often have immediate and substantial transnational impact, including the destabilization of local and global financial and commodity markets. Meanwhile, advances in global communications and transportation have enabled people, goods, and ideas to transcend territorial boundaries with greater ease, not only facilitating cross-border criminal activity but also making the containment of transmittable disease difficult and ecological sustainability challenging.

Correspondingly, states are no longer considered sole agents of threats in the globalized era, where nonstate actors, including individuals and organizations, pose an equal if not greater security risk. The categories of nonstate actors have also broadened to encompass not just such conventional political and criminal security threats as paramilitary guerrillas, drug traffickers, people smugglers, and cyber hackers but also such economic actors as transnational corporations, private equity firms, and currency speculators, whose activities have cross-border impact.

As Cha observes, "The basic transaction processes engendered by globalization—instantaneous communication and transportation, exchanges of information and technology, flow of capital—catalyse certain dangerous phenomena or empower certain groups in ways unimagined previously" (2000, 394). Security in the globalized world is no longer limited to the preservation of state territorial integrity but encompasses the need to guarantee ecological integrity, financial stability, social and cultural cohesion, and environmental sustainability (Scholte 2000, 207–8).

THE ROLE OF THE STATE IN REGULATION

Traditionally, the nation-state has been at the center of regulation at all levels. Only the state had the power to designate and sanction breaches of regulatory norms through its legislative, executive, and judicial arms of government within its domestic jurisdiction and only the state had the power to enter into regulatory obligations at the international level and enforce these norms at the national and local levels.

This form of regulation was based on the conventional organizing principles of interstate relations–notably the principle of sovereign statehood and the territorial integrity of national borders. States are deemed to possess supreme and unqualified rule over their territories and the entities residing within those boundaries. Linked to this is the principle of nonintervention and traditional notions of security premised on upholding the rights of the nation-state to defend its territory against (1) military and other attacks against it by another state and (2) threats to its sovereignty by internal insurgents.

While traditional notions remain largely relevant in the era of globalization, changes in the global economic and political order have seen important shifts in the way regulatory norms are shaped, executed, and enforced. Globalization, as noted, has resulted in the transnationalization and expansion in the scope of security threats as well as in the transnationalization of regulatory norms and institutions. These developments have challenged the traditional dominance of the nation-state as the primary actor setting and enforcing regulatory norms.

In the area of economic governance, the impact of globalization has been to redefine the state's role in the domestic economy. Policies of liberalization and privatization have reduced direct state control over national economic activity and shifted the state's responsibilities away from that of providing goods and services and redistributing economic resources toward that of regulating the activities of private economic actors and facilitating relations between the domestic economy and the external environment.

In some ways, consequently, the state's regulatory role has increased as government functions shift away from the direct provision of such goods and services as water, energy, health care, and education and move toward supervising the activities of private actors who now supply these services. However, liberalization and privatization policies have also resulted in the loss of state autonomy over economic regulation, for many states now have less control over where and how economic resources are distributed within their territories.

The policies have also limited the ability of states to control the flow of goods, services, and capital to and from their territories, making it difficult for governments to regulate the entry and exit of potential threats to human, ecological, and economic security—such threats as genetically modified organisms, speculative capital, and the dumping of surplus food and agricultural products from other state producers, which has an impact on prices within the domestic market.

At the same time, the nation-state itself has become the subject of increasing regional and international supervision of its conduct within its domestic sphere when that conduct affects human, economic, and environmental security. Recognition of the global interconnectedness of domestic policies and the increasing global solidarity in social and political fields have legitimized the international community's scrutiny of the internal action of individual states.

The development of international trade law in the postwar period, as well as the creation of international humanitarian, environmental, criminal, and human rights law, have served to justify external scrutiny of state regulatory practice and legitimized interventions to correct breaches of internationally ascribed regulatory norms. These regulatory mechanisms have also progressively included nonstate actors in international regulatory regimes, both facilitating their participation in the creation, development, and enforcement of regulatory norms as well as enabling their rights to claim against states for violations of these norms (McCorquodale 2004).

Globalization has intensified the reproduction of regulatory regimes across the world, a phenomenon some have termed the "globalization of regulation" (Braithwaite and Drahos 2000; De Sousa Santos 2002, 194; Picciotto 2002, 5–6), involving the spread of regulatory norms and their enforcement mechanisms over territorial boundaries so that "patterns of regulation in one part of the world are similar, or linked, to patterns of regulation in other parts" (Braithwaite and Drahos 2000, 17, 25).

Although some regulatory structures are reproduced through conventional interstate relations like trade or investment agreements or through the accession of states to regional or multilateral organizations, globalization of regulation is increasingly taking place through nonstate mechanisms, including technical and procedural standardization or compliance with arbitration rules of international commercial law (see discussion in next section).

The globalization of regulation can be viewed as both the *source* and the *consequence* of other processes of globalization, facilitating the global spread of local ideas, conditions, or entities, as well as arising out of the need to regulate the aforementioned globalized phenomena in their new locality.

As with other local conditions that have succeeded in extending their influence globally, regulatory globalization may often displace or replace an existing rival condition or entity within its host locality. The effect of this on the ability of traditional state structures to regulate potential security threats has been as significant as the challenges posed by the aforementioned emerging transnationalization of security threats.

BEYOND THE STATE: THE RISE IN SUPRANATIONAL GOVERNANCE

The rise in and novelty of transnational threats to human security–including human and drug trafficking, climate change, spread of infectious disease, cyber crime, currency speculation, and financial contagion–has given rise to the need for states to regulate the conduct of other states as well as nonstate actors outside their territories, which in turn has necessitated greater regulatory cooperation among states, intensified cross-border regulation, and accelerated the rise of transnational and supranational regulatory regimes.

The exponential growth in global markets and transnational production chains has also demanded the establishment of new interstate regulatory arrangements aimed at securing transnational access to resources as well as guaranteeing the rights of nonresident economic actors within a particular jurisdiction. In particular, globalized economic activity has generated the impetus to harmonize or unify conflicting national regulatory norms and structures to better facilitate cross-border transactions. This need has driven the proliferation of bilateral, regional, and multilateral trade and investment agreements made in recent decades to formalize trade and investment relationships between states as well as to enforce commitments made as a result of these relationships.

Signatories to the WTO, for example, agree to be bound by the such multilateral trade disciplines under its auspices as the General Agreement on Tariffs and Trade (GATT), the General Agreement on Trade in Services (GATS) and the Trade-Related Intellectual Property Rights (TRIPS). Enforcement of rights and obligations under the WTO framework is conducted through its adjudicative arm, the Dispute Settlement Unit (DSU). States are bound by the decisions of the DSU, which allows the injured member to take retaliatory action against the offending member.

International regulatory regimes compensate for the lack of state capacity to regulate extraterritorially by creating forums for state parties to mutually undertake commitments to implement agreed regulatory reforms within their national borders. Often, as demonstrated, this includes an undertaking to devolve some, if not significant, authority to an international organization to act on its behalf and on the behalf of other member states. Most intergovernmental organizations possess "international legal personality," which confers upon them the right to enter into agreements or arrangements with governments or other international organizations in pursuit of their organizational mandate without reference to their member states.

Consequently, studies have indicated that in the era of globalization, international organizations have collectively expanded their influence in the globalization of regulation, increasingly setting universal standards and administering regulatory instruments on an ever-widening range of issues (see Braithwaite and Drahos 2000, 486). Governments borrowing from international financial institutions, such as the World Bank or the IMF, also subject themselves to the regulatory jurisdictions of these organizations by accepting policy and regulatory reforms in exchange for financing.

The growing interdependence between states resulting from greater global integration has also created the need for their regulation at the international level to prevent the negative social, economic, and political cross-border externalities associated with their unilateral action at the domestic level. For example, under the United Nations Framework Convention on Climate Change (UNFCC) and the Convention on Biological Diversity (CBD)—two multilateral environmental agreements aimed at combating the problems human activity has caused on the world's ecology—state parties undertake commitments to reduce greenhouse gas emissions and conserve biological diversity within their jurisdictions. In this regard, states remain primary actors in the regulatory process, although regulation occurs at a supranational level. International agreements are negotiated and entered into by state organs, and the absence of such authority renders the obligations void under international law; consequently, states must undertake the responsibility to ensure that the obligations entered into are complied with within their national borders.

Accession to international regulatory frameworks therefore means that the internal policies of states will have to be consistent with state obligations under those regimes, compliance of which is monitored by the institutional focal point of each regime. This includes translating supranational norms into national law and policy and providing the requisite enforcement mechanisms for breaches of such norms. States can bring claims against other states for not complying with their obligations under such international mechanisms; in some instances, this right has been extended to such nonstate actors as individuals under certain human rights regimes and corporations under international commercial arbitration.

The rise in supranational governance also reflects the prevailing thinking in postwar international relations—namely, that states are no longer responsible solely for their acts or omissions directed at other states or entities within those states. Instead, they are also accountable for their conduct in relation to entities within their own jurisdiction, and these may include foreign investors as well

Figure 19.1 United Nations. Photo: Paul Trimmer.

as minority ethnic groups. Technologies of globalization have also generated transnational social and political movements that have mobilized greater awareness of state practices that create human insecurity, economic instability, or ecological unsustainability.

International law now justifies military or other intervention into sovereign territories for humanitarian reasons under specific circumstances. Meanwhile, the international human rights regime reflects the recognition that the promotion and protection of human rights is a legitimate concern of the international community and that a state's treatment of people within its territorial boundaries "is no longer a matter for that state alone ... no matter what may be its wishes" (McCorquodale 2004, 487).

Human rights concerns have generated a plethora of regional and international instruments regulating state conduct on a wide range of issues, among them the International Covenants on Civil and Political Rights (ICCPR), focusing on human rights; the Convention on the Elimination of All Forms of Discrimination against Women (CEDAW), addressing gender discrimination and reproductive rights issues; the Convention on the Rights of the Child, concerned with children's welfare; and the Indigenous and Tribal Peoples' Convention, aimed at asserting the rights of indigenous peoples.

> **Box 19.3 Peace and Security Regulations**
>
> Militarization
> - UN Charter
> - Hague Conventions
> - Non-Proliferation of Nuclear Weapons Treaty (NPT)
> - Comprehensive Nuclear Test Ban Treaty
> - ILO Indigenous and Tribal Peoples' Convention
> - Biological and Toxin Weapons Convention
> - Chemical Weapons Convention
>
> Humanitarian Affairs
> - Geneva Conventions on the Protection for Victims of War
> - Geneva Convention Relating to the Status of Refugees
>
> Human Rights
> - European Convention on Human Rights (ECHR)
> - International Covenant on Civil and Political Rights (ICCPR)
> - International Covenant on Economic, Social and Cultural Rights (ICESCR)
> - Convention on the Prevention and Punishment of the Crime of Genocide
> - Convention against Torture and Other Cruel, Inhuman or Degrading Treatment or Punishment
> - Convention on the Rights of the Child
> - Convention on the Elimination of Discrimination toward Women (CEDAW)
>
> Crime
> - European Convention against Human Trafficking
> - International Convention against the Taking of Hostages
> - International Convention for the Suppression of Terrorist Bombings
> - Convention on Offenses and Certain Other Acts Committed on Board Aircraft

Regulatory cooperation is also taking place outside formal interstate organizational structures, instead using informal networks of government officials and discussion forums between policy makers and the private sector. Meetings of the G7 industrialized countries, for example, have become important sites of regulatory initiatives on issues ranging from money laundering and terrorism to Third World debt and climate change. In the financial sphere, the Basel Committee on Banking Supervision has emerged as a leader in banking regulation, through adoption of its concordats of banking standards by more than 75 nations, even though the organization is technically an advisory committee to the G10 countries and "not a legal body" (Braithwaite and Drahos 2000, 117).

Box 19.4 Health, Environment, and Social Welfare Regulation

Health
- International Health Regulations under the World Health Assembly (WHA)/World Health Organization (WHO)
- ILO Occupational Safety and Health Convention
- WTO Agreement on the Application of Sanitary and Phytosanitary Measures

Environment
- Convention on Biological Diversity (CBD)
- United Nations Framework Convention on Climate Change (UNFCCC)
- Basel Convention on the Control of Transboundary Movements of Hazardous Wastes and Their Disposal
- Vienna Convention for the Protection of the Ozone Layer
- Stockholm Convention on Persistent Organic Pollutants (POPs)
- Equator Principles on Environmental and Social Risk in Project Financing

Social Welfare
- International Labor Conventions, e.g., Freedom of Association and Protection of the Right to Organize Convention, Right to Organize and Collective Bargaining Convention, Abolition of Forced Labor Convention, Indigenous and Tribal Peoples' Convention
- Equator Principles on Environmental and Social Risk in Project Financing

---

NEW PLAYERS IN THE GAME: NONSTATE ACTORS IN REGULATION

Globalization has not only led to the proliferation of bilateral, regional, and international regimes governing the conduct of states but also expanded the range of actors involved in influencing, setting, and enforcing these regulatory frameworks nationally and internationally. States are now seen as only one of the many players involved in the contemporary governance of social, economic, and political life that includes subnational, supranational, and transnational actors, public and private (Braithwaite and Drahos 2000, 479–85; De Sousa Santos 2002, 198–200; Scholte 2002, 143–44).

Such new actors as transnational corporations, business associations, and civil society groups (CSOs) have emerged on the world stage and have become increasingly influential in the design and enforcement of regulatory policy. Although the doctrine of international legal personality reserves official lawmaking rights, including the aforementioned right to enter into international treaties, for states and their representatives, private actors are significantly influencing the creation of regulatory norms for global economic and other transactions through other means of norm creation (Cutler 2003, 195–96).

Quasi-official and private regulatory regimes for setting and enforcing regulatory norms are emerging beside state-constituted supranational and transnational regulatory organizations. This occurs through two primary mechanisms: (1) standard-setting and enforcement by networks of such quasi-governmental authorities as competition authorities or customs unions and by such international private associations as trade organizations; (2) the global replication of business practice.

Nonstate regulatory regimes have emerged partly as a result of the increase in transnational production, trade, and investment that has necessitated standardization of global business practices, which have progressively attained the status akin to customary law.[1] What may have started out as best-practice guidelines have become almost binding regulatory norms for economic actors operating within a particular regime.

The International Air Transport Association (IATA), for example, an organization representing some 250 airlines globally, has emerged as a "significant private international economic regulator" in air transport regulation in the postwar period, establishing the machinery for standardizing fares, rates, and ticketing procedures among air transport companies and wielding the power to levy fines for breaches of industry standards (Braithwaite and Drahos 2000, 455).[2]

The increase in cross-border economic activity has also meant the rapid transnationalization and standardization of business relationships, leading to the "modelling of business practice across national borders" (Braithwaite and Drahos 2000, 491). Private economic actors, among them lawyers, accountants, and bankers, are primarily responsible for such replication, usually asserting that business in the host country is conducted by adhering to the transnational investor's or trader's practice in the home country, normally an economically significant country.

In finance, for example, "Anglo-American corporate governance standards have become the de facto norm of international capital markets" because "anyone who wants to access global capital on attractive terms will have to observe certain basic tenets" (Plender 2003, 237). It follows that the rules of international stock exchanges, like those in New York or London, "also sets global rules because other actors choose to model its policies" upon these rules (Braithwaite and Drahos 2000, 158, 492).

Meanwhile, such international accounting and consultancy firms as Price Waterhouse Coopers or Ernst and Young, or such ratings agencies as Moody's or Standard and Poor's, play important roles in laying down ground rules for financial health of states. The ratings and successful audits by these entities affect the ability of domestic financial markets to attract external resources (Braithwaite and Drahos 2000, 492).

Moreover, as Claire Cutler has shown, private actors routinely "participate in the creation of international law in the establishment of customs that subsequently acquire the status of customary law through repeated usage" (2003, 196). This process of harmonization and unification of commercial law has occurred as transnational parties to a contract bypass local mechanisms for enforcing commercial bargains, instead opting to insert delocalized contractual obligations and references to international arbitration tribunals as dispute settlement forums rather than local courts (2003, 182–84).

Other nonstate actors play a similarly important role in influencing regulatory policies at the national and global levels, albeit not to the same extent. Civil society and other interest groups that use legal and political strategies to lobby governments and advocate their causes are increasingly influential in shaping regulatory norms.[3] Charitable foundations and private philanthropists, as well as large international nongovernmental organizations, are also influencing regulatory structures in recipient countries in the same way that international financial institutions and official aid donors have, that is, through the policies attached to their financing.

Nonstate organizations have also been instrumental in establishing codes of conduct and regulatory standards for fair trade,[4] as well as for environmentally sustainable production and consumption. The certification for such international fair trade products as coffee, tea, cocoa, and cotton is regulated by fair trade labeling initiatives—Max Havelaar and the Fairtrade Foundation, for example—established by commercial or charitable fair trade organizations to guarantee that products retailed under the label meet certain labor and environmental standards and that producers are paid a fair price for the goods.

WEBS OF REGULATION AND MULTILAYERED GOVERNANCE

Globalization has resulted in what scholars have described as diffused, decentered, or multilayered governance in which regulatory authority has been dispersed across a range of public and private entities at all levels (De Sousa Santos 2002, 198–200; Scholte 2002, 22). Although this result has helped to strengthen the state's regulatory role in some areas, it has also weakened the state's capacity to regulate in others.

The circumscription of absolute sovereignty in state regulation has had positive effects in addressing traditional security threats, as well as some less traditional security concerns of the globalized era, including environmental degradation, breaches of human rights, and cross-border criminal activity. Yet there have been negative repercussions from the erosion of state control over other areas, notably that of the economy, which has affected how well states tackle such other sources of global insecurity as food shortages, economic and financial insecurity, and inadequate access to essential services.

The globalization of regulation, accompanied by the ceding of state autonomy to international regulatory authorities, has led to the shrinkage of national policy space. Such "globalization of policymaking"—in which domestic policies are increasingly set, not by national governments, but by global institutions and external entities—has often had the converse effect of generating, rather than overcoming, insecurity as governments and their peoples lose the capacity to implement policies most suited to their economic, social, cultural, and political circumstances.

The uneven process of globalization and the asymmetrical structure of the globalized world economy also mean that the process has weakened the regulatory capacity of some states more than others. While powerful states are able to maintain regulatory monopoly within their own borders and shape regulatory rules at the international level, less powerful states are unable to assert the same regulatory authority and face significant pressures to cede control to international regulatory regimes and to initiate externally driven regulatory reforms within their borders.

States' regulatory policies are also influenced by the legally binding decisions of international commercial arbitration in cases brought against states by transnational corporations (McCorquodale 2004, 491). These corporations often wield economic power far greater than that of many states, especially developing countries, and they have more capacity than state governments to shape the outcomes of regulatory contests in courts and tribunals (Braithwaite and Drahos 2000, 488–97).

In addition, the devolution of regulatory functions to quasi-autonomous agencies and private actors has meant that in many areas, regulatory authority has been delegated to regulatory actors that may or may not be directly accountable to the elected representatives of the state in which they operate. This, coupled with policies of decentralization in which regulatory authority is increasingly delegated to such subnational entities as local authorities or quasi-governmental agencies, can sometimes make it difficult for national governments to formulate consistent and cohesive regulatory norms in a particular area.

WHO GOVERNS WHOM? REGULATION IN A GLOBALIZED WORLD

Globalization, as discussed, has been an imbalanced and polarizing process. Investment resources, economic growth, technological advances, and social development in the globalized economy have been concentrated in a few countries, mostly in North America, Europe, and East and Southeast Asia; in turn, this process has been dominated by an even smaller number of individuals and entities within those countries (Khor 2000, 9–10).

Given the resulting distribution of gains and losses from the uneven globalization process, the differences among nation-states have widened income disparities and social inequality among the world's population. The UN Development Programme has shown that income inequalities between countries now account for the bulk of global income inequality, making up about two-thirds of overall inequality.[5] It argues that "reproduced at a national level, the gap between rich and poor countries would be regarded as socially indefensible, politically unsustainable and economically inefficient" (UNDP 2005, 38).

Unequal participation of states and peoples in global regulatory policies has compounded the problems of a polarized global economy. Globalization has benefited states and transnational entities that have either had a hand in shaping the mechanisms of globalization or had the capacity to take advantage of the opportunities globalization has presented. At the same time, globalization has marginalized those states or entities without the resources or political clout to direct the process or their own participation in it (De Sousa Santos 2002, 179; Stiglitz 2002, 7).

International regulatory regimes are, correspondingly, largely constitutive of the interests of powerful state actors and influential nonstate actors. Historically, since the colonial era, most developing countries have been excluded from taking part in forming international law and engaging in global governance, and this pattern has continued in the postcolonial period. Many important international organizations either suffer from asymmetrical governance structures that are a legacy of the immediate postwar international political alliances or have their representation mechanisms subjected to the economic and military realities of state power.

At the World Bank and the IMF, advanced economies constitute 60 percent of the voting power, with the United States holding an effective veto, although only developing countries who borrow from them are effectively subject to their regulatory disciplines through financing conditions. Meanwhile, the theoretical model of the WTO's one-nation, one-vote and consensus-style decision-making system has routinely been circumscribed by the selective, informal negotiations of powerful states maneuvering to secure concessions from less powerful members (Braithwaite and Drahos 2000, 487; Third World Network 2001, 89–90).[6]

Even at the United Nations, considered the most representative of all international institutions because of its near-universal membership, the existence of the Security Council's five permanent members—China, France, Russia, the United Kingdom, and the United States—with their power to veto the council's resolutions of the Council has been criticized as an anachronistic legacy preventing the United Nations from acting decisively at times of militarized or armed security crisis.

Moreover, as discussed earlier, global regulatory norms are increasingly developed outside formal interstate channels through such groupings of states as the G7 and G10, as well as through quasi-autonomous and private regulatory networks and the reproduction of business practice. These unofficial mechanisms have a significant impact on domestic regulation in a globalized economy, but many governments and other stakeholders subjected to their regulatory impact often have little or no influence in shaping their rules.

Consequently, the way global and transnational regulatory frameworks constrain states results in significant inequalities between states. Critics have argued that current global governance arrangements do not provide for a balanced sharing of regulatory obligations, with one set of countries undertaking greater commitments than the other; further, the areas subject to regulation also prioritize one set of state interests over the other.

The choice of areas brought under multilateral economic disciplines, for example, and the design of regulatory structures within those disciplines have largely reflected the interests of industrialized countries over those of emerging markets and other developing countries (Akyüz 2007, 39). Multilateral trade agreements under the WTO, for example, have been criticized for extracting concessions from members in areas where industrialized countries have competitive advantage, as is the case with the liberalization of industrial products and service sectors; but these have not secured similar commitments in areas of interest to developing countries, as in the liberalization of agricultural markets and reduction of domestic agricultural support in industrialized countries (Khor 2000, 29–38; Third World Network 2001; UNDP 2005, 9–11).

Meanwhile, the establishment of strict intellectual property rights regimes through bilateral, regional, and multilateral arrangements has been viewed as prioritizing private corporate interests of such actors as drug companies based in industrialized countries, with the result that the developmental interests of developing countries have been neglected—which means developing countries have been prevented from accessing industrial technology and life-saving medicines, among others (UNDP 2005, 10).

At the same time, regulation has been weak in the areas of international finance, where global collective action aimed at minimizing financial contagion and supervising the operations of financial institutions and markets has been limited (Akyüz 2007, 4). Despite the heightened risks of cross-border financial crises, nonstate financial actors have provided little global supervision of the domestic financial policies of globally significant economies or cross-border financial flows (Akyüz 2007, 39; Braithwaite and Drahos 2000, 142; Torres 2007, 7–8). This neglect has been attributed to the reluctance of industrialized economies—and private financial actors based in those countries—to subject their financial policies and activities to multilateral oversight (Akyüz 2007).

REGULATORY INEQUALITY AND GLOBAL INSECURITY

The unbalanced nature of global regulation can serve to heighten global insecurity in two ways. First, global regulatory norms that privilege one set of states or nonstate actors over other state and nonstate actors can result in the perpetuation of social, economic, and political inequalities that are the underlying sources of other security concerns. Second, nonrepresentative regulatory regimes can lead to a loss of confidence in multilateralism in general, with repercussions for global regulatory cooperation.

The unequal nature of global regulation can serve to entrench hierarchies of geopolitical and economic power, as discussed. This, in turn, leads to disparities in the capacity of different states to manage security threats. Economically powerful states with robust regulatory and enforcement regimes are able to respond quickly and efficiently to novel as well as conventional security threats.

However, many developing countries lack the financial and technological resources to regulate against such threats.

Aside from the inability to meet the cost of deploying sophisticated surveillance systems and establishing human resource-intensive security infrastructure necessary to prevent and regulate criminal activity, such as cyber fraud or money laundering, many states also lack the resources to mitigate ecological threats; they lack the means of policing forest reserves to prevent illegal logging or enforcing water and air pollution regulations. Lack of enforcement resources weakens states' capacity to regulate against the spread of infectious disease and transfer of illicit goods and services to and from their borders.

The limitations of state regulatory capacity are reinforced by the asymmetries in global regulatory mechanisms today. Imbalanced multilateral rules not only pose a risk of regulated entities repudiating their obligations under international regulatory arrangements but also may lead to international institutions, and multilateral regulatory cooperation losing credibility and legitimacy in general. This situation leads to the risk of states resorting to potentially destabilizing and destructive unilateral protectionist measures to address their security concerns rather than working through multilateral channels to resolve conflict, thereby heightening global insecurity.

The lack of cooperation between states in the area of monetary policy, for example, has cost states and their citizens dearly in the event of a financial crisis (Braithwaite and Drahos 2000, 142). The absence of multilateral rules on international financial flows and adequate international mechanisms available to countries facing financial crisis have, for example, led to countries to establish either policies of self-insurance (through the accumulation of current account surpluses) or regional mechanisms for pooling reserves (see Torres 2007, 12–13).

Consequently, in the absence of preventative regulation, states have resorted to establishing safety nets to cushion the economic and social effects of unregulated financial markets. The concerns with such ad hoc compensatory mechanisms, however, is that they fail to constrain the activities of financial market participants; they also fail to regulate the financial policies of globally significant economies and consign individual states or collectives of states to taking unilateral action, which may affect the financial health of the international financial community as a whole.

The efficacy of regulatory systems is also in question when dominant subjects of the regimes possess the power to move the regulatory agenda to a different forum if the current framework does not suit their interests. This process, known as forum shifting, is a common strategy used by powerful and well-resourced actors, usually states in the international arena, to move the site of regulation from one organization to another or from one regulatory process to another (Braithwaite and Drahos 2000, 564–65).

Braithwaite and Drahos cite the United States as the biggest user of forum shifting, arguing that when the state "is staring at defeat on a given regulatory agenda in a given international forum it shifts that agenda to another forum or simply abandons that forum" (2000, 564). Forum shifting has occurred, for example, in international regulation of intellectual property rights. The regulation of intellectual property was moved away from the United Nations

Conference on Trade and Development (UNCTAD) and the World Intellectual Property Organization (WIPO) and to the WTO's TRIPS Agreement because the United States had perceived that given the one-country, one-vote decision-making structure of both organizations, regulating in their own interests would be difficult at the former venue (Braithwaite and Drahos 2000, 566). Regulatory authority has since shifted back to the WIPO as in recent years the United States and other industrialized countries find their proposals in the TRIPS negotiations increasingly opposed by developing country members.

Without the certainty of a regime's long-term sustainability, the regulatory authority of the system is quickly circumscribed. Again, this affects weaker players in the system, including weaker states and such smaller nonstate actors as civil society groups, since moving from one set of regulatory norms and enforcement mechanisms to another requires resources and technical capacity to engage effectively with new rules, procedures, and institutions. The participation of these actors in the new regulatory forum may therefore be limited or inadequate, leading once again to asymmetrical allocation of regulatory rights and duties under the new regime.

CONCLUSION

Regulation is an important constituent in maintaining human and territorial security in a globalized world. Changes in the organization of the global economy, political structures, and social and cultural processes brought about by globalizing forces have both demanded and enabled new forms of regulatory interventions to maintain social, economic, and political order at the local, national, and international levels.

States are no longer considered the primary source of regulation, by choice or by design, because of the interconnected nature of the world we live in today. The transnationalization of security threats, coupled with greater economic, social, and political integration of states and communities, has given rise to the need for greater international regulatory cooperation and more global regulatory frameworks. At the same time, the proliferation of globalized regulatory networks and international regulatory organizations has also impinged on states' capacity to manage internal security concerns, including addressing issues of human security, economic stability, and ecological sustainability.

Consequently, one of the main challenges of regulation in the context of globalization and security is how to ensure that states are subject to international regulation governing their own acts or omissions that affect security while also ensuring that they retain the capacity to regulate the acts or omissions of domestic or external forces threatening the security of the people within their jurisdiction.

However, the challenge of global regulation cannot be divorced from the attendant challenge of tackling the inequities of the globalized economy and the asymmetrical nature of international relations, exacerbated by the processes of globalization. For regulatory structures to be effective, they have to be legitimate and credible in the eyes of those to whom regulation applies. International regulatory regimes therefore need to be made more responsive to the security concerns of all stakeholders; as well, they need to be made more coherent and consistent with the wider security needs of the globalized era.

NOTES

1. Customary law is a legal term usually used in reference to custom or practices that have acquired the status of legal norms through repeated usage but do not derive their force from treaty, statute, or common law. In public international law, this could refer to such state practice as the prohibition against genocide or slavery; in municipal law, this could refer to such social practice as indigenous communities' land use.

2. For more details, see IATA's official Web site: http://www.iata.org/about/mission.

3. The globalization of communications has meant that citizens' groups and nongovernmental organizations have been able to network and mobilize across territorial boundaries and form coalitions to lobby for causes of common concern (Braithwaite and Drahos 2000, 497; De Sousa Santos 2002, 163).

4. "Fair trade" is started out as a form of trading partnership between nonprofit importers, retailers in industrialized countries, and small-scale producers in developing countries aimed at counteracting the effect of depressed commodity prices and dependence on commercial intermediaries who did not pay a fair price for the agricultural produce used in the manufacturing of consumer products. It is now a multi-million-dollar global initiative, including both large-scale commercial as well as nonprofit retailers on one side and transnational agricultural businesses and small-scale farmers on the other, but with the aim of guaranteeing a fair price for agricultural producers (that is, a price not dependent on market fluctuations) and ensuring that goods retailed under its label meet certain labor and environmental standards.

5. One in every two people in sub-Saharan Africa is now located in the bottom 20 percent of the world's income distribution compared with one in five people in East Asia and one in four in South Asia. Meanwhile, 9 out of every 10 of their citizens in industrialized countries ranked among the richest 20 percent of the world's population, with OECD countries accounting for 85 percent of the world's income distribution (UNDP 2005, 36, box 1.5). Also, the richest 20 percent of the population hold three-quarters of world income, whereas the poorest 40 percent hold 5 percent of the world's income and the poorest 20 percent hold just 1.5 percent. The world's richest 500 individuals have a combined income of more than the poorest 416 billion (UNDP 2005, 4, 36).

6. In fact, Braithwaite and Drahos argue that consensus decision making is in itself a means by which major players deal informally with the formal obstacles that the one-nation, one-vote system may pose as the "crucial feature of consensus as a decision rule is that abstention counts as an affirmative rather than a negative vote" (2000, 487). Furthermore, the major states within the WTO have established an informal system of "Green Room" meetings in which

decisions have been undertaken in meetings with limited participation to secure maximum consensus (see Khor 2000, 27–28; Third World Network 2001, 89–90).

FURTHER READING

Aginam, Obijiofor. *Global Health Governance: International Law and Public Health in a Divided World*. Toronto: University of Toronto Press, 2005.
Alexander, Kern, Rahul Dhumale, and John Eatwell. *Global Governance of Financial Systems: The International Regulation of Systemic Risk*. Oxford: Oxford University Press, 2004.
Braithwaite, John, and Peter Drahos. *Global Business Regulation*. Cambridge: Cambridge University Press, 2000.
Scholte, Jan Aart. *Globalization: A Critical Introduction*. Basingstoke, UK: Macmillan Press, 2000.
Speth, James Gustave, and Peter M. Haas. *Global Environmental Governance*. Washington, DC: Island Press, 2006.
Trebilcock, Michael J., and Robert Howse. *The Regulation of International Trade*, 3rd ed. London: Routledge, 2004.
UN Development Programme (UNDP). *Human Development Report 2005: International Cooperation at a Crossroads: Aid, Trade and Security in an Unequal World*. New York: UNDP, 2005.

REFERENCES

Akyüz, Yilmaz. 2007. Global rules and markets: Constraints over policy autonomy in developing countries. Paper prepared for the Institute for Labor Studies, International Labor Organization.
Braitwaite, John, and Drahos, Peter. 2000. *Global business regulation*. Cambridge: Cambridge University Press.
Cha, Victor D. 2000. Globalization and the study of international security. *Journal of Peace and Security* 37: 391–403.
Cutler, A. Claire. 2003. *Private power and global authority: Transnational merchant law in the global political economy*. Cambridge: Cambridge University Press.
De Sousa Santos, Boaventura. 2002. *Toward a new legal common sense: Law, globalization and emancipation*, 2nd ed. London: Butterworths Lexis-Nexis.
Khor, Martin. 2000. *Globalization and the South: Some critical issues*. Penang, Malaysia: Third World Network.
May, Peter J. 2007. Regulatory regimes and accountability. *Regulation and Governance* 1:8–26.
McCorquodale, Robert. 2004. An inclusive international legal system. *Leiden Journal of International Law* 17: 477–504.
Picciotto, Sol. 2002. Introduction: Reconceptualising regulation in the era of globalization. *Journal of Law and Society* 29: 1–11.
Plender, John. 2003. *Going off the rails: Global capital and the crisis of legitimacy*. Chichester, UK: John Willey and Sons.

Scholte, Jan Aart. 2000. *Globalization: A critical introduction*. London: Macmillan Press.
Stiglitz, Joseph. 2002. *Globalization and its discontents*. London: Penguin.
Third World Network. 2001. *The multilateral trading system: A development perspective*. New York: UNDP.
Torres, Hector R. 2007. Reforming the International Monetary Fund: Why Legitimacy is at Stake. *Journal of International Economic Law* 1–18.
UN Development Programme (UNDP). 2005. *International cooperation at a crossroads: Aid, trade and security in an unequal world*. Human Development Report, 2005. New York: UNDP.

20

Terrorism

Richard Jackson, Marie Breen Smyth, and Jeroen Gunning

TERRORISM IN THE TWENTY-FIRST CENTURY

Terrorism, if defined as the use or threat of violence against civilians that is intended to influence an audience for political purposes, has a long history going back thousands of years. From the Assassins and the Ku Klux Klan, to Al Qaeda, the dictators of the nineteenth and twentieth centuries and a surprising number of liberal democratic states, different actors have tried to achieve their political aims through the use of exemplary violence aimed largely at civilians. Although it is generally agreed that the era of modern terrorism began in the late 1960s, it was the devastating attacks of September 11, 2001, that transformed terrorism from a relatively minor, typically localized security issue to one of major international significance. Since these attacks, unsurprisingly, terrorism has become a major focus of public and scholarly interest, and thousands of new books and articles are published on it every year. It is also a topic of great cultural and political importance, as well as an overriding concern for security officials.

The aim of this chapter is to explore some of the main issues of the scholarly study of terrorism from a "critical" perspective, which can be defined most simply as an approach that does not take commonly accepted knowledge about the subject for granted. In the following sections, we begin by outlining how orthodox and critical approaches to terrorism differ. Next we explore some of the central issues in terrorism research—such as how much of a threat terrorism currently poses, what types of terrorism can be identified, the preconditions and facilitating factors or causes of terrorism, and the options available for responding to terrorism—to highlight how a critical perspective differs from orthodox perspectives in its approach to these important questions. The chapter ends with a brief summary of the main contributions and some of the central commitments and concerns of critical terrorism studies. Throughout the chapter, our main aim is to demonstrate how a critical approach can provide a more thorough and satisfying understanding of the subject than traditional or orthodox accounts.

ORTHODOX APPROACHES TO TERRORISM

For many years, the study of terrorism has been dominated by what some scholars have called a problem-solving approach (Gunning 2007b). Such an approach "takes the world as it finds it, with the prevailing social and power relationships and the institutions into which they are organized, as the given framework for action" (Cox 1981). In contrast to critical approaches, the problem-solving approach does not reflect upon the origins of prevailing power relationships or on how these might have contributed to the problem under consideration, in this case, terrorism. In other words, the primary concern of a problem-solving approach to terrorism is to strengthen the status quo, delegitimize the terrorists and give assistance to the counterterrorist effort. It may seek to improve counterterrorist measures and, as such, can often be critical of aspects of the status quo. But it tends not to question the sharp division between good and evil or legitimate and illegitimate that is established by the authorities, nor does it concern itself overly with how opponents or victims of the status quo might regard the latter's claim to legitimacy.

A number of well-documented methodological flaws flow from the adoption of such perspectives (see Burnett and Whyte 2005; Ranstorp 2006; Schmid and Jongman 1988; Silke 2004). At its worst, orthodox or problem-solving terrorism research has been criticized for ignoring the historical and political context of terrorism and, in particular, the role played by the state and its repressive apparatus in creating an environment in which terrorist actions may be viewed as an attractive option for some actors. Methodologically, it has been criticized for relying heavily on secondary sources, avoiding face-to-face contact with terrorists and their communities (even where access was straightforward and safe), and demonizing them through emotive and condemnatory language. It has also been condemned for failing to reflect adequately on the politics of naming someone a terrorist and how terrorism research has been used to marginalize alternative perspectives and bolster the status quo. The discipline of orthodox terrorism studies has also been attacked for its lack of theoretical rigor and for failing to challenge simplistic explanations that frequently suit the existing social and political order. Last, it has been censured for equating state security with human security and for largely ignoring the many instances of state terrorism carried out in the name of the national interest.

Of course, not all orthodox terrorism research is guilty as charged. Terrorism studies has always had its critical voices, if we take "critical" to mean "not tak[ing] institutions and social and power relations for granted but call[ing] them into question by concerning [one]self with their origins and how and whether they might be in the process of changing" (Cox 1981). In addition, among those orthodox scholars who have remained within a problem-solving framework, there are quite a few who have produced outstanding research that to this day challenges dominant knowledge and understanding of terrorism (see, among others, Crenshaw 1981; Bjorgo 2005; Horgan 2005; Pape 2005; Richardson 2006; Sageman 2004).

THE CRITICAL STUDY OF TERRORISM

The critical study of terrorism, sometimes called critical terrorism studies (CTS), is an emerging movement within the broader study of terrorism that seeks to challenge the dominance of orthodox, problem-solving approaches. It has its roots in the work of such critical scholars as Joseba Zulaika and William Douglass (1996), Michael Stohl and George Lopez (1986), and Ronald Crelinsten (1987). More recently, it has been spearheaded by, among others, a group of scholars within the British International Studies Association who have, among other initiatives, founded a new academic journal called *Critical Studies on Terrorism*. The development of CTS has its intellectual roots in the work of the aforementioned earlier critical scholars who published studies that challenged accepted assumptions and knowledge within the broader field. To a certain extent, the current evolution of CTS mirrors the 1990s emergence of critical security studies (CSS), which strove to redefine security beyond state security to include human security (see Booth 2004; Krause and Williams 1997). Similar to the critical turn within security studies, since 2005 CTS scholars have set out to deepen and expand key debates about terrorism and offer challenges to orthodox views about our common understanding of the terrorist threat, the preconditions and roots of terrorism, the importance of state terrorism, and the methods of countering terrorism.

In contrast to the orthodox approach, which since September 11 has tended to focus solely on the terrorism of nonstate actors, particularly Islamic groups, CTS scholars have argued that there is a need to redress the current imbalance by also examining the much greater and more serious problem of state terrorism (Blakeley 2007; Sluka 2000). The critical approach also aims to provide a more grounded appraisal of the place of terrorism in contemporary life and challenge fear-mongering approaches that encourage moral panics about terrorism—as we discuss in the following section (see Jackson 2007c; Mueller 2006).

Methodologically, critical scholars hold to a number of key commitments. First, they do not a priori take the legitimacy of the status quo for granted but try to look beyond the terrorism label. Following from this, they are committed to contextualizing political violence within its broader social and political context in order to better understand how existing "institutions and social and power relations" have contributed to its emergence (cf. Gunning 2007b; Toros and Gunning 2009). They seek to de-essentialize violent behavior, locating it within the wider web of nonviolent behavior and remaining sensitive to the possibility of transformation (which is why they typically refrain from the totalizing practice of labeling organizations or people terrorist, reserving the term "terrorist" to describe certain types of acts). Second, they are committed to making the study of terrorism more theoretically robust (Toros and Gunning 2009). Third, they endeavor to be transparent about their own allegiances and affiliations so that others can critique their work accordingly. They also actively seek more effective ways, such as the use of coresearchers and intersubjective analysis, to interrogate their own subjective stances. Fourth, while taking into account the impact of secrecy and difficulties in access to sources and data and the limitations this places on scholarly work on terrorism, critical scholars take seriously the need to "talk to terrorists" and their supporters in order to more fully understand their perspectives and motivations.

Most important, following from the focal shift from state to human security, a critical approach entails a commitment to "doing no harm" to either themselves or those they work with; further, any risk is assessed and willingly undertaken by those exposed to it. Recognizing that terrorism research impacts on a variety of different groups, including policy makers, security practitioners, the public, and the so-called "suspect communities" from which terrorists are drawn (Hillyard 1993), critical scholars are committed to engaging with all these end-user groups, rather than privileging only policy makers (Gunning 2007a, 2007b). While critical scholars have sometimes been attacked for being sympathetic to terrorists, they themselves see the goal of their work as the eradication of the use of political terror by any actor, through striving to challenge the assumption that terrorist violence can be an effective way of achieving political goals (Breen Smyth 2007).

In contrast to some orthodox scholars, critical scholars argue that political violence, both terrorism and violent forms of counterterrorism by the authorities, tends to produce a dynamic of bifurcation. Critical scholarship, they argue, should strive not to reproduce such bifurcations—between traditional and critical studies of political terror, state and nonstate actors, and dominant and suspect communities, for example—since these intellectual ghettos created by the dynamic of violence tend to reproduce the conditions under which violence first emerges. A critical approach, in other words, aims to break cycles of violence and avoid totalizing analyses of power relations that allocate the blame or responsibility solely to either state or nonstate actors. Instead, critical scholars advocate an analysis that reflects the complexity of power relations at state, substate and suprastate levels and the ubiquity and involvement of all these parties in malevolence, abuse of power, and breaches of human rights.

In contrast to some recent orthodox scholarship that takes the September 11, 2001, events as the starting point for the analysis of terrorism, critical scholars argue the importance of recognizing that the political use of terror is a consistent historical pattern and that there is much to be learned from the long and varied history of terrorism. In a similar vein, they argue that the experience of the United States on September 11, 2001, was not so removed from the experience of other societies that have experienced sustained terrorist attacks; it is crucial, they contend, to avoid exceptionalizing the experience of any society, historical period, or set of events.

Almost uniquely in the broader terrorism studies field, critical scholars have argued the importance of the gendered nature of political violence and terror. In the study of political violence and terror, the neglect of gender analysis and lack of attention to such issues as masculinity is problematic, according to them, and they advocate a greater incorporation of gender analysis into scholarship in the field (see Sylvester and Parashar 2009). Last, critical scholars have pointed to the legal environment in which scholarship on terrorism takes place, in which certain rights have been eroded and such new offenses as the glorification of terrorism have been created. Critical scholars hold that it is their duty to defend as far as possible the ethical and intellectual integrity of their work within this challenging legal environment.

Having outlined some of the main differences between orthodox and critical approaches to the study of terrorism, we turn now to some of the key issues at the heart of terrorism studies. The following sections briefly describe what a critical perspective brings to the question of the nature of the terrorist threat, the causes of terrorism, and the responses to terrorism.

THE TERRORISM THREAT IN CONTEXT: RHETORIC AND REALITY

Since the 1980s, terrorism has been viewed as a very serious threat to the security of Western countries. For many years, and particular since the September 11, 2001, attacks, politicians, media commentators, and many orthodox scholars have suggested that terrorism is the most serious security threat in the world today; that it threatens the functioning of democracy and the stability of the international system. They have argued that terrorists can strike anyone, anywhere, and with virtually any weapon; that it is only a matter of when, not if, terrorists will attack using weapons of mass destruction; and that the new forms of religiously inspired suicide terrorism are far more dangerous than the old forms of nationalist or ideological terrorism because they are aimed at causing mass casualties. These arguments can be found in numerous speeches by politicians, in media reporting, in public reports by think tanks and in a great many academic books and articles by orthodox scholars (see Jackson 2005, 2007a, 2007b; Mueller 2006).

Critical scholars do not take popular arguments regarding the terrorism threat at face value simply because they are widely accepted; they argue, instead, that the terrorism threat has been greatly exaggerated. In the first place, they point out that year-by-year terrorism is responsible, on average, for a few hundred deaths over the entire world. While still a tragedy for the victims, this number does not add up to more than a minor risk to personal safety. Certainly, the deaths caused by terrorist violence are dwarfed by the 40,000 people who die each day from hunger, a half million annual deaths caused by hand guns, two million annual traffic-related deaths, three to four million killed by influenza and HIV/AIDS every year and the tens of millions killed by state repression. It has been estimated that governments have deliberately killed nearly 200 million of their own and other states' citizens during the past century in repression, mass murder, forcible starvations, and genocide. Using such statistics, it has been calculated that the risk of any particular individual being killed in a terrorist attack ranks somewhere near the risk of being killed by home repair accidents, lightning strikes, meteors, or bee stings (Jackson 2007c; Mueller 2006).

Second, critical scholars point out that the vast majority of terrorist attacks take place in a relatively small number of countries beset by intense political conflict, among them Israel-Palestine, Russia-Chechnya, Kashmir, Colombia,

Algeria, Iraq, Afghanistan, Pakistan, and Spain. The reality is that most countries in the world experience little to no terrorism at all. In addition, an analysis of terrorist attacks over many decades shows that they tend to strike at symbolic targets in major cities. This means that while it is strictly true that terrorists could strike anywhere and at any time, it is much more likely that their attacks will be confined to a small set of specific targets.

Third, the attacks on the Twin Towers in 2001 raised the issue of mass casualty terrorism and the threat of what has been called superterrorism or catastrophic terrorism. As a consequence, many politicians and scholars have suggested that there is a real risk of terrorist groups using such weapons of mass destruction as dirty bombs or chemical attacks. They point to the Tokyo underground sarin attack and the attacks against New York and Washington as evidence of increasing terrorist ruthlessness. Many critical scholars, by contrast, argue that, despite a small number of purported attempts, terrorists are unlikely to use weapons of mass destruction because the risks and costs are too great: such weapons are extremely difficult to obtain and deploy effectively compared with conventional weaponry; the risk of massive retaliation by the target state is very high; and the use of such weapons would undoubtedly undermine support and sympathy for the group (see Jenkins 1998; Mueller 2006; Sprinzak 1998). This explains why despite the existence of hundreds of terrorist groups and tens of thousands of terrorist attacks over the past forty years, there have been no more than a handful of attacks using weapons of mass destruction that have killed a little over a dozen people.

Other facts and arguments that contradict popular perceptions of the major threat posed by terrorism include these: the number of terrorist attacks around the world has remained steady or even declined in recent decades (depending upon the data source); as a whole, the great majority of terrorist attacks are against property rather than persons; mass casualty terrorism is extremely rare (out of more than 10,000 recorded terrorist attacks since 1968, only around 20 or so have caused more than 100 fatalities); and so-called rogue states are unlikely to provide weapons of mass destruction to terrorist groups because the risk that they would lose control of the situation is too high. Critical scholars also point out that no country has ever been seriously threatened by terrorism, although a number of states have experienced severe instability when violent counterterrorist campaigns have undermined social and political order.

What the aforementioned facts and arguments point to is a large and puzzling gap between the perception and the reality of the terrorist threat. In spite of the low probability of being hurt in a terrorist incident, people are far more frightened of terrorism than they are of much more common risks, including vehicle or work-related accidents, disease, crime and the like. Critical scholars argue that this gap needs to be interrogated: how does a relatively minor risk to personal safety and social stability become the basis for a global "war on terrorism," the enacting of numerous new laws and the spending of vast public funds on counterterrorism?

The answer lies in the realms of psychology, sociology, and politics. From a psychological perspective, it can be shown that people fear violence from other humans, particularly if it seems random, more than they do the violence of accidents or natural processes. Such fears are enhanced by the continuous and graphic coverage of the media. In addition, sociologists have noted that many Western countries have developed a "culture of fear," despite the fact that people in these societies have never lived longer, safer, and more secure lives than at any time in history. From this perspective, the fear of terrorism is part of the broader fear of crime, youth delinquency, global pandemics, immigrants, cell phone towers, flesh-eating diseases, and the like (see Furedi 2002; Glassner 1999).

For critical scholars, however, the most important answer comes from an analysis of the actors who directly benefit from people's fears of terrorism (see Kassimeris 2007). For example, politicians who exploit the public's fear of terrorism can benefit from reelection, silencing critics, creating a more docile public, and bringing in such measures not directly related to terrorism as requiring identity cards and limiting civil liberties. Similarly, the military and the security services can all claim greater resources and respect in the fight against terrorism, while the media and many academics may achieve a greater profile, sell more books and documentaries, and receive funding for research. A great many private firms also benefit from the fear of terrorism–among them the pharmaceutical companies who provide vaccines and decontamination suits, private security firms who provide airport security, military contractors who resupply the military, and the like. In combination, all these actors have a vested interest in exaggerating the terrorist threat.

TYPES OF TERRORISM

In contrast to popular perceptions and the work of many orthodox terrorism scholars who tend to equate very different groups and events around the world into a single phenomenon, there are, in fact, a great many differences between campaigns of terrorism, depending upon the actors who engage in it, the primary strategies they employ, their intended aims and ideological motivations, and the historical, political, and social contexts within which they emerge. Critical scholars of terrorism argue that the unique context and features of different groups are more important than their similarities and that treating terrorism as a generic phenomenon, as many orthodox scholars do, usually does more to obscure than illuminate its nature and causes. For example, there is very little important knowledge to be gained by comparing Al Qaeda with the Unabomber, or the European Red Brigades with the Argentinian death squads.

At the broadest level, if a typology is to be devised, a distinction can be made between state terrorism and nonstate terrorism or between "terrorism from above" and "terrorism from below" (see Martin 2003). State terrorism includes the use of open or clandestine violence against domestic opponents, as well as the direct or indirect involvement in terrorism against foreign or external enemies. Typically, state terrorism involves the widespread use of torture, death squads, disappearances and extrajudicial killings to terrorize the state's own people into submission; and the sponsorship of terrorist groups, the use of civilian-directed aerial bombing, and the direct use of secret agents to terrorize the citizens of other states (see Stohl and Lopez 1986). Importantly, the state's attempt to counter terrorism can itself become terrorism if it is disproportionate, indiscriminate, above the law, and abuses human rights (Goodin, 2006, 69–73). Nonstate terrorism, on the other hand, refers to groups or individuals acting outside of the authority of the state, usually directed at a particular government and in pursuit of nationalist or ideological aims.

Within the basic division of terrorism from above or below, the problem of state terrorism appears to be far more serious than that of nonstate terrorism, as terrorism by governments has killed tens of millions of people in the previous century, while terrorism from below has resulted in tens of thousands of deaths (Sluka 2000). Critical scholars note, however, that the traditional or orthodox terrorism studies field remains almost solely focused on the subject of nonstate terrorism. They also note that many governments, including Western governments, have defined terrorism as actions engaged in by nonstate actors, which means that states by definition can never be accused of terrorism no matter what they do. Critical scholars argue that this failure to analyze state terrorism means that the field is politically biased toward states; more important, it creates the impression that Western states do not engage in terrorism and that they do not need to take care in ensuring that their counterterrorism actions do not cross the line into terrorism. Consequently, they argue, there is an urgent need to "bring the state back in" to terrorism research (Blakeley 2007).

Within the category of nonstate terrorism, a distinction is sometimes drawn between professional and amateur terrorism. In the former category are those groups with sophisticated networks and support structures who are fighting for clearly articulated nationalist or ideological causes and who have accumulated tactical experience over a long period of sustained struggle. The Northern Ireland paramilitaries like the IRA and UVF, Basque nationalists in Spain, Palestinian militant groups, the Tamil Tigers, Al Qaeda, and a great many other nationalist and ideologically driven groups would fall into this category. Amateur terrorism, on the other hand, refers to such lone individual terrorists as the Unabomber, Timothy McVeigh, and Richard Reid or to millennial groups like the Aum Shinrikyo cult in Japan. These groups lack the tactical experience and support networks of professional terrorists and often have only rudimentary political programs.

Within the professional terrorism category, it is common to distinguish between nationalist, ideological, and more controversially, religious groups. Nationalist terrorism most often emerges from an ongoing struggle for self-determination or regional autonomy: Palestinian, Northern Irish, Kurdish, Basque, Tamil, Chechen, Armenian, Iraqi, Sikh, and Kashmiri terrorism are all examples. Ideological terrorism reached its zenith in the 1970s, although there are still plenty of contemporary examples. Motivated by extreme right-wing or left-wing ideologies, such groups typically hope to provoke social revolution through violent acts: the Red Brigades in Italy, the Weathermen in America, the Japanese Red Army, the Tupamaros in Uruguay, Shining Path in Peru, and Action Directe in France are examples.

The notion of religious terrorism is a recent addition to existing typologies and refers to groups with primarily religious motives for their violence. The term is usually applied to "Islamic fundamentalist" groups like Al Qaeda, although it is also used to describe right-wing antiabortion groups as well as cults like Bhagwan Shree Rajneesh in Oregon and the Lord's Resistance Army in Uganda. Controversy surrounds whether religion acts as a primary motive or whether it is simply a mobilizing tool for what are essentially political goals (see the next section). In addition, many critical scholars feel that the religious terrorism label is often employed as a political tool to paint certain groups as fanatics lacking genuine political grievances and the capacity to compromise, thus legitimizing exceptional counterterrorism measures (see Gunning, 2007c; Jackson 2007a).

Other typologies and subcategories frequently applied to terrorist groups include revolutionary terrorism, dissident terrorism, nihilist terrorism, communal terrorism, criminal terrorism, narco-terrorism, ecoterrorism, cyber terrorism, and international terrorism. What they illustrate, apart from the highly contested domain of the field, is that terrorism covers an incredibly diverse array of actors, contexts, motivations, strategies, and tactics. In an important sense, it is crucial to acknowledge how each terrorist group emerges from a unique combination of historical and political contexts.

THE CAUSES OF TERRORISM: PSYCHOLOGY, POLITICS, AND RELIGION

Numerous causes have been suggested for nonstate terrorism, ranging from mental illness and religious indoctrination to poverty and political exclusion. Critical approaches to terrorism do not have a unified stance on the origins of terrorism. While some critical scholars are skeptical of the entire notion of causation, regarding it as too embedded in the positivist, problem-solving perspectives they are seeking to critique, others accept the notion of causation but are wary of monocausal explanations. What they all share is a skeptical approach to accepted explanations and an acute awareness of the way causal explanations can be used to depoliticize terrorists and legitimate specific counterterrorism policies. If, for instance, terrorists can be shown to be mentally ill or motivated solely by greed, there is no need to take their political demands seriously, thereby legitimizing a coercive response that eschews direct negotiations.

One set of orthodox explanations focuses on psychological factors. At one end of this spectrum is the by-now widely discredited argument that terrorists are psychopathological deviants, driven to violence by mental disorders. Both critical and orthodox scholars have pointed out that the evidence for this argument simply does not add up and that the dominant characteristic of terrorists is their normality (see Horgan 2003; Silke 1998). In other words, while psychopathological factors may play a role in isolated individual cases, as a broader explanation for why political violence occurs, it is an inadequate model.

A related set of explanations revolves around religious beliefs and the notion that religion can be particularly effective at suspending psychological barriers against killing. One popular theory holds that "religious terrorists" are more likely to kill with abandon and less likely to compromise because they are imbued with the belief that the killing is part of a divine plan, thus rendering pragmatic and political concerns largely irrelevant (e.g., Hoffman, 2006). Here, too, critical scholars and some orthodox scholars have pointed out that the evidence is not conclusive (see Copeland 2001; Duyvesteyn 2004; Spencer 2006). Ideologically motivated terrorists have been just as indiscriminate and intransigent as religiously motivated terrorists, and many religiously motivated organizations engaged in terrorism have ended up compromising on their end-goals for pragmatic, this-worldly reasons (for a critical analysis of the role of religion in Hamas's behavior, see Gunning, 2007c). The nonstate organization that has carried out most suicide bombings, a tactic typically associated with religious fanaticism, is not religious but Marxist-nationalist (Sri Lanka's Tamil Tigers); furthermore, most conflicts in which suicide tactics have been used are characterized not by religious conflict per se but by occupation (see Pape 2005). At the same time, religion often plays a role in motivating insurgents and demonizing the enemy, particularly in conflicts where the religion of the occupying force differs from that of those being occupied.

More credible models can be found among psychosociological approaches that look at the impact of the wider political and socioeconomic environment on terrorists (see Bjorgo 2005). Among the most enduring models are "relative deprivation" theories, according to which political violence is more likely when certain population groups feel deprived socially, economically, or politically relative to other population groups (Gurr 1970). Such theories have been critiqued for their assumption that the frustration of expectations leads to aggression and hence to political violence (Horgan 2003). The reality is that not all those who feel aggrieved or deprived turn to political violence or even have the opportunity to do so. Yet in many cases a perception of relative deprivation can be found to have played a role, particularly when coupled with "social distancing" or "social polarization." One merit of these alternative theories is that they neither depoliticize those who turn to violence nor exonerate the status quo from having potentially contributed to the violence.

A fourth set of explanations has come from those who focus on economic factors (for an overview, see Lia 2004). One subset of such approaches concurs with those who critique relative deprivation theories, arguing that the presence of grievances alone cannot explain political violence. Grievances exist everywhere, yet political violence, and particularly terrorist violence, is actually relatively rare. What explains the occurrence of political violence, then, is the presence or absence of material and organizational resources. While a useful corrective to the grievance-based models, these so-called greed models have served both to depoliticize nonstate insurgents and to ignore such other aspects as the importance of political and ideological factors.

Economic and psychosociological explanations overlap in the argument that poverty is linked to terrorism. A number of quantitative studies suggest that violent conflicts are more likely to occur in or between poor or underdeveloped countries, whereas an increase in wealth has been found to lead to a decrease in support for political violence (see Collier and Sambanis 2002; Cramer 2003; Fearon and Laitin 2003). Explanations offered range from the argument that economic development, especially if accompanied by democratic transition, fosters domestic peace—that is, those who are wealthier have more to lose from participating in an insurgency—to the notion that richer states have more resources to deter insurgencies. Critical scholars and some orthodox scholars, however, point out that those engaged in terrorist violence are not predominantly poor but often better educated and better off than the rest of the population; in addition, they note, terrorism often occurs in states that have experienced rapid economic development and political liberalization, as well as in economically developed mature democracies. In addition, levels of poverty cannot always explain levels of violence. Algeria, for instance, experienced less urban poverty than Egypt in the early 1990s, yet it saw far worse violence during that decade than did Egypt (Hafez 2003). In sum, poverty and economic inequality clearly do play a role, but a more robust explanation needs to include an analysis of such political opportunity structures as the relative strength of opposition groups, existing ideological and cultural frameworks, and the nature of the state, including its relative openness and its repressive capacity.

A number of political explanations focus on the nature of the state. One such argument is that political exclusion is a key cause of terrorism. Political exclusion, whether it concerns ethnic, religious, or socioeconomic groups, plays a factor in a number of conflicts, and nonstate actors engaging in terrorism are often from outside the political elite. However, as with explanations of poverty or relative deprivation, critical scholars point out that political exclusion in itself is not an adequate explanation (Dalacoura 2006). Not all those who are politically excluded turn to terrorism, and, in some cases, political inclusion can also lead to an increase in terrorism. Much depends on the type of political in- or exclusion, the repressive nature of the regime, and the subculture and resources of the violent opposition, among other things. If political exclusion is accompanied by a strong repressive apparatus, the opportunity for terrorism may not exist. Conversely, political inclusion may generate expectations that cannot be met, which, if accompanied by greater political freedoms, can increase opportunities for terrorism—particularly if those advocating violence cannot rally the masses to protest en masse. This is one of the reasons some scholars have argued that democracy itself can be a cause of terrorism.

RESPONDING TO TERROR: OPTIONS AND ALTERNATIVES

Contrary to popular perceptions, responses to terrorism range along a spectrum from the "hard" iron fist approach, which entails punitive and extraordinary security measures, through to intelligence gathering, law enforcement, and the "soft" velvet glove approach advocated by those who prioritize the countering of political disaffection through what has sometimes been referred to as a hearts-and-minds approach. More specifically, soft approaches include such measures as entering into direct negotiations with violent groups, promoting dialogue and understanding with suspect communities, acknowledging and rectifying grievances, and enacting a range of social and political reforms. A great many, but not all, orthodox scholars appear to support such hard approaches as increasing security measures, restricting civil liberties, killing and capturing terrorist group members, using harsh interrogation, engaging in military disruption, instituting policies of deterrence, and using coercive diplomacy against state sponsors of terrorism. They often dismiss direct negotiations with groups engaging in terrorism as being naïve or too soft, in spite of the (varying) success of protracted secret negotiations with such groups in the South African, Palestinian, and Northern Ireland cases, among others.

Critical approaches recognize that responses to terrorism are often driven by such political imperatives as the need for politicians to be seen as proactive against the terrorist threat, especially in the wake of an attack. Consequently, many hard counterterrorist measures have been introduced in the immediate aftermath of high-profile terrorist attacks. Arguably, such measures, while fulfilling the political need, not necessarily effective or rooted in evidence-based assessments. The declaration of the War on Terror, wars in Afghanistan and Iraq, restrictions on civil liberties, the use of torture and assassination against terrorist suspects, and the formation of the Department of Homeland Security in the United States, for example, all of which followed the attacks on the World Trade Center in September 2001, have arguably not only failed to improve security—despite some short-term achievements—but also entailed the loss of many American and British troops, increased opposition to U.S. foreign policies, and increased the likelihood of further attacks.

Some commentators argue that while legislation may be necessary for political or practical policing reasons, it is the hearts-and-minds approach, particularly opening negotiations with terrorist groups, that brings about an end to terrorism and ultimately saves lives (see, e.g., Breen Smyth 2008). Not only have some seen the softer approaches as more effective in improving both human and state security, but others have argued that hard punitive approaches that undermine human rights are counterproductive in that they increase political alienation and drive more recruits into the arms of terrorist organizations (Foot 2007). An example of this is the impact of the policy of internment without trial and the Bloody Sunday shootings in 1970s Northern Ireland, which increased recruitment into the IRA. More recently, when asked about factors that led to the London bomb attacks in 2005, British Muslim students reported that the war in Iraq and British foreign policy were the two most important factors (FOSIS 2005). Similarly, Human Rights Watch, in their briefing paper *Neither Just nor Effective* (2004), argued that counterterrorism measures had diminished the confidence of the Muslim community in the security services and the police, the level of cooperation which these services could enjoy in Muslim areas was reduced, and overall, the new measures were counterproductive to counterterrorism (see also Human Rights Watch 2007).

In contrast to the military-dominated U.S. model, counterterrorist operations in Britain have largely followed the law enforcement model of counterterrorism where the police perform a dual role, that of the prime counterterrorist agency alongside that of ordinary civil policing. While the two roles overlap, for example, in relation to extortion or money laundering and terrorism, there are also some difficult tensions in fulfilling these roles simultaneously. In their antiterrorist mode, police collect intelligence about certain communities, thereby affecting the relationship between the community and the police and often reducing that community's willingness to engage with or assist the police.

In Britain, the law in relation to terrorism and counterterrorist measures has evolved over time (see Table 20.1). The modern-day Metropolitan Police, under Sir Ian Blair, created a single Metropolitan Police Counter-Terrorism Command by combining the investigative parts of the Special Operations Units SO12 and SO13 to form Counter-Terrorism Command, and a Muslim Contact Unit to perform community relations and community liaison functions. However, counterterrorist policing in England, Scotland, and Wales has its origins in the late-nineteenth-century when the Metropolitan Police established the Special Irish Office in response to what Frank Gregory (2007) refers to as "the Irish problem of the period."

Critical scholars point to the inherent problems of some current legislative responses to terrorism and, in particular, their erosion of historical protections of human rights and their failure to recognize evidence-based research relating to effectiveness. Part IV of the Anti-Terrorism, Crime and Security Act (2001), for example, was held by the Law Lords in 2004 to be incompatible with Britain's obligations under the European Convention on Human Rights. Similarly, legal challenges to the Prevention of Terrorism Act (2005) led to an Appeal Court ruling in 2006 that a number of control orders were contrary to Article V of the European Convention on Human Rights. Following the London bombings in July 2005, the British government proposed to extend the period suspects could be detained from 14 to 90 days and defined three new offenses: carrying out acts preparatory to terrorism, indirect incitement, and giving training or receiving training in the use of hazardous substances for terrorist purposes. Later, even more restrictive measures were proposed, including the offense of glorifying terrorism, a revisiting of the maximum permissible period of detention for suspects, the proscription of the Islamist group Hizb ut Tahir, and the closing down of mosques where radical views were expressed. However, the extension of the period of detention to 90 days faced parliamentary resistance, and there was skepticism about the workability of the offense of glorifying terrorism.

Critical scholars argue that the development of such measures demonstrates a need for governments to avoid trading off security and liberty and for rigorous research into the relative effectiveness of different kinds of counterterrorism measures. In particular, there is a real need for solid evidence about the effectiveness and consequences of both the harder and the softer approaches to counterterrorism. They also argue that historical studies on such other cases as Northern Ireland, Canada, Sri Lanka, and Spain, as well as elsewhere, could furnish important lessons for when governments come to designing and implementing current policies.

CONCLUSION

There is little doubt that terrorism is and will continue to be a subject of tremendous importance over the next few decades, particularly in the field of security. What we have attempted to do in this short chapter is demonstrate how a critical approach to the study of terrorism can fill in important gaps, raise new

Table 20.1 The Evolution of British Counterterrorist Legislation

The Evolution of British Counterterrorist Legislation

Date	Legislation	Target	Measures
1800–1921	At least 105 separate Coercion Acts introduced in Ireland	Irish insurrection and terrorism	Various
1922 renewed annually	Civil Authorities (Special Powers) Act (Northern Ireland), 1922	Irish insurrection and terrorism	Authorizes government "to take all such steps and issue all such orders as may be necessary for preserving the peace and maintaining order," including the death penalty for explosives offenses
1926	Emergency Powers Act (Northern Ireland), 1926	Irish insurrection and terrorism	Provides for the declaration of a state of emergency
1954	Flags and Emblems (Display) Act (Northern Ireland), 1954	Irish insurrection and terrorism	Protects the display of the Union flag and provides for removal of "provocative emblems"
1973	Northern Ireland (Emergency Provisions) Act 1973	Republican terrorism in Northern Ireland	
1974	Prevention of Terrorism (Temporary Provisions) Act	"The Irish problem" in Britain	Authorizes powers of arrest, detention, and proscription
2000	Terrorism Act (2000)	Irish and international terrorism	Consolidated and made counterterrorist legislation permanent; defined terrorism and established permanent mechanisms for proscription

(*Continued*)

Table 20.1 (*Continued*)

The Evolution of British Counterterrorist Legislation

Date	Legislation	Target	Measures
			of terrorist groups; created new offense of inciting terrorism abroad; expanded definitions of "receiving or providing weapons training"; empowered police to establish cordons in counterterrorist operations and to detain suspects for up to 14 days
2001	Anti-Terrorism, Crime and Security Act (2001)	Islamist groups	Froze terrorist assets; promoted information sharing about counterterrorism; (Part IV) allowed indefinite detention in Britain of foreign nationals suspected of involvement in terrorism; proscribed incitement of religious and racial hatred and violence; provided for security of aviation and nuclear industries; consolidated security of dangerous substances; extended police powers to the British Transport Police and Ministry of Defence Police; requires the United Kingdom to meet international protocols on countering bribery and corruption

2005	Prevention of Terrorism Act (2005)	Islamist groups	Established 12-month control orders, which could be made with the approval of a judge against any person suspected of terrorism, thereby imposing a range of restrictions short of house arrest
2006	Terrorism Act (2006)	Islamist groups	Established new offenses of committing acts preparatory to terrorism, encouraging terrorism, disseminating terrorist publications, and giving or receiving training in terrorist techniques; extended police power of entering and searching property owned or controlled by terrorist suspects; extended permissible period of detention of suspects from 14 to 28 days; created capacity to proscribe organizations that glorify terrorism

Source: Authors.

kinds of questions, and challenge dominant ideas. In particular, there are four main contributions that critical terrorism studies can make to our understanding of this important phenomenon. First, it contributes new knowledge and theories that help to deconstruct and debunk many of the popular myths and misconceptions about terrorism. Second, it reveals the ways in which language—that is, discourse, and particularly the naming of terrorism—is not a neutral process but has political consequences for the terrorists, their communities, and those that do the naming. Third, it brings in a number of neglected aspects to the study of terrorism, including the importance of history and context, gender analysis, state terrorism, and the like. Finally, critical approaches to terrorism open up new ways of thinking about responses to terrorism, in part by questioning dominant assumptions about security itself, the failure to take note of history, and the efficacy of violence and force.

Although it could be argued that critical terrorism studies is simply a call for better and more rigorous research on terrorism, it involves far more than this. Instead, we suggest that critical approaches to terrorism entail a series of important theoretical and methodological commitments (see Breen Smyth 2007; Gunning 2007a, 2007b; Jackson 2007b). First, critical scholars begin with an acceptance that the term "terrorism" is a political label and a socially constructed category. Second, critical scholars accept that knowledge of terrorism can never be wholly objective but will always have political consequences. In other words, they accept that knowledge always works for someone and for something. Third, critical scholars are committed to transparency about their own values and political standpoints, particularly as they relate to the interests and values of their own states. Fourth, critical scholars are committed to contextualizing political violence and examining how the status quo contributed to its emergence. Fifth, they are dedicated to expanding the focus of research to include the use of terrorism by states, including Western states; to examining the wider nonviolent aspects of violent organizations; and to integrating gender as a key area of focus. Sixth, critical scholars are committed to responsible research ethics, including a refusal to cooperate with state counterterrorism projects that include the use of torture, such illegal practices as rendition, or the victimization of entire suspect communities. Lastly, critical scholars share a broad commitment to normative values that reject all forms of civilian-directed violence and that promotes a broad notion of human security. These commitments, we believe, give critical terrorism studies a distinctive profile among the broader terrorism studies field.

FURTHER READING

Goodin, R. *What's Wrong with Terrorism?* Cambridge: Polity Press, 2006.
Martin, G. *Understanding Terrorism: Challenges, Perspectives, and Issues*. London: Sage, 2003.
Mueller, J. *Overblown: How Politicians and the Terrorism Industry Inflate National Security Threats and Why We Believe Them*. New York: Free Press, 2006.
Ranstorp, M., ed. *Mapping Terrorism Research: State of the Art, Gaps and Future Directions*. London: Routledge, 2006.

Silke, A., ed. *Research on Terrorism: Trends, Achievements and Failures*. London: Frank Cass, 2004.
Zulaika, J., and W. Douglass. *Terror and Taboo: The Follies, Fables and Faces of Terrorism*. London: Routledge, 1996.

REFERENCES

Blakeley, R. 2007. Bringing the state back into terrorism studies. *European Political Science* 6: 228–35.

Bjorgo, T., ed. 2005. *Root causes of terrorism: Myths, reality and ways forward*. London: Routledge.

Booth, K., ed. 2004. *Critical security studies and world politics*. Boulder, CO: Lynne Rienner.

Breen Smyth, M. 2007. A critical research agenda for the study of political terror. *European Political Science* 6: 260–67.

———. 2008. Lessons learned in counter-terrorism in Northern Ireland: An interview with Peter Sheridan. *Critical Studies on Terrorism* 1, 41–123.

Burnett, J., and Whyte, D. 2005. Embedded expertise and the new terrorism. *Journal for Crime, Conflict and the Media* 1: 1–18.

Collier, P., and N. Sambanis. 2002. Understanding civil war: A new agenda. *Journal of Conflict Resolution* 46: 3–12.

Copeland, T. 2001. Is the new terrorism really new? An analysis of the new paradigm for terrorism. *Journal of Conflict Studies* 21: 91–105.

Cox, R. 1981. Social forces, states and world orders: Beyond international relations theory. *Millennium: Journal of International Studies* 10: 126–55.

Cramer, C. 2003. Does inequality cause conflict? *Journal of International Development* 15: 397–412.

Crelinsten, R. 1987. Terrorism as political communication. In *Contemporary research on terrorism*, ed. P. Wilkinson and A. Stewart. Aberdeen, Scot.: Aberdeen University Press.

Crenshaw, M. 1981. The causes of terrorism. *Comparative Politics* 13: 379–99.

Dalacoura, K. 2006. Islamist terrorism and the Middle East democratic deficit: Political exclusion, repression and the causes of extremism. *Democratization* 13: 508–25.

Duyvesteyn, I. 2004. How new is the new terrorism? *Studies in Conflict & Terrorism* 27: 439–54.

Fearon, J., and D. Laitin. 2003. Ethnicity, insurgency, and civil war. *American Political Science Review* 97: 75–90.

FOSIS (Federation of Student Islamic Societies in the UK and Ireland). 2005. The voice of Muslim students: A report into the attitudes and perceptions of Muslim students following the July 7th London attacks: Results from the FOSIS Muslim students' survey. FOSIS. Available online at http://www.fosis.org.uk/resources/ (accessed December 26, 2007).

Foot, R. 2007. The United Nations, counter terrorism and human rights: Institutional adaptation and embedded ideas. *Human Rights Quarterly* 29: 489–514.

Furedi, F. 2002. *Culture of fear: Risk-taking and the morality of low expectation*. Rev. ed. London: Continuum.

George, A. 1991. The discipline of terrorology. In *Western state terrorism*, ed. A. George. Cambridge: Polity Press.

Glassner, B. 1999. *The culture of fear: Why Americans are afraid of the wrong things*. New York: Basic Books.

Goodin, R. 2006. *What's wrong with terrorism?* Cambridge: Polity Press.

Gregory, F. 2007. Police and counter-terrorism in the UK. In *Homeland security in the UK: Future preparedness for terrorist attack since 9/11*, ed. P. Wilkinson. London: Routledge.

Gunning, J. 2007a. Babies and bathwaters: Reflecting on the pitfalls of critical terrorism studies. *European Political Science* 6: 236–43.

———. 2007b. A case for critical terrorism studies? *Government & Opposition* 42: 363–94.

———. 2007c. *Hamas in politics: Democracy, religion, violence*. London: Hurst.

Gurr, T. 1970. *Why men rebel*. Princeton, NJ: Princeton University Press.

Hafez, M. 2003. *Why Muslims rebel: Repression and resistance in the Islamic world*. Boulder, CO: Lynne Rienner.

Hillyard, P. 1993. *Suspect community: People's experience of the prevention of terrorism acts in Britain*. London: Pluto Press.

Horgan, J. 2003. The search for the terrorist personality. In *Terrorists, victims and society: Psychological perspectives on terrorism and its consequences*, ed. A. Silke. Chichester, UK: John Wiley & Sons.

———. 2005. *The psychology of terrorism*. London: Routledge.

Human Rights Watch. 2004. Neither just nor effective: Indefinite detention without trial in the United Kingdom under part 4 of the Anti-Terrorism, Crime and Security Act 2001. Human Rights Watch Briefing Paper. Available online at http://hrw.org/backgrounder/eca/uk/index.htm (accessed December 26, 2007).

———. 2007. UK: Counter the threat or counterproductive? Commentary on proposed counterterrorism measures. Human Rights Watch. Available online at http://www.hrw.org/backgrounder/eca/uk1007/1.htm#_Toc 180299933 (accessed December 26, 2007).

Jackson, R. 2005. *Writing the war on terrorism: Language, politics and counterterrorism*. Manchester, UK: Manchester University Press.

———. 2007a. Constructing enemies: "Islamic terrorism" in political and academic discourse. *Government & Opposition* 42: 394–426.

———. 2007b. The core commitments of critical terrorism studies. *European Political Science* 6: 244–51.

———. 2007c. Playing the politics of fear: Writing the terrorist threat in the war on terrorism. In *Playing politics with terrorism: A user's guide*, ed. G. Kassimeris. New York: Columbia University Press.

Jenkins, B. 1998. Will terrorists go nuclear? A reappraisal. In *The future of terrorism: Violence in the new millennium*, ed. H. Kushner. London: Sage, 225–49.

Kassimeris, G., ed. 2007. *Playing politics with terrorism: A user's guide*. New York: Columbia University Press.

Krause, K., and M. Williams, eds. 1997. *Critical security studies*. Minneapolis: University of Minnesota Press.

Lia, B. 2004. *Causes of terrorism: An expanded and updated review of the literature.* FFI Report. http://rapporter.ffi.no/rapporter/2004/04307.pdf.

Martin, G. 2003. *Understanding terrorism: Challenges, perspectives, and issues.* London: Sage.

Mueller, J. 2006. *Overblown: How politicians and the terrorism industry inflate national security threats and why we believe them.* New York: Free Press.

Pape, R. 2005. *Dying to win: The strategic logic of suicide terrorism.* New York: Random House.

Ranstorp, M., ed. 2006. *Mapping terrorism research: State of the art, gaps and future directions.* London: Routledge.

Richardson, L. 2006. *What terrorists want: Understanding the enemy, containing the threat.* New York: Random House.

Sageman, M. 2004. *Understanding terror networks.* Philadelphia: University of Pennsylvania Press.

Schmid, A., and A. Jongman. 1988. *Political terrorism: A new guide to actors, authors, concepts, databases, theories and literature.* Oxford: North Holland.

Silke, A. 1998. Cheshire-cat logic: The recurring theme of terrorist abnormality in psychological research. *Psychology, Crime and Law* 4: 51–69.

———, ed. 2004. *Research on terrorism: Trends, achievements and failures.* London: Frank Cass.

Sluka, J., ed. 2000. *Death squad: An anthropology of state terror.* Philadelphia: University of Pennsylvania Press.

Spencer, A. 2006. Questioning the concept of "new terrorism." *Peace, Conflict & Development* 8: 1–33.

Sprinzak, E. 1998. The great superterrorism scare. *Foreign Policy* 112: 110–24.

Stohl, M., and G. Lopez, eds. 1986. *Government violence and repression: An agenda for research.* New York: Greenwood Press.

Sylvester, C., and S. Parashar. 2009. The contemporary "Mahabharata" and the many "Draupadis": Bringing gender to critical terrorism studies. In *Critical terrorism studies: A new research agenda*, ed. R. Jackson, M. Breen Smyth, and J. Gunning. London: Routledge.

Toros, H., and J. Gunning. 2009. *Exploring a critical theory approach to terrorism studies.* In *Critical terrorism studies: Framing a new research agenda*, ed. R. Jackson, Breen Smyth and J. Gunning. London: Routledge.

Zulaika, J., and W. Douglass. 1996. *Terror and taboo: The follies, fables and faces of terrorism.* London: Routledge.

21

Trade

Jens L. Mortensen

THE WORLD TRADE ORGANIZATION, SECURITY, AND GLOBALIZATION

One of the high points of globalization was the establishment of the World Trade Organization in 1993 (Saul 2005, 133). One of its main architects called the WTO "a defining moment in modern history" (Sutherland 1993). He continued:

> There are those, not without some reason, who find the post–Cold War world full of new risks and tensions. They posit the choice of whether their security is better assured by erecting defensive barriers against the external world or alternatively by engaging in a broader system of international co-operation and interdependence. . . . Today, the world has chosen openness and co-operation instead of uncertainty and conflict. (Sutherland 1993)

The architects of the WTO had high expectations, perhaps too high. Pro-traders hailed the WTO as a new center of globalization. Critics feared its power. The hype about the WTO has today dampened considerably.[1] The rise of the emerging trading powers and persistent fears of recession in the global North cast shadows on most trade issues today. Energy prices threaten to disrupt global production chains. Food costs have soured. Bubbly property markets make consumers insecure. Investors flee from uncertain markets. Economic globalization is inescapably linked to the provision of security in the positive and negative sense. Among academics and practitioners, there is a growing realization that trade produces insecurity as well as prosperity. Against this background, this contribution to the encyclopedia focuses on how trade and security are linked together in the WTO, that is, in its rules and its governance activities.

The WTO tends to be overlooked in the study of global security. This is increasingly difficult to understand. Trade is one of the key shapers of globalization. As such, it also produces fears and anxieties within governments as well as around the family kitchen table. It cuts across "high" and "low" politics, transcending the domestic and the global spheres of politics. Trade governance is about risk management. The WTO plays a growing role in the management of trade risks. Trade is intrinsic to most contemporary security issues, from underdevelopment, poverty, and food shortage to systemic financial instability and climate change (WEF 2008). Trade is one of the traditional foreign policy tools of states. Today, when confronted with a worsening of the world economy, it is worth recalling that trade is a security provider as well as insecurity generator. Trade often entails a delicate balancing act between prosperity and security.

Trade is indispensable to the analysis of how security and globalization relate to each other. "Security" is an ambiguous term, however. It leaves unanswered such questions as secure from what and security for whom. It is even more complex when security is considered through the lenses of economic globalization. Are trade sanctions legitimate instruments of foreign policy? Or are they thinly disguised protectionism? Should states be allowed to put export restrictions on strategic raw materials? Should states be allowed to selectively tax imports from polluting countries?

This chapter falls into three sections. After a short review of the relevant theoretical perspectives on trade and security—realist, liberal, and constructivist international political economies (IPEs)—the analysis proceeds to focus on how global insecurities are dealt with within WTO dispute settlement. The first part looks at state security. Does the WTO put limitations on the defense of the national interest? Is foreign policy within WTO's jurisdiction? Are governments free to use trade to whatever end they desire? The debate has been intense on these issues. The second part moves beyond traditional conceptions of security and asks how the WTO handles global insecurities of individuals and societies. Are governments allowed to protect their citizen against the human risks from global trade?

THEORETICAL PERSPECTIVES ON TRADE-RELATED SECURITY THREATS

Security and trade can be understood in different ways. Theories on international political economy do not agree on what constitutes trade-related security issues. This chapter understands the concept of security in its broadest sense as a discursive framing of politics, that is, as "the move to take politics beyond the established rules of the game and frames the issue either as a special kind of politics or as above politics" (Buzan, Wæver, and de Wilde 1997, 23). Security is a claim of "exceptionality," a political assertion of the right to do whatever is necessary. Thus, a security framing legitimizes a situation of political exceptionality. It used to be the prerogative of the state to declare such emergencies in the international realm of politics. Today, a host of different actors are making different security claims in order to promote or resist a particular policy.

Trade is also a dynamic concept. It no longer refers exclusively to tariffs and import quotas on cross-border movement of goods. It covers products and services, patent laws and tax policies, domestic as well as international safety and environmental regulations and agreements, and so forth. Most IPE theories see trade as a function of power or the market. This chapter sees trade as something slightly different. Trade is defined not only through negotiation between governments or by the functional need of the global market but also by adjudication. Its precise meaning is hammered out in legal practice by experts and WTO panels as particular policies are tested and examined in the disputes settlement system. Especially in such new and technically complex matters as tax law and environmental or product standards regulations, experts and legal actors have a large measure of "knowledge power," that is, the power to define meanings of the rules (Finnamore and Barnnet 2004).

Most theory operates with much less fluid conceptualizations of trade and security. Historically, realists points out, trade has always been subordinated to the interests of state power. As Michael Mastanduno (1998, 829) writes, "The use of economic instruments to promote security goals was a matter of routine as the leading states sought to exploit asymmetries in their economic and strategic relationships with each other and lesser powers." Security concerns will always triumph over societal ones. It is a manifestation of power. Today, economic nationalist discourses are rarely used openly, whereas liberal economic discourse seems to prevail (see Table 21.1). Yet, ongoing debates concerning China, sovereignty funds, and loss of national competitiveness reveal the continued potency of economic nationalist thinking in politics.

Power *through* trade, not the power *of* trade, is the emphasis of realist IPE.[2] Trade power is exercised through trade embargoes (sticks), through favorable trade agreements with friends (carrots), and through export restrictions on strategic products. Realists see no ethical or legal constrains on the use of national

Table 21.1 Three Perspectives on Trade and Security

	Realist IPE	Liberal IPE	Constructivism
Basic proposition	Trade is subordinated to foreign policy objectives	Free trade facilitates specialization and maximizes the wealth of individuals	Trade and security are given meaning through interaction
Understanding of the WTO	An arena of struggle between states	A contract between governments, firms, and societies	A governance process
Risks of globalization	Existential security of states	Economic threats to societies and individuals	Different risk definitions are possible

Source: Author.

economic power. The WTO is an arena for power struggle. Security of the state ranks above economic welfare of individuals. Consequently, the pursuit of security objectives justifies any economic losses to society or individuals. Realists are commonly criticized for ignoring the economic realities of globalization. This is not entirely correct. For instance, Robert Gilpin (2001) explains the persistence of nonliberal trade policy practices despite the globalization of technology, investment, and trade. Realists are very pessimistic as to what can be expected of trade in politics.

The power *of* trade is the emphasis of liberal IPEs.[3] Trade generates prosperity and therefore also security. Liberals have traditionally been less concerned with the insecurities of trade. Trade is an absolute gain. A state should liberalize regardless of what other states do. Liberal IPEs do implicitly acknowledge the realist claim that systemic insecurity in the international system is a barrier to trade liberalization. International institutions can effectively solve this collective action problem by improving policy transparency and intergovernmental communication.

Liberal IPEs pay more attention to individual and societal insecurities than to political insecurities between states. Such economies see trade and security in much broader terms than do realists; they see trade and security as something more than the sticks and carrots of economic diplomacy. Such economies relate to all kinds of societal and individual insecurities stemming from globalization. Liberal IPEs are more concerned about the costs of trade-restrictive foreign economic policy. Sanctions are the last resort rather than a first choice. To liberal IPEs, trade-related security issues include such policies as import bans on dangerous products as well as antidumping duties or subsidies that protects societies against perceived risks of globalization unfair competition. To liberal IPEs, globalization has broadened the security agenda. Firms and states are now partners throughout the dense risk management networks that transcend territorial borders and international organizations.

Box 21.1 Societal Security Framings: U.S. Steel Tariffs

On March 5, 2002, U.S. secretary of the treasury Robert Zoellick justified the imposition of steel tariffs in this manner: "This safeguard remedy gives the American steel industry some temporary relief from years of import surges and unfair trading practices that have hurt its ability to compete and to prosper. . . . They need to use this breathing space to restructure and to regain competitiveness" (USTR 2002). In November 2003, after the WTO made a final ruling against the United States upon which the steel tariffs were terminated, Robert Zoellick congratulated the steel industry for using its "breathing space well, to the benefit of many families and communities around the country" (USTR 2003). What economists call protectionism may also be understood as societal security policy.

Alternatively, from a constructivist perspective, trade and security are best understood as discourses and policy framings—or more precisely, as "securitizations"

(Buzan, Wæver, and de Wilde 1997; Waever 1995). Securitizations are speech acts that transform the normative structures of policy domains whenever situations of emergency and urgency are used as justifications of emergencies. In this formulation, securitization explains when governments can successfully frame certain trade issues as items on the foreign policy agenda. This happens when states refers to plausible existential threats. Economic interests are then subjugated to a security-driven foreign policy agenda. Economic policy became more nationalist than globalist in its orientation. This could also explain why the Bush administration so overtly protected its steel industry in 2003 (see Box 21.1) or why the United States initiated a new generation of bilateral trade agreements around that time.

There are also instances of "reverse securitizations" of a trade-related security issue, that is, when businesses are successful in persuading a government to let foreign policies or societal regulation become global trade issues. The term "trad'zation" is here used to denote this reconstruction of the meaning of trade-related security issues (see later discussion). Trade politics is taken back into the sphere of economic politics. It resembles what critics call the neoliberalization of politics. I argue that the WTO's governance activities, in particular the dispute settlement system, are crucial components in successfully reversing a securitization of security issues to trade issues.

Box 21.2 Trade Security Policy Framings

- *Securitization* of trade issues: converting economic policy issues into matters of national urgency and taking these outside the WTO process
- *Trad'zation* of security issues: asserting pressure to take existing trade-related security issues outside the existing policy domain and into the WTO

As a constructivist approach, security and trade cannot be separated in a meaningful manner but have to be understood in the context of each other. They are forged together in different policy framings, supported by different constellations of actors. Realism and liberalism are policy framings. A realist framing prioritize national security threats over other types of threats. A neoliberal framing would prioritize the market over national or environmental security, for instance. The societal and individual insecurities generated by globalization are very much part of a social-liberal or green-liberal framing. The remaining sections focus on how interplay between these two framings, the state-centric securitizations and the market-orientated trad'zations, have shaped some of the dramas in contemporary WTO governance.

THE WTO: AN OVERLOOKED SECURITY ORGANIZATION

The WTO is normally not considered a security organization. Yet, it can nevertheless be understood as one of the risk managers of globalization. The WTO cannot prevent power politics. It forces governments to justify their use of economic instruments in foreign policy. Nor does the WTO deteriorate the global environment. Yet, governments cannot automatically punish polluters by restricting imports from them. The WTO does not prevent states from making effective environmental agreements, but it require governments to use the least-trade-distorting instruments. Governments can no longer decide on their own when to restrict imports of harmful products without considering the scientific consensus on the issue. A security or risk claim can no longer suffice. Any policy that involves the use of trade restrictions has to be balanced against its disruptive effects on trade.

Box 21.3 The WTO and the Embargo of Cuba

United States foreign policy toward Cuba has caused a lot of friction in the WTO (Paemen 2003). In 1997, the EU complained about the extraterritorial effects of the Helms-Burton Act, which strengthened the U.S. embargo of Cuba in response to the shooting down of a civilian airplane over Cuba. The complaint infuriated hardliners in Washington. At a House Committee meeting, it was stated that "this is clearly a matter of U.S. foreign policy and national security in which the WTO has no jurisdiction or authority" (Subcommittee on International Economic Policy and Trade 1997, 7). The problem was the extraterritorial effects of the Helms-Burton law. It targeted individuals working for businesses who had invested in what the United States considered to be illegally confiscated pre-revolution property. These individuals would be denied entry into the United States. The case was eventually settled by diplomacy. The EU suspended the panel before a ruling could be reached, and President Clinton suspended the controversial sections of the legislation. Business successfully reversed the securitization of the issue, highlighting the economic costs of toughening the embargo. The exterritorial reach of tougher unilateral sanctions against Iran may create similar problems in the future, however.

The WTO makes it costly for governments to use trade instruments to tackle insecurities. Governments are constrained in their use of economic sanctions as a part of their foreign policy. If foreign businesses are indirectly hit by a unilateral embargo, it is no longer a foreign policy issue. Likewise, governments have to prove that import restrictions, tax breaks, or loans to troubled domestic industries are necessary, temporary, and fair. They also have to demonstrate that their environmental policies do not unnecessary interfere with trade flows.

Trade governance is about balancing security risks with economic growth. The WTO is interesting because it is a global, multilateral institution. Any claim of national security interests is potentially subject to a legal test or a transparent debate. Conflicts are difficult to contain behind closed doors. However, filing a dispute against a trading partner requires a lot of political will, especially if the trading relationship is unbalanced. Moreover, strategic trade issues are kept outside the WTO for political reasons. Oil and energy are considered to be of strategic importance to all states. Such other sectors as agriculture, high-tech products, or civil aircrafts have also been shielded from global market forces for similar reasons. These sectors are now being brought under WTO auspices. More than 95 percent of world trade is subject to WTO disciplines and procedures. The interesting question is whether the various security exceptions are gaining importance as the ultimate safeguard for states against the risks of globalization.

Box 21.4 outlines the most relevant security-related WTO provisions, ranging from those directly regulating the use of trade-related foreign policy measures like sanctions to sector-specific rules on the use of subsidies and import safeguards in the context of economic security. For instance, the WTO rules on anti-dumping seem to provide states with legitimate tools for defending their "societal security" against the "threats" of globalization in specific sectors of the economy.

Box 21.4 Links between WTO Agreements and Security Issues

- National Security Exception: GATT Art. 21
- General Exceptions: GATT Art. 20
- Export Prohibitions: GATT Art. 11
- Agricultural Agreement: food security
- Agreement on Sanitary and Phytosanitary Measures (SPS): food safety
- Agreements on Antidumping and Safeguards: temporary shields against unfair competition
- Agreements on Subsidies: temporary support to troubled industries

---

Many of the security risks associated with globalization are, of course, also dealt with by other international agreements as well. For instance, the Cartagena Protocol of the Convention on Biological Diversity deals with trade in genetically modified organisms (GMOs). Yet, the relevance of this arrangement is seriously undermined by the WTO because the United States is not a party to the agreement.

The WTO's global membership makes the organization a global security provider. Its membership has soared to 153 members. Its agreements cover most sectors of the global economy, from agriculture and industrial goods to electronic commerce, financial services, and intellectual property rights. Surprisingly, the WTO itself is a small, member-driven organization (Blackhurst 1998; Nordstrom 2005). Its total staff of 650 dwarfs alongside that of the IMF and OECD (around 3,000) and the World Bank (10,000), for instance. Yet, its dispute settlement system is by many considered one of the most powerful adjudicatory bodies in international law (e.g., Abbott et al. 2000; Esserman and Howse 2004). The WTO is a contract between states on how to keep liberalizing trade. Because businesses need predictability in the operation of the global market, governments have uploaded some of their sovereignty to the WTO by creating a binding set of rules. Yet, governments do not want to create a supercourt either. The problem is that the WTO cannot be both strong and weak at the same time. The balance between national sovereignty and continued trade liberalization has been difficult to strike. Indeed, the clash between sovereignty and strong legalization is a constant source of tension in the WTO. The debate between supporters and critics of the legal powers of the WTO has been ongoing since its creation.[4] The WTO cannot itself initiate any cases. Only members can file legal complaints. Once the process is initiated, however, it cannot be blocked other than by consensus. It is a unique organization.

Despite the seeming impasse in the Doha Round, of talks that began in 2001, the WTO continues to be a cornerstone of the rule-based, multilateral global governance system that shapes the balance between prosperity and security in globalization.

SECURITY-RELATED TRADE WARS IN THE WTO

Trade disputes are ideal pathways into understanding the complexities of the trade-security conflicts. Table 21.2 outlines five thematic categories of illustrative trade-related security WTO cases. The first cluster concerns the WTO's legal constraints on the use of trade-related foreign policy. Only a few but dramatic cases exist. When development policy is considered part of a foreign policy, a second cluster of potential conflicts exists over the use of preferential trade agreements. These illustrate how states are no longer free to use trade policy as carrots in their foreign policy. In terms of states' provision of economic security for their citizens and industries, the Bush administration's imposition of steel tariffs in 2002 is a good example of an economic nationalist securitization of trade. The tariffs were justified as a necessary move against the threats of global oversupply and underpricing of steel imports. The third category relevant for consideration concerns using import bans other than those justified as national security threats, as mentioned earlier. These have been more frequent in the WTO. The food war across the Atlantic on the validity of the EU food safety regulations on hormone-treated beef and genetically modified food (GMOs) illustrates how governments' individual security provisions are limited by WTO rules, thus, critics say, making effective consumer protection impossible in a global economy. Finally, the ongoing Boeing-Airbus dispute also illustrates the dilemma of how to balance national security with global trade liberalization. This trade dispute remains one of the most explosive ever to have entered into the trade system, having become a legal test of the validity of the national interest exemption.

Some of the most significant security-related WTO disputes and listed in Table 21.2, which should be considered an outline of a future research agenda on trade and security in WTO governance. This chapter focuses on a selected few of these disputes, namely, trade sanctions and import bans that illuminate the contrast between the state-centered, realist understanding of security and the broader understanding of IPE liberals.

Table 21.2 Trade Wars and Security Links in WTO Dispute Settlement

Issue	Contested issue	Illustrative cases[i]
Economic sanctions	Extraterritorial effects of trade and investment embargo	US - *Cuban Liberty and Democratic Solidarity Act* (Helms-Burton case) (DS38): EU complaint about possible commercial restrictions on Cuba-investing European businesses following a tougher U.S. embargo. Diplomatic settlement. (May 1996- April 1997)
Preferential trade arrangements	Unintended trade distorting effects on non-economic motivated policies	*Regime for the Importation, Sale and Distribution of Bananas (Bananas III)* (DS 27): U.S. complaint (together with Ecuador, Guatemala, Honduras and Mexico) against EU banana import regime. EU lost after appeal. Sanctions imposed. New EU banan regime still disputed. (Feb. 1999 -) EC - *Conditions for the Granting of Tariff Preferences to Developing Countries* (DS246): Indian complaint about EU trade preferences to countries with effective policies against drug production and trafficking. EU lost after appeal. (March 2002- Sept. 2004)
Trade defense	Use of antidumping or safeguards to domestic industries	US - *Steel safeguards* (DS248, 249, 251, 252, 253, 254, 258, 259): Multiple complaints about U.S. tariffs discrimination of steel imports. The US lost after appeal. (March 2002- Dec. 2003)
Import bans	Import and production bans on harmful products or production processes	EC – *Measures Concerning Meat and Meat Products (Hormones)* (DS26, DS48):U.S. complaint about

Table 21.2 (*Continued*)

Issue	Contested issue	Illustrative cases[i]
		health-related import ban on hormone-treated beef to the EU market. The EU lost after appeal. U.S. sanctions (annual US $116.8 million) authorized, still in force (Jan. 1996 – April 1999). EC - *Measures Affecting the Approval and Marketing of Biotech Products* (GMO case) (DS291, 292, 293): US complaint against import (and production) ban on genetically modified foods in the EU. The EU lost and did not appeal. U.S. request for sanctions pending but suspended by mutual agreement for now. (May 2003- Sept. 2006)
Subsidies	Financing domestic industries (tax breaks, illegal R&D support, favorable loans)	EC – *Measures Affecting Trade in Large Civil Aircraft* (Airbus case) (DS 316): U.S. complaint about alleged illegal government loans to Airbus industries. Ruling delayed but expected in late-2008. US – *Measures Affecting Trade in Large Civil Aircraft* (Boeing case) (DS 317): EU complaint of alleged illegal subsidies (financed by defense contracts and R&D spending) to the Boeing Corporation. Ruling delayed but expected in late 2008.

[i] At the time of writing 376 complaints have been issues to the WTO since 1995; 108 cases have been completed; 30 complaints are under investigation. For a good overview, see WTO Dispute Settlement: One-Page Case Summaries (2008 Edition). For continuous updates, see http://www.wto.org/english/tratop_e/dispu_e/dispu_e.htm.

However, the disputes focused upon here are no more than illustrations of how security-related trade conflicts are being multilateralized in the WTO. Trade issues are more commonly securitized outside the WTO. They will remain so as long as no other WTO member files an official complaint. Yet, the step from bilateral power politics to WTO-governed, multilateral desecuritization is not what IR theory expects us to find. Realists expect securitized trade issues to remain outside the WTO. It is precisely why the unusual step of openly challenging a trade partner on what is an extremely sensitive problem is so interesting. We should not expect conventional security issues to surface in this manner, since they are normally dealt with by diplomats behind closed doors. The move to turn a security issue into an open trade dispute is a critical test of IR realism's relevance today.

BOEING, CUBA, AND HIGH-TECH TRADE WITH CHINA: LIMITS TO THE NATIONAL INTEREST IN THE WTO?

Foreign policy arguments are frequently used as justifications for trade sanctions. However, the WTO restricts the use of economic sanctions. Article 21 (see Box 21.5) is very flexible and imprecise. It has rarely been tested. When can states securitize a threat without fearing a WTO challenge? First of all, the most indisputable exception concerns sanctions authorized by the UN Security Council. In continuation of the Cuba case (see Box 21.3), an Iranian challenge of U.S. sanctions against Iran will not win a hypothetical WTO case, since sanctions have already been authorized by the UN Security Council following earlier IAEA recommendations. Article 21 would safeguard the national security interest. Yet, the extraterritorial effects these sanction on trading partners doing otherwise legitimate business in Iran is a different matter. Second, trade in weapons and nuclear technology is clearly exempted. Third, it appears that all trade in times of war is exempted from WTO rules. Finally, with respect to disclosure of information, it appears that governments themselves are entitled to define what is necessary to protect their national security. It is obvious that anything involves the use, threat, or control of military force is beyond the scope of WTO disciplines.

Box 21.5 Article 21: World Trade Organization's Security Exceptions

Nothing in this Agreement shall be construed

(a) to require any contracting party to furnish any information the disclosure of which it considers contrary to its essential security interests; or

(b) to prevent any contracting party from taking any action which it considers necessary for the protection of its essential security interests

> 1. relating to fissionable materials or the materials from which they are derived;
> 2. relating to the traffic in arms, ammunition and implements of war and to such traffic in other goods and materials as is carried on directly or indirectly for the purpose of supplying a military establishment;
> 3. taken in time of war or other emergency in international relations; or
>
> (a) to prevent any contracting party from taking any action in pursuance of its obligations under the United Nations Charter for the maintenance of international peace and security

Article 21 appears to safeguard the national interest. There are many unknowns in the wording of article 21, however. What about a "war on terror" or "terrorism" as an emergency in international relations? The precise meaning of such terms has never been established by the relevant bodies or tested in practice. No government has ever justified a policy on these grounds. The scope and content of this assurance remains, therefore, unknown. There are best understood as open-ended assurances that allow WTO governments to make binding commitments in the WTO without fearing loss of control over their foreign policy.

Beyond the use of trade embargoes, article 21 is vague about the permissibility of other trade-related foreign policy measures. The case of export restrictions on strategic resources provides a good illustration of this. The control over exports has always been an instrument of power. Chinese emperors banned on exports of iron ore or silkworms. In principle, article 11 outlaws the use of export restrictions on all raw materials. In practice, certain products of obvious strategic importance have always been excluded from the trading system. Oil is the most obvious case. It is not and has never been traded freely. The global supply is influenced by a cartel of oil producers, OPEC, or individual states. The oil-producing countries have been outside the trading system until recently, with Saudi Arabia becoming a member in 2005 and Russia still not a member. Challenging OPEC as a WTO-illegal export restriction would be possible, but such a move has always been considered politically imprudent. The shortage of raw materials and energy and food supplies has force resource-dependent economies to reconsider this position and use the WTO to counter a possible surge in export restrictions on strategic resources.

Export restrictions on high-tech products with potential military applications have also been common trade-related foreign policy instrument. Globalization has made such restrictions controversial and of limited value. The U.S. restrictions on high-tech trade with China are a good illustration of how business tries to reverse a securitized trade issue. China is a historic opportunity for everyone today. Yet, American high- tech firms cannot trade freely with China. High-tech products are core comparative advantages for the U.S. economy, which struggles with a chronic trade deficit with China. American businesses have also frequently complained about competitors who are less restricted in their relations with China.

The U.S. government has only limited, nominal trade with China. The Bush administration renewed the ban but softened it by permitting trade between prescreened firms. As Commerce Secretary Carlos Gutierrez explained, the new policy got the balance right in the "complex relationship" with China, making it easier for U.S. firms to sell their products to prescreened customers in China, at the same time denying access to U.S. technology that would contribute to China's military. This softening of the policy was no longer justified in terms of national interest alone: "The steps we are taking today are good for national security, and for American exporters and jobs" (reported by *China Daily* July 19, 2007). The United States also used its diplomatic clout to persuade the Europeans not to lift the weapons embargo on China.

> We believe the E.U. has not made a compelling case for why the embargo should be lifted, and our government is united in the belief that there are compelling national security reasons for maintaining the embargo. . . . And so our view is that the E.U. should seek to align itself to this mutual interest, strengthen our export control regimes, so that we can limit sales to China that put those interests at risk." (Bums 2005)

The Chinese were not pleased at all. Sun Zhenyu, former Chinese ambassador to the WTO, complained that the United States prevented foreign companies from seeking merger and acquisition within China: "By interpreting and applying WTO national security clauses in an excessive way, it has again seriously undermined the credibility of the multilateral trade regime, over which China is highly concerned" (as reported by *Xinhua* March 23, 2006). The tensions are still lurking in the background, although the Doha crisis overshadows the tensions.

Export controls are not a thing of the past. Indeed, the EU fears that restrictions on essential raw materials are spreading. The EU Commission is concerned about future access to raw materials and, thus, the future competitiveness of its economy.[5] Estimates are that about 20 countries have put in place at least 450 restrictions on more than 400 imported products of strategic importance to the EU economy (EU Commission 2008). These restrictions take the form of export licenses, subsidies, investment conditions, subsidization schemes, price fixing, double-pricing systems, and export taxes—about which "a great majority of European industrial sectors" are concerned (EU Commission 2008). In April 2006, the EU proposed WTO rules on export taxes, which unlike export bans, are not covered by GATT article 11. Althoug EU diplomats emphasized that financial and food crises measures were not included in the proposal, the European idea received a hostile reception in Geneva (see EU Commission 2006). Many developing countries did not considered the proposal to be an item on the current negotiation agenda.

The Airbus-Boeing case contradicts the realist doctrine that the national interest is firmly above the WTO. It is a perfect illustration of how firms are active players in the WTO game, trying to reverse securitizations within the WTO or shielding themselves behind past securitizations. The issue concerns possible misuse of the national security exception norm in the WTO. Did U.S. defense and NASA budgets provide a cover for illegal subsidies to the American aircraft industry? At the core of the conflict lies the allegation that Boeing deliberately shielded itself behind article 21 to gain unfair marked domination, doint this as a strategic trade policy to cover research and development expenses involved in its aircraft development.

Steven Staples and Miriam Pemberton (2000) suggests that "the security exception shields the war industry from challenges to the WTO, it works to spur military spending by governments. Governments can use the military to promote jobs, new emerging industries, and high-tech manufacturing." Are governments shifting resources away from subsidy to military programs precisely because doing so could not be challenged in the WTO? This is precisely what the EU is suggesting. The case must be seen as a countermove to a U.S. complaint about unfair support to Boeing's main rival, Airbus Industries. A WTO panel has been investigating the case but has been delayed by "technical complexities." The WTO wants to keep all options open for a political compromise. The United States has not securitized the conflict, which it considers a "normal' commercial war between the only two remaining producers of large aircrafts in the world. The battle is about the future domination of the entire industry. The U.S. Department of theTreasury dismisses the EU allegations. Technically speaking, the EU complaint alleges that research and development contracts between Boeing and the U.S. Department of Defense results in dual-use technology—that is, military-sponsored research is applied to civil aircraft production. The United States maintains that its defense research and development support programs are intended to apply civilian Boeing technology to military aircraft production, that most of these programs are of minor importance, that most military research is not relevant to civil aircraft, and finally, that strict U.S. export restrictions on dual-use technology prevents the misuse of military technologies in civil aircraft production. The Americans are normalizing the conflict, rebutting all allegations against the agreement, and avoiding any mention of the national security exception.

Nonetheless, openly challenging the United States on grounds of misusing the WTO security exception norm is unexpected, if not hazardous. That is not what IR theory expects would happen. Yet, it is also striking to note that almost every security-related trade dispute in the history of the WTO has been fought between the United States and the European Union. At least until very recently, only Europe and the United States had enough economic and political muscle to challenge each other on explosive security issues. Today, however, India, Brazil, and China are tilting the power balances within the WTO dispute settlement as well as in the world economy. It seems as though parity of economic power is a necessary condition for testing the system and trying to "trad'ze" of a security problem or "securitze" of an economic problem.

SOCIETAL AND INDIVIDUAL THREATS OF GLOBALIZATION

It can be difficult to distinguish between "protection," as against threats of globalization, and "protectionism," as in unfair trade. As mentioned, in 2003 the Bush administration deliberately violated WTO rules by making explicit references to the economic security of the U.S. steel industry and its workers in 2003. Yet, the tariffs were also removed after the WTO ruling. It is noteworthy that the United States did not claim that the U.S. steel industry was of strategic importance to the economy during the so-called War on Terror. President Bush referred not to national security interest but to unfair practices. The remarks were not about securization of trade but an illustration of societal and individualist understandings of security in the WTO.

The WTO quickly dismissed the steel tariffs as protectionism, however. Whereas tariffs are transparent policy instruments, other trade restrictions are much more difficult to identify as protectionism. For instance, is the EU precautionary approach to food safety an illegitimate form of protectionism, or is legitimate protection of society and individuals? The decade-long food war between Washington and Brussels illustrates well the broadening of security in WTO governance. The first food war started in the late 1980s when a food scandal involving growth hormones made the EU Commission impose a production as well as import ban throughout Europe. The problem was that some of these growth hormones had been approved in the United States, and therefore U.S. meat exports were hurt by the EU ban. As a result of the Uruguay Round, the WTO was equipped with a new agreement on trade-related health safety standards, the SPS agreement (see Box 21.6). For the first time, the trading system had rules on when and how governments could protect their citizens against inflows of potentially dangerous foods. The WTO had become the risk manager of societal and individual threats from globalization. The rules are at best a blunt, if not altogether useless, instrument for effective dispute resolution. Their imprecision left a lot of room for competing interpretations.

Box 21.6 Science and Risk Management in the SPS Agreement

Consider two risk-related provisions in the World Trade Organization's SPS agreement:

SPS article 3.3 reads: "Members may introduce or maintain [SPS] measures which result in a higher level of sanitary or phytosanitary protection than would be achieved by measures based on the relevant international standards, guidelines or recommendations, if there is a scientific justification, or as a consequence of the level of sanitary or phytosanitary protection a Member determines to be appropriate."

SPS article 5.1 reads: "Members shall ensure that their [SPS] measures are based on an assessment, as appropriate to the circumstances, of the risks to human, animal or plant life or health, taking into account risk assessments techniques development by the relevant institutional organizations."

The first provision confirms the sovereign right of a government to choose the level of security it wants to provide for its citizens. The second provision requires that a government provide scientific evidence in support of the chosen level of security. The WTO rulings in the hormones case dismissed the EU defense of its ban on grounds that the EU's precautionary approach to food safety lacked scientific support. It operated on a restrictive, hard-science understanding of scientific evidence. The WTO appellate body reversed this interpretation and emphasized that food safety science is about actual, real-life health risks to individuals. Accordingly, it declared, risks are "not risk ascertainable in a science laboratory operating under strictly controlled conditions, but also risk in human societies as they actually exists, in other words, the actual potential for adverse effects on human health in the real world where people live and die" (*Hormones Appellate Report* 1998, para. 187).

The EU lost the case. It had not provided, and still has not, a WTO-acceptable risk assessment. Whether the EU has complied with the ruling remains unclear. The United States wants the EU to open up for beef exports. The EU rejects this interpretation, however, and wants to provide evidence of uncertainty instead. It has submitted new evidence, but thus far WTO experts have rejected the data. Consequently, the EU is still targeted by U.S. tariffs amounting to about $120 million worth of exports.

The other food war, the GMO case, dates back to April 1990 when EU Directive 90/220 established an approval process for products of agricultural biotechnology. Brussels had not resisted the biotech revolution before then. By 1998, a total of nine GMO crops were approved in the first wave of commercial GMO seeds. In February 1997, however, the Austrian government banned Novartis Bt176, although the drug had already been approved by the relevant EU scientific committees. Luxembourg, France, Greece, Germany, and Italy also banned several other GMO seeds. The EU Commission wanted to avoid a conflict with member states on what had become an extremely sensitive domestic issue. In May 2003, the United States complained to the WTO (Department of Agriculture 2003). Many were angered by European double standards. The EU requires U.S.-produced soybean oil to be labeled, whereas European cheeses and wine made with genetically modified enzymes would not be covered (Paarlberg 2000). The United States does not require special approval or labels for GMO products; only produce certified "organic food" is completely GMO-free in the U.S. market. The EU defended its policy in terms of consumer confidence and the precautionary principle. To the EU, the approval delay was about a new food safety regime, a policy that had lost credibility after repeated food scandals. To the United States, however, the issue was the spread of hidden protectionism—the denial of market access to U.S. agricultural products not only to Europe but also to other markets (the leading firm in global biotech agrobusiness is Missouri-based Monsanto).

Was the GMO ban protectionism or protection? The EU lost the case on grounds of "administrative delay." The WTO did not make a decision on the substance of the ban issue, that is, on whether the precautionary principle could justify the EU policy or whether harmful effects of GMO consumption were scientifically proven. The EU policy was perhaps not protectionism as such, but neither was it acceptable protection. Surprisingly, the EU declined to appeal the case. The EU has since opened up for new GMO approvals, although the food safety concerns remain intact in Europe.

CONCLUSIONS

The governance of economic globalization is intrinsically and increasingly linked to security in one way or another. This chapter has illuminated how the WTO, one of the key sites of global economic governance, also plays a role in globalization of security, linking security and trade issues together in ways that are often overlooked in security studies and international relations.

Sitting at the interface of two opposite processes of security and market liberalization, the WTO is formally restricting traditional economic warfare between states by allowing other governments to tests the legality of economic sanctions, favorable terms of trade, or other foreign policy–motivated trade policies. In practice, however, numerous escape clauses effectively ensure that most trade-related foreign policy practices are beyond WTO jurisdiction. Indeed, since the end of the Cold War, WTO members have seemed to share an understanding to keep security-related trade conflicts firmly outside the WTO. Only unilateral trade embargoes, in particular Cuba, have threatened to ignite a broader trade war inside the WTO.

Throughout most of its brief existence, the WTO institution has been shielded from security-related, foreign economic policy conflicts. If a security-related trade issue is securitized, it is treated as a non-WTO issue. It has been a taboo to legally challenge the national security exception. Yet, this situation is changing. What independent observers may have suspected for years is now openly said within the WTO. The EU is accusing the United States of misusing defense budgets to fund research and development that is boosting Boeing's civilian competitiveness. The EU tries to convert formerly securitized policy issues into trade issues. Although the outcome of the Boeing case is unknown at the time of writing, the dispute itself bears witness to the importance of WTO foreign economic politics.

If security is treated in broader terms, however, the WTO has already been converting global insecurity issues into trade issues. Governments are obliged to justify how they regulate individual and ecological risks in terms of their effects on trade flows. Governments are also curtailed in the policy space of shielding troubled domestic industries from foreign competition, even if the WTO retains surprisingly many of the GATT loopholes.

The WTO is coping with global insecurities. It has done so on many of the defining moments of late-20th century globalization, and it seems poised to continue to do so in the future. Certain trade issues are now perceived in terms of their strategic value to the national economy and not as sources of global wealth. Supplies of foods, raw materials, and energy are on top of the national agenda, though at the expense of liberal ideals. If the securitization of trade is to become the dominant trend of the future, the WTO is heading into fatal troubles. It will be forced to cope with securitized foreign economic policies without a clear mandate or sufficient support.

NOTES

1. Commenting on the relationship between globalization and trade, current director-general Pascal Lamy admitted in a recent WTO publication that fears and insecurities are on the rise: "Misgivings about the consequences of globalization have grown over the years. Increased anxiety about disruption, displacement and exclusion has become more apparent" (WTO 2008, xvi).

2. Gilpin (2001) is a key work of realist IPE. See also Balaam and Veseth (2001) for an introduction to mercantilist, realist-inspired IPE.

3. Liberal IPE is here used to differentiate it from neoliberals in neoclassical economic theory. It is also known as "neoliberal institutionalism" (Keohane 1989) or "neoliberalism" (Martin 2007). Both terms covers different contractual approaches to IPE, primarily explaining economic and rule-governed cooperative behavior in international economic relations as coordination problems. There are many different liberalisms in IPE, however. Republican liberalism, social liberalism, and liberal internationalism are more idealistic approaches than what is referred to here as liberal IPE.

4. Others disagree. For a moderate, pro-WTO critique, see Howse and Esserman (2003), Pauwelyn (2005), or Mortensen (2006). For a radical critique, see Wallach and Woodall (2003) or Peet (2003).

5. The EU's import dependency rate for minerals ranges from 74 percent for copper ore, 80 percent for zinc ore and bauxite, 86 percent for nickel, to 100 percent for such materials as cobalt, platinum, titanium, and vanadium (EU Commission 2008).

FURTHER READING

Balaam, David, and Michael Veseth. *Introduction to International Political Economy*, 2nd ed. Englewood Cliffs, NJ: Prentice Hall, 2001.
Gilpin, Robert. *Global Political Economy: Understanding the International Economic Order*. Princeton, NJ: Princeton University Press, 2001.
Peet, Richard. *Unholy Trinity: The IMF, World Bank and WTO*. London: Zed Books, 2003.
Stubbs, Richard, and Geoffrey Underhill, eds. *Political Economy and the Changing Global Order*, 3rd ed. Oxford and New York: Oxford University Press, 2005.

REFERENCES

Abbott, K. W., R. O. Keohane, A. Moravcsik, A-M. Slaughter, and D. Snidal. 2000. The concept of legalization. *International Organization* 54: 17–35.
Balaam, David, and Michael Veseth. 2001. *Introduction to international political economy*. 2nd ed. Upper Saddle River, NJ: Prentice Hall.

Barnett, Michael, and Martha Finnemore. 2004. *Rules for the world: International organizations in global politics.* Ithaca, NY: Cornell University Press.

Blackhurst, Richard. 1998. The capacity of the WTO to fulfill its mandate. In *The WTO as an international organization,* ed. A. Krueger. Chicago: University of Chicago Press.

Burns, R. N. 2005. Comment by R. Nicholas Burns, Under Secretary for Political Affairs, during a testimony to the House Committee, April 2005. World Trade Report 2008, p. xii. World Trade Organization. Available online at http://www.wto.org/english/res_e/booksp_e/anrep_e/world_trade_report08_e.pdf

Buzan, Barry, Ole Wæver, and Jaap de Wilde. 1997. Security analysis: Conceptual apparatus. In *Security: A new framework for analysis,* 21–47. Boulder, CO: Lynne Rienner.

EU Commission. 2006. Market Access for Non-Agricultural products. Negotiating Proposal on Export Taxes, Communication from the European Communities (TN/MA/W/11/Add.6.), April 27.

EU Commission. 2008. Trade and Raw Materials: Looking Ahead. Report available online at http://ec.europa.eu/trade/issues/sectoral/industry/raw/index_en.htm.

Gilpin, Robert. 2001. *Global political economy: Understanding the international economic order.* Princeton, NJ: Princeton University Press.

Howse, R., and S. Esserman. 2003. The WTO on trial. *Foreign Affairs* 82: 130–40.

Keohane, Robert O. 1984. *After hegemony: Cooperation and discord in the world political economy.* Princeton, NJ: Princeton University Press.

Martin, Lisa. 2007. Neoliberalism. In *International relations theory,* ed. T. Dunne, M. Kurki, and S. Smith, 110–26. Oxford: Oxford University Press.

Mastanduno, Michael. 1998. Economics and security in statecraft and scholarship. *International Organization* 52: 825–54.

Mortensen, Jens L. 2005. WTO and the governance of globalization: Dismantling the compromise of embedded liberalism? In *Political economy and the changing global order,* ed. Richard Stubbs and Geoffrey Underhill. 3rd ed. Oxford: Oxford University Press.

Nordstrom, Håkån. 2005. The World Trade Organisation Secretariat in a changing world. *Journal of World Trade* 39: 819–53.

Paarlberg, Robert. 2000. The global food fight. *Foreign Affairs* 79: 24–38.

Paemen, Hugo. 2003. Avoidance and settlement of "high policy disputes": Lessons from the dispute over "the Cuban Liberty and Democratic Solidarity Act." In *Transatlantic economic disputes, The EU, the U.S. and the WTO,* ed. Ernst-Ulrich Petersmann and Mark Pollack. Oxford: Oxford University Press.

Pauwelyn, Joost H. B. 2005. The transformation of world trade. *Michigan Law Review* 104: 1–66.

Peet, Richard. 2003. *Unholy trinity: The IMF, World Bank and WTO.* London: Zed Books.

Saul, John Ralston. 2005. *The collapse of globalism.* London: Atlantic Books, 2005.

Staples, Steven, and Miriam Pemberton. 2000. "Security exception" & arms trade. FPIF Policy Report, April 24. Available online at http://www.fpif.org/papers/globmil/index_body.html.

Subcommittee on International Economic Policy and Trade. 1997. Interfering with U.S. national security interests: The World Trade Organization and the European Union's challenge to the Helms-Burton law. Hearing before the Subcommittee on International Economic Policy and Trade of the Committee on International Relations, House of Representatives, March 19.

Sutherland, Peter. 1993. Uruguay Round negotiations conclude successfully. GATT doc. NUR 081, December 21.

U.S. Department of Agriculture. 2003. U.S. and cooperating countries file WTO case against EU moratorium on biotech foods and crops. Press Release 0156.03, May 13.

U.S. Trade Representative. 2002. USTR briefing on Stefel. Available online at http://www.whitehouse.gov/news/releases/2002/03/print/20020305-10.html.

U.S. Trade Representative. 2003. Statement by U.S. Trade Representative Robert Zoellick on termination of steel safeguards, April 12. Available online at http://www.ustr.gov/Document_Library/Press_Releases/2003/December/Statement_by_USTR_Zoellick_on_Termination_of_Steel_Safeguards.html.

Wallach, Lori, and Patrick Woodall/Public Citizen. 2004. The WTO's operating procedures and enforcement system: World government by slow-motion coup d'etat. In *Whose trade organization?* New York: New Press.

World Economic Forum (WEF). 2008. Global risks, 2008. http://www.weforum.org/pdf/globalrisk/report2008.pdf.

Xinhua. 2006. China assails U.S. trade policies. March 23.

22

Transnational Corporations

Grazia Ietto-Gillies

The transnational corporation, or TNC, as we know it today has developed mainly since World War II. Nonetheless, its antecedents can be traced to more than a century ago; it might even be possible to go back much earlier—to the Medici Bank in Renaissance Italy or to the trading companies of the seventeenth, eighteenth, and nineteenth centuries. However, the specificity and localization of their operations and their monopolistic charters make these very early enterprises poor forerunners of the modern TNC. Most historians see the establishment of the joint stock company as the real breakthrough toward the later formation of companies that could operate directly abroad.

Before clarifying what is special about the TNC, let us clear the terminology issue. The most common expression for the corporation we are interested in is *multinational corporation or company* (MNC); "international" and "transnational" are also widely used descriptors, and at times the terms "firm" and "enterprise" are used instead of "corporation" or "company." They all denote the same institutions. Throughout this chapter, therefore, the terms "company" and "corporation" are used interchangeably; the descriptor "transnational" is used throughout unless in reference to authors who use a different terminology. Why is "transnational" preferred here? The reason is twofold: first, because the descriptor highlights how corporations operate across nation-states and not just in many of them; second, because it is the term used by the largest research and policy institution dealing with TNCs—the Geneva-based United Nations Conference on Trade and Development, or UNCTAD, who publishes regular studies on the TNCs.[1]

The next two sections deal with definitional issues and with the salient characteristics and activities of TNCs. The fourth section gives a broad perspective on theories of the TNC, specifically discussing the following theories: Stephen Hymer's theory, the international product life cycle (Raymond Vernon), the internalization theory, John Dunning's eclectic approach, the evolutionary theory, and the Scandinavian School theory. The section ends with a discussion of some key elements in the theories and a brief analysis of efficiency versus strategic approaches; this leads to the presentation of a theoretical approach in which the role of nation-states and of companies' strategies toward labor play a very significant part in the explanation of TNCs' activities. The possible effects of TNCs' activities on the countries in which they operate are analyzed in the fifth section. Finally, the sixth section discusses the role of TNCs in the globalization process; this leads to an analysis of the integration versus fragmentation roles of TNCs, their activities and their strategies.

THE MODERN TNC: SOME DEFINITIONS

What makes a corporation transnational? What specific characteristic(s) should a company have to be considered a transnational? The first thought that comes to mind is that they must be corporations that operate across national borders; however, here we have a problem because there are many ways of conducting cross-countries business: the oldest and most relevant is through trade that is through the importation and/or exportation of goods and services across national boundaries. This modality of business activity across frontiers has been in existence for thousands of years, well before the emergence of nation-states. However, though many TNCs are involved in trade across frontiers, this type of activity per se does not make them transnationals. The defining characteristic of the TNC is linked to another type of activity: direct business or production activities, accompanied by the ownership of assets, in at least one foreign country.

Exports involve production in the home country and sales abroad; this is a business activity in which many national and trasnational firms engage. However, some firms produce not only in their home country but also directly in one or more foreign countries with a view to selling their products in the host country or in other countries—a process that at times includes the very home country of the TNC if the goods produced in the host country are exported back home. The *home country* is usually the country of origin of the corporation, the one where the main headquarters—the parent company—are located and where the company is legally registered; a few companies have more than one home country: Daimler-Chrysler is listed in both the United States and Germany, whereas Unilever has the United Kingdom and the Netherlands as home countries. The *host country* is the foreign country in which the TNC locates direct business activities.

Direct production abroad requires the ownership of assets abroad, and these are acquired through investment in the foreign country. Investment in host countries can be made through *greenfield* or *brownfield* investment or through *mergers* and *acquisitions*. Greenfield investment means the creation of new productive capacity, for example, by building a completely new factory; the term "brownfield" is reserved for a situation in which the new productive capacity emerges, not from a greenfield, but from rebuilding where something was already in existence. (In practice, however, the term "greenfield" is used comprehensively to include both brownfield and strictly greenfield investment.) In both cases the essential point to note is that it is investment that leads to the creation of new productive capacity. When the investment takes place through a merger or acquisition (M&A), the TNC does not create new productive capacity but acquires capacity already in existence in the host country. This means that the investment does not lead to new capacity in the host country, though the acquired company forms new capacity for the acquiring corporation.

From the standpoint of the home country, the *foreign direct investment (FDI)* is called *outward;* whereas from the point of view of the host country, it is an *inward FDI.* Data for FDI are available as flow or stock.[2] Through foreign direct investment—whether of the greenfield or M&A type—the parent company located in the home country establishes *affiliates* abroad. Affiliates can be designated as *associates,* when the parent's ownership stake in it is between 10 and 50 percent, and as *subsidiaries,* when the stakes are over 50 percent.

TNCS: THEIR CHARACTERISTICS AND ACTIVITIES

The popular view of transnational corporations is that they are huge and powerful companies; on the whole this is true, though it is not the whole truth. Let us probe a little further into the characteristics, patterns of development, and activities of modern TNCs. The very first type of TNC can be seen in the nineteenth-century so-called *freestanding enterprise,* by which term the business historian Mira Wilkins (1988) denoted those enterprises established abroad with foreign capital—from Britain or the Netherlands—and managed by people trusted and appointed by the parent; they were run with little interference or control from the home country. These affiliates had to be freestanding because the communication system from the home to the host country was too poor for company headquarters to be able to exercise direct managerial control. Here, we come to the key issue of control.

There are two meanings of control: ownership control in terms of the parent's equity stake in the affiliate. What percentage of equity is necessary to exercise control over another enterprise, in this case over an affiliate? It partly depends on how fragmented the ownership is. If it is very fragmented, a relatively small stake is enough to exercise control; if ownership is concentrated, a larger stake is necessary. For the purpose of data collection and for the inclusion of foreign investment into the FDI category, at least a 10 percent stake is necessary. The other meaning of control refers to managerial decisions: can the owners or top managers of the parent company exercise managerial control over an affiliate? Necessary conditions for this are the existence of (a) good communication and transportation infrastructures and (b) an efficient organizational structure within the corporation. Since World War II, both conditions have applied and, indeed, greatly improved, particularly in the last two decades with the development of information and communication technologies (ICTs); this has made possible the development of a variety of patterns and characteristics to which we now turn.

Geography

The number of companies with direct business operations in at least one foreign country has increased tremendously since World War II from a few thousands to 78,411 by 2007, a year for which host economies exhibit a total of 777,647 affiliates located in them. In terms of geographical pattern, 74 percent of parent corporations are based in developed countries. However, the developing and former communist countries' contribution to the total is increasing rapidly particularly because of additions from countries like China, India, and Brazil. The developing and former communist countries are in receipt of the largest number of affiliates, with 67 percent of the world total.

When we look at the FDI situation, however, we see a slightly different pattern. In 2006 the largest share of outward FDI originated from developed countries (86 and 84 percent of stocks and flows respectively), with the share from developing and transition countries increasing steadily. The largest share of inward FDI is to be found also in developed countries (respectively 70 and 66 percent for stocks and flows).[3] This means, in effect, that companies from developed countries invest mainly in other developed countries. The discrepancies between the location of affiliates and the inward investment into developing and transition countries (with shares of, respectively, 67 and 34 percent) can be explained by the fact that most affiliates in nondeveloped countries may be very small and entail small amounts of investment.

Size

Most large companies are transnational, and most transnational companies are indeed large. However, an increasing number of medium to smallish companies are branching out to invest directly into foreign countries: this development is accelerating as a result of the positive impact of ICTs and of the general globalization trends in the economy and society. The large TNCs have affiliates in many countries (Ietto-Gillies 2002, pt. 2).

Modalities

Direct production abroad, as well as the ownership of assets abroad, through FDI and the establishment of foreign affiliates is the main modality of the TNCs' internationalization, as discussed. When analyzing the effects of TNCs' activities, we will reconsider the two main FDI modalities of greenfield and brownfield versus mergers and acquisitions. Among the other modalities of business operations already discussed are imports and exports: these are modalities of internationalization that do not characterize the TNCs as transnational but are nonetheless of great relevance to TNCs. Most TNCs are involved in trade, and most of the world trade originates with TNCs (on which more in the fifth section of this chapter).

Other modalities of operations abroad are evident in the TNCs' organization of production and businesses. The TNC can operate directly or through such contractual arrangements as *franchising, licensing, subcontracting,* and *joint ventures.* All such collaborative agreements have increased in relevance in the last 25 years, within a single country as well as across countries, providing the rationale for trends toward company downsizing (Ietto-Gillies 2005, chap. 2). The overall result is that companies, and TNCs in particular, can now be seen as network institutions in which the network extends geographically to many parts of the same country and to many countries and localities within them; it can also extend to several collaborators who may be dependent on the main company, to whom they are linked by contracts as franchisees or licensees or suppliers, subcontractors, or distributors.

THEORIES OF THE TNCS AND FDI

The scale of postwar growth of transnational corporations and their activities was made possible by the development of specific favorable conditions (see in Box 22.1).[4]

Box 22.1 Conditions Favorable to TNC Development and Activities

Political environment. The postwar settlement reversed the prewar protectionist policies and led to the dismantling of many international barriers to business; cooperation became the order of the day, at least in theory, among developed countries.

Technological environment. The development in the technologies of communication and transportation made it possible to manage units in faraway countries. The changes have greatly accelerated in the last 25 years with the developments in ICTs.

Organizational developments. The internal organization of private and public institutions has changed considerably in response to the need and desire for the growth of business and its geographical expansion. The changes have been made possible by the technological advances.

Such conditions have led to a favorable environment for the expansion of transnational business activities; they may indeed be considered as the necessary conditions for such large expansion to take place. They help to explain why it was possible for TNCs to increase their direct business activities abroad; however, they do not tell us much about why the companies wanted to take the direct international route. On this issue we do not have ready-made answers; we have a series of theories explaining why companies find it profitable or necessary to invest abroad. To these we now turn by giving a brief sketch of the main theoretical explanations for FDI and the TNC.

Stephen Hymer and Market Power

The theory of the TNC originated after World War II with the work of Stephen Hymer, a Canadian economist doing research in the United States at the Massachussets Institute of Technology (MIT). His theory (Hymer 1960, published 1976) was developed as part of his doctoral dissertation and published after his premature death. Hymer starts by criticizing existing theories of international investment and draws a distinction between portfolio investment, led by a desire for speculative financial gains, and direct investment, motivated by a desire to control profitable business activities. This demarcation is a major key to our understanding of transnational direct business activities. It is a demarcation used today in identifying FDI. Hymer then goes on to specify the following two main determinants of direct investment abroad: (1) the existence of firm-specific advantages that can be exploited abroad in the search for better investment opportunities and (2) the removal of conflicts with rival firms. The conflicts arise from the market power held by firms; by acquiring assets abroad through foreign direct investment, our firm acquires further power over its rival and thus removes the conflict, at least temporarily. Thus, Hymer's theory is developed by looking for motives in imperfect market structures, specifically in the oligopolistic[5] structures characteristic of many of the industries in which U.S. international firms operate. His theory emphasizes how one way to get ahead of rival firms is to invest abroad. Hymer's work is considered seminal, and many of his points are still debated and further developed.[6]

Raymond Vernon and the International Product Life Cycle Theory

Raymond Vernon's theory (1966), like Hymer's, was also developed at Harvard University, in the same town where Hymer was working: Cambridge, Massachusetts. Vernon took the product as the basis for his analysis; specifically, he was interested in product innovations. According to Vernon, the innovative firm will have a monopoly over the new product at least in the initial stages before imitations begin; this position will give the firm an advantage over its rivals. Developments throughout the life of the product are an essential element of Vernon's theory, known as International Product Life Cycle Theory (IPLCT). The new product is developed in the United States, an economy with (1) a very large market; (2) consumers who have high incomes per capita; (3) a production environment in which there is abundance of capital and labor scarcity leading to high unit labor costs. The product will be developed, produced, and first marketed in the United States. It will then be exported to other rich countries in Europe; this will soon be followed by direct production in European countries for which our innovative firm will have to invest directly in Europe. Meanwhile, other firms will gradually start imitating the product and our firm will lose its monopolistic position; it is then likely that it will try to compete through cost reduction achieved by shifting production facilities into developing countries—a move designed to take advantage of low labor costs and made possible by the gradual standardization of the product. The product will then be exported from the host developing country to developed countries where the markets are located; this may include importation into the United States, the country in which the product first originated.

Vernon's theory is based on the product and its innovations; issues of market structure and its changing configuration are also considered. The theory tries to explain both direct investment with production abroad and international trade: the product is exported from the United States to Europe and later from the host developing country to developed countries; FDI from the United States is directed first to Europe and then to developing countries. The theory is very dynamic because within it the situation changes constantly: firm's and countries' advantages in the product are eroded, and this leads to new strategies of location. The dynamic pattern follows changes in the life of the product from innovation to maturity to standardization.

The focus on the product means that the theory fails to cover the cases of multiproduct firms and their potential for getting ahead of rivals by using multiproducts strategies.[7] Moreover, historically the changing macroenvironment in Europe has led to erosion in the initial advantages that the United States had over Europe in innovation and production facilities: this is a point made by Vernon himself in an excellent self-critical article (1979). Changes in the international environment have also led to shorter life cycles for products and to shorter imitation lags on the part of other firms. The international innovation environment has changed so much since the 1960s that the theory may have a more limited applicability (Cantwell 1995). Nonetheless, it has been an important and influential theory merging various strands of thought from innovation to life-of-the-product, to countries' comparative advantages, to the dynamics of firms' strategies.

The Internalization Theory

In 1937, Ronald Coase published an article characterizing the firm as an institution in which the allocation of resources takes place through planning and central command. He asked why, if the market is the best allocator of resources, as claimed by neoclassical economic theory, are not all resources allocated by means of the market; in other words, he asked, "Why do firms exist?" The answer: though he saw the market with its price mechanisms as the best allocator of resources, he found that market operations are subject to transaction costs—that is, such costs as those for gathering information on the price and quality of the product or the trustworthiness of the supplier or the legal costs of stipulating contracts. Within the firm, such costs disappear or are minimized because the managers know what to expect from their own products and production processes. It is therefore the existence of transaction costs that explains the existence and growth of the firm. Williamson (1975 and 1981) further developed the case for why firms grow and why high levels of resources are allocated internally to the firm rather than through the market and the price mechanism.[8]

It is from these bases that John McManus (1972), and Peter J. Buckley and Mark C. Casson (1976) developed a theory of the multinational enterprise (MNE) based on internalization. In effect, Coase sparked off a trend toward explaining why more and more resources are internalized—that is, allocated internally—within the firm. McManus and Buckley and Casson used internalization to explain why firms grow across frontiers. The starting point again is market imperfections; however, the imperfections on which Buckley and Casson concentrate are not structural imperfections (market imperfections characteristic of noncompetitive markets) but transactional market imperfections (imperfections stemming from transaction costs arising from imperfect knowledge, low trust between buyer and seller, and legal costs). Products that are knowledge and research intensive are particularly susceptible to internalization because the sellers want to make sure they retain the monopoly over their knowledge. The postwar development of direct production has indeed been largely in products requiring considerable research and development. Buckley and Casson write on this issue: "There is a special reason for believing that internalization of the knowledge market will generate a high degree of multinationality among firms. Because knowledge is a public good which is easily transmitted across national boundaries, its exploitation is logically an international operation" (1976 45).

Buckley and Casson's conclusion, therefore, is that markets are imperfect in a transactional sense and therefore generate incentives to internalize; the market for knowledge is highly imperfect, so there are strong benefits in internalizing it. *Knowledge is a public good within the firm*: this means that it can be used in various branches of the firm at little or no extra cost. Moreover, knowledge is easily transmittable across national boundaries, so products that are knowledge intensive will tend to be produced internally to the firm rather than through external contracts. The theory is therefore designed to explain why the firm may produce all components of a product internally rather than buying some from external suppliers and why the modality of direct production is preferred to licensing. The theory cannot explain, however, why the firm does not use the export modality for servicing foreign markets; why, in other words, it does not internalize production at home and sell abroad through exports.[9]

John Dunning's Eclectic Framework

John Dunning, based at the University of Reading in Britain, had been working on issues of international business since the 1950s. In the 1970s, he came out with a wide-ranging theory that he characterized as "eclectic" and that was later referred to as a "framework" or "paradigm." Dunning (1977) tries to explain the why, where, and when of international production: why and when companies prefer the direct investment and production route to exportation or licensing; how they decide on location of production. Dunning's approach requires an analysis of three types of advantages: owneship advantages specific to a particular company, locational advantages, and internalization advantages, together known as OLI advantages (see Box 22.2).

Box 22.2 John Dunning's OLI Advantages

- *Ownership advantages* are *specific to a particular company*. They constitute competitive advantages toward rivals and enable the company to take advantage of investment opportunities wherever they arise.
- *Locational advantages* are those advantages *specific to a country* that are likely to make it attractive for foreign investors.
- *Internalization advantages* are all those benefits that derive from producing internally to the firm; they allow it to bypass external markets and the transaction costs associated with them. They are, essentially, benefits of operating internally within an institution rather than through the market.

Dunning gives a long list for each of the three types of advantages. Ownership (O) advantages may relate to such elements as the availability of superior technology, special access to inputs, superior organizational knowledge, or acquired experience of operating abroad; on this point there is an analogy between the works of Dunning and Hymer. In the locational (L) advantages Dunning lists all those elements that make a country more attractive as an investment location compared to others. The elements are linked to the geographical and political space and include quality of transportation and communication; legal and commercial infrastructure; government policies; quality and price of inputs. The internalization (I) advantages are the same as those in the theory of Buckley and Casson, who were, at the time, working at the same university as Dunning.

The OLI framework has been very successful in the academic international business community partly because it gives a ready-made set of rules or elements that can be applied to a variety of industries, companies, and locations. In a way, this wide-ranging application is also a weakness of the theory; indeed, Dunning (2002b) himself has recognized the danger of slipping into a shopping list of variables. To face up to this problem, he recommends operationalization and contextualization of the various variables linked to his OLI framework (Dunning 1993, 2002a).

The Evolutionary Theory

The vision of the firm as an evolutionary institution goes back to Richard R. Nelson and Sydney G. Winter's work in 1982. Evolution is linked to the accumulation of knowledge, to technological capabilities, and to the ability to exploit those capabilities by using organizational knowledge. In this vein, Bruce Kogut and Udo Zander (1993) critique the internalization theory for its view on knowledge, which they see as one that can easily be packaged and transferred to other locations. Indeed, Kogut and Zander see knowledge largely as tacit knowledge—that is, knowledge that is embedded in people's skills and experiences, including the experience of teamwork. In their view, it is knowledge that cannot easily be transferred outside the human, social and technological environment in which it was developed. In this vision, internalization and the growth of the firm emerge, not so much because of costs of transaction and the inefficiency of markets, but because the firm is a superior institution from the point of view of the development and utilization of knowledge.[10]

The evolutionary approach, in conjunction with some of Dunning's elements, was further developed in John Cantwell (1989), who sees the firm as an active generator of ownership advantages, particularly by means of research and innovation. Cantwell also sees a strong interaction between ownership and locational advantages. Successful innovators tend to invest in innovation activities in several centers or countries; as they do so, their investment generates spillover effects to the location and the industry, thus encouraging more investment and innovative activities by other firms. Each innovating firm brings external benefits to the locality in which it invests. Conversely, the investors benefit from the favorable technological environment that develops in the locality. Agglomeration scale economies—that is, those economies of scale arising from the geographical proximity of several related businesses—are generated, and they further strengthen the centers and the position of the firms operating in them. Thus, according to Cantwell, locational advantages should be seen as largely endogenous, or generated from within the system itself and from the interaction between companies and countries, and not as exogenous, or arising from outside the production system and linked to a country's resources endowments. His approach leads Cantwell to conclude that in innovation, there is a hierarchy of companies though not necessarily a hierarchy of countries: this is one of the elements on which he criticizes Vernon's theory of the international product life cycle.[11]

The Scandinavian School

Vernon's and the evolutionary theories are the ones that exhibit the strongest elements of dynamism: situations change, and firms adapt to changes as well as generating them. Dynamism is at the center of another theory developed by various Scandinavian economists and marketing experts on the basis of applied case studies. Drawing on the works of E. T. Penrose (1959), of R. M. Cyert and J. G. March (1963), and of Y. Aharoni (1966), a group of Swedish academics explored the dynamics of internationalization in their attempt to explain what motivates firms to move from domestic-only production and sales to foreign sales (Johanson and Vahlne 1977, 1990; Johanson and Wiedersheim-Paul 1975). The authors study the organization of sales and marketing in one or more foreign countries and come up with the idea of *stages in the internationalization process*. Two patterns of internationalization need explaining. The first pattern is designed to explain the increase in business involvement in a specific foreign market or country. The pattern develops according to an *establishment chain* characterized by the following sequence: exports through independent representatives (agents); sales subsidiaries; and finally, production subsidiaries. The authors bring in various theoretical and applied elements to explain how and why the sequence evolves.[12] The second pattern relates to involvement in several foreign countries. This proceeds in a time sequence related linearly to the psychic distance from the home country. The psychic distance is defined as "the sum of factors preventing the flow of information from and to the market. Examples are differences in language, education, business practices, culture and industrial development" (Johanson and Vahlne 1977, 24).

Psychic and spatial distances tend to be very closely related. Firms start by operating in closer foreign countries and later use their knowledge of internationalization to branch out into locations that are psychically and spatially more distant. In both types of patterns—within a single foreign country and across many—we see internationalization as a result of a *series of incremental decisions*. It proceeds dynamically and linearly: from one stage to the next; from small to large resources commitment; from a single foreign country to several.

Key Elements in the Theories: The Role of the Nation-State

The different theories presented here—and, indeed, others not discussed here[13]—are developed by emphasizing one or more of the following elements:

(1) different modalities of operations and the stages within them (as in the Scandinavian School); (2) different aspects of market imperfections: structural (Hymer, Vernon) versus transactional (internalization); and (3) strategy versus efficiency as a general approach to companies' objectives.

Consider further the third element: the strategic-versus-efficiency approach to explanations of TNCs' behavior and activities. Most theorists accept that firms' behavior is motivated by the desire to increase or maximize profits; however, in reality it is not easy to define what maximizing behavior means; for example, over what time period does the firm maximize? In practice, some theories emphasize the efficient use of resources as the main route to profits; others see the firm as led by such strategic objectives as eliminating rivals or defending from rivals' aggressive behavior.

The internalization and the evolutionary theories are dominated by efficiency criteria: efficiency in dealing with transaction costs and/or in using and developing knowledge. This approach has been further developed in the so-called New Trade theories of the multinational companies.[14] Strategic approaches usually deal with strategies toward rival firms; elements of this can be found in the theories of Hymer, Vernon, and Dunning.[15] However, firms and, in particular, TNCs can improve their position and profits by also developing strategies toward dealing with other players in the economic system and specifically toward labor and governments. Transnational corporations are best positioned to develop such wider-ranging strategies because they operate across national frontiers. To understand this point, we must look at the role of nation-states vis-à-vis TNCs.

Paradoxically, when analyzed closely, most theories about TNCs have very few elements that can be considered inter-national; that is, very few theories have elements specific to nation-states and what differentiates them from each other. In considering such elements, we start by identifying three dimensions of operation across nation-states.[16] First is a spatial or geographical dimension, then a cultural cum linguistic dimension, and finally a regulatory regimes dimension. Regarding the latter, the following elements of nation-states' regulatory regimes can be identified: (1) currency regimes; (2) fiscal regimes; and (3) social security regimes, in particular, rules and regulations related to labor and its organization.

Let us now assume that companies behave strategically and that strategies can be developed not only toward rival firms but also toward labor and governments. The existence of regulatory regimes gives companies the opportunity to develop strategies toward labor and/or governments with a view to maximize profits and gain stronger market position. The company could develop a location strategy designed to take advantage of the first two types of regulatory regimes. In particular, different fiscal regimes in different countries coupled with the existence of intrafirm trade give the company scope to manipulate transfer prices, thus cutting the company's overall tax liabilities (an issue explained in the next section of the chapter). Different regulatory regimes for labor mean that the workers employed by the same TNC in the various countries in which it operates are subject to differing regulations and thus have difficulty organizing and resisting company management. A company in this situation has a stronger negotiating position toward labor than does a company in which all workers are employed in one country only. The differences in labor regulatory regimes generate scope for specific locational strategies. The conclusion we can draw from this approach is that the existence of different nation-states with different regulatory regimes enables the TNC to develop locational strategies that enhance its profits and put it in a stronger position toward rival firms.

EFFECTS OF TNCS' ACTIVITIES

The activities of TNCs have many effects on their country of origin as well as on the host countries.[17] There are also indirect effects on third countries, that is, on countries that are neither home nor host to the investment of a particular TNC; this happens, for example, if the third country's trade is affected by the TNC's investment decision. Here, however, the focus is on the effects on home and host countries. There are effects on the macroeconomy as well as on the industry of which the TNC is part and on the company's performance. What general effects can we identify regarding the countries and macroeconomies? There are effects on innovation and capacity creation, effects on employment and labor in general, and there are effects on trade and the balance of payments.

Being large companies well endowed with resources, most TNCs tend to be at the forefront of organizational and technological innovation and to spread their innovative practices in the countries in which they operate. Moreover, evidence shows that their internal networks of operations with affiliates in many countries aid the accumulation and spread of innovation and technology (Cantwell 1989; Castellani and Zanfei 2006; Frenz and Ietto-Gillies 2007 and 2009): they learn from the diverse environments in which they operate, and their activities spill over innovation effects on the localities in which they are involved. This means that the total effect is more than the sum of the parts.

Does foreign direct investment generate productive capacity in the host country? If so, under what circumstances? Foreign direct investment of the greenfield type will increase capacity in the host country; this is not necessarily at the expense of capacity in the home country, for it all depends on the specific circumstances of the industry and the home country. However, FDI generated by the M&A variety does not create extra capacity: all that happens is that existing capacity in the host country changes ownership as a domestic firm is bought by a foreign firm. Sometimes capacity may indeed be reduced if plants are closed under rationalization programs following the merger; there is also the possibility, however, that following short-term restructuring the foreign company will invest in new capacity and new technologies in the long run.

Similar effects are possible also with regard to employment; whether FDI generates employment in the host country much depends on whether it is of the greenfield or M&A variety; in the latter case, employment may be reduced if the postmerger rationalization programs lead to layoffs, as they often do. The greenfield type of FDI does generate extra employment in the host country. Affiliates of TNCs worldwide directly employ some 72.6 million people

(UNCTAD 2007, table 1.4, p. 9), which is not a very large number. Several reasons account for this relatively low number, including the following. Being technologically advanced, many TNCs tend to use labor-saving techniques. Moreover, since the 1980s, many companies have been outsourcing many of their activities and production processes. It is not the case that the employment effects on the home country are always the opposite of those in host countries: outward FDI may or may not reduce employment in the home country, for much depends on the conditions at home. There are also indirect employment effects on both the host and home countries.

The activities of TNCs have wider effects on labor over and above any direct and indirect effects on employment. There are effects on productivity, on skills acquisitions, and on labor relations. Recall that workers of a company operating in several countries have weaker bargaining power in disputes with management than do workers of a company that is not international. This is so, as explained earlier, because labor employed multinationally is fragmented; its trade unions are weaker because they are organized and operate country-by-country while facing companies that are truly transnational in their strategic behavior.

The TNCs have wide effects on international trade, that is, on imports and exports of goods and services worldwide. Over 80 percent of world trade originates with the TNCs. Moreover, some of this trade is internal to the company itself though external to the country: this is the so-called *intrafirm trade (IFT)*. It is estimated that IFT amounts to over a third of all world trade. Intrafirm trade originates through the setting up of international vertically integrated production systems. These systems imply that the corporation decides to locate different components of the final product—and therefore different stages of the production process—in different countries in order to take advantage of different skills availability and different labor costs. The whole strategy is designed to minimize the production cost of the product as a whole. This means the various components have to be transferred from country to country for further processing. Such transfers are internal to the company, with components moving from affiliate to affiliate or between parent and affiliate, though they cross national boundaries.

Intrafirm trade is significant for various reasons. It highlights the relevance of strategy and planning across countries, that is, transnational operations, within the company. It affects the utilization of resources, particularly labor and the development of labor skills or lack of it, and it does this for the various countries involved, both the home and the host countries. It also gives scope for the so-called manipulation of transfer prices (a topic addressed later in this section). Consider yet another type of effect also relevant in this context. Trade generates balance-of-payment effects as currency moves in opposite direction to goods and services to pay for them. Balance-of-payments effects are also generated by currency movements resulting from investment. Indeed, the funding of investment, be it greenfield or M&A, is likely to require currency movements from the home to the host country, though not always because some FDI is funded from the accumulation of past profits or through capital raised directly in the host country. Balance-of-payments effects are also generated by the movement of profits and dividends following investment in the host country: the currency movements of profits and dividends go in the opposite direction to those of the investment; moreover, an initial investment may give rise to profits for many years in the future. Such balance-of-payment effects provide countries that have a long history of outward FDI with a large and steady flow of inward profits (Ietto-Gillies 2000).

One specific effect of intrafirm trade comes from the so-called transfer prices or, rather, the manipulation of transfer prices by companies. Such prices are charged by one part of the company, usually a parent or one of the affiliates, to another part, which could be any of the affiliates or even the parent, for the internal transfer of goods and services. Thus the prices are those charged on invoices for internal transfers within the same company. The word "manipulation" here refers to the fact that the prices charged for internal transfers are set at levels different from actual or potential market prices. The scope for manipulation of transfer prices can be quite wide in the case of transfers internal to the company but external to countries, as in the case of intrafirm trade.

Box 22.3 Possible Reasons for Manipulating Transfer Prices

- To minimize tax liabilities for the company as a whole.
- To circumvent restrictions to the transfer of profits from those host countries that pose strict ceilings and constraints to such transfers.
- To take advantages of expected appreciation or depreciation of currencies.
- To record low costs of components in a country or market the company wants to penetrate through low prices. This is essentially a strategy designed to gain competitive advantages over rivals.
- To record relatively low profits in countries where it is feared labor and its trade unions might demand wage increases if high profits were disclosed.

Why might TNCs manipulate transfer prices? The reasons are many (see Box 22.3). The most common reason for the manipulation of transfer prices, however, and the best known, is that doing so minimizes the overall tax liability of the company. A company faced with tax liabilities in many countries is likely also to be faced with different tax rates in different countries (referred to earlier as different fiscal regimes). If the company manages to declare most of its profits in the country with the lowest tax rate, it will avoid the charge of higher tax rates on some of its profits, thus minimizing its overall tax liability. This aim can partly be achieved by a deliberate strategy of manipulating transfer prices such that the higher profits are recorded in the country with the lowest tax rate; and the very low profits, in countries with high tax rates. Thus, where the profits are transferred depends on the tax rate of the countries, not on whether those countries are hosts or homes or whether they are developed or developing countries. The practice of manipulating transfer prices is illegal but difficult to detect because there are no market prices for many of the components being transferred internally; in fact, many transfers relate to services from one part of the company to another.

TNCS AND GLOBALIZATION

Cross-border transactions are nothing new in the history of humankind, but can we say that the present globalization is something special? If so, why? The present process is special in terms of both quantitative and qualitative elements. Regarding quantitative elements, all types of cross-border transactions—from trade to FDI, to portfolio investment, to collaborative agreements, to movements of people—have been increasing. As regards the qualitative aspects, the current process is underpinned and enhanced by the political and social environment; the breath of change that involves most aspect of modern life—from culture to production processes, to consumption, to the military; the technological basis and, specifically, the ICTs; and the role of TNCs in the process.

The transnational corporations are involved in, or fully responsible for, all types of international transactions and therefore all quantitative aspects of the globalization process; they also drive most of the qualitative elements. Our decades can, indeed, be seen as a new phase of capitalist development in which the TNCs are the "dominant cause" of the globalization process (Ietto-Gillies 2002, chap. 9). It is often argued that the globalization process leads to economic, social, and cultural, if not political, integration. It is certainly the case that consumption patterns are becoming more homogenous; that markets, particularly financial market, are more global; and that concerns over faraway parts of the worlds are increasing. However, to the concept of integration can be attached an additional meaning, one related to production and production processes and their organization.

Transnational corporations are increasingly planning production on a multi-countries, and on occasions global, basis. The planning takes account not only of the location of markets but also of the required productive resources, that is, where the materials and labor needed for production are located. Not only this, but the production process can be adapted to fit the availability and cost of resources in various locations. The production process can be split into various parts in which different components are so designed as to require different skills intensity; such division allows companies to locate production in different countries according to the skills required by the production process. The overall result is that components requiring low skills for their production will be located in labor abundant countries, usually developing countries with low labor costs; components requiring workers with high levels of skills will be located in developed countries. Several firms may be involved in the process, with some working as subcontractors to the large ones. The overall cost of the product will be minimized in this process, known as international vertical integration of production. It is precisely such a strategy that leads to growth in intrafirm trade.

The aforementioned process leads to greater integration of countries and companies; the large TNCs develop not only internal networks across borders but also networks with several external enterprises. However, it can also be claimed that the same process leads also to the disintegration of the production process, since no single country becomes responsible for the whole process and product. Moreover, there is a process of fragmentation of the labor force employed in the overall production process: different groups of laborers work on different components in different countries under the TNC's overall strategy. The labor force has increasing difficulty organizing, through their trade unions, in such a fragmented structure, particularly because workers' solidarity tends to be weaker across borders. The problem arises from the fact that a truly transnational organization—the TNC, with its ability to control, manage, and devise strategies across countries—confronts organizations that are unable, or have so far been unable, to organize themselves transnationally. Whether this asymmetry and imbalance in the power of social forces will continue in the future remains to be seen; regional integration across many area of the world may change the situation. Indeed, the social, economic, and political consequences of such fragmentation are issues that merit further discussion and research. Moreover, the impact of the current recession on the activities of the TNCs and on their relationship with other actors need much analysis and research.

NOTES

1. See, in particular, their annual *World Investment Report* and their quarterly academic journal *Transnational Corporations*.

2. Foreign direct investment flow and stock data for each country are given in the UNCTAD *World Investment Report,* where further details on definitions can also be found. See also Ietto-Gillies (2005, pt. 1) for further analysis of the contents of the first two sections of this chapter.

3. All data in this section from UNCTAD 2007: Annex, table A.I.5, p. 217; Annex, table B2, p. 255.

4. A wider treatment of this is in Ietto-Gillies (1997).

5. An oligopolistic structure is one in which the market is dominated by a few large firms each striving to get ahead of its rivals.

6. See, among others, *Contributions to Political Economy* 21 (2002) and *International Business Review* 15 (2006): 2. Hymer's theory is further analyzed in Ietto-Gillies (2005, chap. 5).

7. See Ietto-Gillies (2005, chap. 6) for more on the theory and critiques.

8. A summary of Williamson's contribution is in Ietto-Gillies (2005, chap. 9, sec. 2).

9. Various criticisms and appreciations of this theory are developed in Ietto-Gillies (2005, chap. 9).

10. For a clear and critical exposition of the evolutionary theory see Forsgren (2007, chap. 4).

11. See Cantwell (1995) for the whole critique, and see Ietto-Gillies (2005, chap. 6, sec. 5, and chap. 12, sec. 2) for selective points.

12. See Ietto-Gillies (2005, chap. 11) for a summary of these and other points related to this theory.

13. Forsgren (2007) presents several theories with emphasis on different aspects of the TNC. See, in particular, his discussion of networking multinationals in ch. 6.

14. Many authors have contributed to this approach in the last 20 years. A clear exposition of these theories is in Barba Navaretti and Venables (2004, chaps. 3–6); see also Ietto-Gillies (2005, chap. 13) for a summary and critique.

15. The strategic approach is very pronounced in Knickerbocker (1973) as well as in Cowling and Sugden (1987). Their theories are considered in Ietto-Gillies (2005) in chap. 7 and chap14, respectively.

16. For a full development of the points made in this section, cf. Ietto-Gillies (2005, chap.15).

17. See Ietto-Gillies (2005, pt. 4) for a longer discussion of the theoretical frameworks and of methodological issues in the assessment of effects; Barba Navaretti and Venables (2004, chaps. 7–9) analyze the empirical results of several studies.

FURTHER READING

Barba Navaretti, G., and A. J. Venables. *Multinational Firms in the World Economy.* Princeton, NJ: Princeton University Press, 2004. See chaps. 7, 8, and 9 on effects.

Cantwell, J. "A Survey of Theories of International Production." In *The Nature of the Transnational Firm,* edited by C. N. Pitelis and R. Sugden. London: Routledge, 2000. See chap. 2 on theories, 10–56.

Forsgren, M. *A Multifarious Creature: Six Tales of the Multinational Firm.* Uppsala, Sweden: Uppsala University, 2007. See chaps. 4 and 6 on theories.

Ietto-Gillies, G. *Transnational Corporations: Fragmentation amidst Integration.* London: Routledge, 2002. See chaps. 1, 9, and 10 on globalization and the TNCs.

———. *Transnational Corporations and International Production. Concepts, Theories and Effects.* Cheltenham, UK: Edward Elgar, 2005. See pts. 1, 2, and 4 on concepts, theories, and effects.

REFERENCES

Aharoni, Y. 1966. *The foreign investment decision process.* Cambridge, MA: Harvard University Press.

Barba Navaretti, G., and A. J. Venables. 2004. *Multinational firms in the world economy.* Princeton, NJ: Princeton University Press.

Buckley, P. J., and M. C. Casson. 1976. A long-run theory of the multinational enterprise. In *The future of the multinational enterprise,* ed. P. J. Buckley and M. C. Casson, 32–65. London: Macmillan.

Cantwell, J. 1989. *Technological innovation and multinational corporations.* Oxford: Blackwell.

———. 1995. The globalization of technology: What remains of the product cycle model? *Cambridge Journal of Economics* 19: 155–74.

———. 2000. A survey of theories of international production. In *The Nature of the Transnational Firm,* ed. C. N. Pitelis and R. Sugden. London: Routledge.

Castellani, D., and A. Zanfei. 2006. *Multinational firms, innovation and productivity.* Cheltenham, UK: Edward Elgar.

Coase, R. H. 1937. The nature of the firm. *Economica* 4: 386–405. Reprinted in *Readings in price theory,* ed. G. J. Stigler and K. E. Boulding, 331–51 London: Allen and Unwin, 1953.

Contributions to political economy 21, 2002.

Cowling, K., and R. Sugden. 1987. *Transnational monopoly capitalism.* Brighton, UK: Wheatsheaf.

Cyert, R. M., and J. G. March. 1963. *A behavioral theory of the firm.* Englewood Cliffs, NJ: Prentice Hall.

Dunning, J. H. 1977. Trade, location of economic activity and the MNE: A search for an eclectic approach. In *The international allocation of economic activity,* ed. B. Ohlin, P. O. Hesselborn, and P. M. Wijkman, 395–431. London: Macmillan.

———. 1993. *Multinational enterprises and the global economy.* Wokingham, UK: Addison Wesley.

Dunning, J. H. 2000a. The eclectic paradigm as an envelope for economic and business theories of MNE activity. *International Business Review* 9: 163–90.

———. 2000b. The eclectic paradigm of international production: A personal perspective. In *The nature of the transnational firm,* ed. C. Pitelis and R. Sugden, 119–39. London: Routledge.

Forsgren, M. 2007. *A multifarious creature: Six tales of the multinational firm.* Uppsala, Swed.: Uppsala University.

Frenz, M., and G. Ietto-Gillies. 2007. Does multinationality affect the propensity to innovate? An analysis of the third UK Community Innovation Survey. *International Review of Applied Economics* 21: 99–117.

———. 2009. The impact on innovation performance of different sources of knowledge: Evidence from the UK Community Innovation Survey. *Research Policy* 38: 1125–35.

Hymer, S. H. 1960 [1976]. *The international operations of national firms: A study of direct foreign investment.* Cambridge, MA: MIT Press.

Ietto-Gillies, G. 1997. The environment of international business. In *Global business strategy,* ed. R. John, G. Ietto-Gillies, H. Cox, and N. Grimwade, 73–89. London: Thomson.

———. 2000. Profits from foreign direct investment. In *European integration and global corporate strategies,* ed. F. Chesnais, G. Ietto-Gillies, and R. Simonetti, 71–91. London: Routledge.

———. 2002. *Transnational corporations: Fragmentation amidst integration.* London: Routledge.

———. 2005. *Transnational corporations and international production: Concepts, theories and effects.* Cheltenham, UK: Edward Elgar.

Johanson, J., and J-E. Vahlne. 1990. The mechanism of internationalization. *International Marketing Review* 7: 11–24.

Johanson, J., and F. Wiedersheim-Paul. 1975. The internationalization of the firm: Four Swedish cases. *Journal of Management Studies* October: 305–22.

Knickerbocker, F. T. 1973. *Oligopolistic reaction and alultinational enterprise.* Cambridge, MA: Division of Research, Graduate School of Business Administration, Harvard University.

Kogut, B., and U. Zander. 1993. Knowledge of the firm and the evolutionary theory of the multinational corporation. *Journal of International Business Studies* 4th quarter: 625–45.

McManus, J. 1972. The theory of the international firm. In *The multinational firm and the nation state,* ed. Gilles Paquet amd Don Mills, 66–93. Ontario: Collier-Macmillan.

Nelson, R. R., and S. G. Winter. 1982. *An evolutionary theory of economic change.* Cambridge, MA: Harvard University Press.

Penrose, E. T. 1959. *The theory of the growth of the firm.* Oxford: Blackwell.

UN Conference on Trade and Development (UNCTAD). 2007. Transnational corporations, extractive industries and development. World Investment Report. Geneva: United Nations.

Vernon, R. 1966. International investment and international trade in the product Cycle. *Quarterly Journal of Economics* 80: 190–207.

———. 1979. The product cycle hypothesis in a new international environment. *Oxford Bulletin of Economics and Statistics* 41: 255–67.

Wilkins, M. 1988. The freestanding company, 1817–1914. *Economic History Review* 61: 259–82.

Williamson, O. 1975. *Markets and hierarchies: Analysis and anti-trust implications.* New York: Free Press.

Williamson, O. E. 1981. The modern corporation: Origins, evolution, attributes. *Journal of Economic Literature* 19: 1537–68.

Glossary

Biopower   Term coined to describe the way in which states or nations control human bodies; power is exercised to protect life through the regulation of individual behavior and groups.

Bretton Woods   Monetary management system set up after World War II to govern financial and commercial relations among the major industrial relations. By 1968, the policy of pegging the dollar to gold was proving untenable.

Civil society organizations   Various voluntary, civic, and social organizations and institutions falling outside the remit of both market and state.

Commodification   Transformation of all social and natural elements to commodities that can be bought and sold in the marketplace—thus, for example, commodification of knowledge. Cf. **neoliberalism**.

Complexity approach   Focus on nonlinear complex systems and how these systems interact and form relationships with their environment. Globalization can be viewed as such a complex system. Cf. **reductionist approach**.

Conjunctural factors   Those factors pertaining to the here and now as against underlying structural causes.

Connectivity   Reference to the huge growth of information in the 1990s through the Internet, in particular, which has connected people across space.

Contingently related   Opposite of necessarily related. A proposition is contingently related to another if it can be affirmed and another denied at the same time. So, the world is becoming more international but not necessarily global. Cf. **reductionist approach.**

Cosmopolitanism   Understanding that all humanity belongs to one world community; despite our differences, "we are the world."

Critical security   Approach that argues that security theory needs to challenge inequitable power structures and seek human emancipation.

Culture Human capacity to classify and communicate our experience through symbolic means. Culture, in this sense, is a way of life, of seeing the world around us.

Cyber attacks Security challenges through the Internet (cyberspace) ranging from hacking to full military intent.

Debt crisis of the 1970s Major problem for the developing world where massive financial borrowing following the 1973 oil crisis led to indebtedness resulting from many factors, including high interest rates.

Deregulation Approach to the economy that argues for a withdrawal of the state (and state regulation) from all economic offers and transactions. Cf. **neoliberalism.**

Economic determinism Belief that the economy is ultimately the cause of social and political transformations. As in "It's the economy, stupid."

Emancipatory theory Approach that argues the need for identifying social structures that are detrimental to human development and to develop coherent and stable alternatives to them.

End of history Term that became popular in the early 1990s as communism imploded and it seemed that a new global era of peace and prosperity in Western lives would ensue.

Eurocentrism Practice of viewing the world from a European perspective, even denigrating the achievements of other civilizations.

Fixed exchange rates Type of pegged exchange rates in which a given currency is matched to a basket of other currencies or against gold or a standard measure. Cf. **gold standard.**

GATT General Agreement on Tariffs and Trades. Set up in 1948 to govern international trade in the postwar period, GATT was the predecessor of the WTO. By 1986, GATT was straining to meet the demands of the new globalizing world economy. Cf. **WTO.**

Global compact Framework created by the United Nations for business committed to what we might call "globalization with a human face." Cf. **global governance.**

Global governance Complex formal and informal mechanisms between states at the level of the state, the market, citizens, and organizations. Global governance is deemed necessary to regulate full market globalization. Cf. **governance.**

Global media Global spread of digitalized and computerized media in the 1990s.

Global North Term now widely used to describe such different industrialized societies of the West as North America, Western Europe, and Japan.

Global South Term now widely used to describe the developing countries of the Third World, comprising the poorer countries of Africa, Asia, and Latin America.

Global terrorism Term that became common after the 9/11 attacks in the United States seeking to discern a coherent pattern in international terrorist attacks. Cf. **terrorism.**

Global warming Increase in the Earth's air and ocean temperature since the mid-twentieth century. The current projection is that this trend will continue.

Glossary

Globality Increasingly interconnected international marketplace, where national boundaries no longer impede trade.

Globalizers Individuals who believe the world is heading inexorably toward a more global future where nation-states might well disappear. Cf. **skeptics.**

Glocalization Amalgam of the terms "globalization' and "localization." Glocalization refers to the practice developed since the 1970s to "think globally and act locally," whether by a corporation or an environmental group.

Gold standard Global monetary system through which a nation's currency could be converted into gold as a universally accepted measure. The gold standard era stretched from the 1870s to World War I.

Governance System different from government insofar as it implies an element of collaboration between institutions to allocate resources to steer the economy and society in a global direction. Cf. **global governance, statist.**

Grand narrative Metanarrative that refers to the underlying ideas of science, religion, or politics that provide a coherent story for human history. Cf. **poststructuralism.**

Great Crash of 1929 One of the most significant crises of modern capitalism, resulting from the failure of the U.S. stock exchange. The financial fiasco led to the worldwide depression and massive unemployment of the 1930s.

Hard power Term describing power within international relations based on the military or economic strength of a state. Cf. **soft power.**

Hobbesian Term relating to the seventeenth-century English philosopher Thomas Hobbes, who argued that states believe in the international arena as individuals do in a state of nature.

Human development index Comparative measurement of development based on life expectancy, literacy, education, and standards of living seeking to capture well-being.

Human security People-centered understanding of security stressing the need to diminish human vulnerabilities as a means of enhancing state security. Cf. **societal security.**

Humanitarian war Seemingly contradictory term coined during the breakup of Yugoslavia in the 1990s to describe a military intervention in pursuit of humanitarian goals. Related to the notion that human rights can override national sovereignty.

Hybridization Term used in globalization theories. Hybridization refers to the ongoing blending of cultures as a result of greater connectivity.

ICT Information and Communication Technologies. The term includes such telecommunications technologies as telephone, cable, satellite, and radio systems as well as the Internet. The so-called ICT revolution of the 1980s is widely seen as setting the way for globalization.

Identity Term used in the social sciences to describes how an individual perceives him- or herself, which may indicate identification with a given nation or religion.

Information Age Term coined to describe the world emerging out of the Internet where emphasis shifts from the production of goods toward the ownership and control of knowledge. Hence, "knowledge economy" and "knowledge society."

Keynesianism Set of economic policies designed by John Maynard Keynes in the postwar period. Keynesianism, based on economic growth and stability in a mixed public- and private-sector economy, entered a crisis in the mid-1970s. Cf. **neoliberalism.**

Knowledge society Social system where knowledge, rather that capital, labor, and land. is the primary production resource. Cf: **Information Age.**

Liminal(ity) Term meaning "betwixt and between," or on the threshold to another state. Identities dissolve, and this process can lead to disorientation. Liminal(ity) may be a side effect of globalization.

McDonaldization Reference to how the methods of the fast food outlet—efficiency, calculability, predictability, and control—have percolated throughout contemporary society.

Methodological nationalism Concept taking for granted the nation-state as the paradigm within which politics or international relations are understood. Globalization operates a paradigm shift.

Modernization theory Approach that emerged in the 1950s to systematically chart the integrated economic, political, social, and cultural advancement of the postcolonial reforms of the world.

Multilateral economic institutions Term given to the various international organizations charged with governance of the new global order. Cf. **IMF, World Bank, WTO.**

National security Requirement to maintain the integrity of the nation-state through economic, financial, and military power as well as diplomatic means.

National sovereignty Exclusive right of a state to govern a given national territory and its people. Part of international law, this principle ruled unquestioned until the era of globalization.

New international division of labor Feature of the 1970s, during which the old colonial era division of labor between the industrialized countries and the agricultural or raw materials–producing countries was transformed through the partial industrialization of the latter.

Neoliberalism Set of economic policies that gained prominence in the 1980s based on the presumption that government control of the economy is both inefficient and corrupt. Such free market economics is currently being questioned. Cf. **Keynesianism, Washington Consensus.**

Paradigms Theoretical frameworks that define a scientific discipline over a period of time, defining its terms of reference and the questions asked. Thus, globalization theory can be said to have operated a "paradigm shift."

Poststructuralism View that encompasses a series of social theories or philosophies that reject the classic pursuit of absolute truth to focus on how structures are culturally conditioned.

Glossary 433

Reductionist approach Focus on simplification. The reductionist approach seeks to reduce a complex system to a sum of its parts and find a simple causality underlying it. Cf. **complexity approach.**

Reflexivity Self-reflection and bidirectionality in relationship, with cause and effect affecting each other. Globalization can be seen as a form of reflexive modernization.

Repressive tolerance A 1960s term that argued that tolerance was an illusion because what the state really wished to achieve was co-optation of the counterculture movement.

Revolution in military affairs (RMA) Theory about the future of warfare focused on the potential of information and communication technologies and the need for total systems integration in contemporary armed forces organizations.

Securitization As distinct from the financial definition of securitization, a term used here to describe the process whereby an issue (e.g., migration or trade) becomes subject to the attention of national security.

Securocrats Term used by critics of the security forces to describe the new security bureaucracy in charge of surveillance and internal security.

Skeptics Individuals doubtful that globalization is either a new phenomenon or a force fundamentally undermining the power and continued role of the nation-state. Cf. **globalizers.**

Societal security Term used in contrast to state security to capture the need for a society to maintain its own collective identity if it is to survive. Cf. **state security.**

Soft power Term used in international relations theory to describe the influencing of politics or state behavior through cultural or ideological means. Cf. **hard power.**

State security Concept that stresses the priority of preserving the integrity and power of the state and society as a whole over individual rights. Cf. **societal security.**

Statist Politics that implies a form of government with significant state intervention in personal, social, and economic matters to the detriment of individual freedoms. Cf. **governance.**

Substate politics Nationalism or political involvement that operates at a level below that of the nation-state, e.g., in a religion. Substate politics may be increasing with globalization. Cf. **suprastate politics.**

Suprastate politics Any process that occurs at a level above that of the nation-state, whether through transnational institutions or protests. Suprastate politics is increasing under globalization. Cf. **substate politics.**

Supraterritoriality Effect of globalization creating transworld or transborder relations that are no longer restricted to national spaces.

Teleological theories Approaches that posit a predefined point of arrival for a given process. Thus, modernization theory argued that all nations could eventually arrive at modernity.

Terrorism Systematic use of fear or terror as a means of political coercion. The term ay also refer to unlawful wars, as in "state terrorism."

Theory-practice nexus Critique of the notion that social theory and human practice operate in different domains: our actions are guided by theory, and our theories need to be practiced to be relevant.

Third-way politics "Radical center" approach to contemporary global politics that rejects both socialism and classic free market politics. In terms of globalization, it may lead to support for global governance.

Time-space compression Way information techniques and advances in transportation closed up both temporal and spatial distances in the 1990s. The world become both "smaller" and time moved "faster."

Transformationalist Approaches to globalization that stress the ongoing, open, and contingent nature of its processes under way, the outcome of which is not certain. Cf. **globalizers, skeptics.**

Virtual Term that can mean fake but in the Internet era refers to the new worlds being constructed in virtual domains where Web technologies allow for multiple economic, social, and cultural interactions.

Washington Consensus Term deployed during the 1990s to describe the dominant approach to economic reform advocated by the main international economic bodies.

Wicked issue Problem that is messy and not amenable to simple solutions. As against the relatively tame problems of mathematics, planners always face such aggressive problems as AIDS or global warming.

World music Traditional or indigenous music that has gained in influence through globalization. The term has replaced the more common expression "folk music"; it is also referred to as "non-Western music."

WTO World Trade Organization. The WTO was created in 1995 to supervise the liberalization of international trade and set the rules for trade between nations at a global level. Many protests have been mounted against the WTO, most notably in Seattle in 1999.

Index

Aarhus Convention, 133
The Accumulation of Capital on a World Scale, 194
aerial bombing, 207, 208
affiliates and associates, 412
Afghanistan, 71, 76, 113, 140, 147, 149, 159, 190
Africa, 63, 67, 71, 73, 82, 140, 144, 177, 192, 241, 279
African Charter of Humans and Peoples' Rights, 176, 185
African National Congress (ANC), 157
Aganben, Giorgio, 7
Agenda 21, 94
age of terrorism, 29
agglomeration scale economies, 418
Agnew, John, 140, 144
Aharoni, Y., 419
Ahmed, Shamima, 305
Airbus-Boeing case and WTO, 402–3
Alexander, Jeffrey, 33
Algeria, 196
Alliance for Progress, 66
alluvial diamonds, 240–41
Almaty, 339
Al Qaeda, 2, 7, 8, 82, 115, 209, 215
Althusser, Louis, 229
amateur terrorism, 377
American Convention on Human Rights, 176
American immigration law, 30
Americas, regionalism in: characteristics, old and new, 318–22; democracy and, 323–4; examples, 313–14; and regionalization, 312–17; struggling over, 317–18; target groups, 322–3
Amin, Ash, 13
Amnesty International (AI), 177, 243, 295–6
amoral state, 174
Amsden, Alice, 72, 73
Andean Community, 324
Andean Group (AG), 320
Andean Promotion Corporation, 324
Anglo-American corporate, 360
Anglophone world and geopolitics, 139
Angola, 113, 240, 242–3, 248, 250, 284
anti-money laundering (AML): and CFT regime, politics of, 116–17; criminalization of laundering, 110–11; global, 109–10; national, 110–12; network, 106–9; policies to prevent laundering, 112–13; principal actors, 113–14; private sector role, 116; regional, 110;

anti-money laundering (AML) (*Continued*)
  strengthening of, 111; structure, 114; terrorist financing, combating, 114–15
Anti-Terrorism, Crime and Security Act, 382, 384
Antwerp, 240, 242
aquaculture, 127
Arafat, Yasser, 145
Argentina, 21, 143, 151
Argonauts, 38
armed conflicts, 163
Arquilla, John, 8
Arrighi, Giovanni, 198, 200, 201
Asal, Victor, 8
Asia, 63, 67, 140, 144, 177; culture and human rights, 185
Asian financial crisis, 21
Asia-Pacific, 71
Asia's Next Giant: South Korea and Late Industrialization, 73
Astana, 339
Atkinson, Anthony, 266
atrocity, 285
Australia, 47, 127, 151
Autor, David, 265
Autor-Levy-Murnane (ALM) hypothesis, 265–266
Axworthy, Lloyd, 4

balance-of-payments effects, 422–3
Balassa, Béla, 319
Ballentine, Karen, 75
Bancroft Treaties, 30
Baran, Paul, 67
Barnett, Thomas, 137, 150
Basel Committee on Banking Supervision, 101, 359
Basque Spain, 126
Battle of Kursk, 209
Bauman, Zygmunt, 10
Beck, Ulrich, 23, 83, 84, 263
Becker, Ian Dew, 266
Becoming a Citizen, 37
Behnabib, Sheyla, 183

Belarus, 338, 340
Belgium, 121
Belize, 133
Belovezhe agreements, 336
Benhabib, Seyla, 31, 32
Bentham, Jeremy, 175
Bhagwati, Jagdish, 21
Biafran War. *See* Nigerian civil war
Billon, Phillipe Le, 82
Bin Laden, Osama, 147
biopolitics, 7
biopower, 7
Black Ice, 212
Blair, Sir Ian, 382
Blair, Tony, 145
Bloemraad, Irene, 37
Blood Diamond, 249
blowback, 147
Blue Cascades, 212
Bobbio, Norberto, 181
Boli, John, 299
Bolivarian Alternative for the Americas (ALBA), 318
Bolivarian regionalism, 318
Bookchin, Murray, 87
Booth, Ken, 1, 9
The Borderless World, 12
Bosnian war, 286
Botswana, 248
Boulding, Kenneth, 156
Brandt Commission, 68, 156
Braudel, Fernand, 198
Brazil, 21, 143, 403, 413, 240, 246
Brenner, Robert, 198
Bretton Woods Conference (1944), 226
Bretton Woods institutions, 16, 17–18, 101, 196, 197
British counterterrorist legislation, evolution, 383–5
British International Studies Association, 372
Broad, Robin, 21
Brownfield investments, 411
Bruntland Report, 93
Brzezinski, Zbigniew, 68
Buckley, Peter J., 416, 417

Bujagali dam project, World Bank, 306
Bukharin, Nikolai, 194
Burke, Edmund, 224
Burkina Faso, 246
Burton, John, 156, 160
Bush, George W., 7, 71, 140, 328
business associations, 360
Buzan, Barry, 4
Bycatch fish, 129, 133

Campaign for Access to Essential Medicines, 300
Canada, 4, 35, 36, 63, 167, 248
Cantwell, John, 418
capital intensiveness, 127
Capitalism and Underdevelopment in Latin America, 67
capitalism, 91, 222, 234; and democracy, 49; casino, 18; consumer, 87; corporate, 49; crony, 73; entrepreneurial, 49; global, 32; and imperialism, 192–6; industrial, 195; internationalization of, 13; and liberalism, 224; moral acceptance of, 21
Capitalism, Socialism, and Democracy, 48
CARE, 305
Carey, Henry, 199
Cartagena Protocol of the Convention on Biological Diversity, 396
Carter, Jimmy, 68
casino capitalism, 18
Cassin, Rene, 177
Casson, Mark C., 416, 417
Castells, Manuel, 233, 260
Catholicism, 222
Center for Economic Policy Research, 304
Central African Republic (CAR), 246
Central America, 69, 71
Central Asia, 141, 147
Central Asian Bank of Cooperation and Development, 337
Central Asian Commonwealth, 338

Central Intelligence Agency (CIA), 141, 147
Cerny, Phil, 20
Cha, Victor, 308, 353
Chandler, David, 275
child-soldiers, 283, 288; Uganda, 283–4
Chile, 131, 132, 142
China, 15, 62, 64, 71, 72, 81, 141, 196, 201, 244, 344, 392, 403, 413; digital divide, 269; high-tech trade with, 401–2; offshoring, 270; and Russia, 342–3
China National Petroleum Corporation (CNPC), 342
Chinese Cultural Revolution, 288
Chrismar, J. Von, 142
Chung, C-P., 141
citizenship of residency, 32
citizenship, 28. *See also* dual citizenship: disaggregation of, 32; modern, 33; revoking, 35
city-state, 28
Civil Authorities (Special Powers) Act, 383
civil conflict, 74
Civil Defense Force militia, 287
civilians, victims of war, 286
civilization and state, 145
civil rights, 178, 179
civil society, 23, 33, 56n5, 294, 361
civil society organizations (CSOs), 23, 360
The Civil Sphere, 33
civil war, 50, 159, 193, 282
Clarke, Gerald, 294
classic dependency theory, 64–66
classical modernization theory, 64–66
Clausewitz, Carl von, 276, 285
Clinton, Bill, 70, 71, 146, 215, 258
Coase, Ronald, 416
Coercion Acts, 383
Cold War, 35, 36, 46, 51, 62, 142, 144, 176, 196, 200, 209; end of, 2, 23, 70–71, 139, 140, 145; legacies, 147
collective security, 3

Collier, Paul, 74, 285
Colombia, 74, 82, 113
colonialism, 92, 177; and imperialism, 191
combating terrorist financing (CFT), and AML regime, politics of, 116–117
The Coming Anarchy, 145
Commission of Human Security, 6
Commission on Global Governance, 6, 22
Commission on Human Rights. *See* Human Rights Council
Commission on Human Security, 160
Common Agricultural Policy, Europe, 122
Common Fisheries Policy (CFP), EU, 121–2, 134; failings, and fisheries crisis in Europe, 122–5
Common Frontiers, 323
common pool resources (CPR), 121
Commonwealth of Independent States (CIS), 329, 336–7, 341
The Communist Manifesto, 199
Community of South American Nations (CSAN), 324
Community of Sovereign Republics, 340
competitiveness, 9
Complex interdependence, 102
complexity approach and globalization, 12, 13
Concept of Economic Integration and Development, 337
Conference on Security and Confidence-Building Measures in Asia, 340
conflict, 6, 145, 160, 176; armed, 163; civil, 74, 75; environmental. *See* environmental insecurity; interstate, 81–82; intrastate, 30; security issues and potential for, 132–3; violent, 158, 164
conflict diamonds, 249–50, 251; versus illicit diamonds, 249–51
Congo, 34, 148
Connectivity. *See* interconnectedness

constructionists, 393–4; IPEs, 393–4; view on regionalism, 335
consumer capitalism, 87
Contadora Group, 318
contingently related tendencies, 13
Convention on Biological Diversity (CBD), 356
Convention on the Elimination of All Forms of Discrimination against Women (CEDAW), 357
Convention on the Prevention and Punishment of the Crime of Genocide, 175
Convention on the Rights of the Child, 357
The Cool War, 210
Copenhagen School, 5
corporate capitalism, 49
corporate social responsibility, 21
Corporate Watch, 304
corporations, 11, 12
cosmopolitan systems, 172
Côte d'Ivoire, 248, 250
Council for Trade in Goods (WTO), 244
Counter-Terrorism Command, 382
counterterrorism measures, 7
Cox, Michael, 141
Cox, Robert, 10, 137
Crelinsten, Ronald, 372
crime, peace, and security regulations, 358
criminalism, 10
crisis management, 280
The Crisis of Democracy, 50
critical security, 3, 5
critical security studies (CSS), 372
Critical Studies on Terrorism, 372
critical terrorism studies (CTS), 372–4, 386
crony capitalism, 73
cross-border transactions, 424
crypto, 213–14
Cuba, 66, 139, 318; embargo of, and WTO, 395
Cuban Revolution, 67
culturalists, view on regionalism, 335
Customary law, 367n1

Cutler, Claire, 361
cyber defense initiative (CDI), 217
"cyber jihad", 211
Cyber Storm, 212
cyberwars, 208. *See also* information war: low entry costs, 209–10; misinformation in, 210–11
Cyert, R. M., 419

Dahl, Robert, 227
Dalby, Simon, 84, 87, 140, 143, 150
Daqing, 343
De Beers, 240, 242
Debrix, Francois, 138
Declaration of the Rights of Men and of the Citizen, 174
Declaration on the Rights of Indigenous People, 179
Declaration on the Rights of Person Belonging to National or Ethnic, Religious and Linguistic Minorities, 179
decline-of-the nation-state thesis, 19
decolonization, 196, 197
deep ecology, 87, 88
deepening of security paradigm, 4–5
deforestation, 304
democracy, 42; and Cold War and America, 46–49; history and crisis of, 50–53; liberal democracy, beyond the limits of, 53–56; Schumpeter's perspective on, 48, 54; toward post-autistic perspectives on, 43–46; Western, 12
Democratic Republic of the Congo, 240, 248
democratization, 50, 51, 52
denial deterrence model, 213
Denmark, 121
Department of Homeland Security, U.S., 111
Deudney, Daniel, 80
developing countries: and ICT, 271; and international law, 363
development: and classical modernization theory, 64–66; and developmental state, 72–74; and early Cold War, 61–64; and end of Cold War, 70–71; and new Cold War, 68–70; nexus with security, and classic dependency theory, 67–68; and return of nation building in collapsed states, 74–76
developmental state, 72–74; and development economics, 72
Devereux, Stephen, 83
Devlin, Robert, 320
dialogic universalism, 183–184
Diamond Development Initiative (DDI), 252
diamond industry, 239–40, 284; conflict diamonds, 241, 242; conflict versus illicit diamonds, 249–51; and development, 251–2; Kimberly Process Certification Scheme (KPCS), 244–5; Kimberley Process (KP) meeting, 242–4; laborers, 252; lessons learned, 252–4; strengths, 245–8; wars, 240–41; weaknesses, 248–9
Diamond, Larry, 51
Dickens, Peter, 91
Diem, Ngo Dinh, 64
digital divide, 266–8; global, 268–9
digital Pearl Harbor, 216
digitization, 258, 259
Dirty War, 143
Dispute Settlement Unit (DSU), 355
division of labor: gendered, 91; international, 17
Dobson, Andrew, 87
Doctors without Borders. *See* Medecins Sans Frontiers
Doh, Jonathan, 293
Domask, Joseph, 304
Domhoff, G. William, 227
dot-com boom, and new economy, 258–9
Douglas, Ian, 22
Douglass, William, 372
Dower, Nigel, 155

dual citizenship, 29; beyond 9/11, 34; as concern, 30; contemporary developments, 31–32; in heightened security concerns period, 38–39; historical excursus, 30–31; impacts of, 37–38; and solidarity, 32–34; valorization of, 37
Dubai, 240
Duffield, Mark, 6, 151, 290
Dunning, John, 17, 417–18
Dye, Thomas, 227
Dyer, Hugh, 80
dynamism, 419

East Asia, 68, 71, 72, 73
Eastern Europe, 199
East Slavic Union, 339
Eckersely, Robyn, 96
eclectic framework and John Dunning, 417–18
ecofeminism, 89–90, 91
Economic Commission for Latin America (ECLA), 67
Economic Commission for Latin America and the Caribbean (ECLAC), 319–20
economic determinism, 15
economic globalization, 148, 390
economic internationalization, 16, 18, 22
economic, social, and cultural rights, 179
Economic Union Treaty, 337
ECOSOC, 302
ecosocialism, 87, 88–89, 91
Edwards, Jenny, 83
Egmont Group of Financial Intelligence Units, 109
Egypt, 69, 70, 71
Eisenhower, Dwight D., 64
Eizenstat, Stuart, 298
Eligible Receiver, 212
elite theories, 227–8, 229
El Salvador, 69, 70
emancipatory theory, 10
embedded autonomy, 230–31

embedded liberalism, 225–7, 232
Emergency Powers Act, 383
The End of the Nation State, 12
The End of Work, 261
Enhanced U.S. Border Security and Visa Entry Reform Act (2002), 148
Enloe, Cynthia, 143
Enterprise for the Americas Initiative (EAI), 319
entrepreneurial capitalism, 49
environmental conflict. *See* environmental insecurity
environmental insecurity, 79; conflict views in media and politics, 81; ecologism, 87; international politics and 93–96; global environmental change, environmental problems, global qualities of, 84–86;, environment as a site of global risk, 83–84; resource wars, 80–83; ôtypes, 87–92
environmental regulations, 359
environmental right, 181
Enzensberger, Hans Magnus, 277
Ernst and Young, 361
Estevadeordal, Antoni, 320
ethics free zone, 21
ethnicity paradox, 37
Eurasian Economic Community (EurAsEC), 329, 337, 338
Eurasian regionalism, 328–329; agreements and institutions, 330–34; Eurasian economic community, 336–338; explained, 329–336; Shanghai Cooperation Organization (SCO), 341–4; single economic space, 338–41, 345
Eurocentrism, 5
Europe, 71, 134, 147, 164, 165, 403
European Community, 248
European Convention for the Protection of Human Rights and Fundamental Freedoms, 176
European Convention on Human Rights, 382
European Council, 130
European Court of Human Right, 176

European Recovery Program. *See* Marshall Plan
European Union (EU), 29, 127, 132, 319
Evans, Peter, 230
exclusive economic zones (EEZs), 121, 130
external dependence, 3

failed states. *See* weak states
fair trade, 367n4
Fairtrade Foundation, 361
Faist, Thomas, 36
Falk, Richard, 344
FAO Code of Conduct for Responsible Fisheries, 133
Federal Bureau of Investigation (FBI), 110, 115
feudalism, 221–2, 235n1
fighting flights, 206
finance, 101; actors, 103–5; AML network, 105–16; deregulation, 17, 21; global, 101–3; key debates and twenty-first century issues, 105; lessons for IPE, 116–17; regulation, 352; and security, linkages and interactions, 103
Finance Capital, 194
Financial Action Task Force (FATF), 105, 111, 113, 114; establishment of, 109
financial capital, 18, 194
Financial Crimes Enforcement Network (FinCEN), 111, 115
Financial Sector Assessment Program, 104
First Gulf War, 71
First World, 62
fisheries security: CFP failings and fisheries crisis in Europe, 122–5; EU fisheries crisis, 125–7; global crisis, 128–30; historical problem, 120–21; impact on global South, 130–32; industrial-scale fishing and global fish markets, 127–8; new fisheries security governance, need for, 133–5; security issues and potential for conflict, 132–3; stock management problems, 121–2
fishing down of marine food webs, 129
fixed exchange rates, 18
Flags and Emblems (Display) Act, 383
food security, defined as, 120. *See also* fisheries security
Ford Foundation, 304
Foreign Affairs, 145
foreign aid, 69, 70
Foreign Assistance Act, 68
foreign direct investment (FDI), 17, 412
Forest Stewardship Council (FSC), 304
Foro Consultivo Económico y Social, 323
forum shifting, 365–366
Foucault, Michel, 7, 22
Fourth-Generation warfare, 278
fragmented pluralism, 34
France, 71, 121, 196
Frank, André Gunder, 67
Franks, 221
free market, 20–21
Free Trade Area of the Americas (FTAA), 316, 318, 321
freedom, 11
freestanding enterprise, 412
French Revolution armies, 288
Fukuyama, Francis, 23, 52, 75, 76, 144

G7, 358–9
Galtung, Johan, 156
Garrett, Geoffrey, 18
GATT. *See* General Agreement on Tariffs and Trade
Gaulin, Ted, 82
Gazprom, 338, 343
General Agreement on Tariffs and Trade (GATT), 16, 355
General Agreement on Trade in Services (GATS), 355

geopolitics, 137; critical, 137–8; orthodox, 137; and security, 141–4; during intense globalization period, 144–7; and War on Terror, 147–50
Gerdes, Jürgen, 36
Germanic tribes, 221
Germany, 35, 36, 71, 121, 139, 193, 194, 195
Gerteis, Joseph, 34
Ghanaian diamonds, 248–9
Gibson, William, 207
Giddens, Anthony, 12, 233
Gilpin, Robert, 393
Global 200 agenda, WWF, 303
global capitalism, 32
global civil society, 9–10
global compact, 22
global consciousness, 3
Global economic integration, 19
global environment for competitiveness, new economy, 260
global ethics. *See* human security perspective
global finance, 101–3
global governance agenda, 6, 21, 22
globalization, 10–15, 308, 309; capitalism's internationalization and, 13; of communications, 367n2; complexity approach and, 12; conjunctural factors and, 14; and economy, 15–19; effect on nation-state, 225, 226, 232–3; as grand narrative, 11; leading to commodification of life, 11; and new economy 258; and new war, 275, 279–82, 288; novelty of situation and, 12; political, 298; and politics, 19–23; and regionalism, 336; and security, 350–51, 353; techno0428ies of, 357; time-space compression and, 14; transformationalist approach to, 14–15
Globalization in Question, 13
Globalization Institute in Brussels, 304
globalizers, 11, 14
globalizing force, war as, 8

global justice, 155, 163
global North, 3
global ordering, 12
global security, 2–4
global social movements (GSMs), 23
global society, 180–81
global South, 3, 178, 184; fisheries security and impact on, 130–32
global terrorism, 3, 10
global warming, 3, 20, 83, 85, 165
Global Witness, 246
gold standard era, 16, 17
Goodin, Robert, 95
Goodson, Larry, 76
Gordon, Robert J., 260, 266, 294
Gothic tribes, 221
governance, 19–20; and crisis management, 52
Grameen Bank, 297
Gray, Colin, 139
Great Britain. *See* United Kingdom
Great Crash of 1929, 16
Great Depression, 47
Great North Whale Fishery, 120
Great Transition project, 168, 169
Great War, 195
Greece, 63
greed and grievance, 75
greenfield investments, 411
Greening Earth Society, 307
Greenpeace, 125, 132, 302
Gregory, Frank, 382
Grenadines, 133
Guantanamo, 185
Guatemala, 70
guerrilla warfare, 288
Guha, 92
Gulbenkian Commission, 161
Gulf War, 71
Gutierrez, Carlos, 402

Haas, Ernst, 335
hacktivism, 211–15; nation-states and, 215–16
Hague Convention, 31, 35
Harcourt, Wendy, 159

Hartmann, Douglas, 34
Hartshorne, Richard, 139
Harvey, David, 14
health impact, 164
health regulations, 359
hearts-and-minds approach, against terrorism, 380–81
hegemony, 198, 200
Heidegger, Martin, 14
Held, David, 3, 14, 18
Helms-Burton Act, 395
Hemispheric Social Alliance (HSA), 316–17
Hepple, Leslie, 142
Hettne, Björn, 328
Hewson, Martin, 102
Higgott, Richard, 21, 22
High-Level Group (HLG), 339–40
Hilferding, Rudolf, 194, 195
Hirst, Paul, 13, 16
Hizb ut Tahir, 382
Hobbes, Thomas, 155, 174
Hobson, John A., 192, 194, 195, 231
Hoeffler, Anke, 74
Holsti, Kalevi, 282, 285
home country, 411
Home Depot, 304
Homer-Dixon Thomas Fraser, 74, 80, 82, 83
Honduras, 133
Hong Kong, 72
host country, 411
human development index (HDI), 6
Human Development Report 1994, 156
human dignity, 174
humanitarian affairs, peace and security regulations, 358
humanitarian war, 10
human rights, 172, 177–80; evolution of, 173; globalization and, 180–81; interpretations of, 184–6; origin, 173–5; peace and security regulations, 358; third and fourth-generation rights, 181–2; Universal Declaration of Human Rights (UDHR), 175–7; universalism versus relativism, 182–4; violation of, 175
Human Rights Council, 179
Human Rights Watch, 381
human safety perspective, 167
human security, 5–7; and global governance agenda, 6; and human control, 6–7
human security and rights language, 167
Human Security Network, 167
Human Security Now, 6, 166
human security perspective: characteristics, 157–8; definitions, 158–9; framework, 155–7, 159–62; global ethics issues, 163; rational comparison, appeals to, 166–8; Rwanda, 162–3; self-interest and mutual interest, appeals to, 163–5; sympathy and identity evolution, appeals to, 165–6
Huntington, Samuel, 50, 66, 137, 145, 335
Hussein, Saddam, 149, 207
hybridization, 13
Hymer, Stephen, 414–15

identity, 5
ideological terrorism, 377
Ignatieff, Michael, 277
Ikea, 304
illegal, unreported, and unregulated (IUU) fishing, 132
illicit diamonds, 249; versus conflict diamonds, 249–51
IMF. *See* International Monetary Fund
immigrants, naturalization of, 37
imperialism: capitalist, and classical theorization, 192–6; dependency and world system theory, 198, 199; new, 200–201; twentieth-century US, and nation-state, 196–200; in twenty-first century, 190–92
Imperialism: The Highest Stage of Capitalism, 194

Imperialism and the World Economy, 194
import-substitution industrialization (ISI), 319, 324–5n6
India, 15, 240, 403, 413; offshoring, 270
Indigenous and Tribal Peoples' Convention, 357
indigenous people and human rights, 179
individualism, and social contract, 174
Indonesia, 21, 72
industrial capitalism, 195, 223–4
industrial long-lining, 127
Industrial Revolution, 206
industrial-scale fishing and global fish markets, 127–8
inequality, social, 70, 74
Information age, 15
information and communications technology (ICT), 257, 266, 269, 271–2; critical views, 271; and economic development, 270–71; national economies and new economy industries, 270; and productivity growth, 260
information society, and new economy, 260
information wars, 206; cyberwars. *See* cyberwars; deterring, 216–17; hacktivism, 211–15; information revolution, 207; nation-states and hacking, 215–16; offense–defense balance, 208–9; technology and warfare, 206
in-group membership, 33
Initiative on Regional Infrastructure of South America (IIRSA), 324
insecurity and security, 9–10
instability, and dual citizenship, 31
instrumentalism, 228–229
insurgency model, 210
insurgency, 280
intellectual property, 352, 365
Inter-American Bank, 324

Inter-American Development Bank (IADB), 318, 320
interconnectedness, 13, 166, 167; of social fates, 14
intercontinental ballistic missiles (ICBMs), 209–10
Intergovernmental Panel on Climate Change, 85
internalization theory, 416–17
International Air Transport Association (IATA), 360
International Association of Insurers Supervisors (IAIS), 101
International Campaign to Ban Landmines (ICBL), 305
International Convention on the Elimination of All Forms of Racial Discrimination (1965), 177
International Covenant on Civil and Political Rights (ICCPR), 178, 357
International Covenant on Economic, Social and Cultural Rights (ICESCR), 178, 179
International Criminal Court, 4
International Development Agency, 103
International Financial Corporation, 103
international financial institutions (IFIs), 103, 279–80, 281. *See also* IMF and World Bank
international financial order, 16, 17–18
internationalization, 13
International Monetary Fund (IMF), 63, 101, 103, 104, 114, 144, 162, 234, 279, 318
international NGOs (INGOs), 295
International Organization of Securities Commissions (IOSCO), 101
international political economies (IPEs), 102; constructionists, 393–4; lessons for, 116–17; liberals, 393; realists, 392–3
international politics and environment, 93–96

Index 445

International Product Life Cycle Theory (IPLCT) and Raymond Vernon, 415–16
international regulatory framework, 355–9
international terrorism, 149
International Tribunal for Rwanda (1994), 177
International Tribunal for the Former Yugoslavia (1993), 177
International Union for the Conservation of Nature & Natural Resources (IUCN), 304
Internet, 267–8. *See also* cyberwar
interstate conflict, 81–82
Inter-state Council, 337
intrafirm trade (IFT), 422–423
intrastate conflict/war, 30, 282
Iran, 146, 148, 149, 196
Iraq, 34, 76, 82, 140, 149, 190
Ireland, 4
Iriye, Akira, 294
Islam and human rights, 185
Islam and West, 8
Islamic radicalism, 149
isolated state autonomy, 230
Israel, 69, 70, 71, 240; diamond industry, 247
Itzigsohn, José, 37, 38

Jackson, Richard, 279, 280
James, Paul, 9
Japan, 47, 64, 71, 72, 73, 127, 164, 192, 193, 200
Jefferson, Thomas, 211
Jintao, Hu, 338
Johnson, Chalmers, 72, 147
joined-up thinking, 161
Jolly, Richard, 10, 161
juridical positivism, 175
jus soli principle, 36

Kagan, Robert, 137
Kaldor, Mary, 10, 277, 286
Kamajors militia, 282
Kant, Immanuel, 182

Kaplan, Robert, 137, 145, 277
Karimov, President, 343
Kautsky, Karl, 195
Kazakhstan, 337, 339, 340, 344
Keating, Michael, 233
Keck, Margaret, 301
Keen, David, 281, 284–5
Kennedy, John F., 64
Keynesian development economics, 197
Keynesian economic policies, 18
Khmer Rouge, 288
Kimberley Process (KP) meeting, 242–4
Kimberley Process Certification Scheme (KPCS), 244; lessons learned, 252–4; strengths, 245–8; weaknesses, 248–9; working groups, 248
Kissinger, Henry, 139
Kjellen, Rudolf, 137
Klare, Michael, 81, 82
Klein, Naomi, 11
knowledge employment, 262
Kobayashi, Audrey, 38
Kogut, Bruce, 418
Kokoshin, Andrei, 340
Koppel, J., 308
Korean War, 64
Kosovo, 145, 146
Kosovo War, 215
Krasner, 102
Kravchuk, President, 336
Kropotkin, Peter, 139
Kuan Yew, Lee, 185
Kuwait, 140
Kyoto Protocol, 29
Kyrgyzstan, 337

Lacoste, Yves, 139
Lal, Barbara Ballis, 37
Laski, Harold, 227
Latin America, 20, 51, 63, 65, 66, 67, 68, 71, 73, 140, 144, 151, 319; debt crisis in, 21; geopolitics and, 141, 142–143; latifundia, 199

Latin American Free Trade Association (LAFTA), 320
Latin American Integration Association (LAIA), 320
Leadbeater, Charles, 262
Lebanon, 247
LeBon, Gustave, 224
legitimacy, 10, 16, 49, 151, 201
Lenin, V. I., 191, 195
Less Developed Countries (LCDs), 69
Levy, Frank, 265
Levy, Mark, 79
Libdblom, Charles, 227
liberal democracy, 46–47, 51
liberal globalization, 11
liberalism, 224, 279, 280, 335, 354
liberalization, 36
liberal justice, 184
liberals, 393, 407n3
liberal social contract theory, 177
liberation ecologism, 90, 92
Liberia, 243, 250
Libicki, Martin, 211
Lindberg, Leon, 335
liquid fear, 10
List, Friedrich, 199
Living on Thin Air, 262
Locke, John, 174
Lome Peace Accord, 281
London bombings, 381, 382
The Long Twentieth Century, 198
Long War, 7–8
Lopez, George, 372
Lord's Resistance Army (LRA), 283
Lovelock, James, 85
low-intensity warfare, 282
Luxemburg, Rosa, 194, 198

Mackinder, Halford, 138
Macklin, Audrey, 34, 35
MacNamara, Robert, 167
Maitland, Frederic, 227
Malaysia, 65, 72
Mallaby, Sebastian, 306
Malta, 133
Manufactured risk, 84

March, J. G., 419
marine protected areas (MPAs), 126
market power and Stephen Hymer, 414–15
Marshall, T. H., 33
Marshall Plan, 63, 71, 337
Marx, Karl, 22, 191, 198
Marxian state theory, 228–30
Marxism: and human rights, 184; political, 199
Mastanduno, Michael, 392
Mathews, Jessica, 2
Matthew, Richard, 82
Max Havelaar, 361
McDonald, Bryan, 82
McManus, John, 416
Medecins Sans Frontiers, 299, 300–301, 305
Meiji Restoration, 193
mercantile capitalism, 222
mercenaries, 288
Merchant, Carolyn, 91
MERCOSUR, 312, 321, 323, 324
mergers and acquisitions (M&A), 411
methodological nationalism, 15
Metropolitan Police Counter-Terrorism Command, 382
Mexico, 21, 157
Michel, Louis, 242
Middle East, 63, 69, 71, 141, 144, 147
Mies, Maria, 91
migration, 350
Miliband, Ralph, 228–9
militarization, peace and security regulations, 358
Military Assistance Command Vietnam (MACV), U.S., 65
Millennium Challenge Account (2004), 150
Millennium Development Goals, 166
Mills, C. Wright, 227
Mine Ban Treaty (1997), 305
minimum universalism, 183–4
MITI and the Japanese Miracle, 72
Mitrany, David, 335

Index

Mlambo-Ngcuka, Phumzile, 242
mobile phone technology, 270–71
modernization theory, 13, 197, 198
money laundering. *See* anti–money laundering (AML)
money service businesses (MSBs), 115
Monroe Doctrine, 318
Moody's, 361
Moonlight Maze, 212
moral autonomy, 174
morality, 174, 183
moral rights, 175
moral virtues, 11
multilateral economic institutions (MEIs), 23
Multilateral Investment Guarantee Agency, 103
multinational corporations (MNCs), 15, 17
Multinational Resource Center, 304
Murnane, Richard, 265
Muslim Contact Unit, 382
Myers, R., 129

Napoleonic Wars, 288
narrative, 11
national citizenship, 28, 31
National Constituent Assembly, 174
national identity, 30, 34, 36
nationalism, 233–4
nationalist terrorism, 377
nationalization of capital, 194
National Liberation Front's (NLF), 65
national protectionism, 20–21
national security doctrine (NSD), 142–3, 146–7, 403
National Security Strategy, 3, 148, 149, 150
National Socialism, 139
national sovereignty, 2, 19, 175, 182
National Union for the Total Independence of Angola (UNITA), 284
Nation-Building: Beyond Afghanistan and Iraq, 76
nation-state, 12, 13, 15, 19, 28, 35, 145, 162, 193; of Central America, 69; civil conflict and, 74, 75; and Cold War era, 61–62; crisis of, 225; decline, 232–4; elite and pluralist theories, 227–8; embedded liberalism, 225–7, 234; fiscal strategies, 224; history of, 221–3; industrial capitalism, 223–224; Marxian state theory, 228–30; modern, 29, 31; neoliberalism, 226; resurgent nationalism, 233–4; security, 234–5; social welfare strategies, 224; state-centered theory, 230–32; transnational corporations, role in, 419–21; twentieth-century US imperialism and, 196–200
NATO (North Atlantic Treaty Organization), 141, 146
natural law, 173–5, 178
natural resources, warfare to control, 284
natural rights theory, 174
Nazarbayev, Nursultan, 340, 341
negative rights, 178
Neither Just nor Effective, 381
Nelson, Richard R., 418
neocolonialism, 197
neofunctionalist, and European integration, 335
neoliberal framing, 394
neoliberal globalization, 9
neoliberalism, 226, 232, 320
neoliberal-led globalization, first wave, 20
neoliberal policies, 15, 19
neorealists, view on regionalism, 335
Nepal, 159, 160
nested citizenship, 32
Nestle, 304
Netherlands, 121, 412
network states, 55
Neuromancer, 207
New and Old Wars, 290
new economy, 257; characteristics of work, 262–4; definition of, 258–61; digital divide, 266–8; global, 268–9; and dot-com boom, 258–9;

new economy (*Continued*)
as economic restructuring, 261; economic risk, 264; effect on work, 261–2; ICT. *See* information and communications technology; and information society, 260; productivity growth, 259–60; technology and labor market, inequality, 265–6; winner-takes-all effect, 266
new international economic order (NIEO), 68
newly industrializing countries (NICs), 68
new war, 275, 276–8; actors, 282–84, 288; challenges to, 287–90; economy, 284–5; globalization and state, 278–82; in Sierra Leone, case study, 281–2; methods of, 286–7; and old war, comparison, 277–8; politics of, 285–6
NGOs. *See* nongovernmental organizations
Nicaragua, 69, 70
Nigeria, 150; civil war, 289–90; offshoring, 270
Nike, 304
9/11 attack, 7, 373
Nixon, Richard, 226
non-cooperative countries and territories (NCCTs) report, 109, 111, 113
nondiscrimination, 183
nongovernmental organizations (NGOs), 22, 23; accountability challenges, 307–8; advocacy, 301; challenges and future, 306–9; characteristics, 294; conceptualizing, 293–7; and diamond industry, 243–4, 247, 252; growth in, 297–9; international recognition, 305–6; international security, 305; monitoring agents, 304–5; political role of, 301–3; public education, 303–4; relief and social economic development, 299–301; representation challenges, 307; role in international politics, 299–306; security challenges, 308; strategy challenges, 306–7
nonstate actors, 148, 293
nonstate terrorism, 377
Nordhaus, William, 260
North Africa, 157
North America, 47, 63, 66, 127, 164
North American Free Trade Agreement (NAFTA), 301, 312, 315, 321
North American Securing Perimeter, 323
Northern Ireland (Emergency Provisions) Act, 383
Northern NGOs (NNGOs), 296
North Korea, 146, 148, 149
North Sea, 120, 121, 123
North Vietnam, 67
Norway, 121, 126, 167, 245
nuclear freeze movement, 301
nuclear power, 206
Nuremberg War Crimes Tribunal, 175

O'Brien, Richard, 144
Offe, Claus, 47
offshoring, 270
Ogata, Sadako, 166
Ohmae, Kenichi, 12, 225, 232
old war, 276; and new war, comparison, 277–8
OLI advantages, 417–18
One World Trust, 307
On War, 276
open regionalism, 320
Operation Desert Storm, 207
organizational developments and TNC, 414
organizational forms, new economy, 260
Organization for Economic Cooperation and Development (OECD), 63, 104
Organization for European Economic Co-operation (OEEC)
Organization of American States (OAS), 318

Index 449

Organization of Central Asian Cooperation, 337
Organization of Petroleum Exporting Countries (OPEC), 68
Otpor, 210
Our Common Future, 93
Our Common Neighbourhood, 6
overfishing, 123, 129
overlapping consensus, 185–6
Ovetz, R., 131
Owen, Robert, 224
Oxfam International, 243, 296, 299, 305

Paarlberg, R. L., 135
Pakistan, 141
Palme Commission, 156
Panama, 133
Pan-America, 318
Papua New Guinea, 133
Paraguay, 142
Parsons, 33
Partnership Africa Canada, 242, 246, 249
Peace of Westphalia, 222
Pemberton, Miriam, 403
Penrose, E. T., 419
Pentagon, 138
People, States, and Fear, 4
People's Republic of China, 129
permanent security, 7
Perrons, Diane, 261, 264
personal integrity, 183
petroimperialism, 82
PetroKazakhstan, 342
Philippines, 21, 192
Picciotto, Robert, 158
Pinochet, 142
Pion-Berlin, David, 142
pirate fishing, 132–133
Plata Basin Financial Fund, 324
pluralist theories, 227–8
Pogge, Thomas, 155
Pohl, Frederik, 210
Point Four Program, 64
political authority, 174

political environment and TNC, 414
political exceptionality, 391
political exclusion/inclusion, 380
political globalization, 298
political Marxism, 199
political opportunity structure, 298–9
Political Order in Changing Societies, 66
political rights, 178
political society, 184
political sovereignty, 19, 22
political stability, 66
political violence, 372
Polsby, Nelson, 227
positive rights, 178
post-9/11 world, 29, 70
post-Enlightenment European culture, 183
postnationalism, 29; impact on dual citizenship, 32
poststructuralism, 9
Potter, David, 305
Poulantzas, Nicos, 229
poverty, 21, 148; and terrorism, 379
Powell, Colin, 147
power: politics, 395; of trade, 393; through trade, 392
Prebisch, Raul, 67
premoral state, 174
Preston, Valerie, 38
Prevention of Terrorism (Temporary Provisions) Act, 382, 383, 385
Price Waterhouse Coopers, 361
Private Enterprise Initiative (PEI), 69
private military companies (PMCs), 288
privatization, 280, 281, 354
problem-solving approach, terrorism study, 371
professional terrorism, 377
protectionism, 234
psychic distance, 419
public goods, 164, 165
public health, 164
punitive model, 215
Putin, Valdimir, 328, 340, 343

Quah, Danny, 266

Rabin, Yitzhak, 145
radio electronic combat (REC), 207
RAND Corporation, 208
Rawls, John, 155, 184
Ray, Deepayar Basu, 161
Reagan, Ronald, 217
realist framing, 394
realists, 392, 393, 400
Red Cross, 299, 305
reductionism and globalization, 12
reflexive modernization, 23
reflexivity, 23
refugee, 286
regional advisory councils (RACs), 124, 134
regionalism, in Eurasia. *See* Eurasian regionalism
regionalism, in the Americas. *See* Americas, regionalism in
regulation: definition, 351; in globalized world, 362–4; and globalization, 349, 351–3; inequality and global security, 364–6; multilayered governance, 361–2; nonstate actors in, 359–61; peace and security regulation, 358; state's role in, 353–5; supranational governance rise, 355–9; trade and finance regulation, 352
Reimann, Kim D., 298
Reinert, Erik, 199
relativism and human rights, 183
religious terrorism, 377–8
Renner, Michael, 82
Reports on the Observance of Standards and Codes, 104
repressive tolerance, 22
reprivatization of war, 35
Republic of Congo (Brazzaville), 247
resource curse, 284
resource wars, 80–83
Resource Wars, 81
reverse securitizations, 394, 402

Revolution in Military Affairs (RMA), 8
Revolutionary United Front (RUF), 241, 281, 287
Rich Man, Poor Man, 252
Richani, Nazih, 74
Rieple, Beate, 36
Rifkin, Jeremy, 261–2
rights primacy, 185
Rio Declaration, 94, 95
The Rise of "The Rest": Challenges to the West from Late-Industrializing Economies, 72
Rodney, Walter, 67
rogue states, 148
Rona, Thomas, 207
Rorty, Richard, 183
Rousseau, Jean-Jacques, 174, 184
Russia, 21, 51, 62, 63, 64, 71, 113, 141, 147, 401, 248, 337–9, 344; cyber attacks in 212–13
Russia-Belarus Union, 339
Russian Revolution, 196
Rwanda, 34, 140; conflict, 305; human security perspective and global ethics in, 162–3

St. Jorre, John De, 290
St. Vincent, 133
Salamon, Lester, 294, 298
Sanitary and Phytosanitary Measures (SPS) agreement, science and risk management in, 404–5
Saudi Arabia, 71, 147, 401
Save Britain's Fish slogan, 126, 127
Save the Children, 299
Savimbi, Jonas, 241
Saving Private Ryan, 276
Saxons, 221
Scandinavian School and TNC, 419
Scandinavian countries, 184
Schaffer, K., 165
Schmitt, Carl, 35
Schmitter, Philippe, 335
Scholte, Jan Aart, 3, 15, 20
Schumpeter, Joseph A., 48, 192

second serfdom, 199
Second World, 62
securitization, 393–4; affecting dual citizenship, 34–35
Security and Prosperity Partnership for North America (SPP), 323
security norms, post 9/11, 35
securocrats, 9
self-determination, 62, 181
self-interest, 165, 166; and mutual interest, appeals to human security perspective, 163–5
self-regulation, 111
Semmel, Bernard, 191
Sen, Amartya, 166, 185
Serbia, 10
Shanghai Cooperation Organization (SCO), 329, 340, 341–4, 345
Sheppard, Stephen, 258
Sherman, Jake, 75
Shining Path, 288
Shiva, Vandana, 91
Siemiatycki, Myer, 38
Sierra Leone, 113, 240, 248, 250; new war, 281–2, 284, 287; ordeal in Yiraia, 287
Sikkink, Kathryn, 301
Silent Horizon, 212
Sinclair, Timothy, 102
Singapore, 72
single economic space, 338–41, 345
Sinopec, 338
skeptics, 13, 14
Skills Biased Technological Change (SBTC), 265
Skocpol, Theda, 230
Small Boys Unit, 283
Smart Border Agreements, 323
Smith, Al, 50
Smith, Brian, 299–300
Smith, S., 5, 165
Snow, Donald, 277, 278
social contract, and individualism, 174
social ecology, 87, 88
social embeddedness, 231

social exclusion, 91
socialism, 195
socialist states, 62
social responsibility, shift to, 21–22
social welfare regulations, 359
societal security, 4–5
solidarity, 165, 168; and dual citizenship, 32–34; human, 183; nationalistic, 35, 36; rights, 181
Solow, Robert, 259
Somalia, 133, 140
Soros, George, 21
South Africa, 157, 163, 164, 240, 248
South American Peace Commission, 156
South Asia, 71
Southeast Asia, 144
Southern NGOs (SNGOs), 296
South Korea, 64, 71, 72, 73
South Vietnam, 64, 65, 67, 69
Southwest Asia, 71
sovereignty, 5, 149; national, 2, 19, 175, 176; political, 19, 22; state, 31, 32, 145, 174, 199
Soysal, Yasemin, 29
Spain, 127, 157
Sparke, M., 150
Special Irish Office, 382
Special Recommendations on Terrorist Financing, 114
species biodiversity, loss of, 86
spirit of democracy, 51
Spiro, Peter, 30, 32, 34
stability, 16
Standard and Poor's, 361
Staples, Steven, 403
state, 179; actors, 39; authority legitimization, 174; autonomy, 230; and national security, 145; organic theory of, 142; power, 392; security, 5; sovereignty, 31, 32, 145, 174, 199; terrorism, 376–7
The State in Capitalist Society, 228
Stevens, Siaha, 281
Stiroh, Kevin, 260
Stockholm Environment Institute, 168

Stockholm Intergovernmental Conference on the Human Environment (1972), 93
Stohl, Michael, 372
Strange, Susan, 18, 102
strategic defense initiative (SDI), 217
Strategic Hamlet Program, 65
Strategic Information Warfare, 208
strategic-versus-efficiency approach, for TNC, 420
Straw, Jack, 275
strong states, 279
structuralism, 228, 229
sub-Saharan Africa, 150
subsidiaries, 412
substate, 20
suprastate, 20
supraterritorial phenomena, 20
supraterritoriality, 15
sustainable development, 93
Swatuk, Larry, 79
Sweden, 121
Switzerland, 111
sympathy and identity evolution, appeals to human security perspective, 165–6
Syria, 146

tabloid geopolitical culture, 137
Taiwan, 64, 72, 73, 127, 133
Tajikistan, 337
Tanzania, 133
Taylor, Charles, 185, 186, 241, 281
technological environment and TNC, 414
technology: impact on work, 261–2; and labor market, 265–6; and warfare, 206
technology transfer, 148
Teegan, Hildey, 293
territorial sovereignty, 225
terrorism: causes, 378–80; critical study of, 372–4; fear of, 376; from above and below, 377; orthodox approaches to, 371–2; responding to, 380–82; threat, 374–6; in twenty-first century, 368–71; types, 376–8
Terrorism Act, 383, 385
Terror on the Internet, 211
Teschke, Benno, 199
Tet Offensive, 67
Thailand, 21, 72
theory-practicve nexus, 10
third-way politics, 21
Third World, 62, 64, 66–69, 73, 144, 197, 198, 199
Thirty Years' War, 222
Thomas, George, 299
Thompson, Grahame, 13, 16
Tilly, Charles, 28
time-space compression and globalization, 14
Titan Rain, 212
Tooze, Roger, 9
total allowable catch (TAC), 122, 123
trad'zation, 394
Trade at Hand project, 271
trade barriers, removal of, 21
trade politics, 394
trade regulation, 352
Trade-Related Intellectual Property Rights (TRIPS), 355
traitors, 30
transcender logic, 1
transcultural consensus, need for, 184
transfer prices, manipulation of, 423
transformationalists, 14
Transnational Capitalist Class, 232
transnational citizenship, 37–38
transnational corporations (TNC), 12, 360, 410; activities, effects of, 421–4; characteristics and activities, 412, geography, 412–13, modalities, 413–14, size, 413; definitions, 411–12; and globalization, 424–5; theories of, and FDI, eclectic framework and John Dunning, 417–18, evolutionary theory, 418–19, internalization theory, 416–17, International Product Life Cycle Theory and Raymond Vernon, 415–16,

Index

transnational corporations (TNC) (*Continued*)
  market power and Stephen Hymer, 414–15, nation-state, role of, 419–21, Scandinavian School, 419
transnational migrants, 28, 33
transnational social movement networks, 172
Trans-Saharan Counter-Terrorism Initiative (2005), 150
trawler fishing, 127
Treasury Department authority, U.S., 111
Triadafilopoulos, Phil, 35, 36
tribalism, 10
Trilateral Commission, 50–51
TRIPS Agreement, 366
trophic level (TL) of global marine landings, 129
Truman, Harry. S., 63
Truman Doctrine, 63
Tuathail, Gearoid O., 140
Turkey, 63
Turkmenistan, 337
Tuvalu, 133

Ukraine, 71, 338, 339–340
ultra-imperialism, 195
Uncivil Wars, 277
União Nacional para a Independência Total de Angola (UNITA), 241, 250
United Kingdom, 34, 35, 48, 71, 120, 121, 126, 141, 151, 195, 196, 200, 201, 264, 412; counterterrorist operations, 381–2; productivity growth, 266
United Nations, 63, 93, 217, 271, 302; Commission on Environment and Development, 93; Committee on Non-Governmental Organizations, 302; Conference on Environment and Development (UNCED), 94; Conference on Trade and Development (UNCTAD), 366; Convention on the Law of the Sea, 121; Declaration on the Right to Development, 182; Development Programme (UNDP), 4, 6, 159, 160, 362; Framework Convention on Climate Change (UNFCC), 356; Global Program against Money Laundering, 110; Human Development Report (1999), 180; Mission in Sierra Leone (UNAMSIL), 281; Scientific and Cultural Organization (UNESCO), 163, 182
United States: cyber attacks in, 212; productivity growth, 266
Universal Declaration of Human Rights (UDHR), 168, 173, 175–7; covenants, 176; against gender discrimination, 179–80; for protection of children, 180; state-centric approach, 177
Universal Declaration on Bioethics and Human Rights (2005), 182
universalism and human rights, 183
Urdal, 82
Urry, John, 12
Uruguay, 143
U.S. Agency for International Development (USAID), 65, 68, 69, 70
USA Patriot Act (2001), 148, 149
U.S. Declaration of Independence (1776), 174
Uzbekistan, 337

Venezuela, 250
Vernon, Raymond, 415–16
Victorian Internet, 206
Vienna Declaration, 178
Vietnam, 139, 196
violence, 29, 284–5; in Argentina, 143; privatized, 70

Waddell, Nicholas, 6
Wade, Robert, 271
Wallerstein, Immanuel, 198
War of the Triple Alliance, 142
War on Terror, 140, 375, 404; global, 7–8; security and geopolitics and, 147–50

Warren, Bill, 199
wars, economic benefits from, 285
Washington Consensus, 20–21, 104, 320
weak (failed) states, 278–9, 280–81, 284
Weimann, Gabriel, 211
Weiss, Linda, 230, 232
welfare state, 56–57n9
West Africa, 150
Western Europe, 47, 63, 200
What Is Information Warfare?, 211
Wheeler, Nicholas, 1
wicked issues, 20
Wilkins, Mira, 412
Williamson, O., 416
winner-takes-all effect, of new economy, 266
Winter, Sydney G., 418
Wolf, Aaron, 82
Wolf, Martin, 11
Wolfsberg Forum, 116
Wolfsberg Group of Banks, 116
work, impact of technology on, 261–2
World Bank, 63, 74, 103, 144, 172, 194, 234, 279, 318
WorldCom, 259
World Diamond Council (WDC), 243, 246
World Heritage Convention, 304
World Intellectual Property Organization (WIPO), 366
world system theory (WST), 198
World Vision, 243
World War I, 16
World War II, 16, 36, 47, 144, 412
World Wild Life (WWF), 303
Worm, B., 129
WTO (World Trade Organization), 17, 244, 301, 355; Doha Development Round, 321; limits to national interest in, 400–403; as overlooked security organization, 394–7; as overlooked security organization, 394–7; power of trade, 393; power through trade, 392–3; and security and globalization, 390–91; security-related trade wars in, 397–400; societal and individual threats of globalization, 403; trade-related security threats, theoretical perspectives, 391–4

Yiraia, ordeal in, 287
Young, Iris Marion, 10
Yugoslavia, 34, 62, 140
Yunus, Muhammad, 297

Zander, Udo, 418
Zhenyu, Sun, 402
Zulaika, Joseba, 372

About the Editors and Contributors

EDITORS

G. Honor Fagan is a senior lecturer in sociology and is currently Dean of Graduate Studies at National University of Ireland, Maynooth. She has written widely on gender, conflict, and cultural issues in globalization. She has carried out European- and nationally funded research projects on democracy.

Ronaldo Munck is theme leader for internationalization, interculturalism, and social development at Dublin City University and is visiting professor of political sociology at the University of Liverpool. He has written widely on globalization and its discontents, focusing on social movements, social exclusion, and development issues. He is currently working on migration and security in the context of globalization and governance.

CONTRIBUTORS

Shamima Ahmed is a professor in the Department of Political Science at Northern Kentucky University. She is also the director of the MPA program at Northern. Her teaching and research interests include human resource management, nonprofit organizations, and organizational behavior. She has contributed numerous articles to such journals as *Public Personnel Management, State & Local Government, International Journal of Public Administration, Journal of Management Development,* and *Journal of Public Affairs Education* and has published a book on NGOs in international politics.

John Arquilla is professor of defense analysis and director of the Information Operations Center at the U.S. Naval Postgraduate School. His research interests extend to Information Age conflict, irregular warfare, and the impact of the rise of networked organizations on society and security.

Mark T. Berger has been a Visiting Professor in the Department of Defense Analysis at the Naval Postgraduate School (Monterey, CA USA) since July 2006. Since September 2009 he is also concurrently Adjunct Professor (History/Politics) in the Irving K. Barber School of Arts and Social Sciences, University of British Columbia—Okanagan (Kelowna, B.C., Canada). He is author of Mark T. Berger, *The Battle for Asia: From Decolonization to Globalization* (2004). He is editor of Mark T. Berger, Ed., *From Nation-Building to State Building* (2008). Mark T. Berger (and Douglas A. Borer), Eds., *The Long War: Insurgency, Counterinsurgency and Collapsing States*, (2008). Mark T. Berger, Ed. *After the Third World?* (2009). Heloise Weber and Mark T. Berger, Eds. *Recognition and Redistribution: Beyond International Development* (2009). Mark T. Berger (and Heloise Weber), Eds. *War, Peace and Progress: Conflict, Development, (In)Security and Violence in the 21st Century* (A Special Issue of *Third World Quarterly*, Vol, 30 No, 1. 2009). Mark T. Berger and Heloise Weber, *Rethinking the Third World: International Development and World Politics* (Forthcoming, 2010).

Cory Blad is assistant professor of sociology at Manhattan College. His research interests generally focus on globalization studies, including state institutions, national culture and legitimacy, national movement mobilization, and global political economic structures.

Chiara Certomà is research fellow in political philosophy at Sant'Anna School of Advanced Studies in Pisa. Her research interests are environmental politics, global justice and human rights, science and societies studies, and noninstitutional politics.

Erika Cudworth is senior lecturer in international politics and sociology in the School of Social Sciences, Media, and Cultural Studies at the University of East London. Her research interests include social and political theory, particularly feminisms, ecologisms, and complexity theory, and human relations with nonhuman animals. She is author of *Environment and Society* (2003), *Developing Ecofeminist Theory: The Complexity of Difference* (2005), and *The Modern State: Theories and Ideologies* (with Tim Hall and John McGovern, 2007).

About the Editors and Contributors

Harry F. Dahms is associate professor of sociology at the University of Tennessee, Knoxville, and editor of *Current Perspectives in Social Theory*. His primary areas of interest are social theory, sociological theory, and critical theory, economic sociology, globalization, and basic income. His articles have appeared in *Sociological Theory, Current Perspectives in Social Theory, Soundings*, and *Soziale Welt*. His other publications include a volume titled *Transformations of Capitalism*.

Radhika Desai is professor at the Department of Political Studies, University of Manitoba, Winnipeg, Canada. She is author of *Slouching towards Ayodhya: From Congress to Hindutva in Indian Politics* (2004) and *Intellectuals and Socialism:"Social Democrats" and the Labour Party* (1994), a *New Statesman and Society* book of the month, and editor of *Developmental and Cultural Nationalisms* (2008). She has also authored numerous articles in *Economic and Political Weekly, New Left Review, Third World Quarterly*, and other journals and in edited collections on parties, political economy, culture, and nationalism. She is working on two books: *When Was Globalization? Origin and End of a U.S. Strategy* (forthcoming, 2009) and *The Making of the Indian Capitalist Class* (forthcoming, 2010).

Helen Dexter is a teaching fellow in the School of Politics, International Relations, and Philosophy and an affiliated member of the Research Institute for Law, Politics, and Justice at Keele University. Her research addresses competing conceptualizations of warfare, the logic of violence, and the relationship between the politics of ethics and violent conflict.

Klaus Dodds is professor of geopolitics at Royal Holloway, University of London. His latest books include *Geopolitics: A Very Short Introduction* (2007) and as coeditor *Spaces of Security and Insecurity: Geographies of the War on Terror* (2009). His research interests include geopolitics, the polar regions, and media.

Des Gasper lectures at the Institute of Social Studies in The Hague, a postgraduate institute for international development studies within Erasmus University, Rotterdam. His research interests include well-being, international development ethics, and the human discourses of human rights, human development, and human security.

Liza Griffin is a research fellow on the Governance and Sustainability Program at Department of Politics and International Relations at the University of Westminster. She is interested in debates about power and space in relation to the governance of sustainable development.

Jeroen Gunning is deputy director of the Center for the Study of Radicalization and Contemporary Political Violence (CSRV), coeditor of *Critical Studies on Terrorism*, and lecturer in Middle East studies and (critical) terrorism studies at the Department of International Politics, Aberystwyth University. His research focuses on the interplay between Islamist social movements, violence, religion, and democratization in the Middle East, with a particular emphasis on Hamas and Hezbollah, and has included extensive fieldwork in the area. His publications include *Hamas in Politics: Democracy, Religion, Violence* (2007–2008), and with Richard Jackson and Marie Breen Smyth he has coedited, *Critical Terrorism Studies: A New Research Agenda* (2009).

Stephen Hobden is senior lecturer in international politics at the University of East London's School of Social Sciences, Media, and Cultural Studies. His main areas of interest are international relations theory, China in world politics, and North-South relations. He is the author of *International Relations and Historical Sociology: Breaking Down Boundaries* (1998) and together with John Hobson has edited *Historical Sociology of International Relations* (2002).

Rosalba Icaza is an international studies scholar specializing in the international political economy of transborder civic activism on regionalism, democracy, and gender with a particular emphasis on Latin America and Mexico. She currently holds a European Commission Reintegration Grant (ERG) to develop a two-year research on alternative regionalisms in Latin America (2007–2009). This research develops a systematic and comparative South-South analysis of key initiatives promoted by civil society groups in Latin America as alternatives to overcome socioeconomic deficits embedded in contemporary regionalism; it also examines the practices of governance that are emerging for the implementation of such alternatives.

Grazia Ietto-Gillies is emeritus professor of applied economics and director of the Center for International Business Studies at London South Bank University. She is also a visiting professor at Birkbeck, University of London, and King's College London. Her main research interests are in the activities of transnational companies. She has published several books and many articles in academic journals.

Richard Jackson is editor of the journal *Critical Studies on Terrorism* and co-convenor of the British International Studies Association (BISA) Critical Studies on Terrorism Working Group (CSTWG). He is deputy director of the Center for the Study of Radicalization and Contemporary Political Violence (CSRV). His latest book is *Writing the War on Terrorism: Language, Politics and Counter-Terrorism*.

About the Editors and Contributors

Peter Kivisto holds joint appointments at Augustana College, where he is the Richard Swanson Professor of Social Thought, and the University of Turku, where the Finnish Academy has awarded him a Finland Distinguished Professorship. He is currently working on an edited book on migration and development and is beginning a major project on multiculturalism in comparative perspective.

Neil Lee is a PhD candidate in the Department of Geography and Environment at the London School of Economics. He is also a senior researcher at the Work Foundation. His research interests are cities, economic change, and inequality.

Mikhail A. Molchanov is associate professor of political science at St. Thomas University in Fredericton, Canada. Dr. Molchanov has taught at several universities in Ukraine and Canada and has published books and articles on various aspects of postcommunist transitions in Russia and Ukraine. His current research focuses on regionalism and globalization, Russian foreign economic policies, and politics of energy in Eurasia.

Jens L. Mortensen is an associate professor in the Department of Political Science at the University of Copenhagen, Denmark. He has published on trade and WTO-related topics in various journals and books, contributing articles in *Political Economy and the Changing Global Order* (2006) and *The European Union and International Organisations* (2008). His current research interest concerns the framing power of international organizations in global trade and emerging climate governance.

Ian Smillie is an international development consultant and author who was one of the initiators of the Kimberley Process, which today certifies the world's trade in rough diamonds. His latest book is *Freedom from Want: The Remarkable Story of BRAC, the Global Grassroots Organization That's Winning the Fight against Poverty.*

Marie Breen Smyth is director of the Center for the Study of Radicalization and Contemporary Political Violence (CSRV), coeditor of *Critical Studies on Terrorism*, and reader in international politics in the Department of International Politics, Aberystwyth University. She was 2002–2003 Jennings Randolph Senior Fellow at the United States Institute of Peace. In 1994, she founded the Institute for Conflict Research and initiated The Cost of the Troubles Study, the first study to document the impact of political violence on the population (including children) of Northern Ireland. She has worked with the special representative of the secretary general of United Nations for Children and Armed Conflict.

Her latest books are *Truth and Justice after Violent Conflict: Managing Violent Pasts* (2007) and *Critical Terrorism Studies: A New Research Agenda* (2009), a work jointly edited with Richard Jackson and Jeroen Gunning.

Celine Tan is lecturer in law at Birmingham Law School, University of Birmingham. Her research centers on exploring aspects of international economic regulation with a focus on international economic law, development financing law, policy, and governance.

Eleni Tsingou is research fellow at the Center for the Study of Globalization and Regionalization, University of Warwick. Her research focuses on global banking regulation and transnational private governance, transnational policy communities, and the global anti-money-laundering regime and the fight against terrorist financing. She is also program manager of GARNET, an EU-funded project on the EU's role in global governance, regionalization, and regulation.